9, An. Ar   9

THE ARCHITECTURE OF ENGLAND

Salisbury Cathedral from the south-west.
West front c. 1258; tower and spire c. 1334

THE ARCHITECTURE OF ENGLAND

from Prehistoric Times to the Present Day

DOREEN YARWOOD

B. T. BATSFORD LTD
London

To
Sir Basil Spence, OM, RA, RDI, PPRIBA
with his kind permission
in appreciation and recognition of his services to
British Architecture

FIRST PUBLISHED 1963

© DOREEN YARWOOD 1963

Made and printed in Great Britain
by William Clowes and Sons, Limited, London and Beccles
for the publishers
B. T. BATSFORD LTD
4 Fitzhardinge Street, Portman Square, London W.1

PREFACE

In this book a serious attempt has been made to cover the field of English architecture, from the earliest times to the present day, as comprehensively as space permits. Nearly 300 pages of line drawings and 70 pages of photographs illustrate the examples chosen. It is not easy to make a selection of buildings to illustrate, particularly in more recent periods when there is a quantity of work from which to choose. It was considered important to include the majority of famous and masterly works, both in their own right and in order to illustrate the designs of their individual architects whose careers are summarised in the text. In addition, the author has included a number of lesser-known buildings which are essentially typical of their age and has endeavoured to take these from all over the country and not, as sometimes happens, only from London and the south of England. The book covers primarily English architecture, but, in view of the serious omission it would have caused in the discussion of Medieval military architecture, Welsh castles have been included and also, in modern work, Scottish bridges.

In order to use copyright-free material for the drawings, to present varied aspects of buildings different from those so commonly depicted and, above all, to make a personal study, the author has visited over 95 per cent of the buildings illustrated. Mr John Yarwood has then taken numerous photographs of complete views and of architectural details, and the drawings have been made from these photographs. This method of approach has made it possible to produce a drawing from a combination of five or even eight photographs pinned together, supported, where available, by the architect's original drawing or a contemporary print; by this means, many buildings have been illustrated which it is not possible to photograph well. Such examples include a number of Wren's city churches, the complete Royal Crescent in Bath and the new Runcorn–Widnes bridge over the Mersey. For this purpose, nearly 5,000 photographs of 750 buildings have been taken and printed.

The remaining five per cent of drawings, not resulting from the author's personal on-the-spot research, are chiefly of buildings which are considered important but which do not now exist: for instance, Old St Paul's Cathedral, Coleshill House and Nash's Regent Street. Also covered are a few important and famous schemes which were designed but for various reasons never carried out: for example, Wren's earlier designs for St Paul's Cathedral and Lutyens' Metropolitan Cathedral at Liverpool. In such instances the author has worked where possible from the architect's original drawings or model or, failing these, from contemporary prints.

In England at the present time, in common with other countries, many old and valued buildings, generally of eighteenth- or nineteenth-century design, are disappearing. Road widening and construction is responsible for much of this demolition, but it is in our cities, particularly London, that the greatest changes are taking place. Fine buildings are disappearing faster than many of us realise, often despite genuine attempts to find alternative solutions for the individual land or road problem which makes demolition necessary. The author was surprised and somewhat shocked to discover, on completing this book after seven years of travel and study, how many of the buildings, which she had earlier photographed and visited, no longer existed. There are, of course, much publicised examples such as the Euston Arch, but there are also instances of buildings threatened or being completely surrounded and overshadowed by larger schemes which render the earlier construction incongruous. Among these might be numbered the Imperial Institute or the Hyde Park Screen. It is useless to sigh for the past and we cannot retain everything from earlier ages in a modern world. It does seem, however, that so often the overriding factor in the question of to demolish or not is the economic one rather than the architectural worth of the building concerned.

It is hoped by this wide coverage in period and county that readers will find their interest aroused to go to visit some of the buildings illustrated here. Such a work can, despite its size, only be an introduction to the subject. In order to experience and enjoy the buildings around one more fully, it is necessary and absorbing to see them for oneself. Many of the examples shown in this book are still in private hands, but the properties owned by the National Trust and those opened to the public by their private owners are very numerous and, in many cases, easy of access.

London, 1963   DOREEN YARWOOD

CONTENTS

IV Perpendicular Gothic 1375-1509

V Tudor 1509-1603

VI Stuart 1603-1660

VII Restoration Stuart & Queen Anne 1660-1714

CONTENTS

CONTENTS

XI Victorian 1850-1900   452

XII The Twentieth Century 1900-1945   514

XIII Modern Architecture 1945 onwards   577

LIST OF ILLUSTRATIONS

COLOUR PLATES

MONOCHROME PLATES

ACKNOWLEDGMENT

The drawings of the buildings and of architectural details for this book were made by the author from about 5,000 photographs taken by Mr John Yarwood when he and the author visited and studied the actual buildings. The author would like to express her appreciation of the kindness shown by the present owners of the properties who readily gave their permission for such photography and, in many instances, offered further acceptable advice and assistance.

Particular thanks are due to the National Trust for their unvarying courtesy and helpfulness. Among the properties owned by the Trust and included in this book are: The Old Soar Manor House, Kent; Bodiam Castle, Sussex; Smallhythe, Kent: Stoneacre, Otham, Kent; the Old Wool Hall and the Guildhall, both in Lavenham, Suffolk; Great Chalfield Manor, Wiltshire; Coughton Court, Warwickshire; Little Moreton Hall, Cheshire; Montacute, Somerset; Lacock Abbey, Wiltshire; Ightham Mote, Kent; Bourne Mill, Colchester, Essex; Willington Stables and Dovecote, Bedfordshire; Ham House, Richmond, Surrey; Bateman's, Burwash, Sussex; Petworth House, Sussex; Uppark, Sussex; No. 42, Queen Anne's Gate, London (Headquarters of the National Trust); Mompesson House, Salisbury; Hanbury Hall, Worcestershire; Fenton House, Hampstead; Princes Risborough Manor House, Buckinghamshire; Clandon Park, Guildford; Nostell Priory, Yorkshire; Cliveden, Buckinghamshire; Lyme Park, Cheshire; Osterley Park, Middlesex; West Wycombe Park, Buckinghamshire; Attingham Park, Shropshire and Ickworth, Suffolk.

The Universities of Oxford and Cambridge have also expressed interest and rendered assistance. Grateful thanks are due to:

The Bursar of All Souls College, Oxford; the Bursar of Balliol College, Oxford; the Dean of Christ Church, Oxford; the Bursar of Corpus Christi College, Oxford; the Bursar of Exeter College, Oxford; the Bursar of Jesus College, Oxford; the Warden and Fellows of Keble College, Oxford; the Principal of Lady Margaret Hall, Oxford; the Bursar of Lincoln College, Oxford; the President of Magdalen College, Oxford; the Bursar of Mansfield College, Oxford; the Bursar of Merton College, Oxford; the Warden of New College, Oxford; the Treasurer of Oriel College, Oxford; the Bursar of the Queen's College, Oxford; the Principal of St Anne's College, Oxford; the President of St John's College, Oxford; the Bursar of Trinity College, Oxford, the Dean of University College, Oxford, and the College Clerk of Clare College, Cambridge; the Master of Corpus Christi College, Cambridge; the Bursar of Downing College, Cambridge; the Bursar of Emmanuel College, Cambridge; the Manciple of Jesus College, Cambridge; the Bursar of King's College, Cambridge; the Principal of Newnham College, Cambridge; the Bursar of Pembroke College, Cambridge; the Bursar of Peterhouse, Cambridge; the President of Queens' College, Cambridge; the Bursar of St Catharine's College, Cambridge; the Bursar of St John's College, Cambridge; the Bursar of Selwyn College, Cambridge, and the Chief Clerk of Trinity College, Cambridge.

The author would like to express her gratitude to the following owners and custodians of private properties and to various municipal, educational and institutional bodies. Buildings are listed in chronological order approximately as they appear in the book.

To the Glastonbury Antiquarian Society for permission to use information in the late Dr Bulleid's book on 'Lake Villages'; to Mr John Lunn, Director of the Verulamium Museum and to Lord Verulam for Roman remains at Verulamium, St Albans; to the Master of the Armouries, H.M. Tower of London; to H. E. Wallbrook, Rector of St Bartholomew-the-Great, Smithfield, London; to the owners of Markenfield Hall, Yorkshire; to Viscount de L'Isle for Penshurst Place, Kent; to the Matron, St Osyth's Priory Convalescent Home, Essex; to Lord Astor for Hever Castle, Kent; to Mr S. H. Barnett for Ockwells Manor, Bray, Berkshire; to the owners, Paycockes, Coggeshall, Essex; to Mr D. R. Greig for Rumwood Court, Langley, Kent; to Lord Darnley for Cobham Hall, Kent; to Mr Richard L. Vernon for Keevil Manor, Trowbridge, Wiltshire; to the Marquess of Northampton for Compton Wynyates, Warwickshire; to the Curator of the Natural History Museum, Wollaton, Nottingham, for Wollaton Hall; to the Duke of Rutland for Haddon Hall, Derbyshire; to the Principal, Mrs M. E. Massey, Brereton Hall School, Sandbach, Cheshire; to the Rev D. Whyte for Barlborough Hall School, Derbyshire; to Mr B. G. Brocklebank for Gifford's Hall, Stoke-by-Nayland, Suffolk; to Mrs Campbell for Layer Marney Hall, Essex; to Mother Aloysius of the Assumption Convent, Hengrave Hall, Suffolk; to Sir George Binney for Horham Hall, Thaxted, Essex; to Mr Raymond F. Bawtree, Proprietor, Country House Hotel at Studley Priory, Oxfordshire; to Mr J. Goring, Wiston Park, Steyning, Sussex; to Major Morton for Fritwell Manor, Bicester, Oxfordshire; to the Marquess of Bath for Longleat, Warminster, Wiltshire; to the Ministry of Works for Hampton Court Palace, Middlesex; to the Duke of Devonshire for Hardwick Hall and for Chatsworth, Derbyshire; to the Duke of Sutherland for Sutton Place, near Guildford, Surrey; to the Secretary for the Royal Naval College, Greenwich; to the National Maritime Museum for the Queen's House, Greenwich; to Lord Sackville for Knole, Sevenoaks, Kent; to the Marquess of Salisbury for Hatfield House, Hertfordshire; to the Town Clerk, Mr Harold Whetstone, for Charlton House, Greenwich; to Chief Superintendent E. Barker, Assistant Commandant, Police College, for Bramshill House, Hartley Wintney, Hampshire; to the Ground Secretary, London Postal Region Sports Club for Swakeleys, Ickenham; to Mr G. Jell for Broome Park, near Canterbury, Kent; to Miss M. M. Wingate, Principal, Balls Park Training College, Hertford; to the owner of Grimshaw Hall, Knowle, Warwickshire; to the Duke of Marlborough for Blenheim Palace, Woodstock, Oxfordshire; to Mr F. Scurr, Custodian of the Muniments Room, for Morden College, Blackheath; to the Lieutenant Governor and Secretary for the Royal Hospital, Chelsea; to the Secretary, Royal Blackheath Golf Club, for Eltham Lodge, Kent; to the Divine Mercy College at Fawley Court, Henley-on-Thames, Oxfordshire; to the Secretary, Richmond Golf Club for Sudbrook Lodge, Petersham, Surrey; to the Headmaster, the Alexander Duckham Memorial School, R.A.F. Benevolent Fund, for Vanbrugh Castle, Blackheath; to Lord Brabourne and the Caldicott Community for Mersham-le-Hatch, Ashford, Kent; to the Viscount Scarsdale for Kedleston, Derby; to Lord Harewood for Harewood House, Yorkshire; to the Hon. A. A. Vanneck for Heveningham Hall, Suffolk; to the Headmaster, Woodhall Park (Boys' Preparatory School), Hertford; to the Matron, Grovelands Hospital, Southgate, for Southgate Grove, N.14; to Mrs Arthur Hill for Denton

Hall, Yorkshire; to the Australia and New Zealand Bank Limited for Tyringham Park, Buckinghamshire; to the Headmaster, Park House School, for Peper Harow, Godalming, Surrey; to Mr Simon Whitbread for Southill Park, Biggleswade, Bedfordshire; to the Mother Superior of St Joseph's for Croome Court, Worcestershire; to the Manager, Mr H. G. Cornford, for the Macclesfield Card Factory of Messrs Henry and Leigh Slater Ltd; to the Rev J. S. Cammack, Manresa College, Roehampton, for Harlaxton Hall, Lincolnshire; to the Principal, Richmond College, Surrey; to the Bursar, Mr Bernard L. H. Alder, for Ashridge Park, Berkhamsted, Hertfordshire; to Mr B. P. Dolan, St Mary's, Toddington, for Toddington Manor, Gloucestershire; to Lord Carnarvon for Highclere Castle, Newbury; to the Principal, St Katharine's College, Liverpool, for Scarisbrick Hall, Lancashire; to the Matron, Park Hospital, Moggerhanger, Bedfordshire; to Sir Christopher Codrington for Dodington Park, Gloucestershire; to the High Master, Mr A. N. Gilkes, for St Paul's School, West Kensington, W.14; to the Head Master for Lancing College, Sussex; to the Matron, Grim's Dyke, Harrow Weald, Middlesex; to the Headmaster, Mr F. G. R. Fisher, Bryanston School, Blandford, Dorset; to Mrs Mary Ling, the Orchard, Chorleywood, Hertfordshire; to the Principal, Royal Holloway College (University of London), Englefield Green, Surrey; to the Headmaster of St Cuthman's School, Stedham, Midhurst for 'Wispers'; to the Warden, House of the Sacred Mission, Kelham, Newark, Nottinghamshire, for Kelham Hall; to Mr C. J. Pethed, Managing Director, N. G. Bailey and Co. Ltd, for Heathcote, Ilkley, Yorkshire; to Mr Lacon for Great Maytham, Rolvenden, Kent; to Mr Pollen for the Deanery, Sonning, Berkshire; to the Warden, Mr J. B. F. Brackenbury, for the Village College, Impington, Cambridgeshire; to Sir Roger Conant for the 'Pastures', North Luffenham, Rutland; to Miss Mary Parker for Feathercombe, Hambledon, Godalming, Surrey; to the Boots Pure Drug Co. Ltd for their factory at Beeston, Nottinghamshire; to the Abbot for Nashdom Abbey, Burnham, Buckinghamshire; to Mr and Mrs Hall for Goddards, Abinger Common, Surrey; to Lady Manton for Plumpton Place, Sussex; to the Assistant General Manager, National Provincial Bank Limited, for Middleton Park, near Bicester, Oxfordshire; to Miss Constance Chapman for Tigbourne Court, Hambledon, Surrey; to the Headmistress, Miss M. Miles, for Mayfield Comprehensive School, Putney, S.W.15; to the Headmaster, Mr F. A. Hobart for Churchfields Comprehensive School, West Bromwich; to Messrs Mott, Hay and Anderson, and in particular to Mr A. E. Temple and to Mr Hamilton (Resident Engineer, Forth road bridge) for the new Forth road bridge and the Runcorn–Widnes road bridge; to Sir Basil Spence for Coventry Cathedral; to Mr Arthur Ling, City Architect and Planning Officer for the Coventry City Centre; to Mr K. H. Saunders, Assistant Chief Architect for Crawley New Town, Sussex; to Mr R. H. Coates, Divisional Controller, Central Electricity Generating Board, for Marchwood Generating Station, Southampton; to the Central Electricity Generating Board, and in particular to Mr P. J. Field and Mr Magee for Berkeley and Bradwell nuclear power stations; to the Headmistress of Fairlawn Primary School, Honor Oak, London; to the Headmaster, Mr M. W. Williams, for Hallfield Junior Mixed School, London, W.2; to the Principal, Mr C. Chew, for the Leeds College of Technology; to the Principal, Mr J. Hiles and to the architects, Messrs Gollins, Melvin, Ward and Partners, for the Sheffield College of Technology; to the Principal, Mr W. F. Stephenson, for Luton College of Technology; to the Principal, Mr C. Whitworth, for the Royal College of Advanced Technology, Salford, Lancashire; to the Bursar, University of Sheffield; to the

Manager, Mr Bradshaw, for the Seed Warehouses of Messrs Cooper, Taber and Co. Ltd, at Witham, Essex; to the British Broadcasting Corporation for the Television Centre, London; and to Mr Frederick Gibberd for supplying a photograph of the model of his design for the Metropolitan Cathedral, Liverpool, and for giving his permission for the author to make the drawing in figure 1435b from this photograph.

The author would also like to thank the publishers Messrs B. T. Batsford Ltd and especially Mr Samuel Carr for the quantity of invaluable material placed at her disposal from the Batsford book collection. Further useful material has been provided by Mr McColvin from the library at The Polytechnic, Regent Street, W.1. The opportunity to study and to borrow books from the library at the Royal Institute of British Architects has proved extremely helpful. Finally, grateful thanks are due to Mr John Yarwood for his inexhaustible patience in taking and printing photographs and in editing the manuscript and to Miss C. Waight for typing it.

The Author and publishers wish to thank the following for permission to reproduce the photographic illustrations included in this book:

Aerofilms and Aero Pictorial Ltd for plates VI, XII, XIII and XXXIII; Stewart Bale Ltd for plate LIX; British Broadcasting Corporation for plate LXIV(a); British Travel and Holidays Association for colour plate 4; J. Allan Cash, F.R.P.S., for plates III, XI and XIV; *Country Life* for plates XXVII and LIII; Eric de Maré for plates IV, L and LXII; Herbert Felton, F.R.P.S., for plates I and XX; F. Frith & Co. for plate XV; Central Electricity Generating Board for plate LXIV(b); A. F. Kersting, F.R.P.S., for colour plates 1–3, 5 and 6, and for plates VII, XVI, XXIV, XXVI, XXIX, XXXII, XXXVII, XXXIX, XLIV, XLVII, LI, LII, LIV–LVI, LVIII, LX, LXI and LXIII; Ministry of Public Buildings and Works (Crown Copyright reserved) for plates V and XXIII; National Buildings Record for plate XXXV; Kenneth Scowen, F.R.P.S., for plates VIII and XXI; Edwin Smith for plates II, IX, X, XVII–XIX, XXII, XXV, XXX, XXXIV and XLI–XLIII; Warberg Institute for plate XXXVIII; A. C. K. Ware for plate XXXI.

Plates XXVIII, XXXVI, XL, XLV and XLIX are from the publisher's collection.

NOTE

The figures in parentheses in the text refer to the illustrations: line-drawings are denoted by Arabic numerals, photographic plates by Roman numerals.

CHAPTER I

Early Architecture in Britain until 1066

PREHISTORIC TIMES: STONE AGE TO A.D. 43

The tangible remains of the homes, forts, temples and burial chambers of the prehistoric period (i.e. before the existence of written records) are more of archaeological than of architectural value. In order, therefore, to present even a tentative picture of the activity in building of these times, it is necessary to consider in outline what is known of the history and life of the early inhabitants of Britain. Moreover, in attempting to obtain a clearer view of our predecessors, useful evidence results from the study of those peoples of the world who are still living in a primitive manner at the present time, as, for example, the various tribes in New Guinea.

In the latter part of the **Palaeolithic Age**, many peoples came westwards and northwards to Britain from the Continent as the Ice Age was ending, and while the land bridge still spanned what is now the English Channel. Such newcomers settled in the south-east of Britain and gradually moved west and north as more immigrants came after them. It was still very cold in winter and mankind lived in **caves** with, perhaps, a branch and bracken, or turf and heather 'door' acting as a lean-to shelter (1). In summer, a wind-break or primitive **hut**, open at each end, would probably be built of branches, bracken, mud, turf and heather (2).

With the **Mesolithic Age** (from about 10,000 years ago to 3000 B.C.) came a warmer climate and consequent melting of the ice. This, together with a land subsidence, produced the English Channel and the North Sea. Though Britain was then cut off by water from the Continent, the south and east coasts were still low-lying, the rivers navigable and the land a fertile plain. The influx from the Continent therefore continued in successive stages, while the mountains and forests situated in the north and west provided shelter as earlier inhabitants dispersed before the advent of newcomers. Thus, Britain became a mingled race or races with many different ideologies and ways of life. **Caves** were still in use in winter time, and examples of these can be found, with evidence of successive periods of habitation, in Yorkshire, North and South Wales, Devonshire and, particularly, the Mendips where the famous Wookey Hole is situated. **Huts** were often used, of various constructions, and of materials which differed from one part of the country to another, according to what was most easily available. Foundations and traces of stone huts have been found, but in the majority of areas wood, turf, branches, etc., were still in more common use, and these have, of course, disappeared. Some idea of their construction, however, can be gained from the cave drawings on the Continent, particularly in France and Spain. The tent design was apparently in general use (2) with branch ridge pole and open ends, while the beehive shape in stone or branches

SUGGESTED RECONSTRUCTIONS OF PREHISTORIC HUTS
20,000 B.C.–A.D. 43

1 Cave with lean-to cover of brush, heather and branches   2 Upper Palaeolithic type of hut of branches, turf, bracken and mud   3 Neolithic style of hut of branches, saplings and turf set in an earth bank—central pole   4 Beehive hut of branches, saplings, turf and mud   5 Later Neolithic style of hut built on dry stone walls   6 Dry-stone beehive hut   7 Iron Age hut on pattern of Glastonbury lake village—central poles, wattle and daub walls, turf and thatch roof   8 Iron Age version of farmhouse—similar construction to Fig. 7   9 Hut with ridge-pole, earth mound base

and turf was another early pattern (4, 6). Both these constructions lacked headroom; they had no walls, and the branches were pushed into the ground or into an earth wall.

Neolithic man (*c.* 3000–1800 B.C.) began to farm land, whereas his predecessors had lived solely by hunting and fishing. He was consequently more settled in one locality, until a new group of peoples came from the Continent to displace him. Little more than foundations and post holes have been found of his dwelling places. It is probable, however, that huts of the earlier design were used but, it is thought, with more headroom provided by digging a circular pit first and inserting the supporting branches in the earth mound created by the diggings which surrounded the hut. The hut was thus partly below ground and gained in stability. A central pole was likely as support (3).

By the **Bronze Age** period (*c.* 1800–500 B.C.) more solid dwellings were being built in south-east England where few caves were available; winter huts were built also. The general plan was to dig a pit first, and set the supports into an earth bank, or stone wall if the material was available. Covering for the branch structure was provided by fur skins, grass sods or turf, bracken, heather and thatch (5). In areas where stone was plentiful, numerous **hut circles** have been found, also foundations of different hut designs on a courtyard plan. The simplest form of dry-stone hut was of beehive shape, containing one room, and a small door-way with two stone uprights and a lintel, generally only about 3 feet high. The diameter of the hut varied from 8 or 9 feet to as much as 20 feet. They were often in groups with surrounding low stone walls for protection. Cattle pounds were also enclosed by walls. Floors were of beaten clay and hearths of clay or stone. Roofing was provided by thatch and turf on top of the stone (6).

With the **Iron Age** in Britain (from about 500 B.C. to the coming of the Romans) more varied hut designs were in use. The circular plan was frequently adopted in stone or wood. In the latter case, instead of digging a deep pit, a wall of dry-stone construction was built, and the supports set into it (5). Alternatively, a tent shape was used, with ridge-pole and a vertical support at each end (9). Thatch was in general use for roofs, and walls were constructed on firm vertical stakes of wood using wattle and daub, the wattle or branching being plaited across the stakes, whilst the coating of daub in the form of mud or clay became hard on baking in the sun. A farmhouse of a similar type of construction can be seen in Fig. 8. During this period, numerous waves of newcomers arrived from the Continent, and brought new skills and ways of life with them. Each successive contingent drove the previous immigrants west and north. Consequently, throughout the country, there is a considerable variation in plan and design of inhabited sites of which we have knowledge through the excavations and investigations of archaeologists.

Stone dwellings were sometimes now on a more complicated plan, comprising a central open courtyard with rooms arranged round it and roofed with turf and branches. This appears to be modelled on the Roman villa design, but pre-Roman examples are known, particularly in Cornwall, though later examples are found in Wales and Anglesey. The simple, circular, dry-stone hut was still in use, built both singly and in groups, and remains of many of them are to be found on Dartmoor.

One of the most interesting forms of community living of which evidence is available is that of the **lake-dwellings**. These flourished on a large scale on the Continent, especially in France and Germany. The relics of those in Switzerland and Austria are famous; outstanding examples are those that existed on Lake Zürich. The majority of Continental lake-dwellings were of the Neolithic and Bronze Age periods. These were usually erected on a wooden platform supported on piles sunk into the actual lake bed. In the British Isles, lake-dwellings were most common in the Iron Age; remains of many examples exist to this day. In Scotland and Ireland they generally took the form of crannogs, or artificial islands made of wood, trees, earth, brushwood and stone and surrounded by a stockade of wood piles. They were constructed in swamp or marsh areas and on the edges of lakes, with often only a few dwellings in each case. In England it was more usual to build up from shallow water or marshy ground on a wood platform resting on piles or layers of brushwood and small trees, and kept in place by piles round the edge, sunk into the lake bed. Remains of such sites have been found, especially in East Anglia and in Holderness in East Yorkshire—both marshy lake areas in this period—but our best examples are those of **Glastonbury** and **Meare** in Somerset, where the community dwellings were inhabited from about 300–250 B.C. onwards. At Glastonbury, a palisade of posts enclosed an area of some 2–2½ acres. A platform of 3–4 feet in thickness rested on peat, clay and brushwood over the whole enclosure. This platform was made of logs with extra strengthening under the actual hut sites. Of these sites, 89 have been found, but it is thought that only 60–70 of them were occupied by huts for human habitation. The huts were circular in plan and varied in diameter from 14 to 40 feet. The floors were of clay on the wooden platform. The walls were formed by wood posts driven into the clay floor and made solid with wattle and daub. The roofs were supported on a central post—or two or three posts set near to the centre of the hut—and were thatched. The hearth was of clay or stone with a hole in the roof above it as a smoke exit. Hearths varied in size from 2½ to 5½ feet across. Subsidence into the peat took place in time, so that further floors and hearths had to be superimposed when necessary. The hut area was often enlarged at the same time. In some instances as many as 10 floors have been found on top of one another. Hut walls were about 6 feet high surmounted by wall plates to bear the rafters, and it is presumed that huts had cross timbers to counteract the outward thrust of the roof. It is not known if the huts had windows, but there were doors of wood or hurdle work. The width of the doorways varied from 4 to 6 feet. The entrances to huts were paved on timber foundations.

Little trace of the hut superstructures have been found, only charred remains, presumably the result of later destruction of these homes. Whether this was due to attack from other peoples, or whether the site was razed before the inhabitants moved elsewhere, is not known. Certainly these areas were becoming less wet, and therefore unsuitable for safe habitation; for without doubt, these sites were built and inhabited in this way as a protection from other tribes and peoples. Fear must have been strong and real to demand the labour of bringing materials to the spot, and erecting homes, and keeping them safe from the ever-present suction from beneath. Trees and brushwood were available *in situ*, but clay and stone must have been brought by canoe. A pier or landing stage was built on to the outer palisade, and contact with their agriculture on dry land was maintained by these canoes, while withdrawal to the village could be swift if need arose.

A bird's-eye-view reconstruction of the Glastonbury lake village can be seen in Fig. 14; a suggested reconstruction of a typical hut there in Fig. 7; a hut foundation in Fig. 11.

Prehistoric **hill-forts** provide further evidence of the building activities of man, and, as

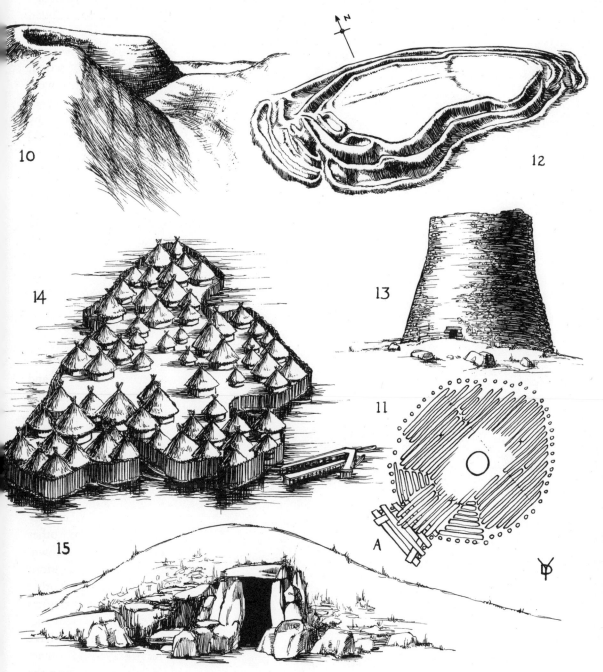

10 Earthworks at Maiden Castle, Dorchester. Iron Age   11 Plan of foundation of usual hut design in Glastonbury lake village. Centre circle represents hearth and surrounding area the clay floor. Timber foundation and wall posts are marked around these. Entrance at A. Diameter of hut *c*. 25 ft
12 Bird's-eye view of the Maiden Castle hill-fort. Length from east to west approx. 6/10 mile
13 Dry-stone Scottish broch or castle. Iron Age   14 Bird's-eye-view reconstruction of Glastonbury lake village. Iron Age   15 Entrance to Bronze Age round barrow

in the case of lake villages, it was an effort inspired by fear. These hill-forts were defensive in character, designed to safeguard those living within from outside attack. Most of these forts in Britain, particularly those of complicated design and monumental scale, are from the Iron Age. They were on carefully selected sites on eminences which provided uninterrupted views of the surrounding countryside, and with good grazing land for the cattle. The earthworks comprising the fort were often dug on an impressive scale, especially considering the primitive tools available. They consisted of ditches and ramparts with protected entrances and exits. The bottoms of these ditches were sometimes protected by sharpened stakes, and the rampart tops with palisades. Within the earthworks were hut circles and storage accommodation, also shelter for the stock. Examples of these forts can be seen in many parts of Britain, in North Wales and on the South Downs, but Dorset provides the principal sites, the most impressive of which is that of **Maiden Castle**, near Dorchester. It is not the largest of such forts, but has defensive lines on a massive and complicated plan. The site was inhabited by Neolithic and Iron Age settlers, though the chief contribution of the former took the shape of small-scale ditches, and an immense mound or barrow, 1,790 feet long and 60 feet wide, now set in the middle of later earthworks. The Iron Age contributions were chronologically in several phases from about 300 B.C. until the final storming and taking of the fort by the Romans about A.D. 45–50. By the first century B.C., the fortifications were enlarged greatly in defence against the chief weapon of the period—the sling. Several lines of defence were constructed with ditches 8–9 feet deep and 70 feet wide, providing an outer sloped ramp of some 80 feet at an angle of 40 degrees—a formidable obstacle to scale at speed while being attacked from the ramparts above. Approaches were also remodelled at this time and in the first century A.D. to give a complex system of interlocking outworks with entrances adequately covered by fire from the ramparts. In fact the defence system was so proof that it was not defeated until the Romans came to attack with quite different weapons. Within the fort were innumerable hut sites and storage pits. A bird's-eye view of Maiden Castle, and a portion of the ramparts, can be seen illustrated in Figs. 12 and 10.

In the Neolithic and Bronze Ages, great effort in building and digging was devoted to burial mounds or **barrows**. Neolithic burial mounds were in the form of long barrows, roughly egg-shaped in plan, but varying greatly in size. Inside these, burial chambers were constructed with large stones or monoliths, and the bodies were covered with earth. Bronze Age barrows were generally round with similar store-chambers inside. Examples of these can be seen in Figs. 15–17.

Finally we come to the remaining form of constructional effort by prehistoric man: that of **standing stones**, either singly or in sacred circles. Examples of single standing stones— **monoliths** as they are termed—are very common in Britain, particularly in stone and mountain areas, and as far afield as in the Hebrides. There is still considerable speculation as to their purpose and meaning. Some are natural formations left behind by retreating glaciers, but others may have been placed to mark burial sites or land divisions (19). Groups with two or more upright standing stones and a horizontal stone or lintel supported on them were also common. These are known as **dolmens** or **cromlechs** (18). The most interesting and impressive standing stones are those arranged in circles, again for an unknown purpose, but generally taken to be for some kind of worship, so they are termed sacred circles. The largest of these is the circle at **Avebury**, Wiltshire, which is set inside a ditch and bank. The ditch has now silted up a good deal, but is still on a grand scale, the circumference of the site being some 4,440 feet. A road now cuts the circle in two parts, and some of the stones are missing, but even so the general view is imposing (24). Avebury is considered to be dated about 1800–1500 B.C. Other good examples can be seen at **Windmill Hill**, near Avebury, and **Keswick**, Westmorland, while on the Island of **Lewis** in the Hebrides is the Callanish stone circle.

The best-known of these circles is **Stonehenge**, which stands in windswept loneliness on Salisbury Plain. Though smaller in circumference than the circle at Avebury, the stones are larger and the design more elaborate. It is composed of two circles of stones enclosing two smaller horseshoe stone formations. The outer circle, known as the **Sarsen** ring, originally had 30 standing stones some 10 feet apart (centre to centre) and standing $13\frac{1}{2}$ feet above ground. On top of them were 30 lintel stones, cut to the curve of the circle, and fitted by mortise and tenon joints. The diameter of the circle was 97 feet. Within this was a circle of some 76 feet diameter, of smaller, standing **bluestones**. The larger horseshoe comprised originally five sets of **trilithons** (three stones) increasing in height to the centre trilithon, which was $25\frac{1}{2}$ feet from ground to top of lintel. Within this was a smaller horseshoe of 19 bluestone standing stones. The famous **altar stone** (now partly buried below other fallen stones) was set at the foot of the great trilithon. As can be seen in the plan of Stonehenge in Fig. 20, outside the stone circles are some holes called Y and Z holes, set in a rough circle

BRYN CELLI DHU, ANGLESEY: BRONZE AGE TUMULUS *c.* 1500 B.C.

16

17

16 Entrance from exterior   17 Interior of barrow. Walls and roof of rock

18 Dolmen 19 Monolith at Avebury 20 Plan of Stonehenge showing ditch, bank, Aubrey holes, Z and Y holes, and stone circles. Altar stone is marked A, standing stones ■, fallen stones ▨, missing stones ▢. Diameter bank to bank *c.* 320 ft 21 Granite clapper bridge 22 Stonehenge, Wiltshire 23 The two trilithons at Stonehenge with smaller, bluestones of inner horseshoe in front 24 Avebury village, Wiltshire: stone circle, bank and ditch in foreground

some 5–15 feet and 35 feet respectively outside the Sarsen circle, but there is no evidence about their purpose. Further out again came the Aubrey holes, named after the antiquary who mentions them in 1666. From measurements on radioactive carbon taken in 1950, they are dated at about 2123–1573 B.C. A bank and ditch surround the monument and the bank measures 320 feet in diameter. A single entrance breaks this in the form of an avenue with parallel pairs of ditches and banks some 70 feet apart. There is still great controversy regarding the date and purpose of Stonehenge and over the method of transport of the stones themselves. The best evidence seems now to date the monument at about 1800 B.C. but, like many great building achievements, it is not all of the same period. The earliest features are the bank, ditch and Aubrey holes with entrance, while the Sarsen circle and trilithons were erected later, and the bluestones later still. The stones were dressed by pounding with a round stone, but this was not done at the site. They are thought to have been erected by being slid down an incline into the ready-dug hole, and then being pulled upright. The lintels must have been pulled up on a wooden ramp into position. All the stones were brought some distance—the sarsens from north Wiltshire, the bluestones from Pembrokeshire, and the altar stone from Glamorgan, but it is not established by which route or method. The sacred circle is thought to be a temple, presumably connected with sun worship, judging by its alignment, but it is difficult to confirm this because the exact date is not known, and so evidence is lacking of the position of the sun at the time that the temple was erected. It is nevertheless certain that its building was not connected in any way with the Druids, to whom it was once popularly attributed, as they were Iron Age peoples of much later date (20, 22–3).

Two miles away from Stonehenge is the similarly planned circle known as **Woodhenge**, consisting of a shallow, broad ditch, with outer bank, and within this the socket holes of timber posts arranged in six oval rings one inside the other.

The most usual way of crossing or **bridging** a river in prehistoric times was by a large tree, which may have fallen or have been cut down for the purpose. Rope bridges were used later and, by the Iron Age, bridges with log platforms supported on wood piles sunk into the river bed, in the same fashion as for the lake-dwellings. **Stepping stones** were an alternative method (62). The usual design for **stone bridges**, which were comparatively rare, was the **clapper-bridge** type of which a few examples still exist. They are difficult to date, but the use of large monolithic slabs, laid on dry-stone piers is reminiscent of the work on the sacred stone circles (21). A famous English version, thought to be some 1,500–2,000 years old, is the **Post Bridge** over the Dart on Dartmoor. The granite slabs used are massive, some 14–15 feet in length. Other examples can be found in Devonshire, also in Yorkshire and Lancashire.

ROMAN BRITAIN A.D. 43–410

From A.D 43 until early in the fifth century, Britain became a province or colony of Rome. Julius Caesar had made two landings in 55 and 54 B.C., but these were only small-scale raids and had no perceptible effect on Britain's way of life. From 54 B.C. to A.D. 43, southern Britain and Rome were on friendly terms and Romans came from Gaul to visit and trade. When the long-expected invasion came in A.D. 43, the south and east of Britain quickly fell to the advancing legions of Claudius; the Britons were ill-organised, at loggerheads with one another, and outmatched in tactics and arms. Within a short space of time the Romans had occupied the south of England and the midlands but, as others before them, met rebuffs in the mountain and forest areas of Wales and the north. However, they were persistent, and although their occupation of these areas meant constant military surveillance and adequate fortification, held them during their stay. Many attempts were made to conquer Scotland but, in general, failed completely, while Ireland was left alone. The area of **Roman occupation**, therefore, was more or less that of present-day England and Wales, but it was the south and east which became Romanised and, with a mixture of stock, evolved into a Romano-British population, while Wales and the north continued in a state of intermittent fighting with little or no mingling of races or ideas. It is largely due to this fact that there are so few Roman architectural remains in Britain today, and that the imprint of Roman civilisation vanished almost as if it had never been. For, during 400 years of occupation, the Romano-British in southern England ceased to fight or quarrel amongst themselves, and the only soldiers were the Roman professional ones. When the legions were withdrawn in the early fifth century this area of England was left helpless, and became an easy prey to invaders from the Continent. These invaders came to settle, occupy, massacre and destroy—unlike the Romans who had come to enslave, tax and administer—and southern England suffered numerous waves of such invaders between A.D. 410 and 1066. In Wales and the north, the invaders did less damage for the same reasons that the Romans had less effect there also.

A few years after A.D. 43, the Romans began to settle in their new colony. They started work in lead mines in the Mendips; they took advantage of the waters at Bath; they established London as a commercial city on the Thames; in Wales and the north they built roads, forts, walls and made a network of communication for military occupation and suppression. The three great fortresses at Chester, York and Caerleon were centres of this occupation, and from A.D. 124 Hadrian built his famous stone wall from Solway to Tyne (73 miles) to mark the northern, fortified boundary-line of the Empire. The wall was 8 feet thick and 12 feet high, built with 80 forts and 320 watch-towers set at intervals to house the soldiers and for use in communication.

The Romans lived in cities and laid out and built several of these in Britain during their stay. The principal ones were Colchester, York, Gloucester, St Albans, London and Lincoln, though many smaller towns were erected also. It is probable that much remains to be excavated from such cities, for during the ensuing years many generations have rebuilt on the same site, covering the Roman remains to a depth of feet with rubble, dust and masonry. During the rebuilding subsequent to the bombing of World War II, more has been discovered in such cities, but the chief discoveries have come from towns where the modern site has been displaced from the Roman choice. Such towns include Verulamium (St Albans), Silchester (near Reading), and Wroxeter (near Shrewsbury). The Romans built **city walls** with gateways for entrance and exit, and it is fragments of these walls which constitute one of the commonest type of Roman remains today. The most complete and clear examples are at Lincoln, Leicester, Silchester, Caerwent, Colchester, London and York. Roman walls were commonly built of concrete or rubble with bonding layers of bricks (like flat tiles) at intervals. The Roman mortar was very hard, and was made of pulverised brick mixed with lime. Many walls were faced with cut stone; alternatively, in a smaller number of instances, the walls were entirely of large, squared stone blocks. In some areas flint facings were used. Some city walls were 9–10 feet wide at the base, but generally lessened by sets-off towards the top which

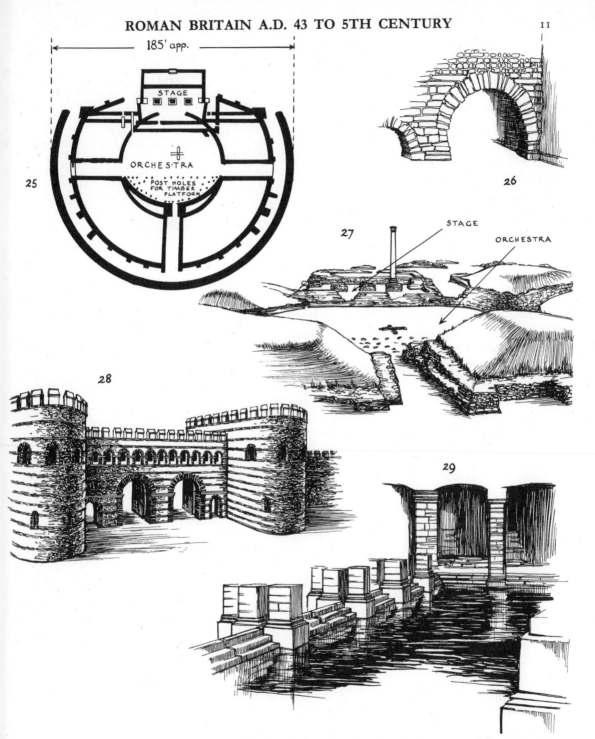

25 Simplified plan of Roman theatre at Verulamium, 2nd and 3rd centuries A.D.   26 Roman gateway   27 Remains of Roman theatre at Verulamium   28 Suggested reconstruction of typical Roman town gate. Bonding courses and arch openings of brick, 2nd century A.D.   29 Great Roman bath at Aquae Sulis (Bath), 1st century A.D. The bath has lead lining. Water surface area 82 ft × 40 ft. Hot springs still functioning

30

31

would be up to 20 feet above the ground. Additional security was provided by a ditch dug outside the wall. Watch-towers and gateways were set at intervals. Arch openings of windows, doorways, entrances, etc., were generally turned with Roman bricks. Examples of Roman walling and fortification can be seen in Figs. 26, 28, 30–1 and 39.

The Romans were good builders and made the best use of **materials** to hand, while preserving similar styles of work over the whole of their domain. In Britain, there were fewer examples of larger buildings than in Italy or the rest of the Continent, and work was less lavishly decorated. The country was a northern outpost of the Empire, and, being colder and damper than the other regions, was less suited to open-air courts. The Romans used **brick-work** a considerable amount, both for bonding courses, arch facings, and in the form of complete walls. Their bricks were flat, like tiles, and were therefore distinctive from the early Medieval bricks which appeared in the thirteenth century. Roman bricks found in Saxon work were simply a re-use by the Saxons of Roman materials to hand, as at Brixworth Church, Northamptonshire. The Romans used **plaster** in abundance; it was red in colour, made from pulverised bricks and was thus very hard. They used it for walls and floors chiefly. Many of their floors were of fine **mosaic**; the *tesserae* were of stones and/or small cubes in vivid colours to form most decorative and complicated designs. They were used in villas and all public buildings (32–4).

Towns were laid out carefully, often in rectangular blocks, and were highly symmetrical. Streets divided these blocks. Silchester was one example of such planning, whilst traces can be seen in Chester, Exeter and Gloucester.

The Roman **arch** was round, made with cut stones or bricks. In the latter instance, bricks were generally in two rows, set edgeways, one above the other. Sometimes brick and stone were combined to make the arch. Roman **vaulting** was of concrete rubble or of stone blocks and mortar. Their groined vaults were constructed on brick arches whose under sides were plastered and decorated with colour. Roman vaults were heavily and solidly made, and often covered very great spans.

In larger buildings, particularly the **basilica**, colonnades were built, using a modified version of Roman Doric or Corinthian capitals with Attic bases (40–1). The Roman basilica was a large hall used as a market. At one or both ends was the semicircular tribune, where the judge sat to dispense justice. The hall was generally rectangular in plan, and divided lengthways by a row of columns on each side, giving a wide centre space flanked by aisles. The Roman **forum** was the town market place, generally square in plan, with the shops and stalls arranged round the sides.

The houses or **villas** constituted one of the chief contributions of the Romans to our architecture, but their destruction has been so complete that all that is left to us is their foundations, plans, mosaic pavements and heating systems. However, from what is left, together with our knowledge of contemporary houses in Italy and other Roman provinces, we can gather a fairly clear picture of them. Houses of the first and second centuries A.D. were comparatively small and simply planned, while the third century was a time of unsettlement and raids. So it is the fourth century which primarily produced the very large country houses so typical of the wealthy Romano-British population. The Roman villa at **Chedworth** Gloucestershire, was one of this type. Most houses in town and country were planned on a corridor basis or round one or more courts. In Italy, the idea was to have corridors opening into such courts, and to be thus shielded from the sun's glare; in Britain, this plan seems to have prevailed, though it is thought that the court or **atrium** would be roofed over in many instances. The courtyards were often colonnaded in larger homes, with a good deal of stonework used in construction. In the corridor-designed homes, the windows still faced the back of the house and opened on to a colonnaded veranda. The foundations were of concrete,

EXAMPLES OF ROMAN MOSAIC PAVEMENTS

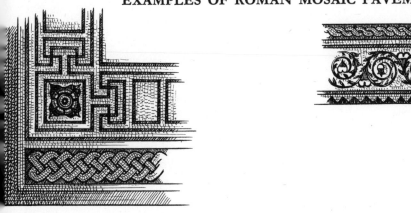

32

33

34

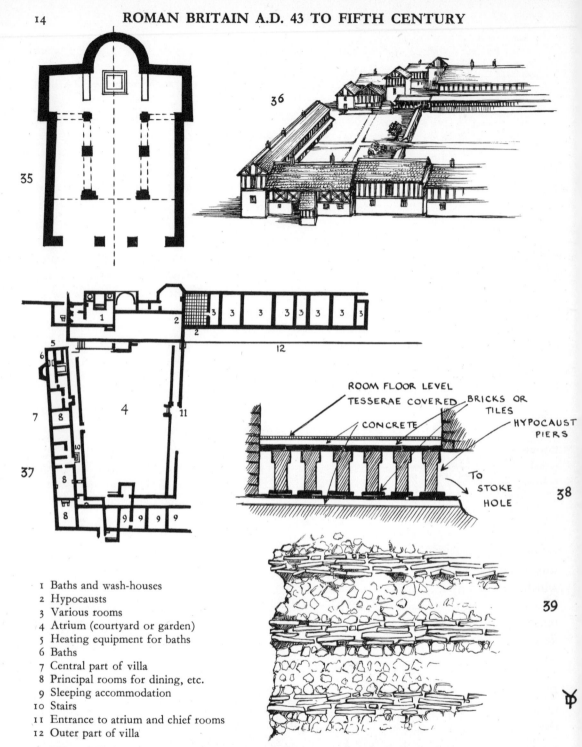

1 Baths and wash-houses
2 Hypocausts
3 Various rooms
4 Atrium (courtyard or garden)
5 Heating equipment for baths
6 Baths
7 Central part of villa
8 Principal rooms for dining, etc.
9 Sleeping accommodation
10 Stairs
11 Entrance to atrium and chief rooms
12 Outer part of villa

35 Plan of Christian church at Roman city of Silchester, 4th and 5th centuries A.D.   36 Suggested reconstruction of villa in Fig. 37   37 Plan of larger type of Roman villa, 4th century A.D.   38 Hypocaust method of heating. Section below floor level   39 Example of Roman rubble walling with bonding courses of brick, Verulamium

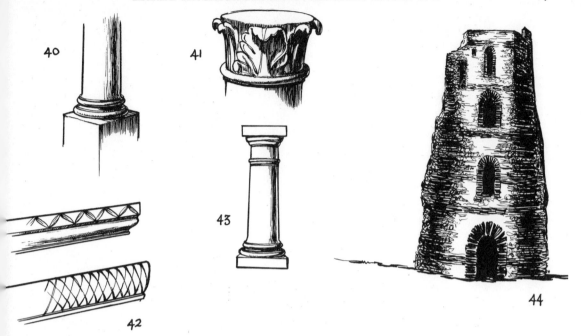

40 Roman column base   41 Part of Roman Corinthian capital (Verulamium)   42 Roman mould-ings and decoration   43 Roman small column or shaft   44 Roman lighthouse (Dover)

stone and brick, but in the majority of homes the superstructure, or at least the upper floors, were of timber and plaster. Roofs were generally covered by small stone slates. Inside, the floors were commonly covered by *tesserae* and the white walls were plastered and usually painted. The layout of the rooms included drawing and dining rooms and other large recep-tion rooms, bedrooms, kitchen and a system of baths. Larger houses had three bathrooms: a cool, warm and hot room—like our system of 'Turkish baths'—called respectively the *frigidarium*, the *tepidarium* and the *calidarium*. These were heated by the general hypocaust method. A water plunge bath was also installed.

Even smaller houses were heated, or at least part of the house. To do this, a hypocaust was situated under the floors. The *tesserae* were laid into a concrete bed on large bricks below which were the hypocaust piers, which in turn were supported on further bricks and con-crete, leaving an air passage between the piers. This passage was connected to a stoke hole outside, kept constantly fuelled. Hot bathrooms generally had the stoke place under the floor itself (38). Other amenities provided by the Romans included drainage, water pipes and window glass.

Apart from Chedworth, notable remains of other Roman villas have been excavated at Bignor, Sussex, Brading, Isle of Wight, Winchcombe, Gloucestershire, and North Leigh, Oxfordshire. A plan of a typical large country villa is shown in Fig. 37, and a suggested reconstruction of it in Fig. 36.

There is little indeed of an architectural nature in Britain to show the growth of the **Christian church** at this time. It is presumed that here, as elsewhere on the Continent, churches were built, especially after the conversion of the Emperor Constantine in A.D. 312, as subsequently Christianity became the dominant religion of the Roman Empire. Presumably such churches were, in general, of timber and have perished. All that has been definitely discovered so far is the foundation and lower walls of a small church at the Roman city of Silchester. This consists (35) of a nave and side aisles with small transeptal projections and one apsidal end. The church is paved with red *tesserae*. The date is uncertain, but the plan coincides with what is accepted as the Roman design for such churches, which were based on that of the *basilica*. At the Roman city of Caerwent another possible example has been discovered.

We have the remains of only one Roman **theatre** in Britain—that at Verulamium. This theatre was added to and altered in various periods after its original construction in about A.D. 140–50. It consisted of an orchestra—the central area—which was sunk below the earth level, and the soil from these excavations was piled up round the outside. Thus the surface all round the orchestra sloped down towards it. From the tiers of wooden seats on these slopes the audience had a good view of the proceedings. At the present time this soil bank has largely disappeared and we can only see the orchestra sunk below normal ground level. The auditorium bank enclosed two thirds of the orchestra, while the stage was set on the open side. It had piers to support columns which were surmounted by Corinthian capitals. The floor was of wood and wood steps led down to the orchestra. The auditorium bank was divided by three gangways leading down into the orchestra. These would have been origin-ally vaulted over to take seats above. In the centre of the orchestra is a cross-shaped cut indentation in the ground, presumed to have been fitted with two cross pieces of wood and a vertical post, but whether for fettering animals or not, we can only surmise. By A.D. 160, nearly half the orchestra space was covered by seating placed on a wood platform; the post holes of the supports are still visible. This gives rise to our name for similar seating—the orchestra stalls. A plan of the Verulamium theatre is shown in Fig. 25 and a sketch of the theatre as it is today in Fig. 27.

A great deal of Roman **bridge** building was thought to be of timber, as so few traces of it are left. Remains of examples of Roman stone bridges on a quite magnificent scale can be found on the Continent, but in Britain we have only pier supports and fragments of arches. Semicircular arches were built and these were supported on massive piers. Some remains have been excavated in Britain while newer bridges were being erected and foundations dug; this applies to both Rochester (Medway) and Newcastle (Tyne). Fords were used by the Romans a great deal for crossing rivers, particularly in country areas.

The principal spa, quickly utilised by the Romans, was Aquae Sulis, the modern city of **Bath**. The Great Bath was further excavated in the nineteenth century, and today can be seen with the steps and pilaster bases, while the original lead lining is still in place. The hot springs there are still functioning as they did for the Romans. The original Roman plan for the bath was of open-air design surrounded by a colonnade. Later this was vaulted over with concrete supported on stone piers. In addition to the bath, there were heated rooms at various temperatures with the usual hypocaust method of construction. Although Bath possesses the most imposing remains of baths, all Roman towns possessed them in larger or smaller degree according to their wealth and population (29).

Britain, or rather England and Wales, was occupied by the Romans for nearly 400 years and their influence on architecture and the arts was tremendous. The question as to why this influence left little or no permanent imprint has been a subject for lively debate for many years. The theory has been advanced that the Roman workmanship here was of poorer quality than on the Continent and the constructional work inferior so that little remains. This is possible, but the writer suggests, however, in common with many others, that 300–400 years of looting, burning and destruction, and of removal of stone and brick for later building by the Saxons and other tribes who overran Britain subsequent to A.D. 410, provide more than adequate reason why so little of the great civilising influence of Rome has survived, and why it was over a thousand years before some of their lost arts and crafts were re-discovered and again applied and appreciated.

SAXON AND CELTIC BRITAIN A.D. 410–1066

From the departure of the Roman legions until the arrival of William of Normandy was, for Britain, a period of mingling and establishment of the British race. Successive waves of invaders came to our shores from late in the third century until 1066. While the Roman occupation lasted, raids by the Saxons from the Continent, the Picts from Scotland and the Scots from Ireland were kept within bounds. But, from the time in A.D. 409 when the Roman Emperor notified Britain that henceforth her towns must defend themselves because Rome itself was threatened, the British Isles were an easy prey to all invaders. In the years till the early part of the seventh century—well named the Dark Ages—when a constructive Saxon way of life began to emerge, Britain was one large battlefield with intermittent fighting, destruction, looting and massacre, both amongst her own peoples and with invaders from overseas. The south and east coasts were constantly assailed from the Continent by the Germanic peoples—themselves being pushed westwards—in particular, Angles, Saxons and Jutes who settled respectively in East Anglia, Mercia, Northumbria; Essex, Sussex, Wessex; Kent and the Isle of Wight. These waves of invaders spread gradually, as had their predecessors, westward and northward, while the earlier Celtic peoples were confined more and more to Cornwall, Wales, Scotland and Ireland.

During the seventh and eighth centuries the Dark Ages receded and a new way of life emerged. Raids became sporadic and almost died out. It is from this time that some of our few earlier Saxon and Celtic examples of architecture have survived to show us a little of the life and work of the times. Monasteries were founded and built whilst learning began more and more to be cultivated and followed.

The ninth century saw the savage and reiterated raids of the Norsemen, plundering all round our coasts, burning and looting. The Saxons were unprepared and ill-equipped to fight; monasteries especially were unprotected, and offered tempting riches at little cost in battle. The destruction at Lindisfarne in A.D. 793 was followed by that at Jarrow in 794 and at Iona in 795. These early raids were precursors of longer and more adventurous visits which increased in intensity till 850. By 865, a Danish invasion army arrived, and was only finally controlled by King Alfred later in the ninth century.

The tenth century was a time of comparative peace and much of the best Saxon architecture dates from this period, but Viking attacks were renewed at the end of the century to culminate in Danish rule from 1016–42. However, building flourished again under this regime, continuing in various fields until the advent of Norman architecture soon after mid-century.

In England, the spread of **Christianity**, which had been gradually seeping into Romanised Britain, was rudely halted and largely destroyed by the Saxon invasion of the fifth and sixth centuries. It was not until A.D. 597 that St Augustine, sent by the Pope, reached Kent, and from his centre at Canterbury began his re-Christianisation of southern England. The belief slowly took root once more, so, despite later set-backs due to Viking invasions, Christianity —and with it the building of churches and monasteries—grew and spread northwards and westwards. In Scotland, Cornwall, Wales and Ireland, where Romanisation had had little or no effect, and which lands largely escaped Saxon onslaughts, Christianity came earlier and spread more steadily. In Scotland, the Celtic church was established and spread chiefly by St Columba and St Ninian. The latter built his church in A.D. 397 in Galloway—a small, un-pretentious church, made of local stone and slate, with clay. From here he went on long and adventurous journeys to convert the people of Scotland, as far as the Orkneys and Shetlands. St Columba, in the sixth century, founded the monastery at Iona, and from here helped to convert the people of southern Scotland and northern England. Later, St Aidan left Iona and founded his monastic settlement at Lindisfarne. Ireland, which was not touched by Roman influence or the Saxon invasions, yet received the spread of Christianity, and her church slowly but steadily expanded. Many monastic centres were founded.

The great majority of **Saxon churches** were constructed of timber, or even timber with wattle and daub, particularly before the tenth and eleventh centuries, so we have only a rough idea of what such buildings were like. The early churches continued to be based on the Roman basilican plan. At first, the altar was at the west end, so the priest faced the east and the congregation. Later the altar was transferred to the east, where it is placed now. Remains of Saxon cathedrals and monasteries are very scanty indeed. This is predominantly because, during the tremendous activity in building instigated by the Normans after their conquest, almost all cathedrals were rebuilt from the foundations, and, in most cases, on the same site as the Saxon predecessor. At Ripon we have a Saxon crypt, possible Saxon work at Gloucester, late Saxon in Westminster Abbey, but little else except foundations and records. In the comparatively numerous examples of smaller, Saxon, stone churches left to us there has been, in the past century, considerable discussion as to whether the work is Saxon or Norman, and of what date. Many churches previously thought to be Saxon are now estab-lished as Norman workmanship and vice versa. In order to assist the reader in recognising Saxon workmanship, its chief characteristics are listed here:

1 **Walls**: not as thick as most Norman examples, generally 2–2½ feet. **Pilaster strips** were often used. These are not buttresses, as Saxon walls are commonly unbuttressed. They are flat, vertical bands of stonework, 6 inches to 1 foot wide, set at intervals on the wall and projecting very slightly. They are for decoration only (47, 49, 54, 55b, 68).

2 **Quoins**: generally treated with **large stones** or long-and-short work. In the former instance, very large, squared stones, up to 3 feet in width, are placed one on top of another with the longest dimension set alternately on one face then on the other (52). In **long-and-short work** a tall, squared stone of up to 4 feet high is put vertically and alternately with a flat slab set horizontally into the wall. This gives a very strong quoining, which has a key in each alternate stone (47, 66, 68). Both pilaster strips and long-and-short quoins are very typical of Saxon work. In each instance, the wall face is set back only an inch or half an inch, and is then plastered to be flush with the quoining.

3 **Plinths**: not always used. Square or chamfered section when seen.

ANGLO-SAXON CHURCHES 7TH TO 11TH CENTURIES A.D.

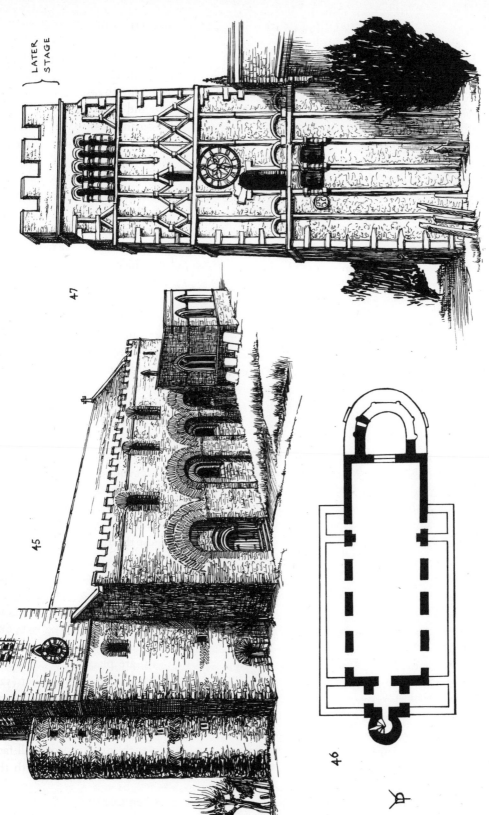

45 Brixworth Church, Northamptonshire, from the south-west. Founded 7th century. Some of work 10th and 11th centuries. A 14th-century spire on top of tower, also later east end addition. Roman bricks used for arches and wall corners set in rubble walling 46 Plan of Brixworth Church. Length c. 120 ft   47 Earl's Barton, Northamptonshire: west tower, south face, early 11th century. Long and short quoins, pilaster strips. Height c. 69 ft

4 **Towers** : generally unbuttressed, square in plan, and set at the west end of the church. Sometimes diminished by sets-off to the top. Lofty in proportion. Inside, the storeys are divided by wooden floors. Stone vaulting is rare. Wooden ladders used from floor to floor.

5 **Windows** : often double-splayed. Arch opening round or triangular. Turned baluster shafts.

The **plan of Saxon churches** now extant varies somewhat. The most typical has a rectangular nave with smaller, rectangular chancel added at the east end. Some churches were very simple indeed, consisting only of a rectangular nave or oratory. Examples of the former design are at Escomb, Co. Durham, Wittering, Northamptonshire, Boarhunt, Hampshire, and Bradford-on-Avon, Wiltshire. **Escomb** (52) has a long, high nave. Typical of Saxon workmanship, its walls, some $2\frac{1}{4}$ feet thick, have quoins made up of large, rectangular blocks of stone, while the windows are internally splayed. A plan of **Boarhunt** is shown in Fig. 51. The church of St Lawrence at **Bradford-on-Avon** is a well-known and fine Saxon example of church building. It is built from local stone in large blocks, well cut and closely fitted. The walls are some $2\frac{1}{2}$ feet thick, rising from a square plinth. Indicative of Saxon decoration is the shallow arcading with reeded pilasters (48).

Another variation in Saxon church plans is the design with rectangular nave and apsidal added chancel, following the plan of the Roman *basilica*. The church of St Pancras, Canterbury, was of this type, but only the foundations and lower walls now remain.

Not many Saxon examples still exist with side aisles to the nave. It is thought that numbers of these were built originally on the basilican plan, especially larger churches in the later Saxon period, for example, the Saxon Canterbury Cathedral, but little remains to see of such churches. **Reculver**, Kent, was one such example on a small scale, but was largely destroyed in the early nineteenth century. From later excavation we can see that it consisted of a nave with apsidal chancel. **Wing**, Buckinghamshire, has retained its basilican plan inside, though the exterior has been greatly altered. It has a polygonal apse and preserves its side aisles. The naves of both these examples are divided from the side aisles with walls pierced by arched openings, rather than by columns supporting the arches. The finest example of a Saxon church on basilican plan is also probably the oldest, that of **Brixworth**, Northamptonshire (45–6). It is a seventh-century church, founded about 680, with a long, rectangular nave, narrow side aisles, an apsidal east end and a square western tower. The church was badly damaged by Viking attacks, and was built up again in the tenth and eleventh centuries, when the west-end stair-turret was added, the side aisles with lean-to roof removed and arcades blocked. The church is large, with a nave 100 feet long and 30 feet wide. It is plainly but well constructed of small pieces of red rag-stone—laid in herringbone manner in places—and with the arches of doors and windows turned with one or two rows of Roman bricks. This workmanship, however, is certainly not Roman as can be seen in the non-radiating brick arches (65). The principle of the radiating arch was not fully understood until Norman building began in England. The western tower is surmounted by a fourteenth-century spire; only the lower stages are Saxon. Set in the nave walls above the original arcade arches are clerestory windows—an unusual feature of this early architecture. These windows are internally splayed. The apse is of semicircular plan inside but polygonal outside.

There are numerous examples of Saxon churches with western towers; in many cases, it

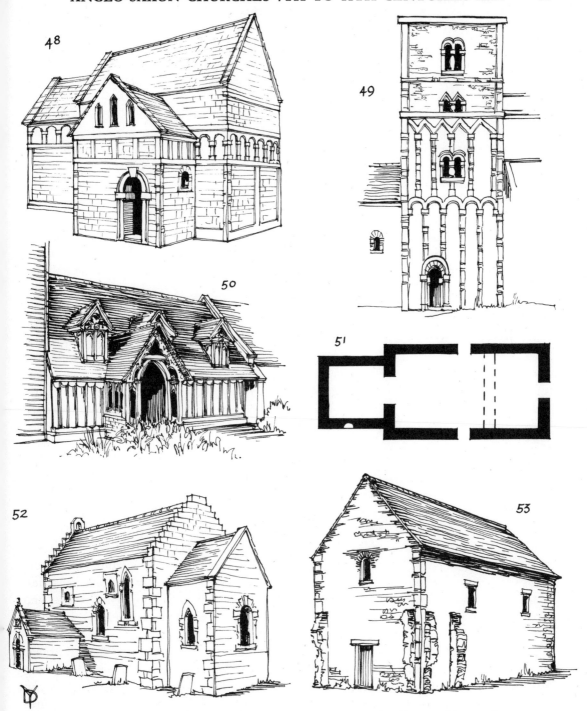

48 Bradford-on-Avon, Wiltshire, 10th century: large stone blocks. Pilaster strips   49 Barton-on-Humber, Lincolnshire, 10th century: tower, belfry stage later   50 Greensted, Essex, 10th century: timber church. Original nave timbers. Other work later   51 Boarhunt, Hampshire, 11th century: plan. Length *c.* 60 ft   52 Escomb, Durham, 7th century: stone blocks   53 St Peter-on-the-Walls, Bradwell, Essex, 10th century: stone, rubble and brickwork

is only the towers that remain to show the Saxon workmanship in such churches, as the remainder has since been altered and enlarged. Among such examples are Earl's Barton, Northamptonshire, Sompting, Sussex, Barnack, Northamptonshire, Barton-on-Humber, Lincolnshire, Dunham Magna, Norfolk, St Benet's, Cambridge, St Michael's, Oxford, and Monkwearmouth, Durham.

Earl's Barton is one of the most famous of these examples as its tower is large, elaborately decorated and in fine condition (47). It is nearly 69 feet high with faces of about 24 feet across. The walls of plastered rubble rise from a square plinth and are 4 feet thick at ground level, decreasing in thickness by sets-off towards the top. The corners have long-and-short quoins, and pilaster strips decorate the faces, though not symmetrically. The western doorway is Saxon and of fine workmanship (63). The fourth stage of the tower—the belfry stage—has an opening on each face, divided into five spaces by turned baluster shafts. Belfry stages in this work generally had such openings for transmission of the sound of the peals, but the Earl's Barton examples are exceptionally large and decorative. The thickness of the wall—some $2\frac{1}{2}$ feet here—is carried on single, square stone pillars, while the baluster shaft support is set forward to the front edge of the opening. This is typical of Saxon design. The top stage of the tower is of later workmanship.

Sompting is noteworthy as it is the only Saxon church tower to have preserved its original top storey, and in this case is of Continental design known as 'German helm' pattern. It is pointed with four flat gable faces 100 feet above the ground. The tower is of plastered rubble with long-and-short quoins and pilaster strip decoration (54).

Barnack also has stone quoins and pilaster strips, but has lost its belfry stage and now possesses an Early English spire. Like **Barton-on-Humber** (49) it is constructed of Barnack stone. The latter example has similar long-and-short quoins, pilaster strip decoration, and both round and triangular-headed windows.

The cruciform plan was not common in Saxon church architecture. The most perfect example we possess is that of **St Mary in Castro** (Dover Castle). **Worth**, Sussex, has a good deal of Saxon work left, and is of this plan with an apsidal east end (55a, b).

The remains of one example of Saxon **timber church-building** still exists at **Greensted**, Essex. In the tenth century a small timber chapel was built there from trunks of large oaks, split and roughly hewn. These were set upright closely together, and let into a sill at the bottom and a plate at the top to form nave walls. They were fastened with wood pins. These timbers still form the nave walls of the little church, although they had to be removed in the nineteenth century, shortened, and set in a brickwork plinth, because of decay at the foot. The original size of the church nave was nearly 30 feet long and 17 feet wide. A later tower, spire and roof have been added (50).

Although the majority of Saxon churches and other buildings must have been of timber of which we have little trace, stone and other fairly permanent materials were used, particularly in the late Saxon work of the tenth and eleventh centuries after the worst Viking raids. **Barnack stone** was used a great deal, quarried in Northamptonshire, and **Roman stonework** from the ruins of their buildings was re-used by the Saxons, as also were **Roman bricks** for quoining and arch turning. In the chalk areas of Britain, **flint** was found and used in building. It had the disadvantage of only being found in smallish pieces and was uncarvable, but is very hard and durable as it is nearly pure silica. Various ragstones were in use,

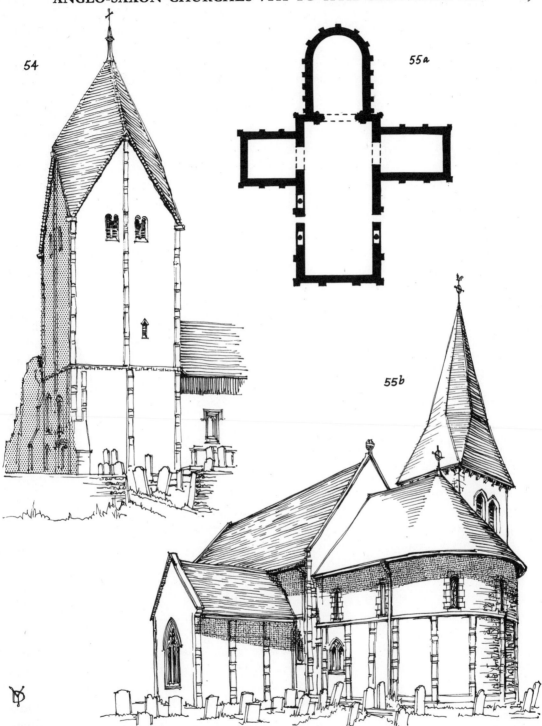

54 Sompting, Sussex, early 11th century: west tower, plaster covered rubble. Pilaster strips and quoins of stone. *c* 100 ft high   55a, b Worth, Sussex, late 10th century: plan and view. Tower later addition. Cruciform and apsidal plan. Pilaster strips and long-and-short work quoins

of better quality in some counties than others. **Roofing** was commonly of thatch or of timber shingles.

From the **Celtic** areas of Britain, architectural remains are chiefly in three categories: chapels or cells, round towers and high crosses. Examples of these can be found in Scotland, Cornwall, Wales and Ireland. Cornwall and Wales have only a few fragmentary remains, Scotland has more, but Ireland possesses them in greatest number and most complete condition. The **chapels** are generally of the simple cell type, made in dry-stone fashion, and often of beehive or near beehive shape. Fine examples are found in the ruins of monasteries where the church is a larger building, and the monks' cells, of beehive shape, cluster round it. One of these is on the island of Skellig Michael—the remains of a monastery of the sixth century. Some monasteries had a group of small chapels instead of one larger church, while a stone wall generally enclosed the community. Stone buildings on a rectangular plan came later, often shaped like an inverted boat, with small doors and windows, having large stones for the lintels and uprights. From the seventh century onwards, mortar was employed, and larger stone oratories and chapels were built. Some of these then had high gable ends and stone roofs, though roofs were also of thatch or timber shingles. Later churches and chapels had a rectangular nave and chancel, and were not single-celled. Barrel vaulting was constructed by using a framework of wattle and daub of the desired completed section, then mortar was poured on to it and stones set in the arch. The framework was removed—usually by burning —when the mortar had set. The gable roof was constructed over this. The best Irish remains are on the lonelier parts of the coast or on the islands, where succeeding civilisations have disturbed them less. Of the dry-stone oratories and chapels, a famous example is the 'Gallarus Oratory' in County Kerry, dated about A.D. 700. On rectangular plan, it has walls leaning inwards in boat shape, while window (3 feet 4 inches high) and door (5 feet 7 inches high) lean in at the same angle (60). The later development is seen in the oratory in Fig. 57, which has tall gables projecting beyond the wall face at each end; this oratory is in Connemara. In coastal areas, some cells were cut into the rock face, and then built with stone on to this.

The **round towers** date from the periods of Viking raids and are thought to have been primarily a defence for persons and valuables; they are mostly of the late ninth and early tenth centuries. The towers are dignified, slender erections, often having a slight inward curve and a conical top. The windows are merely slits and the doorways narrow with round arches. The latter are generally placed some distance up from the ground, about 9 feet or more, and were reached by ladder, which could be withdrawn in event of attack. Inside, the towers were divided into several floors, also served by ladder (59). Such towers were not confined to Ireland, though the majority of examples are there; some are in Scotland, others in England.

Carved standing stones and **high crosses** are found in Ireland and Scotland; there are also some in England. These vary a good deal in size, but are usually ornately carved, often all over, in all kinds of design and motifs from the fret and interlacing patterns to animals, birds, flowers and religious scenes. A number have a wheel or circle enclosing the cross. The majority date from the tenth and eleventh centuries (56, 58, 61).

Saxon **window openings** were round or triangular-headed, set singly or in pairs. They were often double-splayed, that is, had a narrow opening which splayed inwards and outwards. Earlier examples were generally set in the centre of the wall; later versions nearer the

ARCHITECTURE AND DECORATIVE ORNAMENT IN THE BRITISH ISLES
7TH TO 11TH CENTURIES A.D.

56 Saxon cross, England, 8th century 57 Early stone chapel or oratory, Ireland, 8th century
58 Celtic cross, Scotland, 10th century 59 Stone round tower, Ireland 60 Dry-stone building
'Gallarus Oratory', Ireland, 8th century 61 Celtic cross, Ireland 62 River crossing by stepping-
stones

outer face, and then commonly splayed inwards only. In the double-window style, the two lights were generally divided by a shaft or baluster which supported the impost; the latter was a long, rectangular stone carried through the whole thickness of the wall, while the baluster was set nearer the outer face. Some windows had narrow, scroll-mouldings over the round arch, and, as at Earl's Barton, a central cross carved in low relief.

Belfry openings were cut straight through the wall thickness, and were subdivided into two or more openings, each of which was covered by a round arch. A shaft or pilaster separated these openings. The shafts were often turned in baluster form with horizontal decorative bands; alternatively, they were octagonal, oblong or square in section. Capitals were generally cubical, or later, scalloped, while a few were of volute style (64, 67, 70, 72–5).

Doorways, like windows, were round or triangular-headed. Some examples were very plain, others have a framework of stones, or simple mouldings, while a number were turned with Roman bricks (65). The doorways were narrow in proportion to their height. At Earl's Barton tower (63), vertical pilaster strips are taken round the arch, with the arch mouldings set inside them. Square blocks form the imposts.

There are only a few Saxon **crypts** in England; those at Repton and Hexham are the best-known examples, both of the seventh century. Barrel vaulting is used, while both walls and roof are plastered. An illustration of one of the supporting pillars can be seen in Fig. 69.

Bridges were of timber except for the stone clapper designs which were still being made. There is mention of the timber bridge at London in the Anglo-Saxon Chronicle of the eleventh century, but we have little evidence of what it was like.

The Saxons dug **earthworks** to protect their important homes and village groups, particularly after the beginning of the Viking raids. The chief hall or house was of timber, and surrounding huts of timber and wattle and daub. A wood palisade then enclosed these, and the whole site was on top of a natural hill or artificial mound, which in turn was surrounded by a circular ditch or two concentric ditches. The earth from these provided the mound, or alternatively a bank beyond the ditch. Often a double palisade was constructed with a space for cattle in between. Water filled the ditch, which would be spanned by wood planks, removable as necessary.

The Saxons lived in small communities and so did not make use of the Roman houses. They built **homes** almost entirely of timber and wattle and daub, none of which have survived. They used a style of building, however, which was common until Medieval times and which can still be seen in some of the Continental areas from whence it originated. The hall of the Saxon *thegn* was of wood with thatch or wood shingled roof. It was built in bays, each of which was some 16 feet wide, while the number of bays varied according to the wealth of the owner. The bays were divided by and supported on crucks or forks of massive timber, in pairs; these crucks were bent tree trunks meeting at the top to support a ridge-pole. Smaller timbers in between, called rafters, helped to hold up the roofing. Such buildings lacked headroom as the walls and roof were in one piece. Inside, the hall was divided into sleeping and living space for the family, servants, farm-workers and animals. The large majority of people lived in small **huts** of straw or branch framework, covered in turf, bracken, mud and heather, much as their prehistoric ancestors had done. Such huts could be abandoned and rebuilt as the inhabitants were harried to another part of the country by invaders and barbarian raids. **Wattle and daub**—as this method is commonly called—was

DETAILS OF ANGLO-SAXON ARCHITECTURE 7TH TO 11TH CENTURIES

63 Earl's Barton Church, Northamptonshire: western doorway of tower. Height 8 ft 7 in.   64 Earl's Barton Church: belfry opening on south side of tower. Turned balusters   65 Brixworth Church, Northamptonshire: small doorway on south side of tower. Roman bricks used   66 Long-and-short work quoins at Earl's Barton tower   67 Double-splayed window opening, using Roman bricks   68 Pilaster strips at Earl's Barton tower   69 Pillar support from crypt at Repton, Derbyshire   70   Double belfry window. Triangular type   71 Saxon mouldings   72 Baluster shaft   73–4 Saxon capitals   75 Impost and shaft

constructed by a row of vertical stakes or larger branches which were then interwoven horizontally by smaller branches and reeds. Mud was then plastered on one or both sides and left to bake in the sun. The method was in use for houses and huts all through the Medieval period, although, in later times, laths replaced branches and surfaces were plastered and painted on top of the mud. Hair or straw was then mixed with the mud to give greater strength and durability.

CHAPTER II

Norman and Early English Gothic
1066 - 1275

The architecture of Britain during the Middle Ages, from the time of the Conquest to the Reformation, has been classified and designated in numerous and varied ways. In the seventeenth and eighteenth centuries, all such architecture was considered to be 'without just proportion or beauty' and 'dark and melancholy'. It was termed **Gothic** architecture—a label which has been perpetuated—and many scholars hold the view that this name is derived from that of the Goths who sacked Rome in A.D. 410, thus indicating the barbarous quality of this new evolution which replaced classical architecture.

In 1817, **Thomas Rickman**, writer and ecclesiastical archaeologist, considered that this period of Gothic architecture extended from A.D. 1066 to the middle of the sixteenth century, and introduced a classification under period names, which, in general, are still used, though with reservations, by students of architecture at the present day. His terms were Norman, Early English, Decorated English and Perpendicular. These subdivisions replaced the earlier division, into centuries, which was less accurate and less useful.

Since the time of Rickman, many writers, both Victorian and twentieth-century, have given different classification, names and dates to Gothic architecture, but this early description and nomenclature has survived, and is still the one most often used. We have learnt, however, by later study, that it is inaccurate to be too dogmatic in applying specific dates to these subdivisions, because one style merged gradually into another, with a steady evolution as masons, designers and craftsmen became more skilled in the use of their materials. The general architectural style that we call Gothic moved inexorably forward from its massive, clumsy but magnificent beginnings in Norman building, through the dignified simplicity of Early English grandeur to the complexity and wonder of Perpendicular tracery and vaulting, gaining from, and influencing in its turn, activity on the Continent. Each period was merged with the next by a Transitional time, the best-known of which we designate as Transitional Gothic: that which links Norman architecture to the Early English style. In different parts of Britain the onward progress was made at different speeds and in different stages; thus, at Durham Cathedral we have the first use of a stone high vault over the nave, while in the Cloisters of Gloucester Cathedral is an early example of fan-vaulting. Both these are famous and noteworthy patterns, but there are many cases, especially of lesser buildings, which could be discussed to show that one style of Gothic architecture did not prevail over the whole country at any given date.

In this book, therefore, it has been decided to employ the dates and nomenclature most commonly in practice, but the student should bear in mind that, in the use of dates, a hard and fast line should not be drawn. It is considered that the period of **Norman** architecture extended from 1066 to 1150, the **Transitional** style from 1150 to 1200 and the **Early English** from 1200 to 1275. The term Norman is used in preference to Romanesque as it is thought to be simpler and more expressive of the style than the latter, somewhat misleading term. In fact, the Norman style of architecture had been used in England from about 1050 onwards due to the not inconsiderable Norman influence over the English king and nobles during this time. An example of such early Norman-style work can still be seen in Westminster Abbey (founded by Edward the Confessor in 1050) in the dormitory substructure. However, 1066 has been indicated as a starting point because the majority of Norman building was commenced after the Conquest.

The second half of the eleventh and all the twelfth century was a time of prodigious building activity in Britain, and, due to their massive and durable character, a great deal of these buildings remain today, in the form of cathedrals, abbeys and priories, castles and parish churches; only domestic buildings are scarce because these were made primarily of wood, or even less durable materials, or were fortified for defence purposes and are what we should term castles. Tremendous effort was expended on the building of cathedrals; in nearly all cases, the Saxon cathedral was pulled down and a new edifice erected, either on the same site or elsewhere; the Normans began again from the foundations upwards. In the same way monasteries were founded and erected, showing the same tremendous effort and energy. Much of the work was done by Saxons but was supervised by the Normans. Castles and other fortified buildings were vitally necessary to dominate and hold down a people who for some years to come were not as passively inclined as their conquerors could wish. This applied particularly to the west and north of England, where timber castles went up quickly to be replaced in a more leisurely manner by stronger, stone versions. One of the Conqueror's first stone buildings was the **White Tower**, keep of the **Tower of London**, built to show clearly to all his dominance of the capital. Parish churches arose in larger numbers still, though, in many cases, a great deal of the work was Saxon; there are today many English villages which boast their Norman church with squat, square tower and ageing, massive, creeper-covered walls.

In general, the **Norman buildings** were much larger than their Saxon counterparts, and, in some cases, even greater in size than the Continental equivalents. Church and Cathedral naves were long, but the width was governed by the size of timbers to span the roof—nearly all Norman nave roofs were of timber as yet, except for Durham Cathedral, as mentioned earlier. In contrast to this long nave, the eastern arm was short, ending in a round apse or apses. There are few cathedrals and churches in Britain today whose eastern arm has not been lengthened more than once—or completely rebuilt—in later periods to provide greater chapel space, and re-fenestrated to give more adequate light.

The Normans were much better **masons** than the Saxons, but, even so, early Norman workmanship in England was often crude and clumsy. The masonry was wide-jointed and decoration was not often used. The mortar was generally poor and this, together with weak construction, resulted, in some instances, in the collapse of towers and other features within a few years of building. Earlier Norman work is generally very massive in character, with walls of an excessive thickness of up to 20 feet at the base. Windows were small, partly for defence purposes and partly in order not to weaken the wall. The Normans did not fully understand the strength of the materials they used, and employed such massive features to avoid early collapse. In numbers of instances they have been so successful that the buildings are standing today with little apparent damage from weather, time or successive wars.

Later Norman work of the middle and later twelfth century, when the style was becoming transitional in character, was generally of less massive construction, with slenderer columns and piers, thinner walls and larger windows, while most of the impressive and finely executed decorative carving on arches, mouldings and doorways dates from this period. At this time also the masonry was fine-jointed, and capitals and mouldings showed the use of the chisel. As the knowledge and art of the mason advanced, enabling him to use less material to imbue the same strength to the building, it was also learnt how to vault larger and wider spans. Gradually stone vaults began to replace wooden roofs and the pointed arch made its appearance, used in conjunction with the Norman round one to construct the groined and ribbed vaults over aisle and nave. The pointed arch also appeared side by side with its round predecessor in window openings and doorways. Some of the finest examples of **Transitional** work can be seen in the choir of **Canterbury Cathedral, Durham Cathedral, Byland Abbey**, Yorkshire, and **Oakham Castle Hall**, Rutland.

From 1200 to 1275 the **Early English** style was generally paramount. This is the earliest of the styles of Gothic architecture and is likened by some writers to the Spring or 'budding' time of the style. Thirteenth-century architecture presents a great change of appearance from Norman building design; the massive walls have become thinner, the thick piers slenderer, the semicircular arch evolves into a pointed one and, in general, the horizontal emphasis is replaced by vertical lines. Roofs are pitched more steeply and towers become less squat, while many are topped by elegant, slender spires. Simplicity is the keynote of the finest Early English buildings, but this does not constitute emptiness; decoration is provided, but in an austere, dignified manner. The lofty piers sweep upwards into simple, ribbed vaulting, and the small Norman windows in the spaces between piers are gradually replaced by the elegant Early English lancets and, later still, by wider windows with early tracery. One of our Cathedrals, that at **Salisbury**, is a unique example of the work completed almost entirely in this style, and provides a uniform whole rare in English Cathedrals, which, in evolution and of necessity, have become a mixture of styles and standards of workmanship.

Various **building materials** were in use from 1066 to 1275. The Normans introduced Caen stone from Normandy, and continued to import it for many years for their important buildings, especially for quoins and interior work. Caen stone is white and easy to carve, so it continued in use during the Medieval period. It is still used today, particularly in sculpture. However, transport constituted a problem, and the Normans began to use local stone where it was available in quantity and quality, reserving Caen stone for special work. Among local stones used were Bath stone, various limestones and oolites, also sandstones, though the latter lacked durability. Kentish ragstone was still in use among other ragstones, but primarily for less important work in walling. Chalk and flint were also still employed. However, stone was, as yet, much less in evidence for building than timber. Stone was more costly to work, acquire and transport; moreover many parts of the country were still well wooded. In such areas nearly all building was of wood, or wattle and daub or, perhaps, a mixture of timber and stone. The only exceptions were cathedral churches, abbeys, monasteries and some of the castles.

Among the **tools** in use by building workers in the Gothic period would be included an axe, various types of saw for stone and wood, an adze, the chisel later in the period, a hammer, a pick, a crowbar, trowel and shovel. Carvers used bellows to blow out dust from their work.

CATHEDRALS

Before commencing a discussion of **Norman** and **Early English** cathedrals, it may be useful to append here a list, with brief notes, of the more important parts of a large church or cathedral.

Nave—Western limb of a cathedral; for assembly of congregation. Often separated from the choir by a screen.

Choir (*Quire*)—Eastern limb; part occupied by clergy.

Transept(*s*)—Northern and southern limbs of a cruciform church. More than one transept is possible on each side. Where transepts join the nave and choir is called the **crossing.**

Aisle—Lateral divisions. Can be applied to nave, choir and transepts.

Lady Chapel—Chapel dedicated to the Virgin, placed east of the high altar, and generally a projection to the main cathedral.

Presbytery—Eastern termination of choir, where high altar is placed.

Chapels—Situated in various parts of cathedral. Often added later.

Chapter-house—Often polygonal and generally vaulted. Place of assembly for dean and canons for transaction of cathedral business.

Cloisters—A covered way round a quadrangle in a monastic church. Bounded by the cathedral church on one side.

Crypt—A vault beneath the building, partly or wholly below ground. Used for burial, as chapels, and for services.

Apse—Semicircular or polygonal termination to choir or transepts, and occasionally, to nave.

Vestry (*Sacristy*)—Room attached to choir in which sacred vessels and vestments are kept, and where priests robe themselves.

A great deal of **Norman workmanship** remains extant in English cathedrals; almost all have some Norman building remaining, while others like Durham, Rochester, Gloucester and St Albans are, particularly in the interior, still predominantly Norman in character. The Norman cathedral, like other Norman constructions, was massive in the extreme, but this did not preclude beauty and grandeur. The Normans relied on massiveness to ensure the stability of the fabric, as they had only an elementary knowledge and understanding of abutment. But the quality of size in itself created grandeur, as can be seen today in the nave piers of Durham or Gloucester, while the abundance of carved ornament gives the lie to any charge of dullness or emptiness. In Norman times the cathedrals must have been dark, gloomy places with the few, small windows providing quite inadequate lighting to the fabric. These windows have been replaced in later years by larger traceried openings, so, today, the cathedrals can be seen to advantage.

Many Norman Cathedrals were built on the **cruciform plan** with a long nave, short choir, and one or more transepts on the north and south sides. A squat, square, heavy tower was then usual over the crossing, while the piers and arches on each of the four sides below took the stress and thrust of the tower. Western towers were also erected in a number of

Plate 2   Durham Cathedral, from the south-west. Upper stages of western towers c. 1220; lower stage of central tower 1465–75, upper stage c. 1483–9

cases, and in later times they were terminated with spires or lanterns, though in a number of instances Norman towers have subsequently collapsed, to be completely replaced by towers and spires of later design. The cathedrals were partly aisled though, in most instances, aisles were added later where previously absent, particularly in the transepts. The cathedral was generally built in three stages: nave arcade (ground floor), triforium arcade and clerestory. The windows of the latter illuminated the cathedral, while the triforium (or blind-storey) had a passage behind which backed on to the sloping roof extending from the bottom of the clerestory to the top of the aisle arcade. The thrust of the high vault was then diverted downwards by the weight of pinnacles, and transmitted to the flat aisle buttresses by flying buttresses constructed, generally, under the aisle roof. The thrust was then conveyed to the ground at the base of the aisle buttress. However, at this time, the chief stability was provided by the massive walls rather than by abutment, and stone vaulting of high vaults was very rare, and was generally confined to side aisles and small rooms, while larger spans were covered by timber roofs with tie-beams across.

In their original form, the eastern limbs of Norman cathedrals were **apsidal**. This might be in the plan of a single apse, or with a central apse and lateral apses in the form of tangential chapels. The central apse was generally designed inside in the form of an ambulatory, where a vaulted aisled passage encircled the eastern end of the choir and high altar. **St Bartholomew-the-Great, Smithfield,** has now been restored to its original plan in such a design. However, in the case of English cathedrals, most eastern arms have been extended once or several times, or even completely rebuilt, and the apsidal ends have in most instances disappeared.

Many Norman cathedrals were built with **crypts**; in some cases, this part of the cathedral is all that remains of the original Norman work today. Crypts were then often used to house the relics of saints, which pilgrims came to see and touch and to be cured of their ailments. Two of the finest examples of crypts of this period can be seen at **Canterbury** and **Rochester** (120, 123).

Cathedral building in these times was often ascribed to a bishop or prior, but this is only a courtesy description. The work was done for, and on behalf of, a certain bishop who probably had the difficult task of finding the money, but the building was designed by the master mason in drawing or model form. In many instances, cathedral records give us information about such masons, though, unfortunately, the designs have not survived.

The majority of our cathedrals are fine examples of Norman and Gothic architecture and it is invidious to compare one with another on points of merit. It is proposed, therefore, to give here brief comments, without comparisons, on those of our cathedrals which show adequate remains of their Norman workmanship.

Durham is one of the cathedrals with an almost completely Norman scheme. It occupies a commanding site on a bluff, surrounded on three sides by the river Wear (Colour Plate 2). It was built, as were many such cathedrals in Norman times, not only as a monastic centre but as a fortification, in this instance against the Scots. The cathedral was begun in A.D. 1093, on a cruciform plan, with a low, central tower and two western towers. The principal changes subsequently have been a later central tower and choir. As referred to earlier, the vaulting is Norman, nave and aisles being completed in 1135. In this instance, the pointed arch was used over the shorter spans whereas the longer diagonal ribs were in the form of round arches. Flying buttresses are hidden under the triforium sloping roof, to transmit the thrust of the nave vault to the outer wall buttresses. Both the vault and abutment system at Durham are early examples of such construction. The cathedral interior is magnificent in its massiveness, with incised decorated, round piers, and the usual three stages of nave arcade, triforium and clerestory (128, 190, 193; I).

The interior of **Gloucester Cathedral** is predominantly Norman, with plain but massive, cylindrical nave piers. The nave is early twelfth century, though the high vault belongs to the thirteenth century (76–7). **Peterborough** also shows a largely Norman interior and this impression is emphasised by its retention of the timber roof over the nave. Much of the great apse remains also to give the original design.

Rochester Cathedral contains an interesting crypt, part of which is early Norman dating from the cathedral built by Bishop Gundulph, c. 1080–1100. The remainder of the crypt is a fine example of later work (123). The nave shows middle and later Norman work with varied piers of this style, also triforium, while the west front illustrates late Norman workmanship including a fine west doorway (78–9).

St Albans, earlier a Benedictine abbey church, but which became a cathedral in 1877, presents an unusual but good example of Norman work. The Norman church was built by Abbot Paul of Caen, and work commenced in 1077. Roman bricks from near-by Verulamium were used, and coated with plaster, but today these bricks are plainly visible as the plaster has now largely disappeared. The nave is extremely long, aisled, and the supports are very plain, huge nave piers, plastered and painted. A good deal of reconstruction and alteration has taken place in more recent times, but among the unaltered parts of the cathedral is the large, square central tower of Roman brick at the crossing, rising 144 feet to the top (127).

Considerable remains of Norman workmanship can still be seen in many other English cathedrals. Amongst these, good examples of such work exist at **Hereford**, in the nave arcade; **Chichester**, also in the nave; **Norwich**, which has a fine interior, and late Norman tower (131); **Lincoln**, with Norman workmanship still extant of different periods on the west front (169, II); **Winchester**, showing a late Norman tower, rebuilt soon after the collapse of the original tower in 1107; fine interior work at **Ely** in late Norman style, and further examples of interior work at **Carlisle**. **Canterbury** shows evidence of several periods of Norman work; Archbishop Lanfranc began building a new cathedral after the previous one had been burnt down in 1067. The work was completed quickly, and soon showed signs of damage and weakness. After further alterations and additions to the eastern arm by Prior Ernulf and Prior Conrad, the work was completed in 1130, but, once again, largely destroyed by fire in 1174. We can see today the earlier Norman work of this period in the crypt and parts of the monastic buildings (120–1).

One very fine example of Norman cathedral building, which, unfortunately, is not now standing, was **Old St Paul's, London.** Our knowledge of this cathedral is from fragments of masonry, drawings and written accounts, of which the seventeenth-century engravings of Wenceslaus Hollar and the *History of St Paul's Cathedral* by Sir William Dugdale, published 1658, are the best known. The rebuilding of St Paul's Cathedral was begun after a London fire had destroyed the Saxon cathedral in 1087. The work continued over many years, intermittently throughout the twelfth century. From Hollar's drawings, we can see that the Norman nave was little altered in later periods, though much of the rest of the fabric was rebuilt and changed. This nave was divided into the customary nave arcade, triforium and

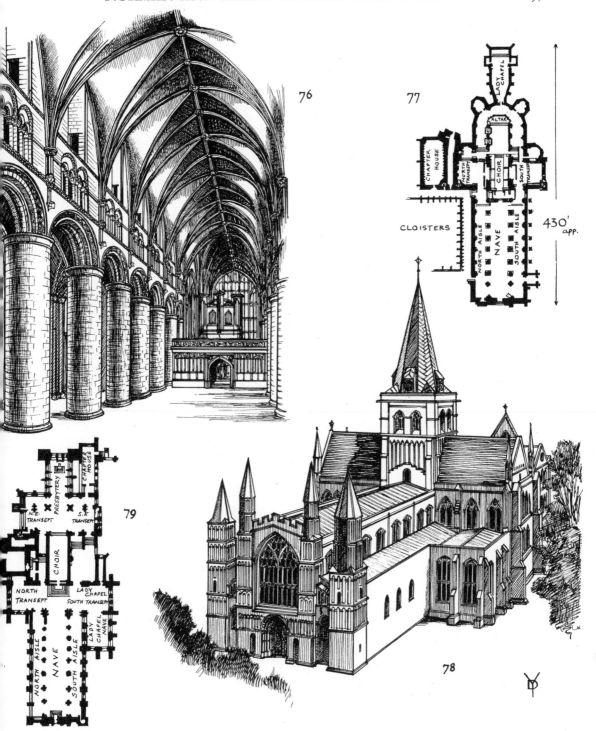

76 Gloucester Cathedral, nave looking east. Norman, *c.* 1100–60; vault Early English, *c.* 1242
77 Plan   78 Rochester Cathedral, from the Castle keep south-west of Cathedral. West façade late
Norman *c.* 1150–60, central tower reconstructed later   79 Plan

clerestory and was long—12 bays—and aisled. Extant engravings present an impressive vista with vaulting shafts rising from the ground at the pier bases, in unbroken line to clerestory level, showing a lofty as well as extensive cathedral interior. An excellent and most interesting book, *Old St Paul's Cathedral* by Mr G. H. Cook, was published in 1955. It provides more detailed information with contemporary illustrative material.

The best known and most extensive example of **Transitional** work in English Cathedrals is at **Canterbury**. When the cathedral was largely rebuilt after the fire of 1174, William of Sens (so called because of his association with Sens and its cathedral) was asked by the monks to restore the choir as far as possible to the previous design, which had been named after the prior as 'Conrad's Glorious Choir', and was famed at that period. He did so, and work continued from 1175 to 1184, though his fall from the scaffolding and subsequent death in 1179-80 necessitated that the work be completed by another William—known as the 'Englishman' to differentiate. The choir resulting shows clearly the change in style from the Norman work of Conrad's time. Parts of Conrad's choir were retained and the rest rebuilt, while the difference in style in pillars, capitals, arch mouldings and ornament can be seen between the two periods of work. The French influence of William of Sens is apparent and is particularly shown in the peri-apsidal planning of the chapel to the cathedral saint, Archbishop Thomas Becket, which terminates the eastern arm, and is known as the corona or Becket's crown—a most unusual feature in English cathedrals.

Other cathedrals showing good examples of **Transitional** work include the **Christ Church, Oxford**, in particular, the nave and tower dating from 1160 onwards (132); the Galilee at **Durham** (190); and work at **Ely, Rochester, Chichester** and **Peterborough.**

In discussing **Early English** Cathedral workmanship the name of **Salisbury** is synonymous with this period of Gothic architecture. This is not only due to the quality of the work, but to the unusual fact of the unanimity of style of the cathedral, which was mainly constructed in one continuous building operation. The work commenced on a new site for a new cathedral in 1220, and by 1258 much of it was complete. This is rare in the story of the building of English cathedrals, and gives to Salisbury a unity so often lacking in other examples (Frontispiece). The west front, central tower and spire are of rather later date, but the rest of the structure gives a clear impression of Early English ecclesiastical architecture.

Another cathedral famed for its Early English workmanship is **Wells**, whose west front has been described in glowing and extravagant terms by many writers. The doorways of this façade are not large, and almost the whole area is devoted to a display of sculpture, originally painted and gilded, and completed by the middle of the thirteenth century. Such a display is more common in France than England, and Englishmen are justly proud of the magnificent façade (III). Other first-class Early English workmanship can be seen in the interior—in particular in the nave, whose piers and capitals show the style to great advantage and in variety (189, 200).

Two other impressive but completely different west fronts of the style can be seen at **Peterborough Cathedral** and **Ripon Cathedral** (80-3). In the former example, the porch and spires are of later date, but the general effect of the façade is imposing in an architectural rather than sculptural scheme. Ripon is much simpler and possesses a sedate and dignified appearance.

Another cathedral with extensive Early English workmanship is **Lincoln**, set in a com-

I Durham Cathedral: the nave looking east, 1093-113

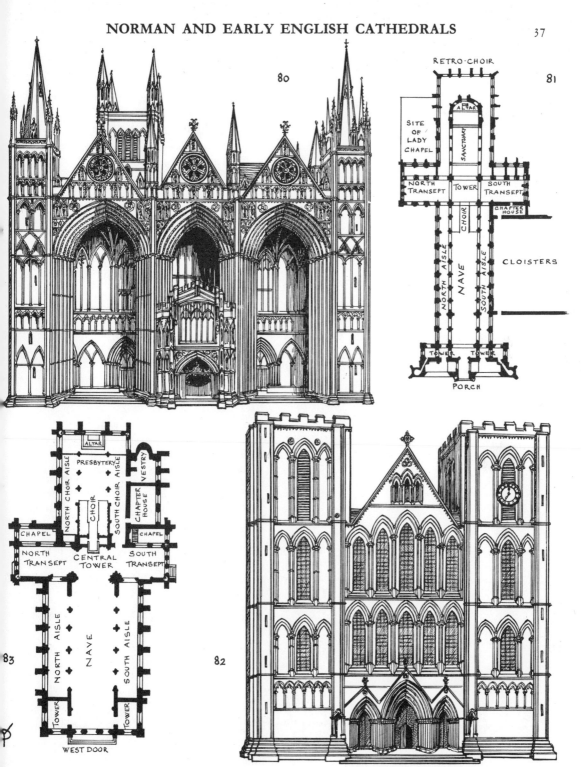

80 Peterborough Cathedral, Early English: west front, 1195–1220 Porch late 14th century; Left spire 15th century; Right spire 14th century 81 Plan 82 Ripon Cathedral, Early English, west front, 1230–45 83 Plan

Lincoln Cathedral: the west front, c. 1225–1400

manding position on Lincoln Hill, and having a west façade largely of this period, built into the Norman work of earlier date. The combination of styles is not unfortunate, and the result has a grandeur all its own (II). In the interior, the Angel choir is justly famous (141; Colour Plate 3).

Further examples of Early English work are visible at **Glasgow, Rochester, York**—chiefly transept work; **Durham**, particularly in the transeptal chapel of nine altars begun in 1242; **St Albans**, where the nave was still further lengthened, and parts of the triforium rebuilt; **Carlisle, Southwell** (84), **Chichester** and **Ely.** At **Lichfield**, the choir and transepts show Early English work while the nave dates from about 1250.

In **Old St Paul's** work on the nave and transepts was completed in this period; lancet windows were inserted, and the high ribbed vaults of nave and transepts constructed on quadripartite plan. The west front was also completed at this time. A famous Medieval London landmark was provided by the tall, tapering timber spire set on its central tower. This suffered various assaults by storm and fires, but the final spire was only destroyed in the sixteenth century.

Although not strictly relevant to this work, the reader who has visited the Continent may

84 Southwell Minster (Cathedral), from the north-west: west front *c.* 1130. Later perpendicular window. Spires modern but based on original style. Chapter house, *c.* 1290

like to compare the contrasting styles and decoration of cathedrals there, of this period, with those already mentioned in England. For example, in France, the present **Amiens** was begun in 1220—a great deal of the work being done 1220–88; **Chartres** was largely rebuilt 1194–1260 after destruction by fire; **Rheims**—the Coronation Church of the Kings of France—was also partly rebuilt 1211–41, with further work later in the century, while work on the Cathedral of Notre Dame in **Paris** can also be seen of this time, particularly in the south transept. In Germany, **Cologne** was begun in 1248, but work was very slow due to lack of funds, and only the choir was completed at this time, while the cathedral was not consecrated until 1320.

ABBEYS AND PRIORIES

One of the largest contributions to the architecture of the Middle Ages was made by the monks: from 1066 onwards, and particularly from then until mid-fourteenth century, there was a steady monastic expansion and growth, with a tremendous outburst of energy in the eleventh and twelfth centuries. During the Middle Ages the monastic communities provided education, shelter and guidance, and the monks themselves were the chief members of society who were educated and learned. Until the twelfth century, nearly all monastic building was by the **Benedictine Order**, introduced into England in the late sixth century, and flourishing from 1066 onwards. Numerous other orders later made their appearance, but architecturally, the other predominant influence was given by the **Cistercians**, a more ascetic branch or order, who felt it incumbent upon them to depart into the more remote parts of Britain to build, or have built for them, their monasteries. They lived under excessively hard conditions, particularly in the early years after the individual site was chosen, but before the stone building was completed, living in wattle and daub huts of their own construction in beautiful but—especially in that period—desolate countryside. It is these Cistercian monasteries that have become one of the tragedies of architecture, for, after the Dissolution of Monasteries by order of Henry VIII in the sixteenth century, such monastic churches could not, by reason of their remoteness, be used as cathedral or parish churches as were those of so many other orders, which had been set nearer to towns and villages. For centuries these monasteries fell into ruin, the stone being taken for local building, and time and weather completing the dissolution. Since the late nineteenth century this decay has been halted, and magnificent repair work has been carried out on such fine architectural examples as Glastonbury Abbey, Somerset, and Fountains Abbey, Yorkshire, but their original glory is lost to us for ever. Other orders which were responsible for interesting monastic building include the Augustinian Canons, the Cluniacs, the Carthusians, the Gilbertines and the Premonstratensians. In the first two centuries after 1066, nearly 500 abbeys and priories were founded or re-established, due to the religious revival sweeping the Continent and Britain at that time, and a resurgence resulting from the Crusades.

A monastery was often built first of all in wood, then, over a period of years, rebuilt, part by part in stone. The church was converted into stone first, and other buildings followed later. Often large portions were left in timber, with thatch and wood roofing, for many years, and this was the primary reason for the periodic, serious damage and destruction by fire.

The most important building of the monastic settlement was the **church**; built as soon

85 Glastonbury Abbey, Somerset, 1184–1216: Lady Chapel 86 Fountains Abbey, Yorkshire: 1135–50: nave looking west 87 St Botolph's Priory, Colchester, Essex: the Norman nave 88 Tintern Abbey, Monmouthshire, 13th century: from the south-west

III Wells Cathedral: the west front, c. 1230–60

as possible of stone, it was generally of cruciform plan with a central tower. In numerous instances, all over the country, the monastic church is all that now remains—together with scanty, desolate ruins—of the old monasteries. These surviving churches have been repaired and are used today, serving as cathedral and parish churches for the area. Some of these churches were of cathedral status in the Middle Ages, others have been created cathedrals in later times. **Canterbury Cathedral, Westminster Abbey, Winchester** and **Worcester Cathedrals, Sherborne Abbey, Ely, Rochester** and **Norwich Cathedrals** and **Boxgrove Priory Church**, Sussex, are a few examples from the large number which have survived in this way from this particular period of building.

The **domestic buildings** of the monastery were generally arranged round a quadrangle, one side of which was formed by the nave of the church, while its transept provided one right-angle corner of the quadrangle. In the centre of the quadrangle was usually a lawn—the cloister-garth—while on all four sides was a stone-flagged walk with open stone screen and lean-to roof: this was called the **cloister**, and is a part of the monastic construction generally in best repair in most cathedrals and abbeys. The cloister was often built on to the south side of the church nave to face the sun and to give protection from the north-east wind. Among the domestic buildings was the **dormitory**, which was commonly built next to the church transept to facilitate frequent attendance in church, particularly in the middle of the night; monks could, by means of the night-stairs, gain easy, undercover entrance from one building to the other. Further planning included the **refectory**, the **chapter-house**, the **vestry**, the kitchen and offices and the **infirmary**, the **almonry**, the **calefactory** or common room, the **library**, the guest-house and the **Abbot's lodging** which generally had its own kitchen and hall for entertaining guests. An interesting example of an Abbot's kitchen is preserved at Glastonbury Abbey; it is built of stone, with fourteenth-century vaulted roof (241). Sanitation was good and, in general, far ahead of its time. Lead pipes conducted running water to lavatories, bath-house and kitchen.

There are numerous examples of Norman and Early English workmanship among the monasteries of this period, where the surviving church is still in use but not of cathedral status, and some monastic buildings remain, despite later alterations and the ravages of time. Examples include **Dorchester Abbey,** Oxfordshire, **St Botolph's Priory, Colchester** (87, 168), founded in 1102 and built chiefly of Roman bricks, **St Bartholomew-the-Great, Smithfield,** founded 1123, **Kelso Abbey,** Scotland, 1128, **Waltham Abbey**, Essex (93), and **Christchurch Priory**, Hampshire, 1093, where the nave presents an impressive example of Norman architecture (319). **Tewkesbury Abbey,** Gloucestershire, has a magnificent Norman nave, west front and central tower (130), in various periods of the work, while **Westminster Abbey** in London contains a monks' dormitory built in the pre-Norman period, about 1050–60, and later Norman and Early English work in the Church itself.

Among the **ruined monasteries** the most complete example, particularly for the domestic buildings, is that of the Cistercian monastery at **Fountains Abbey**, Yorkshire (IV). Founded in 1132, and said to be named after the springs on the near-by river Skell, the new buildings suffered a fire in 1140, and rebuilding began. In the church, the nave and transepts are of later Norman work from 1147 (86), while the work of the first half of the thirteenth century —when the choir was extended—and also the ruined Chapel of the Nine Altars (185) give us some impression of the high quality of the Early English workmanship which existed

Fountains Abbey, Yorkshire: the 12th-century south aisle

89 Typical 13th-century church with tall stone broach spire   90 Boxgrove Priory Church, Sussex, 12th century   91 Church at Dover, Kent, late Norman (restoration later)   92 Glastonbury Abbey, Somerset: pier of central crossing, late 12th and early 13th century   93 Waltham Abbey Church, Essex: tower from the west

here. The fifteenth-century tower still dominates the Skell valley; many domestic buildings remain in whole or in part, including the undercroft illustrated in Fig. 124 with its excellent stone vaulted roof.

Unfortunately, much less remains of the other Yorkshire Abbeys: **Kirkstall, Rievaulx** founded 1131 (201), **Jervaulx** (167), and **Roche**, 1147. In other ruined abbeys, some fine Norman workmanship can still be seen in the Lady Chapel at **Glastonbury**, Somerset, 1184–1216—the first part of the Abbey to be rebuilt after the fire (85) while Early English work is visible in the remains of the crossing (92)—also at **Buildwas**, 1135, and **Lillieshall**, 1145, in Shropshire and **Malling Abbey**, Kent, 1090–1103. In the last case, the Abbey building is still inhabited by the religious order.

CHURCHES

As with cathedrals and monasteries, the Norman period of architecture was a time of great activity in **church building**; many Saxon churches were rebuilt, while equally numerous were new churches constructed on new sites. There was considerable variation in plan, but similar ideas prevailed to those in cathedrals, though on a much more modest scale. Very simple church plans consisted only of a nave and chancel; others had nave, chancel and sanctuary, but a very common Norman plan, especially in the twelfth century, was the cruciform type with nave, chancel, transepts and a central tower. Some churches had aisles to their various limbs, while in many cases only one aisle was made, and its companion followed at a later date. The popularity of the central tower made the use of transepts advisable for abutment purposes. Such a tower had to be supported on the four piers of the crossing within the church, and transepts were needed to provide abutment in all four directions of thrust, not just east and west by chancel and nave. Many Norman chancels were apsidal-ended, though these were often altered in later times when the east end was extended. There are many examples of Norman churches in Britain, though most of these have been altered to a varying degree in later periods. Comparatively untouched specimens of Norman church building can be seen at **Old Shoreham** and **New Shoreham**, Sussex, though the latter is mainly transitional workmanship (95, 97–8), **Caistor**, Northamptonshire, **Iffley**, Oxfordshire, where the decoration is very rich and varied (94, 170, 179), **St Giles', Oxford**, the **Temple Church, London**—which includes transitional examples—and **Newhaven**, Sussex.

Norman church **walling** was very thick, generally constructed with a rubble cove faced by squared stones. The walls were often crowned by a cornice supported on corbels, and string courses were constructed inside and out. Herringbone masonry was used sometimes, rather in Saxon fashion (165–6).

Roofs were of timber but little or nothing remains of these now. It is presumed that they were built with heavy oak tie-beams which rested on wall plates. From these would be constructed a roof of timber rafters. Exterior roofing was of thatch or wood shingles, and later, of tiles and/or lead.

In the **Early English** period the cruciform church was still built, but central towers were more slender and often topped by spires. Many churches possessed a western tower, or towers, instead of a central one, and a rectangular instead of cruciform plan. The apsidal end of the Norman church was frequently rebuilt in this period, as the chancel was lengthened

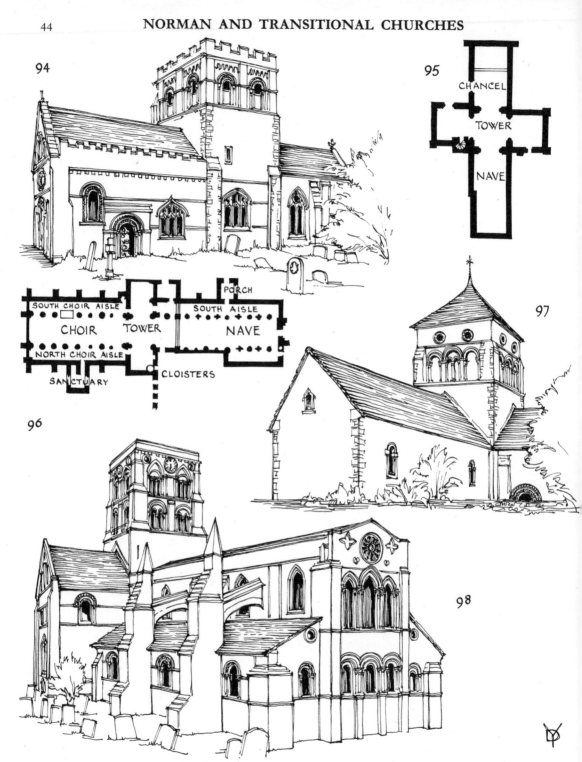

94 Iffley, Oxfordshire, late Norman, *c.* 1170. Some later windows and chancel   95 Old Shoreham church: plan   96 Boxgrove Priory Church, Sussex, 12th century: plan   97 Old Shoreham, Sussex, late Norman   98 New Shoreham, Sussex, Transitional

to give more room for chapels, and a square end with lancet windows replaced the apse. Aisles were added to some naves, and, when these were roofed, it became necessary to raise the nave wall to a greater height, and insert clerestory windows to give more light to the church. However, this was a lengthy process, and clerestories are comparatively rare until Decorated Gothic times. Roofs were of steeper pitch in Early English churches and the timbers and wall thicknesses less massive, while buttresses were more common providing strength in lieu.

CASTLES

The Normans were also industrious builders of **military architecture**; in the years immediately following the Conquest, it was important for the king, his barons and other nobles to keep and increase the power and possessions which they had obtained at that time. **Castles** were hastily erected all over the country to protect these nobles, their riches and property, both from the insurgent British and from one another, for life was turbulent and insecure. Most of the castles of this time, **1066–c. 1150**, were of necessity built of timber, and, for protection, were of the **motte-and-bailey** type. The motte or mound was the important feature of defence, and was either natural, if this could be found, or artificial. These mounds were large and, for further protection, a deep ditch was dug round the base. Round this was the bailey—the enclosed land—with its wooden stockade which was generally further encircled by an earth rampart and another, outer ditch. On top of the motte was built a house or tower, enclosed by a wood fence, for the lord, his family and servants. Inside the bailey were the timber buildings of hall, chapel, kitchen, storehouses, barns, etc., and in times of attack the house or tower on top of the motte would serve as a retreat for all. Entrance from without was afforded by a bridge over the outer ditch as the latter was generally full of water.

From about **1150 onwards, stone castles** were more often built to replace those timber and earthwork erections which were so easily subject to destruction by fire. A few notable stone examples were built before this: the keep of **Malling Castle**, Kent, now called St Leonard's Tower, built about 1070 (103) by Bishop Gundulph who was also responsible for the **White Tower**, keep of the **Tower of London**. This latter keep—one of the best examples of the period—was built about 1080. It has four storeys, is some 92 feet high and has massive, thick walls (V). On the third floor is **St John's Chapel**—a first-class example of early Norman architectural work, with its nave, narrow aisles in the wall thickness, and ambulatory encircling the apsidal end. The piers, capitals, bases, barrel-vaulting and arches are of high quality for such early work and the whole has been retained in an almost perfect condition (108–9, 194–5, 206). Other examples of early stone castles include those at **Castle Heding-ham**, Essex, c. 1130, **Castle Rising**, Norfolk, c. 1140, and Rochester Castle Keep, c. 1130. At **Rochester**—a typical example—the keep is some 125 feet high with a square plan of 70 feet on each face. The walls are 12 feet in thickness. The floors are divided vertically by a wall, giving two rooms on each floor of 46 feet by 21 feet each. On the second floor is the Great Hall where the dividing wall is pierced by arches and piers to make one large room (108, 111–13).

The period **1150–89** was one of the great ages of castle building, and the most prolific in Norman stone castle construction. Henry II organised the building of new castles but

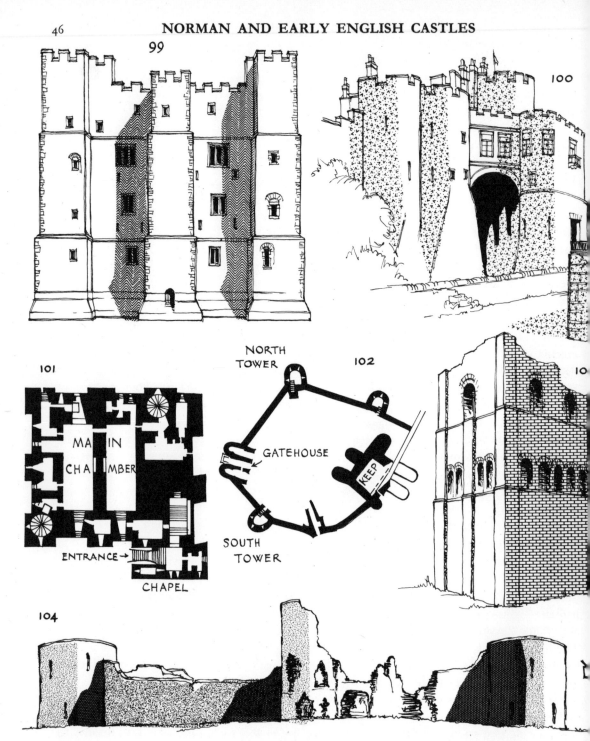

99 Dover Castle, Kent: the keep, 1180–6, height 83 ft. Caen stone, local ragstone, flint and rubble. Windows enlarged 15th century   100 Dover Castle, Constable's Gate, 1230–40. Also later reconstructions   101 Dover Castle: plan of the keep   102 Pevensey Castle, Sussex: plan. 13th century curtain walls. Norman keep in right corner   103 Malling Castle, Kent: the Norman keep (St Leonard's Tower), *c.* 1070   104 Pevensey Castle: curtain walls

also, and predominantly, the replacement of timber castles by stone ones on the same or near-by sites. His nobles followed his example.

There were two chief designs of Norman stone castle: those with a **rectangular keep** and those with a **shell keep**. Both were built in large numbers, but the latter were more fragile, and have not, in most instances, survived in good condition. The **rectangular keep** was a very strong, heavy building and therefore had to be erected on solid ground—if possible on an eminence or natural hill; it was not safe to build it on an artificial mound. The highest natural site within the outer walls was chosen and the keep

105 Exterior castle staircase, 13th century

erected there. The plan of the keep was generally square, and walls were plain except for flat, pilaster buttresses of about 6 inches projection and 7–8 feet wide, set at the ends and centre of each face. The keep was generally divided at each floor level by string courses and often had a set-off at each stage, decreasing slightly in thickness towards the top. Walls could be as much as 20 feet or more at base, but generally lessened in thickness to the top by the external sets-off and by interior ones as well. Apart from solidity and strength, the excessive thickness was to provide space in which to construct wall passages and rooms. Larger keeps were, like Rochester, divided by a cross wall, often extending the whole height of the keep, and pierced at levels as required by doorways and arches. Such keeps were built with basement floor and two or three floors above this before reaching the roof and battlement walk. The **basement floor** was only a little below ground level, if at all, and was for storage purposes only. Thus its walls were solid, pierced only by slits for air. The **first floor** was occupied by the garrison and servants and also had only slit windows. The **second floor** was for the lord and his family; it contained the Great Hall for everyone to dine in. It had large windows opening into passages and rooms in the walls, which, in turn, had large windows also, on the exterior walls. The hall would be about 25–30 feet in height and would have several wall fireplaces with exists for flues to the outer walls, set at an angle. The top floor was generally reserved for sleeping accommodation. A **chapel** was built into the second or third floor. **Floors** were of timber planks resting on heavy beams some 12–14 inches square, set in joist holes in the walls. The **roof** was of moderate pitch to allow the water to drain off, but the gable did not rise above parapet level. It was covered by shingles or lead. **Staircases** were constructed in angles to the keep with their exits in turrets at the top. The stairs were of newel design, of stone, and very narrow and dark, lit only by slit windows (106–7). As in the monasteries, sanitation was well provided for; in this case by garderobes built into the wall thicknesses. They had stone seats, and a vent to the wall outside or to a cesspool below.

Although the well-built, rectangular keep was immensely strong, and well-nigh impregnable in its period with the weapons employed, it was further guarded from without. The entrance to the keep was in turn covered by another building or tower which was connected—usually by an inside stair—to a second outer tower. The **main doorway**, of considerable size, had one or two heavy oak doors, with iron fittings held in place by massive oak bars across the door, which slid into wall sockets on each side. An oak and iron portcullis often protected the doorway, and a drawbridge spanned the gap between the two outer towers. On the roof of the keep, the **parapet**—now absent on most keeps—was about 5 feet high and 2 feet thick. A walk was provided all round to join up the four angle turrets. Keeps were built of a variety of materials: from Roman brick, rubble, flint, Caen stone, chalk and ashlar. Most had ashlar quoins and facings to buttresses.

There are many examples of rectangular keeps extant in Britain in various stages of repair or ruin. Some of the most interesting and well preserved include those at **Colchester**, Essex (116), **Richmond** and **Scarborough**, Yorkshire; **Dover**, Kent (99, VI); **Chester; Rochester**, Kent (111); **Castle Hedingham**, Essex; **Guildford**, Surrey and the **White Tower**, keep of the **Tower of London** (109, V).

Very large numbers of **shell keeps** were also built in Norman times, based on the earlier motte-and-bailey castle plan. However, they lacked the strength and solidity of rectangular keeps, and comparatively few remain today, even in a state of ruin. Examples can be seen, with considerable later rebuilding, at **Carisbrooke**, Isle of Wight (233), **Lincoln** and **Arundel**, Sussex. Like the motte-and-bailey castle, the stone version was always placed on a mound, natural or artificial; stone walls of 8–10 feet thick were then built on a polygonal or circular plan round the top of the mound, enclosing an area of 40–100 feet in diameter. This was the shell keep, and within its walls, in the open court, were then erected the buildings for residence of stone and/or timber. The shell keep walls were generally of rubble with ashlar plinth and quoins, and reached a height of 20–25 feet above the ground.

The change in architectural style from Norman to Early English was less apparent in military architecture than in ecclesiastical. Castles built between 1189 and 1225 were on similar lines to the Norman examples, only indicating the change of building design and methods in the increased projection of buttresses, the more finely jointed stonework and the increased use of stone vaulting, in the ribbed and groined construction, to replace timber roofing. From about 1225–30, however, castle design began to

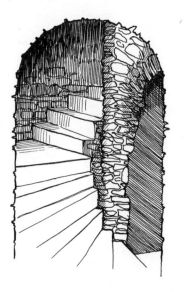

106–7 Newel staircase—turret of Rochester Castle keep. Norman

108 White Tower, Tower of London: plan of third floor of keep, *c.* 1080   109 White Tower, *c.* 1080: St John's Chapel, length 55 ft   110 Rochester Castle, Kent: plan of second floor of keep 111–13 Rochester Castle second or hall floor of keep, Norman, *c.* 1130. Note holes in walls for floor joists, dividing wall on left pierced by arches. Shaft passes through central pier with openings on each floor

evolve from the square keep to the **cylindrical tower keep**. This was due to the need to overcome the main weakness of the square keep—its angles—which could be undermined by tunnelling, so that partial collapse was achieved. The newer towers were sometimes polygonal on the exterior and circular inside; alternatively, they were circular in exterior plan also, but were reinforced by flat but boldly projecting, stone buttresses. The examples of this type of keep are not numerous, as castle design was changing considerably in this century; one of the most typical is that at **Conisborough**, Yorkshire. This castle stands on a natural hill, and its cylindrical tower, 70 feet in height and 50 feet in diameter, is strengthened by six interior buttresses. Its entrance is on the first floor, well above ground level, reached by wall staircases.

In the second half of the thirteenth century, additional efforts were made to defend the outer walls of the bailey, thus further protecting the interior keep. Greater success was achieved in this aim by building **mural towers** in this outer wall, from which attackers could be spotted and fired upon. Such towers were commonly circular or semicircular, giving, by the insertion of four or five in the complete wall, a better field of view and fire, than from the earlier keep design. This was the beginning of the revolution in castle design which took place in the late thirteenth and early fourteenth century, and from this time onwards, the necessity of an impregnable keep was obviated. As a result, there was more room for living quarters within the bailey than in the smaller keep, and greater comfort as well as security was realised (100, 102, 104).

HOUSES

Very few examples of **domestic building** of the **Norman** period are still extant, even in a ruined or altered condition. This is due to the fact that few houses were of stone, but were mainly built of timber, or wattle and daub, even in towns. The Normans spent their building effort and architectural design on cathedrals, abbeys and castles; all of these being inhabited by those with power and wealth. From the remains available, together with written records, it appears that the larger town houses generally had two rooms; the lower one used for storage, and the upper open to the roof as a hall, with curtained-off sleeping quarters at one end. Fires were common in towns, and the wood houses with thatch roofs burnt so easily that, by the end of the twelfth century, a few stone houses were being built, and stone party-walls to many of the others, up to 16 feet in height. In the country, where there was more space, there were some manor houses of stone, but only a few as yet; anyone wealthy enough to build a stone house would fortify it for protection.

The majority lived in wattle and daub huts as the Saxons had done, with one room, no windows, a hole for a doorway, and a mud floor with central hearth. Among the few examples of stone houses of the twelfth century are the two houses at **Lincoln**: that of **St Mary's Guild**, and the **Jew's House** (114), the **manor house** at **Boothby Pagnell**, Lincolnshire (118), and ruined remains at Southampton (the King's House) and at Christchurch, Hampshire. **Oakham Castle** in Rutland still has a late twelfth-century hall with timber roof and transitional pillars, capitals and bases.

In the **thirteenth century** the vast majority of homes were, as before, made of timber and plaster, wattle and daub, and with little or no added space or amenities. For the more

114 The Jew's House, Lincoln Hill, mid-12th century (later alterations particularly windows) 115 Ypres (Baddings) Tower, Rye, Sussex, mid-13th century 116 Colchester Castle keep, Essex: main entrance on first floor. Norman, late 11th century. Roman bricks used in construction 117 Little Wenham Hall, Suffolk, c. 1270–80: early domestic brickwork 118 Manor House, Boothby Pagnell, Lincolnshire, c. 1180 (some later alterations)

119 Norman stone entrance staircase

well-to-do, in country areas, more **manor houses** were being built, usually with some fortification, small windows except on upper floors, and entrance at first floor level as a safety measure. The hall continued to be the main room, open to the timber roof, which was now of higher pitch, and covered by tiles, wood shingles or thatch. Glass was still very rare for windows. **Staircases** were of newel stone type in a turret as in castles, or of wood ladder design, but more commonly of stone or wood steps up the exterior wall face (105, 119).

Examples of Early English domestic building are more numerous than Norman but still only a few exist. One of the most interesting of these is the early specimen of Medieval brick building at **Little Wenham Hall**, Suffolk, *c.* 1260–80 (117)— an art lost in Britain since the departure of the Romans. It is built on a rectangular plan with a tower at one angle, and has a hall, chapel, and good period examples of doorways and window openings. There is a house at **Charney Basset**, Berkshire, *c.* 1270–80, which still shows the solar and chapel of the period; and original parts remain at **Cottesford Manor House**, Oxfordshire, **Parsonage House, West Tarring**, Sussex, and the **Manor House, Crowhurst**, Sussex. The **Bishop's Palace** at **Wells** has some fine workmanship of the Early English period as does also the **King's Hall, Winchester**.

BRIDGES

Throughout the country, the majority of rivers were crossed by means of **fords**; the number of place names in which ford is incorporated are a testimony to this practice. **Bridges**, when they were built, were of timber, thus we have scarce extant remains of them. The best-known example of bridge-building in Medieval times was that of **London Bridge** across the Thames. This also was of timber, and was altered, repaired and rebuilt on several occasions between Saxon times and the late twelfth century when the first stone bridge was begun there. Building of the new bridge, established to the west of the wooden one, continued from 1176 to 1209. It was London's only bridge over the Thames until the eighteenth century, due to the commercial influences which thrived on the restriction to one crossing and subsequent control of trade from the Continent and southern counties. The bridge was a remarkable structure for its period; it lasted until 1832 when it was pulled down in order to build the present bridge. It was supported on 18 stone piers which were built on to oak planks and bedded in pitch. The planks themselves rested on elm piles, filled with rubble and driven into the river bed. The piles were shaped into 'starlings' which protected the piers from the scour of the tide, which at that time was excessively strong. The bridge itself with its starlings acted as a dam, holding back the ebb tide; this caused the river to freeze above the bridge in cold winters on many occasions—conditions accentuated by the lack of the embankments which are now present. The roadway was supported on these piers, which were connected by pointed arches of differing size to accommodate vessels of varying tonnage. On the roadway were built the Chapel of St Thomas of Canterbury (rebuilt in the fourteenth century) and the timber-framed houses and shops whose rent paid for the upkeep of the bridge. These houses suffered by fire from time to time and were rebuilt, generally larger than before, so, although the bridge roadway was 20 feet wide, only 12 feet of free passage remained, and the houses jutted outwards over the river.

ROOFS AND VAULTS

The **exteriors** of Norman **roofs** were covered by tiles, stone slates, wood shingles or thatch. The pitch was fairly steep in order to drain off water and snow, generally 40 to 50 degrees, but Early English examples were, on the whole, steeper, up to about 60 degrees. In the later Norman period, lead was more often used, in which case roofs were flatter, as lead tends to tear under its own weight because of the frequent expansions and contractions on temperature changes. Roofs generally overhung the walls to some extent to avoid damage by water to the stonework beneath. These were supported by a **cornice** at the wall top, which in turn was strengthened by **corbels** or projecting stones; these were frequently decoratively carved, especially after mid-twelfth century. The whole member was referred to as a **corbel-table**.

The **roof interior** was constructed in stone or wood. In the former case, **vaulting** was employed, but in **Norman** times this was generally confined to the smaller spans such as church aisles and crypts, rather than the more ambitious high vaults of cathedral naves and choirs. The early Norman designs were of **barrel-vaulting**—a method which had been used by both Romans and Saxons. This consisted of a continuous round arch of stone constructed by centering, that is, by building a wooden frame on the underside to the required shape, and setting stones and mortar in position. When these had set, the framework was moved on to the next section. This type of vaulting can still be seen in **St John's Chapel** in the **White Tower, Tower of London**, where the nave and upper aisles are treated in this way (109). This method, however, was too costly in labour and time to use over large spans, and the next stage evolved—that of the **groined vault**. In this instance, also similar to Roman designs, the result was like two barrel-vaults meeting at right angles, giving four arches with different direction faces. The massive supporting pillars were then set under the points of intersection. This type of vaulting was used a great deal in the eleventh and early twelfth century in aisles and crypts, particularly the latter, which, in view of the low roofing, were suited to the method, and pillars could be placed where required. Good examples can be seen in the earlier section of **Rochester Cathedral** crypt (known as Gundulph's crypt), and in Ernulf's crypt in **Canterbury Cathedral** (120). In the twelfth century, designers and builders were seeking a method by which they might safely span the wider spaces with stone vaults, and so avoid the serious damage from fire to which the existing timber structure was so prone.

The problem was finally solved by means of **ribbed vaulting**, wherein a skeleton of ribs for six arches was thrown over the span, supported on the pillars below; two of these arches

120 Canterbury Cathedral, Ernulf's crypt, c. 1096–1107: groined vaulting 121 Canterbury Cathedral, monastic buildings, 12th century: Norman ribbed, quadripartite vault 122 Typical Early English ribbed quadripartite vault, c. 1230–40 123 Rochester Cathedral crypt, c. 1201–24: ribbed vault 124 Fountains Abbey, vaulted undercroft, 12th century: ribbed vaulting

crossed diagonally the square vault space, and the others crossed from side to side of the span, making four compartments in between. These arches could be created separately by centering. This was a great constructional advance, but still limited the vaults to a square, or near square, area, and often the space to be spanned was rectangular, as the nave and aisles were not of equal width. This problem was eventually dealt with by the use of the pointed arch, or as the French call it, the *arc brisé*—a more suitable name as it indicates a broken, round arch, which, with the two ends abutted, gives the pointed arch. By the use of pointed and round arches together in one vault, the differing spaces could then be adequately covered. The earliest example of a high vault over a wide span was that of the choir of **Durham Cathedral**, which was completed by 1104, but subsequently rebuilt. However, the nave high vault, finished in 1133, remains today as the earliest example extant on such a scale; a suitable tribute to Norman construction and ingenuity (I). A smaller version of Norman ribbed vaulting is illustrated in Fig. 121, and is taken from the monastic buildings of Canterbury Cathedral.

In the early part of the thirteenth century, the use of the **ribbed quadripartite vault** continued, using pointed arches of different widths; this was a vault in four sections provided by the two diagonal cross ribs over the span. However, in this period, the ribs were simple in section, narrower than the Norman, made up of round and hollow mouldings with, some-times, dog-tooth decoration. The vault was lighter, requiring less massive piers than before, and was constructed of a layer of washed stone supported on the ribs, instead of the earlier stone and rubble vault. Where fracture or damage occurred, it could then be dealt with in its individual compartment, without reconstructing the whole vault (122–3). In the later part of the Early English period, more ribs were introduced giving a **sexpartite vault**. In this, an extra transverse rib was inserted on each side of the vault leaving narrower spaces in between. A still lighter construction could then be used, but with even stronger effect. A **ridge-rib** was then employed down the centre to receive all transverse ribs and at these intersection points a boss was carved to cover the joints. This was a common design for nave and choir high vaults in the cathedrals and large churches of the time (Fig. 76 shows the nave of **Gloucester Cathedral**). Other examples can be seen in the nave of **Salisbury Cathedral**, also in **Lincoln Cathedral**. A vaulted undercroft at **Fountains Abbey**, showing a plainer version of Early English vaulting, is illustrated in Fig. 124.

The majority of **Norman interior roofing** over larger spans was by **timber** construction, which, in general, was left open showing the rafters, but in cathedrals and larger churches, a flat, boarded ceiling would be erected underneath. In most cases, the roof timbers were only roughly trimmed and were heavy baulks; tie-beams extended from wall to wall to counteract the outward thrust of the roof. Although a few cathedrals and some churches still have timber roofs, these are replacements; true examples of Norman construction are very scarce. In the **Early English** period, cathedrals, abbeys and castles were being built more and more with stone vaulting, but timber roofs were generally adopted for other buildings. The tie-beam method was in use all this time, but later in the thirteenth century it tended to be superseded by a lighter construction, particularly in areas where massive and lengthy baulks of timber were not available in quantity. These lighter roofs were, in cases of small spans, constructed without cross support, common rafters only being used. In larger spans, the outward thrust was too great for stability so diagonal ties were employed, or alternatively, collar-beams. Ridge-pieces were inserted longitudinally, and the rafters tenoned or pinned into these to prevent sagging. Vertical king- and queen-posts were introduced, to assist in support, on to the tie-beam, in cases where the latter was still in use. Again, few examples of thirteenth-century timber roofs remain extant, but numbers have been repaired or rebuilt in the same style.

STEEPLES, TOWERS AND SPIRES

Norman steeples were generally in the form of heavy square **towers**, only rising to a square, or less, in height above the roof; this was particularly so in the case of central towers, in order to restrict the weight placed on the piers of the crossing below. Later Norman work, especially in the Transitional period, was highly decorative with carved ornament and window and belfry openings. A number of central towers of cathedrals and large churches collapsed comparatively soon after building, due to inadequate foundations and their excessive weight; in such instances, they were often replaced by one or twin western towers, which had ground foundations on three sides; alternatively, these were added and a new central tower built with better abutment. Squat, pyramidal spires, often of wood, generally surmounted these towers, but the majority of these have since disappeared. Later Norman towers, especially those at the west end or on transepts were generally higher and were ornate. Many fine Norman towers are extant on cathedrals and churches: outstanding are the central tower, **Tewkesbury Abbey Church** (130), the south-west tower at **Durham Cathedral** (128, Colour Plate 2), the transeptal towers at **Exeter** (129), and the central tower at **St Albans** (127), **Norwich** (131), **Oxford** (132) and **Winchester Cathedrals**; and those in smaller churches at **Iffley**, Oxfordshire (94), **Old Shoreham** and **New Shoreham**, Sussex (97–8) and **Dover Church**, Kent (91).

With the advent of the **Early English** style of architecture came the tall, graceful **spire**, set on a taller, decorative tower. The spire was of Gothic introduction and is typical of the style itself. As a feature it is not essential, but highly decorative, particularly in the best examples in which tower and spire are finely proportioned and one acts as a foil to the other. Two principal types of design were in use—the spire with a parapet, and the spire without parapet, often in the form of a broach-spire. This is a broad division, for there were many variations on the theme. The chief problem in design was that, whereas spires had eight sides, towers only had four. In the first type the **parapet** acted as the support, and was generally constructed with pinnacles and buttresses, later, of flying buttress design (131). In the second type, where there was no parapet, squinches, or small arches, were built across the tower corners, inside, at the top, to support the remaining four sides of the spire; from these, in many cases, pyramidal buttresses, called **broaches**, followed up the spire sides for some distance. Where tower and spire met, a tablet finished the junction (126). One of the earliest examples of Early English spires can be seen on **Oxford Cathedral**, dated *c.* 1225, which is still rather squat and Norman in character (132). Apart from **Norwich** (131), that at **Chichester Cathedral** is very fine, although rebuilt on the same pattern by Scott because the original spire collapsed in the nineteenth century. There are numerous specimens of Early English church spires in country areas, and their design varies from county to county. Some are of timber, others of stone, but the latter tended to replace the former in the later Middle Ages because of the danger from fire, particularly if struck by lightning.

125 Canterbury Cathedral: Norman tower on south side, *c.* 1100   126 Broach spire. Parish church, *c.* 1260   127 St Albans Cathedral: central tower, *c.* 1077–88. Roman brick construction; 144 ft high 128 Durham Cathedral: south-western tower, early 13th century   129 Exeter Cathedral: north transeptal tower, *c.* 1112–40. Upper storey and crenellation Gothic   130 Tewkesbury Abbey Church: central tower, *c.* 1123–45. Wooden spire collapsed 1559. Pinnacles built 1660. Height of tower 148 ft, each face 46 ft wide. Original roof levels still apparent   131 Norwich Cathedral: central tower and spire. Tower Norman, 1121–45. Wooden spire collapsed 1361. Present spire Gothic   132 Oxford Cathedral: tower and spire. Tower, *c.* 1170. Spire, *c.* 1225, one of oldest extant in England

TRIFORIA AND CLERESTORIES

It has been mentioned earlier in this chapter that the majority of large Norman churches and cathedrals were built in three stages. These stages are now called the pier arcade—nave and choir—triforium arcade and clerestory. The word **triforium** is thus applied to the middle or second stage. The term seems to have been first applied to Canterbury Cathedral in the twelfth century, then referring to the passage or chamber behind the arcade, that is, the space between the flooring on the top of the ground floor aisle vault and the lean-to roof above. This is now generally termed the triforium chamber, while the openings into the interior of the cathedral are triforium arcades. In a few instances, this wall is not pierced by arcades but is solid, to give greater strength to the construction. The triforium is also designated the blind-storey, indicating that it has no window outlet to the exterior, in comparison with the clerestory (clear-storey) window above. In fact, in some cases, usually later in the period, windows have been inserted into the wall between the exterior aisle roof and the interior aisle vaulting, to give extra light to the interior of the church. In such instances, the arcades would be of slenderer columns with pierced tympana to allow the light to shine through the triforium wall. The triforium chamber, or wall passage, varied in area and had sundry uses. Altars were erected there for worship; processions passed through, and access was provided for the work of cleaning and repair to the cathedral fabric. Today, many such triforium chambers are walled in as unsafe or are used only for this repair and cleaning work, particularly where the aisle vault has not been covered by wood-flooring. In a few cases, it is possible to visit triforium chambers and to circumnavigate the church at first-floor level. The chamber then provides further congregational space for special services. **Norman triforium arcades** were commonly arranged with one or two containing arches to each bay of the cathedral, and these were then subdivided into two or four smaller arches with plain or decorated shafts and Norman capitals and bases (139, 140; I). In other cases, there was no containing arch but an arcade of small, round-headed arches to each bay. In both these designs, the bays were marked by the vertical vaulting shafts. Some examples, however, had continuous arcading without such demarcation. In **Early English cathedrals**, the height of the triforium was often reduced in order to increase the clerestory height to give greater light. (Early English triforia are illustrated in Figs. 141–2.)

The term **clerestory** was at one time applied to windows in many different parts of a church, but is now generally taken to refer to the top line of windows above the aisle roof along the nave and choir of a church. In **Norman cathedrals** the windows were very small indeed, and were often limited to one window per bay. This was because the clerestory also had a passage through its walls for repair and cleaning purposes and the Normans did not want to weaken their wall further by constructing larger windows in greater numbers. This accounts for the excessively gloomy appearance that the interior of Norman cathedrals must originally have possessed. In **Transitional** building the windows were increased in number, often to two per bay, while in **Early English cathedrals** the clerestories had lancet windows and later, larger openings with simple tracery. By this time, abutment was more fully understood and the walls were less massive but more adequately supported by projecting buttresses. Most of our churches and cathedrals today possess a clerestory which has large windows giving adequate light to the interior, but these have been replaced, probably several times,

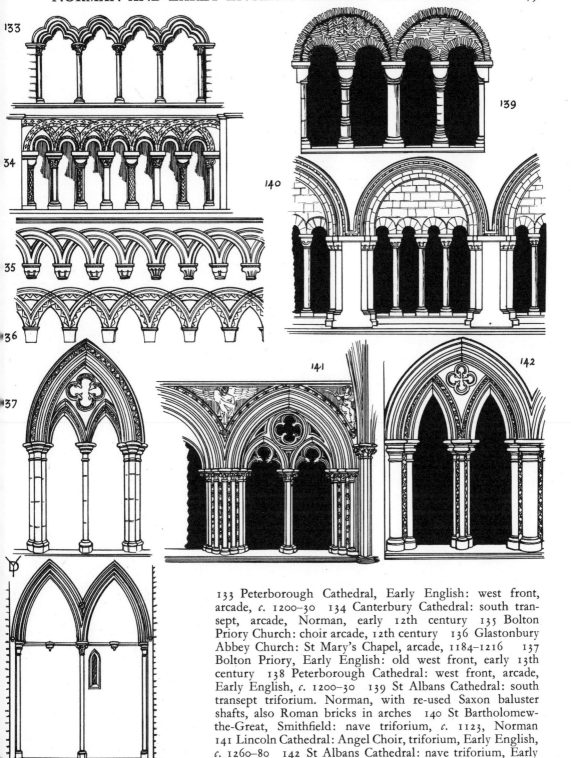

133 Peterborough Cathedral, Early English: west front, arcade, c. 1200–30 134 Canterbury Cathedral: south transept, arcade, Norman, early 12th century 135 Bolton Priory Church: choir arcade, 12th century 136 Glastonbury Abbey Church: St Mary's Chapel, arcade, 1184–1216 137 Bolton Priory, Early English: old west front, early 13th century 138 Peterborough Cathedral: west front, arcade, Early English, c. 1200–30 139 St Albans Cathedral: south transept triforium. Norman, with re-used Saxon baluster shafts, also Roman bricks in arches 140 St Bartholomew-the-Great, Smithfield: nave triforium, c. 1123, Norman 141 Lincoln Cathedral: Angel Choir, triforium, Early English, c. 1260–80 142 St Albans Cathedral: nave triforium, Early English.

since the first Norman or Early English building, and are generally of Decorated or Perpendicular design.

WALLS AND BUTTRESSES

Norman walling was invariably thick, but often, especially in earlier work, crudely constructed with wide joints. The common practice was to make double walls of stone and fill with rubble and mortar, leaving passages as and where required. The same method was used in all stone buildings whether cathedrals, churches or castles. The exterior face was undecorated, but in later work the interior, and sometimes the exterior, was decorated by interlaced arcading. In **Early English** workmanship, with a greater accent on buttressing, the walls were rather less massive, and more worked stone was used in comparison with rubble coring; joints were finer and better finished.

A **buttress** is a reinforcement and projection to a wall; its use renders unnecessary the building of a thicker wall to provide the same stability, and, at the same time, increases the aesthetic appeal of the structure, whilst economising in building materials. As window openings weaken a wall still further, buttresses are provided between them. The primary need for abutment comes from the thrust and pressure from the roof: with a timber roof, this outward thrust is partly counteracted by the tie- and collar-beam construction; with stone vaulting the design problem to maintain a balanced construction is more severe. The early barrel-vaulting produced a uniform thrust along the whole length of the wall, and the Norman constructional method of making an excessively thick wall without buttresses was adequate. With groined and ribbed vaulting, however, the maximum thrust is exerted via the diagonal ribs to give maximum resultant forces at points on the walls somewhat above the arch-springing; at such a point the buttress must supply the necessary counter-thrust. In between, the wall could safely be weakened by windows. Therefore, early **Norman** buttresses, when used, were merely flat pilasters, plain and projecting only a very little from the wall face (103, 159). Later Norman versions had rather greater projection and, often, a slender shaft, with capital and base, at the angles (160).

In **Early English** construction, walls were thinner; stone vaulting was more often used and over larger spans; this made stronger abutment necessary. Various buttress designs evolved; some were flat like the Norman but less broad, and terminated with a sloping top; others stood up above the parapet and had greater projection; a further variant was a slender buttress with narrow face but considerable projection. Early English buttresses were often divided into stages, diminishing in projection upwards and terminating in a triangular head or pinnacle. Later versions had three stages, each set back more than the last to give a general tapering effect from ground level (117, 161–3).

Flying buttresses were not yet common. They had been in use in Norman building, but were then generally hidden from exterior view, being constructed under the triforium roofing. In Early English work they were used outside the building and provided decoration as well as abutment. A flying buttress consists of a half arch which spans the space between the aisle wall buttress and the clerestory wall above the aisle roof. Its purpose is to convey the outward thrust of the nave and choir high vault over the aisle roof and down the aisle buttress to the ground. It is only in large buildings of this type of design that a flying buttress becomes necessary, and the weaker the wall construction due to window openings, and the higher

V   Tower of London: the White Tower, 1078–

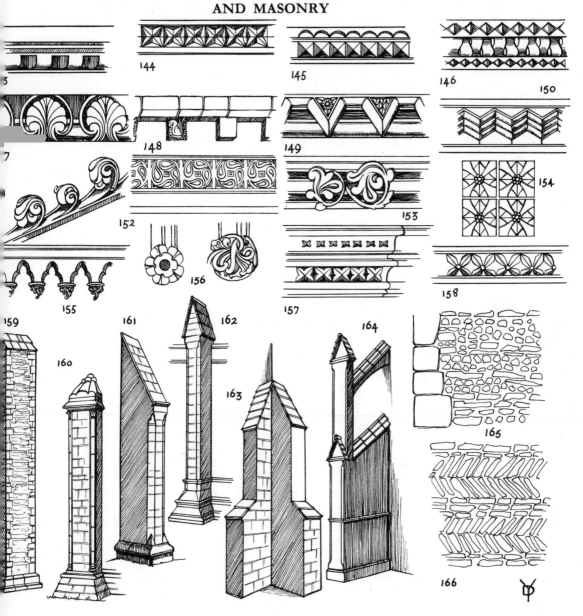

143 Norman billet design 144 Norman star decoration 145 Norman nail-head ornament 146 Norman billet and lozenge ornament 147 Decorative Norman moulding 148 Norman corbel-table 149–50 Norman chevron ornament 151 Early English crockets 152–3 Early English decorative ornament 154 Early English diaper ornament 155 Early English corbel-table 156 Early English dripstone termination 157–8 Early English dog-tooth ornament 159–60 Norman buttresses 161–2 Early English buttresses 163 Early English angle buttress 164 Early English flying buttress 165 Norman masonry: rubble with ashlar quoins and bonding courses of brick 166 Norman masonry with herringbone courses

Dover Castle, Kent: the keep (centre) c. 1179–91;
Mary-in-Castro and Pharos (top right)

and wider the vault, the more it becomes essential (164). One of the chief problems which faced the builders of these early exterior flying buttresses was at which point on the clerestory wall to place the buttress head. The greatest thrust was generally found to be at some point between the rib springing and half-way up the interior vault. The exact point varied with each vault and had to be calculated by mathematics and experience before success was obtained. Numbers of buttresses were placed too low or too high before the best point was established, sometimes with unfortunate results. The problem was solved in some instances by setting the buttress arch on to a smaller buttress built on to the clerestory wall, thus distributing the abutment over a safer margin of wall area.

DOORS AND DOORWAYS

Norman doorways constitute one of the most highly decorated features in their architectural style, particularly in cathedrals and churches. Early examples were fairly plain with simple mouldings, but later work was most ornate. The doorways had round arches, but the door was often square-headed, leaving an intermediate stone panel—called the **tympanum**—which, in later work, was lavishly carved, often in high relief, in a design of sculptured figures representing some biblical scene. These later doorways had many mouldings, most of which were carved with Norman ornament; they were either carried down the sides of the doorway, or were finished at the arch springing by an impost-moulding, then designed in decorated shafts with appropriate capitals and bases, numbered to fit in with the arch-moulding scheme above. The doorway was deeply recessed, and the shafts were inserted on an outward splay on each side. The chief decoration was on the exterior of the doorway so that the door was set in the wall nearer to the interior face than the exterior. Norman doorways, many in fine condition, survive in considerable numbers in Britain, as, unlike window openings, it was not found necessary to enlarge them later. They were already of fair size, indeed in cathedrals and large churches some examples were very large, and, with profusion of decoration, shafts and mouldings, became proportioned as a square instead of a rectangle. Among the finest examples is that on the west front of **Lincoln Cathedral** (169), that on the west front of **Rochester Cathedral**, and one at **Peterborough** (174), also those at **Ely, Durham** and **Worcester Cathedrals**, while outstanding specimens amongst the many on small churches are at **Iffley**, Oxfordshire, whose several doorways show great variety of decoration and a high standard of craftsmanship (170). Other examples can be seen in Figs. 167–8. In **Transitional** work the decoration was at its most profuse and the carving excellent. Some doorways began to show the pointed arch as a replacement for the semicircular, as in Fig. 173.

Norman doors have, unfortunately, survived in far fewer numbers. They were of oak and of simple construction. On the outside they had narrow vertical boards; these were fastened to wider, horizontal ones on the inner side. They were strengthened by horizontal, ironwork bands which were sometimes only plain straps, or, more often, were finished in curved scrolls. Most doors were square-headed.

Early **Norman porches** were usually of shallow projection, sometimes terminated by a gable. Later examples projected much further, and in large churches and cathedrals, the outer

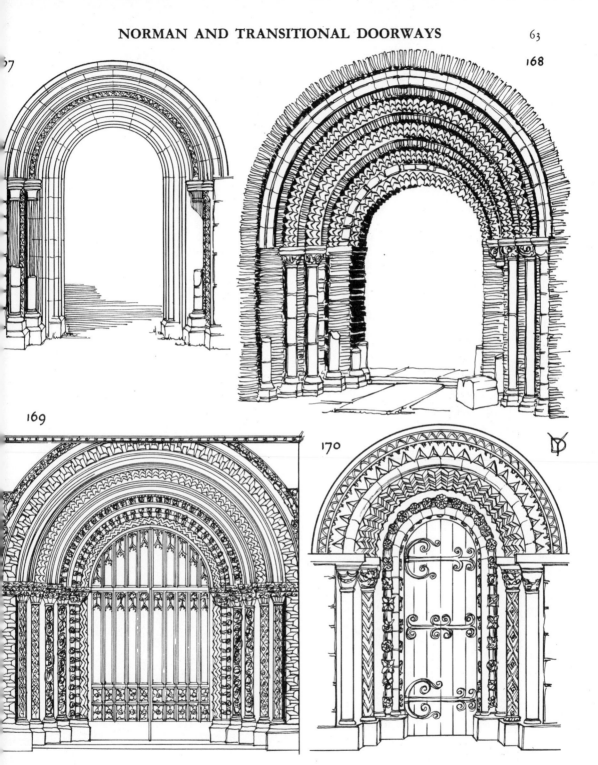

167 Jervaulx Abbey, Yorkshire, Transitional, late 12th century: early dog-tooth ornament   168 St Botolph's Priory Church, Colchester, Norman: chevron ornament   169 Lincoln Cathedral, c. 1150: west front entrance   170 Iffley Church, Oxfordshire, Norman, c. 1160: south doorway

171 Ripon Minster, Yorkshire, Early English, c. 1220–50: west front   172 Bolton Priory Church, Yorkshire, Early English, early 13th century: west front   173 Transitional doorway: chevron ornament and pointed arch   174 Peterborough Cathedral, late 12th century: Norman doorway

archway is designed like other Norman doorways, while the sides of the porch are arcaded. Some very fine examples still exist (175).

The majority of **Early English doorways** had pointed arches, though some still retained the round arch, and others, usually the small examples, had square heads with a shouldered arch on each side. Foiled heads were also commonly designed, generally trefoil, but sometimes cinquefoil; in larger doorways only the first order of mouldings was foiled. Some patterns had continuous mouldings but the majority were shafted;

175 Canterbury Cathedral: Norman porch and staircase, *c.* 1150–65

these shafts usually stood free, and were of contrasting marbles or stones to the rest of the doorway; Purbeck marble with its rich, dark polish presented the most frequent appearances; shafts were often banded for further stability. The double- or even treble-arched doorway was used in this period on cathedrals and large churches. Alternatively, it was common to see a double door under a single-arched doorway; in this case, the door-heads would be trefoiled, and a quatrefoil opening appeared in between as in window design. The gabled doorway was also still seen. There are many good examples extant, for instance at **Chichester, Salisbury, Lincoln** and **York Cathedrals**. Other versions are illustrated in Figs. 171–2. The ironwork on **Early English doors** was finely executed and of attractive design in foliated scrollwork; it was more free and flowing than Norman decorative ironwork. The larger examples of double doors were usually separated by a stone shaft.

Early English porches were, in general, larger than the Norman; in cathedrals and large churches, the outer doorway was deeply recessed with a multiplicity of shafts and mouldings, while the side walls were arcaded and traceried. Examples can be seen at **Salisbury** and **Lincoln Cathedrals** and in the Galilee at **Ely**.

WINDOW OPENINGS

Early **Norman** window openings were very narrow and little more than round-headed slits, a few inches wide and 2–3 feet high. They had no glass, only wooden shutters, though they have been glazed in later times, in which case the glass is set almost flush with the outer wall. Inside, the window openings were deeply splayed. Most examples were quite undecorated

(176). In later work, windows were made wider (177) and were decorated by mouldings which had carved ornament; some windows had shafts at each side as in doorway design. At the same time, a dripstone was added. Examples of Norman windows are much scarcer than those of doorways as most of them have been replaced in later years by larger openings, but fine examples can be seen in the churches at **Iffley**, Oxfordshire (179), **Castle Rising**, Norfolk (180), and **Waltham Abbey**, Essex (178). Some later windows were divided into two lights by a central shaft; this was especially typical of belfry openings. These have not been glazed later but are protected from birds by louver boards. Small circular windows were also fairly common, particularly at clerestory level.

Transitional work shows round and pointed arch window openings often side by side in the same building. Norman decoration and mouldings are still used, though, from *c.* 1170, the lancet window made its appearance. However, this design is more commonly associated with Early English workmanship.

The earlier examples of **lancet windows** were generally single lancets; these were in use from *c.* 1170 to the end of the thirteenth century and were thus common all through the Early English period. The lancet opening was tall and narrow, with acutely pointed arch on the exterior wall face. The most usual proportion was for the height of the opening to be eight or nine times its width, but in some examples this ratio was as much as 11 : 1. Inside, the opening was widely splayed, and, as the walls were still thick, the internal arch opening was as much as four or five times wider than the exterior one. The inside arch was generally much flatter so the shaft of light was thrown downwards, leaving the roof in darkness (185). From the single lancet design come the multiple lancets for which the Early English period is renowned. These were in groups of two, three (most commonly), five and seven, even numbers over two being rarely used; the centre light was generally taller and wider than the others. The dripstone moulding sometimes covered them in one single arch (184), or covered each lancet separately with appropriate horizontal moulds in between as needed.

The origin of **window tracery** can be followed back to Norman work when two lights were placed under one arch moulding. In the Early English period this idea developed, and as two or more lancets were grouped under one arch, the remaining space—called the spandrel—was felt to present an awkward design, so quatrefoil and trefoil shapes were carved to fill it. In course of time these shapes were pierced, giving **plate tracery**, a term applied to a plate of stone pierced by one or more holes. In plate tracery, the area of the apertures is less than that of the stone; on the other hand, the reverse is true of the later bar tracery. Plate tracery evolved slowly from this simple pattern of two lancets and a quatrefoil head. It was modified by the introduction of **cusping**, that is a plain, outer arch and a cusped inner one, giving quatrefoil and trefoil shapes. The earlier cusping is referred to as **soffit cusping**, as the cusps spring from the soffit or lower surface of the arch and not, as in later work, from the arch-side chamfer. Further variations were provided by the introduction of a transom, which made a four-light window from the two-light version by a horizontal dividing bar (183, 186).

The majority of **Early English window openings** were of lancet or plate tracery design, but in houses, castles and small churches, the square-headed window was in use. This often had an arch over it while the tympanum was plain or carved with ornamental decoration. There were also circular windows as in Norman times; some of these were simple, quatrefoil

176 Guildford Castle keep, Surrey, Norman, mid-12th century: window slit opening   177 Malling Castle keep, Norman, *c.* 1070   178 Waltham Abbey Church, Essex, Norman: chevron ornament. Billet decoration on dripstone   179 Iffley Church, Oxfordshire, Norman, *c.* 1160: chevron decoration   180 Castle Rising Church, Norfolk, Norman, *c.* 1160   181 Quatrefoil window opening in circular panel, *c.* 1220   182 Lincoln Cathedral: circular window, *c.* 1220. Plate tracery   183 Castle Hall, Winchester: window with plate tracery, *c.* 1250–60. Quatrefoil in head   184 Oundle Church, Northamptonshire: five-lancet window, Early English, *c.* 1200   185 Fountains Abbey Church: window opening in Chapel of Nine Altars, Early English, *c.* 1204–47   186 Little Wenham Hall, Suffolk, Early English, *c.* 1260–80

openings (181), or had more elaborate plate tracery like the fine example at **Lincoln Cathedral** (182).

ARCHES

The **Norman** arch was **round**, but several versions of this were built. All of these had one centre: in the **semicircular** arch, this was on the diameter; in the **stilted** arch, the centre was above diameter level; in the **segmental** arch, the centre was below diameter level; in the **horseshoe** arch, the curve was carried below the semicircle. In earlier Norman work, the arch was not usually recessed and its edges were square in section and undecorated. Later work showed deeply recessed arches with many mouldings, most of which were covered with carved decoration (139–40, 190). **Arcading**, often of intersecting variety, on wall surfaces for decorative purposes illustrated the prevailing architectural style (134, 136). Constructional members of an arch have various names which it may be useful to mention here. The arch's under-surface is called its **soffit**, while its upper surface is its **extrados**. The wedge-shaped blocks which form the arch are called **voussoirs**, of which the central one is the key or **keystone**. The lowest voussoirs are called **springers**; this is where the arch springs from the capital.

The **Early English** arch is predominantly pointed, but again there are variations of this. A pointed arch has two centres; the **lancet**, the acutely pointed arch commonly in use, has its centres on the diameter line but outside the arch. Alternatively, in the **equilateral** arch, also much used, the two centres coincide with the diameter limits. The **obtuse** or wide arch, where the centres are inside the arch, on the diameter level, was rarely used in Early English work. Most Early English arches were richly moulded with simple, dignified decoration (137–8, 141–2, 187–8).

PIERS, CAPITALS AND BASES

Norman piers, or pillars were extremely massive, particularly the early examples such as the nave piers at **St Albans Cathedral**. They were of various forms of which the most common was the circular pillar, which could be plain as at **Gloucester Cathedral** nave and **Tewkesbury Abbey** (76), or incised with chevron, spiral or network decoration as at **Durham Cathedral** (193, I). Other variations were the square pilaster design, the multiangular pier (191), and the recessed angle pier with shafts (192). **Transitional** examples were similar but slenderer (190, 192). **Early English piers** were much more slender and were divided up into shafts. Sometimes these were very numerous and were connected together by fillets as at **Wells Cathedral** (189) and **Glastonbury Abbey** (188). Perhaps more common were those with separate shafts, generally four or eight, arranged round a central column, only joined to it at capital, base and intervening banding. The shafts were then often of different material, usually Purbeck marble. Examples can be seen at **Lincoln, York, Ely** and **Salisbury Cathedrals** (Colour Plate 3, 187).

The purpose of a **capital** is twofold: to provide a larger area than the pier from which the arch may spring, and to decorate the joint between arch and pier. **Norman** capitals, therefore, were always massive, heavy members, to match the piers and to support the arch. In some instances, where the pier and arch had equivalent mouldings, the capital was omitted

187 Ely Cathedral, Early English: arch and piers from the choir   188 Glastonbury Abbey Church: arch and piers from the crossing and sanctuary, Early English, late 12th and early 13th century   189 Wells Cathedral: nave pier, early 13th century; 24 shafts on cruciform plan   190 Galilee, Durham Cathedral, c. 1170: arch and piers   191 St Bartholomew-the-Great, Smithfield, Norman: nave pier, c. 1123   192 Rochester Cathedral, Norman: nave pier, chevron ornament   193 Durham Cathedral, Norman: nave pier

194 Tower of London: St John's Chapel, *c.* 1080, Norman capital 195 Tower of London: St John's Chapel, *c.* 1080, Norman capital 196 Boxgrove Priory, Sussex: Norman capital 197 Canterbury Cathedral: monastic buildings, Norman capital 198 Westminster Abbey: Early English capital 199 Lincoln Cathedral: Early English capital, *c.* 1220 200 Wells Cathedral: Early English capital 201 Rievaulx Abbey Church, 13th century: Early English pier capital 202 St Alban's Cathedral: Norman chamfer moulding, *c.* 1080 203 Peterborough Cathedral: Norman bowtel moulding 204 Early English arch moulding (rounds and hollows) 205 Early English arch moulding (rounds, hollows and pear-shapes) 206 Tower of London: St John's Chapel, *c.* 1080, Norman base 207 Boxgrove Priory, Sussex: Norman base 208 Lincoln Cathedral: Early English base, *c.* 1220 209 Peterborough Cathedral: west front, *c.* 1200–30, Early English base

and the mouldings continued downwards. The top member of the capital was called the **abacus** and in Norman work was a distinctive feature, being square in plan with vertical sides, chamfered off and sometimes decorated in the lower portion (191, 194–5). Later Norman abaci were alternatively circular or octagonal in section (193, 196). Early Norman capitals were of simple **cushion** design or were roughly voluted at the corners. The former were rounded off at the lower angles to give the cushion shape, while the latter were voluted in a crude imitation of the Ionic design; the central space on each of the four faces was decorated by a plain Tau cross, as in **St John's Chapel** in the **White Tower** (194). From about 1090, the **scalloped** capital evolved from the cushion, though the latter was also in use all through the Norman period (195–6). Later Norman work also produced **foliated** capitals, including figure and animal carving. Some of these were very rich in decoration (197). In their original form, capitals were generally gilded and painted, though few traces of this are visible now. **Transitional** capitals still showed the square abacus, and were of cushion, scallop or foliated types. Among good examples of these are those in the choir of **Canterbury Cathedral. Early English** capitals were very varied but commonly of **moulded** or **foliated** design. The abacus was usually round in section, in contrast to the square Norman and Transitional versions, and was composed of one or more round mouldings separated by hollows. Below the abacus, the capital was either moulded or carved into foliage. The latter was, at first, rather vertical in design, but later was arranged in heavy, falling clusters. Foliated scrolls, leaves, flowers, animals, birds and figures were used as motifs. Below the capital came the **astragal** and necking (198–200). In some instances, the mouldings of the capital continued round the pier to make a single capital (201). Other versions had octagonal or poly-sided abaci (189).

Early Norman bases were insignificant in comparison with the capitals, consisting only of a quarter-round moulding standing on a square plinth (193). Later examples were more weighty and elaborate but all had round pier mouldings on a square plinth. In later work, the angles between the square and round sections were filled by carved decorative foliage or animals: these were called **spurs**. Such examples resembled the Attic base, having two round mouldings, or one round and a quarter round separated by a hollow or chamfer. There were variations on this as can be seen in Figs. 206 and 207. **Early English bases** were also commonly on the Attic principle, but in later work, a multiplicity of mouldings were used on a deeper pedestal (208–9).

OTHER ARCHITECTURAL FEATURES, ETC.

The **ground-course**, like the dripstone and string course mouldings, was primarily to protect the wall fabric and window tracery from damage by water. The ground-course also provided a means of completing the building with suitable architectural members, and gave greater stability to it. **Norman** ground-courses had rectangular mouldings, or, more often in later work, chamfered edges. **Early English** versions were much taller, like the bases, and had a greater number of mouldings.

String-courses marked the different storeys of a building and were horizontal mouldings which projected, and therefore kept the rain from the wall beneath. Later **Norman** examples were carved, while **Early English** versions were moulded with two or three mouldings in use.

A **dripstone** was like a string course in arch form, round the outside of a doorway or window opening, and had the same function of protecting the carved mouldings beneath from wear by water. In many cases, particularly in the **Early English** period, the string moulding was continued uninterruptedly round the arches of doors and windows with horizontal banding in between. When the dripstone was not a continuation of the string course, it generally terminated in a **corbel** on each side of the arch. Many Early English examples were in the form of heads (and were thus termed corbel-heads), usually those of kings, queens or bishops. Other corbel terminations were of floral or animal motifs. Early **Norman** work did not have a dripstone; the walls were massively strong, and there was little or no carved decoration to harm. Later work was often carved with ornament. Interior dripstone mouldings were generally called **hood-molds**. Dripstones of rectangular shape over square-headed doorways were termed **labels**.

The **table** was a projecting, horizontal stone course which carried the parapet front of a building. It was supported on corbels—hence **corbel-table**—and these were, in early examples, merely square blocks of stone, but in later **Norman** work were carved into figure, animal and floral sculpture (148). **Early English** examples were often round in shape and were generally carved with floral designs; trefoiled arches spanned the intervening spaces (155).

Parapets were built to facilitate access to the high roofs; they were in the form of an inner and outer wall with a lead-lined passage between. The outer wall generally projected over the main wall face and was supported on the cornice and corbel-table. The parapet was then pierced at intervals to let out the water which had collected in the passage or channel, and, as it was desirable to dispose of this water away from the wall face, the exit openings for the water were lead spouts fixed into the ends of long, projecting, stone blocks. These blocks were in later work carved into grotesque shapes which are called **gargoyles**. The shapes were formed into birds, animals, devils, monsters, etc. The theory is widely held that these figures represented the evil spirits which were captured and rendered harmless in stone by the Christian building on which they sat. Often buttresses were used as sites for gargoyles so that the water might be thrown off at even greater projection from the wall face.

MOULDINGS AND ORNAMENT

Norman mouldings, particularly in the early work, were very simple: generally rectangular courses like the abaci, and shallow hollows, chamfers and fillets. Later work shows wide rolls or rounds which were profusely carved with ornament. The mouldings were cut more deeply at this time (202–3). **Early English mouldings** provided a great contrast: they were deeply cut in suites of rich, bold rounds and equally rich hollows, with fillets in between. The mouldings were often cut on a sloping surface and none of the plain square masonry was left free. In later Early English work, the mouldings became more numerous and therefore thinner, while the rounds were very much undercut. The hollows were carved with ornament in many instances (204–5).

Early **Norman** work was sparing of decoration, and capitals, corbels, mouldings and walls were left, in general, in plain blocks with slight chamfering by an axe. Later work, however, showed a profusion of ornament, particularly from 1140 to 1200 when almost all surfaces of these members were carved with decoration. **Sculpture** in the round and in high relief was carved, especially on tympana and to fill niches and tabernacles. The most frequently used subject was Christ. Among the varied forms of geometrical decoration, the chevron and the billet were most often used. The **chevron**, or zig-zag as it is also often called, was used singly or in rows, and in later work, was often used facing different directions on consecutive mouldings (149–50). The **billet**, like the chevron, was one of the earliest forms of Norman decoration and in use all the period: it consisted of cylinder-shaped stones placed alternately with spaces in a hollow moulding (143, 146). Among other varieties of Norman decoration were the **beak-head** ornament, in which the heads of birds and beasts were carved in a hollow moulding while their beaks and tongues encircled the following round moulding; the **nail-head** ornament, which had pyramidal projections (145); the **star** ornament which was a four-pointed star cut into the moulding (144); the **lozenge** ornament, a diamond-shaped decoration (146); the **cable** ornament, the **scallop** and **floral** designs (147).

Just as the chevron ornament was the most typical of all Norman decoration and was to be found on nearly all examples of Norman workmanship, so the **dog-tooth** ornament was typical of the Early English period. It consisted of a small pyramid cut into four leaves which met in a projecting centre. The ornament—also called shark's tooth—can be found on nearly all Early English work in many different forms and sizes (157–8). **Diaper** decoration is also typical of this time; it is divided into squares which are filled with leaf and flower designs (154). **Crockets** were introduced in this period; they were formed into conventional foliage and projected from the main surface which they decorated. The name is derived from crook, after the shepherd's crook, and was adopted by the bishops as being a symbolical emblem of their office (151). **Early English carved foliage** decoration is an important feature of the style. It was used particularly on the capitals, but also in window and doorway mouldings, cornices and in bosses. It is called stiff-leaf foliage because of the stiff stalks which rise from the pier moulding then fall over in clusters of flowers and leaves. Much of it was based on the trefoil type of leaf, but considerable variation of form is derived from this (189, 199–200).

CHAPTER III

Decorated Gothic 1275 - 1375

As in the case of the introduction of Early English designs into Gothic architecture (see Chapter II) it is unwise to quote specific dates for the next change to the Decorated Gothic style. The transition was gradual and occurred at various times and rates in different parts of the country. In general, the Decorated work became established in the last quarter of the thirteenth century, particularly in the case of larger edifices such as cathedrals and churches. There is, however, a subdivision of the Decorated style which is noticeable. The earlier work is primarily of what is termed **Geometric** design. This is seen, in the main, in window tracery. Window openings are larger now, especially in width, designed with a greater number of mullions, and the window head—constructed in bar tracery—is predominantly divided geometrically, in circles and part circles. The later Decorated work is termed **Curvilinear** or Flamboyant, and in it the ogee shape in arch tracery largely supersedes the circle, leading to flowing designs of complicated, lively pattern. At the same time, ornament shows similar trends, becoming naturalistic, and presenting a riot of undulating, thrusting foliage, often later in globular shapes.

The trend which is apparent in Early English workmanship towards lighter construction and away from the massiveness of Norman work, is continued in Decorated Gothic building designs. The area covered by windows, doors and arches increases whereas the wall area diminishes; the resultant lack of solidity is compensated by increased use, accompanied by an improved knowledge, of exterior buttressing. Flying buttresses became more common. Simultaneously, stone vaulting construction develops and becomes more ambitious, and is typified by an increased number of ribs. We can thus see its evolution into tierceron, star and lierne-vault patterns, which are both aesthetically pleasing and constructionally sound.

Larger buildings, in particular, show a simplicity of basic design but a greater ornamentation of surfaces and individual members. In cathedrals and churches, clerestory windows are inserted or enlarged, while a corresponding diminution of the triforium storey is seen. It is difficult to find individual buildings entirely of this style, but for considerable quantity and distinctive quality in this work the cathedrals of Exeter, York and Lincoln should be studied.

In the fourteenth century, building work of all kinds was almost halted by the terrible visitation of plague, commonly called the Black Death, of 1348–9. This was one of the many recurring waves of infection which swept Britain and Europe in the Middle Ages; in this instance, it was so severe that more than a third of the population died. It is common to find, therefore, in cathedrals, churches and colleges work of the two styles of Decorated architecture, where part of the construction was effected before 1348, and the remainder continued about 1360 or later.

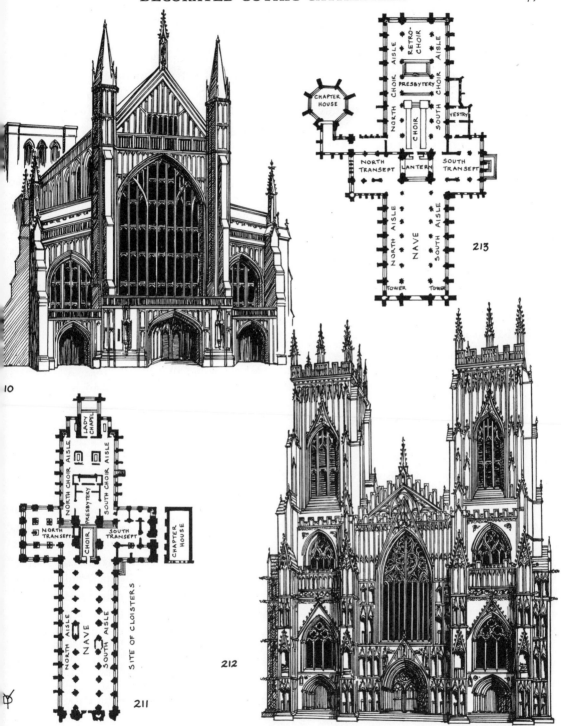

210 Winchester Cathedral: west front, *c.* 1360. Gable and parapets, *c.* 1400 211 Winchester Cathedral: plan. Length, *c.* 560 ft 212 York Minster: west front, *c.* 1291–1345. Towers later, *c.* 1432–74 213 York Minster: plan. Length approx. 505 ft

CATHEDRALS

As individual examples of Decorated Gothic workmanship in English cathedrals, Exeter and York are outstanding. Much of the construction of **Exeter Cathedral** is of this period and is some of the finest work extant. Particularly fine is the west front, in three stages, with its rich abundance of sculptured figures set in niches and carved ornament (VII); above these is the great window with Decorated tracery. This work is mid-fourteenth century, while the entrance screen of sculptured figures dates from later in the century. Also of this style are the east end, 1275–1308, the nave, 1328–42, and the choir, 1288–1308. The nave and choir with high vaults of simple, uninterrupted design are particularly good examples of the work (253, 255), as also are the plain but dignified nave piers of Purbeck marble with stone arches (287, 289). In **York Minster** the west front also presents a first-class example of Decorated work, but is a completely different mood from Exeter. There is much less sculptural decoration: the emphasis is on window tracery (with a fine central window of curvilinear design), buttresses, niches and crockets, all composed into a design of vertical lines, sweeping upwards to the fifteenth-century towers. The west front (212) was constructed 1291–1345, while at the same time the nave was built with its lofty piers and impressive high vault (285, 291; IX). Work on the choir and also on the Lady Chapel was continued subsequently.

Extensive workmanship of the Decorated period can also be seen at Lincoln, Lichfield, Carlisle, Bristol, Gloucester and Winchester cathedrals. At **Lincoln**, the famous Angel choir (Colour Plate 3) is largely of early Decorated pattern, while the outstandingly tall central tower, c. 1240–1311, provides a stately landmark in the Lincolnshire countryside (260, VIII). The west front of **Lichfield**, c. 1280 to early fourteenth century, like that of Exeter, is richly adorned with carved sculpture and ornament, although it has suffered from the Civil War and the weathering of the soft red sandstone employed, with consequent heavy restoration work (XI). The nave also shows early Decorated work, c. 1260–80; so does the Lady Chapel of later construction, 1320–35. **Carlisle** is particularly noted for its exceptional nine-light east window of mid-fourteenth curvilinear workmanship; it was designed when the east end was rebuilt 1352–95, following a disastrous fire (281). **Bristol** is largely of Decorated design except for a Perpendicular tower and a much later nave. The choir of **Gloucester** is of this period, 1337–50; it has a particularly fine high vault (X). The cloister of mid-fourteenth century shows one of the earliest examples of fan vaulting in England. The west front of **Winchester** (210) illustrates the later type of Decorated work where it has almost merged into the Perpendicular. This façade was begun c. 1350–60, but was not completed until the early fifteenth century. The choir at Winchester is also of Decorated workmanship.

Further specimens of Decorated Gothic work are extant at **Salisbury** in the chapter-house (277) and the gracefully proportioned central tower and spire (259; Frontispiece); **St Albans** in the Lady Chapel and nave (263); **Wells** central tower (258), the choir high vault (254) and the chapter house; **Hereford** central tower (257), the north transept and chapter house; **Worcester** central tower (261), and work in **Norwich, Chichester** and **Ripon Cathedrals** (282), and **Westminster Abbey, London.**

Interesting and extensive Decorated Gothic craftmanship was lost in **Old St Paul's, London**. Here, in this period, the eastern arm was completed, being remodelled and added to so that it consisted of 12 bays in length, with three-stage construction, roofed by a tier-

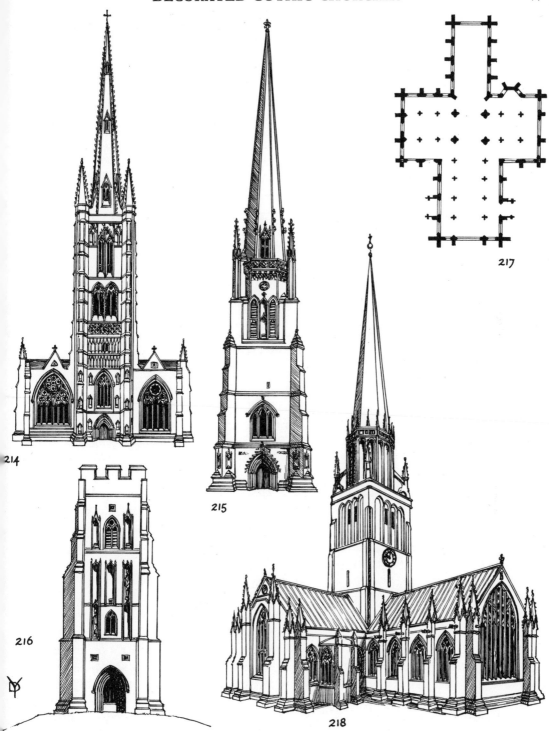

214 St Wulfram, Grantham: west front. Height 231 ft   215 Bloxham, Oxfordshire, height 198 ft
216 Chapel of St Michael, c. 1360. Summit of Glastonbury Tor, Somerset   217 Patrington: plan.
Length c. 125 ft   218 Patrington, Yorkshire

VIII   Lincoln Cathedral, from the east. Central
ver c. 1240–1311; Angel Choir, late 13th century

ceron vault, and with exterior flying-buttress support. The famous east window, a circle some 40 feet in diameter and known as 'Paul's rose' was designed above seven slender, tall lights. The whole was outstanding in Decorated tracery, and must have presented an inspiring sight.

CHURCHES

The average parish church was continuing its evolution and expansion, and, by 1300, was commonly in the form of an aisled nave, a longer eastern arm than previously, but generally without aisles or chapels, and with a western tower. In the following 75 years, chapels and/or aisles were added to the chancels of most churches, while the chancels were extended still further, and the east end then terminated in one flush wall with windows of Decorated tracery. Clerestories were added, or larger windows inserted in existing ones. A number of churches were still of cruciform plan, with the central tower now topped by a slender spire. In many cases, aisles and chapels were added to chancel, nave and transepts, giving a more rectangular plan. Stone, flint and timber were used in building, with timber roofs still prevailing, covered by tiles, lead, wood shingles or thatch. Many fine examples of church building and expansion in this period exist; among them are **St Wulfram, Grantham**, Lincolnshire (214), with its tall, graceful tower and spire, **Heckington**, Lincolnshire, **Patrington**, Yorkshire (217–18), and **Holy Trinity Church, Hull**.

CASTLES

The last quarter of the thirteenth century and the first half of the fourteenth century comprised the golden age of castle building in Britain. Commonly, the castles of this time are referred to as **'Edwardian'**, after Edward I who used the concentric method in erecting his castles to establish firmly his rule in Wales and Scotland, particularly the former. This type of design, recognisable by its several lines of defence, one outside the other, its dispensing with a keep or strongpoint, and its concentration on equal fortified strength in all quarters, was actually being used in castle building before Edward became king. The finest example that we have, in this respect, is at Caerphilly, South Wales, which immense, imposing structure was erected in the latter days of Henry III. However, Edward's name has long been associated with such castles as he built the fine Welsh and Border examples such as can be seen at Caernarvon, Conway, Beaumaris and Harlech. This type of design was used in Britain as a whole until *c.* 1350, after which time the need for castle defence in warfare diminished, because of the greater unification of Britain and the introduction of more 'open-field' methods of fighting. Castles continued to be erected, but in smaller numbers and with greater emphasis on the domestic rather than the military viewpoint. Gradually, as the building of castles declined, the fortification of towns was increased and elaborated, and many gatehouses and walls remain to us of such work.

The principle involved in building the concentric or quadrangular castles of the Decorated period was that no part of the structure should be undefended or weaker than another. The protective lines, in the form of walls and towers, were constructed one within another, giving two, or more usually three, rings of defence. The walls were less thick than formerly;

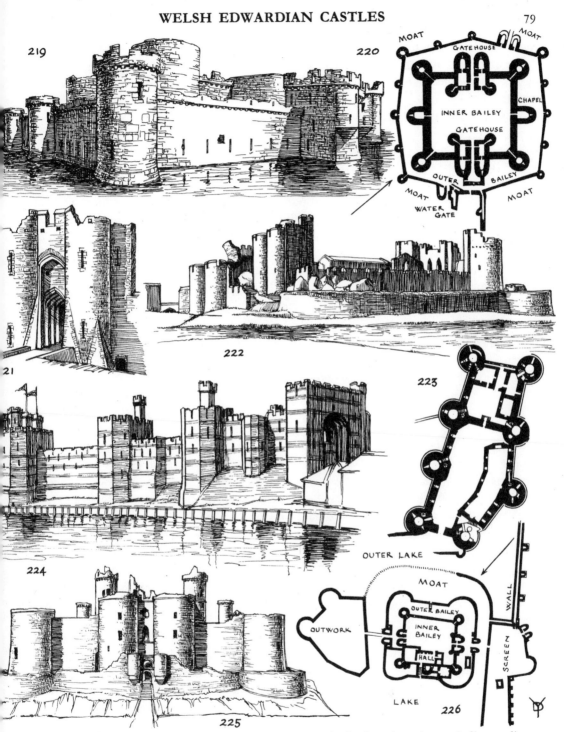

219 Beaumaris Castle, Anglesey, 1295–1325   220 Beaumaris Castle: plan. Arrow indicates direction of viewpoint shown in Fig. 219   221 Caerphilly Castle: gatehouse, outer screen wall   222 Caerphilly Castle, South Wales, 1267–77   223 Conway Castle, North Wales: plan   224 Caernarvon Castle, North Wales, 1283–1383, viewed from river   225 Harlech Castle, Merioneth, North Wales, 1286–90   226 Caerphilly Castle: plan. Arrow indicates direction of viewpoint shown in Fig. 222

more reliance was placed on the greater skill and accuracy of the defenders. Each section of the castle could be held independently and was covered by fire from the others. The keep—now superfluous—was replaced by an open courtyard in the centre of the castle structure. In this court, which was strengthened at its sides and angles by gatehouses and mural towers, were built the hall and other domestic accommodation. Round the open court were constructed the inner wall with its mural towers, and between this and the second wall was space for accommodating various offices, while in the third and outer bailey, generally very large, were established the garrison, stables, peasants and cattle, with the necessary buildings. Outside the outer wall was generally dug a ditch or moat; often a lake or stream was dammed for this purpose.

Caerphilly is the earliest and one of the finest and largest of such castles in Britain (XII). It has a rectangular inner ward of some 70 by 53 yards, with a drum tower at each corner and a gatehouse in the centre of each end wall. The hall is 72 by 33 feet, flanked by a chapel and private apartments. Further accommodation is available in the gatehouses. The second ward, of some 106 by 90 yards, is also rectangular with gatehouses on the same sides. The wall of this ward descends 20 feet into the water, where use has been made of the lake, supplemented by a man-made moat. A further ward is defended by gatehouses, towers and portcullis and was connected to the second by bridges. The castle is now partly ruined, and the outer ward and bridges particularly have been affected, but the whole structure still presents a remarkable picture of this type of fourteenth-century military construction, rendered more convincing by the lake which still ripples outside the walls. A plan of Caerphilly castle is given in Fig. 226, a view showing the middle ward in Fig. 222 and a gatehouse in Fig. 221. **Harlech Castle**, in an impregnable position on the coast of North Wales, rises out of the sea on rock, and is approached from the landward side over a bridge which once spanned its moat. Like Beaumaris Castle on the Isle of Anglesey, it is of similar design to Caerphilly (225, 227). At **Beaumaris** the moat is still full of water on two sides, and entrance is gained over a wooden bridge to the gatehouse (219–20). The **Tower of London** was also converted into a concentric castle at this time. The Norman keep and Early English inner ward were ringed by a further ward (228). Outside this was constructed a moat on three sides, while the river Thames provided water defence on the fourth. It was on this side that the strongly fortified water tower (St Thomas's Tower) was built, the lower portion of which came to be known as Traitor's Gate. The gate was used as an entrance to the Tower of London from the busy Thames highway. It gained its name from its use as a landing place for prisoners who had been tried at Westminster.

As in the purely domestic architecture of this period, the **hall** was the principal feature of living accommodation. It was large and lofty, open to the timbers of the roof, while the domestic apartments led off from the daïs end, and the kitchen and other offices from the 'screens'. The **kitchen** itself was also large, with immense fireplaces and ovens for cooking and baking. A **chapel** was included in the group of buildings inside the inner ward.

Gatehouses were now most important centres of defence; a large castle might have several of these, but generally there was one principal gatehouse, larger and stronger than the others. Outside this, across the moat or alternative defence, was another gatehouse—often called the **barbican**—which constituted the outer point of protection from attack, and could be abandoned if necessary. Gatehouses were generally rectangular in plan, and were flanked

227 Harlech Castle, Merioneth, Wales: great gatehouse and smaller outer gate, 1286–90   228 Tower of London: the Bloody Tower gateway and the Wakefield Tower, 13th and 14th centuries   229 Landgate, Rye, Sussex, 1329   230 Battle Abbey, Sussex: gatehouse, c. 1340   231 Lewes Castle, Sussex: barbican, first half 14th century   232 Canterbury, Kent: west gateway, c. 1378   233 Carisbrooke Castle, Isle of Wight: gatehouse, 14th century

in front (and often in the rear also) by drum towers, which might contain staircases. The first floor of the gatehouse was generally designed as a spacious room. In the centre of the gatehouse, at ground level, was a Decorated Gothic entrance arch, defended by a portcullis, and behind this, a thick double door of oak, secured by iron bars fitted into sockets in the walls on either side. Iron studs were usual on the door framing. In the rear of this door was often a small wooden roofed room with a further portcullis behind it. A doorway then opened on either side at the back of this into the guard room and perhaps a small prison cell (221, 227–33).

The **portcullis** itself was of iron, or oak with iron spikes. It was suspended by ropes or chains fitted in side grooves. These chains were either worked from a winch or were fastened to a counterpoise. The **portcullis chamber**, into which the portcullis was drawn, and from which it was worked was either a special small room or use was made of the first-floor chamber, as in larger castles (271).

Further protection to the main gatehouse was provided by a **drawbridge** over the moat which often acted as a link between the gatehouse and the outer barbican. The drawbridge was a stout wooden platform drawn up and down on chains and operated by counterpoise weights or by hand. When in the 'down' position, the drawbridge rested on a pier sunk in the bed of the moat or ditch; when up, it concealed the entrance portal.

Castle **walls**, now much thinner, were about 6–8 feet in thickness and of 30–40 feet in height. A rampart walk, called the **allure**, formed a circuit round the top of these walls and their mural towers set at intervals. The towers were half-round, rectangular, polygonal or completely circular, projecting in front and behind. They varied greatly in size. The exterior wall top and allure were protected by an **embattled parapet** which often projected over the base of the walls and towers so that the defenders could hurl down missiles or pour boiling tar or other liquids on to the attackers. This architectural feature is known as **machicolation**. Gatehouses were equipped with similar machicolations, or projecting apertures (229, 231–3). Ovens and flues were situated above these for heating the pitch or lead.

Adequate accommodation for sanitation was provided, and some mural towers were equipped as garderobes.

In addition to those already mentioned, good examples of castle building in this period are those at **Flint, Pembroke** and **Carew**; while fine gatehouses or barbicans exist at **Lewes, Carisbrooke**, Isle of Wight, the **Tower of London, Battle Abbey**, Sussex, and **Canterbury** (231, 233, 228, 230, 232). The two famous castles of Edward I at **Caernarvon** and **Conway** in North Wales are rather different in plan from the concentric designs at Caerphilly and Beaumaris. They were built as part of a scheme for town defence and are roughly rectangular in plan with strong mural towers set at intervals in the main wall. At Caernarvon these towers are polygonal, at Conway, circular. Both castles occupy a commanding position. Caernarvon (XIII) is almost encircled by the river estuary, and Conway rises above the harbour edge (223–4). At **Windsor Castle**, which today presents an extensive, heterogeneous mixture of the work of various periods, considerable quantity of new building and alteration was carried out at this time.

TOWNS

In the Middle Ages, town planning varied according to the foundation period of the individual town. Those which originated in Roman times, such as Colchester and Chester, were of rectangular plan, built within city walls which had an entrance gate on each face. Others, of Norman or twelfth-century origin, had grown up round the castle or monastery, as this provided the greater security and means of livelihood; the houses were clustered in narrow streets round the outside of the moat. Some towns, however, founded in the thirteenth and fourteenth centuries, were more symmetrical in planning with wider main streets arranged in parallel lines intersecting at right angles. Houses were then packed tightly on to the remaining rectangular plots. Near the centre of the town was a large market place into which the main streets emptied, with usually one corner site reserved for the church. Numbers of such towns exist on this plan on the Continent; in England, however, few examples remain. Winchelsea is one of these, planned as a seaport by Edward I, on a new site, as the sea had encroached on the old town. Three of the town gates remain—for Medieval towns were strongly fortified by walls and gatehouses—made from Kentish ragstone with drum towers at their corners. Few of the original houses, however, are extant. Another town also founded by Edward I is Kingston-upon-Hull, in which a harbour was created where the river Hull flows into the Humber estuary. The harbour was completed in 1299 and much of the town grew up quickly around it, while roads were built across the low-lying marshes to the present-day suburbs (then villages) of Hessle, Anlaby, Holderness and Cottingham. The imposing church of Holy Trinity in Hull is an extant architectural achievement of this development. The streets were paved and the town fortified by walls, towers and gates, with adequate ditch protection; the cost for this was met by toll charges; the principal remains today of town buildings of the Decorated Gothic time are **gatehouses** and town walls. Numbers of the former exist in different parts of the country, of similar architectural character, and all of strong construction. However, today they are gradually disappearing (as are also Medieval bridges) in face of an urgent need to widen town roads to accommodate the increased motor traffic, except in the all too few instances where the main road has been built to by-pass the town. Examples of such gatehouses can still be seen at **Canterbury** (232), **Rye**, Sussex (229), and of abbey gatehouses at, for example, **Battle**, Sussex (230, 269).

DOMESTIC BUILDINGS

A greater number of **houses** of the Decorated Gothic period remain than those of previous centuries; although such examples are predominantly in country areas; few town houses have survived due to the prevalence of fire in the closely packed timber structures and the necessity for rebuilding in later times on the same site. In the southern part of England, dwellings were becoming more domestic and peaceful in appearance—manor houses, town houses and cottages—while those in the north and border areas were still heavily fortified and more like castles than houses. However, most homes, other than those in towns, were still protected by a barbican or gatehouse, with portcullis and drawbridge, and were encircled by a moat or defence walls; the moat often lapped the house walls. Town houses were of similar plan to country manor houses, although more restricted in area, and with the gable end facing the street to economise in space. These gables were decorated by barge boards, carved and crocketed. The homes of poorer people were still very primitive; they were made of wattle and daub with thatch or rush covering.

In general, the appearance of houses was still castellated and this was most apparent in the barbican and towers. Most houses of any size had small, square towers attached; these were partly for defence and asylum in case of attack and partly to indicate wealth and rank. In less peaceful areas, the ground floors possessed no windows, only loopholes; the ceilings were stone vaulted and the space used for storage, while the living accommodation was on the upper floors. The entrance was frequently via an exterior staircase which led from the courtyard to the hall door; the latter was often covered by an entrance porch of wood or stone. Ground floor entrances were now more common in towns, however, with just a few steps leading up to a wooden porch.

The general **manor-house plan** was in the form of a rectangle with or without the addition of wings. The hall continued to be the principal living-room and occupied the whole height of the house. In the wing or wings, generally of two storeys, were accommodated the solar, chapel, private rooms and other offices. The whole, with stabling and kitchen, was arranged round an open quadrangle or courtyard, or at least three sides of it. The hall was in the centre of the main front and the gatehouse faced the open side opposite to it. Many manor houses were of wood, but if stone was used for the main building, wood was employed for the outbuildings.

Roofs were covered with wooden shingles or thatch most commonly, although tiles and slates were used more as time passed. The ridge crest was often ornamental. The roof pitch became less steep later in the fourteenth century. A **louvre** was usual, of decorated lantern structure over the hall or kitchen roofs (311), but **chimneys** were becoming more common as wall fireplaces were installed in other rooms. These chimney shafts were round or octagonal in shape; they were of various heights and had apertures on all sides for the escape of smoke. They were set on the roof-ridge or gable-peak and had crocketed or crenellated tops (242–3).

Town houses extended vertically rather than horizontally and a third storey was often added, especially in London, at this time. The lower storey was half underground and was commonly stone vaulted over and used for cellarage and storage. The rest of the house was usually of wood. The upper storey overhung the lower to give greater space and stability. The high-pitched gable roof surmounted the top storey and a window was set in the gable, while the space within was often used for grain storage.

The **hall** roof was open to the timbers. It was a large rectangular room with a central hearth, and louvre above or, occasionally, a wall fireplace with chimney. At one end was a slightly raised daïs with a window at one side of it and a doorway at the other, leading to the accommodation in that side of the house. At the other end of the hall was the passage or 'screens', above which was the minstrels' gallery. Access to this and upper rooms at this end of the house was by step-ladder or small staircase. At each end of the 'screens' was a doorway to the exterior, while behind them, doorways led to the kitchen, pantry and buttery.

The **solar**, the private room of the owner and his family, was on the upper floor, reached by staircase from the daïs end of the hall. It also had an open timber roof, but generally a wall fireplace (256). Nearly all homes, even the smaller ones, had a room used as a **chapel**. It usually had an east window with ecclesiastical-type tracery.

The **kitchen** was commonly a separate building—due to fear of fire—connected to the 'screens' by a covered passageway. Larger kitchens were of stone with vaulted roof, others were of wood, laths and plaster. Both types had a central louvre in the roof for the escape of

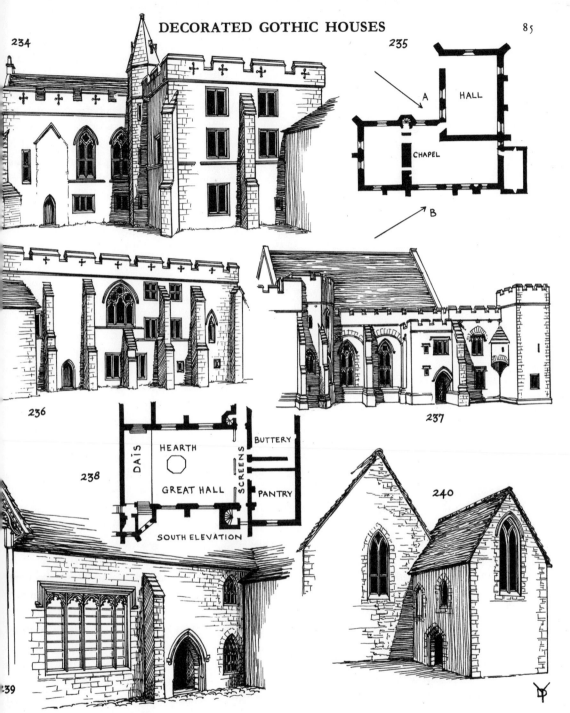

234 Markenfield Hall, Yorkshire, c. 1310. Hall is on first floor; original entrance was a doorway also on first floor reached by external staircase—see remains of this   235 Markenfield Hall: plan, first floor. Arrow A indicates view in Fig. 234, arrow B that in Fig. 236   236 Markenfield Hall from the east, showing traceried chapel window   237 Penshurst Place, Kent: elevation of Great Hall, c. 1340   238 Penshurst Great Hall: plan   239 The Mote House, Ightham, Kent: east wing showing Great Hall, c. 1340–50   240 Old Soar Manor House, Plaxtol, Kent, c. 1290. Solar and chapel windows now restored to original design

241 Glastonbury Abbey: the Abbot's kitchen, early
14th century

smoke and steam. They were equipped with several large fireplaces and ovens (241). The pantry, buttery, larder and store rooms were adjacent.

A small washing-room or lavatory was situated near to the bed-chambers, and fitted with a laver or cistern of lead, marble or stone. In larger houses, garderobes provided adequate accommodation; in stone buildings these were often in a garderobe tower, as in a castle, with two or four per floor. Smaller versions were garderobe turrets. Outlets were to the moat or to a cesspool pit.

The **staircase** was often as yet in the form of stone steps on the exterior of the house (244). Internal staircases were becoming more common and took the form of stone newel-stairs in a turret, or straight wood stairs or ladders (245).

Architectural details such as window openings, arches, porches, doorways, mouldings and buttresses were based on those designed for churches and cathedrals, although in domestic architecture, simpler, less ornamental forms were used. Window glass was still expensive and uncommon in houses; wood window shutters were more usual.

Among the outstanding examples of domestic architecture which possess portions of Decorated Gothic work still in existence are Penshurst Place, Kent, Markenfield Hall, Yorkshire, Stokesay Castle, Shropshire, Old Soar Manor House, Kent and The Mote, Ightham, Kent. At **Penshurst**, the earlier Medieval house has been enlarged and added to in later periods but the fourteenth-century hall (*c.* 1340) is still intact with its fine timber roof, Decorated Gothic windows, daïs and central, open hearth. At the daïs end of the hall, an archway opens into a staircase leading up to the other apartments (237–8, 245). **Markenfield Hall**, a manor house still surrounded by a moat, has a hall and chapel of this period (*c.* 1310) in an L-shaped plan. The Decorated Gothic windows are in good condition (234–6). **Stokesay Castle** is primarily a domestic building, despite its name, and was strengthened and crenellated in 1291. A moat encircles the buildings and courtyard. A tower adjoins the house at one end and is connected to it by a covered passage. This tower is an irregular polygon of three storeys; its battlemented parapet is pierced by loopholes, and a staircase in the wall leads to the upper storeys. The hall, occupying much of the main building, is large and spacious, with open, timber, collar-braced roof and several fine window openings. The main entrance is by an arched doorway at the north end of the hall from the courtyard, while at the opposite end of the hall, another doorway leads to the other apartments. Stokesay is a fine example of thirteenth-century domestic architecture. At **Old Soar Manor House** the site of the Medieval hall is now occupied by an eighteenth-century farmhouse, but the solar, chapel, small chamber and garderobe remain from the late thirteenth-century manor house. The building is in Kentish ragstone, and all these rooms are raised above ground level, with a barrel-vaulted undercroft beneath the solar. Restoration, particularly of the window openings, has been carried out by the Ministry of Works, using the old remains and preserving the early character of the building. The original windows were not glazed, with the exception of the northeast chapel window, but were fitted with wooden shutters. The interior, particularly the solar, gives an interesting picture of late thirteenth-century domestic architecture with its early timber roof and window seats. There is also an early fourteenth-century piscina (293) and a fine carved stone corbel (300). The whole is a relatively unspoilt, good example of its period and of this type of house (240). **Ightham Mote** shows several periods of domestic architecture, blended pleasantly and successfully into a Medieval and Tudor whole with the moat still encircling the house. The hall, which is entered from the interior courtyard, is the fourteenth-century part which still remains (239).

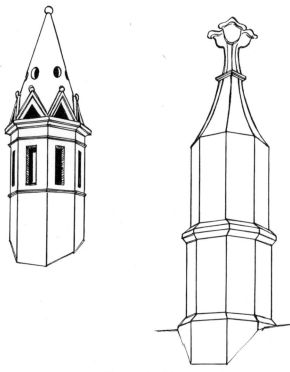

242–3 Domestic chimneys

Other examples of domestic architecture of this time can be seen in different parts of the country. Most notable and interesting examples are at **Sutton Courtenay Manor House**, Berkshire—a fourteenth-century hall and external staircase; two houses at **Meare**, Somerset —the **Manor House** with hall and cellarage and the **Fish House** near by, which is small but in good condition; also **Martock Manor House**, Somerset.

Timber-framed Houses

This method of domestic building was in use all through the Medieval period and later. The technique and workmanship improved with time but the basic design was fundamental. It has been mentioned in a previous chapter that early timber framing was based on cruck foundation, but, in general, from the thirteenth century onwards, vertical walls were built, at least in the larger homes. The main framework was constructed on to a rectangular base of timber baulks (ground sills) mortised to one another. These ground sills were often set on to a low wall of stone or brick to avoid damp and rot. Vertical posts were then mortised into the sills at the corners and extended the full height of the house. On these were supported the horizontal wall plates which, in turn, carried the roof timbers. Smaller homes consisted only of this one rectangular room with one or two storeys; larger versions were subdivided by more timber baulks which supported the floor timbers. Walls were then constructed with

244 Beaumaris Castle, Anglesey: stone steps inside outer curtain wall, leading up to parapet

245 Penshurst Place, Kent: staircase from Great Hall to Solar

horizontal and vertical wood framing, and, later, diagonal braces were added to these. The spaces between were filled with wattle and daub or plaster. Window and door openings were framed with wood, and windows were generally fitted with wood shutters, but were later glazed. The roof, of timber, was generally a simplified version of the ecclesiastical design (p. 94). In smaller buildings, floor joists were supported on the wall plates, but when the floor span was too large for this, one or more baulks called 'summers' would be fastened across, and the joists would then be supported lengthwise across them. This was common in two-storey buildings where the upper floors were extended and overhung the lower. The joists were mortised into the summers and plates. All the main construction beams in a house were mortised and pegged together, although the timbers might be cut and measured some distance away and assembled where required. This also facilitated house moving, which could be and was carried out quite literally. Oak was the usual material, being in generous and ubiquitous supply. Pargetting was employed in timber-framed houses; this was a method of applying plaster to cover wall surfaces and was either finished smoothly or rough-cast with the addition of small stones.

Barns

These, built in considerable numbers throughout the country, were often large and solidly constructed. The same architectural features appeared as in other building, except that windows were generally small and solely for ventilation. Many barns were of wood, but in stone versions also the roof was of open timber framing, as in houses and churches. Some larger

246 Tithe Barn, Bradford-on-Avon, Wiltshire, mid-14th century

247 The Abbey Barn, Glastonbury, Somerset, c. 1330

examples were divided into nave and aisles like a church, and were strongly buttressed. Fine specimens still exist of this time, notably the **tithe barn** at **Bradford-on-Avon**, Wiltshire (246), and the **Abbey barn** at **Glastonbury**, Somerset (247).

BRIDGES

A number of **stone bridges** exist of fourteenth-century construction. These were usually jointed on timber piles, which were reinforced with iron and driven into the river bed. A starling of piles was built round each main pile and filled in solid. The starling tops were boarded and a stone platform was laid to support the actual bridge which was generally constructed of ashlar blocks laid with mortar. Examples can be seen at **Newbridge**, over the Thames (248), **Aylesford** and **East Farleigh** over the Medway (249–50), **Bideford** in Devon over the Torridge and at **Huntingdon** over the Ouse. The pointed arch is predominant in such designs. Numbers of Medieval bridges were built with a **chapel** on them. In this, a priest would bless travellers, hold services and collect alms. Most of these chapels have now disappeared but one remains at **Bradford-on-Avon**, Wiltshire (251), and also at **St Ives**, Huntingdonshire. In troubled areas war bridges were common, wherein a fortified

248 Newbridge over River Thames, near Oxford 249 Aylesford Bridge over River Medway, Kent 250 East Farleigh Bridge over River Medway, Kent 251 Chapel Bridge at Bradford-on-Avon, Wiltshire

IX *York Minster: the nave, looking east, 1291–1*

252 Monnow Bridge with military gateway, Monmouth, late 13th century

gatehouse was constructed in the centre of the bridge to control the passageway. Again, most of these gateways have gone, but a good example can be seen at **Monmouth** over the Monnow (252).

ARCHITECTURAL FEATURES

Vaults and Roofs

The **stone vaulting** of the Decorated period becomes more complicated than earlier work, and intricate star and net patterns are produced. At first, a more complex design than the Early English ribbed vaulting is achieved by the introduction of an added number of ribs called **tierceron ribs.** These are introduced in pairs, rising from the same capital and ascending to the ridge rib, where the joint is covered by a small boss. They do not, however, rise to the central and larger boss. A vaulted roof of this type, therefore, would consist of transverse, diagonal, ridge and tierceron ribs. **Bosses**—beautifully carved, generally with natural foliage—are usually at all the intersections, and particularly on the ridge. There are many fine examples of **tierceron vaulting,** notably the nave and choir high vault at **Exeter Cathedral** (253, 255). In the development of this theme of increasing the complexity of ribbed vaulting, but not necessarily strengthening the construction, **lierne ribs** were introduced. This term, taken from the French *lier,* meaning to bind or connect, is used to indicate

Gloucester Cathedral: the choir, 1337–50

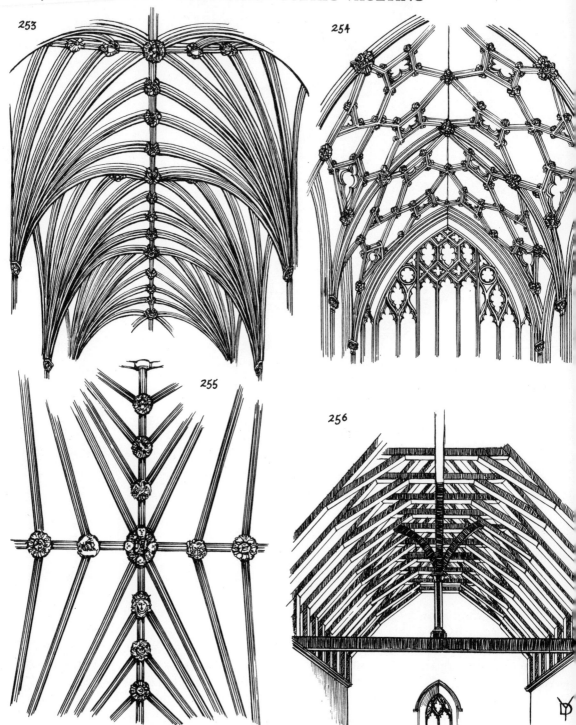

253 Exeter Cathedral: nave high vault, ribbed tierceron style, c. 1353–69   254 Wells Cathedral: choir high vault, lierne style, c. 1329   255 Exeter: high vault: plan view   256 Timber domestic roof—typical example of solar roofing, 14th century. Tie-beam and king post

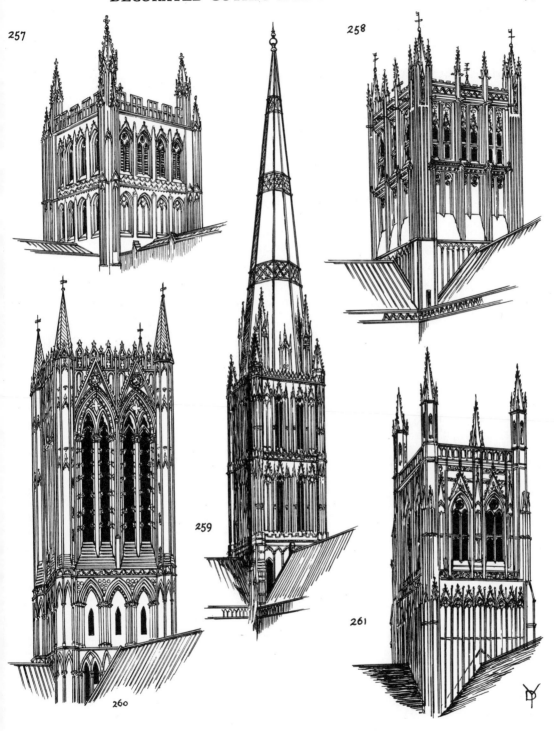

257 Hereford Cathedral: central tower, *c.* 1325　258 Wells Cathedral: central tower, *c.* 1321–3
259 Salisbury Cathedral: central tower and spire, *c.* 1334　260 Lincoln Cathedral: central tower.
Lower stage *c.* 1240, upper stage *c.* 1306–11　261 Worcester Cathedral: central tower, *c.* 1365–74

a rib which does not spring from the capital or arch springing, or rise to a central boss, but which merely crosses and connects from rib to rib, giving the star and net designs of the time; these are termed **stellar vaulting**, and can be seen particularly in **Wells, Gloucester, Canterbury, Ely** and **Winchester Cathedrals** (254, IX, X, XVII). The problem of vaulting was being appreciated and understood better as time passed. Consequently, while these vaults are more interesting than earlier patterns, they were also designed bearing in mind the weakening of the structure by the use of larger windows and the resulting necessary increased abutment. The design and placing of vaults and piers are essentially concerned.

Examples of **timber open roofs** of this time are somewhat scarce, and the best specimens are usually found in domestic halls rather than churches. **Penshurst Place** and **Old Soar Manor House** are two examples, as mentioned earlier. In general, there are two main designs: that based on **tie-beam** construction and the **collar-beam** pattern. The majority of remaining roofs are of the former variety, where the tie-beam is frequently cambered and forms a low arch with curved braces to support it on corbels. **King-** or **queen-posts** rest on the tie-beams and are braced to the **ridge-piece** (256). In most timber roof construction, pairs of **principal rafters** are set at intervals into the ridge-piece and wall plates. Two extra, massive principals form the gable at each end. The tie-beam is to prevent these principals from spreading, **Purlins** are placed horizontally from principal to principal and carry the common rafters. Hammerbeam designs of timber roof were introduced late in this period, but are more typical of the fifteenth century so are described in Chapter IV.

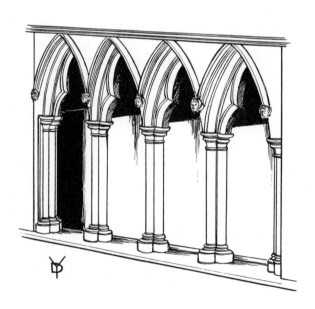

262 Exeter Cathedral: nave triforium   263 St Alban's Cathedral: nave triforium

XI   *Lichfield Cathedral: the west front, c. 1280–13.*

Spires and Towers

It is in the Decorated period of Gothic architecture that **spire** building and design, initiated in the thirteenth century, comes to fruition. Fourteenth-century spires and towers are, in many instances, finely proportioned one to the other, and present a tapering graceful silhouette, reaching high into the sky, and making many a church and cathedral a landmark over great distances in the countryside. **Lichfield Cathedral** has three spires (XI), and among the truly great steeples should be included that of **Salisbury** (259; Frontispiece), and the churches at **Grantham** (214), **Newark**, and **Patrington** (218). There are also noteworthy examples of central and western **towers**, such as those at **Wells, Lincoln, Worcester** and **Hereford Cathedrals** (257–8, 260–1).

Triforia

During this time, the triforium in larger churches and cathedrals diminished in height to make more room for taller clerestory windows and give a more lofty nave arch with consequent taller piers, higher vaults and larger aisle windows (262–3). These alterations provided much better illumination in the cathedral, although at the expense of rather stumpy triforium arcades. Towards the end of the fourteenth century the triforium stage was often omitted altogether. As the **clerestory windows** became taller, they also increased even more in width to accommodate the geometric and curvilinear tracery of the period; they commonly reached from buttress to buttress.

Buttresses

A great variety of architectural forms can be seen in the buttresses of Decorated work; many are quite plain, in stages with sets-off and terminating in a slope. Others are topped by a gable, pediment or crocketed finial. Most angles are chamfered. Richer designs have carved niches and canopies, with pinnacle decoration above, crocketed and terminating in a finial. Gargoyles are set over many buttresses. **Corner buttresses** are fitted diagonally or face in both directions. **Flying buttresses** are now much more common, particularly in cathedral workmanship (264–8).

Doorways

The Early English designs wherein the shafts of door jambs were detached and often of different stone or marble were gradually discontinued in Decorated Gothic work, and shafts became slender but had capitals of varied pattern, commonly foliated with naturalistic foliage. The size of **doorways** varied greatly and with it the amount of decoration. Many small church and domestic examples were quite plain, having only a dripstone and round moulding. In other instances, the mouldings continued round the arch and door jamb without separate shaft, capital and base (270, 273). **Dripstone terminations** were generally in the form of heads, often royal or of bishops; others were foliated. **Doorway heads** varied also: many were of ogee pattern, others in pointed arches of different proportions, while some were square-headed. Interior mouldings to the arch were frequently trefoiled or cinquefoiled (269, 272, 275). Most doorways were single but larger versions were in double form and many examples were gabled. In the more important specimens a great deal of decoration was used

I   Caerphilly Castle, Glamorganshire, late 13th century

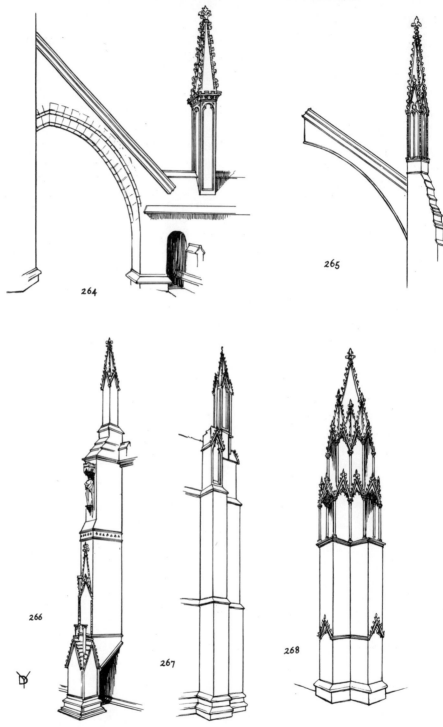

264 Exeter Cathedral: flying buttress   265 Salisbury Cathedral: flying buttress   266 Gloucester Cathedral: nave buttress   267 Bolton Abbey, Yorkshire: corner buttress   268 Church corner buttress

269 Battle Abbey, Sussex: gatehouse doorway, *c.* 1340   270 Chapel of St Michael, Glastonbury
Tor: doorway, *c.* 1360   271 Beaumaris Castle, Anglesey: an entrance gateway showing portcullis
positioning, *c.* 1295–1325   272 Small church doorway with ogee-shaped head   273 Church doorway with ball-flower ornament. Carved wood door   274 Carved wood church door   275 Larger
doorway. Timber door with iron scroll work

276 Church porch of timber

in the form of richly carved crockets, finials, foliated cusps, decorated spandrels and ball-flower and other ornament.

Doors were still designed with elaborate ornamental ironwork, although many plain, boarded and panelled examples also exist. In the fourteenth century, wooden doors carved with tracery and panelled designs began to supersede the iron work decoration, while iron was used for lock fittings (273–4).

Porches were of stone or wood—predominantly the latter—and of bold or shallow projection. The designs and ornament, the windows and side arcades followed the prevailing architectural fashion (276).

Window Openings

The form of window **tracery** became much more complex in the fourteenth century; windows were divided by one or more vertical **mullions** to give a number of lights, and five, seven or even nine were frequently seen in larger buildings. **Transoms** were also used, but more sparingly and generally for domestic work, where only two or three lights occupied the width of the window. There were four main planes of construction: on the exterior face there was first the plane of the wall, then, working inwards, the mullions plane, the tracery plane and lastly the cusping plane. **Bar tracery** was in general use, and a far larger area of glass in proportion to stone wall surface and tracery was now an accomplished fact. The window arches were pointed or ogee in shape; in the former instances the arch varied in width from a sharp pointed design to a very obtuse one. The inner arch was commonly of different shape and proportions from the outer. Square-headed windows and segmental designs were also in use. As referred to earlier in the chapter, there were two chief types of Decorated Gothic tracery, although an almost infinite number of variations were played on either theme. The earlier type of tracery— **Geometric**—employed circles, trefoils and quatrefoils predominantly in its designs. These were often most complicated in pattern, particularly when a large number of mullions was used. Among the best examples are the east window of **Ripon Cathedral** (282), many windows in **Exeter Cathedral** (VII), and those in the chapter-houses at **York Minster, Southwell Minster** and **Salisbury** and **Wells Cathedrals** (277). The later work was predominantly **Curvilinear** or flowing tracery, although the two styles overlapped a great deal and were often used side by side in the same building. Designs in Curvilinear tracery varied tremendously but they can be classified roughly into three categories: those in which the window is subdivided into two detached sub-arches, often ogee in shape, and

277 Salisbury Cathedral: chapter-house, c. 1270–80. Geometrical tracery   278 Segmental-headed church window, c. 1320–30   279 Penshurst Place, Kent: window from Great Hall, c. 1340   280 Circular church window, c. 1320   281 Carlisle Cathedral: east window of choir, mid-14th century   282 Ripon Cathedral: east window of choir, c. 1300

separating or intersecting, with a centrepiece of design; those in which the window is divided into two engaged sub-arches, wherein the outer sides are identical with the main arch, and pointed arches are used; and, thirdly, where there are no sub-arches, and **net** or **reticulated tracery** patterns are employed. In such designs, the stonework in the head is formed in waved lines crossing one another in each direction, giving quatrefoils all over the window head. With the use of five or more lights, a diaper effect is produced as in examples at **Westminster Abbey**. Fine specimens of Curvilinear tracery can be seen in the east window of **Carlisle Cathedral**, which has nine lights (281), and in the central, west window of **York Minster** (212).

Circular windows are fairly common in churches and cathedrals of this time and give a fine opportunity for Decorated Gothic tracery designs. A number of famous rose windows in cathedrals belong to this style, although some of these do not exist now. A particularly great example was in **Old St Paul's**—the east window known as 'Paul's rose'. A typical position for such windows is at the end of the transepts, as at **Lincoln Cathedral** and **Westminster Abbey**, although in smaller churches they are more commonly set in the west front (280).

283–4 Decorated Gothic arcades

Windows were frequently inserted into spires and were known as **spire lights**. They became larger and more decorative as the fourteenth century advanced (214–15).

Arches

The arch most generally employed in Decorated work is the **equilateral arch**, although **obtuse** and **drop arches** are also in general use. The **ogee** form of arch is prevalent, particularly for door and window heads and arcading. This design is a four-centred construction; its two upper curves are concave and the two lower convex. The **shouldered arch** is also often seen. All designs can be multi-foiled; the commonest being the trefoil and cinquefoil. In Decorated work, the arch mouldings often continue unbroken down the jamb or pillar without a stop being provided by an impost moulding or capital.

285 York Cathedral: nave pier, *c.* 1310–30 286 Salisbury Cathedral: cloister opening, *c.* 1265–85
287 Exeter Cathedral: nave pier and arch, *c.* 1328–42 288 St. Alban's Cathedral: nave triforium,
foliated capital 289 Exeter Cathedral: pier base, early 14th century 290 Southwell Minster: foliated capital, *c.* 1295–1300 291 York Cathedral: nave capital, *c.* 1310–1320

Arcades followed the architectural style and were used to decorate the richer, more ornamental buildings (283–4).

Piers, Capitals and Bases

The most usual arrangement of shafts to make up a **pier** is in a diamond-shaped plan. The shafts are set close together with only a fillet moulding or small hollow between them. Often, the central shaft is larger than the side ones, (285, 287; IX). In smaller churches, only four

292 Winchester Cathedral: west front, niche

293 Old Soar Manor House, Kent: piscina

294 St Alban's Cathedral: holy-water stoup

shafts might be employed with wider spaces in between, occupied by a fillet and bold hollow. Alternatively, the multi-angular flat-faced pier is in use.

Decorated **capitals** are generally of two main types: the **moulded** and the **foliated**. In the former instance, the abacus is generally in the same block of stone as the rest of the capital, unlike the earlier work when it was often separate. It is broader now, in roll form, and is a part of the mouldings of the capital, which consists of rolls, hollows and scrolls, with small fillets. Ogee-curved mouldings are also used (287). In foliated capitals, the foliage is naturalistic and free; leaf shapes are larger, less stalk is apparent and flowers and fruit are used abundantly (285, 288, 290–1).

Bases are composed of triple rolls, but these were replaced later in the fourteenth century by the use of ogee mouldings. The bases tend to become taller and are often set on an octagonal plinth (285, 287, 289).

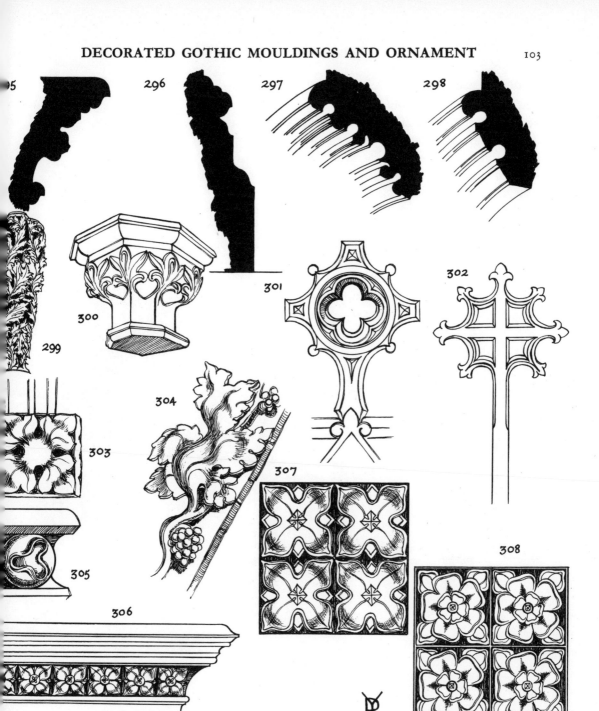

295 Typical capital moulding section   296 Typical base moulding   297 Arch moulding   298 Arch moulding   299 Exeter Cathedral: carved stone corbel   300 Old Soar Manor House: carved stone corbel   301 Church roof stone cross   302 Church roof stone cross   303 Carved stone dripstone termination   304 Winchester Cathedral: carved crocket decoration   305 Ball-flower ornament 306 Carved decorated moulding   307–8 Diaper decoration

Other Features

The ogee and scroll mouldings are also used profusely in **string-** and **ground-courses, cornices** and **dripstones**. The latter is often itself in an ogee curve, crocketed and terminating in a carved finial. **Battlements** are still constructed; these are pierced, and carved with decorative panels in quatrefoil and ball-flower ornament.

Niches provide one of the chief forms of decoration of the style and often possess great beauty of design and workmanship. Some are panelled, wherein the frontal canopies are flush with the wall or buttress in which they are set, while the interiors are square or semi-hexagonal in plan. Others have projecting canopies and have triangular,

309

310

309 Tewkesbury Abbey: west front, turret, 14th century

310 Gloucester Cathedral: transept, turret

311 Westminster Hall: louvre

ogee or pinnacle heads, with crocket and carved finial decoration. Such niches also have a projecting base set on a corbel or a basement pedestal carried up from the projecting face below. They are often flanked by small buttresses and pinnacles (292).

Like the niches, **piscinas** show the decorative features of the time and are often richly carved, with canopies and crockets. They are water drains and are set in churches and chapels (293–4).

XIII   Caernarvon Castle, North Wales, 1283–c. 1.

Mouldings and Ornament

Mouldings are now less deeply cut, but are more complex in grouping. The double ogee and roll are most typical, and there is a greater use of fillets. Chamfers are also in use (295–8).

The typical form of **decoration** in this style is the **ball-flower ornament**; it is comparable with the dog-tooth ornament in the Early English period. The ball-flower is a globular flower, partly opened to show a small sphere. It is used profusely in all buildings; it is generally set in a hollow moulding on arches, cornices and canopies (273, 305). Another common form of decoration is the **four-leaved flower**, which has four petals in high relief and a raised or depressed centre. It also is generally set in a hollow moulding (306). **Diaper patterns** are still used a great deal; they are richly carved, predominantly with foliated decoration (307–8). **Foliage** in all forms is used extensively as ornament; on corbels, dripstones, terminations, wall surfaces, crockets, finials, etc. (299, 300, 303–4). The commonest patterns are the vine, maple and oak, carved in a riot of naturalistic abundance. **Sculptural forms** are also more realistic, both in figure and drapery compositions, and in the use of animals, birds and insects.

CHAPTER IV

Perpendicular Gothic 1375 - 1509

The final phase of Gothic architecture extended over a long period. It began, in a transitional stage, at the time of Richard II in the last quarter of the fourteenth century. The main characteristics of the style were paramount for much of the fifteenth century, while, in Tudor form, **Perpendicular** Gothic, as it is termed, continued to evolve until the Dissolution. Thus, architecturally, the Tudor dynasty is divided into two sharply defined styles: Tudor Perpendicular Gothic lasting until about 1540–50, followed by Elizabethan until the end of the century. However, the scope of this chapter is confined to a study of late fourteenth-century and the fifteenth-century Perpendicular Gothic. During this time were created buildings which still illustrate for us the beauty of silhouette, fine craftsmanship in carving and soaring majesty of buttress, tracery and vaulting which were the fruits of over 300 years of development of the Gothic architectural theme.

The predominating characteristic of this style—as its name suggests—is perpendicularity. This can be seen in the window tracery, where vertical lines have replaced the flowing and geometric shapes of Decorated Gothic, and in the stone and wood panelling which covers many surfaces from buttresses and walls to vaulting and timber roofs. There is a slenderness and delicacy, both in exterior silhouette and in the detail of pinnacles and turrets. This lightness in structural appearance has been made possible by improved knowledge of vaulting and abutment, generally manifested at this time by the flying buttress, gracefully spanning the choir and nave aisle roofs, and transmitting the thrust to the ground far below. Another factor which gives an airiness and added illumination is the further enlargement of window area in comparison with that of the walls. In Chapter III the increased size of windows was discussed with reference to the evolution from the Early English lancet openings to Decorated traceried examples. Here again, a further increase in size has taken place so that in a building like **St George's Chapel, Windsor**, for example, almost the entire wall area is divided into windows. This weakening of the wall structure is then typically offset by a greater number of mullions and transoms and further buttressing (323).

In addition to the window size, silhouette characteristics and the perpendicular effect of panelling, pinnacles and mullions, Perpendicular Gothic can also be recognised by the specific shape in arch design. The equilateral and obtuse shapes of the Decorated period give way, particularly in the later fifteenth century, to the **four-centred arch**. This is a flattened version, still with a pointed centre, but of very much lower construction.

In cathedrals and large churches the triforium storey has now almost disappeared; the clerestory windows are much larger and are divided from the nave arcade by a band of carved decoration in sunk and/or pierced panelling.

The whole style of Perpendicular Gothic is the product of trial and error, ingenuity and experience gained from the 300 years of Gothic design. In this final phase is shown the

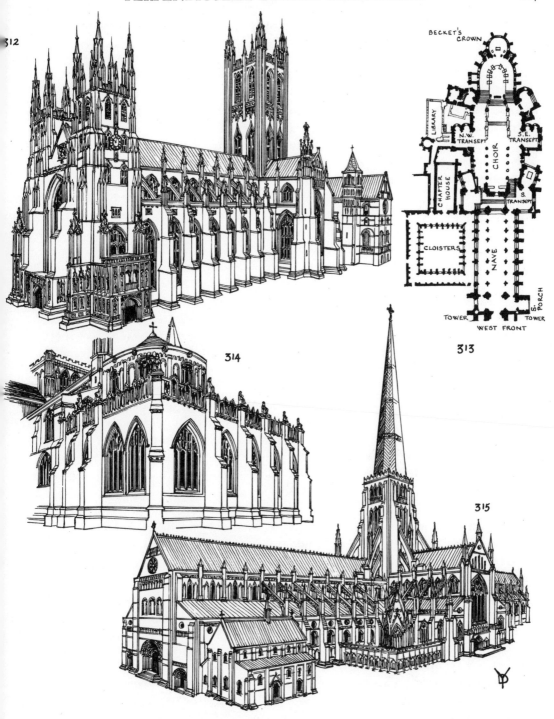

312 Canterbury Cathedral from the south-west: nave 1378–1405, south-west tower 1423–34, central tower 1490–7 313 Canterbury Cathedral: plan, length *c.* 540 ft 314 Peterborough Cathedral: apsidal east end, with 15th century retrochoir, *c.* 1496–1508 315 Old St Paul's Cathedral, London, viewed from the south-west as it appeared in the 15th and 16th centuries

culmination of these years of effort and creation, likened by some writers to the summer or flowering period of this architectural form.

ECCLESIASTICAL BUILDINGS

Cathedrals

Although we have extant much fine workmanship in Perpendicular design in our cathedrals, no example is available which is entirely of this style. However, in Canterbury, Winchester and Gloucester the Perpendicular achievement is of such extent and blends so fortunately with the earlier and later designs, that we can get a clear picture of the unity and singleness of purpose which is so characteristic of Perpendicular work in cathedrals and large churches. Decoration and small architectural features fall into their correct perspective and the emphasis is on the complete design. At **Canterbury** the rebuilding of the nave and western transept was begun in 1378 and continued into the early fifteenth century. Typically, the clerestory was enlarged at the expense of the triforium and the perpendicular emphasis was made apparent. A lierne vault was built over the nave, aisles and transepts. On the exterior, flying buttresses span the aisle roofs; a sculptured porch and Lady Chapel were built and the south-west tower was finished by 1458. (The north-west tower is a nineteenth-century addition.) The crowning glory of Canterbury is its 'Angel Steeple' or central tower which adorns the crossing in graceful, dignified fashion, rising to 235 feet. It was completed by 1503 (312–13, 361, Colour Plate 4). At **Winchester** the finest Perpendicular work is in the rebuilt nave, which was completed in 1450 (XVII). The west front is mainly of earlier work, although it was not finally finished until mid-fifteenth century (210). **Gloucester** (as mentioned in Chapter III) illustrates one of the earliest examples of Perpendicular design in its reconstructed choir and cloisters, carried out in the middle of the fourteenth century. It is on the exterior, however, that its magnificent central tower, *c.* 1450–7, shows such fine Perpendicular form; it is dignified, solid, yet indisputably delicate and graceful. Also on the exterior can be seen the west façade with its great west window, 1421–37, the Lady Chapel, 1499, and the fine, sculptured south porch, *c.* 1420 (376, XVI).

Among other cathedrals with extensive Perpendicular work are York, Norwich, Oxford, Durham, Peterborough, Chester, St Giles', Edinburgh, and Beverley Minster. At **York Minster** can be seen the great east window, 1405–8, the twin west towers, 1432–74, the central tower, 1389–1423, and the Lady Chapel and choir, 1361–1400 (212). **Norwich** has a rich fan-vault over its centre aisle and transept, and at **Oxford** the nave has been revaulted (XX). The central tower at **Durham** was rebuilt 1465–90, after the Norman one had been struck by lightning in 1429. The new tower is lofty and inspiring, rising above the wooded heights of the river Wear. At **Chester** the new nave was completed in 1492; at **Peterborough** the retrochoir is of late fifteenth-century design (314), and much of **St Giles', Edinburgh**, was built in the fifteenth century. One of the finest Perpendicular west fronts is that at **Beverley Minster**; it has all been constructed in the one style and consists of a great west window of nine lights and two western towers. The whole front is panelled and the buttresses and doorways are richly decorated. The tympanum of the gable is filled with beautiful tracery.

In 1444 the spire of **Old St Paul's** was once again struck by lightning and in 1462 this was repaired. A drawing of the cathedral as it appeared in the fifteenth and sixteenth centuries is given in Fig. 315.

316 Sherborne Abbey, Dorset: south aspect, *c.* 1475–90   317 Fountains Abbey Tower, Yorkshire, from the east, *c.* 1494–1526   318 St Osyth's Priory, Essex: gatehouse, *c.* 1475–80. Flint and stone construction   319 Christchurch Priory, Hampshire: west tower, 120 ft high, late 15th century to *temp.* Henry VIII

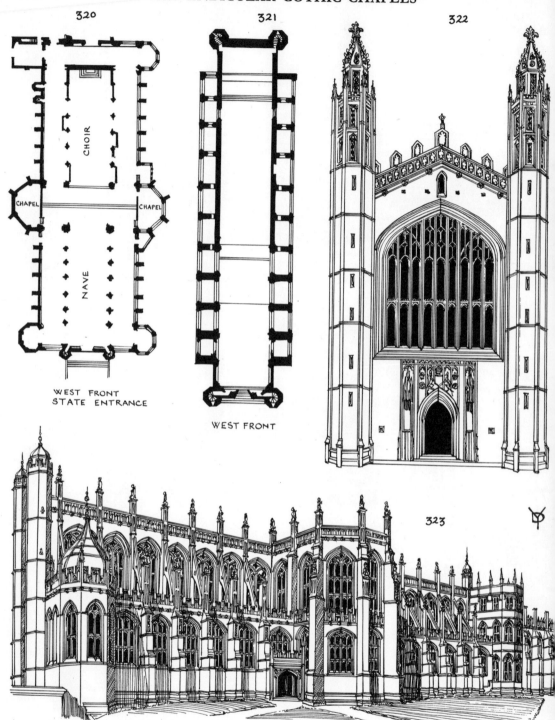

320 St George's Chapel, Windsor Castle: plan, length *c.* 230 ft   321 King's College Chapel, Cambridge: plan, length *c.* 300 ft   322 King's College Chapel, Cambridge, west front 1466–1515   323 St George's Chapel, Windsor Castle: south aspect, 1475–1509

Abbeys and Priories

The fifteenth and early sixteenth centuries saw the final phase in the building of, and additions to, English abbeys and priories. A most complete example is the church of **Sherborne Abbey**, Dorset, of which the south aspect, *c.* 1475–90, is shown in Fig. 316. It has exceptionally fine large Perpendicular windows and interesting flying buttresses, gargoyles and Perpendicular ornament. Two extant towers of this period are the ruined tower of **Fountains Abbey**, Yorkshire, *c.* 1494–1526 (317), and the west tower of **Christchurch Priory**, Hampshire (319). Among the specimens of flint and stone construction in eastern England is the impressive gateway to **St Osyth's Priory**, Essex, *c.* 1475–30 (318).

Royal Chapels

Among the finest contributions of Perpendicular Gothic architecture, and illustrating the essentially English quality of the style, are the chapels of the period, in particular, the three examples: King's College Chapel, Cambridge, and the two royal chapels, one at Windsor and the other at Westminster Abbey. All three chapels provide first-class illustrations of fan-vaulting, which, at Westminster, is in pendant fan-design. **King's College Chapel, Cambridge**, has a beautiful setting: on the west side the green lawn slopes down to the river Cam, while the east front rises majestically above the twentieth-century traffic, rumbling past on the main road. Much of the work is mid-fifteenth century, *temp.* Henry VI, although it was completed under Henry VII in the early sixteenth century. The great end windows, the turrets and finials, buttresses and doorways, all give evidence of the high standard of design and craftsmanship (321–2, 375; XVIII). Work at the royal chapel of **St George** at **Windsor** extended over several reigns. An earlier royal chapel was in a ruinous state when Edward IV ordered its rebuilding in 1476. The work was not completed until the early sixteenth century under Henry VII. The state entrance on the west front is most impressive; steps are ascended to reach the doorway under its great west window which occupies so much of the façade. The south aspect is shown in Fig. 323, with its buttresses topped by sculptured finials and its multiplicity of windows. The interior is vaulted in a manner akin to King's College Chapel. The third of these chapels, that of **Henry VII, Westminster Abbey**, was largely completed by his death in 1509, although much of the decorative work, particularly that by Torrigiano, was carried out in Henry VIII's reign. The interior of the chapel is illustrated in Plate XIX.

Parish Churches

One of the commonest features of parish churches of the fifteenth century was the clerestory, which was introduced above the nave arcade, with a consequent lowering of the aisle roof. Until about 1375 this had been primarily a feature of cathedrals and larger churches; in this period it became general. Not many new churches were built; by this time most parishes had their own, but alterations and repairs were carried out as required. Another such alteration was to add aisles where this had not already been done, particularly to transepts to give the squarish plan in the manner of some cathedrals and large churches. Among the chief characteristics of the period, as evidenced in churches, are the carved stone panelling of wall areas, buttresses, doors, doorways and vaulting (both exterior and interior), the embattled

324 Church of St John, Glastonbury, *c.* 1485   325 Thaxted Church, Essex   326 Louth Church, Lincolnshire, *c.* 1465–1514: steeple   327 Lavenham Church, Suffolk, *c.* 1485–1525

XV *St Michael's Church (later the Cathedral), Coventr*
1373–1433. (Partly destroyed by enemy action 194

and panelled parapets and the finely decorated porches. There are first-class examples of Perpendicular towers and spires still standing in different parts of the country. **Materials** in use for church building varied greatly, largely according to the region concerned. **Stone, Cornish granite**, flint and brick were the most durable materials in general use. **Flint,** especially, was used on a large scale and the flints were now more carefully selected and graded for size. **Flush-work** was introduced into East Anglian church building: stone blocks were cut into thin slabs for economy of the imported material and the flints were arranged round them to produce patterns and designs between the panels, but they were set in flush with the stone, not raised above it. Simple designs were used at first, but soon much more elaborate patterns were created, especially on porches and towers. The method spread quickly to other counties, for example, Essex, Sussex, Wiltshire and Berkshire. **Brick** was used far less than the other materials, as yet. It is particularly seen in work of this period in Essex, Norfolk and Suffolk due to lack of stone there. For this same reason, the majority of **timber** work in churches survives in Essex, and also because this county was, at that time, a heavily wooded region. The wood—predominantly oak—is seen mainly in belfries set on stone towers; also steeples, porches, turrets and, of course, for roofs. The pitch of these roofs was now nearly flat and they were supported on horizontal tie-beams which rested on the wall plates. Designs of timber roofs are described more fully later in the chapter in the appropriate section. A selection from the many fine examples of Perpendicular Gothic parish churches are illustrated: **St John's, Glastonbury** (324), **Thaxted**, Essex (325), **Lavenham,** Suffolk (327), **Louth** (326) and **Boston** (364) in Lincolnshire, **St Mary's, Oxford** (362), **Shepton Mallet**, Somerset (363), **St Mary's, Taunton** (365), and **St Michael's, Coventry,** which was partly destroyed in 1940 (XV).

PUBLIC BUILDINGS

Under the auspices of Richard II, **Westminster Hall, London**—originally built by William Rufus in the eleventh century—was considerably altered. Although it was extensively repaired in the early nineteenth century, we still owe to the late fourteenth century the exceptional hammerbeam roof—among the best extant—also the windows (384). Among other work of the period are the **Guildhall, London**, and the **Guildhall, York**. The London example was a fine building on which work commenced in 1411. The Great Hall (1411–39) had a vaulted chamber below. However, it has undergone many changes with the years, as it was partly burnt in the Great Fire of 1666, was altered by Wren, restored to its original design in the nineteenth century, destroyed in 1940, and Sir Giles Gilbert Scott has now carried out the latest restoration. The Guildhall, York, has an attractive Perpendicular room with an open timber roof and two rows of octagonal wood pillars with four-centred arches. The **Guildhall** at **Norwich**, rebuilt 1407–13, is a good example of flint-work. However, much of the work is of later date.

EDUCATIONAL BUILDINGS

Universities

At **Oxford** and **Cambridge** the Medieval halls of residence give a clear impression of the house plan of the Middle Ages, as they contain a hall, chapel and rooms grouped round one

I Gloucester Cathedral, from the south-east. Tower 450–7, west window 1421–37, Lady Chapel (right) 1499

328 Merton College Chapel, Oxford, *c.* 1450 329 Jesus College, Cambridge: main gateway, *c.* 1497–1500 330 Magdalen College, Oxford: tower, 145 ft high, *c.* 1490–1509 331 New College, Oxford: front quadrangle, late 14th century

or more quadrangles. A number of the Colleges were founded before 1509 and, although some of these have been restored or rebuilt, part of the original work is still extant. At **Oxford, Merton College** contains some fourteenth- and fifteenth-century work, in particular the chapel (328). **Magdalen College**, built by the Bishop of Winchester in the second half of the fifteenth century, still contains much of its original workmanship. Especially and justly famous is the college tower (1490–1509) which stands high above the busy High Street, though its dignified proportions show to best advantage when viewed from the river (330). **New College Chapel** was one of the earliest buildings erected in Perpendicular style (1380–6). It was built by William of Wykeham, Bishop of Winchester, whose work at Winchester Cathedral and College is of great repute. At **Cambridge, King's College Chapel** has already been referred to. In addition, there is

332 Jesus College, Cambridge: brick gateway, late 15th century

the later Perpendicular work at **Jesus College** where attractive brick gateways with ogee and four-centred arches foreshadow the Tudor work at other Colleges such as **Trinity** (329, 332). Other specimens of good, late fifteenth-century brickwork can be seen at **Queens' College** (333), while at **New College, Oxford**, the front quad still exists in its late fourteenth-century style, although some window openings have been altered at a later date (331).

Schools

Work was begun on **Eton College** in 1442 but was interrupted by the death of the founder, Henry VI. It was recommenced in 1476 and much of the late fifteenth century and early Tudor work still exist.

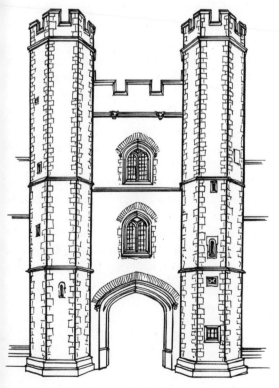

333 Queens' College, Cambridge: brick gateway, 15th century

The school presents a good example of brickwork of the period in the form of two quads and a gateway tower. The stone chapel is of the time of Henry VII. **Winchester College** was built after New College, Oxford, by William of Wykeham in 1387–93.

CASTLES

Castles and fortified residences continued to be built during the whole of the fifteenth century, but gradually the purpose and function of these great erections was changing. The old, military traditions lingered on, however, and, even when the need for excessive fortification had almost died out, castles were still constructed on Medieval lines, although inside they began to resemble palaces. By stages the great house was beginning to emerge from the older castle form of planning. During the Hundred Years' War, many English noblemen, who had spent much of their time in France, brought back ideas which they had assimilated there, so that a number of English castles acquired a French architectural flavour.

As the military importance of the building decreased, its domestic comfort and spaciousness was increased. In outward appearance, the gatehouses, battlements, water defences and towers remained, giving a façade of fortified strength, but within this was enclosed the spacious, wealthy, great house. However, in the border country and on the sea coasts, strong military fortification continued to be essential, and such castles were erected on the older, Medieval plan during the whole period. Here, as in Scotland and Ireland, Peel towers were built: these were plain and roughly fashioned but very strong. In the lower stages, windows were still only loopholes; above were the more comfortable state apartments and private rooms. Such towers were built until the sixteenth and even seventeenth century.

In England, the quadrangular plan had, in general, superseded the Edwardian concentric arrangement. **Bodiam** in Sussex is a fine example of such castle building. Although of late fourteenth-century design, it is typical of fifteenth-century workmanship. It is approached over an oak bridge, which spans the moat, to the octagon. During such an approach the intruder would be under fire from the towers and would then have to pass the barbican, cross a 10-foot moat (over which the drawbridge could be dropped as required) and storm the main gatehouse. This was fitted with three portcullises with their individual doors and chambers. Bodiam presents the shell of a great Perpendicular castle. Its outer walls are in good condition and the moat still laps them. The barbican is in ruins but the main gatehouse is in a good state of preservation. Entering here, one steps into the quadrangular court which is surrounded by buildings, with a round tower at each corner and a square one in the centre of each face. The doorway into the Great Hall is opposite the gatehouse and this was still the focal point of castle life. Other buildings included the chapel, private chambers and the kitchen, which, by this time, was considered of greater importance than hitherto (334–5, 374).

Among other good fifteenth-century examples remain those at Hurstmonceux, Sussex, Warwick, Berkeley, Raglan, Monmouthshire and Hever, Kent. **Hurstmonceux** (XIV) presents an imposing façade of magnificent brickwork of the time of Henry VI and VII but, unfortunately, the interior has been badly damaged. The moat is partially dry and is spanned to reach the principal gatehouse which is well preserved (339). The castle interior, built over a long period, extends into three courts. **Warwick Castle** was built in the late fourteenth

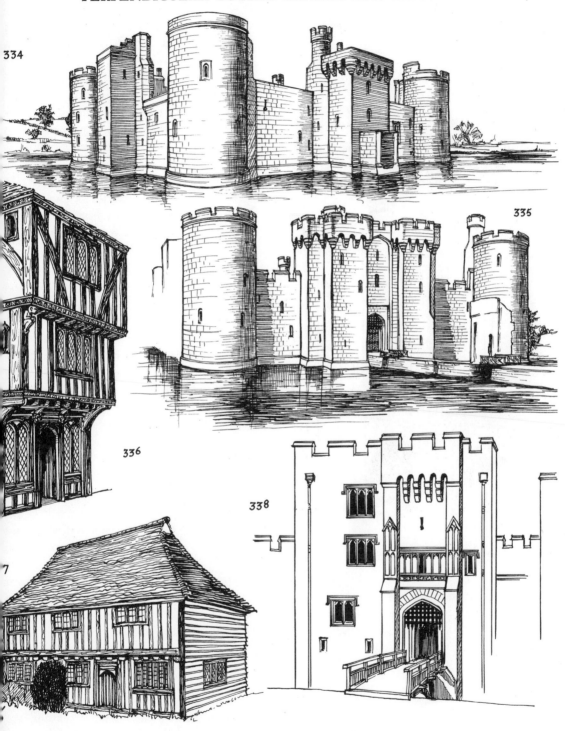

334 Bodiam Castle, Sussex, 1385, from the south-west   335 Bodiam Castle from the north, showing great gatehouse with ruins of barbican in front   336 Half-timber house, Canterbury, c. 1495
337 Half-timber cottage at Smallhythe, Kent, c. 1490   338 Hever Castle, Kent, rebuilt 1462

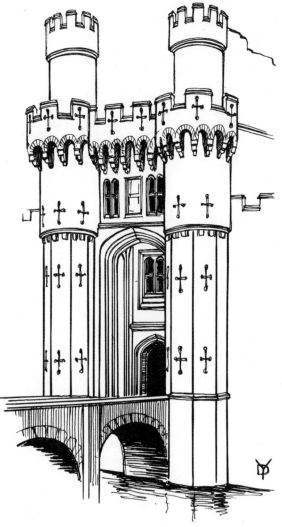

339 Hurstmonceux Castle: gatehouse, c. 1445

and early fifteenth century. It is in a good state of preservation and provides an excellent illustration of the fifteenth-century achievement of an external fortress combined with internal extensive but comfortable apartments. **Hever Castle**, rebuilt in 1462, is a small, quadrangular, castellated house with a surrounding moat. Considerable later additions and alterations have been made but much of the exterior is unchanged, as exampled by the gatehouse (338).

In the fifteenth century **sanitation** was provided by similar methods to those in use earlier, but more adequate accommodation was provided. At Bodiam, for example, there were a score of garderobes. Such garderobes possessed outlets which emptied into the moat below the water level, but, if the castle had no moat, the garderobe was constructed in a projecting turret and soil was dropped from here into a depository below, which could be emptied as required. Streams running under castles and houses were utilised for cleaning purposes.

In the north of England, Scotland and Ireland, in addition to the Peel (or Irish) towers mentioned earlier, large castles were also built at this time. These were all still heavily fortified, as the areas were more unsettled than southern England; even the manor houses were yet built in the form of castles. A number of examples remain, such as those at **Doune**, Perthshire, **Rothesay**, Bute, and **Glamis**. These have a Scottish national character which is distinctive and is enhanced by the use of local materials.

TOWNS

Cloth-making, one of the principal industries of the fifteenth century, was responsible for the expansion of some towns and villages and the contraction of others. Essex and the Cotswolds were two such areas of expansion; in evidence of this, in the former are many half-timber houses built by well-to-do cloth-merchants, while stone houses are more common in the latter. Few new towns were established; rebuilding and planning were carried

FIFTEENTH-CENTURY MARKET CROSSES

340 Chichester Market Cross   341 Salisbury Market Cross   342 Winchester High Cross, 1422–61, restored 1865

out in existing ones. However, the necessary fortification by town walls and gateways hindered a good deal of expansion and, often, only houses of sufficient importance to be fortified separately were built outside the walls. Main streets were fairly wide, but the minor ones very narrow. Upper storeys of houses overhung into the streets to make passageway almost negligible. Street paving was now becoming more common in large towns. A number of **market crosses** have survived from this date; in particular, those at **Chichester, Salisbury and Winchester** (340–2).

DOMESTIC BUILDINGS

Manor and Country Houses

As the fifteenth century advanced, the fortification of such houses was gradually abandoned, especially in the midlands and southern England. The drawbridge and portcullis gave place to a bridge and a decorative, but less military, gatehouse; in the upper storey of which the chapel was often built. Beyond the gateway was an outer court, around which were situated the farm buildings, stables and barns. Through an archway in an inner gatehouse, one entered the inner court which was often a quadrangle completely enclosed by buildings, as for example, at the Medieval Oxford and Cambridge colleges. The main buildings were generally built over cellars and storerooms, which were partly underground. The **hall** still occupied the centre of the house and extended upwards to cover two storeys. At the upper end of the hall, behind the daïs, a staircase ascended to the **solar** and private apartments, while at the other end the wing of the house was devoted to domestic rooms and servants' quarters. These side wings were usually two or three storeys high and accommodated several smaller rooms. **Passages** were still generally constructed in the thickness of the walls and were lit by loopholes or windows. In timber houses they were often external, forming a double cloister, one above the other. The main entrance into the hall was covered by a **porch** at the top of the steps which ascended from the courtyard. Other **staircases** were still in newel form in turrets or were of wood or stone steps, often built externally. One staircase usually led up from the hall to the musicians' gallery, while another descended from the 'screens' into the kitchen. The **kitchen** itself was now commonly part of the main building and frequently had a room above it. In this case, the kitchen roof would be stone vaulted for protection from fire. The kitchen was equipped with very large fireplaces having projecting hoods. A number of kitchens of this period exist, such as those at New College, Oxford, and Warwick Castle. Glass was in more common use in **windows** by this time and some casements were made to open and close. Heraldic, coloured glass was also employed. **Oriel** and **bay windows** were designed for larger rooms; the oriel window was generally on an upper floor, supported by a stone corbel or pillar outside. Both types were many-sided and had fan-vaulted ceilings within. **Chimneys** became one of the decorative features of a house by the late fifteenth century, in single shafts or clustered into groups. Earlier examples were of stone, but by 1500, brick chimeys were coming into use.

The **peasants' homes** were yet only hovels, built of mud and covered with reeds and straw. There was only one room where the family lived, ate and slept round a central, turf fire, which filled the room with smoke as there was no louvre above. By 1500, cottages were larger and were more adequately planned and built.

Materials used for building houses varied according to district; little attempt was made

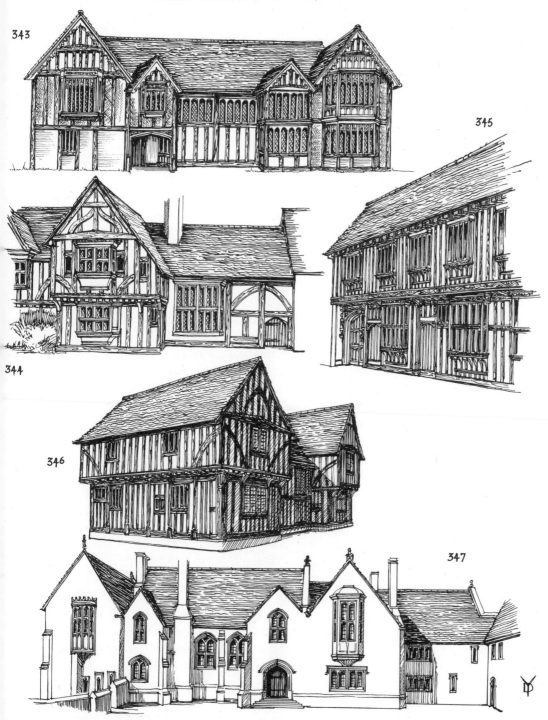

343 Ockwells Manor House, Bray, Berkshire, 1466. Timber and brick, original heraldic glass
344 Stoneacre, Otham, Kent, *c.* 1480. Half-timber 345 Paycocke's House, Coggleshall, Essex,
temp. Henry VII. Half-timber 346 The Old Wool Hall, Lavenham, Suffolk, 15th century. Half-
timber 347 Great Chalfield Manor House, Wiltshire, *c.* 1480. Stone, moated house

to transport stone or other fabric any distance. Thus, in areas where stone was in plentiful supply, it was used for many types of house. This can be seen in such counties as Gloucestershire, Wiltshire and Somerset where houses in the enduring stone have been preserved. In the eastern counties, particularly Norfolk and Suffolk, brick was used, but only in comparatively rare examples until the time of Henry VII. Brick is a more typical material of the sixteenth century. In the chalk areas of Kent, Sussex and Norfolk, houses can be found which are faced with flints, which have been cut and trimmed to present pleasing designs in this durable material. Timber and half-timber houses were built in all areas, as this material was in abundant supply almost everywhere still, and was quicker and cheaper to use for building than anything else.

In many types of timber house design can be seen the **overhanging upper storey**. In some instances this is supported on bold corbels and joists; in others, it is carried on an open arcade of wooden arches in cloister form. The timbers on the front of the house are often decoratively carved and/or panelled.

Among the fifteenth-century stone houses still extant are **Great Chalfield Manor House** and **South Wraxall Manor House** in Wiltshire; **Ashleworth Court, Gloucester**, another manor house; and **Lympne Manor House**, Kent, which has been modernised inside but retains a characteristic exterior. **Great Chalfield** is a fine example of a fifteenth-century manor house. It was built about 1480, and its moat and grounds are attractively situated (347). **Oxburgh Hall**, Norfolk, is a late fifteenth-century specimen of brickwork, unfortunately partly destroyed. However, a magnificent brick gateway remains. In the half-timber type of house the best-preserved larger house is that of **Ockwells Manor House** at **Bray**, Berkshire. It was built about 1466, and was allowed to become dilapidated in the late nineteenth century. However, it is now in good condition, and with its richly carved barge-boards, window tracery and heraldic glass, presents a good example of fifteenth-century timber construction (343). Another famous and well-preserved timber house is that of **Paycocke's** at **Coggleshall**, Essex. This also has richly carved boards, beams and door-frames, with a linenfold panelled double door, typical of the time of Henry VII (345, 371). Other interesting timber examples are those of **Gainsborough Hall**, Lincolnshire, late fifteenth century; **Stoneacre, Otham**, Kent, c. 1480 (344); and **Smallhythe Cottage**, Kent, c. 1490 (337), formerly the home of Ellen Terry.

Town Houses

In towns, timber was still the chief building material; as a result of this and the constant rebuilding on a limited site, together with the prevalence of fire in houses packed closely together, far fewer examples of houses are available for study in towns than there are in rural areas. This is particularly so in large towns, especially in London. Timber houses were built on stone party walls and with a greater number of storeys than hitherto, to increase the available accommodation. Floor joists were heavy beams laid flat across the house. In order to avoid too great a springiness from lengthy joists, the upper floors were constructed to overhang the storey below and to rest on its projecting joists. Carved and decorated cornices aligned the two floors. The angle posts which joined one wall to its next-door neighbour were massive baulks of timber which were carved ornately, especially when occupying a corner site. Brackets and corbels spanned the space between the angle posts and the projecting joists; they were carved also. The carving generally took the form of foliage or flowing tracery. The ground floor of a house was often fitted as a shop, while above this was built the hall and other living-rooms. In other town houses the hall was on the ground floor, with solar and bed-chamber above. Town houses still existing include the **Old Wool Hall** at **Lavenham**, Suffolk (346), and examples at **Canterbury** (336), **Thaxted** in Essex, **York, Gloucester** and **Shrewsbury**. Some of the Oxford and Cambridge colleges contain interesting examples of fifteenth-century domestic halls.

Inns

A number of fifteenth-century **inns** still exist and many of these are functioning as such. The **George Inn** at **Glastonbury** is an example; it was built in 1475, originally to accommodate pilgrims to Glastonbury, and is now an hotel. It is stone-fronted with the whole surface divided up into panels, pierced for windows. On one side a bay window rises in three stages to the whole height of the building. The main coaching gateway is placed almost centrally; it has a four-centred arch with a decorative carved panel above (348). Another stone-fronted building is the fifteenth-century **Angel Inn** at **Grantham**. This also has a central gateway with four-centred arch, which is surmounted by an oriel window. Two-storeyed bay windows flank either side of the arch (349). A half-timber example can be seen

in the **Mermaid Inn** at **Rye**, Sussex. Here the coaching entrance is set to one side of the house (350). Other examples include the **George Inn** at **Salisbury** and the **Star** at **Oxford**.

Barns

Several tithe **barns** of this period exist in different parts of the country. There is the **West Pennard Court Barn** near **Glastonbury**—a buttressed stone example (351), and the barns at **Abbotsbury**, Dorset, and **Ashleworth**, Gloucestershire.

348 The George and Pilgrim's Inn, Glastonbury, *c.* 1475

349 The Angel Inn, Grantham, 15th century. Window frames of later design

350 The Mermaid Inn, Rye, Sussex, 15th century. Half-timber

351 West Pennard Court Barn, near Glastonbury, 15th century

BRIDGES

Among the stone bridges of this time is the late fourteenth-century bridge at **Radcot** over the Thames; this has three pointed arches (352). The most beautiful bridge of the time is probably that spanning the Wye at **Bakewell**, Derbyshire. It is a five-arched stone bridge, with strong, pointed buttresses; the arches are low, wide and pointed (353). Another stone bridge is that at **Stratford-upon-Avon** called the **Clopton Bridge**. This was built about 1480 and is remarkable for its length (354).

352 Radcot Bridge over the Thames, Oxfordshire, 14th century

353 Bakewell Bridge over the Wye, Derbyshire

354 Fourteen arches of Clopton Bridge, Stratford-upon-Avon, *c.* 1480

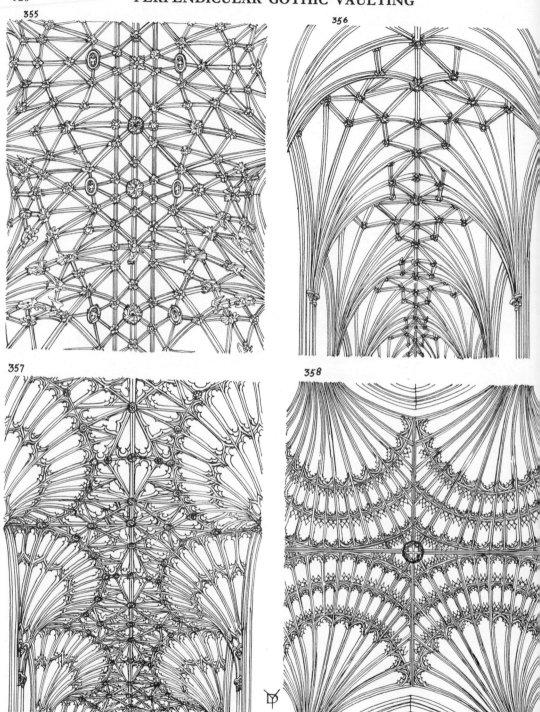

355 Gloucester Cathedral: plan view of complicated lierne vault in presbytery, *c.* 1350. Floral and angel bosses   356 Canterbury Cathedral: nave, lierne vault, *c.* 1390–1405   357 Sherborne Abbey, Dorset: nave, fan-vault, *c.* 1475–1500   358 Peterborough Cathedral: plan view of fan-vault in choir, *c.* 1496–1508

XVII   Winchester Cathedral: vaulting of the nave, 1394–1

359 Eltham Palace; Great Hall, 1475–80. Timber roof, false hammerbeam type

VIII *King's College Chapel, Cambridge: fan-vaulted roof, 1446–1515*

360 Tie-beam style of roof with king-post and braces, *c.* 1450

ARCHITECTURAL FEATURES

Vaulting

During the latter part of the fourteenth century and the early fifteenth century the **stellar** and **network** rib designs in stone vaults became yet more complex. **Lierne vaults** were constructed in many of our cathedrals over nave, choir and aisles, and also in larger churches. **Bosses** were carved at each intersection of the vault and were designed in a variety of shapes: floral, animal, human and angelic. From the many examples available the lierne vault at **Gloucester Cathedral** is illustrated in Fig. 355 and Plate X, the nave of **Canterbury** in Fig. 356, and the nave of **Winchester** in Plate XVII. This developed into the peculiarly English form of vault—the **fan-vault**. It resulted from the need to provide a type of vault which would accommodate ribs of different curves as they sprang from the capital. In a fan-vault, the radiating ribs are of equal length, and the bounding line of these ribs is shaped into a semi-circle. Each rib is formed at an equal angle with its neighbours, and the whole is fashioned into an inverted, concave cone. Such vaulting is alternatively called palm or conoidal vaulting. The radiating ribs are crossed at certain levels by horizontal, lierne ribs so that the panels remaining between ribs are smaller than hitherto, while the ribs themselves are thinner and plainly moulded. The whole vault is delicately designed in small panels; these panels or spandrels can be flat but are more commonly slightly arched, and cusped. A fan-vault has little thrust: each inverted conoid meeting the thrust of its adjacent and opposite conoids and supporting between them the spandrels of masonry. As a result, buttressing could have been greatly diminished, but in most cases, builders were reluctant to do this, partly for the appearance of the exterior design and partly due to timidity. As the panels are so small in fan-vaulting, they and the ribs are often made from the same piece of stone, and thus the ribs have lost much of their constructional value, and have become decorative panelling similar to the wall ornamentation and window tracery of the time. There is a plethora of magnificent examples of fan-vaulting in England. Perhaps the most justly famous are at **King's College Chapel, Cambridge** (XVIII), and **St George's Chapel, Windsor**. Other fine vaults can be seen at **Sherborne Abbey**, Dorset (357), and **Peterborough Cathedral** (358). Some fan-vaults were constructed in pendant form; these pendants sometimes descend as low as the springing line of the fans. **Henry VII's Chapel** in **Westminster Abbey** provides a wonderful example of this (XIX), while that at **Oxford Cathedral** is also exquisite (XX).

Timber Roofs

The fifteenth century marked a zenith of craftsmanship in the construction of timber roofs. These varied considerably in design, but were almost all of first-class workmanship; they were constructional achievements, while, at the same time, satisfying decorative and aesthetic needs. Roofs built after the fourteenth-century fashion with **tie-beam, collar-beam** and **king-post** construction continued to be made, particularly for domestic usage (360). However, the **hammerbeam** design is that which is most typical of fifteenth-century roofing. This style developed from the collar-beam and arch-braced roof. The hammerbeam itself is a horizontal piece of wood which is bedded on the wall plate and extends outwards almost to the outer face of the wall, whilst inwards, it projects to approximately one-fifth of the width of the main opening. It is braced underneath to a wall strut which, in turn, is supported on a stone corbel, thus transmitting the thrust down the wall. The hammer-post then rises

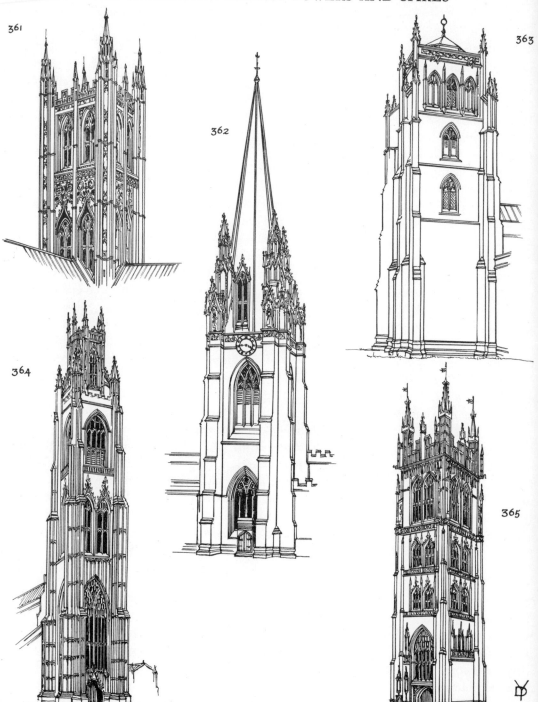

361 Canterbury Cathedral: central tower ('Angel Steeple'), *c.* 1490–1503, 235 ft high   362 St Mary's Church, Oxford: tower and spire. Total height 188 ft   363 Shepton Mallet, Dorset: church tower, *c.* 1380   364 Boston Church, Lincolnshire: tower, 1425–1520, 266 ft high   365 St Mary's Church, Taunton, Somerset: tower, *c.* 1500

XIX   Henry VII's Chapel, Westminster Abbey: fan vaulting, 1503–

vertically from the inner end of the hammerbeam to support the principal rafter which is
tied in by the collar, and also strengthened by the curved braces. The weight from the
hammer-post on the inner end of the hammerbeam is balanced by the weight of the rafter
post resting on the outer end of this beam, thus giving a cantilever action. There are variations on this theme, the most usual of which are the **false hammerbeam roof**, wherein the
hammer-post is tenoned into the end of the hammerbeam instead of resting upon it, giving
a weaker construction; and the **double-hammerbeam roof**, wherein there are two sets of
hammerbeams, one above the other. In the latter instance, there are usually two sets of curved
struts but only one set of hammer posts. The best known and the greatest example of hammerbeam roofs, also one of the earliest, is that of **Westminster Hall, London**, constructed in
the last years of the fourteenth century. Many other examples still exist, especially as the
style of roofing continued in use well into the sixteenth century. A false hammerbeam roof
was built at **Eltham Palace**, Kent, in the Great Hall, 1475–80 (359). A third type of timber
roof construction is provided by the almost flat design. This is more commonly used in

366 Sherborne Abbey, Dorset: flying buttress, 15th century

367 Winchester Cathedral: nave
buttress, *c.* 1394–1450

Oxford Cathedral: choir 1158–80. Vault 1478–1503

churches where stone vaulting has not been applied. Alternatively, the roof has a slight pitch or is coved. There are a ridge rib, wall plates and principal rafters, while in between, the rectangular or square wood panels are either painted or filled with tracery and carved decora-

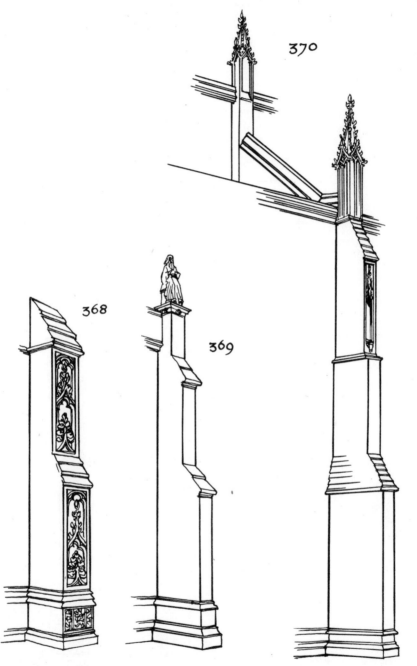

tion. In all types of wooden roofs, carving is abundant: angels and other forms of decoration ornamented the hammer-posts, beams and corbels, while the surfaces of large beams were also carved in high relief. Colour has been much used, but, of course, it has now largely worn off. In a few instances, stone vaulting designs have been imitated in wood, particularly fan-vaulting. Oak was still the principal timber employed and construction continued to be by mortise and tenon, with oak pins to secure. No metal was introduced.

Towers and Spires

England is indeed rich in the number and quality of **towers** still standing and built during this period. Perpendicular towers are generally elab-

368 Lavenham Church, Suffolk: buttress, c. 1500 369 Peterborough Cathedral: buttress, eastern arm, 15th century 370 Canterbury Cathedral: nave, flying buttress, c. 1380–1400

371 Paycocke's House, Coggleshall, Essex: carved oak door and doorway, *temp*. Henry VII   372
Chester Cathedral: doorway west front, *c*. 1500–20   373 Magdalen College Chapel, Oxford: door-
way, *c*. 1475–80   374 Bodiam Castle, Sussex: main entrance, doorway, late 14th century   375 King's
College Chapel, Cambridge: doorway, *c*. 1446–1510

376 Gloucester Cathedral: south porch, c. 1420

orate in design, erected in four or five storeys, and having large window openings and decorative canopies, pinnacles and tabernacles. Double buttresses are set at the angles, and the corner turrets have small flying buttresses attached. Parapets are deep, richly ornamented, and are pinnacled and crocketed. The stairway is usually built within an angle of the tower, though in some cases, a newel stair is contained in a projecting turret at one of the angles, when the turret usually rises higher than the remainder of the tower. Among the greatest examples of fifteenth-century church towers are the central towers of **Canterbury Cathedral** (312, 361, Colour Plate 4) and **Gloucester Cathedral** (XVI); **St Mary's Church, Taunton** (365); **Boston,** Lincolnshire—an exceptionally tall tower (364); the chapels of **Magdalen** (330) and **Merton Colleges, Oxford** (328); **Lavenham Church**, Suffolk (327); **St John's, Glastonbury** (324); the central tower of **York Minster; Fountains Abbey,** Yorkshire (317); **Christchurch Priory**, Hampshire (319); and **Shepton Mallet**, Somerset (363).

   Spires were added to a number of towers, particularly after the height of churches had been increased by the addition of clerestory windows, and the tower had then lost its dominant quality. Many such spires were of elegant construction, decorated by pinnacles, crockets, lantern lights and flying buttresses. Examples illustrated here include **St Michael's, Coventry,** later the Cathedral and partly destroyed in 1940 (XV); **St Mary's**, Oxford (362); **Thaxted,** Essex (325); **Louth**, Lincolnshire (326); and **Old St Paul's Cathedral, London** (315).

Buttresses

Fifteenth-century buttresses are often panelled; their sets-off are in the form of bold, but plain slopes; the buttress becomes slender towards the top and commonly terminates in a pinnacle which rises above the parapet. Few large buildings are without flying buttresses:

Plate 4   Canterbury Cathedral, from the north-west. South-tower 1423–34, central tower 1490–7, north-west tower 1834

indeed, in a number of cases, two or three arches or bars leave the wall to join the main buttress at different levels and help to transmit the thrust towards the ground. The flying buttress arches are often pierced and some examples are richly traceried (366–70, 402–3).

Doorways

The main characteristic of Perpendicular doorways is the square hood-mold over the arch, which is generally of flattish equilateral or four-centre type. The spandrels between are filled with carved tracery, shields, angels or foliated decoration. The door jambs are ornamented by shafts, which are small with plain capitals and tall, octagonal bases. Richer examples—and there are many of these—have flanking niches also (371–5).

377 Lavenham Church, Suffolk: porch, 15th century

Doors, of wood, are frequently panelled in traceried design. In the time of Henry VII linenfold panelling appears. Ironwork is confined to strap hinges and closing latches (371–3).

Porches of Perpendicular design are, in general, very fine indeed. Several of our cathedrals and many churches have had fifteenth-century porches added. Such examples are richly decorated by panel work, buttresses and pinnacles, while sculpture can be seen in profusion, filling niches and in all-over decoration. In the later period, in particular, the entire area is decorated as in **Henry VII's Chapel, Westminster Abbey**. Other beautiful porches are those at the cathedrals of **Gloucester** (376), **Canterbury** and **Chester** (378), **Beverley Minster**, and **Lavenham Church**, Suffolk (377).

Window Openings

It is in window design and tracery that the essence of the Perpendicular Gothic style is apparent. Earlier Perpendicular windows are divided into sub-arches as in Decorated work, and such sub-arches rise from the centre or side mullions. In later versions, all mullions continue through vertically to the main arch without being subdivided into curves and geometric patterns. Transoms, which had been used in a limited manner in Decorated windows, are now augmented in number, as are the mullions also, giving a tremendously increased number of lights where the two intersect at right angles. For example, in the west window in **St George's Chapel, Windsor**, with four transoms and a considerable number of mullions

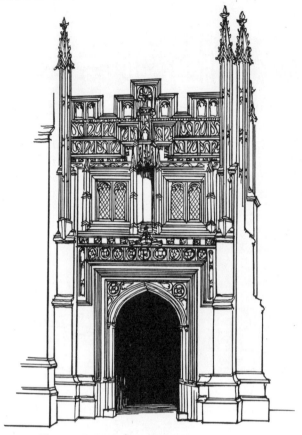

378 Chester Cathedral: south-west porch, *c.* 1490–5

there are 75 individual lights, not counting the head tracery (383). As time passed, windows, particularly those of the clerestory, became larger, in width rather than height, and the four-centred arch was used more and more to accommodate these proportions. Thus, the area of window head decreases in proportion to the remainder. A peculiarly Perpendicular design can also be seen in which the central light in a five-light window presents a continuous panel from top to bottom, and sub-arches spring on either side from its mullions in the head. An example is in **Henry VII's Chapel, Westminster Abbey** (381). In later designs, the transoms are often decorated with small battlements or flowers, as in the two examples already mentioned (381, 383). Square-headed, segmental-headed and circular windows are also used, but generally for small window openings (382). Stained glass is much in evidence, both in ecclesiastical and secular buildings, though much of this has unfortunately disappeared. The majority of Gothic windows extant today are of fifteenth-century origin, so the examples available of this period are very numerous. Among some of the best may be mentioned those at **York Minster; Winchester Cathedral**; the three royal chapels, **St George's, Windsor** (383), **Henry VII's, Westminster Abbey** (381), and **King's College, Cambridge** (322); **Canterbury Cathedral** (379); and **Westminster Hall** (384).

Arches

The type of arch chiefly associated with Perpendicular architecture is, of course, the **four-centred arch**. As its name suggests, it is struck from four centres; two of these give a small, quickly curving arc, and the other two a large, flat arc; the former at the sides and the latter at the top. The **ogee arch**, as described in Chapter III, is also of four-centred construction but, in this instance, the arrangement is reversed. However typical the four-centred arch may be of this period, its use is more generally confined to the later time, and many other types of arch were in common usage also. These include the **equilateral**—ranging from narrow to wide—the **ogee**, and the **square-headed**. The last-named is more commonly seen in aisles and in smaller buildings. Mouldings frequently continue round the arch from the base without a capital stop; in other instances, there is one shaft and capital while the other mouldings

379 Canterbury Cathedral: nave aisle window, *c.* 1390–1430   380 Lavenham Church, Suffolk:
window, *c.* 1485–1525   381 Henry VII's Chapel, Westminster Abbey: clerestory window, *c.* 1500–5
382 Corpus Christi College, Cambridge: Old Court, window   383 St George's Chapel, Windsor:
west window, *c.* 1485–1509   384 Westminster Hall: window, late 14th century

385 Fountains Abbey, Yorkshire: arch at the crossing, c. 1490–1526   386 Rochester: gateway arch, 15th century   387 Typical perpendicular style, pier section 388 Winchester Cathedral: part of nave pier, c. 1394–1450   389 Carved foliated capital   390 Plainer moulded perpendicular capital   391 Perpendicular pier base

continue round unbroken. In window arches, shafts are seldom used. Triforium arches are now commonly omitted altogether and their place is taken by decorative panels or niches (385, 386).

Piers, Capitals and Bases

Piers are now thinner in the dimension between the arches and wider from nave to aisle (section in Fig. 387). This is accentuated because the shafts which continue up to the vault are added front and back; they do not form part of the mouldings of the arch but have a bold hollow between them. This can be seen particularly at **King's College Chapel, Cambridge**, and **St George's Chapel, Windsor**. Pier mouldings are shallow and simple (385, 388).

Moulded capitals are common and vary in design. Some are very angular, others softer.

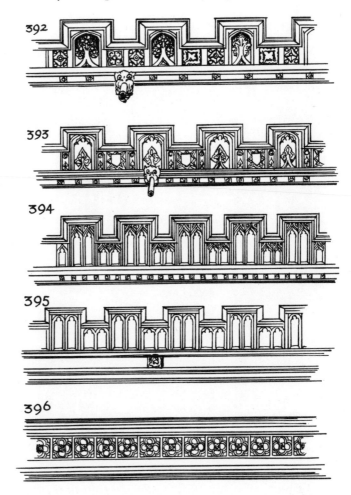

392 Lavenham Church, Suffolk: parapet 393 Lavenham Church, Suffolk: parapet 394 Chester Cathedral: parapet 395 Gloucester Cathedral: parapet 396 Sherborne Abbey, Dorset: parapet

Often octagonal capitals are set over circular piers and columns. Capitals are sometimes formed separately for each shaft but more commonly are continued round the whole cluster of shafts (385, 388, 390). In larger buildings **carved capitals** are used. These are decorated with foliage or figures in the form of angels. The foliated capital is now shallower in relief, and less natural in form (389).

Bases are tall, slender and finely proportioned. It is usual to have a roll moulding at the top, then a double ogee, and further rolls. Bell-shaped bases are common. Below this is the octagonal plinth in one or more members (391).

Parapets, Niches and Canopies

Parapets are in use on most buildings and in larger examples are panelled and generally pierced with tracery and trefoil or quatrefoil decoration. Castellated battlements are common. Foliated ornament is also used, and gargoyles with their lead spouts

397 Chester Cathedral: a section of the canopy of the choir stalls, *c.* 1390   398 St Osyth's Priory, Essex: gatehouse, stone niche, 15th century   399 Chester Cathedral: west front, carved niche, *c.* 1500–10   400 Canterbury Cathedral: choir screen section, *c.* 1400   401 Gloucester Cathedral: pinnacle from the parapet   402 Chester Cathedral: choir aisle buttress pinnacle   403 King's College Chapel, Cambridge: buttress pinnacle   404 King's College Chapel: north-east turret

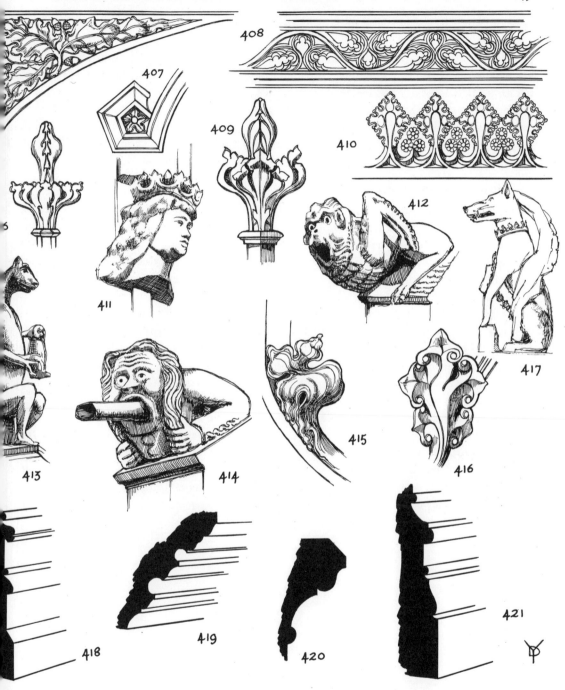

405 Spandrel   406 Carved stone finial   407 Stone dripstone termination   408 Paycocke's, Coggleshall, carved oak beam   409 Carved stone finial   410 Stone ornament   411 St Osyth's Priory, Essex: carved stone corbel   412 Thaxted Church, Essex: carved stone gargoyle   413 Magdalen College, Oxford: carved buttress finial   414 Thaxted Church: carved stone gargoyle   415 Lavenham, Suffolk: carved crocket   416 Carved wood crocket   417 Magdalen College, Oxford: carved buttress finial   418, 419, 420 and 421 Typical Perpendicular mouldings

appear at intervals. Pinnacles are spaced along the parapet in large churches and cathedrals (392–6, 401, 412, 414).

Niches and canopies both present a typical feature of the style and numerous examples are extant. Many niches are merely simple recesses, but others, in larger buildings, have over-hanging, rich ogee or square-headed canopies, with a multitude of tiny buttresses and pinnacles crowning the whole. Both wood and stone are equally used for such carved decoration, the former being restricted to interior work, particularly choir stalls. Especially excellent niches and canopies of this type are at **Canterbury Cathedral** (400) and **Chester Cathedral** (397). Other examples are illustrated in Figs. 398–9.

Mouldings and Ornament

The predominant characteristics of Perpendicular **mouldings** are their shallowness and breadth. The most common mouldings in use include the ogee (single or double), the round and the fillet (387, 390–1, 418–21).

Panelling in its various forms provides the principal means of **decoration** in Perpendicular architecture. This is especially true of larger buildings where entire walls are covered with it so that doors and windows announce their presence only by the pierced openings. Even the vaulting echoes this theme so that very little plain area of wall or roof can be seen. Typical of such ornamentation are the **Henry VII Chapel, Westminster Abbey, St George's Chapel, Windsor**, and **King's College Chapel, Cambridge**. Other designs in ornament include carved foliage, grotesque figures, animals and, particularly, angels. These frequently adorn brackets, bosses and buttress finials (355, 413, 417). **Crockets** are still in common use, now projecting well above the moulding to which they are attached (415–6). Other carved decoration can be seen on **pinnacles, finials, dripstone terminations, oak beams, spandrels** of all types and **cornices** (405–9, 411). Particular designs in foliage include **paterae** and the **Tudor flower**. The latter is so-called because of its prevalence in the sixteenth century, but it was introduced at this time. It consists of a modified *fleur-de-lys* alternated with a small trefoil or ball. It is widely used on screens, niches and parapets as exampled by **Henry VII's Chapel, Westminster Abbey** (410).

CHAPTER V

Tudor 1509 - 1603

For the arts, in Europe, the *cinquecento* is synonymous with the Renaissance. There come to mind the paintings of da Vinci, Raphael and Titian; the sculpture of Michelangelo Buonarotti; the exquisite designs and craftsmanship of Cellini and the architectural glories of Bramante, Peruzzi and Palladio. This re-birth of the arts and learning took shape in Italy and its influence spread outwards and westwards, as it had done in the days of Rome's greatness. For nearly 1,000 years, since the collapse of the Empire and its subsequent obliteration by savagery, knowledge of the arts had remained dormant.

In retrospect, we can see the great quality of art and workmanship in Italy of the *quattrocento*. It is present in the paintings of Fra Angelico, Verocchio and Botticelli and the sculpture of Donatello; while in architecture, Brunelleschi and Alberti, for example, were responsible for building of considerable importance in current designs. At this time, classical learning, or re-learning, spread in Italy with a fervour and vigour associated nowadays only with nationalistic movements. There, the Gothic designs in architecture had never really taken hold or found sympathy and perfection of expression. It was, therefore, with delight and enthusiasm that the Italians endorsed the revival of their ancient art form. From the time in 1414, when Bracciolini discovered the now famous manuscripts of **Vitruvius**—the Roman architect and engineer who wrote *De Architectura Libri Decem* about 50 B.C.—clear fundamentals were enumerated for the guidance of future Italian architects. In these books, covering a wide survey which includes medicine, painting, mathematics, optics, sculpture and grammar, may be found the correct proportions and styles for classical architecture as interpreted by Ancient Rome. Vitruvius puts forward the view that, in architecture, the proportions and symmetry of a building should be regarded as of sacred importance. He provides the orders with capitals and entablature, the ornament, and gives precise details on the unit of measure by which the proportions may be correctly obtained. Information is included on building materials, methods of construction and sites for building.

During the fifteenth century the Italian Renaissance of learning expanded, gaining experience and quality. In architecture, both in construction and ornament, the principles of Vitruvius were used and followed, mainly by a few architects as the manuscripts were not available in an Italian text until 1521. In general, however, this new movement was confined to Italy and its environs. In western Europe, Gothic architecture still held sway. In France, Germany, Spain and, most of all, in England this style had evolved to a high standard of design and quality of workmanship. The time was not yet ripe for change and new ideas. However, by the early sixteenth century, travellers from France in particular, were returning full of the exciting news of the buildings, paintings and sculpture seen in Italy. Slowly the great movement spread westwards. At first it came in the form of ornament, carried out by Italian craftsmen and designers employed by western monarchs and the wealthy.

It was in this form that the Renaissance began to appear in England in the early sixteenth century. Ironically, it was Henry VIII, that then lively, energetic monarch who, by his patronage, was responsible for most of the sixteenth-century Italian Renaissance workmanship which we have in England. It was he also who was responsible for terminating the influx of Italian craftsmen so abruptly on his break with the Papacy. Before 1530, a considerable number of Italians were employed in England, primarily on royal works. Their contribution was in ornamental design, in the crafts of metalwork, marble and stone carving, plasterwork and terracotta. They were not architects and we cannot attribute to their work an actual building. Their activities were, in general, confined to southern England.

After the break with the Catholic Church, and consequent social upheaval in England, the influence of the Italian Renaissance ceased. It had never been a strong force and the innate English conservatism had proved stronger than Henry's desire for the new designs and learning. Gothic architecture, first in its fifteenth-century Perpendicular form, then in its adaptation to Tudor Gothic, with accentuation on flattened arches and plain, vertical lights, continued to be the usual English architectural design for all buildings. Brickwork became a general building material as evidenced by Hampton Court Palace and the great houses of Sutton Place and Layer Marney.

The dissolution of the monasteries brought increased funds to the royal purse. The lands and wealth from the dispossessed monasteries were distributed to loyal followers of the king. When the country had settled somewhat after these storms and crises, a new era of building commenced, inaugurated by those who had benefited from this re-distribution of wealth. In England, the days of the Church as a prime provider, patron and builder, were over. In the sixteenth century building was by royal patronage and the wealth of private individuals. This has left to us an impressive heritage of domestic architecture.

The primary influence on Elizabethan architectural form was a type of classicism brought to England from the Low Countries and Germany. From the 1560s onwards this influence was very strong, and a direct result of Henry VIII's break with the Catholic Church, which led subsequently to England's close association with these countries.

The connection presented a united front against Catholicism. However, this modified classicism was not the same as the purer Italian strain. It represented the Flemish version of the Italian, and, by the time it was further interpreted by English artisans and designers, the final results were very different from the original. Flemish classicism was mannered and ornate; it abounded in strapwork, grotesques, caryatid figures and riotous ornament full of movement and caricature. It came to England as a form of ornament, not as a method of building. English craftsmen took to this version of classical ornament with enthusiasm and used it, as did the Low Countries, for all types of media. It was equally applied to buildings, engravings, metalwork and stone carving. The designs were used in a decorative manner and not, in general, a constructional one.

Our Elizabethan great houses, which today present the chief architectural expression of the time, have been condemned by those who see them only as an early and clumsy attempt to attain the pure classicism of Palladio. They are described as ugly, ornate, crude. It is felt though, that such architectural monuments should not be viewed merely as humble beginnings to the great classical method of the seventeenth and eighteenth centuries. They constitute, in themselves, an architectural form which is wholly and typically English despite the

BATH ABBEY 1501-39

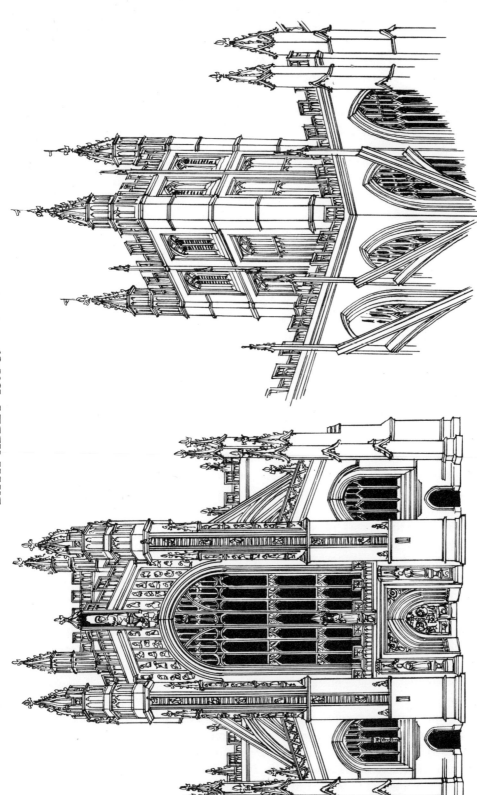

423 Central tower and crossing

422 West front

strong influence from Flemish pattern books. For the Englishmen who designed and built these houses did so to create in each house a single unit and composition. They were not concerned with the proportions accorded to the classical orders which they utilised. They employed such orders, entablature and ornament purely as decoration to the whole design which with its individuality, fascinating skyline and weathered stone or brick makes each house an original, interesting construction. The aim was to show splendour and wealth and, if the result is occasionally a little ostentatious, it is undeniably vital.

The means of introduction into England of Flemish and German styles of classical ornamentation were twofold: by illustrated and written matter, and by craft-workers. The quantity of published material sent abroad from various Continental countries was considerable by 1565. The material took the form of books, folios of drawings—copied and re-designed—and pattern collections. It was produced chiefly in Italy, France, Germany and the Low Countries, though the greatest influence on Elizabethan England came from the last-named. Among the more important contributors in this field were de Bry, de Vries, Dietterlin, Serlio, Alberti, Palladio and, of course, Vitruvius. Both **de Bry**, 1528–98, and **de Vries**, 1527–1608, came from the Low Countries. The former, a good engraver, designed highly ornamented drawings for decorative features. The latter published works which had a great influence on English sculptors and designers. The best known is his *Architectura*, published in 1563. This covers the five orders and also gives designs for chimney-pieces, gateways and interior features. Some of these designs are elaborate and a little overpowering.

Dietterlin, 1550–99, was a German whose published works, *De Quinque Columnarum*, 1593, and *Architectura*, 1594–8, had a profound effect on later Elizabethan work. His drawings are over-ornamented and have a curiously unpleasant quality, in a number of instances, especially when he depicts animals or the human figure. This is so much so that Mr Lees-Milne* refers to them thus: 'In them we may detect the haunting obsessions of a German sex maniac'; or 'his favourite themes are animals in revolting attitudes', and 'limbs grotesquely distorting all physical laws'. This is perhaps hyperbole, and there is no doubt that something in Dietterlin's work appealed to the robust and realistic Elizabethans, while their interpretation of it generally omitted any tendency to obscenity, retaining only the vigour of design.

One of the greatest influences, though, from these written sources was that by the Italian architect and writer **Sebastiano Serlio**, 1475–1552. Serlio spent many years compiling a treatise on architecture in seven volumes which were published over the period 1537–75. He had studied the remains of Ancient Rome whilst he worked there. His books contain accurate information on the remains, and on the details and proportions of classical architecture. They provided a basis of knowledge for builders in England and his work continued to be studied well into the seventeenth century.

The manuscripts of **Vitruvius** were available in Latin, Italian and French by 1547 and exercised the most profound influence on western European architecture. In England, however, the influence was stronger in the seventeenth and eighteenth centuries. In the sixteenth century English builders were less interested in pure classicism than in the lively, ornate decoration provided by de Vries or Dietterlin. For the same reason, **Palladio's** and **Alberti's** works were largely ignored by the majority of English builders. The first English engravings

* *Tudor Renaissance* (B. T. Batsford, Ltd).

XXI Hampton Court Palace, Middlesex: the great west gatehouse, 1515–

424 Trinity College Chapel, Cambridge, mid-16th century

of the orders were published in 1563 by **John Shute**. These were based largely on the work and manuscripts of Serlio and Vitruvius, although Shute did go to Italy in 1550.

In addition to this flood of illustrated literature on ornament which poured into Elizabethan England, there was also a tide of emigrants, largely Flemish, leaving their homeland to escape the Inquisition. These included artisans of many types: painters, glaziers, potters, metalworkers, weavers, surveyors, masons and sculptors. They used Flemish, and sometimes French pattern designs, and their work undoubtedly influenced that of their English colleagues. In architectural forms, this was particularly noticeable in gateways, chimney-pieces, entrance porches, gables and doorways.

Of the **Italian artists** and **craftsmen** who came to England under the patronage of Henry VIII, the greatest was **Pietro Torrigiano**, 1470–1522, a sculptor from Florence. In Italy, he did not rank with the greatest artists of the Renaissance—such as Michelangelo or Cellini—but he was the finest that Henry VIII could persuade to come to England. He designed and carried out, with the aid of English craftsmen, the tomb of Margaret Beaufort in Westminster Abbey. His most famous work, also in the Abbey, is the monument to Henry VII and his queen in the Henry VII Chapel. This work is in the form of an altar tomb and is fashioned from white marble and black touchstone with gilt bronze decoration. The classical design, typical of Italy of the period, incorporates the Corinthian pilastered order, with relief sculptured panels. On the four corners of the tomb are gilt, winged angels. The work was begun in 1512 and was completed in 1518. Other Italian artists who worked in England include **da Verono** and **Giovanni da Maiano**. Da Maiano was responsible for the

II *Bath Abbey, Somerset: fan-vaulted nave, 1501–39*

terracotta plaques of Titus and Galba on the gateway at Hampton Court Palace. They were carried out in 1521.

ECCLESIASTICAL BUILDINGS

In England, in contrast to the Middle Ages, the sixteenth century was a time of secular and university expansion: the ecclesiastical initiative had run itself down. Until 1530, there was still some new building: parish churches for example, and additions or alterations to cathedrals and abbeys. In particular should be noted the rebuilding of **Bath Abbey**, Somerset, 1501–39, the completion of the **Henry VII Chapel** at **Westminster Abbey** in 1512, the Lady Chapel at **Rochester Cathedral**, and a revised nave, porch and tower at **Cirencester Church**. Additions also included carved screens and tombs in many parish churches. All this work was of late fifteenth-century Perpendicular Gothic design. It represented a continuation of the workmanship which England had excelled at for so long and had established as a national style. **Bath Abbey** and the **Henry VII Chapel** are outstanding examples (422–3; XIX, XXII). Within the Universities, **chapels** were still being built and altered. That of **Trinity College, Cambridge**, is most noteworthy. It is interesting to compare it with the earlier chapel of King's College, Cambridge, built at the zenith of the Perpendicular style (424). After the Dissolution, ecclesiastical building virtually ceased, and in the days of Elizabeth all building activity was concentrated on the domestic and educational spheres.

PALACES

Much of the earlier construction was by Cardinal Wolsey, as at Hampton Court and Christ Church, Oxford, and was therefore built in domestic and university method. Hampton Court, for example, was not intended as a palace, but as a large, impressive house to be lived in by a wealthy churchman. It was after 1530 when Henry VIII took over a number of such projects and, with the financial means provided by the sequestration of monastic property, was able to revise them in the form of palaces. Even then, however, the collegiate and domestic plan was retained, but on a more splendid scale. The architectural style was in the last Gothic phase, but with the increased use of brick to replace stonework, the further flattening of arches in doorway and window openings, and a reciprocal flattening of roof and gable, this architectural form is generally referred to as Tudor Gothic, rather than late Perpendicular Gothic.

The gatehouse and hall both retained their importance in the main layout. The former was not now necessary as a means of defence but was built for its value as accommodation and to impress. It was square in plan and had octagonal turrets at each corner and an oriel window was set above the main entrance arch. Generally, as at Hampton Court, there was an outer gatehouse and a second or even third constructed as a bastion between courts. There were usually two courts, the hall and chapel being placed on the inner one. The hall was also in its last phase as an enormous room erected as meeting place, state dining-room and, in general, as a place of entertainment and centre of life for the king, his guests and courtiers. In addition to the hall there were now far more private rooms available in the form of chambers and parlours. A new feature of the plan was the Long Gallery which was incorporated into the largest houses of this time, and which became such an integral part of

425a Hampton Court Palace (Tudor section): the entrance court, showing Great Hall behind, on left. Brick, *temp.* Henry VIII

Elizabethan great houses. This was used for strolling, conversing, making music or playing games. There was also always a chapel included in the plan, but this was not as noticeable architecturally now, as its windows were treated with vertical mullions like the other windows and not traceried as in the fifteenth century.

An important organisation concerned in palace building was that of the King's Works or the Office of Works. The chief official was the Surveyor-General and his second in office the Comptroller. Such men were usually highly skilled masons or carpenters and they gathered around them the skilled men of the country in all trades necessary to building and interior decoration. Supplied with adequate financial resources by the Crown, the Royal Works provided the opportunity to employ the finest craftsmen possible, and important buildings in the land resulted from this nucleus of highly skilled labour. Then men who controlled the erection and built the palaces of Henry VIII were Englishmen, while a comparatively small amount of the work was carried out by foreigners, such as French or Italians who were incorporated into the scheme.

Cardinal Wolsey leased the site of **Hampton Court Palace,** Middlesex, for 99 years in 1514 and began to build in the following year. He made—as was the custom of the time—a rough, general design himself and contracted artisans for each trade, masons, carpenters, glaziers, etc., to carry out the work. It was all executed by Englishmen except for some of the ornamental work which was carried out by Italians. As evidence of some of the latter workmanship is the terracotta roundel decoration on the gateway by Giovanni da Maiano and the still surviving plasterwork ceiling and frieze in 'Wolsey's Closet'. The west front of the house, built by Henry Redman, was completed first (XXI), and a suite of rooms, including 'Wolsey's Closet', can be seen, much as Wolsey left them. The linenfold panelling is particularly fine. In Wolsey's time the plaster panels of the frieze were painted, and many of his walls were hung with rich tapestries. In 1525 he handed the house over to Henry VIII who began to convert it into a palace. Henry's celebrated addition is the Great Hall of 1531–6 with its notable hammerbeam roof. The design is basically Tudor Gothic, but there is a classical flavour about some of the roof decoration. It was the creation of James Nedham, master carpenter, and, from 1532, Surveyor-General (425a, 500–1, 507, 525, 527; XXIII).

Whitehall Palace, London, followed a similar course to that of Hampton Court, but unfortunately does not survive today. It was largely destroyed in the seventeenth century. Wolsey had built a house, including a great hall, at York Place. Henry VIII 'requested' the building in 1529 and expanded it with a palace in Whitehall. He also was responsible for the gateway known as 'Holbein's Gate', in the roadway there, which was completed in 1532. This did not survive the eighteenth century.

St James's Palace, London, was erected 1532–40 and parts are still extant. Included in these is the gatehouse, reminiscent in design of those at Hampton Court Palace (464).

Of Henry's palaces, **Nonsuch** in Surrey was the most extravagant, fantastic and exciting. Sadly for us, our knowledge of it is confined to contemporary drawings and written accounts by those who saw it, such as Pepys and Evelyn. It was wantonly demolished about 1670. The palace was erected on a manor bought by Henry VIII in 1537. It was incomplete when he died 10 years later but was finished a few years after this. The palace represented, to some extent, a stage in Henry's continuous rivalry with Francis I of France, and a Continental influence can be seen in its design. It was built around two courts; the outer one, 132 by 150

XXIII   Hampton Court Palace, Middlesex: the gr
hall, 1531–36. Timber roof designed by James Nedh

feet, was paved with stone and enclosed by slate-roofed, stone buildings. The inner court, entered through a gatehouse with clock-turret above, was the more unusual. A flight of steps was the approach as its level was higher than that of the outer court. It was smaller in area, while its surrounding buildings were only of stone for the first storey and above this were of

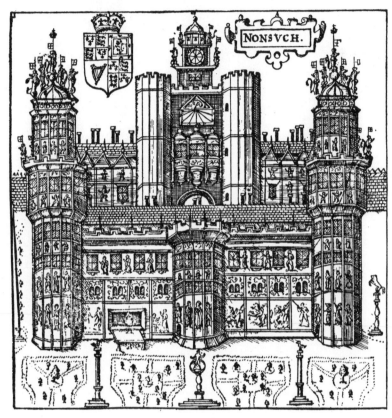

425b Nonsuch Palace, Surrey, begun in 1537
(From John Speed's Map of Surrey, 1611)

half timber. The high-relief plasterwork panels between the timbers were richly and pictorially ornamented and of Italian craftsmanship. The skyline of the garden front of this court was irregular and romantic. It was broken by lead-roofed turrets and pinnacles. Again, as at Hampton Court, the work was essentially English, but with the lavish ornamentation supplied, in Renaissance workmanship, by foreign artisans (425b).

PUBLIC AND MUNICIPAL BUILDINGS

After the Dissolution public building became more necessary; others had to undertake work previously carried out by the monasteries. Two social necessities were education and hospital service. The buildings were often founded and erected by merchants as memorials to themselves. Some of these still exist, for example, **Ford's Hospital** (Almshouse) **at Coventry,**

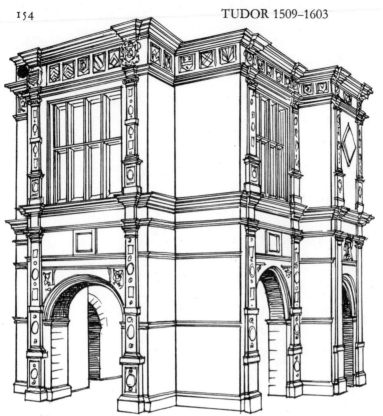

426 The Market Hall, Rothwell, Northamptonshire, Elizabethan

built in 1529. This was unfortunately largely destroyed in the recent war but has now been rebuilt to the original design (458, 488). There is also the **Whitgift Hospital** at **Croydon**, of late Elizabethan construction. Two market houses in particular remain, those at **Rothwell** (426) and **Shrewsbury**. Both are Elizabethan.

A number of halls of the **Inns of Court** were rebuilt in this century, with large open timber roofs. Especially notable were that at **Grays Inn**, 1556–60, and that of the **Middle Temple**, 1562–70. Tragically, both were gutted during the recent war (XXIV).

EDUCATIONAL BUILDINGS

The Universities

At the two universities considerable expansion and alteration were made under the Tudors, particularly at Cambridge. **Trinity College, Cambridge**, was founded in 1546 and much of the building of the Great Court took place in the sixteenth century. The chapel was completed in the 1560s (424) and is in Perpendicular style with a gatehouse entrance. Thomas Nevile was master of Trinity College during much of the building of the Great Court and this included that of the hall, erected at the turn of the century. The hall was modelled on that of the Middle Temple and the hammerbeam roof can still be seen (462).

Another new foundation at **Cambridge** at this time was that by Dr John Caius of **Gonville and Caius**. He returned to his old university in 1565 after studying Renaissance architecture in Italy and France and began to add a new quadrangle to Gonville Hall. Dr Caius was enthusiastic about introducing to Cambridge the new Renaissance architecture which he had seen at first hand. His three famous gates—Gate of Humility, Gate of Virtue and Gate of Honour—show this interesting and fairly successful attempt at the new style. He also introduced a three-sided court, as opposed to the older, completely enclosed court, used in Medieval and early Tudor times. This idea was adopted in Elizabethan house plan. The

427 Queens' College, Cambridge: President's Gallery, mid-16th century. Half-timber work 428 Christ Church, Oxford: Tom Quad, early 16th century. Lower stages of Tom Tower (Great Gate) 1525–9; upper stage by Wren, 17th century 429 Corpus Christi College, Oxford: front quadrangle and gatehouse, early 16th century 430 Gonville and Caius, Cambridge: Gate of Honour, 1573–5

Gate of Honour, 1573–8, has three storeys, greatly decorated and carved with Ionic order pilasters on the ground storey, flanking a four-centred archway (430). The **Gate of Virtue**, 1567, is almost wholly Italian in design. This is rare in Elizabethan architecture (481).

Further sixteenth-century building was carried out at three other **Cambridge colleges**: St John's, Queens' and Emmanuel. At **St John's**, founded 1511, are still extant the wonderful Tudor brick gateways. The entrance gatehouse is early Tudor with rich, painted decoration (479, 505), and the first court is of similar date. The second court is late Elizabethan, also in brick. At **Queens'**, the half-timber work of the long gallery was added about 1540, and though partly altered since, still provides an exceptional college court with sixteenth-century atmosphere (427, 531). **Emmanuel College** was founded in 1584 but most of the early work has been rebuilt.

At **Oxford** the principal Tudor work is at Christ Church and Corpus Christi College. Cardinal Wolsey founded and began building in 1525 his 'Cardinal College', now called **Christ Church**. It was his main architectural achievement apart from Hampton Court, but here, as at the Palace, Henry VIII took over, after Wolsey's fall. Henry moved the see to Oxford and called the college 'The House of Christ's Cathedral in Oxford'. It is still known as 'The House'. Wolsey had built the great hall and kitchen, both on the grand scale in Tudor Gothic style with Renaissance flavour, and part of the enormous Tom quad. This is the largest quad in Oxford, almost 264 feet square. Henry continued the enterprise. Tom Tower was built up to the flanking towers. Wren completed the work in the seventeenth century (428). **Corpus Christi College** possesses a sixteenth-century front quad which is very typical of this time of building. It is simply designed and has a quiet, pleasant, domestic appearance (429).

431 Deal Castle: plan

Grammar Schools

New schools were founded and older, church schools re-founded in mid-sixteenth century to fill the gaps in education caused by the Dissolution.

432 Deal Castle, Kent, c. 1540

Most schools consisted of a library, gallery and one long schoolroom in which two classes were held simultaneously, one at each end of the room. Each class had a master's high desk and forms for the children. **St Paul's School, London**, was founded in 1505 and **Guildford School** in the mid-sixteenth century. **Eton College** possesses a number of Tudor buildings, for example, Lupton's Tower 1516–20—the great gateway with its tall oriel and flanking towers. It was built by Redman and Vertue.

CASTLES

The age of castle building had ended with the Medieval world, but a string of coastal castles was erected by Henry VIII about 1540. These were built as a precaution against invasion from France which Henry feared might come as a result of his break with Catholicism. The design of these castles was different from that of the Medieval buildings. In plan, they possessed a circular court surrounded by concentric circles of semicircular turrets each containing guns and equipment. Among remaining castles of this type are those at Deal, Walmer and St Mawes (431, 432).

BRIDGES

There are not a great number of these extant and most of them display similar qualities of proportion and construction. The examples remaining are of stone, generally undressed and without carving or decoration. They are still heavily built, particularly about the arches and have wide piers and breakwaters. Among existing sixteenth-century bridges of this type are the sandstone bridge at **Stopham** over the Arun, which has seven arches, the central one being much higher than the others (433), the **Bridge of Dee** at **Aberdeen**, which is early sixteenth century, built of granite and sandstone and which is very long; also that at **St Neot's** over the Ouse. The **Sheepwash Bridge** at **Ashford**, Derbyshire, over the River Wye is presumed to be about sixteenth century in date, and is an attractive example in its beautiful tree-lined river setting. Its name is derived from the sheep-dip provided at one end by the curved parapet wall (434).

DOMESTIC BUILDINGS

Great Houses of the Early Tudor Period 1509-1558

A number of large houses were built in these years. Most of them were erected by men who had benefited from the social upheaval resulting from the Dissolution, and who had become wealthy in consequence. The houses were still commonly built on the enclosed courtyard plan, with one or more courts, although the need for defence had now disappeared. The entrance to the courts was by means of a large gatehouse, flanked by octagonal turrets. In many cases, due to the exceptional solidity of building, it is only the gatehouse which remains from such houses. Around the court extended the hall, chapel, offices, living and sleeping accommodation. Some of these houses were of stone, but many were of brick. Tudor brickwork is of high quality and many examples of it still stand. It was in the sixteenth century that the craft of brickwork was fully mastered and comprehended. It became a

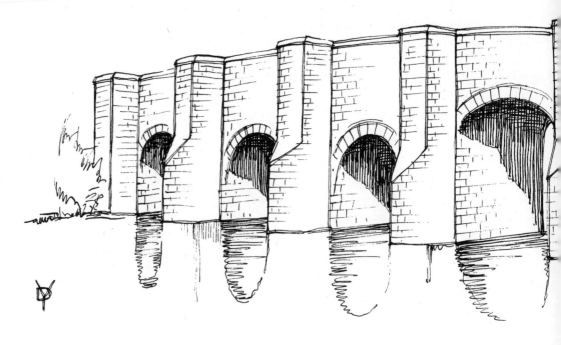

433 Stopham Bridge over River Arun, Sussex, 16th century

fashionable building material, but more particularly in stoneless counties, for example, Suffolk and Essex. Workmanship in these great houses was essentially English, although some owners did employ foreign craftsmen, particularly Italian and French, to carry out ornamental work in terracotta, plaster, etc.

Sutton Place, Surrey, 1523–5, was typically built round a quadrangular courtyard with a gatehouse entrance, but the fourth side, which included the gatehouse, has been destroyed so that a three-sided house remains. It is symmetrical, particularly so for such an early example, and is noted for its fine Italian decoration in the form of terracotta work on the exterior. The terracotta is used for shafts, mullions, finials and door and window opening surrounds. The hall is over 50 feet long and 30 feet high with a central doorway opening leading towards it. There is also a long gallery of more than 150 feet in length (439, 440)

Hengrave Hall, Suffolk (from 1525) is also typical in that it encloses a square court. The plan is almost symmetrical with flanking towers at the corners. The most noteworthy feature is the carved stone entrance gateway which has a curved, triple oriel window. The lower part of this window design is carved in heraldic panels. The workmanship, which is Renaissance in concept, is of exceptionally high quality for such an early example (437, 438, 465, 482, 497, 506, 526).

Layer Marney Hall, Essex, *c.* 1522, is significant for its terracotta work which is contemporary with that at Sutton Place. The workmanship here is also Italian in style and of high quality. The brick gatehouse is remarkable for its great height of eight storeys (461).

There are a number of other large houses built in this period which are still standing and

in good condition. **Horham Hall**, Essex, 1502–20; also a brick building which displays a very fine bay window of some 40 lights (454, 494, 502). **Compton Wynyates**, Warwickshire, built during the reigns of Henry VII and VIII, has been altered and repaired to a certain extent. Its mellowed Tudor brickwork and unsymmetrical planning are seen to advantage in its quiet, wooded setting, at the foot of a hill. It is essentially early Tudor in design, with rectangular window openings and a squat entrance porch (435–6, 496, 532). Other examples include **Lacock Abbey**, Wiltshire, where considerable rebuilding was carried out between 1540 and 1553 (495); **Barrington Court**, Somerset, c. 1530, a more symmetrical design enclosing three sides of a court; **The Vyne**, Hampshire, c. 1530, an impressive brick house with a beautiful long gallery still with its original Tudor panelling, and **Little Leighs Priory**, Essex, where only the large, solid gatehouse remains of the early Tudor work.

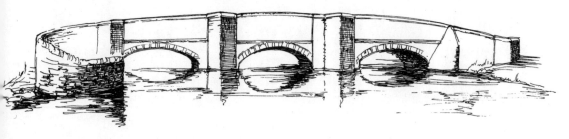

434 'Sheepwash' Bridge, Ashford, over the River Wye, Derbyshire, 16th century

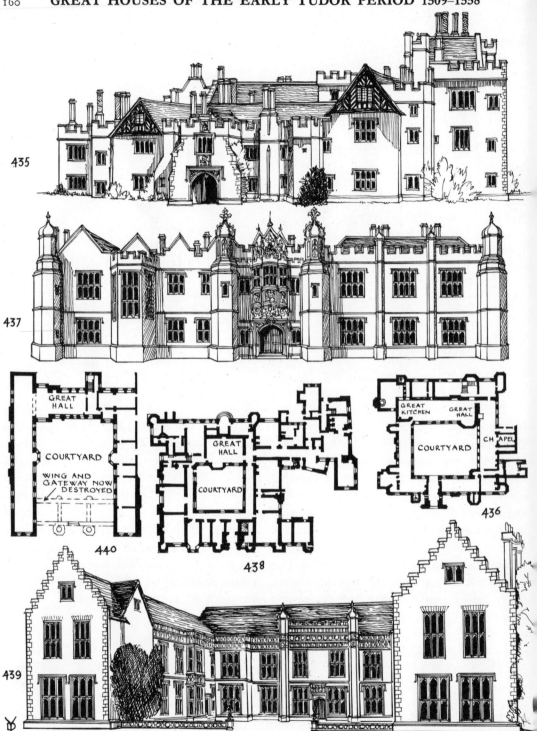

435 Compton Wynyates Manor House, Warwickshire: brick, *temp*. Henry VII and VIII   436 Compton Wynyates: plan   437 Hengrave Hall, Suffolk, 1525-38: stone and brick   438 Hengrave Hall: plan   439 Sutton Place, Surrey, 1523-30; brick and terracotta   440 Sutton Place: plan

Elizabethan Great Houses 1558–1603

Until after the end of the sixteenth century there were no architects as we use the term today. It is difficult, therefore, to assign the building of these mansions to any particular man. The custom practised during much of the Medieval period continued to work well: the client often designed his own house—usually in a sketchy manner—from design books and from houses seen by himself in England or on the Continent. He employed craftsmen in the building trades: masons, carpenters, glaziers, plasterworkers, etc., and these men were directed by a master of their trade, with the whole generally supervised by a master mason or surveyor. The names of many of the latter are unknown to us, largely because complete records are rarely available now. Furthermore, unlike Henry VIII, Queen Elizabeth inaugurated little building effort herself. Thus even royal records are few indeed. The two best-known names in this period are those of **John Thorpe** and **Robert Smythson**. **Thorpe** is remembered chiefly for his collection of drawings now kept in the Soane Museum, London. These show plans, elevations and perspective views of many of the houses of this period, and earlier it was thought that he had designed them. This has since been realised to be untrue. Thorpe was employed for a period at the Office of Works and these drawings represent his work in connection with his survey of such properties. They are helpful in the light that they shed on such buildings but show little of Thorpe's own abilities as a designer. **Smythson** is thought to have been connected with the direction of works at three of the great Elizabethan mansions: Longleat, Wollaton and Hardwick. His connection with Wollaton is proved most conclusively and it is regarded as his principal achievement.

Although Queen Elizabeth was herself responsible for so little building, her way of life had a profound effect on the great houses of her time. For such houses, owned by her ministers and influential subjects, were built by them to accommodate her and her court on its annual summer progress. To provide adequate accommodation of sufficiently high standard for such a large body of persons required a mansion indeed. Each subject endeavoured to outdo his predecessor when building a new house, in architectural style, ornamentation, splendour and scale.

The **plan** of the Elizabethan great house varies, but in general the tendency veered towards greater symmetry, a more compact house and a preference for building round an open rather than a closed, four-sided court. As these ideas evolved, the **E-plan** houses resulted. In these, two wings extended at each side of the house, while, in the centre, the short arm of the E was provided by the projecting entrance porch. The house front was completely symmetrical, with the hall, solar and reception-rooms at one side of the porch, and screens, passage and offices at the other. Often the last of these would be given an oriel or bay window to the full height of the house to balance that of the hall. The large gatehouse, so common a feature of Medieval and early Tudor houses, was abandoned, and the more compact, but decoratively carved entrance porch, took its place.

The **H plan** evolved further from the E version. Here, the side wings were extended as far back as forward. As the century advanced, a greater perfection of symmetry was achieved: bay window matched bay window; gable matched gable; chimney-stack matched chimney-stack. Window area increased in proportion to that of the wall. The skylines of Elizabethan houses are one of their most interesting features. They are varied and lively in silhouette, with

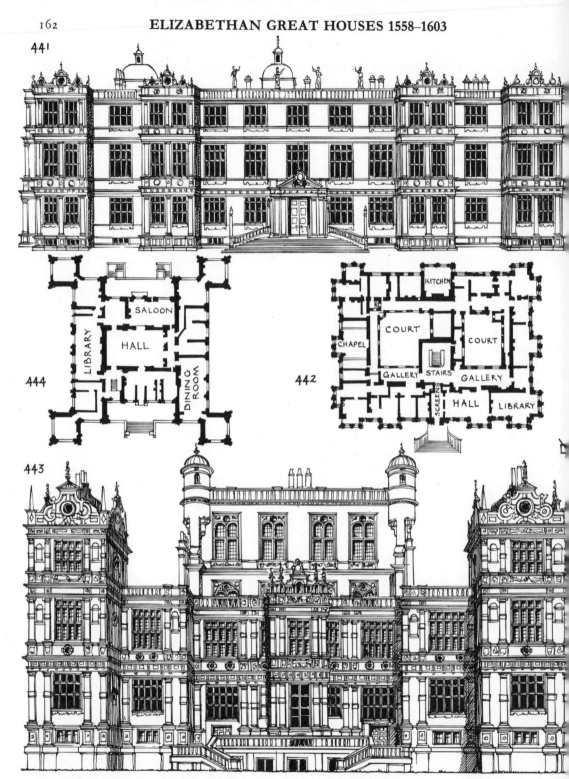

441 Longleat House, Wiltshire, 1550–80; stone   442 Longleat: plan   443 Wollaton Hall, Nottinghamshire: south front, 1580–8. Stone   444 Wollaton: plan

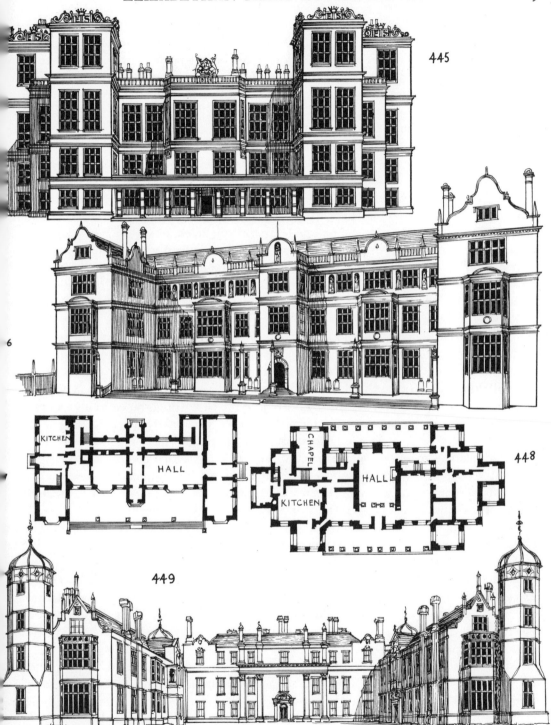

445 Hardwick Hall, Derbyshire: west front, 1591–7. Stone 446 Montacute House, Somerset, 1588–1601; stone 447 Montacute: plan 448 Hardwick Hall: plan 449 Cobham Hall, Kent: west front, 1594–9. Brick and stone. Centre part mid-17th century

projecting gables, cresting and chimney-stacks. At this time also the interior plan was changing. The enormous hall became less fashionable; there were one or two large reception rooms to replace it, with dining parlours, private rooms and bedchambers in greater numbers than hitherto. The long gallery became an established feature of the layout; it generally occupied one long side of the house on the first or second floor. One side faced the outside wall so that it could be fenestrated on the entire length and at each end, while the other, inner side was fitted with two or even three large fireplaces. The staircase, for the first time, became of importance in the domestic plan. A grand staircase was designed to connect the gallery and principal reception-rooms with the ground floor of the house. Such staircases were planned on a commodious scale and had elaborately carved finials, newels and balusters.

Longleat House, Wiltshire, 1550–80, is one of the earlier Elizabethan examples and certainly the most truly classical in conception and decoration. It is one of the finest designs of the period and at the same time is simple and extremely dignified. Its skyline is less flamboyant and interrupted than other examples, having a plain parapet, partly crested and ornamented with sculpture. Sir John Thynne carried out building at Longleat from 1554, but in 1567, when almost complete, the house was burnt down. A new design was made and rebuilding commenced, continuing until 1580. The present Longleat is highly symmetrical; its four sides enclose two courts, and each bay is balanced on the opposite side. On the façade all three orders are represented in pilaster form, one to each storey. The classical proportions are surprisingly accurate for this date. The house is built of pleasantly mellowed stonework, simply carved (441–2, 480, 492, 518–19, 521).

Wollaton Hall, Nottinghamshire, 1580–8, is a great contrast to Longleat. Whereas the latter is greatly influenced by Italian classicism interpreted by Englishmen to give an essentially English house, Wollaton shows a Flemish influence, particularly in decoration, but again the result is very English. In plan, it is original for its period: there are no courts and the house is square, symmetrical and is finished with a block at each corner. Enclosed in the centre is a large hall which is exceptionally high in order to accommodate clerestory type windows, without which it would receive no daylight. The hall timber roof is ornate but typical of late Elizabethan design. The workmanship is good and the carving excellent. The exterior is again embellished with pilastered orders and fenestration is amply supplied. Unlike Longleat, the skyline is extravagantly crested and broken (443–4, 509).

Hardwick Hall, Derbyshire, 1590–7, is one of the later type of Elizabethan designs with great emphasis on symmetry. The entrance porch projects into a colonnaded front. The excessive size and number of windows prompted the contemporary remark that Hardwick had more glass than wall. Certainly the light interiors benefit from this in comparison with Medieval ones. Decoration is limited and the cresting, which includes Bess of Hardwick's initials, is simple (445, 448, 491, 517).

Montacute House, Somerset, 1588–1601, built in pleasantly weathered stone, is one of the simple but very satisfying Elizabethan silhouettes. The plan extends at the wings and has a projecting entrance porch opening on to a short flight of steps which extends the full width of the house. Curved, decorative gables of Flemish design break the plain, balustraded skyline. The bay windows on the façade and wings are two storeys high (446–7, 468, 516).

Other interesting examples of Elizabethan large houses include **Burghley House**, Northamptonshire, which has a broken lively skyline; **Kirkby**, Northamptonshire, of traditional

450

451

452

450 Boughton Malherbe, Kent, *temp.* Henry VIII and Elizabeth 451 Fritwell Manor House, Oxfordshire, late Elizabethan 452 Barlborough Hall, Derbyshire, *c.* 1583

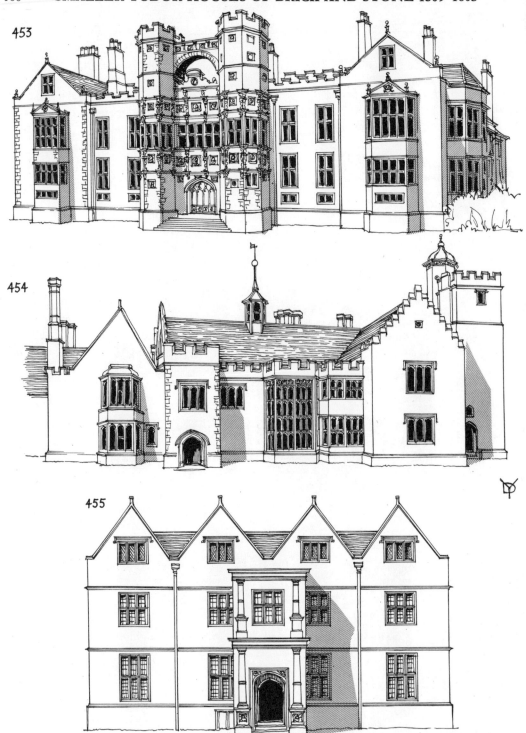

453 Brereton Hall, Cheshire, *c.* 1586. Stone and brick   454 Horham Hall, Essex, 1502–20. Brick
455 Keevil Manor House, Wiltshire, late 16th century

plan enclosing a central courtyard; **Charlecote Park**, Warwickshire, which was altered in the eighteenth century but has a particularly good Elizabethan gatehouse, and **Cobham Hall**, Kent. The last-named has had later work incorporated into the design but the general layout remains Elizabethan, 1594–9, with its long, extended wings, cupola-topped towers and tall bay windows. The three-storey entrance porch is especially noteworthy in Renaissance style with Doric and Ionic columns and superimposed pediment (449, 467, 522–3).

Town Houses

In the first half of the sixteenth century these were still narrow fronted to preserve economy of space. The house plan extended further to the rear to give more accommodation than in the Medieval counterpart. Often the front room was devoted to a shop; living accommodation was at the rear and above. Elizabethan town houses were larger and those of wealthy merchants possessed a much wider frontage than before. The majority of houses were still of half-timber construction; their gables fronted the street and the upper storeys overhung the lower. Not a great number of these survive; many of those which existed until recently were gutted in the last war or have been demolished in order to widen main street thoroughfares. Chester, Shrewsbury and Newark provide the most numerous and high-quality examples. Unfortunately the Coventry half-timber houses were among those largely destroyed in the war. Stone and brick town houses were much rarer, but being more durable, a larger proportion have survived. Examples can be seen at Salisbury, Norwich and Sherborne.

Smaller Country Houses

The wave of domestic building was not confined to large mansions. In the second half of the century new homes were erected by and for the expanding middle class—yeomen and gentry —also the labourers. The proportion of half-timber work in such houses was smaller than in the Middle Ages; the drain of hundreds of years without replanting was beginning to be apparent in England's timber supplies, with a consequent rise in prices. It became cheaper in appropriate areas to build in brick, or even stone. In design, the symmetrical approach of the great houses was passed on to the smaller houses. They were simpler in layout and showed much less influence of the Flemish pattern book or Italian ornament. However, in small ways the Elizabethan Renaissance features could be seen: in entrance porches, plaster gables decorated by cresting, finials and vases, ceilings and fenestration. Like the large houses, though, the courtyard gradually became obsolete and the house was designed with wings on an E, H or simple T plan. For most houses the central hall was still the main feature. With it, on the ground floor, were the kitchen and offices, while the various chambers were above. The top storey was used for servants and storage. The open timber roofs of the hall and solar were now generally replaced by a decorative plaster ceiling. An inside, wooden staircase, often sited in a tower, was becoming more usual than the old exterior or newel stairs. There are a number of smaller Tudor houses still existing in different parts of the country. Among the stone, brick or flint versions are **Barlborough Hall**, Derbyshire, 1583–4 (452), **Boughton Malherbe farmhouse**, Kent, *temp.* Henry VIII and Elizabeth (450), **Brereton Hall**, Cheshire, *c.* 1586 (453), **Fritwell Manor House**, Oxfordshire, late Elizabethan (451, 472, 478), **Keevil Manor House**, Wiltshire, late Elizabethan (455, 469, 533), **Studley Priory**, Oxfordshire (470), **Gifford's Hall, Stoke-by-Nayland**, Suffolk, early Tudor (477, 510), and **Coughton**

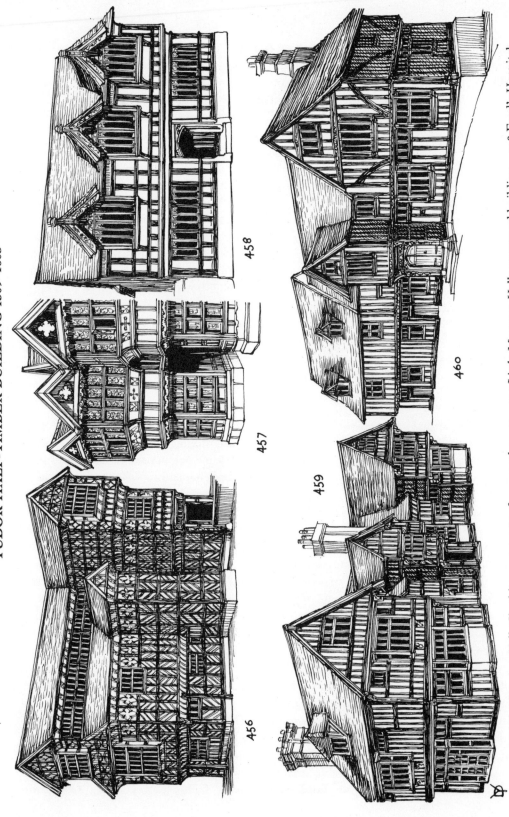

456

457

458

459

460

456 Little Moreton Hall, Cheshire, *c.* 1559–80, from south-west 457 Little Moreton Hall: courtyard building 458 Ford's Hospital, Coventry, 1529 (bombed 1940, rebuilt 1953) 459 Rumwood Court, Langley, Kent, late 16th century 460 The Guildhall, Lavenham, Suffolk, *c.* 1529

Court, Warwickshire, *temp.* Henry VIII (466). Among the half-timber examples, **Little Moreton Hall**, Cheshire, *c.* 1559–80, is perhaps the most justly famous. Now in the hands of the National Trust it is well cared-for and visitors can admire and appreciate the remarkable long gallery, the half-timber work and the carved corner posts, window frames and gables (456–7, 487, 489–90, 530). **Rumwood Court, Langley**, Kent, late sixteenth century, is also in fine condition (459, 486), while the **Guildhall, Lavenham**, Suffolk, presents a good town and municipal example (460, 475).

ARCHITECTURAL FEATURES

The gatehouse is a most typical feature of Tudor architecture, particularly up to 1558. In palace, university and domestic designs alike is found the tall gatehouse of brick or stone, flanked by its octagonal shafts at all four corners. Its military value had almost disappeared but it was retained for its accommodation and its impressive impact in the architectural design. In Elizabethan houses it was smaller and often detached from the main building, as at **Charlecote Park**, Warwickshire. Some town examples still exist and are often richly decorated like the carved stone gateway to **Canterbury Cathedral** (463). Among the exceptionally fine university examples are those at **St John's College, Cambridge** (479), and **Trinity College, Cambridge** (462). **Hampton Court** and **St James's** give us a clear impression of the palace brick gateways (425, 464; XXI), while among the interesting domestic versions are those at **Layer Marney**, Essex (461), **Hengrave Hall**, Suffolk (465), **Coughton Court**, Warwickshire (466), and **Gifford's Hall, Stoke-by-Nayland**, Suffolk (477).

 The frontispiece and entrance porch are, in general, an Elizabethan development from the early Tudor gatehouse. It provided a main entrance to the house or college and gave to the Elizabethan designers their principal opportunity to use the new Renaissance features of ornament. It is in these porches that is visible the Elizabethan interpretation of the classical orders and decoration used, not as structural elements, but in an ornamental form. Sometimes the two or more stages of the entrance porch have single or double columns, but more often are pilastered. There is little attempt to study the correct classical proportions or forms—this was not deemed necessary—but the Elizabethan application of the classical tenets is interesting and shows great vitality. Two or more orders may be used unrelatedly in one porch. **Cobham Hall**, Kent (467, 522–3), and **Studley Priory**, Oxfordshire (470), are excellent examples. See also **Montacute House**, Somerset, and **Keevil Manor House**, Wiltshire (468–9).

 The colonnade is probably Italian in origin and, as an open colonnade, is certainly more suited to a Mediterranean climate. However, a number of Elizabethan houses are designed with such a feature, which in some cases is almost a cloister.

 The Perpendicular Gothic four-centred arch over **window openings** became more flattened in the early sixteenth century; this gave the typical Tudor Gothic window head. By Elizabethan times, the flat, rectangular head was in common use. As the century advanced, fenestration gained in importance and the window area encroached on that of the wall. **Oriel** and **bay windows** were an essential part of the architectural design. Some of these were curved in semicircular section, others were rectangular or chamfered in poly-sided designs. Both bay and oriel windows provide one of the most typical and attractive features of Tudor

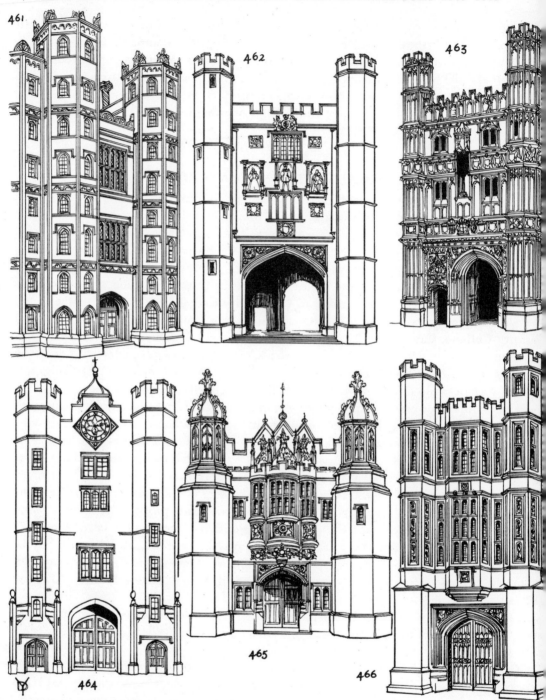

461 Layer Marney, Essex: entrance gateway, south side, 1500–25. Brick and terracotta   462 Trinity College, Cambridge: The Great Gate, 1518. Brick and stone   463 Christ Church, Canterbury; gateway, 1517. Stone   464 St James's Palace, London: gatehouse, *temp*. Henry VIII. Brick   465 Hengrave Hall, Suffolk: gatehouse, 1525–38. Stone   466 Coughton Court, Warwickshire: gatehouse, 1509. Stone

TUDOR ENTRANCE PORCHES 1509–1603

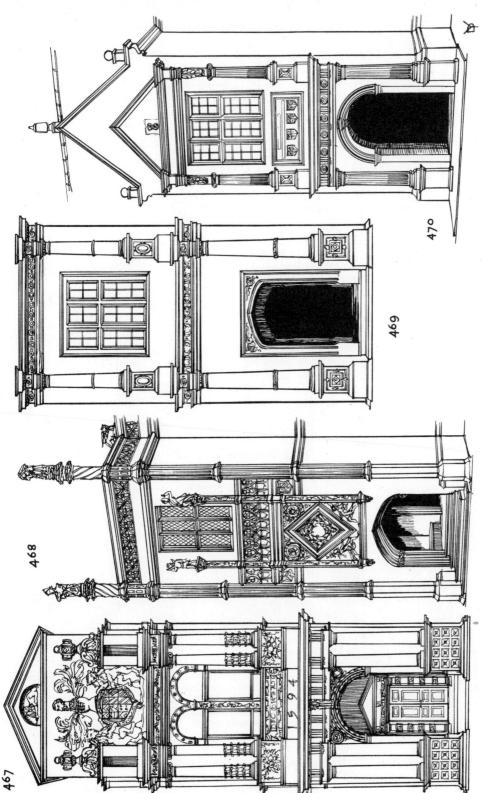

467 Cobham Hall, Kent, c. 1594   468 Montacute House, Somerset (porch removed from earlier house—early Tudor)   469 Keevil Manor House, Wiltshire, late 16th century   470 Studley Priory, Oxfordshire, late Elizabethan

467

468

469

470

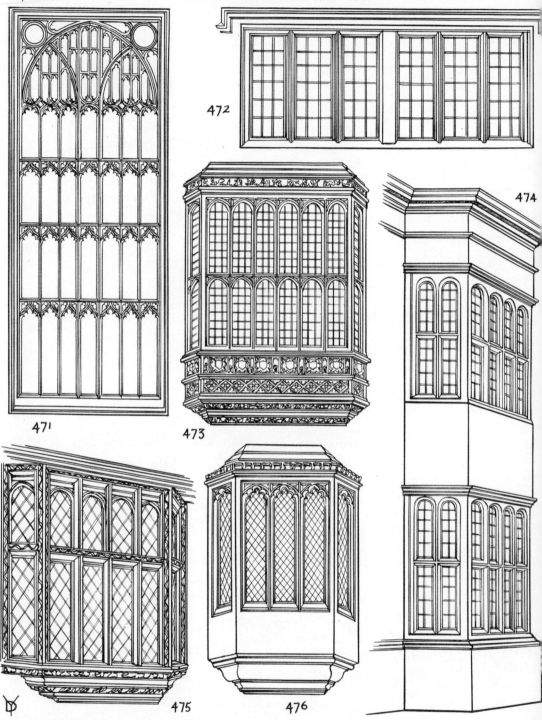

471 Bath Abbey, Somerset: east window, 1501–39   472 Fritwell Manor House, Oxfordshire, late Elizabethan   473 St Osyth's Priory, Essex: oriel window, 1527   474 Wiston Park, Steyning, Sussex: bay window, 1558–78   475 The Guildhall, Lavenham, Suffolk: timber window-frame, early Tudor   476 Compton Wynyates, Warwickshire: oriel window, *temp.* Henry VIII

architecture. Some were plain, but many had richly carved or terracotta decoration. Timber frames on half-timber houses were also often carved with a profusion of ornament showing vine and leaf motifs (472–6). Among the few ecclesiastical examples of the period **Bath Abbey** indicates the continuance of Gothic tracery in its more severe Tudor form; the emphasis is marked on the horizontal transom and vertical mullion (471).

Until about 1570–5 the flattened four-centred arch was in general use for **doorway** heads. This was surmounted by a square heading and the spandrels remaining were filled with carved floral or heraldic ornament. Shafts were small and plain or non-existent (477, 479, 482). As the classical influence increased, doorways were flanked more often by pilasters or columns and a round or flat head was employed (478, 481). At **Longleat House**, Wiltshire, the more Italianate form of classical design can be seen with the Doric columns, entablature and surmounting broken pediment (480). Early Tudor **doors** are generally panelled in linen-fold design while later examples have squarer panels and varied carved ornamentation (477).

In the second half of the century, especially, English **gable design** is diverse, lively and interesting. In stone and brick buildings there are the steeply pointed plain gables as at **Keevil Manor House**, Wiltshire (455), the stepped and finialled Flemish designs as at **Bourne Mill, Colchester** (483), and **Willington Stables and Dovecote**, Bedfordshire (484–5), and the curved and scrolled types as at **Montacute House**, Somerset (446). In half-timber buildings, a simple pointed silhouette is used, but there is infinite variety in carved decoration and form of the **barge-boards** and finials (486–8).

Among the most diverse and attractive features which enliven the Tudor broken skylines are the **chimney-stacks**. These were provided in a tremendous variety of forms, both singly and in clusters. Brick, terracotta or stone is used; the last of these being less traditionally associated with the chimneys of this time. The commonest types of shaft are octagonal or round in plan and are decorated by zig-zags, scrolls, crossed beading, circular holes, honey-comb patterns and fluting. Bases are octagonal, square or diamond-shaped and have intricate mouldings and fluting. Interesting and typical examples can be seen at **Hampton Court Palace, Lacock Abbey**, Wiltshire, **Compton Wynyates**, Warwickshire, **Penshurst Place**, Kent, and **Horham Hall**, Essex (494–501).

In the latter part of the sixteenth century the spacious, wooden **staircase** had begun to take the place of the Medieval stone newel design or exterior steps. Many staircases were planned in 'dog-leg' fashion; that is, with each short flight turning back in the opposite direction from its predecessor. By the end of the century the 'open well' staircase had made its appearance. Here, the newel posts were free. The whole construction was lavish in its use of space, well-suited to accommodate the wide farthingale skirts of the time. Newels, finials, strings and balusters were of carved oak; treads and rises were solid and generous (508b).

In the palace, college and great house, the **hall** retained its importance during the whole century. Many examples were still roofed in the open timber manner, usually in one of the hammerbeam variants of design. They were fundamentally much the same as their late Medieval predecessors but possessed more ornate carving, sometimes with Renaissance motifs. Primary examples include those at **Hampton Court Palace** (XXIII), The **Middle Temple** (XXIV), unfortunately now destroyed, **Trinity College, Cambridge, Wollaton**

TUDOR DOORWAYS 1509–1603

479

482

478

481

477

480

477 Gifford's Hall, Stoke-by-Nayland, Suffolk: gate-house doorway, *temp.* Henry VII and VIII. Brick 478 Fritwell Manor House, Oxfordshire, late Eliza-bethan: stone 479 St John's, Cambridge: outer gateway to first court, early Tudor. Brick and stone, coloured decoration 480 Longleat, Wiltshire, *c.* 1575: stone 481 Gonville and Caius, Cambridge: Gate of Virtue, 1567. Stone 482 Hengrave Hall,

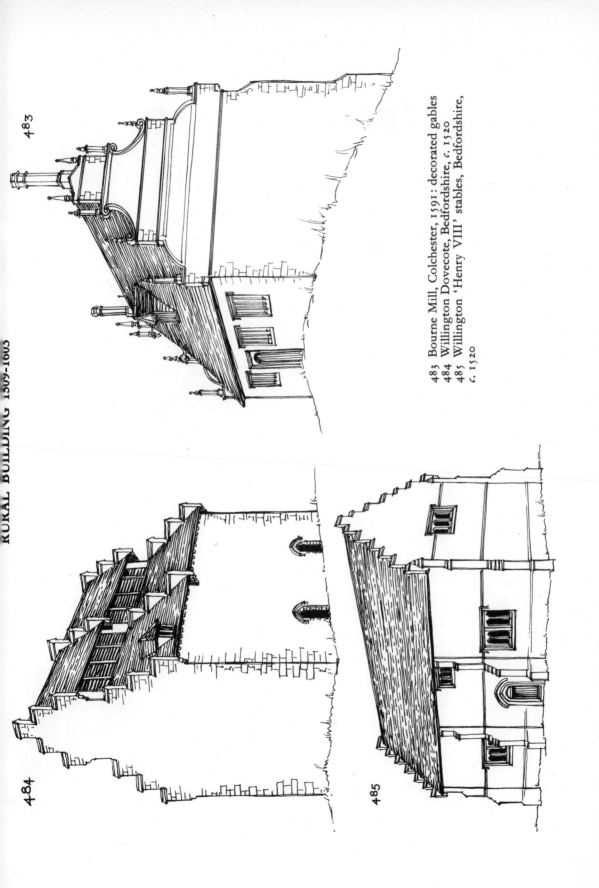

483 Bourne Mill, Colchester, 1591: decorated gables
484 Willington Dovecote, Bedfordshire, *c.* 1520
485 Willington 'Henry VIII' stables, Bedfordshire,
c. 1520

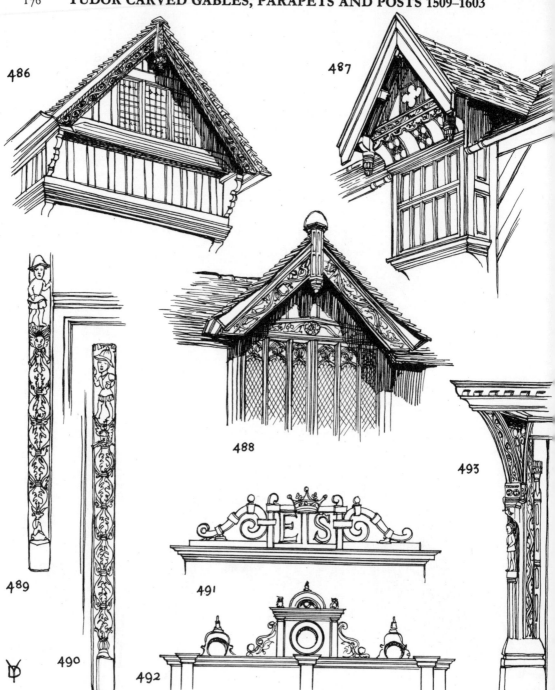

486 Rumwood Court, Langley, Kent: carved timber barge boards and gable, late 16th century
487 Little Moreton Hall, Cheshire: courtyard. Half-timber gable and window, Elizabethan   488
Ford's Hospital, Coventry, 1529: carved timber barge board and gable   489–90 Little Moreton
Hall: carved wood door-posts, Elizabethan   491 Hardwick Hall, Derbyshire: stone parapet crest-
ing, Elizabethan   492 Longleat, Wiltshire: stone parapet cresting, c. 1575   493 The Guildhall,
Lavenham, Suffolk: carved wood corner-post, c. 1529

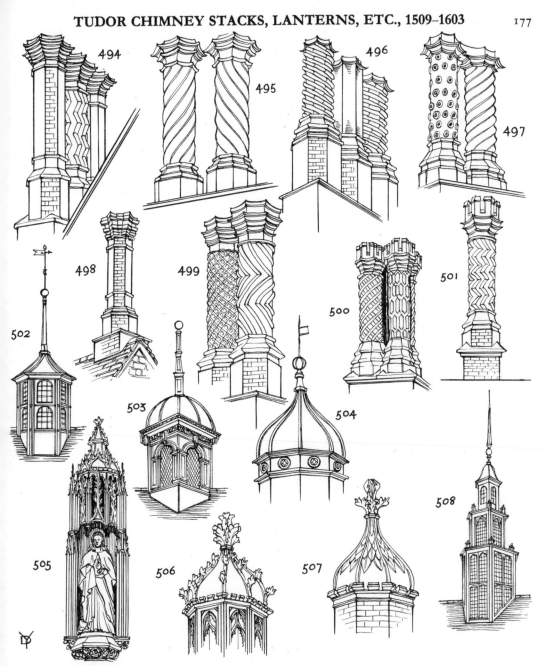

494 Horham Hall, Essex: chimney-stack, early Tudor. Brick   495 Lacock Abbey, Wiltshire: chimney-stack, *temp.* Henry VIII. Stone   496 Compton Wynyates, Warwickshire: chimney-stack, *temp.* Henry VIII. Brick   497 Hengrave Hall, Suffolk: chimney-stack, 1525–38   498 Ightham Mote Manor House, Kent: chimney-stack, Elizabethan. Brick   499 Penshurst Place, Kent: chimney-stack, Elizabethan. Brick   500–1 Hampton Court Palace: chimney-stack, *temp.* Henry VIII. Brick   502 Horham Hall, Essex: hall lantern, early Tudor   503 St John's College, Cambridge: lantern, late Elizabethan   504 Burghley House: stone cupola, Elizabethan   505 St John's College, Cambridge: main gateway, niche, early Tudor   506 Hengrave Hall, Suffolk: carved stone cupola, 1538   507 Hampton Court Palace: cupola, *temp.* Henry VIII   508a Trinity College, Cambridge: hall lantern

Hall, Nottinghamshire (509), and **Gifford's Hall, Stoke-by-Nayland**, Suffolk (510). A flat plaster ceiling with pendant rib or strapwork decoration became more usual in the late Elizabethan period (513–4).

There are early examples of **the long gallery**, as at Hampton Court Palace, but it was the Elizabethan builders who popularized this feature, so that by 1600 it was almost indispensable to the layout of the larger houses. Among the largest galleries are those at **Montacute**, 170 by 20½ feet; **Hardwick**, 166 by 22½ feet, and **Haddon**, 109 by 18 feet. There are many attractive smaller galleries too, such as the one at **Little Moreton Hall** and at **Queens' College, Cambridge**.

Stone vaulting was still employed in the small quantity of ecclesiastical building. It was usually of fan design, and **Bath Abbey** presents an excellent example (511–12, XXII).

Apart from the open timber roofs and stone vaults, the most common method of roofing the average room was now by a flat **ceiling**. This could either be all of plaster, of beams with plaster panels in between, or of wood boards with beam construction. Such beams were frequently made with bold round and shallow hollow mouldings, as in rooms at **Little Moreton Hall**. Where plaster was used it was almost always decorated in rib or strapwork form and often had relief ornament between which was painted in gilt and colour. The strapwork designs were intricate and decorative. Rib patterns were often in pendant form with interlaced ribs in between. Ornament was most varied in motif: flowers, leaves, fruit and animals were utilised as well as pictorial scenes

508b 'Dog-legged' staircase of carved oak, Elizabethan

and figures. In most instances the frieze was also of plaster and continued the ceiling design down to wainscot level. There are some examples extant and two are illustrated in Figs. 513 and 514.

Oak panelling, or **wainscoting** as it was commonly called, was the usual method of covering walls in the sixteenth century. The only exceptions to this are the tapestry-covered walls in the large houses and the painted plaster walls in the very small houses. In the first half of the century **linenfold panelling** was the typical design. The panels themselves were in the form of tall rectangles and the linenfold designs possessed some diversity. Contemporary with the linenfold patterns were the panels which had a central **roundel**, decorated above and below with shields or heads. These panels were usually Italian or French in design if not workmanship and show Renaissance influence. **Elizabethan panelling** was more varied. Both carving and inlay were used. In the latter instance were employed dark or light woods

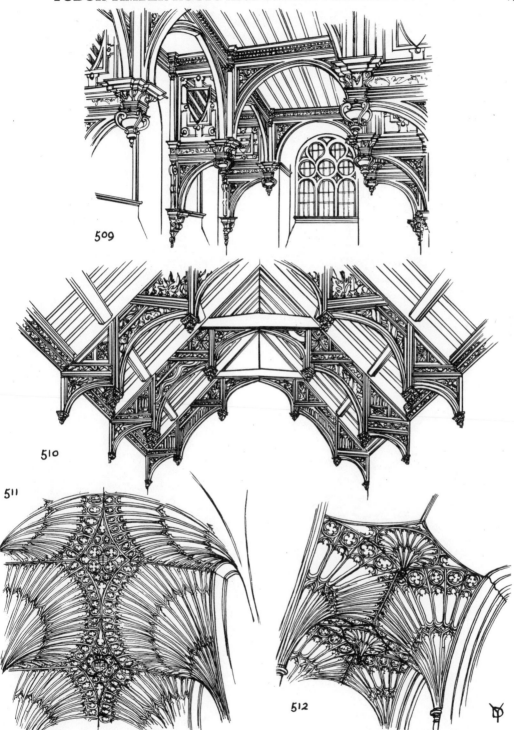

509 Wollaton Hall, Nottinghamshire: the hall, 1580–88. Timber roof   510 Gifford's Hall, Stone-by-Nayland, Suffolk: hall roof, early Tudor. Double hammerbeam style   511 Bath Abbey: nave stone fan vault, 1501–39   512 Bath Abbey: nave aisle fan vault

513 Elizabethan Main Chamber, *c.* 1575–80: ceiling and bay ceiling

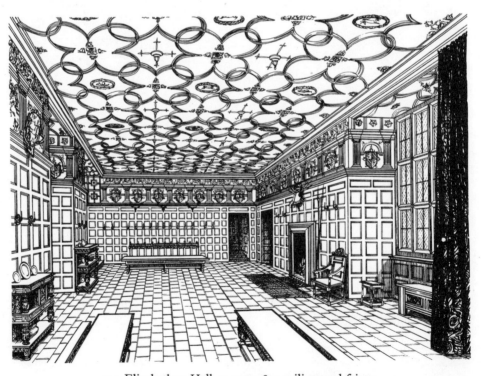

514 Elizabethan Hall, *c.* 1570–80: ceiling and frieze

nd also colour in the form of paint. There are numerous extant examples of sixteenth-
entury panelling. They include walls at Wolsey's Closet at **Hampton Court Palace**, the
ong gallery at **The Vyne**, Hampshire, **Coughton Court**, Warwickshire, **Boughton Mal-
erbe**, Kent, the screen at **King's College Chapel, Cambridge**, the hall screen at **Compton
Wynyates**, Warwickshire, and the inlaid room from **Sizergh Castle**, now in the Victoria and
Albert Museum. (See also 534–8.)

In Elizabethan interior decoration the **chimney-piece** became the focal centre of
ornamental design. This reflected in a similar manner the position of the entrance porch
n exterior design. Elizabethan chimney-pieces illustrated all the new Renaissance motifs
nextricably mixed with the Flemish designs from their pattern books. There were usually
wo stages to the feature, which might be carved or inlaid in wood, stone, marble or
roduced in terra-cotta. The orders were used frequently in pilaster or column form,
ut most favoured were the grotesques and caryatid figures as side supports. Most
lesigns were richly ornate and illustrate the great vigour as well as the naïvety of Elizabethan
lesigners (515a and b).

In early Tudor times the geometrical form of **ornamentation** was still in common use

515a Carved stone fireplace surmounted by
carved oak mantel or chimney-piece, c. 1600-3

515b Oak chimney-piece, c. 1570-5; carved
and inlaid

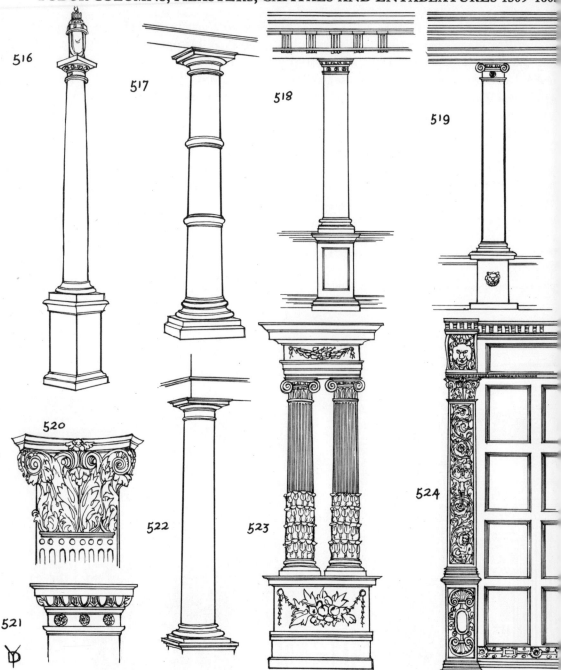

516 Montacute House, Somerset: lantern column, 1588–1600. Doric Order   517 Hardwick Hall,
Derbyshire: porch supporting column, Elizabethan. Doric Order   518 Longleat House, Wiltshire:
pilaster and entablature, first floor, c. 1575. Doric Order   519 Longleat House: pilaster and entablature, second floor. Ionic Order   520 Carved pilaster capital, late Elizabethan. Corinthian order
521 Stone capital, Doric Order. Enlargement of Fig. 518   522 Cobham Hall, Kent: column, lower
stage of porch, 1594. Doric Order   523 Cobham Hall: Ionic columns and entablature, first floor of
porch   524 Carved oak pilaster, panelling and plinth, c. 1600

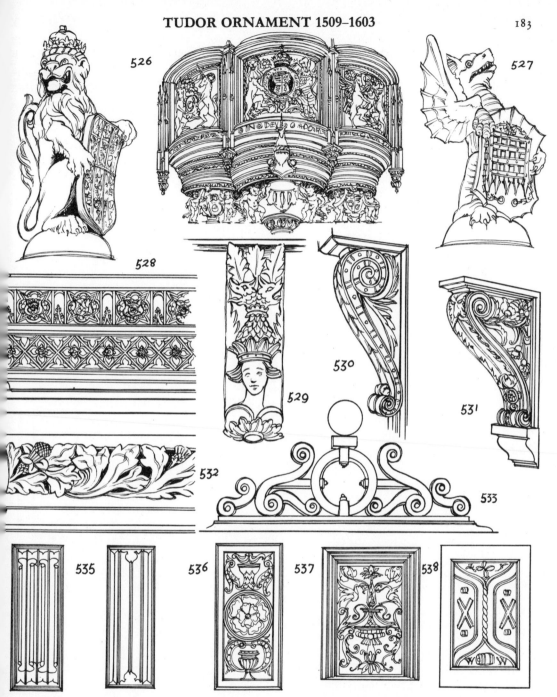

525 Hampton Court Palace: carved stone finial   526 Hengrave Hall, Suffolk, *c.* 1538: ornamental lower part of oriel window   527 Hampton Court Palace: finial   528 St Osyth's Priory, Essex, 527: ornament   529 Little Moreton Hall, Cheshire: carved wood doorway ornament. Elizabethan 530 Little Moreton Hall, Cheshire: carved wood corbel bracket. Elizabethan   531 Queens' College, Cambridge: carved wood corbel bracket   532 Compton Wynyates, Warwickshire: ornament, *temp.* Henry VIII   533 Keevil Manor House, Wiltshire, late 16th century: stone gateway cresting   534 Linenfold panelling, early Tudor   535 Vertical moulded panelling, early Tudor 536 Carved panelling, early Tudor   537–8 Carved panelling, Elizabethan

with cusping and trefoil patterns. Floral designs also were general, particularly the vine, the
rose and the ivy. Heraldic motifs appear frequently, especially as finials and in coats of arms.
With the Elizabethans came the Renaissance motifs—usually of Flemish type. Here were
displayed the orders, grotesques, masks, caryatids, obelisks, vases, balls and fluting. These
were particularly in use as decoration for parapets and gables, chimney-piece and corbel
(516–33).

CHAPTER VI

Stuart 1603 - 1660

Jacobean architecture progressed steadily in continuation of the Elizabethan towards a culmination in about 1620 of the chief features of the style. The fundamental influences continued to be Flemish and German, shown in the mannered, lively ornament and profusely decorated open surfaces. The great houses of the period were not quite the same as their Elizabethan predecessors; they had evolved further towards symmetry, striking silhouettes and splendour of mass formation. Hatfield House and Bramshill House are clear examples of this.

In the second quarter of the seventeenth century, however, the influence of the purer classical strain from Italy made itself felt, primarily in the work of Inigo Jones. Before commencing a description of Jones's life and work, it is proposed to give a brief outline of the contemporary Italian work and the ancient classical architecture on which this, and much of the English architecture up to the end of the eighteenth century, was based.

It has been described in Chapter V how the discovery and study of the manuscripts of Vitruvius had provided inspiration and a solid basis for Italian classical architecture. In the sixteenth century **Andrea Palladio**, the great Italian architect, made a detailed study of those manuscripts, and his *Quattro Libri dell' Architettura*, which was published in Venice in 1570, provided the fundamentals for the guidance of future architects.

In this work (a reiteration of that of Vitruvius), he laid down the rules for proportion, design and ornament, following closely, almost slavishly, on Vitruvius' work. This was emulated zealously by foreign architects, including Englishmen, and culminated in the almost fanatical idolatry shown by the group of eighteenth-century English architects, later to be called Palladians. In Italy, in the sixteenth century, architecture was now regarded almost as a science. The Medieval, somewhat haphazard, method of constructing great buildings by various craftsmen, led by their masters in trade, was abandoned in favour of a central figure or architect, who conceived, designed and directed the whole. Such architects were required to study and practise in many subjects, including sculpture, painting, perspective, mathematics, history and drawing, and all the famous figures of the Italian Renaissance were capable and even outstanding performers at several professions. For instance, Michelangelo was a sculptor, painter and architect; Brunelleschi was both architect and goldsmith; Alberti practised architecture and music; Raphael was a painter and an architect and Bernini was an architect and a sculptor.

ANCIENT CLASSICAL ARCHITECTURE

The Italian classical architecture of the sixteenth and seventeenth centuries as practised and described by Palladio and his colleagues was based directly on ancient Roman forms, as recorded in Vitruvius' manuscripts and supplied by the remains of architecture then being discovered and studied in the native land, particularly in Rome. However, this Roman form stemmed directly in origin from the earlier but purer Greek architecture. **Greek buildings** were simple structures but it was a simplicity produced only by an advanced, well thought-out, scientific method. Columns supported the roofs with entablature in between, and a stepped base at the foot. Various subtle aids were used to correct optical illusions in both the horizontal and vertical plane. For example, the entablature and stepped bases were cambered to produce a straight not hollow appearance; columns were given an entasis for the same reason, and were constructed to lean slightly towards the centre of the building to prevent the appearance of leaning outwards. The spacing between columns was also adjusted and even the slopes of the pediments—the triangular top members above the entablature—were cambered to avoid an impression of hollowness. The fineness of the proportions and these subtle, scientifically designed adjustments are at the basis of the notable beauty of Greek buildings and the satisfaction with which they can be contemplated, even in the more or less ruined condition of those that remain today. The student should not, however, confuse these subtle adjustments to line and curve made by the Greeks, purely to correct and not induce optical illusion, with the distorted over-corrections produced by some eighteenth- and nineteenth-century English architects.

The Greeks designed in three orders: the **Doric**, the **Ionic**, and in later works, the **Corinthian**. The Doric is the simplest of these and is shown to perfection in the **Parthenon**. Each order supported an **entablature**, which in turn was made up of three chief divisions: the **cornice** at the top, the **frieze**, and the lower **architrave**. Each stage of the entablature was composed of certain mouldings which varied from order to order in proportion, type and number. (Descriptions and diagrams of mouldings and other features in classical architecture referred to in the text are given in the Glossary.) The proportions of width and height of column, depth and recession of entablature and frieze, the employment of fluting on columns and the use of bases varied also from order to order and, to a certain extent, on individual examples. A parallel of Greek, Roman, Italian and English seventeenth-century orders is given on page 187. Greek examples may be seen in Figs 539, 542 and 545.

The **Romans** adapted Greek designs to their own use and from the three orders evolved five: **Doric, Tuscan** (a version of the Doric but unfluted), **Ionic, Corinthian** and **Composite**. The last-named is a hybrid of Ionic and Corinthian design. These orders were often employed two or three together on one building, usually one per storey or façade. The Roman versions were more ornate—mouldings were more frequently carved with decoration—the proportions were less subtle and fine and the whole was less simple but full of vitality and movement. The Romans were great engineers but fundamentally lacked the artistry of the Greeks. This is apparent in equal measure when one compares, for example, Greek and Roman sculpture, or Greek and Roman costume. Roman orders are shown in Figs 540, 543, 546 and 549; and Italian Renaissance examples in Figs 541, 544, 547 and 548. To provide comparison, two orders from Inigo Jones's designs are shown in Figs 550 and 551. Apart from the use of orders, columns and pilasters, Roman architecture utilised the semicircular arch for the openings of windows, doors and niches, and also pediments, plain or filled with carved or sculptured ornament. Such pediments were superimposed on the cornices of roofs, doorways and window heads. All these features may be studied in the English interpretations, seen in this chapter and continued through the time of Wren, the Palladians and to the age of Robert

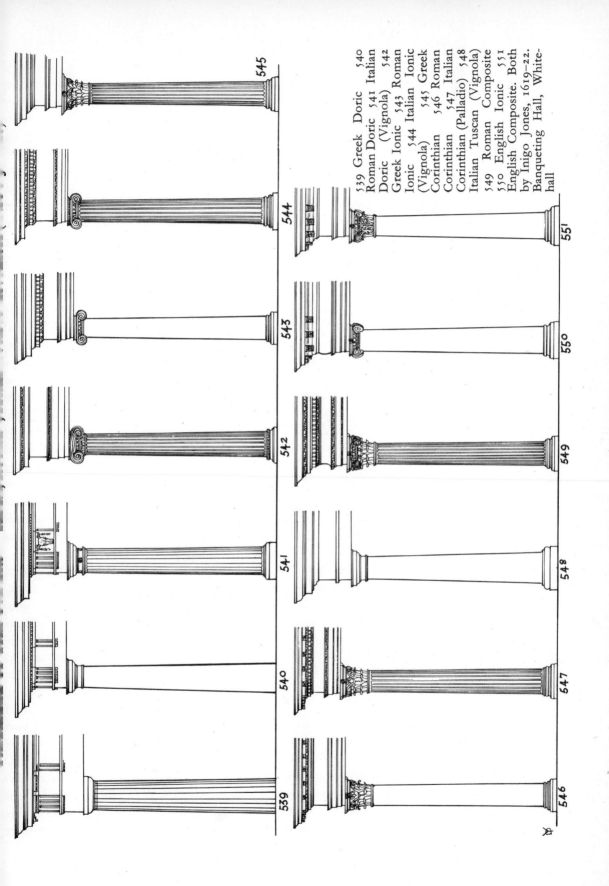

539 Greek Doric 540 Roman Doric 541 Italian Doric (Vignola) 542 Greek Ionic 543 Roman Ionic 544 Italian Ionic (Vignola) 545 Greek Corinthian 546 Roman Corinthian 547 Italian Corinthian (Palladio) 548 Italian Tuscan (Vignola) 549 Roman Composite 550 English Ionic 551 English Composite. Both by Inigo Jones, 1619–22. Banqueting Hall, Whitehall

Adam and his contemporaries in the late eighteenth century. They reappear with nineteenth-century classicism and even our own century possesses many examples of the 'classical building'.

INIGO JONES 1573–1652

The contribution of Inigo Jones to the history of English architecture is invaluable. By the Italian, his work would be considered of good quality for his time, but in England he was an innovator, a harbinger of an entirely new sphere of thought in planning and approach. Here in England, he is commonly regarded as our first true architect, that is, a designer who provided the working drawings and supervised the entire construction of the work from beginning to end. He also pointed the way to later English architects by instituting the true classic proportions and design. He made his own measured drawings from classical buildings and did not take his information at third or fourth hand via Serlio or Flemish sources as designers had done hitherto.

Inigo Jones was born in London, the son of a clothmaker. Knowledge of his early life is scanty; it is presumed that his education was limited, and that he was largely self-taught; his father was poor. He became known at first as a designer of costumes and décor for the masques at Court. Queen Anne of Denmark reintroduced this Tudor custom and Jones, having studied Continental décor, made many designs for her. In the late sixteenth and early years of the seventeenth century, he is thought to have travelled on the Continent and later in Denmark, but little is known definitely of his activities, apart from the masque designs, until 1611 when he was appointed Surveyor to Prince Henry of Wales. After the latter's premature death, Jones toured Italy and France for Lord Arundel in search of works of art. He was away for over one-and-a-half years and visited Rome, Venice, Vicenza, Florence, Naples and Padua. He took with him a copy of Palladio's *Quattro Libri dell' Architettura*, and on the various building sites checked the measurements and information given in this book. He had a great admiration for Palladio's work, but this did not result in him becoming a slavish copier. Indeed, he did not always agree with Palladio, particularly in regard to the Italian's great dependence on Vitruvius. Inigo Jones felt that Vitruvius had not lived to see the later creations of Rome and that his contribution, therefore, had certain limitations. Jones placed great emphasis on going to see for himself the works of Ancient Rome, and preferred to base his own designs on these rather than on the Italian Renaissance buildings, much as he admired them. This insistence on going to the fountain-head for inspiration and study was indeed revolutionary for Englishmen, who hitherto had been quite content to study in England at third or fourth hand via the books of Italy, France and Flanders. Jones studied the writings of other Italian architects, Vignola and Fontana, for example, and met a number of architects in his travels; among these was Scamozzi.

After his return to England, Inigo Jones was appointed in 1615 as Surveyor-General and held this post until the Civil War. It is often remarked that, considering his long period of office, it is strange that there is so little of his building work extant, in comparison with Wren later in the century. It is indeed a great loss to English architecture that this is so. It is due primarily to the fact that Parliament permitted such a small amount of money to be spent on public and official building and hardly any ecclesiastical construction was carried out either. A number of large schemes, such as that for Whitehall Palace, never got far beyond

XXV   Wilton House, Wiltshire: the Double Cube Room, c. 1649. Architect Inigo

the drawing stage. Also, some of the work that Jones did carry out, in London in particular, was demolished later for new building enterprises. It is remarkable, in view of the small quantity of building which was actually constructed to his designs, that his fame and reputation as an architect was so great, even in his own lifetime, not only in England, but also on the Continent. In the last 50 years, a number of buildings, originally ascribed to Jones by tradition or historians, have now been re-ascribed on later evidence to his colleagues or successors. In his long period of office only some 20 buildings are known to have been designed by him and of these only half a dozen still survive to any extent.

The Queen's House, Greenwich, 1616–35, was Inigo Jones's first main work and as such is of great importance in the history of English architecture, for it is our first truly classical building. It was begun in 1616, but, due to the Queen's death, work was stopped in 1618 and did not recommence until 1629, for the next queen, Henrietta Maria. Because of this delay it was not completed until 1635 and thus was finished later than the Banqueting Hall, on which Jones had been working in the meantime. The latter thus became the first *completed* classical building. The Queen's House is essentially simple in design but of fine quality architecturally. It is still regarded as a masterpiece. That it survives today is only due to the intervention of another queen, Mary II. She insisted on its retention in the scheme when the new Greenwich Hospital was planned and erected in the later seventeenth century. Originally the building was devised to span the main road and was erected on a bridge with half of the house constructed on each side. Later, Webb filled in this bridge and made the house a plain rectangle. In Jones's design the plan consisted of two rectangles connected by the bridge. The chief room, the hall, is a cube of 40 feet and has a flat ceiling decorated by carved wood cornices, painted in gold and colour. Around the hall is a gallery which gives access to the Queen's apartments. The house has a circular staircase which was a great innovation at this time (553, 555).

The Banqueting Hall, Whitehall, 1619–22, is generally regarded as Inigo Jones's greatest work. It was built to replace the earlier Banqueting Hall which had been destroyed by fire. It was planned with a much larger scheme in Whitehall and to be part of a great façade. Its cost was over £15,000, and it was the only part of the great Whitehall scheme to be carried out. It is completely classical in conception and treatment, and apart from the necessary nineteenth-century refacing due to city smoke, the building remains much as Jones left it. The exterior façade has two orders, the lower one Ionic (like the Queen's House) and the upper, Composite. Inside, the double cube hall which was designed as a banqueting hall is 110 feet in length, 55 feet wide and 55 feet in height. Its ceiling panels were painted by Rubens at a cost of £3,000. They represent the government of James I (550–2).

The scheme for laying out **Covent Garden,** a square of development in the London fringe, was sponsored by the Earl of Bedford and the King and Council in 1630. It is thought that Jones was responsible for the design of the *piazza* as it was called, also for St Paul's Church, built on the west side. Houses were constructed on two sides, designed by Isaac de Caus and, like the church, were classical in character. The church was destroyed by fire, and, though rebuilt, now bears little resemblance to Jones's design. However, at the time, the scheme did represent a very early attempt at English town planning.

The Queen's Chapel, St James's, 1623–7, is now the chapel at Marlborough House. It was built as a Catholic chapel for Henrietta Maria, and is of classical design. It was Jones's

VI   Hatfield House, Hertfordshire: the staircase, 1607–12

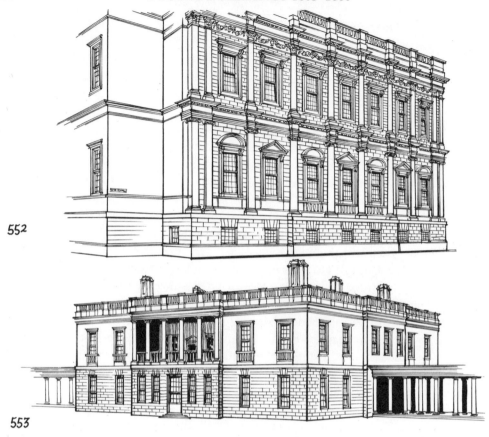

552 The Banqueting Hall, Whitehall, London, by Inigo Jones, 1619–22   553 The Queen's House, Greenwich, south side, by Inigo Jones, 1616–35   554 Kew Palace (in Kew Gardens), 1631. Brick   555 Queen's House: plan of first floor

first ecclesiastical work. It still survives, much as it was designed and is a double cube 56 feet in length. It has no aisles. The ceiling is a barrel-vault with rich decoration.

It is not definitely established that Jones designed **Lindsey House, Lincoln's Inn Fields, 1640**, but the evidence of Colin Campbell points to this. The area of Lincoln's Inn Fields was laid out as a public square from 1618. This particular house has now been divided into two houses, but apart from a duplication of the front door little else on the exterior has been changed. The façade has a giant Ionic order supporting the entablature, which is surmounted by a balustraded parapet. The lower part of the façade is rusticated and has a basement below. It is a fine example of town architecture of the period (579).

Among the large schemes designed by Inigo Jones for the King and never carried out was the ambitious plan for the complete rebuilding of Whitehall Palace. He was also commissioned to do extensive work at Somerset House, then occupied by Henrietta Maria. However, all the work that he did here was lost when Sir William Chambers designed the new Somerset House in 1776.

The Restoration of St Paul's Cathedral was carried out by Jones between 1634 and 1643. Old St Paul's had fallen into decay through the disastrous neglect during Elizabeth's time. In 1620 James I appointed a Royal Commission to investigate the matter. It was decided to try to raise the necessary £20,000, regarded as a minimum figure for rebuilding the steeple and repairing the rest of the fabric. Wealthy men and the King contributed, but sufficient money was not forthcoming and the matter was shelved. Finally, in 1631, when the very existence of the cathedral as a building was threatened, the energetic Archbishop Laud was responsible for the study of the question by a further commission. In 1634, Inigo Jones was appointed as Surveyor to the work and restoration began.

Great variance of views has been shown both then and in later times on Jones's contribution to the fabric of St Paul's. He was entrusted with an almost impossible architectural task —to make the cathedral safe and usable and to incorporate the new classical form of architecture with the older, Gothic workmanship. Some of his contemporaries and many later architects, notably the Burlington group, felt that the work ranked as his masterpiece. Others have thought it a desecration of the Medieval cathedral. In actual fact, Inigo Jones held Old St Paul's in high esteem, but its fabric was so decayed that much had to be done. Moreover, it had been used for some time for various secular purposes and Laud was anxious that this should cease and the building be used for worship only. So Jones designed and built a great portico in front of the old Norman west end, to be used as a public ambulatory. This classical portico, 66 feet in height, had a Corinthian order of 14 columns, while giant scrolls filled in the side angles between the high nave and low aisles. Above the entablature, instead of a pediment, was a balustraded parapet with pedestals set at intervals to receive the statues of benefactors. In addition, he gave a classical covering to the south-west and north-west sides, but did not alter the interior. Decayed masonry was cut away and the new stone facings were in classical style. Money was raised by national appeal, but Charles I himself paid for the portico as a memorial to his father.

In 1643 work on the cathedral ceased owing to the Civil War. Desecration began once more. The balance of the funds collected for the restoration of the cathedral, amounting to some £17,000, was confiscated by the Commonwealth Parliament. Materials were also impounded and workmen were unpaid. The scaffolding of great timbers which had been set up to support the tower and high vaults was cut down, sawn up and sold. As a result much of the vault collapsed. Lead roofing was stolen, gold and silver from church fittings were melted down and sold. The nave was used as a stables and the new portico provided cover for stalls and shops. The chapter-house undercroft became a wine cellar. This sorry history was finally brought to a close in 1666 with the Great Fire. The cathedral was so badly damaged that it was useless to try to restore it again. The portico still stood but Wren deemed it too difficult to incorporate it into his new cathedral. Later Palladian architects have censored him for destroying Jones's work. Despite the quality of this work, which we today can only judge from drawings, it comprised an incongruous classical patchwork on the Medieval building, and it was therefore no service to Jones's memory to retain it.

Wilton House, Wiltshire, **1649–53,** is one of the few country houses where work can be attributed definitely to Inigo Jones. His court life had ended in 1642 with the advent of the Civil War. With it ended also his office of Surveyor-General. From 1649 until his death in 1652 he was assisting the Earl of Pembroke and rebuilt part of the great house at Wilton. The south front still exists, and, ascribed to Jones, it provides a magnificent example of his work. The exterior is simple, without orders but with a central great window flanked by sculptured figures. Behind this front are seven rooms, of which the two great state rooms are justly famed. These, the Double Cube Room and the Single Cube Room are two of the best examples of seventeenth-century apartments extant. The Double Cube measures 60 by 30 by 30 feet and is shown in Plate XXV. The walls are painted white with gold decoration and are hung with Van Dyck portraits. Between the latter are carved oak decorative drops of fruit and flowers, depended from scrolled cartouches. The carved wood doorcase is of the Corinthian order and the doors have deep panels with acanthus leaf decoration. There is a large oval panel in the ceiling design. The chimney-piece is of white marble carved in scrolls and swags. The Single Cube Room is a little less elaborate but is also rather French in character.

JOHN WEBB 1611–1674

There were two other architects of note in the first half of the seventeenth century: **John Webb** and **Sir Roger Pratt**. It is difficult to separate Webb's work from that of his master, Inigo Jones, for whom he worked for 24 years. Webb revered Inigo Jones and kept himself somewhat humbly in the background during these years of service, so that his own work has perhaps not received the credit which it merits. This work was obviously strongly influenced by that of Jones, and Webb carried out many drawings for him. It was only after Jones's death in 1652 that Webb's independent creations are really apparent. Among these are **Lamport Hall**, Northamptonshire, 1654–7 (greatly altered later), **Belvoir**, Leicestershire, 1654 (later rebuilt), and the portico of **The Vyne**, Hampshire, 1654. The last-named example still stands and shows stucco-carved brick columns and pilasters surmounted by a wood pediment.

SIR ROGER PRATT 1620–1684

Pratt received his education at Oxford and later studied law at the Inner Temple. During the Civil War he was touring on the Continent, where he stayed in Flanders, France and Italy. He was in Rome in 1644 where he lived for some time with his friend John Evelyn. Like

XXVII Coleshill House, Berkshire: the staircase l
1662. Architect Sir Roger Pratt. (Destroyed by fire 19

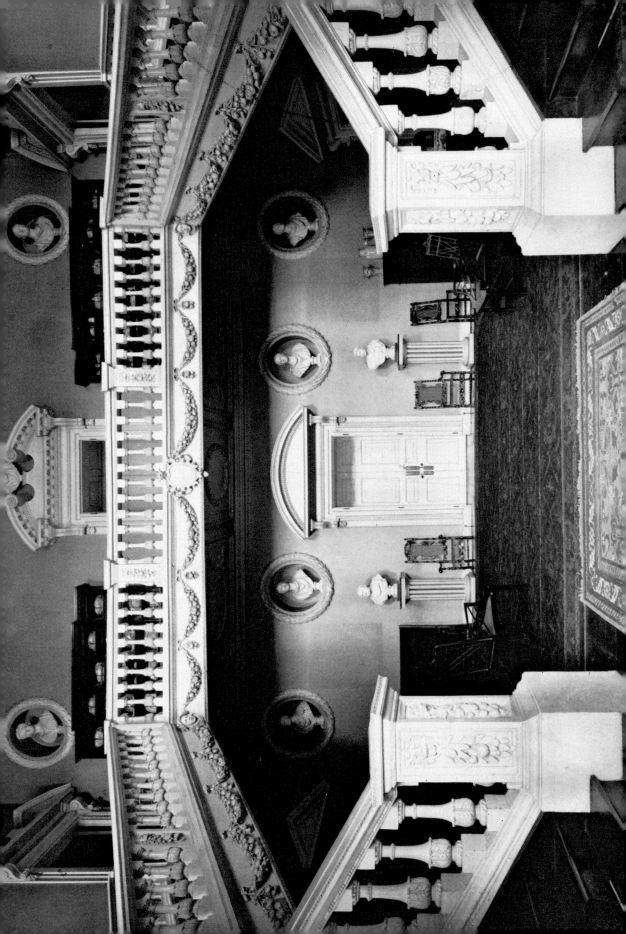

Inigo Jones, he believed that a good architect must study classical architecture at first hand, from Ancient Rome and also from Italian Renaissance works. He made copious notes and drawings and much evidence of this study still exists. When he returned to England in 1649 he began work on redesigning the burnt-out house at Coleshill, Berkshire, for his cousin Sir George Pratt. This was the first of five large houses for which he was responsible in a short but momentous career, important in the history of English architecture. His work was pure classicism and he was intolerant both of Gothic architecture, and of the Flemish style of work so common in England in the first half of the seventeenth century. His houses are strictly symmetrical, simple, long and rather low-built, and consist of a half-basement, two floors and an attic storey with dormer windows. The chimney-stacks play an important part in providing an interesting skyline and emphasising the symmetry.

Coleshill House, Berkshire, **1650–2,** was rectangular in plan divided by a central corridor with the main rooms on each side. On the ground floor was the hall and great parlour, while above, on the first floor, was the upper part of the hall and the dining-room. The staircase was most notable, an original design for its period, and an outstanding feature of the house. It dominated the two-storey hall with its great double flights of stairs and occupied more space than had hitherto been usual. On the exterior there were no orders; the horizontal line was emphasised by the string course, cornice, and balustrade. From the sloping roof above sprang the tall chimneys, all reaching the same level. There was no pediment and no break in the walls except windows and doorways; a flight of steps led up to the latter. Coleshill was destroyed by fire in 1952; a great loss as it was finely executed and represented an important milestone in the history of English architecture (572; XXVII, XXVIII).

OTHER ARCHITECTS

The remainder of the colleagues working at the same time as Jones were still, according to Medieval custom, master masons or carpenters. Among these, of particular note, were Nicholas Stone, Sir Balthazar Gerbier, and Isaac de Caus.

Nicholas Stone, 1586–1647, occupied the position of master mason during much of the period that Inigo Jones was Surveyor-General. He worked under him at the Queen's House, the Banqueting Hall and at St Paul's Cathedral. He carried out other work on his own but was a mason and builder rather than an architect. Like his Elizabethan forebears he worked largely from Flemish pattern books, and in his youth had received a Dutch training in Amsterdam from a Dutch sculptor there. He also worked as a sculptor and is noted for his monument to John Donne in St Paul's.

Sir Balthazar Gerbier, d. 1667, was a friend of Rubens and also came from Flanders. He was a man of many parts and included languages, draughtsmanship and inventions among his accomplishments. He published a number of works, in particular, *Counsel and Advice to all Builders* in 1664. Much of his building has now been altered or destroyed.

Among the constructions variously attributed to Inigo Jones, Nicholas Stone and Gerbier is the **Water Gate** to **York House** in the Embankment Gardens in **London**. The gateway was designed and built for the Duke of Buckingham (with stone originally allocated for the restoration of St Paul's) as an entrance to his York House in the Strand. At that time the gate opened on to the riverside itself. The openings are flanked by rusticated half-columns and

VIII   Coleshill House, Berkshire: the ceiling of the
n. Architect Sir Roger Pratt. (Destroyed by fire 1952)

are surmounted by a curved pediment. Below this are the arms of Villiers and on each side is a recumbent lion. Despite the official notice in front of the gate, it is difficult to believe that this interesting but impure classical gateway was designed by Jones. It is felt that those who claim that this is the work of Stone or Gerbier are more likely to be correct (594).

ECCLESIASTICAL BUILDINGS

Very little activity existed in this sphere before 1660; under James I there was virtually none. Between 1625 and 1640 an impetus was given to building, repairs and rehabilitation of churches by **William Laud**, then **Bishop of London** (p. 191). This Laudian revival, as it was termed, supported no definite architectural style. The work was mainly classical but a mixture of purer and Flemish, mannered design. There were also some Perpendicular Gothic examples. The few churches which were built were very simple in plan, and usually were little more than chapels, having no chancels. Examples include **Groombridge Church**, Kent, **St Mary's, Leighton Bromswold, St John's, Leeds**, and **St Catharine Cree, London**. At **St Mary's, Oxford**, the new porch added in this period shows a Baroque strain which is lively and ornamented (591).

THE UNIVERSITIES

Architecturally, **Oxford** provides the more interesting examples of work at this time, in contrast to the Elizabethan period. The Elizabethan tradition of University building continued, wherein new projects were handled by university staff who employed masons to carry out the building. One such major project was the **Oxford Schools** inaugurated by **Sir Thomas Bodley in 1613.** It consisted of a quad surrounded by three-storey buildings of which the Library Tower was the most outstanding part. This **Tower of the Five Orders** is so-called because all these orders are incorporated into its construction (556).

Canterbury Quad, 1632-6, at **St John's College**, was another major project, again instituted by Laud, when he was Chancellor of the University. This quad is the best-known example of seventeenth-century Baroque architecture in the two universities. The work is rich and splendid; Flemish influence abounds in strapwork and other ornament; the colonnades on the east and west sides each are centred by a frontispiece containing respectively the statues of Charles I and Henrietta Maria (559, 593).

Brasenose College Chapel, 1656-9, provides a strange mixture of Gothic and classical designs incorporated into one building. It has an affinity with Peterhouse Chapel, Cambridge, for this reason. It is the work of a master mason, John Jackson. Geometrical tracery is used in window design while above this is an entablature. At the top is a crocketed, finialled gable. Side windows with pointed arch and tracery are flanked by Corinthian order pilasters.

Further work can be seen at **Oriel College**, which was rebuilt 1600-42. The front quad is of this time, and though restored in the nineteenth century, is largely of the original pattern (560). At **University College**, the front quad is of 1634–77 and is basically Jacobean in design despite the interruption of work due to the Civil War. **Wadham College** was begun 1610-13. The original work has not been appreciably altered and is mainly Gothic in conception with classical decoration.

At **Cambridge** the two wings of the quad of **Clare College** were built at this time: the

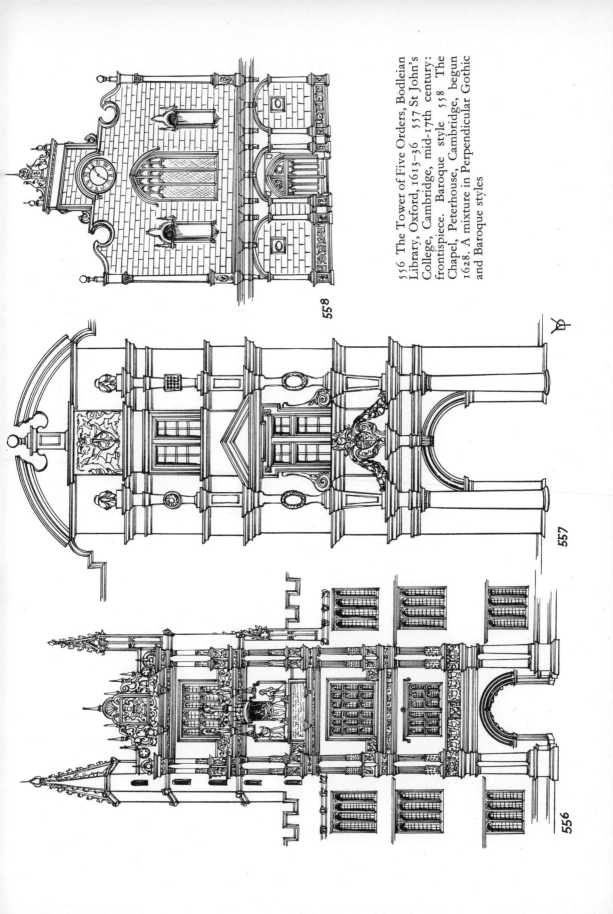

556 The Tower of Five Orders, Bodleian Library, Oxford, 1613–36 557 St John's College, Cambridge, mid-17th century: frontispiece. Baroque style 558 The Chapel, Peterhouse, Cambridge, begun 1628. A mixture in Perpendicular Gothic and Baroque styles

558

557

556

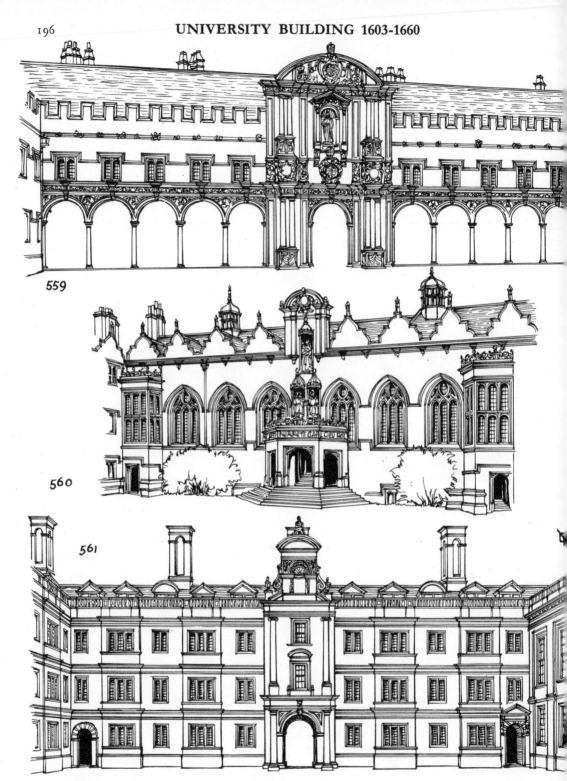

559 St John's College, Oxford: Canterbury Quad, 1631–6   560 Oriel College, Oxford: front quad, 1600–42   561 Clare College, Cambridge: east range, 1638–41

east range in the period 1638–41 and the south, 1640–2. The work is by **Thomas Grumbold**, a mason who also was responsible for the beautiful **Clare Bridge**, over the Cam, 1638–40. This, the oldest of Cam bridges at the University, has three spans. The parapet contains square-faced balusters set diagonally to the bridge (562). In the court the main theme is classical, although in the earlier range, the east, the frontispiece has a Jacobean flavour (561).

562 Clare Bridge, over the River Cam, Cambridge, 1639–40. Stone. Designed by Thomas Grumbold

The **Fellows' Building** at **Christ's College**, 1640–2, is similar to Clare court in design, and the balusters of the parapet are set like those of Clare Bridge. The architect is unknown.

The work on the chapel of **Peterhouse** was begun in 1628 during the mastership of Bishop Matthew Wren (the uncle of Christopher), but was not completed until after the Restoration. Like Brasenose at Oxford it is a classic Gothic/hybrid. The main Gothic window is flanked by canopied niches but the whole façade is rusticated and stands upon an arcade. The cresting is unorthodox but entertaining. One's reaction to the chapel depends on one's architectural views. Ardent classicists seem to regard it as 'beyond the pale'. More tolerant observers see in it a charming, unusual quality which does not submit to over-defined rules of taste (558).

HOSPITALS AND ALMSHOUSES

Abbot's Hospital, Guildford, begun 1619, still stands as an example of this type of building. However, the work, especially the exterior, is a mixture of a tall, Tudor brick gatehouse with wings topped by Flemish, curved gables. It is a pleasing blend of styles in red, mellowed brickwork (563).

DOMESTIC BUILDINGS

Jacobean Great Houses

A considerable number of these were built in the first 25 years of the seventeenth century. They were large, imposing and in the grand manner. In design, they were a continuation of Elizabethan great houses, but the pattern continually evolved further and beyond the sixteenth-century aims. The work was still essentially Flemish and mannerist classical in character; indeed it became more so than in Elizabethan times. More foreign workers were employed, chiefly Flemish craftsmen, particularly carvers. Whereas the pattern books of De Vries had played such a large part in influencing English craftsmen in the late sixteenth century, the present influence was more that of Dietterlin, with a consequent increase in distortion and decoration of classical members and orders. However, this influence was largely by way of the Flemish craftsmen more than by the actual pattern books and therefore differed from Dietterlin's own work. Symmetry, particularly in exterior form, was even more slavishly adhered to than previously. This was often at a cost of the inconvenient interior domestic arrangement of rooms. The H plan was still employed, and alternatively, the rectangular house with gabled projections on all four sides.

By the seventeenth century the use of the **hall** had declined and so even in large houses it became a smaller room, often placed with its length extending from the main entrance, instead of across it as before. The **Long Gallery** was still an essential part of the plan, and was generally to be found on the first floor. Under it, at ground level, was often constructed an open **loggia** to provide the same facilities when the weather was more clement. There were two or more **parlours**, generally adjoining the hall, while above the latter was the **Great Chamber**, used for receiving guests. **Bed-chambers, kitchen** and domestic offices were relegated elsewhere without a great deal of thought or planning.

563 Abbot's Hospital, Guildford, Surrey, 1619. Brick

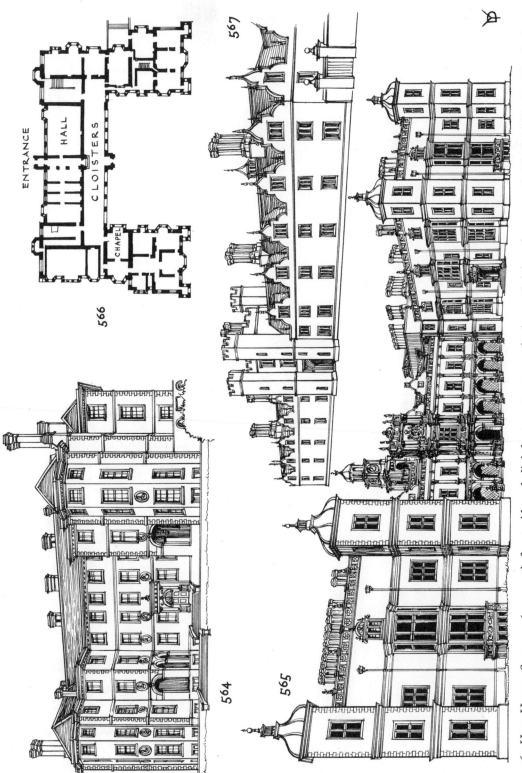

564 Ham House, Surrey, 1610: north front. Altered slightly, turrets removed 1673–5. Brick and stone   565 Hatfield House, Hertfordshire: south front, 1607–12. Brick and stone   566 Hatfield House: plan   567 Knole, Sevenoaks, Kent: west front, 1603–7. Stone

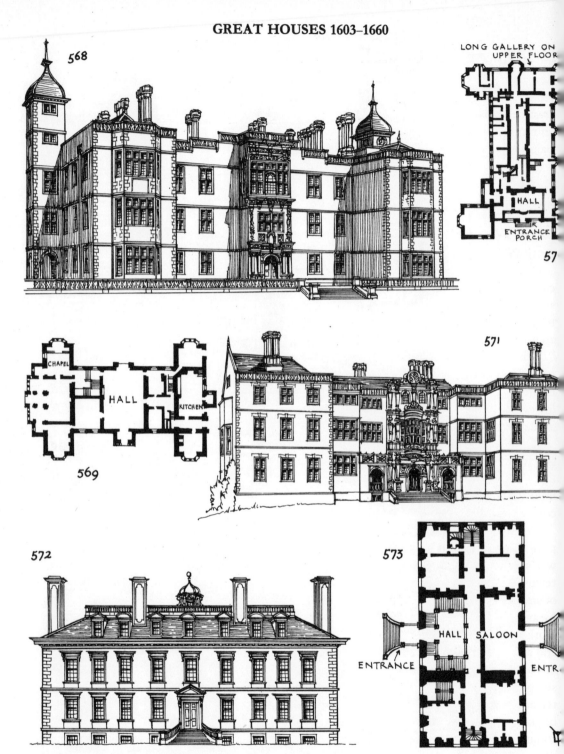

568 Charlton House, Greenwich: west front, 1607–12. Brick and stone   569 Charlton House: plan
570 Bramshill House: plan   571 Bramshill House, Hampshire: south-west front, 1605–12. Brick
and stone   572 Coleshill House, Berkshire, 1650–2: north front. Stone. Designed by Sir Roger
Pratt. Destroyed by fire 1952   573 Coleshill House: plan

Hatfield House, Hertfordshire, **1607-12**, was built near the old palace of Hatfield as a new house for Robert Cecil, Earl of Salisbury. It follows primarily an H plan; the entrance front is fairly plain and square but the south or garden front is more Jacobean in design and treatment. The red brickwork is contrasted by stone facings and the decoratively carved entrance porch. The two projecting wings have ogee-topped towers and an ornamental balustrade. In the centre block there is a loggia on the ground floor and a long gallery above it (565–6, 588, 602).

Audley End, Essex, **1603-16**, was of the largest and most impressive of the Jacobean great houses and was constructed round two courtyards. Unfortunately, now only a portion remains. This is the inner court which contains a fine hall of the period. It is ceiled with flat panels in wood and plaster. The screen is large and most ornate, and of Flemish design and motif.

Bramshill House, Hampshire, **1605-12**, is, like Hatfield, in brick with stone facings and carving. The entrance front, which is Jacobean in treatment, particularly the frontispiece, is seen as a distant vista as one approaches by the very long drive. This frontispiece has three tiers of Flemish style orders and a central, curved oriel window set above the semicircular arched doorway (570–1, 589, 604–5, 621–2).

Charlton House, Greenwich, 1607-12, has a simpler exterior design with bay windows taken the full height of the house on the projecting wings. Towers rise from the sides of the house. Again the central feature of entrance porch is essentially Jacobean in character. The lower stage has fairly orthodox Corinthian order columns, but in the second stage the Flemish influence runs riot. The cornice is richly carved (568–9, 590, 597, 618, 625).

Other examples include **Knole**, Kent, *c.* 1605, which is a fine, large house, richly decorated and furnished in the interior. The staircase remains one of the finest Jacobean examples (567, 608). There is also **Charlton Park**, Wiltshire, *c.* 1607, an H-plan house with a central, ground-floor loggia, and **Blickling Hall**, Norfolk, a very large house, rectangular in shape and with corner towers.

Apart from the public buildings erected by Inigo Jones and Webb on the one hand in pure classical manner and the great houses on the other of Flemish classical character, there was also much building not strongly influenced by either of these sources. Inigo Jones, in retrospect, appears to dominate his period. But, in domestic building in particular, especially of smaller houses, his influence was not felt until much later, and at this time, was considered by average English builders to be 'advanced' and 'undesirable'. It is difficult to classify this work in a definite category of style: influences were various according to material, locality and size of purse. However, certain features were common to most houses, particularly those in country areas. Such features include the use of curved, rather Dutch gables, sometimes stepped and having finialled or pedimented tops; wooden window frames which began to replace stone mullions and rectangular openings, larger than before; a predominance of brick as a building material, especially over stone, although half-timber work was still in common use in certain areas; an emphasis of the horizontal lines of a building by string course and cornice, although in some examples, low projection pilasters emphasised the vertical lines also. Very little building was carried out from 1642 to 1660 due to the Civil War and subsequent Commonwealth rule. Two exceptions to this were Coleshill and Wilton, already described.

Brick Houses

This medium had been used extensively for domestic construction during the sixteenth century, but only with the advent of the seventeenth century was building in brick exploited fully. It was realised that it was more suitable as a medium for the Renaissance style of architecture than half-timber, and thus began to replace wood to a considerable extent, and particularly in areas where stone was expensive or not readily available. The **Flemish bond** was introduced—alternate headers and stretchers on all courses—and it became common to see gauged bricks; that is, bricks were cut to the exact size instead of the joint fillings being thickened to make up space. Decoration was attempted in brick. This generally took the form of pilasters, capitals and bases employed to flank doorway and window openings and niches. A round, moulded arch sprang from the capitals. This new craft gained great popularity in English domestic building and was most suitable for the medium-sized house. Such houses often show further Flemish influence in design. This can be seen in the curved, scrolled and stepped gables, which were generally mixed with purer classical features. In plan the H design was retained, but gradually the wings were reduced in projection and rectangular houses became more common.

There are a number of good examples of brick houses. Among those with curved, stepped or scrolled Dutch gables are Kew Palace, Raynham Hall, Broome Park and Swakeleys. **Kew Palace, 1631,** is a neat rectangular building, rather taller than earlier examples with four storeys. The curved gables are surmounted by pediments. Window and doorway openings have moulded brick features. The brickwork here is of good quality and presents a fine example of its period (554, 598, 603). **Raynham Hall**, Norfolk, **1635-6,** is a large house where the brickwork is faced and decorated with stone. The gables are scrolled and pedimented while the main front has a central classical feature with giant Ionic order. An imposing flight of steps ascends to the front door (574). **Broome Park**, Kent, **1635-8,** presents an exceptionally good example of gauged and moulded brickwork. It is a large house with stepped, decorative gables and pilaster decoration of the wall faces. A deep cornice stresses the horizontal emphasis. Tall, decorative chimney-stacks provide a broken skyline (575). At **Swakeleys**, Middlesex, **1629-38,** there are also stone facings to the brickwork, but here the house is rather more Jacobean than classical in conception. The gables present a riot of curves and scrolls topped by miniature pediments, niches contain busts and ornament, and the chimney-stacks are clustered and diverse in design. The whole is pleasing in effect and illustrates clearly the changing modes of the time (576, 599, 614–15). A slightly later example, but one which is far more advanced architecturally in period is **Balls Park**, Hertfordshire, **c. 1640.** Here, the house shows more of the purer classical strain. It is a square building of two storeys in red brick, with dormers in the roof. The cornice is deep and projecting, supported by carved wood brackets in classical fashion. There is a central pediment over the entrance porch which boasts Ionic columns. This house in its more advanced style points the way to the more typical late seventeenth-century houses (581, 600, 606, 630). In contrast, **Quebec House** at **Westerham**, Kent, early seventeenth century, is a continuation of the late sixteenth-century design in brick, with three pyramidal gables on each face. It is of simple, square plan with wall faces broken only by window openings and flat string-courses (577).

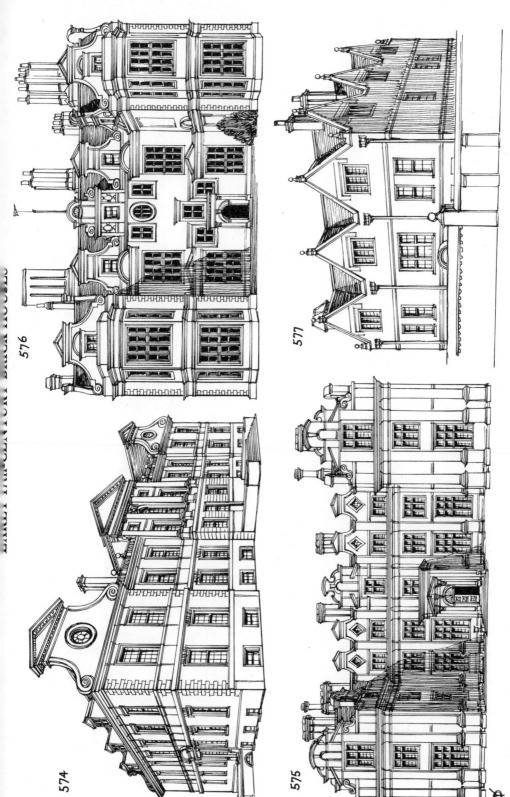

574

576

574 Raynham Hall, Norfolk, c. 1635–6. Brick and stone   575 Broome Park, Denton, Kent, 1635–8. Brick   576 Swakeleys, Middlesex, 1629–38. Brick and stone   577 Quebec House, Westerham, Kent, early 17th century. Brick

575

577

SMALLER HOUSES 1603–1660

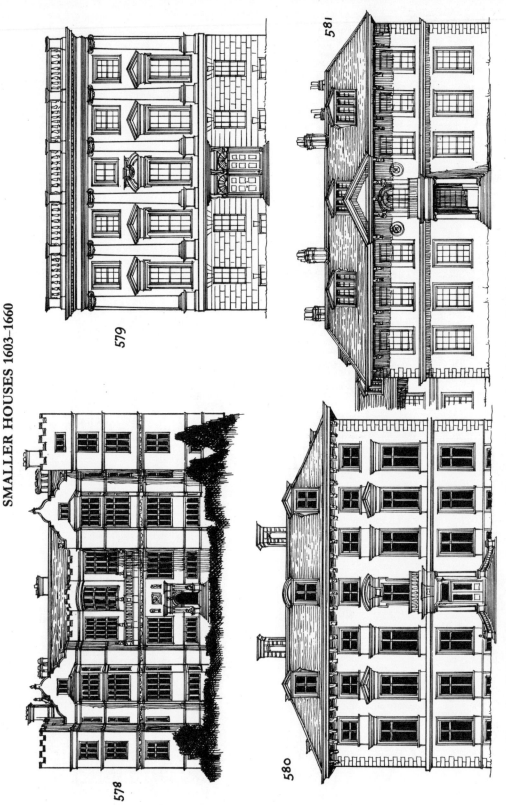

578 Fountains Hall, Yorkshire, 1610. Stone 579 Lindsey House, Lincoln's Inn Fields, London, *c.* 1640. Probably by Inigo Jones 580 Thorpe Hall, Northamptonshire, 1653–6. Stone 581 Balls Park, Hertfordshire, *c.* 1640: south front. Brick

583

585

582

584

582 Chastleton House, Oxfordshire: south front, 1603–12. Stone 583 'Bateman's', Burwash, Sussex: south front, 1634. Stone
584 Grimshaw Hall, Warwickshire, mid 17th century. Half-timber 585 Town house, Chester. Half-timber

Smaller Stone Houses

Two examples which illustrate the Jacobean design in these houses are **Fountains' Hall**, Yorkshire, 1610, and **Chastleton House**, Oxfordshire, 1603–12. Here the late Elizabethan plan is continued with slightly projecting wings on each face terminating at the skyline in decorative gables. The bay windows extend to the full height of the house and are still Tudor in pattern with rectangular openings made by stone mullions and transoms (578, 582). A small but charming stone house of 1634 can be seen in **'Bateman's'**, **Burwash**, Sussex, at one time the home of Rudyard Kipling (583). A later example which shows the complete change which overtook building design during this period is **Thorpe Hall**, Northamptonshire, 1653–6. Here is a house which much more nearly approximates to the classical designs of Inigo Jones or Webb and it has much in common with Pratt's Coleshill, although it is not quite so refined in form. The building is rectangular in plan and consists of three storeys with basement storey below and dormer windows on the hipped roof, giving five floors in all. There are four rusticated chimney-stacks set within the roof platform. The cornice projects strongly and its horizontal line is echoed by the string courses. Prominence is given to the first-floor windows which are classical in pattern, and alternate windows are pedimented. The central doorways on two faces are approached by a flight of steps with curved balustrade (580, 592).

Half-timber Houses

These were still being built in town and country though in smaller numbers than hitherto. In some of our towns there are still extant good examples, particularly in Chester, Tewkesbury and south-west England (585). **Grimshaw Hall**, Warwickshire, illustrates clearly the midseventeenth-century trend in this medium. The house has become large with more commodious rooms and the upper floor overhangs considerably. Carved wood decoration in the

586 Edensor Bridge, Chatsworth, Derbyshire, 17th century. River Derwent. 69 ft span

form of brackets, corner-posts, barge-boards, etc. is widespread and provides a most attractive ensemble. Window area is greater than before, although the actual design in rectangular panels is little altered. Roofs are still steeply pitched and deep (584).

Town Houses

Not many such houses survive in towns today owing to later rebuilding. The majority were gabled and pedimented and 'Dutch' in style, much like the country houses but more compressed with narrower frontage. In classical strain is **Lindsey House** in **Lincoln's Inn Fields**, *c.* 1640, thought to be by Inigo Jones, which foreshadows the town house of later times. Here the classical windows and a giant Ionic order break the plain wall face and the whole is surmounted by a balustraded parapet (579).

BRIDGES

This was not a time of energetic bridge building; indeed in the period 1640–55 more bridges were destroyed than constructed. The main features of stone bridge building continued much as in the sixteenth century, with Gothic arches and heavy buttresses. However, some mid-century examples indicate the beginnings of classical influence in round arches and wider spans, while the depth between arch crown and parapet lessened. **Clare Bridge** over the Cam at **Cambridge** has already been mentioned (562), but there is also the graceful 69-foot single-span bridge at **Edensor** over the river Derwent on the Chatsworth estate (586) and **Llanrwst** bridge over the Conway, *c.* 1636, nearly 170 feet long and most elegant in design. A drawing of **London Bridge** in 1647 (after Hollar's contemporary drawing), shows a view of London's riverside at that time, including Old St Paul's and some of the pre-Fire city churches (587).

ARCHITECTURAL FEATURES

In Jacobean building, particularly at the universities and in the larger houses, the **entrance porch** or **frontispiece** continued to be a predominant feature of the building. It occupied a central position in the quadrangle or building face and generally extended the full height of the construction. Extant designs vary greatly; many show strong Flemish pattern book influence via De Vries or Dietterlin, in the form of distorted classical orders, strapwork, masks and grotesques, cartouches and animal and human figure finials. Two or three stages are usual, surmounted by a pediment, cartouche and/or finials. Plain or oriel windows generally play an important part in the design of the entrance porches to large houses. These are on the second or third stage while the doorway forms the main feature for the lower stage. Illustrations are given of the features at **Hatfield House**, 1611 (588), **Bramshill House**, 1605–12 (589) and **Charlton House, Greenwich**, 1607–12 (590). The more baroque approach of the 1630s and 1640s is shown in the designs for **St John's College, Oxford**, 1631–6 (593), **St John's College, Cambridge**, mid-seventeenth century (557) and the five-order layout of the **Bodleian Library Tower**, 1613–36 (556). In ecclesiastical architecture, the baroque design of the entrance porch is illustrated clearly by **St Mary's Church, Oxford**, 1637, with its barley-sugar twisted columns and scrolled pediments (591). A later, more traditionally

587 View of London from south bank of the Thames, 1647 (after Hollar)

A Old St Paul's Cathedral	B St Laurence Poultney	C St Andrew's Holborn
D St Michael	E Guildhall	F St Dunstan-in-the-East
	G London Bridge	

classical example is provided by **Thorpe Hall**, *c.* 1656, with Doric order of plinth, columns and entablature set on a curving flight of steps (592).

Many houses were built in this period with imposing **entrance** and **exit gateways** to the grounds and gardens. Later on these were of classical design, often with rusticated features. Examples shown include the **York House Watergate, London**, *c.* 1626 (594), **Kirby Hall**, Northamptonshire, *c.* 1640 (595), **Chiswick House**, *c.* 1621 (596) and **Charlton House, Greenwich** (597).

The classical pattern of **doorways** in Flemish or Italianate form prevailed. The majority of doorways were flanked by pilasters or columns, most commonly of the Doric order; in larger examples these supported an entablature and either pediment or cartouche cresting. The doorway arch was round, or perhaps square with a semicircular lunette of glass or carved decoration above. In important buildings the doorway was approached via a flight of steps (598–602).

The classical influence on **window openings** was present but was not so paramount, particularly in domestic architecture. The more classical examples were round- or square-headed, with classical mouldings surrounding the arch and rising from a half column or pilaster at each side of the window. Curved or triangular pediments were superimposed over the window head mouldings. Many other window designs, especially in the Jacobean period, were still predominantly Tudor in character. The wide rectangular window with square-headed dripstone was still in use; also the tall, three-sided bay window of two or more storeys. In addition there was the rectangular or semicircular oriel design with cresting at the top. In all these cases carved, moulded stone mullions and transoms still separated the window opening into rectangular divisions, while lead frames subdivided them further. In the later, more classical window designs, narrower metal frames replaced the stone mullions and transoms (603–7).

The **staircase** had begun to be an important feature in the architectural layout of the house in Elizabeth's time. In the first half of the seventeenth century its prominence was established. These staircases occupied a good deal of space; they were usually of carved oak, and had broad treads, spacious landings and most decorative newels, finials, balusters and

590

589

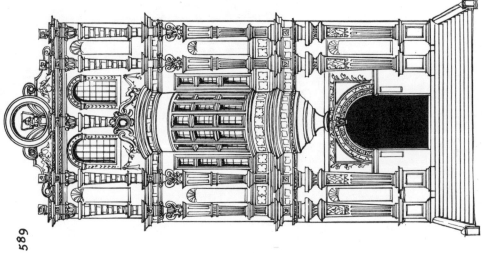

588

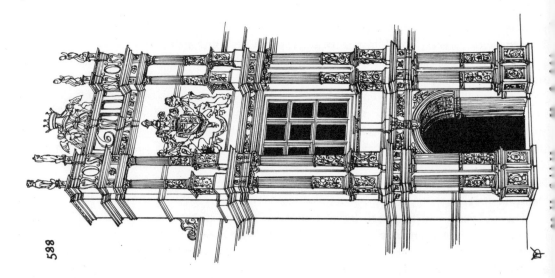

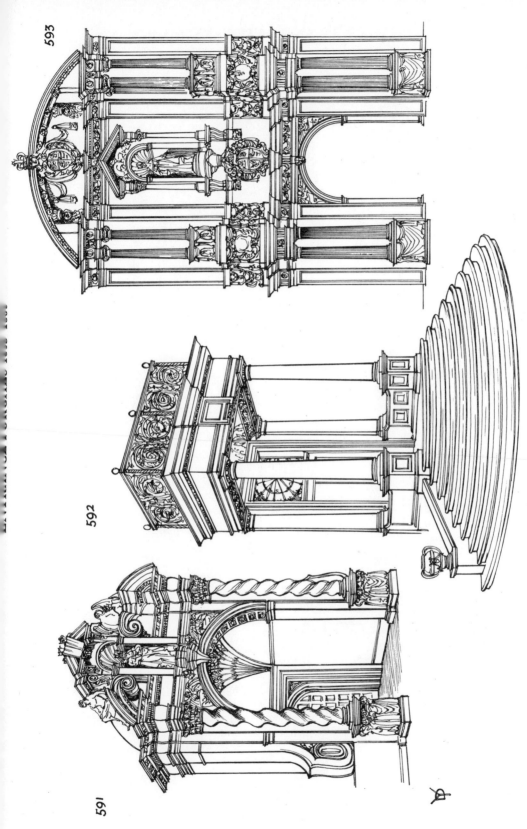

591 St Mary's Church, Oxford: south porch, 1637. Baroque 592 Thorpe Hall, Northamptonshire: south porch, *c.* 1656
593 St John's College, Oxford: Canterbury Quadrangle. Frontispiece, 1631–6

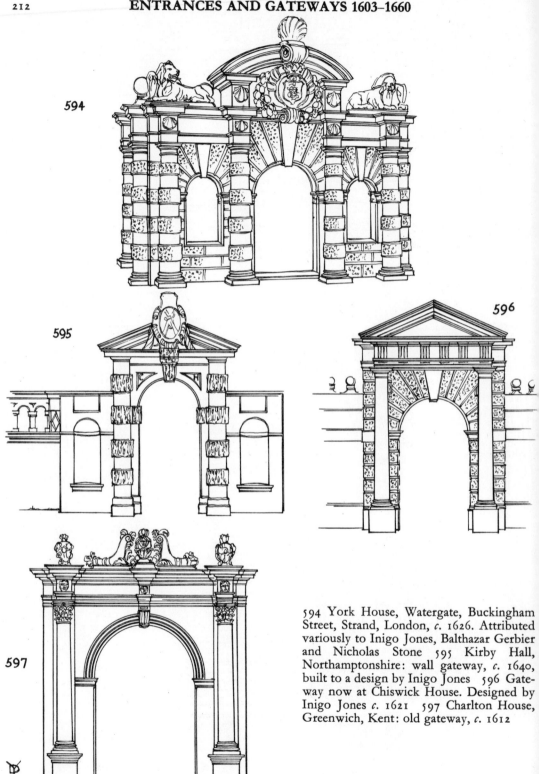

594 York House, Watergate, Buckingham Street, Strand, London, *c.* 1626. Attributed variously to Inigo Jones, Balthazar Gerbier and Nicholas Stone 595 Kirby Hall, Northamptonshire: wall gateway, *c.* 1640, built to a design by Inigo Jones 596 Gateway now at Chiswick House. Designed by Inigo Jones *c.* 1621 597 Charlton House, Greenwich, Kent: old gateway, *c.* 1612

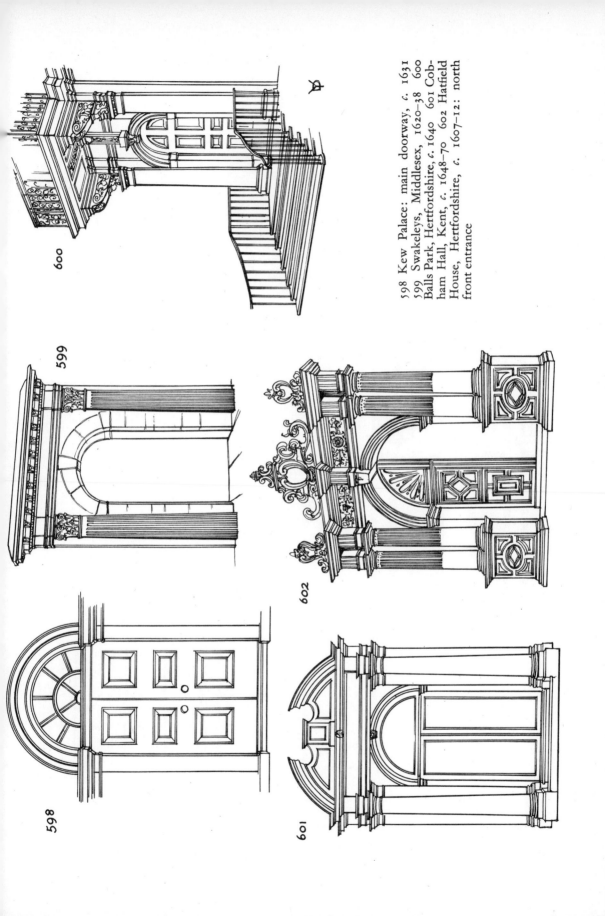

598

598 Kew Palace: main doorway, *c.* 1631
599 Swakeleys, Middlesex, 1620–38 600
Balls Park, Hertfordshire, *c.* 1640 601 Cobham Hall, Kent, *c.* 1648–70 602 Hatfield
House, Hertfordshire, *c.* 1607–12: north
front entrance

600

599

602

601

603   604   605

606

607

603 Kew Palace, 1631. Brick opening, wood frame   604 Bramshill House, Hampshire, *c.* 1605–12:
oriel window. Stone   605 Bramshill House: bay window. Brick with stone frame   606 Balls Park,
Hertfordshire, *c.* 1640: brick opening, stone sill, wood frame   607 Bateman's, Burwash, Sussex,
c. 1634. Stone

608 Knole, Kent: staircase 609 Commonwealth carved staircase: scroll panel balustrade

610 Carved oak chimney-piece with carved stone fire opening, early Jacobean period

string. Among the famous examples are those at **Hatfield House** (XXVI), **Knole** (608), and **Coleshill House** (XXVII). At this time also, the carved, scrolled balustrade often replaced the separate balusters. Here the balustrade was solid wood, boldly carved in complicated designs and pierced all over its surface, as at **Ham House** and **Tyttenhanger** (609).

Plaster **ceilings** were highly ornamented. Jacobean versions were generally decorated all over and divided up into compartments by patterned strapwork. These panels were in turn embellished by floral or heraldic motifs. Towards mid-century this type of design was replaced by a central raised circle or oval which was bordered by intertwined leaves and fruit. The central panel was either left plain or ornamented. A patterned frieze accompanied the ceiling and echoed the design (XXV, XXVIII).

The **chimney-piece**, as in Elizabethan times, was still the focal point of the room. Various media were used: wood, marble or stone. An intricate overmantel was carved and/or inlaid above the fire opening. Jacobean designs were very heavily ornamented so that no part was left undecorated. Motifs included masks, grotesques, flowers, fruit, figures, animals and strapwork. Later chimney-pieces were more classical in appearance. Columns or pilasters flanked the fire opening and a picture was often incorporated into the rectangular space above in the overmantel (610).

Brick or stone was used for **chimney-stacks**, which were constructed separately or in clusters. Many examples were like the Elizabethan designs, usually in brick with octagonal shafts and multi-moulded caps and bases. Later stacks, like those at Coleshill or Thorpe Hall, were plainer, square or rectangular in plan and had classical mouldings (611, 612).

Stone or brick **gables** were most commonly of Flemish pattern with curved sides terminating in scrolls. Other designs were stepped in stages. Many were topped by pediments

611 Charlton House, Greenwich: brick chimney-stack

612 Knole, Kent: brick
chimney-stack

613 Charlton House, Greenwich: cupola and turret

614–15 Swakeleys, Middlesex: stone and brick gables

(614–15). Half-timber gables still had carved, decorative barge-boards and widely projecting eaves (616).

Parapets and balustrades were of carved stone strapwork or pierced designs (617–19). Later parapets had turned balusters which were generally vase-shaped as at the Queen's House, Greenwich, and the Banqueting Hall, Whitehall (620).

Panelling continued to be the most usual method of wall covering. The panels were larger in the seventeenth century with greater projection than hitherto. Oak or pine was employed and was not generally painted. Carved decoration was used, both as a filling for panels and as ornamentation of the mouldings (624). **Ornament** underwent considerable change between 1603 and 1660. In the earlier years the Elizabethan motifs, inspired by the Flemish pattern book, continued to be used in Jacobean buildings with unabated enthusiasm;

616

617

618

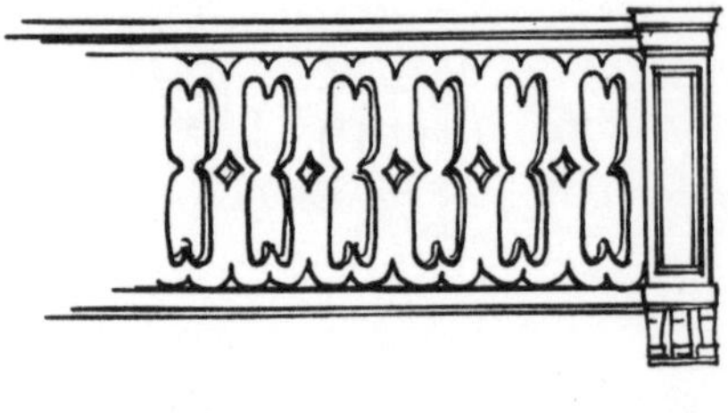

619    620

616 Grimshaw Hall: half-timber gable 617 Hatfield House: parapet 618 Charlton House, Greenwich: parapet 619 Bramshill House: parapet 620 Queen's House: parapet

621 Bramshill House: member flanking doorway   622 Bramshill House: member flanking window
623 Knole, Kent: detail, hall screen   624 Chastleton House, Oxfordshire: panelling   625 Charlton
House, Greenwich: spandrel ornament, doorway   626 Balls Park, Hertfordshire: corbel
627 Charlton House: ornament, doorway   628 Carved staircase newel finial   629 Cobham Hall,
Kent: Corinthian capital   630 Balls Park, Hertfordshire: Ionic capital   631 St John's College,
Cambridge: cartouche over doorway

misrepresented versions of the orders, strapwork, masks, grotesques, animals, flowers,
human figures were all employed, often in one design, with carefree abandon. The effects
were lively and vigorous, if at times a little brash and uncouth. Towards 1650 the effect of
Inigo Jones's work and that of his followers began to affect and stimulate other designers,
and more truly classical motifs emerged. The orders became more traditionally classical in
their use, their proportions and their detail, particularly capitals and entablature; cartouches
decorated with heraldic shields, cornucopiae and scrolls were employed, and acanthus leaves
appeared on carved bolection mouldings. The full metamorphosis into an entirely classical
form of ornament did not take place until after the Restoration but the change was apparent
by 1660 (621–3, 625–31).

CHAPTER VII

Restoration Stuart and Queen Anne 1660 - 1714

From the Restoration in 1660 to the death of Queen Anne in 1714 the name of one man is paramount in the history of English architecture. His achievements as an architect stand out clearly from those of his contemporaries and rank with the great Continental names of the time: Le Vau in France and even Bernini in Italy. **Sir Christopher Wren** is not only our great architect but it was apparent, in his lifetime, that his intellectual capacity was so far above average that he would have gained outstanding success in other fields also. A preliminary study of the architecture of this period at once reveals that the work and influence of Wren—dominant in the foreground from 1670 to 1692, and less strongly in the background from then until 1714—was pre-eminent in almost every sphere. This is shown in the royal works and public building, in cathedral and church construction, in universities and schools. The only field not so covered is that of domestic architecture, and even here, we are told of the 'Wren style of house', although this is in fact a misnomer.

Unlike that of most architects and artists, the reputation of Wren has stood high for 300 years, affected only slightly by the evanescent phases of taste and fashion, while today, in an era of shifting standards of design of all kinds, his name ranks higher than ever before. Stemming from this pre-eminence of Wren in his own field and time, there has been a tendency to attribute to him all buildings of whatever function which appeared to be designed in a similar style to his own, without any documentary or firm evidence whatsoever. This movement is now in reverse, so to speak, and due to the patient work of many scholars, in particular those of the Wren Society, such generalisations are now being refuted, and the earlier attributions (a number of them from the family records published in *Parentalia*) either firmly established or shown to be inaccurate.

It is untrue to suggest that the form and design of Restoration architecture were attributable only to Wren. In fact, the pattern had been clearly set out between 1660 and 1675, before much of Wren's work had actually been created. It was the result of the work of many men, as at that time there were still few architects, and the profession continued to be one for the amateur and/or craftsman. Two names, though, stand out: those of Hugh May and Roger Pratt; while John Webb was also still at work. Especially in the realm of domestic architecture the pattern was firmly established by 1675 and the Dutch style, with free use of brick, was accepted and in general use.

In the later period of Wren's influence, 1695–1714, the names of other architects emerged. These men, in particular, Vanbrugh, Hawksmoor and Archer had been influenced by Wren, but it can never be said that their work was a copy of his; it was more a continuation and expansion which in its turn led to another branch of classical architecture, that of the Baroque. The architectural flowering of the Baroque style in England was short indeed, but in the years 1700–25 it was a vigorous healthy movement. It contrasted with the dignity and reserve of Wren but was full of vitality and showed a new approach to the tenets of classicism.

The three chief names in early Restoration architectural achievement are **John Webb, Sir Roger Pratt** and **Hugh May**. The first two of these had already established themselves by 1660 and a study of their works is made in Chapter VI. **Webb** designed **Amesbury House** in 1661 and **Gunnersbury**, Middlesex, in 1663. His main work, a public building, was the edifice now called **King Charles II's Block** at **Greenwich Hospital**. Here, he had planned an ambitious scheme which incorporated the Queen's House already built by Inigo Jones, but he only succeeded in actually completing a small part of this.

Pratt, as described in Chapter VI, reached his peak of achievement at **Coleshill**; although he designed several houses after this, he did not improve upon it. A man of means and leisure, he did not require to maintain a high output but was able to give great attention to the design and execution of each house, and thus measure up to his own ideas as a perfectionist. In the 1660s he built **Kingston Lacy** in Dorset and **Horseheath** in Cambridgeshire. The former resembled Coleshill in many ways but was altered in 1834 by Barry. The latter house, unfortunately demolished in the eighteenth century, was of a design often referred to as a 'Wren style of house'. This really means a basically English house of the second half of the seventeenth century, with a centre block surmounted by a pediment. Pratt evolved the design as a natural derivation from his architectural studies. This domestic pattern seen here and also in his important commission, **Clarendon House, Piccadilly**, was extensively copied and influenced English building widely until after 1714. The London house was one of the few early classical buildings in this city and regrettably was demolished in 1683. After the completion of these works in 1667, Pratt, after being knighted in 1668, retired to his own house which he built in Norfolk and concluded his successful venture into the realm of architecture.

HUGH MAY 1622–1684

Like Pratt, May designed houses which for many years were called 'Wren-styled'. Also, in common with his colleague, much of his work has suffered demolition. In London, in particular, it has been forced to make way for later buildings. May's chief surviving house is **Eltham Lodge**, Kent, built for Sir John Shaw but now a golf club house. In this one example is shown the design which, allied to those of Pratt, formed a basis for English domestic architecture until the early eighteenth century. The style of work is generally described as **Dutch Palladian** because of its similarity to the work of Dutch architects of the mid-seventeenth century who were basing their designs on those of Palladio. As used in the Netherlands and in May's work, brick with stone were the usual materials; there was generally a central pediment and a simple pilaster feature flanking a central front doorway and steps. At Eltham Lodge there are two main storeys with dormers above and a half-basement below. The pilasters are Ionic with festooned swags. The whole conception is simple, horizontal in emphasis and easy to build and imitate; hence its popularity (691). May himself had been in Holland before the Restoration with the exiled Duke of Buckingham and had studied the architecture there. He built Eltham Lodge in 1663/4 and in 1665 **Berkeley House, Picca-**

dilly (destroyed by fire 1733). Much of May's work was, like Eltham, on medium-sized houses, but in his lifetime, also for many years afterwards, his name was overshadowed by the illustrious Wren.

SIR CHRISTOPHER WREN 1632–1723

It is difficult to separate the study and account of Wren, with his abilities, achievements and very long lifetime of creative activity, from the important architectural schemes of this time, for the two are, in most cases, one. However, in order to simplify as much as possible for classified reference, the descriptions of Wren's contributions to **St Paul's Cathedral**, the **rebuilding of London**, the **City churches, University** and **public building** and the **Royal Palaces** are dealt with individually under these headings.

Christopher Wren was born at East Knoyle, Wiltshire, on 20th October 1632. His father was rector of Knoyle, while his uncle, Dr Matthew Wren, was also a churchman, later being consecrated Bishop of Ely. Wren was thus brought up in a High Church tradition with a university background. He was educated at Westminster School which he left in 1646. Three years later, after some time in London, during which he showed early intellectual activity at the age of 15 by translating into Latin the part of William Oughtred's *Clavis Mathematica* dealing with geometrical dialling, he was accepted at Wadham College, Oxford, as a Gentleman Commoner. He took his B.A. degree in 1650–1 and his master's qualification in 1653.

From his early years at Wadham College he became interested in scientific matters and was associated, both in his studies and social life, with other well-known thinkers in this field. He assisted Dr Charles Scarburgh, the anatomist and mathematician, and, in conjunction with Dr Wilkins, the Warden of Wadham College, Robert Boyle the physicist, then a don there, and others, the Philosophic Club of Wadham was founded. The principal subjects of study of this club were science and philosophy and its membership soon included such famous names as Isaac Newton, Robert Hooke and John Evelyn. In due course, the club became the Royal Society.

From these close contacts with eminent scientists and scientific students Wren's talents and ideas welled forth. His interests were wide, his inventive powers intelligent and lively. He carried out anatomical experimental work with Scarburgh (a disciple of Harvey); he worked on the subjects of submarine navigation, instruments for recording weather, temperature, rainfall, etc., telescope designs, and produced a hard, durable substance for use as paving. The list of Wren's inventions and studies in different subjects is long and varied as can be seen in *Parentalia*. In themselves, the research work and original results are, no doubt, not of great note: what is much more important is the insight which they give into Wren's approach to practical scientific problems.

Wren's chief scientific interest became astronomy and he studied with the Professor of Astronomy at Oxford. He also concerned himself deeply with physics and meteorology. Newton himself considered the young Wren to be an outstanding student. At the age of 25 he was appointed to the chair of Astronomy at Gresham College, London, and two years later in 1659 returned to Oxford to become Savilian Professor of Astronomy.

This background was an unusual one, even in the seventeenth century, as training for an architect. Wren's formative years up to the age of 30 had been spent in practical scientific

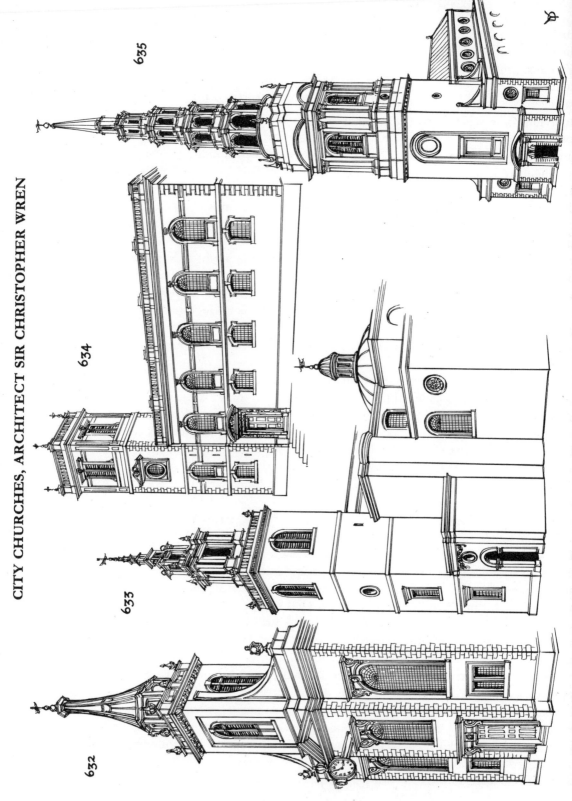

CITY CHURCHES, ARCHITECT SIR CHRISTOPHER WREN

632

633

634

635

tudy. This is generally the period of life when the foundations of a man's future are being
aid down. In the 1660s Wren obviously decided to change his career. Before the time of
Wren, architecture was hardly a profession and his predecessors had been able men in other
ubjects, so this was not as unusual a proceeding as it would be today. His scientific training,
however, had a profound effect on Wren's approach to architecture. He had the faculty of
nvisaging an extensive architectural scheme as a whole before work was begun, and to the
constructional problems of roofing large spans, providing sound structures for support and
buttressing, he brought his fresh, practical approach.

It is not known exactly when Wren became interested in architecture. In 1661, Charles
II invited him to supervise the fortification of Tangier. This Wren declined. However, he
did turn his attention to architectural matters. His first essay in this respect was at Cambridge
where his uncle, the Bishop of Ely, asked him to design a new **chapel** for **Pembroke College**.
In 1663 he did this and produced a competent, purely classical building. It is not of outstand-
ng architectural merit and shows certain inexperience. His second essay in architecture was
he **Sheldonian Theatre** at **Oxford**. This was in 1664 and attracted much attention as Wren
based his design on a Roman Theatre (studied in Serlio). The original building had been
open at the roof and Wren had a difficult problem in covering the English counterpart without supporting the roof on columns. This he solved in typical manner and with the aid of his
colleague the Professor of Geometry, Dr Wallis, by means of a timber trussed roof to carry
he ceiling.

In 1663 a commission had been appointed to undertake the restoration of **Old St Paul's
Cathedral**, which once again was in a deplorable state of disrepair. The commission approached the Surveyor-General, then Sir John Denham, John Webb, Roger Pratt and Wren
with regard to making plans for reconstruction. Such an approach was certainly a tribute to
Wren's mathematical reputation and ability as a draughtsman and model maker, for at that
ime his architectural experience was negligible.

However, in 1665 Wren set out on his only trip abroad. Unlike Inigo Jones before him,
and so many of the great eighteenth-century architects after him, his first-hand knowledge
of Continental architecture was small, and, although he studied Italian and French designs,
his main preoccupation was always to produce classical buildings suited to his own country.
His great fertility of imagination provided endless variations on the classical theme to meet
this need. He went to France as a holiday traveller to see its fine buildings, and spent some
months in 1665 there. He stayed in Paris where he met Bernini, and was particularly interested
in the Palace of Versailles (then only a small portion of the present edifice), also in the
Collège des Quatre Nations in Paris, designed by Le Vau. He visited a number of châteaux and
met Le Brun, Le Vau and Poussin. He was not able to get as far as Italy, but brought back
with him much architectural material in the form of books and engravings. When he returned
to England he had extended his architectural knowledge and enriched his sense of design and
appreciation.

On his return, the problem of **Old St Paul's** had reached a vital stage. Pratt had advocated
leaving the structure alone until it became necessary to demolish and rebuild completely.
Wren put forward a reconstruction plan which was extensive. This included demolition of
the tower and its replacement by a central feature such as a dome or classical steeple. He also
suggested that the nave should be re-cased in classical manner, in keeping with Inigo Jones's

636 Royal Naval College, Greenwich: chapel dome. Begun by Sir Christopher Wren   637 St Mary-le-Bow, London, 1671–80. Bombed 1941. Sir Christopher Wren   638 St Mary Aldermanbury, London, 1711. Sir Christopher Wren   639 St Augustine, Watling Street, London. War damaged (spire destroyed). Sir Christopher Wren   640 Castle Howard, Yorkshire, 1699–1712: dome. Sir John Vanbrugh

west front. In August 1666 his plan was accepted. Six days later the Great Fire settled the problem permanently.

The destruction of so much of the City of London gave Wren his great opportunity. It is not often that a prime need for an outstanding architect occurs at the exact time that such an architect is available. In 1666 the occasion and the man coincided. In the succeeding decades Wren was responsible both directly and indirectly for a prodigious amount of work of varied type but consistently high quality. In some of the projects his genius emerged clearly, for example, in the city church towers and spires and the problems which beset his designs for St Paul's. Posterity, however, has attributed to him an even larger list of works than he actually carried out; for example in the rebuilding of the City of London and particularly with regard to country houses. Stylistic evidence has been accepted, often of a flimsy nature, so that Wren has been credited with many a 'Wren-style' house which is in fact of Dutch Palladian concept. Most of his work was involved with the city churches, St Paul's, Hampton Court and Greenwich Palaces and at the Universities. He designed very few houses and even fewer of these survive.

In 1669 Wren was appointed to the post of Surveyor-General on the death of Sir John Denham. Both Hugh May and John Webb ought to have expected to be considered for this position in advance of the young and architecturally inexperienced Wren, but with the favour of Charles II the appointment was made. Wren had been assisting Sir John Denham for some time and with his new post he turned aside from his other scientific interests and embraced the profession of architecture wholeheartedly.

In 1673 he was knighted and in 1681–3 was President of the Royal Society. He remained Surveyor-General for nearly 50 years and in addition to the administrative and architectural work of the position, he was for some time an M.P., the Surveyor of Greenwich Hospital, Comptroller at Windsor and Surveyor of St Paul's and Westminster Abbey.

Sadly, the end of Wren's career was beset by jealousies and intrigues. The fact was that he had outlived his generation, and, as so often happens, the next generation of architects and patrons desired a change of style and approach. In 1714 when Queen Anne died Wren was 82. He had led the architectural field in all principal appointments for nearly 50 years and younger men who had worked for and with him were breaking new ground. George I, who acceded in 1714, preferred the newer approach. As Wren did not resign his Surveyorship he was somewhat shabbily relieved of his post in 1718, on the pretext of some minor disagreement about the completion of St Paul's. His dignified acceptance of this situation was made with these words: 'having worn out by God's Mercy a long life in the Royal Service and made some Figure in the World, I hope it will be allowed me to die in peace'. This he did at the age of 91 in 1723.

The Rebuilding of London

Before 1666, many attempts had been made since the twelfth century to enforce diverse laws making it compulsory to use stone, particularly in party wall construction for town buildings. In the mid-seventeenth century, however, many buildings, especially the houses, were still of timber. The streets were narrow and the upper stages of the houses projected almost to meet in the centre of the street. The Great Fire, which began on 3rd September 1666 in

641 St Michael, Cornhill, 1672–1721. City church. Sir Christopher Wren   642 Royal Hospital, Chelsea, 1682–92. Sir Christopher Wren   643 Morden College, Blackheath, 1695   644 Christ Church, Newgate Street, 1704. City church. Sir Christopher Wren   645 Staircase finials   647–8 Hanbury Hall, Worcestershire, 1701

Pudding Lane, was at first only a local outbreak. With these conditions of construction and planning, and augmented by a strong wind and the preceding dry, hot weather, the city of London was inundated by the rapid conflagration. Over 400 acres of closely packed buildings were destroyed and the city was bereft of many millions of pounds' worth of public buildings, churches and houses.

After three days the fire was brought under control and the King set up a commission to organise the rebuilding of the city. Several plans were submitted. Among them were those of Wren and John Evelyn. On 13th September the Royal Proclamation announced the proposed rebuilding of the city in durable materials of brick and stone, and promised a new layout with wider streets and better passageway. The Commission appointed to carry out this task comprised Wren as principal architect, assisted by May and Pratt, and three members as city delegates—Robert Hooke, Peter Mills and Edward Jerman. Gradually the area was surveyed and planned for rebuilding. Wren's layout for the new city was based on Ancient Roman design with adaptation from more modern French ideas. It was largely a geometrical plan with focal points or circles to pinpoint such public buildings as the Guildhall and the Mint. These were linked by main thoroughfares which provided vistas to and from them. The city churches were allowed for with suitable area and position, and in front of St Paul's was envisaged a long wedge-shaped space. A key point of the plan was a wide embankment quay along the Thames from the Tower to Blackfriars, based on the Seine design in Paris. Streets were to be much wider and the whole conception would have eradicated the twisting alleyways of varying direction which constricted the city of London before 1666 and still do today. The plan was passed by Parliament, approved by the King and frustrated to final extinction by the city commercial interests as represented by the freeholders, who refused to change their blackened site for another elsewhere in the city, however advantageous the change might appear for the general good. Without this co-operation the matter was stultified and the city rose again on precisely the same plan as before. Students of twentieth-century architecture might care to draw a parallel with the fate of Sir Patrick Abercrombie's plans after World War II.

The new plan was abandoned but much work had to be done. Over 13,000 houses had been burnt, as well as innumerable churches, colleges, halls and other public buildings. There was no insurance or compensation and private enterprise rebuilt much of the city. Among the new buildings which arose first were the **Guildhall**, the **Royal Exchange**, the **Customs House** and many **City Halls**. Some of Wren's colleagues fell by the wayside but, assisted ably by **Robert Hooke,** he spent many years on the reconstruction, notably on the 3 churches which replaced 87 burnt, and on St Paul's Cathedral. Indeed the co-operation between these two men was so close that in a number of instances it is not known who was the guiding influence and who the actual designer. To give two examples: there is the **Monument** erected in 1677 near the site of the start of the fire and in commemoration of it, and the **Temple Bar** built in 1672 in Fleet Street. The former is a fluted Doric column, 200 feet in height, topped by flames coming out from an urn. Relief panels decorating the base were carried out by the sculptor **Caius G. Cibber** (674).

Though Wren's city layout was frustrated, a great advance in building construction was effected by the Fire. A new structural standard was set up for the erection of domestic buildings in brick and the timber gabled pattern was abandoned. This was reflected also in new

649

650

651

649 St Lawrence Jewry, 1670–86
Gutted 1941, now restored 650
St Magnus the Martyr, London
Bridge, 1670–1705 651 St Michael
Royal, College Hill. Extant but
damaged during the war

building work in other towns in various parts of the country, and over a long period was profoundly effective.

The City Churches

In 1670 a tax was ordained by Parliament to be collected on sea coal arriving at the Port of London. The income derived from this tax was designed to pay for the rebuilding of the city churches and St Paul's Cathedral. In the period 1675–1705, which roughly covered this building enterprise, the money thus raised paid for the fabric of the churches, while the individual parishes assumed responsibility for the interior decoration and fittings. Wren built 53 London churches, 51 in the city and two—St James's, Piccadilly, and St Clement Danes in the Strand—outside the city boundary. It is a great architectural loss to London that 20 of these were demolished or allowed to decay between 1700 and 1939; most were demolished in the nineteenth century in the cause of the surge of Victorian commercial city expansion. Of the 33 churches which remained in 1939, a large proportion could not be seen adequately or even at all because of the adjacent offices, warehouses and commercial buildings. In some instances, the new building was constructed with its walls only a foot from the side of the church tower. A further loss was incurred during the recent war when 17 more churches were destroyed or reduced to a shell. In 1945, 15 or 16 remained more or less complete, while the towers and spires of another dozen survived as gaunt city remains. Since 1945 much reconstruction has taken place and many familiar landmarks, such as **St Lawrence Jewry** and **St Mary-le-Bow**, are rising or have risen again, facsimile copies of Wren's designs. However, at the same time, skyscraper office blocks have risen too and the visibility of the city churches (and of St Paul's) is deteriorating once more. It is impossible to photograph well all but five or six of these churches and many present an insuperable problem. As a result, few books on the architecture of this time, even those devoted specifically to Sir Christopher Wren, are able to show many illustrations in this medium, and long verbal descriptions are necessary. For this volume, 12 surviving churches have been photographed in their entirety and the greater proportion of a further 9. It was necessary to take these photographs in several sections and drawings have been made from a reconstruction of these combined with original or contemporary illustrative material. In view of the much larger number of available illustrations than is common, and the plethora of descriptions in print, it is not proposed to discuss the individual churches in detail.

Unlike other buildings in the reconstruction of London, Wren's authorship of the city churches has not been disputed. The standard of design varies. This is due partly to site limitations, the parish funds available for interior work and the fact that Wren was more closely associated in detailed drawings and supervision with some churches than with others. The interior carving, glass- and stonework and church fittings were carried out by craftsmen. Grinling Gibbons was the chief of these, but his work only appears on some examples, and that of many of his colleagues is much inferior. The churches were erected mainly between 1675 and 1705—the central section of Wren's career. Taken all together they illustrate his tremendous vitality, fertility of imagination, ingenuity of solving site problems, and a fresh, live approach to this great enterprise. These qualities are shown most clearly in Wren's designs for his **steeples**. He had no English classical precedent to work upon, but many of the designs were in classical form and ornament based on Gothic construction. Of the very

652 St Benet, Paul's Wharf. Brick and stone   653 St Anne and St Agnes. Stone   654 St Clement, Eastcheap. Stone   655 St Martin, Ludgate. Stone   656 St Margaret, Lothbury. Stone

XXIX   St Bride, Fleet Street, London, 1670–84. Architect Sir Christopher W

tall steeples, **St Mary-le-Bow** was probably the most beautiful. The gradual build-up from square, pilastered tower and decorated parapet, via a central drum with surrounding columns to a slender obelisk, was perfectly proportioned and provided an impressive but delicate London landmark (637). Among the other lofty steeples are the tiered, wedding-cake design of **St Bride's, Fleet Street** (635), with diminishing tiers surmounted by an obelisk, and **Christ Church, Newgate Street**, with a diminuendo in four-faced pattern (644).

Most interesting and unusual are the tall towers surmounted by bell towers and lanterns. These vary from the lofty **St Magnus the Martyr** at **London Bridge** (650), the delicate **St Martin, Ludgate** (655), to the plainer **St Margaret, Lothbury** (656), **St Edmund the King, Lombard Street** (632) and the classical approach in **St Stephen Walbrook** (633), **St Michael, College Hill** (651), and **St Vedast, Foster Lane** (660). Many designs are simple **towers** (although in some instances the tower remains while the upper steeple has been destroyed). Among the towers are **St Clement, Eastcheap** (654), **St Augustine, Watling Street** (639), **St Andrew Wardrobe** (634), and **St Andrew's, Holborn** (658). A simple tower with cupola mounting is **St Benet, Paul's Wharf** (652). It is thought that Wren possibly realised that in later years his church steeples would be hedged in by commercial edifices. At any rate, his focal interest in the designs and principal ornament is on the upper and final stages, while the lower storeys of the tower are generally plain.

Wren varied his building materials considerably to give interest and colour to the church. He used Portland stone and brick, together and separately, and most churches possessed lead belfries and gilded vanes and crosses.

In a few instances he employed **Gothic** designs, or rather, his interpretation of Gothic principles. This was generally because he had been requested to complete an existing, partly damaged Gothic church, and he had the task of adding a steeple. Among these churches are **St Michael, Cornhill**, of Perpendicular Gothic design (641) and **St Mary, Aldermanbury**, which verges more on the Decorated period (638). The most famous example was **St Dunstan-in-the-East** where Wren designed a thin spire on curved supports which arch upwards from the tower corners. Although not unsuccessful this steeple was rather more Wren than Gothic (659).

In general, Wren designed his city churches on the lines of the Roman basilica, for which he drew freely on Vitruvius and Serlio. However, the designs varied a great deal owing to the diversity of size, site and individual conditions. Wren also bore in mind that these were Protestant churches being erected on what had been mainly Catholic sites. He wanted the pulpit to be visible and audible from all parts of the church so as to give a rapport between preacher and congregation. Also, and partly for this reason, the majority of these churches have light interiors, with large flat-topped or semicircular headed classical windows, in contrast to the darker, more mystical Catholic equivalents.

It is not always easy to imagine what these churches were like in 1700 for, although a number of the exteriors have come to us only slightly impaired, this is true of few interiors. These, even when not demolished or war-damaged, were altered in later periods, particularly the nineteenth century, when the Victorian penchant for gloom and over-decoration filled the bright windows with stained glass, replaced the pews with more ornate versions and re-covered the floors with coloured tiling.

Since the Second World War, a serious attempt has been made when rebuilding or restor-

X   *St Stephen Walbrook, London, 1672–9. Architect Sir Christopher Wren*

DOMES, STEEPLES AND TOWERS, 1660–1714, SIR CHRISTOPHER WREN

657 St James Garlickhythe, London, 1678–83: steeple   658 St Andrew's, Holborn, London: tower. Gutted 1941   659 St Dunstan-in-the-East, London, 1698: steeple. Bombed 1941   660 St Vedast, Foster Lane, London, 1698: steeple. War damaged   661 St Paul's Cathedral, 1675–1710: south-west tower   662 St Paul's: the central drum and dome from the south-east

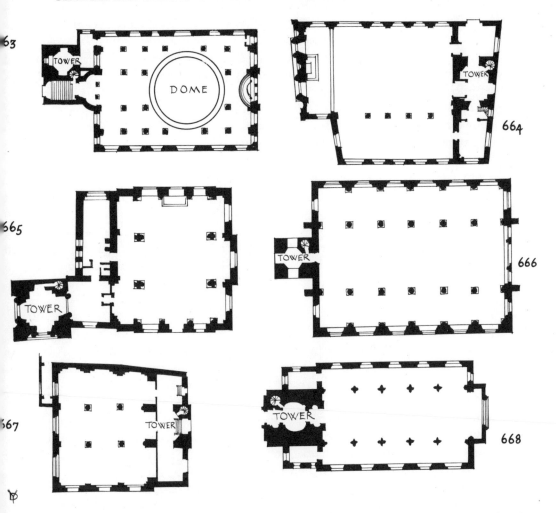

663 St Stephen Walbrook 664 St Lawrence Jewry 665 St Mary-le-Bow 666 Christ Church, Newgate Street 667 St Martin, Ludgate 668 St Bride, Fleet Street

ing such churches to carry out this work architecturally and decoratively as it was when first completed. Such interiors as **St Lawrence Jewry, St Bride** and **St Stephen Walbrook**— three of the best examples—have regained this pristine appearance (XXXIX). The last-named was apparently used by Wren as an experimental precursor to St Paul's. It is one of the larger city churches and, with more money available, was designed with a central domed space in addition to the corner steeple. This dome is carried on eight arches supported on columns, and provided a preparatory exercise in domed spatial covering. The church was built in 1672–87 (633, 663; XXX).

Although many of the churches contained beautiful carving in wood and stone, the richest example was that of **St Lawrence Jewry**, tragically gutted in 1940. Its woodwork was lavishly carved on doorways, gallery and numerous panels. The whole was a worthy tribute to the very high standard of craftsmanship of the period, especially that of carvers and joiners (649, 664). Another church which contained magnificent carved wood by Gibbons and his colleagues was **St James, Piccadilly**, also severely damaged during the war.

One of Wren's greatest problems in designing these churches were the sites. These varied in shape to a tremendous extent, and few had any parallel sides of equal length, while **St Benet, Fink**, was decagonal in plan. Equally, only a few examples possessed a right-angle at the corners, and in some instances, as at **St Benet, Paul's Wharf**, the site was so steeply inclined on a hill that even in this small area there was a variation of ten feet in height. To illustrate his method of dealing with these problems, the plans of six churches are illustrated in Figs 663–8.

The rebuilding of the city churches occupied many years and much of Wren's long life. The first church to be restored and reopened was **St Mary-at-Hill** in 1678. The last was **St Michael, Cornhill** in 1721. Wren was then 89 years old.

Illustrations of **city churches** may be seen in Figs 632–5 and 649–56. **Towers and steeples** are shown in Figs 637–9, 641, 644 and 657–60. **Window design** can be seen in Figs 742 and 744–6; **doorways** in Figs 750–2 and 755; while **ornamental design** is shown in Figs 772, 773 and 776.

St Paul's Cathedral

In the years following upon the Fire (1666) attempts were made, with Wren's somewhat reluctant supervision, to bolster up the remains of the old cathedral and make it usable once more. The Cathedral Commissioners stubbornly refused to admit the hopelessness of this plan. The tower and choir were written off as beyond restoration but the nave was being rebuilt when more masonry collapsed and widening cracks made further efforts useless. Wren himself was asked to design a new cathedral. He had decided that it should be classical in form and submitted a number of designs before satisfaction was unanimously effected.

His **first design** in **1670** was a modest affair and he soon embarked upon a much more ambitious layout. This, for which he prepared drawings and a wooden **model** in **1673**, was his own favourite design. It would have been an unusual and exciting focal centre to London's city architecture if it had been built. Designed in the form of a Greek cross, it bore some similarity to St Peter's in Rome. It had a very large central dome 120 feet in diameter, and in the interior the great circular space formed the nave. On the four sides, short broad aisles led from it to provide chancel and chapels. Between the four arms of the cross, on the exterior, were impressive curved elevations, sweeping in concave planes from arm to arm. The exterior dome rose from a large drum pierced by windows, while the cupola was simple and dignified in its immensity. The whole building was to stand upon a ten-foot-high podium approached on three sides by a flight of steps. This plan, usually called the **Great Model** design, is illustrated in Figs 672 and 673. It was rejected by the Church Commissioners who, despite its impressive grandeur, felt it to be too much of a break with the Gothic tradition of cathedral building in England. Architecturally they wanted a tall spire; ecclesiastically they wanted a Protestant cathedral, not one which savoured so much of Rome. They complained that the floor space was inadequate and there must be a long nave and choir.

Wren tried again. The result in **1675** was the **Warrant Design**, so called because the Royal Warrant was issued for its erection, in the same year. This plan shows an uneasy compromise between Wren's insistence upon a classical cathedral with a dome and the clerical preference

XXXI   St Paul's Cathedral, London, 1675–17
from the south-east. Architect Sir Christopher W

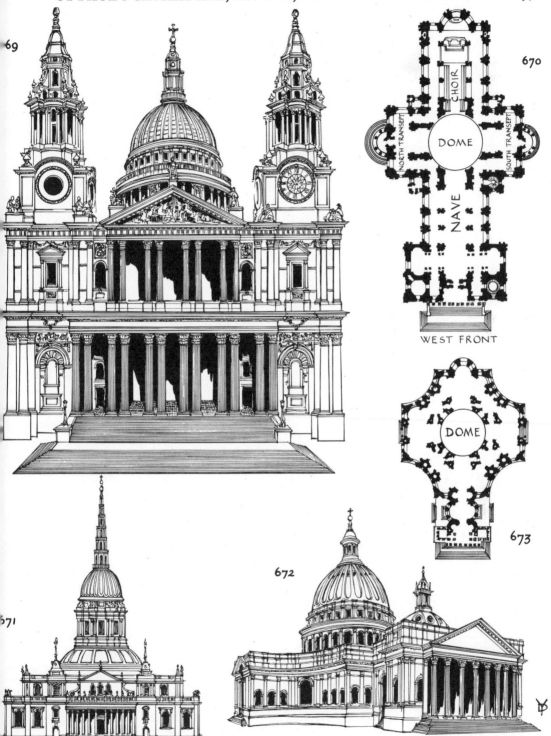

669 West front, present cathedral, 1675–1710   670, Plan, present cathedral   671 Warrant design, 1675   672 Great Model design, 1673   673 Plan of design in Fig. 672

XII *St Paul's Cathedral, London, 1675–1710: crossing. Architect Sir Christopher Wren*

for a cruciform plan with a spire. The ground plan, very similar to that of the cathedral which was finally built, was cruciform with a long nave. But Wren placed his dome over the crossing, then broke it by a drum, and continued with a smaller dome which grotesquely terminated in a six-stage steeple reminiscent of St Bride's Church in Fleet Street (671).

Having received the Royal Warrant to carry out this design, the foundation stone being laid in the same year, Wren proceeded to modify the cathedral considerably between then and its completion in 1710. Among his principal modifications were the substitution of an entirely different dome and abandonment of the steeple, a contraction of the length of the transepts and extensive alterations to the design of the nave. The final cathedral was therefore the outcome of extensive modification and experimentation. The result is impressive and pleasing, if less original and striking than the 1673 design would have been. From the time of its completion in 1710 until today it has remained a cathedral of which London and the rest of England are proud. It is our only classical cathedral in seventeenth- and eighteenth-century tradition. This remarkable fact bears testimony to the different religious spirit of those years compared to the great Medieval era of cathedral building from which we still possess 24 of the original churches.

The ground plan of St Paul's is cruciform in conventional English manner. However, the large circular space at the crossing beneath the great dome provides a break with this tradition. Eight massive piers support the eight arches from whence springs the dome. Each pier is faced with pilasters. The dome itself posed a problem for Wren during its construction. He wanted to have an exterior cupola which would be of dignified proportions and provide a notable London landmark. Such a dome would not create a suitable interior shape as it would be too dark and lofty. He solved the problem (though not until nearly 1700) by the construction of an inner dome surmounted by a brick cone which supports the lantern above, while the exterior dome shape is built out with wood framing and lead construction to give the desired exterior silhouette. Several sectional drawings are available to illustrate this clearly, for example, in Sir Banister Fletcher's *A History of Architecture*. Wren used the Corinthian order on his cathedral and, as in the west front, it is employed in two stages in both column and pilaster form. A clock tower flanks either side of the central pediment on this façade, which is approached from Ludgate Hill, up two flights of steps. The central cross on the lantern is 355 feet above the ground floor of the cathedral (661–2, 669–70, 729, 738, 748, 759, 775; XXXI, XXXII).

The **craftsmanship** in St Paul's Cathedral is of a very high order. The workers in different fields were selected from the best available during the 35 years of building. These craftsmen also carried out other work for Wren and his colleagues in the building projects of this half century as, for example, Greenwich Hospital, the city churches and Hampton Court Palace. Chief among the craftsmen at St Paul's were the painter **James Thornhill**, the mason **Joshua Marshall**, the ironworker **Jean Tijou** and the carvers and sculptors **Jonathan Maine, Francis Bird, Caius Gabriel Cibber** and **Grinling Gibbons**.

OTHER ARCHITECTS AND ARTISTS

Of the architects and artists associated with Sir Christopher Wren in the rebuilding of the City and in other Public Works between 1666 and 1714, the most important were Robert Hooke, Edward Jerman, Jean Tijou, Sir James Thornhill and Grinling Gibbons. **Robert**

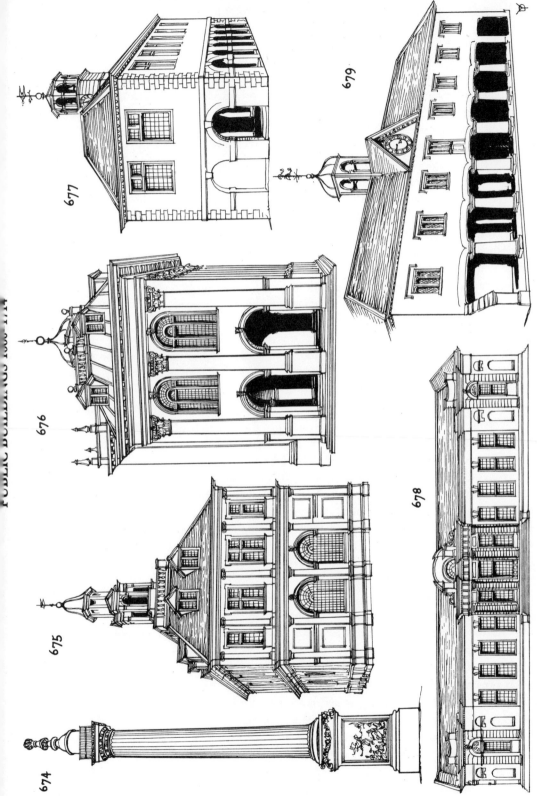

674 The Monument, London, 1671–77   675 The Custom House, King's Lynn, 1681. Henry Bell   676 The Town Hall, Abingdon, Berkshire, 1677–80. Sir Christopher Wren   677 The Town Hall, Amersham, Buckinghamshire, 1682   678 The Orangery, Kensington Palace, begun 1704   679 The Market House, Tetbury, Gloucestershire, 1700

Hooke, 1635–1703 was primarily an experimental physicist. He was appointed Curator of Experiments to the Royal Society in 1662, of which he became a Fellow in the following year. He was secretary to this august body from 1677 to 1683. His experimental work was diverse and included research into optics, elasticity, the wheel barometer, and the spring balance in watches. His constitution was frail and he was often ill, but despite this handicap he led an active, full life which included architectural work. In this field, he also submitted a plan for the rebuilding of London after the Fire, and he was appointed one of the Surveyors for this rebuilding. He worked closely and harmoniously with Wren on this project for many years. Among his architectural achievements were the **Monument, London,** 1671–7 (in conjunction with Wren) (674), the **Royal College of Physicians** 1672–6 (also with Wren's surveillance), **Montagu House,** c. 1680 (now destroyed), **Willen Church**, Buckinghamshire, 1677–80 (696), and **Bethlem Hospital, Moorfields**, 1674–6. The last-named example, later famed as 'Bedlam' and demolished in 1815, was a large building over 500 feet in length. It was constructed in brick and stone and had projecting wings. It was a hospital for the insane. Willen Church has a square tower with Corinthian pilasters on the bell-stage. It bears a resemblance to Wren's simpler church design, especially in the window pattern, but lacks his perfection of proportion and study of detail (696).

Edward Jerman, d. 1668, was appointed to assist in the rebuilding of London. He was concerned with the new **Royal Exchange** (completed 1669) also the **Fishmongers' Hall** and the **Merchant Taylors' Hall.** He died in 1668 and unfortunately all these buildings have since been altered or rebuilt.

Jean Tijou was a French ornamental ironworker who came to England in 1689, having fled from France in the Huguenot exodus of 1685. He was a prime mover in the revival of interest in ironwork in England in the seventeenth century. In the extensive schemes on hand for St Paul's, the city churches and Hampton Court Palace he found full scope for expression in his medium. His influence on English ironwork was very great. Although his own work was often ornate and freely scrolled, later, eighteenth-century ironworkers followed his lead, though in a more restrained form. As a craftsman Tijou's work is outstanding, not only in the seventeenth century, but for all time. His chief masterpieces can be seen at **Hampton Court Palace** in the great staircase, door grilles and the Thames screen; and at **St Paul's Cathedral** are the circular stair in the south-west tower, a number of screens and grilles also wrought-iron coverings for the windows (702).

Sir James Thornhill, 1676–1734, was noted especially for his ceiling and wall paintings, many of which decorated the large building projects of this period. One famous example is the interior of the **dome** of **St Paul's**, for which Thornhill designed scenes from the life of St Paul. His work can also be seen in the great hall at **Blenheim Palace** and apartments at **Hampton Court Palace.** His greatest achievement is generally considered to be at **Greenwich Hospital** where he carried out wall and ceiling paintings for the **hall.** The scale here is particularly suited to his work, which is shown to advantage. He represented the sovereigns of England of this time (William and Mary, Queen Anne, and George I and II) with their families interrelated in an allegorical backcloth with heavenly muse and sky. Thornhill, who became the father-in-law of Hogarth, was knighted in 1715 (XXXIV).

The story of how in 1670 John Evelyn discovered **Grinling Gibbons**, 1648–1720, carving

XXXIII   The Royal Naval Hospital, Greenwich. The Queen's House (top right) 1616–35, by Inigo Jones. F Charles II block completed 1665, by John Webb and Queen Anne's block completed 1715, by Nicholas Haw moor (foreground). Main blocks and colonnades completed 1716, by Sir Christopher Wren, Sir John Vanbr and Nicholas Hawksmoor (centre)

in a cottage, is well known. Gibbons was encouraged by Hugh May and later worked for Wren, when he made his name in his work at **Windsor, St Paul's** and in the **city churches**. Grinling Gibbons was probably one of the most gifted of all the craftsmen who worked for Wren. He carved in stone and worked in bronze but his métier was really wood. In this medium he established a unique style in which he strove to recapture the realism and vitality of natural forms as typified by the great flower painters of the day. His work revolutionised the carving which was then being done in St Paul's and other enterprises. Hitherto the floral forms had been tightly packed and formally arranged. Gibbons carved almost in the round, with projecting sprays of leaves, flowers and fruit rapturously flowing and laid here and there, each being clearly detached from the other. This high-relief work threw deep shadows on to the background and on to the other floral forms so that the whole design became vital, alive and vividly real. This is illustrated most clearly in his magnificent carving on the Stalls and organ case in **St Paul's Cathedral** (773, 777).

ROYAL WORKS AND PALACES

Apart from John Webb's King Charles's Block at Greenwich in 1665 and work by Hugh May at Windsor in 1675, the large, royal schemes for Palace and Hospital building did not get under way until after 1680.

The Royal Hospital, Chelsea, 1682-92, was designed by **Sir Christopher Wren**. Sir Stephen Fox, then Paymaster General of the Army, was the chief promoter of the scheme to build this Army hospital, inspired by *Les Invalides*, Paris, which had been founded in 1670. The enterprise was paid for partly by the Privy Purse and partly by the Army. The site, chosen by Wren, had no restrictions or space limitations but stretched uninterruptedly to the river. The King laid the foundation-stone in 1682 and the hospital was opened ten years later.

The layout is simple. It forms three sides of a quadrangle open to the river. In the centre block are the hall and chapel, and a cupola is set in the centre. The giant Doric order is used in column form in the central portico, surmounted by a pediment. On the north side this is echoed without the portico projection. In the side wings are pilastered, pedimented pavilions. The whole design is simple and austere, carried out in red brick and stone. The three sides have each three storeys with dormer floor above. The hospital design set a pattern for many years in such buildings, while the use of a giant order, the cupola construction and simple portico were repeated well into the eighteenth century (642, 680, 683, 730).

Sir Christopher Wren was also responsible for the replanning of **Hampton Court Palace, 1689-1701.** Henry VIII's Tudor Palace had been neglected for some time when William and Mary (particularly Mary) decided to use the Royal Palace once more and to set in motion extensive plans for rebuilding. The original intention was to destroy the whole Tudor Palace except the Great Hall, but due to the Queen's death, and shortage of funds, the idea was greatly modified. It is very fortunate that this was so. Wren's contribution to Hampton Court Palace is impressive and interesting and was carried out by the finest of craft-workers in wood, iron, stone and paint, but it would have been a tragedy to destroy the fine Tudor brickwork and panelling which today so harmoniously blends with the later buildings. Wren made several designs for Hampton Court. He had planned an imposing central dome and corner pavilions to be connected by low elevations. The Great Hall was to

XIV   *The Royal Naval Hospital, Greenwich: the hall, 1698-*
7. Architect Sir Christopher Wren; painter Sir James Thornhill

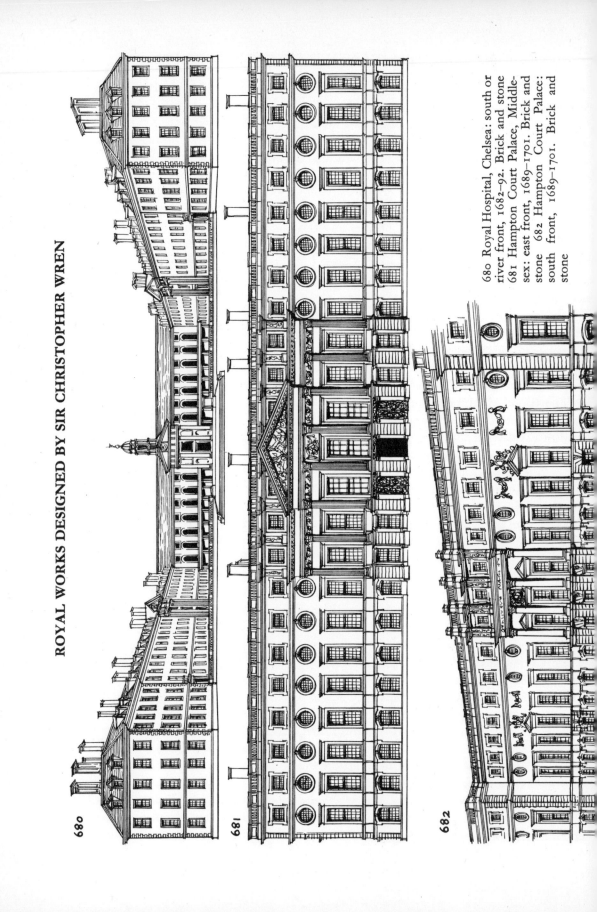

ROYAL WORKS DESIGNED BY SIR CHRISTOPHER WREN

680

681

682

680 Royal Hospital, Chelsea: south or river front, 1682–92. Brick and stone 681 Hampton Court Palace, Middlesex: east front, 1689–1701. Brick and stone 682 Hampton Court Palace: south front, 1689–1701. Brick and stone

be a focal centre with a double staircase to the entrance. There was to be an open colonnade on two sides. The final design to be accepted was a rather severe rectangular building with an uncompromisingly level sky-line. The principal charm of Hampton Court lies in its weathered rose-coloured brick set off by the Portland stone parapet, windows, columns and carving. This attractive combination of materials which we associate so closely with Wren had, up to this time, only been used experimentally on one or two city churches (notably St Benet, Paul's Wharf) and at Chelsea Hospital. Here was Wren's first use of the materials on a large scheme and its success is evident. The great craftsmen of the day are seen at their best at Hampton Court.

683 Chimney-stacks, Royal Hospital, Chelsea, 1682–92. Brick

There is **Tijou's** wonderful staircase, his gates and grilles, and particularly his Thames-side screen (700, 702), and there is the sculpture of **Cibber** and the carving in stone and wood by **Gibbons**. Not least one can see the ceiling and wall paintings by **Verrio** and his colleagues, especially up the grand staircase.

Wren's work at Hampton Court has been criticised for its unsympathetic severity, as typified by the exterior silhouette. This uncompromising plainness, however, is offset to a remarkable degree by the standard of detail handling as evidenced on the frontispiece of the east or south façade, in the window design, the stone carving and the interior magnificence (681–2, 700, 702, 763).

King William requested **Sir Christopher Wren** to enlarge Nottingham House in 1691, as an alternative London residence to Whitehall Palace. The result was **Kensington Palace.** He was assisted by Hawksmoor who was then Clerk of Works. Much of Wren's work here was altered in the eighteenth century, but part of the south side remains as he designed it. **The Orangery**, dated 1704, is a charming building in red brick and stone with a large, simple window design in white. Often attributed to Vanbrugh, it was also much the affair of Wren and Hawksmoor, respectively the Surveyor-General and Clerk of Works at the Palace at the time (678, 760, 771).

The Royal Hospital, Greenwich, 1660-1714, benefited from the knowledge and experience of the greatest architects of the seventeenth century. The overall design was by **Wren,** but **Nicholas Hawksmoor** and **Sir John Vanbrugh** carried out a considerable part of the scheme and showed their respect for their famous colleague by interpreting his design in his manner and not their own.

The Greenwich Palace of Tudor days had been allowed to fall into decay. **John Webb** started an extensive design for a new Palace, but only succeeded in completing one large block, the **King Charles II building**, in 1665. Once more the enterprise was allowed to lapse.

With the accession of William and Mary it was decided to build at Greenwich a naval counterpart to Chelsea Hospital. The sovereigns gave the site of Greenwich Palace and put Wren in charge of the project, which was to be on a much more ambitious scale than Chelsea, as a fitting tribute to Britain's sea power.

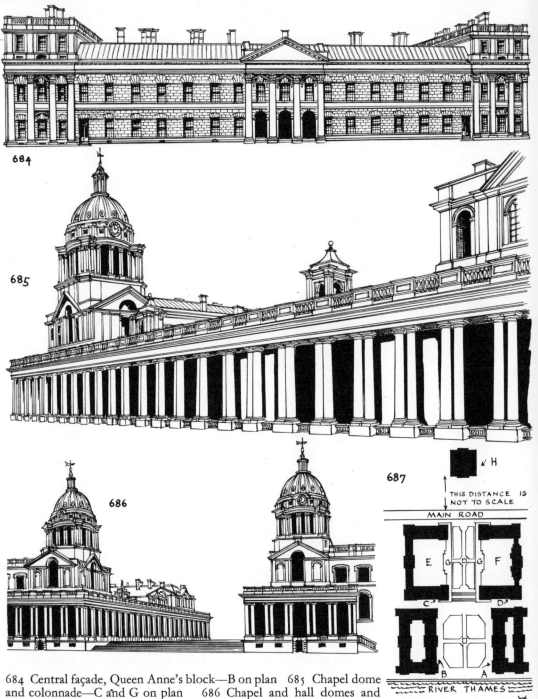

684 Central façade, Queen Anne's block—B on plan   685 Chapel dome and colonnade—C and G on plan   686 Chapel and hall domes and colonnade—C and D on plan   687 Sketch-plan of layout

A King Charles's block, Webb, 1662–9.

B Queen Anne's block, Wren, Hawksmoor, 1696–1729.

C Chapel. Begun Wren, Int. 1779–89.

D Hall, Wren, 1698–1705.

E Queen Mary's block, 1699–1752.

F King William's block, 1698–1723 (part Vanbrugh 1701).

G Colonnades begun 1699.

H Queen's House, Inigo Jones, 1616–35.

In designing the layout for this impressive seamen's hospital Wren had to incorporate both Inigo Jones's Queen's House and Webb's block. The former presented a problem. For, whereas Wren was fully cognisant of the beauty and importance of the building it was difficult to make it part of his scheme. He planned buildings on two sides of an open vista which should terminate in the Queen's House, but he felt, as have many later critics, that the Queen's House was too small in scale to carry off the scheme satisfactorily. The design comprised four blocks; one was Webb's 1665 building and another one was to be built opposite to balance it. Towards the Queen's House were then to be erected two large blocks from which individual domes would roof the chapel on one side and the hall on the other. From these domed structures, open colonnades continued on each side of the central court towards the Queen's House.

Wren, with **Hawksmoor** assisting him, supervised the work until 1702, when **Sir John Vanbrugh** took over. The hall dome, with its ceiling painted by **Thornhill**, was completed in 1704 and the chapel by 1716. The **Queen Anne's block**, facing Webb's earlier building, was completed by **Hawksmoor** in 1715. However, work in enclosing the larger courts continued intermittently through the eighteenth century and into the nineteenth.

Various features of Greenwich Hospital have been criticised; the imposing colonnade vista leading nowhere, the design of the dome drums, for instance. There is, however, a grandeur and spaciousness about Greenwich which is felt particularly when disembarking at the Thames pier, and approaching these elegant, finely proportioned domes and colonnades. As the columns retreat in distant perspective one perceives, far away, that precursor of this classical magnificence, the simple but perfect **Queen's House** (553, 636, 684-7, 734, 757; XXXIII, XXXIV).

WREN'S COLLEAGUES AND SUCCESSORS

William Talman, 1650-1720, succeeded Hugh May as Comptroller of Works in 1689 and made a considerable reputation as a designer of large country houses. Of these the most familiar example is **Chatsworth**, where Talman worked for the Duke of Devonshire on the south front from 1687-96. His achievements here brought him fame, but as an architect he is uninspiring compared with the master. The design of this façade is capable and well-proportioned but lacks interest due to a certain monotony of line and treatment. There is no central feature and the giant Ionic order proceeds unbroken from one side to the other. The quality of carving and enrichment is of high standard and the house, as a whole, possesses dignity and stateliness (689; XXXV). Among Talman's other works is the smaller house at **Uppark** in Sussex, 1688-90. This is a charming, simple house with a well-carved centrepiece on the south front, essentially typical of the period as is particularly clearly shown on the central doorway and pediment (693, 732, 766). A larger, more famous example is that of **Dyrham Park**, Gloucestershire, built between 1698 and 1700. Here Talman designed a house of plain but finely proportioned elevations, situated in a pleasant valley, and looking out upon a balustraded terrace on the garden front. During his term of office as Comptroller of Works, which lasted until he was succeeded in 1702 by Vanbrugh, Talman was closely connected with the work at Hampton Court Palace, and it is here and at Chatsworth that he gained much of his reputation.

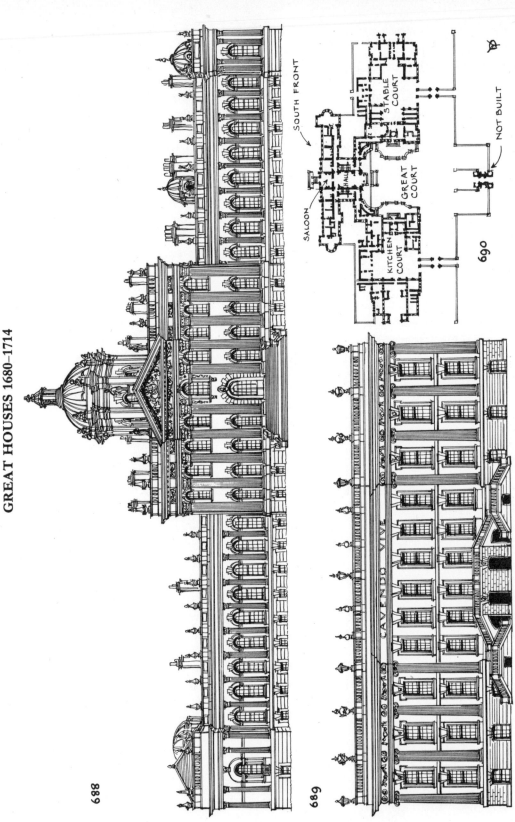

GREAT HOUSES 1680–1714

688 Castle Howard, Yorkshire: south front, 1699–1712. Sir John Vanbrugh   689 Chatsworth, Derbyshire: south front, 1686–96.

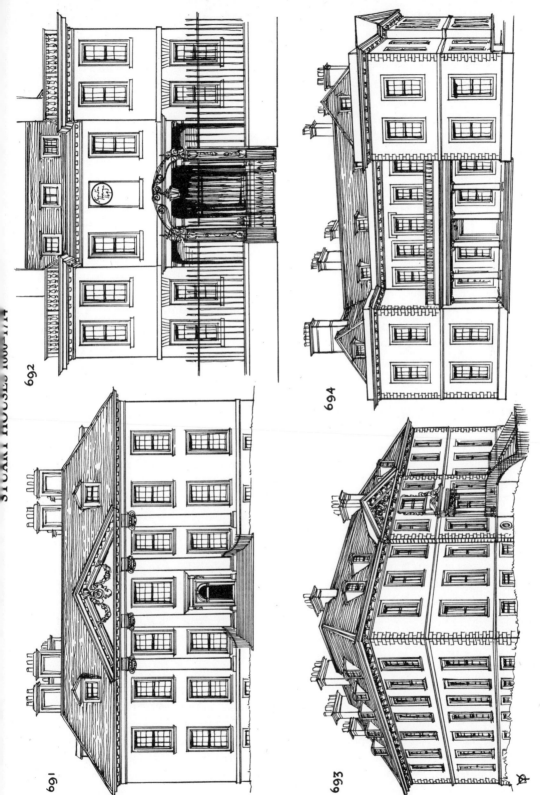

691

692

693

694

691 Eltham Lodge, Kent, 1664. Hugh May. Brick and stone 692 Fenton House, Hampstead, 1693. Brick town house 693 Uppark, Sussex, 1688–90. William Talman. Brick and stone 694 Fawley Court, Oxfordshire, 1684–8. Brick and stone

Henry Bell, 1653-1717, is one of a number of architects of the seventeenth and eighteenth centuries whose life and work was spent in one specific locality. His architectural achievements are not, therefore, famous nationally, and in Bell's case his contributions were made in the district of King's Lynn, where he was twice mayor. His first and most famous work is the **Custom House** there, 1681. It is a most attractive two-storey building of Portland stone. The lower ground floor is adorned by the Doric order and the upper one by the Ionic. Above this is a wooden cornice and a steeply pitched roof with four-sided balustrade. The whole is surmounted by a pleasant and elegant cupola (675). Bell's other works included a market cross, a house in King's Lynn and the church at North Runcton.

William Winde, *d*. 1722, is principally known as the architect of **Buckingham House, London** (later rebuilt as Buckingham Palace). He designed this for the Duke of Buckingham in 1703-5. In style it had Dutch Palladian features and was based on a rectangular, central block plan with flanking arcades curving forward from the sides and forming a three-sided forecourt. The main façade was decorated by an Ionic order. It was a plan which came into general use in the first half of the eighteenth century. Winde was earlier a pupil of Gerbier and spent some of his early life in Holland from whence his interest in Dutch Palladianism presumably stemmed. He also designed **Newcastle House**, 1688-9, in London and **Hampstead Marshall**. Neither of these examples of his work survives.

ENGLISH BAROQUE

Hawksmoor, Vanbrugh and **Archer** all had working connections with Wren, and Hawksmoor, in particular, was engaged with him on a number of projects including St Paul's, Greenwich and Hampton Court. The earlier works of all three were consequently strongly influenced by Wren, but they were sufficient personalities in architecture to branch out later into different spheres of design. They were closely bound together in their interpretation of classical architecture and the main span of their contributions, independent of Wren, covers the period 1700-30. In this time their work was principally in the Baroque style of classical architecture. This school enjoyed a brief flowering only, in England, and these architects provided the larger share of its expression. Much of their work has been criticised, especially by those who admire Wren's buildings. It is, however, invidious to compare the two styles. They are quite different interpretations of the classical theme, and while the work of Hawksmoor and Vanbrugh may appear heavy, ornate and clumsy when compared to the delicacy and lightness of Wren, it has a different function and is designed to give a different impact. Vanbrugh's work, in particular, was on the massive and impressive scale. It should be viewed as a single entity, not as deficient in comparison with other work.

Nicholas Hawksmoor 1661-1736

Hawksmoor spent his whole life in the study of building and architecture. At the age of 18 he came to London and began to work for Wren—at that time as his domestic clerk. He assisted Wren on many projects and quickly absorbed the skill and knowledge needed to make his help invaluable. He was engaged on work at **Chelsea Hospital**, the **City Churches, St Paul's Cathedral, Hampton Court Palace** and **Greenwich Hospital**, and in 1705 became Deputy-Surveyor of Works at **Greenwich**. About 1700 Hawksmoor came into close association with Vanbrugh and worked with him on a number of the great houses on which Vanbrugh was then engaged. Despite this very long and close association, first with Wren and then with Vanbrugh, Hawksmoor developed his own style, and in the first 35 years of the eighteenth century carried out much of his own work, principally in ecclesiastical and university projects. These are discussed in Chapter VIII. His principal works in this present period are his one large domestic building, that of **Easton Neston** near Towcester begun 1706, and the **Library** of **Queen's College, Oxford**, 1692. The latter is a well-proportioned two-storey building with central, pedimented feature (717).

Sir John Vanbrugh 1664–1726

Vanbrugh's introduction to architecture was very different from that of Hawksmoor. He was brought up as a gentleman in London. As a young man he was commissioned in the Army, and after resigning this commission, he travelled extensively. In his thirties he wrote a number of plays. It was not until 1699 at the age of 35 that he turned his attention to architecture. He had studied building while travelling abroad, but his first attempt at design was the stupendous mansion which he built for the Earl of Carlisle: **Castle Howard** in Yorkshire. Work was begun in 1701, and like all Vanbrugh's conceptions was in the grand manner with enormous frontage and impressive hall. Castle Howard set the pattern for his designs which dominated the architectural world until his death in 1726. The arrangement was not rigidly defined, as in seventeenth-century work, but consisted of an impressive central mass with spreading subsidiary buildings, connected to the main unit by arcades or colonnades. Vanbrugh's approach was flamboyant and on a large scale. The detail is often coarse and his work ill-proportioned, but of such forceful grandeur that it cannot be ignored. He initiated a movement which was never adequately followed up, chiefly because the cost became prohibitive. His work suited the wealthy landowners of his time, but with his death there closed the era of large-scale private building of palace proportions. After Castle Howard his fame grew. In 1702 he succeeded Talman as **Comptroller**. He was commissioned to build **Blenheim Palace**, conferred by Queen Anne on the Duke of Marlborough in recognition of his victories in 1704. Vanbrugh also took over the supervision of work at **Greenwich Hospital** from Wren, and in this same district built his own house, **Vanbrugh Castle**.

There has been and still is much controversy over Vanbrugh's work. To many people it appears only to succeed in its stupendous size, while the content of the design is considered ugly and pretentious. To others it presents a scheme full of grandeur and stimulation. The frontages of his buildings are excessively great—at Blenheim, for example, 856 feet. The conception of the whole is imaginative and exciting, but it is often difficult to appreciate this except from a distance or an aerial viewpoint. He sacrificed much to his desire for scale and external effect; thus many rooms are inadequately lighted and badly shaped. Yet at Blenheim Palace, even if the style of work does not appeal, there is much to study and admire (640, 688, 690, 699, 703–7, 709, 728, 733, 743; XXXV).

Thomas Archer 1668–1743

The third contributor to English Baroque architecture, Archer, was educated at Oxford and studied on the Continent for four years before starting his architectural career. He had been able to see for himself in Italy ancient classical buildings and the work of contemporary

695 St Mary's Church, Ingestre, Staffordshire, 1673–7. Attributed to Wren   696 Willen Church, Buckinghamshire, 1677–80. Robert Hooke   697 All Saints' Church, Oxford, 1709. Designed by Dean Aldrich   698 Farley Church, Wiltshire, *c.* 1690

Italian architects. Thus, he possessed certain advantages over his contemporaries in England. Much of his work has been lost, such as his house at **Heythrop** and his **London houses.** He designed the north façade at **Chatsworth** with its imposing curved and pilastered front; also **Roehampton House** in 1712. Later, he carried out a good deal of ecclesiastical work, particularly the **Cathedral** at **Birmingham** and **St Paul's Church, Deptford**.

CHURCHES 1660–1714

It has been mentioned in Chapter VI that few churches were built in the seventeenth century before 1666 owing to the fact that England already possessed so many Medieval churches. For this same reason there were very few churches in the classical style existing prior to this date. The Fire of London made much new church building necessary and Wren established the popularity of the classical form in ecclesiastical building by his city churches. In this period one or two examples were also built outside London. The chief of these were **Farley Church**, Wiltshire, *c.* 1690, **Willen Church**, Buckinghamshire, 1679–80, and **St Mary's Church, Ingestre**, Staffordshire, 1673–7. These are all classical churches in country areas. Willen Church was designed by Robert Hooke and the other two churches were in the Wren tradition of building. All have square towers, parapets with finialled corners and simple, classical window openings (695–6, 698). Two larger churches were also built in towns, to replace ones damaged by fire: **All Saints', Northampton**, 1676–80, and **St Mary's, Warwick**, 1704. The Northampton Church has a central dome and is in classical form, while at Warwick, the Perpendicular Gothic Church is a very late specimen of this style. **North Runcton Church** near **King's Lynn**, by **Henry Bell**, is reminiscent of some of Wren's city churches.

While the Great Fire of 1666 gave impetus to a new era of church building under Wren's initiative and guidance, the Act of 1711 for building Fifty New Churches, provided another such impetus. Here, Hawksmoor was the predominating influence, and these churches are described in Chapter VIII. One particular example was, however, built just previously: **All Saints', Oxford**, 1707–10, designed by **Dean Henry Aldrich** of Christ Church. This church, although not of the stature of Wren's or Hawksmoor's work, does provide a link between the two periods of ecclesiastical building. It owes much to St Lawrence Jewry in its design, while its steeple is reminiscent of that of St Mary-le-Bow. The church itself is, however, more Baroque in style than the city churches, and indicates something of Hawksmoor's later approach. The tower is lofty and has a square base terminating in a balustrade. Within this rises a circular drum with its colonnade in Corinthian style. The panelled steeple is plain and has eight sides. The interior is rectangular and has a gallery (697, 731).

DOMESTIC BUILDINGS

Large Country Houses

The most popular ground plan was a simple rectangle, though a few houses were designed with an interior courtyard, for example, **Chatsworth** and **Hampton Court**. From **1700–14** side wings were attached to the main rectangular block in the form of curving or straight colonnades which projected forwards to provide a three-sided forecourt. The principal floor

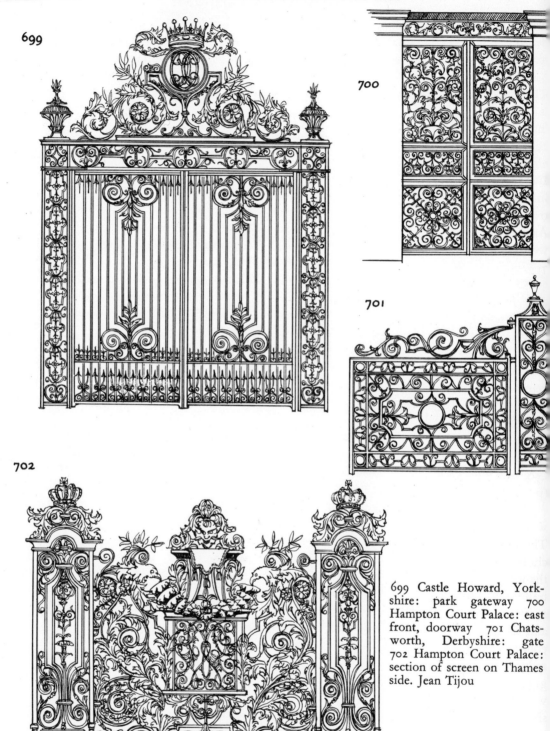

699

700

701

702

699 Castle Howard, Yorkshire: park gateway 700 Hampton Court Palace: east front, doorway 701 Chatsworth, Derbyshire: gate 702 Hampton Court Palace: section of screen on Thames side. Jean Tijou

was the first floor or *piano nobile*. Much of the plan of the rest of the house was sacrificed to the height and nobility of the rooms on this floor. Here were to be found the hall and saloon; exterior stairs led to the front door at this level.

William Talman started work on the south front at **Chatsworth**, Derbyshire, in **1687**. The exterior façade is pleasant and dignified, if unremarkable, though the carved stonework is of the first quality. In plan, it comprises a great block of apartments disposed around an inner courtyard. Inside, there can be seen some of the finest staterooms in England and a chapel of comparable merit. No expense was spared to obtain the services of the most eminent artists and craftsmen. There are outstanding wall and ceiling paintings by **Verrio, Laguerre** and **Thornhill**, while the wood carving in particular is exquisite. The whole interior is richly decorated and superbly finished. The work was carried out with great care over a long period. Talman completed his contribution to Chatsworth in 1697 and **Thomas Archer** designed the north front with its semi-elliptical bow by 1705. It is thought that the west façade was the work of the 1st Duke of Devonshire himself in 1700–4 (689, 701, 736, 758, 767, 770; XXXV).

Castle Howard, Yorkshire, 1699-1712, was **Sir John Vanbrugh's** first country house and, in many ways, his greatest design. On the south front, facing the garden, is a long façade with a higher central block surmounted by a large drum and cupola (688). On the north side curving arcades are advanced to connect with other buildings and form the sides of an open court. These, in turn, are connected to further buildings which are arranged round independent courts, and comprise kitchens, stables, laundry, etc. (plan in Fig. 690). The whole conception is very large and ornamental in treatment, but controlled and symmetrical. The great drum and cupola dominate the design from the exterior. Inside, the great hall is square, while giant Corinthian pilasters support the arches upon which the drum rises. The hall itself is spacious and imposing but, in order to create exterior height, the interior of the dome is too tall and narrow—i.e. 27 feet diameter of dome and 77 feet in height from the floor (640, 688, 690, 699; XXXVI). Wren solved this problem at St Paul's by his artificial inner dome (p. 238).

The creation of **Blenheim Palace**, Oxfordshire, **1705-22**, a combined palace and castle was **Sir John Vanbrugh's** supreme triumph, but presented him with his greatest difficulties. The militant Duchess of Marlborough did not attempt to disguise her disapproval at the choice of architect and design and her relations with Vanbrugh steadily deteriorated during the long period of building of the palace until Vanbrugh was finally excluded from his own building; the work was completed by Hawksmoor after Vanbrugh's death. Blenheim Palace as it stands today is still a remarkable house. The great centre block with Corinthian portico and rising pediment is connected to the stately pavilions by a curving colonnade of Doric columns. The pavilions themselves are castellar; being massive and very tall, they tend to reduce the importance of the central feature. The whole house encloses three sides of a gigantic courtyard and has a total frontage of 856 feet. The conception is heavily Baroque with much rustication and deeply shadowed colonnades. The details are often surprisingly simple, for example, the plain window openings. Inside there are magnificent ceiling and wall paintings by **Thornhill** and **Laguerre** (703–7, 709, 733, 743).

Nicholas Hawksmoor designed, in **1706**, a stone house at **Easton Neston near Towcester**, with a giant order of Corinthian pilasters. Below these is a rusticated base. The two

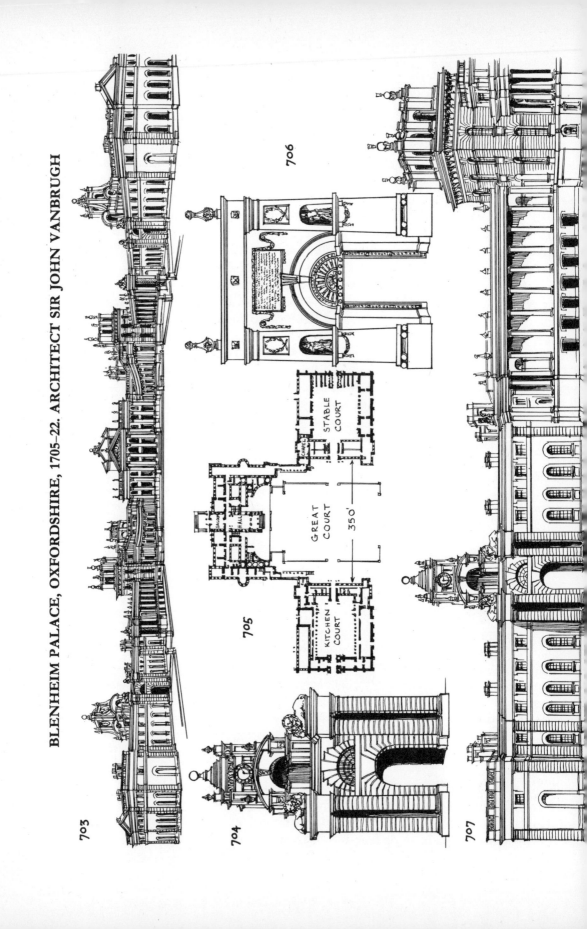

BLENHEIM PALACE, OXFORDSHIRE, 1705–22. ARCHITECT SIR JOHN VANBRUGH

703

704

705

706

707

STABLE COURT

GREAT COURT

KITCHEN COURT

350'

CHAPEL

HALL

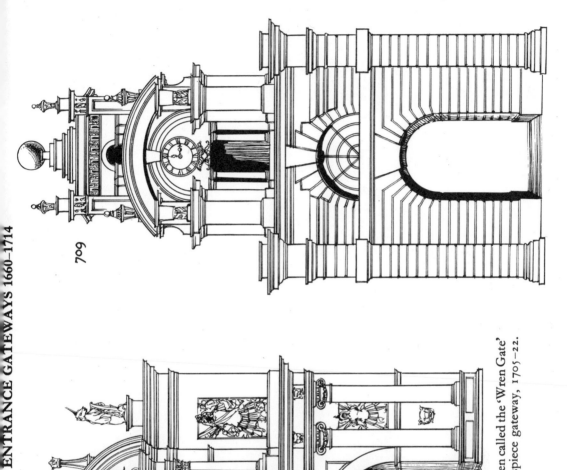

709

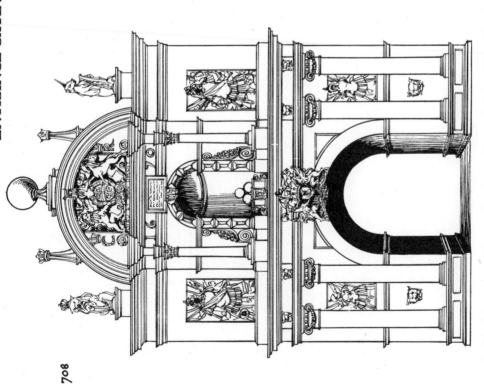

708

708 Citadel gateway, Plymouth, 1670—often called the 'Wren Gate'
709 Blenheim Palace, Oxfordshire; frontispiece gateway, 1705–22.
Sir John Vanbrugh

710   Petworth House, Sussex, 1688–9: the west front   711 Mompesson House, Salisbury, 1701. Town house   712 No. 42 Queen Anne's Gate, London. Town house, *temp.* Queen Anne   713 Hanbury Hall, Worcestershire, 1701. Red brick. Style of Wren

XXXV Chatsworth House, Derbyshire: the state di... room, 1687. Carving by Samuel Watson; ceiling by Verrio,

side pavilions are of earlier date and the house had to be planned to fit between them. Inside is a beautiful staircase with an iron balustrade. The wall paintings are by **Thornhill**.

Among the slightly smaller country houses existing of this period are four very good examples: Fawley Court, Oxfordshire, Petworth House and Uppark in Sussex and Hanbury Hall, Worcestershire. **Fawley Court**, 1684–8, is of H plan with short projecting wings. A loggia with colonnade, and parapet above, connects these wings in the front elevation. The house is of brick with stone dressings and facings and has a sloping roof set inside the parapet (694). **Petworth House**, Sussex, 1688–9, has an imposing long, low west front of this date, with shallow projecting wings and a rusticated central feature. The whole elevation of stone relies for its simple effective design on the window spacing and proportion. Many of these windows are beautifully carved with varied decoration (710, 741). **Uppark**, Sussex, was designed by Talman in 1688–9. It is in the form of a rectangular block. The centrepiece on the south side is unaltered and in good condition. There are two floors, also a semi-basement and dormer level (693, 732, 766). **Hanbury Hall**, Worcestershire, 1701, is a red brick house with stone dressings and decoration which is of a style so commonly described as 'Wren'. It has a rectangular front elevation with projecting wings and a centrepiece of the Corinthian order supporting a pediment. A cupola rises in the centre. There are two storeys with plain, evenly spaced window openings and a dormer floor above. The total effect is pleasing and essentially English (647, 713).

Town Houses

In towns, builders were slow to follow the designs of larger country houses and accentuate the first floor. Thus, most houses of this period have equal-sized windows on first and second floors. These are tall, rectangular openings with key blocks in the centre. Simple bands or string courses divide the floors horizontally. There is generally a deep cornice with perhaps a parapet and a hipped roof. The central doorcase is of carved wood in classical design. If the house is large enough to have seven or more windows across its façade, the central section might be slightly projecting and a pediment be set above. Among the examples illustrated here are **Mompesson House, Salisbury** 1701 (711), **No. 42 Queen Anne's Gate, London**, *temp*. Queen Anne (712) and **Fenton House, Hampstead**, 1693 (692).

THE UNIVERSITIES

The greater part of the building at **Oxford** in the second half of the seventeenth century was by **Wren, Aldrich** and **Hawksmoor**. **Wren's** chief contribution was his first architectural commission: the **Sheldonian Theatre**, intended for general use by the University. He undertook in 1662 the design of this building, which was named after Archbishop Sheldon who shouldered the cost. Wren based his design on that of a Roman theatre, but as the English climate was unsuited to an open-air theatre, he roofed it by means of a timber trussed span in order to avoid obscuring the view with columnar supports. The mythological scenes on the ceiling were painted by Streater. The building typified Wren's scientific approach to his problems and, because of its engineering aspect, a model of the design was exhibited at the Royal Society in 1663 (714, 721). Wren's other work at Oxford was the completion of **Tom Tower** at **Christ Church**. Here, in 1681–2, he had the task of providing a Gothic tower in

XVI *Castle Howard, Yorkshire: the entrance*
1699–1712. Architect Sir John Vanbrugh

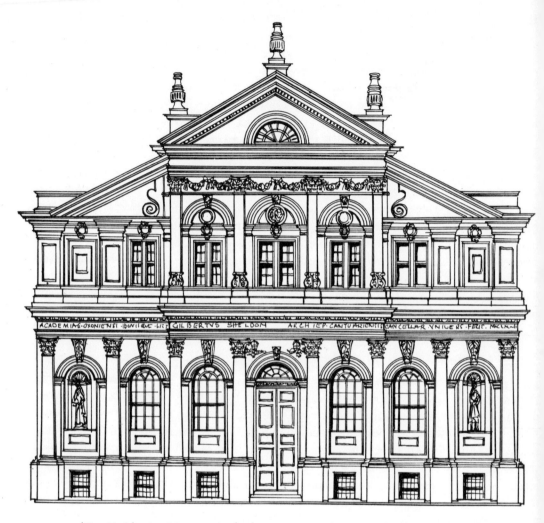

714 The Sheldonian Theatre, Oxford, 1664–9: south aspect. Sir Christopher Wren

keeping with the lower part already built and with Wolsey's quad and hall. The result is successful and architecturally satisfactory, although hardly of the same style of Gothic workmanship presumably envisaged by the builders of the lower stages (428).

Dr Henry Aldrich made extensive architectural contributions to Oxford while Dean of Christ Church. At **Trinity College** he designed the **Chapel**, a most successful and charming work. It is well proportioned in simple rectangular form and has a square tower. Inside is some exquisite carving by **Grinling Gibbons** (716). In addition to the **Fellows' Building** at **Corpus Christi**, 1706–12, **Aldrich** also designed the **Peckwater Quad** at **Christ Church** in 1705–6. Here he planned three virtually identical sides, pilastered in the Ionic order. Each side had a centrepiece with pediment above. The result is a little monotonous but gives an impression of dignity and solidity. The fourth side was not completed until after his death in 1710 (715).

715

716

717

715, Christ Church, Oxford: Peckwater Quadrangle, 1705–11. Dean Aldrich   716 Trinity College Chapel, Oxford, c. 1690. Dean Aldrich   717 Queen's College, Oxford: library, c. 1695. Nicholas Hawksmoor

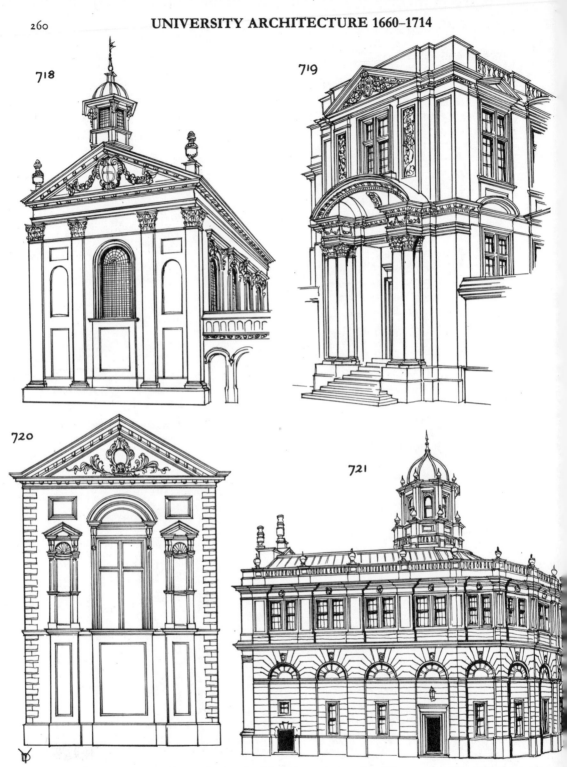

718 Pembroke College Chapel, Cambridge, 1663. Sir Christopher Wren   719 The Old Ashmolean, Oxford, 1678–83   720 St Catharine's College Chapel, Cambridge, 1704   721 The Sheldonian Theatre, Oxford, 1669. Sir Christopher Wren

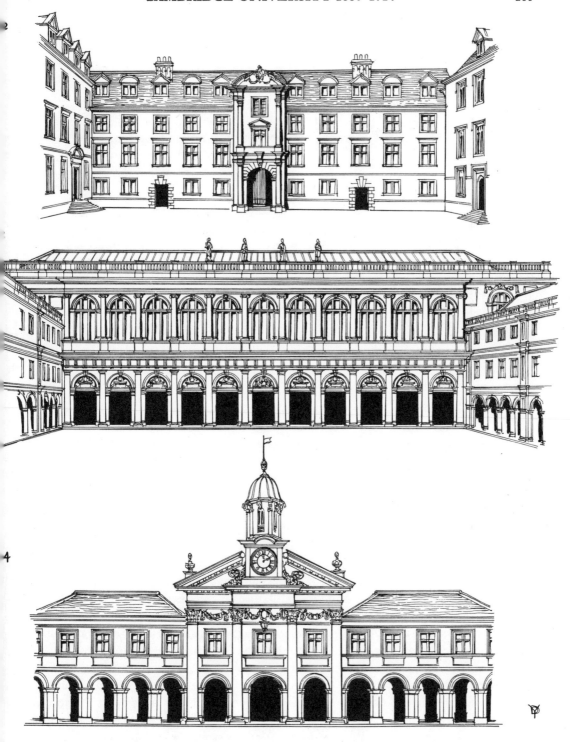

722 St Catharine's College, Cambridge: the principal court begun 1674. 723 Trinity College Library, Cambridge, 1676–84. Sir Christopher Wren 724 Emmanuel College, Cambridge: the gallery, 1668. Sir Christopher Wren

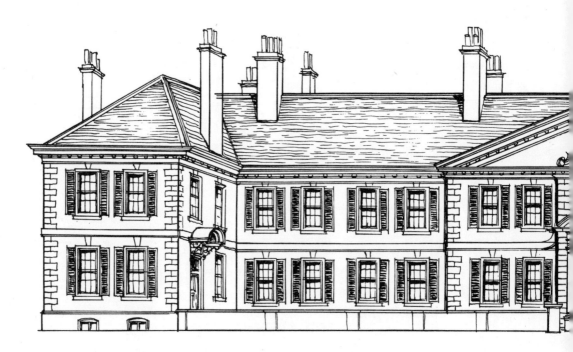

725 Morden College, Blackheath, *c.* 1695

The most important Oxford building project of the late seventeenth and early eighteenth century was that of **Queen's College**. Here, by 1670, the Medieval buildings had become very dilapidated and as the College was now wealthy it was decided to rebuild on an ambitious scale. **Nicholas Hawksmoor** was entrusted with the task and in 1693–6 built a fine **Library**. This is influenced to no small degree by Wren's Library at Trinity College, Cambridge, but it is differently proportioned. The Library at Queen's has a central feature with pediment and is a two-storeyed building with semicircular leaded window openings. It is a gracious composition and was so successful that Hawksmoor was able to continue his scheme on completing the court and main street façade in the eighteenth century (717).

One other very interesting building at Oxford in this period is that of the **Old Ashmolean**. This was erected in 1678–83 but its authorship is in doubt, though, as in so many instances, it is often ascribed to Wren. It is an attractive small work, rather tucked away near the main road. The detail carving and the doorway are exceptionally good (719).

The bulk of architectural work carried out at **Cambridge** at this time is by **Sir Christopher Wren**. He was responsible for **Pembroke College Chapel**, much of **Emmanuel College**, specifically the **Chapel**, and the **Library** at **Trinity College**. At **Pembroke** the **Chapel** is one of Wren's earliest works, and although an interesting and pleasant building, illustrates his immaturity and inexperience. Work was begun in 1663 and it was the first college chapel in completely classical form. It is a rectangular building of brick with stone facing and Corinthian pilasters. There is a pediment with cartouche and swags and the whole

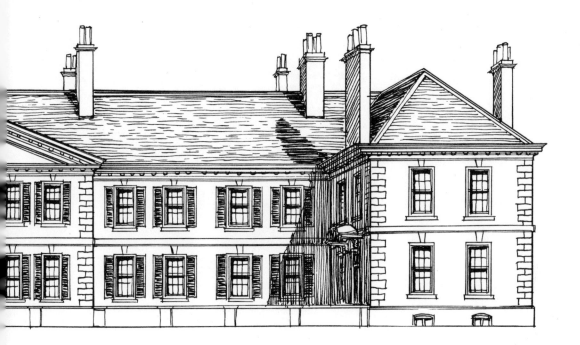

is surmounted by a cupola. Inside, the lower part of the walls is panelled and the ceiling decorated by plasterwork (718, 737, 740, 761, 764).

The **Chapel** at **Emmanuel College** was Wren's third commission carried out in 1666–73. The work still indicates his architectural immaturity; the proportion has not the perfection of his later designs as is shown by the over-heaviness of the cupola and pediment. It is, however, the best part of the college buildings and is designed with a long gallery supported on an open arcade to connect the side ranges. In the centre the chapel front has a large Corinthian order with pediment above (724).

Wren's Library at **Trinity College**, designed 1676–84, is a masterpiece of simple perfection in composition. It is a long rectangular building in two storeys, surmounted by a parapet. The Doric order is used on the lower storey which has an open arcade, and the Ionic order above it, flanking the window openings. The Library sealed off the fourth side in Nevile's Court. The interior, completed in 1695, is magnificently decorated by **Gibbons's** carving, particularly in panels on the bookcases (723, 777).

Further work was carried out at Cambridge at this time at Clare College and St Catharine's. At **Clare** the river front was completed to **Robert Grumbold's** designs and has Ionic pilasters somewhat reminiscent of Trinity College Library. A new court was undertaken at **St Catharine's** in 1674. The **Chapel**, consecrated in 1704, is in simple classical style (720, 722, 739).

726 Winchester College, 1684—school

727 St John's Bridge over the Cam, Cambridge. Late 17th century

OTHER BUILDINGS

There are three noteworthy buildings which are often associated with the name of **Sir Christopher Wren**. The first of these, the **Town Hall** at **Abingdon, Berkshire**, is attributed to Wren, if not certainly at least on sound evidence. Built in 1677–80, the building has a deep cornice with sloping roof, parapet and cupola above. A giant Composite order in pilaster form flanks the window and arcade openings (676). The evidence for the other examples is much less strong, but both are interesting buildings of good classical design. The **School** at **Winchester** built in 1684 is very simple with central pediment and advanced central block (726). **Morden College, Blackheath**, built in 1695 and founded by Sir John Morden, is decorated on the central pediment by the figures of Sir John and his wife. The building is a long, low design, most pleasing in its deep red brick contrasting with the stonework and white paint of the window frames. The central doorway is particularly attractive (725, 754.)

BRIDGES

Two examples are noteworthy: the bridge at **St John's College** over the Cam at **Cambridge** and the **Grand Bridge** over the lake at **Blenheim**. The former, three-arched bridge is by **Hawksmoor**. The parapet is balustraded, while at intervals are set panels embellished with relief sculpture. At the end of the bridge are two piers surmounted by heraldic beasts (727). The park bridge at **Blenheim Palace** is by **Vanbrugh**, and was never completed to his ambitious designs. Even in its unfinished condition it still appears as a pretentious structure to traverse a narrow lake. The stone bridge has a central segmental arch while on either side are narrower semicircular arches. The design reflects the massive scale of the Palace (728).

ARCHITECTURAL FEATURES

Window openings, and **doors** and **doorcases** are illustrated on pages 268 and 269 respectively. Both features are entirely of classical design in this period and numerous examples are available for study. Particularly notable are the designs from Wren's city churches, which vary from the essentially plain and simple to the richer versions with carved, moulded ornamentation and flanked by columns or pilasters. Many examples have an overhanging cornice and/or

728 Vanbrugh's Bridge at Blenheim Palace, Oxfordshire, 1711

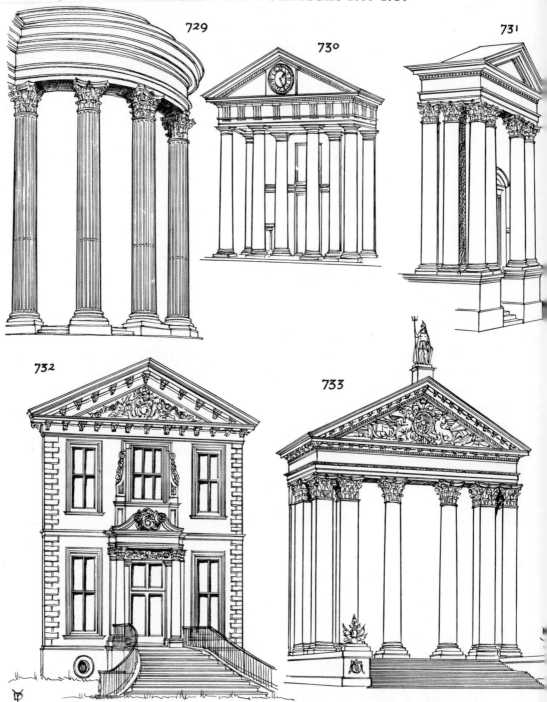

729 St Paul's Cathedral: south porch, 1675–1710. Architect Sir Christopher Wren 730 Royal Hospital, Chelsea: south front portico, 1682–92. Architect Sir Christopher Wren 731 All Saints' Church, Oxford: porch, 1708–9. Architect Henry Aldrich 732 Uppark, Sussex: south front centrepiece, 1688–90. Architect William Talman 733 Blenheim Palace: the north portico, 1705–24. Architect Sir John Vanbrugh

734

735

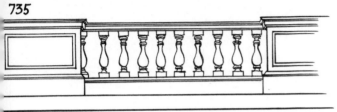

734 Royal Naval College, Greenwich 735 St Margaret Lothbury, London 736 Chatsworth, Derbyshire 737 Pembroke College Chapel, Cambridge 738 St Paul's Cathedral: west front 739 St Catharine's College Chapel, Cambridge

736

739

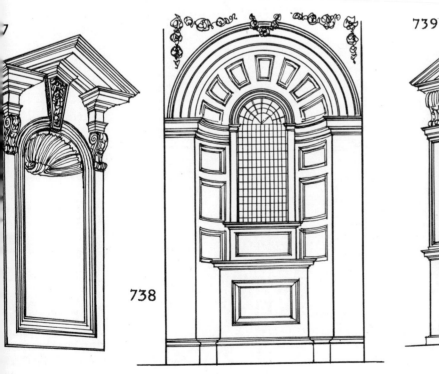

738

WINDOWS 1660-1714

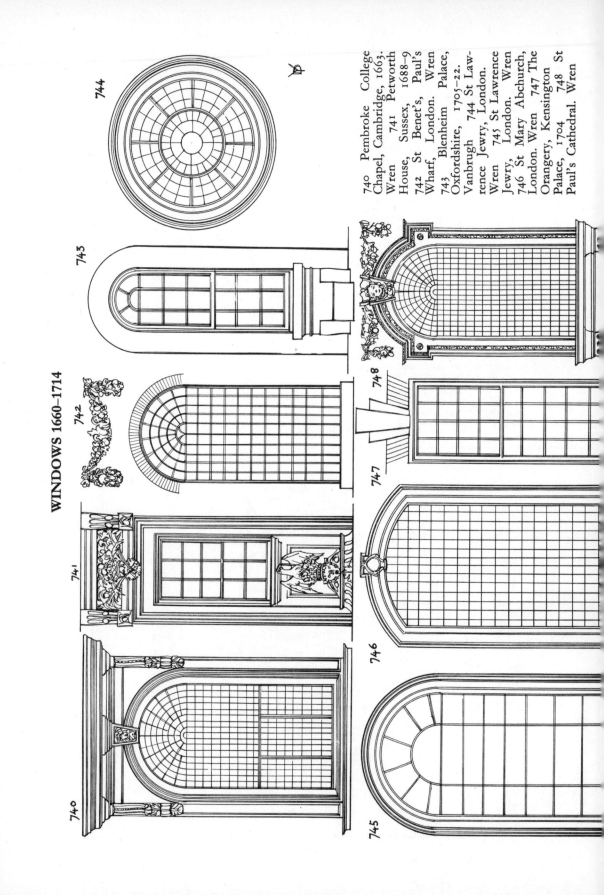

740 Pembroke College Chapel, Cambridge, 1663. Wren 741 Petworth House, Sussex, 1688-9 742 St Benet's, Paul's Wharf, London. Wren 743, Blenheim Palace, Oxfordshire, 1705-22. Vanbrugh 744 St Lawrence Jewry, London. Wren 745 St Lawrence Jewry, London. Wren 746 St Mary Abchurch, London. Wren 747 The Orangery, Kensington Palace, 1704 748 St Paul's Cathedral. Wren

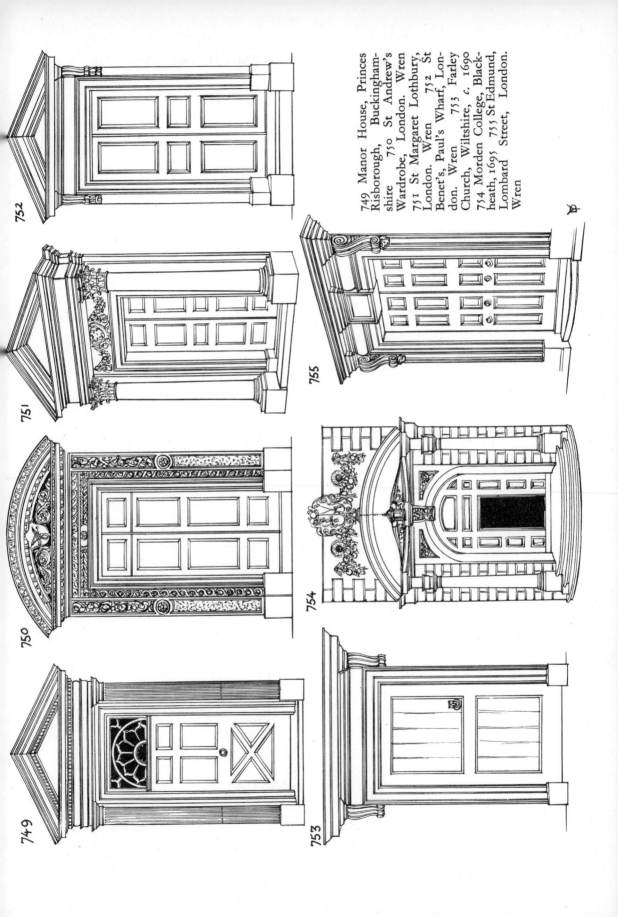

752

751

750

749

755

754

753

749 Manor House, Princes Risborough, Buckinghamshire   750 St Andrew's Wardrobe, London. Wren   751 St Margaret Lothbury, London. Wren   752 St Benet's, Paul's Wharf, London. Wren   753 Farley Church, Wiltshire, c. 1690   754 Morden College, Blackheath, 1695   755 St Edmund, Lombard Street, London. Wren

756 All Saints' Church, Oxford, 1708: Corinthian Order   757 Royal Naval College, Greenwich: colonnade, 1696–1715. Doric Order   758 Chatsworth House, Derbyshire, 1687: Ionic Order 759 St Paul's Cathedral: Corinthian Order. Wren   760 The Orangery, Kensington Palace, 1704: Doric Order   761 Pembroke College Chapel, Cambridge: Corinthian Order base. Wren   762 Blenheim Palace, Oxfordshire: Doric Order. Vanbrugh   763 Hampton Court Palace: Corinthian capital. Wren   764 Pembroke College Chapel, Cambridge: Corinthian capital

765 Morden College, Blackheath, 1695: corbel 766 Uppark, Sussex: entablature and doorway decoration, 1688–9 767 and 770 Chatsworth: finials, 1687 768 Petworth House, Sussex: finial, 1688–9 769 Hampton Court Palace: doorway decoration. Wren 771 The Orangery, Kensington Palace: entablature, 1704 772 St Martin Ludgate: door-head. Wren 773 Carved decoration. Grinling Gibbons 774 Eltham Lodge, Kent: carved staircase panel 775 St Paul's Cathedral: decoration. Wren 776 Typical Wren mouldings 777 Trinity College, Cambridge: panel. Gibbons

778 Carved oak staircase, twisted balusters, 1670–5   779 Carved oak staircase with pierced scroll panel balustrade, 1670–80   780 Open string staircase. Turned balusters—vase shape, 1700   78₁ Stone staircase with wrought iron balustrade, 1700–10

782 Marble fireplace with deep bolection moulding. Carving on chimney-piece in lime wood—Grinling Gibbons's style of work. Picture frame in centre, *c.* 1685–90   783 Carved oak chimney-piece, *c.* 1686–8

pediment supported on columns, pilasters or S-curved corbels. The **casement window** continued in use till late in the seventeenth century, but the frame, transom and mullion were of wood and built into the brickwork or stone surround. By 1680–5 the **sash window** was well established and rapidly superseded the casement pattern in general use (740–55).

The five **Roman orders** were used in architectural design on all forms of building, both in column, half-column and pilaster version. The Doric, Corinthian and Composite orders were most frequently employed and the accuracy of mouldings, proportions and ornament was now established on Roman lines. Detail examples are illustrated in Figs. 756–64.

Ornament also was now entirely in classical form. Natural foliage was employed and, following upon **Grinling Gibbons's** example, a much freer type of carving was adopted.

The designs were open with sprigs of flowers and fruit springing and falling naturally, while birds and animals were frequently introduced. The older, formalised method of floral design was abandoned. **Mouldings** were of classical type—the **cyma recta** and **reversa**, the **dentil**, the **ovolo**, the **fillet**, the **cavetto** and the **corona** were all used frequently, while many were carved with traditional decorative forms such as **egg and dart, bead, acanthus leaf** and **anthemion design**. These decorative forms and mouldings are illustrated in the glossary under 'classical mouldings'. Examples of general ornament and mouldings can be seen in Figs 765–77.

CHAPTER VIII

Early Georgian 1714 - 1760

With the exception of one or two romantic excursions into Gothic design the architecture of this part of the eighteenth century was exclusively classical. Within this concept, there was a certain variation in interpretation, for example, the Baroque of Vanbrugh, Archer and Hawksmoor, and the individual approach of Gibbs; but, predominantly, it was the heyday of the Palladian school. Palladianism was a reaction from both the classicism of Wren and that of the Baroque architects. It was a return to the stricter precepts of Palladio—as evidenced by the name—and the interpretation of Inigo Jones.

The prime movers in establishing this style were members of the aristocracy—Lord Burlington, the Earl of Shaftesbury and Lord Pembroke—and the architects Colin Campbell, William Kent and Giacomo Leoni. The work of these men and their followers is always of a high technical standard and in good taste, but frequently dull. This is partly because they adhered so closely to what they considered to be the correct, ancient classical proportions and construction, while eliminating and suppressing freedom of design and decoration, so that the results are mathematically perfect but artistically cold. This is true of Lord Burlington's work in particular. Buildings designed by Kent and Leoni have more interest as both these men were artists as well as Palladians.

Despite the name Palladian, the architecture of its school is often far removed from that of Palladio himself. It is as if the pupil, in his great anxiety to imitate exactly his master, fails, through over-cautiousness, to achieve the prime purpose of the originator. The essential spark of life, present in the work of most of the Italian classicists of the Renaissance, is lamentably lacking in many of the creations of their English imitators. English Palladianism is based on three sources of inspiration: firstly, upon Vitruvius, who supplied the knowledge of antique classicism in his manuscripts; secondly, upon Palladio himself, who was considered to be the modern exponent of Vitruvius' work and information; and thirdly upon the first English interpreter of this classical theme—Inigo Jones. The results, in the first half of the eighteenth century, were different from all these sources, and, it is to be feared, inferior.

Two factors were greatly influential in determining the architecture of the eighteenth century. One was the custom of sending the sons of the aristocracy and the well-to-do on the Grand Tour of Italy, France and other Continental countries for months and even years. The other was the increasing flood of books and engravings of Continental and British architects published in these years. The aristocratic young men returned from their travels with knowledge gained, and concrete evidence of their studies in the form of antique sculpture and the decorative arts, as well as engravings and drawings of the buildings that they had seen. A number of them designed, often in a dilettante manner, buildings of their own. Others employed and influenced architects of the day. Among the books which had a profound influence on the formation of the Palladian school were *Vitruvius Britannicus*, a folio of 100 engravings of classical buildings in Britain, by **Colin Campbell**; a translation by **Dubois**, illustrated by **Leoni** of Palladio's *I Quattri Libri dell' Architettura*; *Designs of Inigo Jones* by **William Kent**; *Fabbriche Antiche* by **Lord Burlington**; *Designs of Inigo Jones and William Kent* by **Vardy** and, a more individual contribution, **Gibbs's** *Book of Architecture*.

With the aid of such books, many buildings, particularly houses, on classical lines, were put up all over the country by men who were builders rather than architects, for the number of professional architects was still comparatively small. Some of these buildings are dull, some rather heavy and uninspired, but almost all are in good taste and of a high standard of construction. Today we refer to them as Georgian houses and prize them, sometimes rather above their value, perhaps because our standards in the realm of taste have deteriorated.

THE BAROQUE SCHOOL

The work of **Vanbrugh, Hawksmoor** and **Archer** has been considered to some extent in Chapter VII, but many of the achievements of the last two, at least, are pertinent to this section of the eighteenth century also. **Vanbrugh** died in 1726 but continued in practice until this time. Work was still in progress at **Blenheim Palace**, and he succeeded Wren as Surveyor at **Greenwich Hospital** in 1716 and made his architectural contributions there. He designed **Eastbury**, Dorset, from 1716 and **Seaton Delaval** 1720–9. His own house, **Vanbrugh Castle** at **Greenwich**, was begun in 1716. Here he had no fractious client to placate and was able to explore his own ideas without hindrance. On a steeply sloping site he designed his version of a Medieval castle with towers and machicolations (792).

Much of the work upon which **Hawksmoor's** reputation rests was carried out in the eighteenth century. His designs were highly original, with an inventiveness and lively imagination equal to that of Wren, but he never achieved a comparable degree of grace and delicacy. Hawksmoor's architecture showed the massive exuberance of Vanbrugh, but this was tempered by Wren's influence, which remained strong; it had been paramount for so many years of Hawksmoor's working life. To give Hawksmoor his due, his work was always vitally personal and, though showing influence from Wren and Vanbrugh, was entirely his own individual design. The bulk of his contribution to eighteenth-century architecture is at the University and in the ecclesiastical field. At **Oxford** he carried out an extensive rebuilding scheme at **Queen's College** and at **All Souls** (820–2; pp. 293, 295).

In 1716 Hawksmoor was appointed one of the Surveyors for the 50 new churches planned under the Act of 1711 (pp. 290, 293). **Six churches** were built to his designs and all are highly individual, impressive and remarkable in many ways. It is difficult in some instances to see beauty, but they are compelling and refuse to be ignored or overlooked. They comprise **St Alphege, Greenwich, St Anne, Limehouse, St George-in-the-East, Christ Church, Spitalfields, St Mary Woolnoth** and **St George, Bloomsbury**. As four of these are set in London's East End and one in the City, it was inevitable that they should have received severe damage from bombing in the recent war. Due to their massiveness of design and construction, much of the exterior remains, except for St Alphege, which was reduced to a shell (801–804, 817).

Hawksmoor's ecclesiastical work was obviously so original and of such telling standard

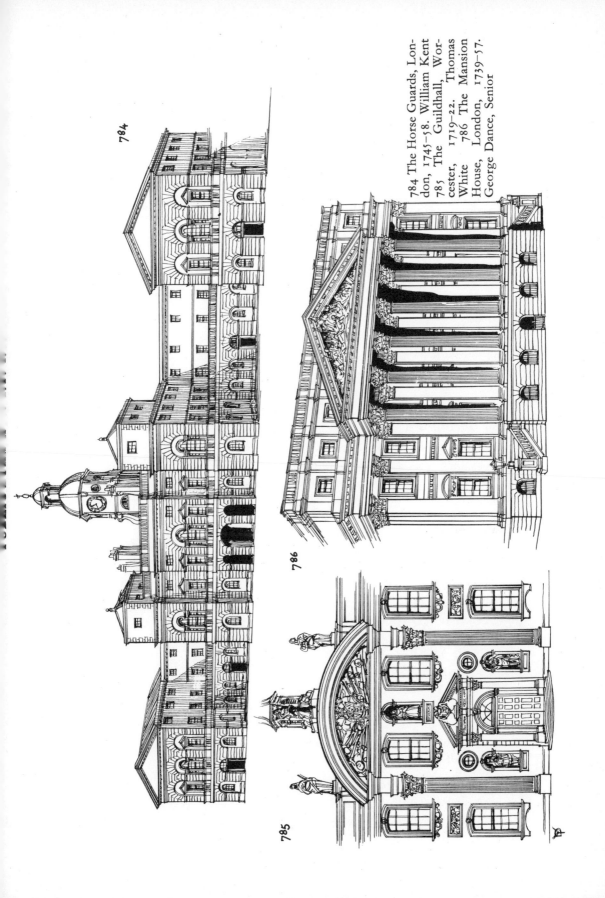

784 The Horse Guards, London, 1745–58. William Kent
785 The Guildhall, Worcester, 1719–22. Thomas White   786 The Mansion House, London, 1739–57. George Dance, Senior

that when Wren died in 1723 Hawksmoor was appointed **Surveyor** at **Westminster Abbey**. Under this Surveyorship the western towers, long under discussion, were at last designed and built. The towers are hardly pure in style, but they have now become a familiar, affectionately regarded, London landmark.

Like Hawksmoor, **Archer's** reputation in eighteenth-century work rests on ecclesiastical architecture. His major design was for **St Philip's, Birmingham**, now the **Cathedral**, 1709–15. In a simplified Baroque manner this large building is finely sited in the middle of a Birmingham square. The tower especially is of interest. Its four faces are concave with belfry openings and twin Corinthian pilasters; the cupola above is graceful and well proportioned (815, 864, 870). The two other churches for which he is known are **St John's, Smith Square, Westminster**, 1721–8, and St Paul's, Deptford, 1730. St John's was gutted in 1940, an event not regretted by many Londoners. It was a massive church, soundly planted in a central position in Smith Square. Of unusual design, it had four large towers and four Baroque elevations (XXXVII). **St Paul's, Deptford**, is in a very different vein. Fortunately it survived the war-time bombing and stands as a graceful building of considerable beauty in pleasant garden surroundings set in a drab district. There is a certain incongruity in the solid body of the church, with its semicircular Doric portico rising to a slender steeple reminiscent of Wren (799, 819, 847).

THE PALLADIANS

Earl of Burlington 1694–1753

Lord Burlington's influence on the eighteenth century in general and on the Palladian school in particular was very great, both as a patron and an artist. He went to Italy in 1714–15 as a young man and on his return became extremely interested in the work of Palladio, as he studied Campbell's *Vitruvius Britannicus*. He went back to Italy in 1719 and spent some months at Vicenza studying Palladio's work there. He met William Kent in Rome, brought him back to England and employed him at Burlington House to carry out decorative painting. He also employed Campbell, whose work he much admired, to transform his Piccadilly home, Burlington House. Gibbs had also worked on the house and later Lord Burlington himself, though much of this joint effort was altered in 1866. Burlington did not design a great deal himself; his chief influence was as a patron of **Kent, Campbell** and **Leoni**, and through them he was largely responsible for the power and influence of the Palladian movement in England. His own work was of professional standard, meticulous in its technical aspect, closely modelled on that of Palladio and Inigo Jones and rather pedantic in approach. In taste it was faultless. Among his designs were the Dormitory at **Westminster School**, 1724, **Stanmer House**, Sussex, 1727, and, with William Kent, he designed and built a **villa** for himself at **Chiswick**, 1727–36. This is modelled closely on Palladio's Villa Capra (the Rotonda) near Vicenza (828). Wings were added by Wyatt in 1788. Lord Burlington's best-known work was the **Assembly Rooms** at **York** where he carefully followed Palladio's 'Egyptian Hall'.

William Kent 1685–1748

Kent was, together with Lord Burlington whose patronage and friendship he enjoyed for some 30 years, the great personality of the Palladian school of architecture in England. He

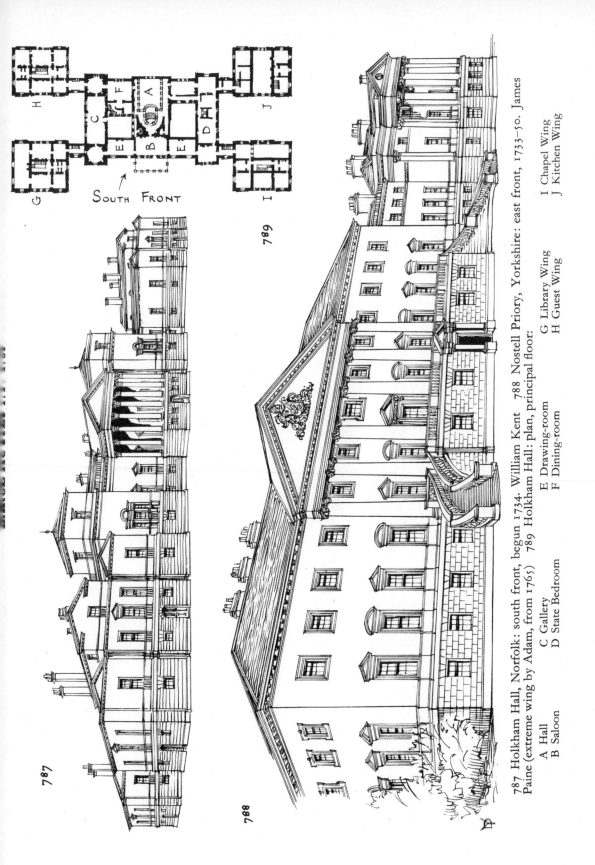

SOUTH FRONT

787

788

789

787 Holkham Hall, Norfolk: south front, begun 1734. William Kent 788 Nostell Priory, Yorkshire: east front, 1733–50. James Paine (extreme wing by Adam, from 1765) 789 Holkham Hall: plan, principal floor:

A Hall
B Saloon

C Gallery
D State Bedroom

E Drawing-room
F Dining-room

G Library Wing
H Guest Wing

I Chapel Wing
J Kitchen Wing

790 Hampton Court Palace: neo-Tudor gateway, 1732.
William Kent

was born at Rotherham in Yorkshire, but came to London, whence he was sent to Italy to study painting. He lived in Rome for nearly 10 years, copying paintings for English patrons. Here, in 1719, he met Lord Burlington and returned to Burlington House with the earl to pass the rest of his life there. At first he was employed to carry out decorative painting, but his work in this field was not outstanding and gradually, under Lord Burlington's guidance, he turned to architecture. Through his patron's influence, he acquired important commissions and became the fashionable architect of the 1730s and 1740s.

In 1734 Kent began work at **Holkham Hall**, Norfolk, a large house of Palladian design (787, 789; XXXIX). In 1742–4 he designed **No. 44 Berkeley Square, London**. This was a successful attempt to make a lavish home inside a London terrace house (833, 851). In 1734 he built the Treasury and in 1745 designed the **Horse Guards, Whitehall**—a project for which he is best remembered. This large-scale work was carried out after his death by Vardy, and is similar in design to Holkham Hall, but with the addition of a clock tower. It is one of the best Palladian buildings extant (784, 859).

Kent's architectural work was rather severe and plain. He used rustication widely and his buildings were arranged in simple, well-proportioned masses. Occasionally he essayed attempts at Gothic or Tudor, as at Hampton Court Palace where he designed a companion Tudor gatehouse to the existing one (790). Kent is also renowned for his interests in other fields and his idea that an architect should also design the interior decoration, chimney-piece and furniture for the rooms of his buildings. He designed a great deal of furniture and was also influential in the development of the less formal layout in landscape gardening of the eighteenth century. This was a necessary complement to the severe house designs of the Palladian architects.

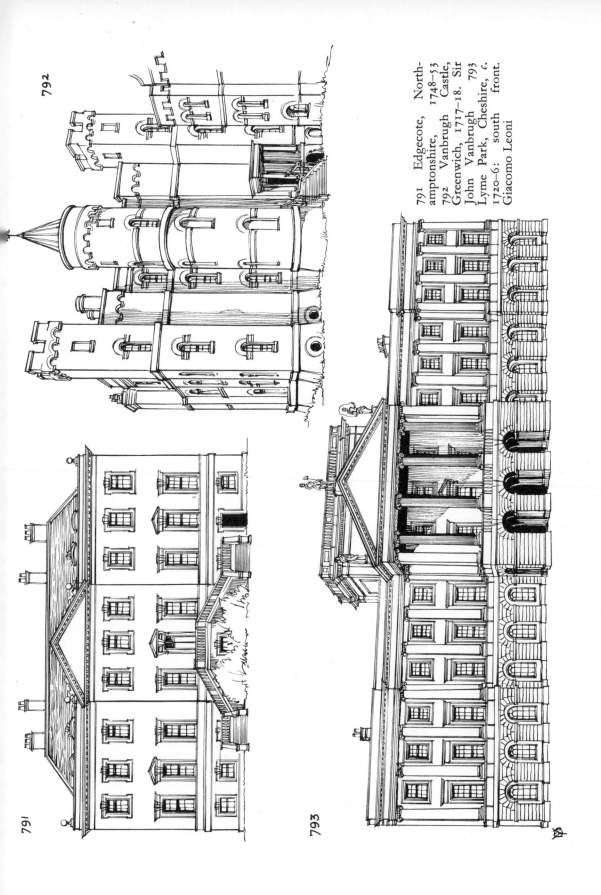

791

792

793

791 Edgecote, North-
amptonshire, 1748–53
792 Vanbrugh Castle,
Greenwich, 1717–18. Sir
John Vanbrugh 793
Lyme Park, Cheshire, c.
1720–6: south front.
Giacomo Leoni

Colin Campbell, d. 1729

Little is known of Campbell's early life until he was commissioned by the Earl of Burlington to remodel **Burlington House, Piccadilly**, in 1717. Just previous to this he had brought out the first edition of his *Vitruvius Britannicus* in which he published a series of plates of works of English architects including many of his own designs. It was this publication that attracted Lord Burlington's attention to his work. He subsequently published two more editions in 1717 and 1725. The main idea was to advertise his own work, but he also performed a great service to architecture by the publication of so many plates of well-known buildings, although their standard was uneven. He modelled his own work very much on that of Palladio and Inigo Jones, and was obviously a Palladian even before Lord Burlington. His villa at Mereworth—**Mereworth Castle** in Kent—is, like Lord Burlington's Chiswick House, based on Palladio's Villa Capra at Vicenza, but it is a closer facsimile than Lord Burlington's design. Ideal though the villa may be for the valley of the Po, it is highly unsuitable for the English climate, with its central hall under a dome 60 feet high and 38 feet in diameter (829). Campbell designed a number of houses of various sizes. Among these were **Newby**, Yorkshire, 1720, square in plan and very Palladian; **Wanstead**, Essex, 1720, an extensive house with a frontage of 260 feet, which was demolished in 1824; and **Houghton Hall**, Norfolk, designed in **1721** for Sir Robert Walpole, and built in the decade up to 1730, a very large house with a central block connected by colonnades to two smaller blocks, the total frontage being 450 feet (XL).

Giacomo Leoni, *c.* 1686–1746

Leoni was a Venetian and came to England to superintend the publication of an English edition of *Palladio*, which appeared in 1715–16 in two volumes. The translation was by **Dubois** but Leoni had spent some years in preparing the illustrations. Second and third editions were published in 1721 and 1742. In 1726, sponsored by Lord Burlington, Leoni published his three-volume translation of *Alberti's* architecture. Leoni remained in England until his death in 1746, but does not appear to have received any public appointment here, although he was responsible for a number of buildings. Among these are **Lyme Park**, Cheshire, **1720–30**, where he designed the south front portico and made other alterations (793, 844, 860); **Queensberry House, Burlington Gardens**, 1721 (reconstructed and altered 1792) (834), and **Clandon Park**, near **Guildford**, 1731–5 (830). Leoni's work was Palladian in style, but less severe and more lively than that of some of his colleagues.

James Gibbs 1682–1754

Gibbs was the most outstanding architect of the first half of the eighteenth century; his work was independent of both the Baroque school and of the Palladians. He was not an innovator, but he showed great brilliance of technical skill in the handling of his materials and in architectural design. As a young man he left Scotland and travelled on the Continent for some time. Later he was accepted in Rome at the Studio of Fontana, who was then at work on St Peter's. Gibbs worked in Rome during the years 1707–9 and thus had the advantage over his British colleagues of having studied both in practice and theory at the fountain-head.

His first important commission on his return to England was the church of **St Mary-le-**

796

795

794

794 St Clement Danes, The Strand. Designed by Wren 1684; steeple by Gibbs 1719 795 St Mary-le-Strand, 1714–17 796 St Martin-in-the-Fields, Trafalgar Square, 1722

Strand, in **London**, 1714–17. Here Gibbs showed himself to be the inheritor of the Wren tradition in classicism. The steeple, in particular, illustrates this clearly, as does also the masterly treatment of the double-stage order. His church reflects his Italian work and style and this influence was not too well received at the time; succeeding generations have appreciated the church more fully (795). In 1719 Gibbs was given the task of completing the neighbouring church of **St Clement Danes**. A Wren church, this was finished by Gibbs from the entablature below the clock upwards, by the addition of a steeple very much in the Wren manner. Unfortunately this church suffered considerable damage during the war, but it is now restored as the Royal Air Force Church (794).

Continuing his ecclesiastical work, Gibbs then designed the chapel, now the church of **St Peter**, in **Vere Street**, in 1721 and went on in **1722–6** to his masterpiece, **St Martin-in-the-Fields**, in **Trafalgar Square**. Without question this is one of the most important buildings of this period and certainly the finest church of the time. Its influence was profound and widespread. Copies, and designs obviously inspired by it, can be seen not only in England (for example, Mereworth Church, Kent), but especially in the U.S.A. where a number of churches in different States were erected to 'Gibbs's designs'. At first, Gibbs designed a circular church, after the Wren city church principle, but this was not carried out, owing to the high cost. The present church has a magnificent Corinthian portico and this order is continued round the building in pilaster form. The steeple displays Gibbs's outstanding mastery of this difficult feature and shows him a worthy successor to Wren in this field. An Ionic order in pilaster form is used on the belfry stage, while above comes the clock, and then a repetition of the Corinthian order before commencing the spire itself. To save space and to provide a compact design, Gibbs built the tower inside the west wall so that it came out from the roof. This is in contradistinction to Wren and Hawksmoor, who had always followed the earlier method of placing the steeple as an adjunct to the church, with the tower base firmly planted on the ground. Gibbs, and the many eighteenth-century architects who followed his idea, have been criticised for this, on the grounds that the tower emerges awkwardly from the portico. Constructionally the method appears quite sound and aesthetically it does not seem to offend. Inside, the church has five bays and is aisled. The ceiling is barrel-vaulted with elliptical section, and the decoration was carried out in plaster by the Italian craftsmen **Artari** and **Bugatti**. The work is of exceptionally high standard (XXXVIII). Enough time had been spent on design and construction and there resulted a quality of workmanship which had not often been reached in Wren's city churches owing to the great haste in which they were erected (796, 816, 866).

Gibbs carried out further ecclesiastical work at **All Saints', Derby** (now the Cathedral), 1725, but here the Gothic tower was retained and the Gothic/classical marriage is not entirely fortunate. His last church was that of **St Nicholas** in his home town of **Aberdeen**. This was also his last commission, begun in 1752. It was a simple design using the Ionic order.

From 1722 onwards Gibbs was much occupied with University work, largely at **Cambridge**. Here he designed the **Senate House**, 1722, the **Fellows' Building** at **King's College**, 1724, and, at **Oxford**, the **Radcliffe Camera**, 1739–49 (823–5, 854; pp. 295, 298). His fame rests far more on his public buildings—in which his skill and brilliance showed to greatest advantage—than in the domestic sphere. Here, his work is sound and well designed though, perhaps, less stimulating. One charming example is **Sudbrooke Lodge**,

797 St George, Hanover Square, 1713–14. John James   798 St Leonard's, Shoreditch, 1736–40.
George Dance, Senior   799 St. Paul's, Deptford, 1730. Thomas Archer   800 St Giles-in-the-Fields, 1731–3. Henry Flitcroft

LONDON CHURCHES, 1714–1730. ARCHITECT NICHOLAS HAWKSMOOR

801 St Anne, Limehouse, 1714–24   802 Christ Church, Spitalfields, c. 1725   803 St George, Bloomsbury, 1720–30   804 St Mary Woolnoth, 1716–27

XXXVII St John's Church, Smith Squ
London, 1714–28. Architect Thomas A

Petersham, Surrey, built in 1718, and now a golf club house. Here, there is a central, flat portico in the Corinthian order, with two columns and two pilasters; a balustraded staircase is designed as an approach. There are two main floors with emphasis on the *piano nobile*, and in the centre a balustraded parapet (827). A larger house is that of **Ditchley**, Oxfordshire, 1720–2, and here the design verges on the Palladian. It is typical of his work in this field, and certainly less impressive and stylistic than his churches.

Although Gibbs is accepted to be 'the man who walked alone', in that he subscribed neither to Hawksmoor's and Vanbrugh's Baroque or Burlington's Palladian school, his influence on later generations of architects was profound. This influence was transmitted partly by his published works, in particular, *A Book of Architecture*, 1728, and *Rules for drawing the several parts of Architecture*, 1732. His name is often coupled with that of Wren, for, alone among his outstanding architectural contemporaries, he was not averse to utilising Wren as a source of inspiration. He studied and was influenced by the work of several architects and schools but remained always an independent individualist.

LESSER ARCHITECTS

John James, 1672–1746, carried out work both at Greenwich Hospital and at St Paul's. He later became one of the surveyors for the building of the 50 new churches. In this connection may be found his best and most famous work, the church of **St George, Hanover Square, London**, 1713–24. The portico with six Corinthian columns is particularly impressive and the cupola-topped tower is competently designed (797, 850, 871, 872, 875). He was also responsible for **St Mary's, Twickenham**, 1713–14, where he built a church on to the fifteenth-century tower, and he completed the tower for Hawksmoor's **St Alphege, Greenwich**.

The chief contributions of **George Dance I, 1698–1768**, were in the City of London, where he was Clerk of the City Works from 1733 until his death. His best-known public building is the **Mansion House, 1739–53**. Not an outstanding building, the Mansion House does, however, stand out from the surrounding architecture (for example, the Royal Exchange), as being competently designed, proportioned and in good taste. The principal elevation comprises a rusticated basement storey which supports a Corinthian pilastered order, with balustraded parapet above. There is a projecting portico with six columns sustaining entablature and pediment (786). Among his churches are **St Luke's, Old Street**, 1732, **St Leonard's, Shoreditch**, 1736–40, **St Matthias, Bethnal Green**, 1741 and **St Botolph, Aldgate**, 1749–50. At St Luke's Dance conceived the unusual idea of adapting an obelisk into a steeple. His most successful church is undoubtedly St Leonard's, Shoreditch, with a steeple reminiscent of St Mary-le-Bow (798, 852, 863).

Following upon Lord Burlington and William Kent came a further group of Palladian designers among whom should be mentioned **Isaac Ware, Henry Flitcroft** and **John Vardy**, while the school was consolidated by a second generation of architects led by **Sir Robert Taylor** and **James Paine**, whose work was largely carried out in the 1760s (788; also Chapter IX).

Isaac Ware, *d*. 1766, is said to have begun his working life as a chimney-sweep. Later he developed his talent for drawing and held various public offices. His best-known work is

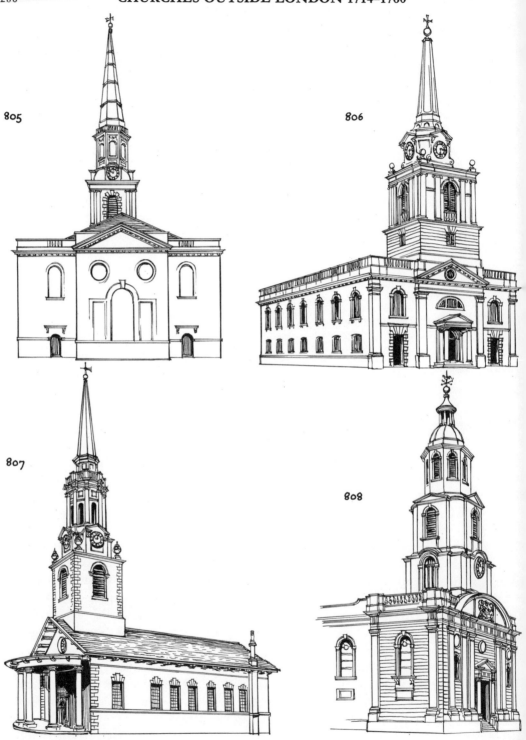

805 St John's, Wolverhampton, 1755–60. William Baker 806 Daventry Church, 1752. William and David Hiorn 807 Mereworth, Kent, 1744–6 808 St Nicholas', Worcester, 1726–30. Thomas White

809 Honiley, Warwickshire, 1723   810 Knutsford, Cheshire, 1744   811 Berkley, Somerset, 1751
812 Blandford, Dorset, 1731–9. John Bastard

Wrotham Park, Middlesex, 1754, which is typically Palladian in pattern. He also designed **Chesterfield House**, 1749, a number of houses in **Dover Street, Hanover Square** and **South Audley Street**, and **Oxford Town Hall** in 1754. Most of this building is now destroyed. In 1756 he published his book *A Complete Body of Architecture*.

Henry Flitcroft, 1697–1769, was a draughtsman for Lord Burlington and later held office as Comptroller. His work was competent but often rather dull. His best known church is that of **St Giles-in-the-Fields**, 1731–3, which he based partly on Wren's work on city churches and largely on Gibbs's St Martin-in-the-Fields. St Giles is less graceful and has no portico, but possesses a tall, elegant steeple which, unfortunately, changes scale too suddenly in the middle (800). He also designed **St Olave's, Tooley Street**, 1737–9 and **St John's, Hampstead**, 1745–7. In the domestic sphere he carried out extensive work at the mansion of **Wentworth Woodhouse** in Yorkshire, *c.* 1740.

John Vardy, *d.* 1765, worked for many years in the King's Works at Greenwich, Hampton Court Palace, Whitehall and Kensington and was closely associated with William Kent. It was after Kent's death in 1748 that Vardy erected the Horse Guards in Whitehall to Kent's designs. He himself designed **Spencer House**, 1756–65.

CHURCHES

It was in 1711 that an Act of Parliament was passed providing for the building of 50 new churches to accommodate parishioners in the expanding suburbs of **London**. This number of churches was not built under the administration set up under the Act, and only a dozen were completed at this time. The two surveyors appointed were Hawksmoor and William Dickinson. The latter was soon replaced by James Gibbs, who in turn was succeeded by John James. **Gibbs's** contribution, as has been described, was **St Martin-in-the-Fields** (796, 816) and **James's** was also one church, **St George, Hanover Square** (797).

By far the largest contribution—six churches—was made by **Hawksmoor**, and his reputation as an architect stands, in no small measure, upon these highly original designs. They are all different, individual conceptions and show vitality and power. They may be criticised for their over-heaviness, especially in the steeples. They lack any sense of grace or delicacy, but provide London with some impressive and most individualistic churches, which unfortunately suffered extensive damage by bombing.

Of the six churches, **St Alphege, Greenwich**, 1712–14, in which the Doric order was used, was unfortunately reduced to a shell during the war. **St Mary Woolnoth**, 1716–27, is the only city church among the six. It is a most original design set upon a square plan. It has a solid-looking, rectangular tower with Corinthian columns in the centre stage. Much of the lower section of the church is rusticated (804). **St Anne's, Limehouse**, 1712–24, has a tall, semicircular porch at one end. The tower rises by diminishing stages to a final multi-sided top feature (801). **St George-in-the-East**, 1715–23, whose interior was badly damaged 1941, has an extremely substantial tower with a weighty upper feature, again multi-sided (817). **Christ Church, Spitalfields**, 1723–9, is the most individualistic of the group. Here, a rectangular tower of great width ascends to a Medieval-styled spire. The projecting porch is in the Doric order with a semicircular arch above it. Like all these other churches, it is large and capacious (802). **St George, Bloomsbury**, 1720–30, is the only church of the six

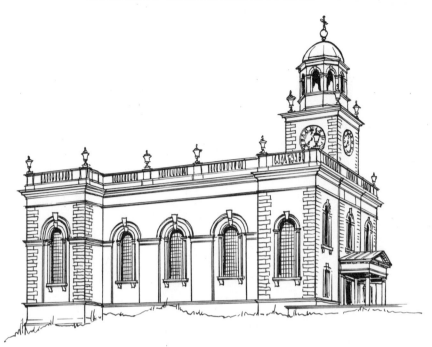

813 Great Witley Church, Worcestershire, 1735

814 Galby Church, Leicestershire, 1741. Wing of Leicester

815 St Philip, Birmingham (now the Cathedral), 1709–15. Thomas Archer (tower finished 1725)
816 St Martin-in-the-Fields, 1722. James Gibbs   817 St George-in-the-East, London, 1715.
Nicholas Hawksmoor   818 St Thomas's, Stourbridge, 1726   819 St Paul's, Deptford, 1730.
Thomas Archer.

built in London's West End. Erected on a square plan, it has a giant Corinthian portico raised on a podium with central steps. The tower is set at the side of the church and the steeple rises in stepped pyramidal form to the statue of King George at the top (803).

Among the other churches built in London under the Act were **St Giles-in-the-Fields** (800; p. 290), **St George's, Southwark**, 1734–6, designed by John Price (861), **St Luke's, Old Street**, by George Dance I (852, 863; p. 287), and **St Paul's Church, Deptford**, and **St John's Church, Westminster**, designed by Archer (799, 819, 847; XXXVII; p. 277).

The greatest influence on the designs of **churches outside London** was Gibbs's work on St Martin-in-the-Fields. This type of church made a wide appeal to provincial architects, far more so than Hawksmoor's style of work. Two very close versions of this pattern are to be seen at **Mereworth**, Kent, 1744–6, a charming country church (807) and **St John's Church, Wolverhampton**, 1755–60 (805). Work of good quality and sound construction with varied design is shown in churches all over the country by provincial architects. There is, for example, the work of **Thomas White** at **Worcester**, as evidenced both in his church of **St Nicholas**, 1726–30, and his **Guildhall**, 1719–22 (785, 808, 856, 858, 869, 880). At **Blandford** in Dorset is work by **John Bastard** of that town. Blandford was largely destroyed by fire in 1731 and Bastard built much of the new town which included the church, 1731–9. This is indeed a good architectural example for a country church (812). At **Daventry** is the church by **William** and **David Hiorn**, 1752, with a fine porch and west end but a rather too heavy, square tower which abruptly diminishes into an over-slender spire (806, 845).

Among the simpler designs, generally with a square tower, are the country churches at **Knutsford**, Cheshire, 1744 (810, 853, 857), **Berkley**, Somerset, 1751 (811), **Honily**, Warwickshire, 1723 (809), **St Thomas's, Stourbridge**, 1726 (818) and **Great Witley**, Worcestershire, 1735 (813). **Galby Church**, Leicestershire, 1741, is designed by **Wing of Leicester** and illustrates an early example of the eighteenth-century approach to Gothic design in the lighthearted marriage of Gothic and classical features in one building (814).

THE UNIVERSITIES

A number of extensive new and rebuilding schemes were carried out at **Oxford** in this period. The largest of these were at The Queen's College, All Souls and the Radcliffe Library. The two principal architects involved were Hawksmoor and Gibbs.

The scheme for rebuilding **The Queen's College** was set in motion in the late seventeenth century with the building of the Library by Hawksmoor (Chapter VII). In **1709** work was begun under **Hawksmoor** for rebuilding the front quad. The plan conceived the erection of a hall and chapel as a symmetrical block with a residential wing on each side, to advance towards the High Street, while the fourth side of the quad, fronting the High, would be filled by a screen and gateway. The hall and chapel block have a central, pedimental feature in the Doric order, while Doric pilasters are continued across the whole elevation. In the centre rises a cupola reminiscent of Wren's design at Chelsea Hospital (820). The screen on to the High Street is terminated at each end by the tall wing elevations, each with surmounting pediment, and these elevations are joined by a rusticated screen which has ten niches placed at regular intervals. In the centre is the gateway, flanked on each side by twin, rusticated Doric columns, and above the entablature is set a large cupola (822, 877). This work at The Queen's College by Hawksmoor, carried on until after his death, is the most

820 Queen's College, Oxford: front quadrangle, 1709–59   821 All Souls College, Oxford: north quadrangle, 1716–34   822 Queen's College, Oxford: façade on to the 'High', 1709–24

typical work in eighteenth-century Baroque at Oxford, and represents some of the finest eighteenth-century architecture at the University.

Nicholas Hawksmoor was also responsible for the rebuilding at **All Souls College, 1716–34.** In 1710 Christopher Codrington, Fellow of the College, died and left his library and money for housing it to his college. It was decided to rebuild the quadrangle with the Library on the north side and a hall and chapel on a different elevation. Hawksmoor was asked to make and carry out designs for this, but, whereas at The Queen's College the medieval buildings had been demolished to make way for a classical scheme, at All Souls Hawksmoor was requested to design in Gothic to fit in with the existing work. The whole quadrangle is thus in the Gothic pattern. The main layout of the design is fairly conventional with tall traceried windows separated by buttresses which have decorative finials set at intervals along the battlemented top of the wall. An arcaded screen with central gateway fronts the High. Hawksmoor's approach here was comparatively modest though not in the true spirit of medieval Gothic. On the fourth side, he erected two large towers, planned on the basis of a Medieval gateway but in this instance, the gateway is absent. As Gothic architecture they are ludicrous, but viewed simply as Hawksmoor architectural design they are majestic and possess a powerful, interesting silhouette, almost on cathedral scale (821).

The third great work of this period at Oxford was **The Radcliffe Library, 1739–49.** Dr Radcliffe died in 1714 leaving the money to build a library at Oxford. Several leading architects were considered for the work but eventually a design by Hawksmoor was preferred. However, due to protracted negotiations over the site and architectural design, Hawksmoor died before the work was begun. **Gibbs** was therefore asked to carry out the project, which he did, in his own interpretation of Hawksmoor's design. Only the basis of the work was provided by the Hawksmoor plan; the approach and handling was entirely in the vein of Gibbs. The building, which is Gibbs's most famous work after St Martin-in-the-Fields, is the finest in Oxford of its period. It is circular, surmounted by a dome, and has a rusticated lower storey and a Corinthian order for the central band. The interior is somewhat elaborate, but, like St Martin-in-the-Fields, is richly decorated in plasterwork by Artari and Bugatti. Eight piers and arches support the drum and dome (823).

Other examples of the first half of the eighteenth century in Oxford include the **Library, Peckwater Quad, Christ Church** where Dean Aldrich's plans for the completion of the quad were carried out after his death. The designs were by **Dr George Clarke** of All Souls. **Worcester College**, having obtained its Charter in 1714, was built over a long period in the eighteenth century. **Clarke** designed most of this but died in 1736 before the work was complete. A more important work is the **Clarendon Building** at Oxford, originally built as the University Printing House in 1713–14. It was designed by Hawksmoor and is a robust classical building with a giant Doric portico and pediment (826, 846).

In **Cambridge** the two most important building projects at this time were both by Gibbs—the Senate House and the Fellows' Building at King's College. **The Senate House, 1722–30,** is one of the finest classical buildings in the university and ranks with Wren's Library at Trinity in this respect. It was originally designed to be only one wing of a three-sided, open court, but the rest of the scheme was never carried out. A giant Corinthian order is used, in pilaster form across the façade, but as part columns in the central portico. The proportions are excellent and the treatment dignified (825).

UNIVERSITY ARCHITECTURE 1714–1760

823 The Radcliffe Camera, Oxford, 1739–48. Architect, James Gibbs 824 Fellows' Building, King's College, Cambridge, 1724. Architect, James Gibbs 825 The Senate House, Cambridge, 1722–30. Architect, James Gibbs 826 The Clarendon Building, Oxford, 1713–15

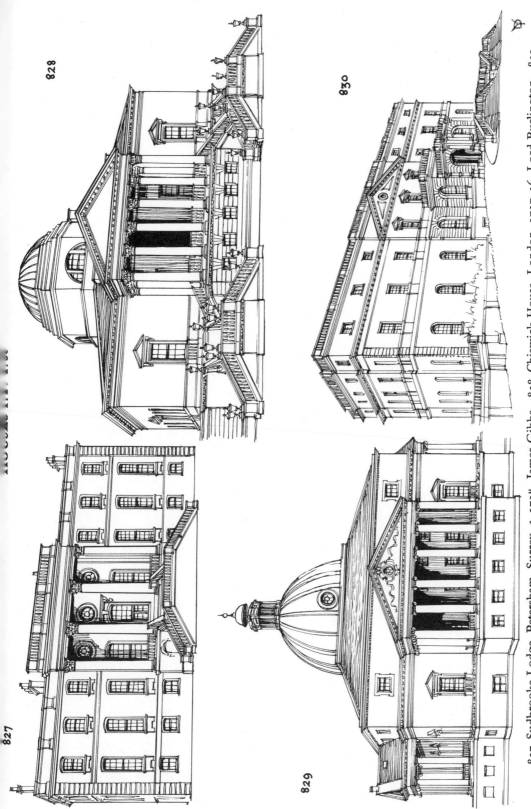

827

828

830

829

827 Sudbrooke Lodge, Petersham, Surrey, c. 1718. James Gibbs   828 Chiswick House, London, 1727–36. Lord Burlington   829 Mereworth Castle, Kent, 1723. Colin Campbell   830 Clandon Park, Guildford, Surrey, 1731–5. Giacomo Leoni (19th-century porch)

The Fellows' Building at King's, 1724, is almost as fine as the Senate House. Here the central feature consists of a Doric entrance gateway with an open archway through it; above is a semicircular window. The whole is enclosed in a slightly projecting, pedimented feature. Apart from this central note, the remainder of the long building is plain, with rustication on the ground floor only (824, 854).

DOMESTIC BUILDINGS

Large Houses

With very few exceptions houses were all built in classical style and the predominant influence was Palladian. In larger houses an order was introduced in the form of a portico, or perhaps a central feature without a projection. A pediment was generally set above the entablature. The ground floor was usually rusticated; excessive prominence was given to the *piano nobile* where the height of rooms had been increased, sometimes disproportionately to the whole. The importance of the main interior staircase decreased as access to the principal floor was generally by means of an exterior approach, with balustraded stone staircase. Two of the very large houses of the period are **Holkham Hall**, Norfolk, begun in **1734** and designed by **William Kent**, and **Houghton Hall** in the same county, designed in **1721** for Sir Robert Walpole by **Colin Campbell**. Both are Palladian houses on the grand scale, with impressive entrance halls (787, 789; XXXIX, XL). At **Lyme Park** in Cheshire, **Giacomo Leoni** carried out extensive alterations in 1720–30. Of particular note is the south portico, where the Ionic order is used above three rusticated archways (793, 844, 860). A further example is at **Nostell Priory**, Yorkshire, largely carried out by **James Paine** in the years 1733–50, although Adam added a wing in the 1760s. The east elevation here is simple but extensive; there is a double stairway leading up to the main floor, which has a central, Ionic order in half columns, surmounted by a pediment (788).

Among the examples of **smaller houses** are the two versions of Palladio's Vicenza villa— the Rotonda—one by **Campbell** at **Mereworth** (829) and the other by **Lord Burlington, Chiswick House** (828). There is **Edgecote House**, Northamptonshire, 1748–53, a symmetrical and typical example with pleasant aspect (791) and **Clandon Park** near **Guildford**, designed by **Leoni** in 1731–5 (830). Here, a porch has been added at a later date, although the entrance flight of steps is of the earlier period. In contrasting styles are **Gibbs's Sudbrooke Lodge** (827), a beautiful example of eighteenth-century domestic classicism at its best, and **Vanbrugh's** castle Gothic at **Vanbrugh Castle, Greenwich** (792).

Town Houses

The influence of the design of larger country houses is now adapted to the town house. In the latter instance, the building is necessarily taller and narrower, but there is the same insistence on predominance for the first floor, where an order is indicated if not built. Where the order is actually designed, it extends up from the first floor, through two or three storeys to support the entablature above; surmounting this is usually an attic floor; if there is no order, its non-existence is noted by a horizontal band at first floor level. This Palladian style of town house was in general use, first in London, and later in other large towns, from about 1730 onwards until the early nineteenth century. Examples built prior to 1760 include

XXXIX   Holkham Hall, Norfolk: the hall, begun 1734. Architect William K

831 No. 68 The Close, Salisbury, *c.* 1735–40   832 The Circus, Bath. Architects, the Woods. Three
Orders used. Begun 1754   833 No. 44 Berkeley Square, London, 1744–5. Architect, William Kent
834 Queensberry House, London, 1721. Architect, Giacomo Leoni (incorporates later work)

Houghton Hall, Norfolk; the stone hall, 1721–30.
hitect Colin Campbell; plasterwork by Artari

Queensberry House, Burlington Gardens (later altered and now the Bank of Scotland) designed by **Leoni** in 1721 (834), **No. 44 Berkeley Square**, designed by **William Kent**, 1744–5 (833), and **No. 68, The Close, Salisbury**, *c.* 1735–40 (831).

Street Planning

It was in this period that there was initiated, on a considerable scale, the designing of houses by the street and not merely individually or in groups or two or three. This had been tried before in isolated instances, but from 1740 to 1760 town expansion began to go forward at a speed which made this method architecturally desirable. Thus, ground landlords began to let their sites in a larger block instead of space adequate for only one or two houses. A few London streets and squares were built in this way, for example, part of Grosvenor Square, but the primary experiment at this time was made in Bath in Somerset.

In the early years of the eighteenth century **Bath** was still a small town. It was between 1720 and 1730 that the value of its waters was rediscovered and popularised for their medical properties. With royal support and patronage, Bath soon became fashionable as a summer health and amusement resort; a redesigning of its architecture was imminent. The leading personality in this replanning was **John Wood I**, 1704–54. Wood had designed buildings in London and in the north of England, but in 1727 he moved to Bath and lived there for the rest of his life. By his work he helped to revive the popularity of Bath stone from the local quarries. He had a masterly conception of town planning in terraces, streets and squares. He did not visualise houses simply as individual units but as part of a complete architectural

835 Queen Square, Bath, 1728–35. John Wood, Senior

Plate 5   Hatfield House, Hertfordshire, 1607–11: the south

layout for the city. He built **Queen Square** in **1728–35**. The entire square is designed in the Palladian manner. In the aspect illustrated in Fig. 835 can be seen the Corinthian order used in pilaster form along the whole elevation, two storeys in height, and changing to columns for the central, pedimented feature.

Wood discovered something of the Roman history of the city and planned ambitious layouts, including a sports arena and a forum. From the former idea comes the famous **Circus**. The sports arena idea was abandoned owing to the unsuitable climate, but the Circus represents a landmark in the history of English town architecture. Here is a circle of 33 houses, divided at three points by incoming streets. The design is repeated in identical manner all round the circle and comprises three stages using different orders—Doric for the ground floor, Ionic for the centre and Corinthian for the top stage (832, 868, 873; XLIII). This simple but great conception was not completed in John Wood's lifetime, but work went on into the 1760s under his son John Wood II. Wood also built **South Parade** in 1743,

836 Liverpool Town Hall, 1748–55. The Woods of Bath

837 Palladian Bridge at Wilton Park, Wiltshire, 1736-7

which was to have been an essential part of his forum. This did not, however, succeed as an enterprise and the Parade today is pleasant, though not inspiring.

The influence of these examples of terrace architecture in Bath was far-reaching and encouraged architects in London and many other towns, for example, Brighton, Cheltenham and Hastings, in the second half of the eighteenth century and Regency period, to develop the theme when presented with the opportunity, in the rapidly expanding urban areas. John Wood II went on in the Bath district to explore the possibilities of his father's ideas, after the latter's death in 1754, and was responsible for some good and interesting work there (see Chapter IX). One other architectural enterprise by the Woods, which illustrates their capabilities in the field of public building, can be seen in **Liverpool Town Hall**, 1748–55. This is one of the early examples of such public edifices which became commonplace in the nineteenth century. The Liverpool example, however, retains the eighteenth-century

838 Queens' College, Cambridge: timber bridge, designed 1749–50. (This example is a modern replica)

839–43 Early Georgian staircases

approach to classicism in its proportion and treatment, and despite the city grime, has not developed into the massive monumentality of its later counterparts. It has a rusticated lower storey and a central Corinthian portico surmounted by a pediment. Above this rises a large drum and cupola with use of the same order (836).

BRIDGES

There is a scarcity of good bridges built at this time. In Palladian vein can be seen the covered bridge in **Wilton Park**, Wiltshire, 1736–7, which has an Ionic colonnade supporting entablature and roof (837). There is also the modern copy of the teak **Mathematical Bridge** at **Queens' College, Cambridge**, over the Cam. This truss bridge was designed by **James Essex** in 1749 (838). Perhaps the most beautiful bridge is that at **Pont-y-Pridd** in Glamorganshire, *c.* 1750. Here is a simple, broad, single-spanned bridge built by William Edwards.

844 Lyme Park, Cheshire: south front, portico, 1720–6. Giacomo Leoni   845 Daventry Church,
1752: porch. William and David Hiorn   846 The Clarendon Building, Oxford, 1715: north façade,
portico   847 St Paul's Church, Deptford, 1730: portico. Thomas Archer

ARCHITECTURAL FEATURES

Staircases were of wood or stone with wood or, usually narrower, iron handrails. Open string staircases were usual with slenderer newels and balusters. Spiral or barley sugar balusters were most common, often arranged in groups of two or three. The ends of the treads might be decoratively carved (839–43).

For **doorways** the classical pattern prevailed throughout, generally in impeccable Palladian proportions and detail. The more elaborate examples were flanked by columns or pilasters and had an entablature and pediment or lunette above. The carved ornament was almost invariably of high standard and was generous in scale. The earlier **doors** were still in two panels, but towards 1750, mahogany replaced the previous use of oak or pine, and doors were six-panelled (849–56).

Chimney-pieces varied immensely from monumental marble designs to quite simple pilastered types. The later, Rococo chimney-pieces were generally carved in pine and then painted; mirrors were incorporated into the design (865).

Windows, like the other architectural features, were in classical vein. Domestic patterns were generally rectangular, with six or nine rectangular panes to each half of the sash window. Circular windows were still employed in ecclesiastical building. In the more elaborate examples, as in Kent's Horse Guards in Whitehall, an outer arch enclosed the use of an order

848 Trumpington Street entrance, Peterhouse, Cambridge, 1751

and flanking columns on each side of the semicircular headed window (857–64).

The types of classical **mouldings** and **ornament** employed were the same as in the seventeenth century. The proportions differed, and were based carefully upon those of Palladio. Entablatures and cornices were often heavy in scale, especially prior to 1750. Rococo ornament, emphasising shells, scrolls, flowers and birds, was paramount in mid-century, especially for interior decoration (866, 868–73, 875, 880).

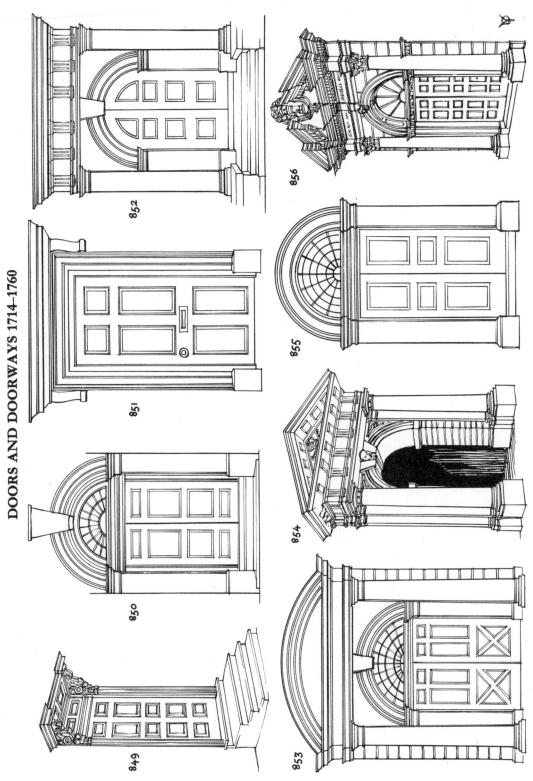

DOORS AND DOORWAYS 1714–1760

849 Lamb House, Rye, Sussex, 18th century   850 St George's Church, Hanover Square, London, 1713–14.   John James   851 44 Berkeley Square, London, 1744–5.   William Kent   852 St Luke's Church, Old Street, London, 1727–33.   George Dance I   853 Knuts-

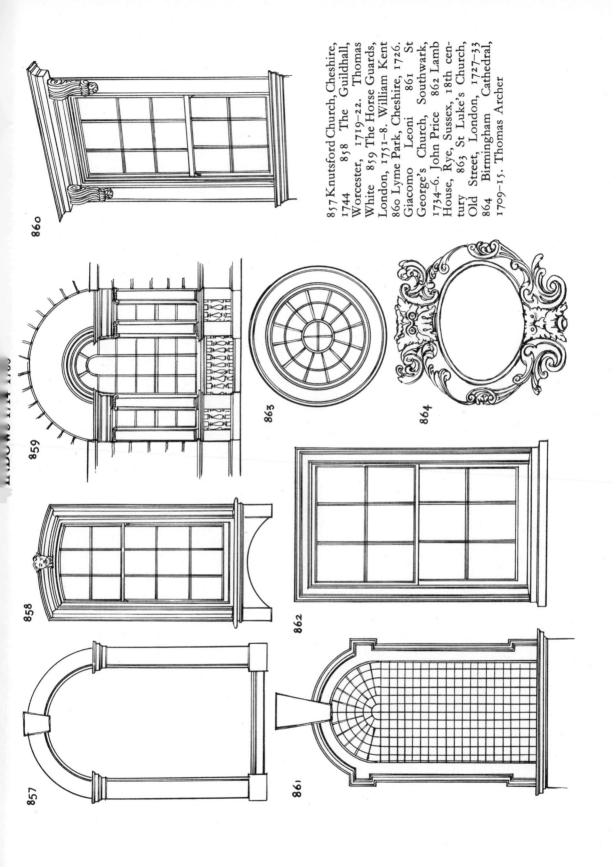

857 Knutsford Church, Cheshire, 1744   858 The Guildhall, Worcester, 1719–22. Thomas White   859 The Horse Guards, London, 1751–8. William Kent   860 Lyme Park, Cheshire, 1726. Giacomo Leoni   861 St George's Church, Southwark, 1734–6. John Price   862 Lamb House, Rye, Sussex, 18th century   863 St Luke's Church, Old Street, London, 1727–33   864 Birmingham Cathedral, 1709–15. Thomas Archer

860

859

863

864

858

862

857

861

865　Chimney-piece with mirror, 1756—carved and painted pinewood. Rococo design

866 St Martin-in-the-Fields, 1722: Corinthian column and entablature. James Gibbs   867 Market
Cross, Colston Bassett, Nottinghamshire: Doric column, 18th century   868 The Circus, Bath: Doric
columns and entablature, ground floor. Begun 1754 by the Woods   869 Guildhall, Worcester: Composite pilaster and entablature, 1719–22. Thomas White   870 Birmingham Cathedral: Doric pilasters,
1709–15. Thomas Archer   871 St George's, Hanover Square: Corinthian capital, 1713–14. John
James   872 Base as in Fig. 871   873 The Circus, Bath: Ionic columns and entablature, first floor

874 The Guildhall, Worcester: cupola, 1719–22. Thomas White   875 St George's Church, Hanover Square: pediment ornament, 1713–14. John James   876 St Leonard's Church, Shoreditch: clock ornament   877 Queen's College, Oxford: cupola over entrance screen, 1709–59. Nicholas Hawksmoor   878 Carved decoration, 1754–60   879 Daventry Church: parapet, 1752. Hiorn   880 The Guildhall, Worcester: panel, 1719–22

881

882

881 The Guildhall, High Wycombe, Buckinghamshire, c.
1757–60   882 The Blenheim
Pavilion, 'Cliveden', Buckinghamshire, from 1735. Giacomo
Leoni

CHAPTER IX

Late Georgian 1760 - 1800

Classicism was the dominant theme in art and architecture until the close of the eighteenth century. As a fundamental basis for design it was undisputed. A fierce controversy raged, however, during some 30 to 40 years about which type of classicism provided the finest inspiration for eighteenth-century architects and artists. The nation which made the first moves towards questioning the hitherto unchallenged supremacy of Roman classicism was the French, followed, to a much lesser extent, by the Italian. The latter, quite naturally, viewed as unwelcome any suggestion that Rome was not the original founder of the classic artistic form.

These trends, which led to a new concept of classical origins and thus to a new appreciation of architectural values, were generally referred to as the neo-classical movement or the classic revival—both somewhat inaccurate expressions. The French began to query the Palladian assertion that Vitruvius and his disciple Palladio should constitute the only, or even the best, interpretation of classic form and decoration. With this inquiry came a more revolutionary theme: had classicism even originated in Rome? From Germany also came the—to the Italians at least—heretical pronouncement that it was to Greece, not Rome, that men must look for the cradle of this architectural conception.

Italy admitted the historical eminence of Etruscan art and architecture, but patriotic opinion was for some time unwilling to concede the origins of the style to Greece, although eventually, of course, this recognition had to come.

By 1760, this controversy, so far chiefly limited to words and drawings, inspired in a number of Europeans the desire to go to see for themselves, and an ever-growing stream of travellers set out from England, France, Germany and Italy to countries where Ancient Rome and Greece had held dominion. Exhaustive studies on the spot were made, particularly by the English and the French (the Italians then as now being less interested in travel abroad). As time passed it became more apparent that Greece was to be accepted as the originator of classic art and architecture and was identified more and more with the ideals of political and moral liberty.

One of England's noted contributions to the expansion of European knowledge in this field was by way of the Dilettanti Society, founded in 1732 for the purpose of artistic encouragement and patronage of excavation and research, particularly in Greece. A number of students went to study in Greece, Yugoslavia and Italy under the auspices of the Society, and on their return published their work. Members who had made the Grand Tour helped to make this a convivial and social club to sponsor interest and study of the antique, and to collect specimens of sculpture, ornament and detail from actual sites.

Among the contributors to this research into the antique were **Robert Wood**, 1716–71, who went as a private gentleman with two friends to Palmyra and published in 1753 *Ruins of*

Palmyra and in 1757 *Ruins of Balbec*; also **James Stuart**, 1713–88 and **Nicholas Revett**, 1721–1804, who together visited Naples, Paestum, Athens and Corinth. On their return to England they published in 1762 their famous work *The Antiquities of Athens*; also, after further expeditions, *Ionian Antiquities*.

Such works as these aroused great interest and controversy in both England and France. From England came more artists, architects and private gentlemen to make the Tour. Many of the famous English architects of the latter part of the eighteenth century did this and spent varying periods of time up to several years in 'on the spot' original study.

This period in England is often described—sometimes nostalgically—as the 'golden age of architecture', and there is justification for the title. Since the days of Inigo Jones English classical architecture had moved steadily forward to higher standards of design, proportion and decoration. Indeed, by way of the work of such men as Wren, Hawksmoor, Vanbrugh and Kent, English classical architecture arrived at the superlatively high achievements of this period, as evidenced primarily in the buildings of Adam and Chambers. All this classical design had been based on the Roman prototype. Now came the Greek phase. The majority of English architects took one side or the other and designed particularly in the Roman or Greek style. Sir William Chambers, for example, was determinedly a Roman scholar, while Adam, although taking ideas from several sources, often veered towards the Greek. Architects of the last years of the century tended more to the Greek forms, although they often streamlined to adapt the ornament to their own needs of design. Much of this over-emphasised 'battle of the styles' was perhaps superfluous 'hot air', but it did introduce into the somewhat placid Palladianism from the first half of the century the creative vitality and variety which was noteworthy in the second.

By 1760 it had become apparent to many that the older conception, of classical architecture having continued in a general sequence since the days of Rome, with a retrogressive break for Gothic design in the Middle Ages, was not a true picture. It was slowly realised that there were three dominant architectural periods: Ancient classical architecture, as evidenced first by Greece, then by Rome; secondly the long and, in its turn, varied Gothic phase; and lastly a Renaissance of classical forms which, although in certain periods related to Ancient Classicism, was basically different from it in treatment, origins and achievement. This realisation brought a new approach to the architecture of the present, and, although the dominant form continued to be classical, its actual results were much more varied than hitherto and of the highest standard so far achieved then or since.

As Wren dominated the architecture of the second half of the seventeenth century so do **Robert Adam** and **Sir William Chambers** together dominate this period. Although their work is strongly contrasted there is much in common between their individual careers. They were almost exactly contemporary and the working lives of both span the same period, 1760–90. They came from similar well-to-do middle-class backgrounds and both enjoyed a long period of foreign travel and study before starting in practice. Both men were very ambitious and both were equally convinced that their approach to classical architecture was the true and only way. Both achieved many of their ambitions and the influence of their work, in different ways, on English art and architecture, has been profound and lasting. Chambers was the official architect of his period: the man of principle, scholarship and conservative, meticulous classical design on Roman lines. Adam was the bright new star, the innovator, the experimenter. Both had their admirers, imitators and supporters, but they were both architects of a class which stands far above their contemporaries and successors. It is to be regretted that since their deaths, only one architect of such high order has appeared—Sir John Soane. Their work can only be classed with that of such men as Inigo Jones, Wren and Vanbrugh.

A new generation of architects of note was working in the period 1770–1800: George Dance II, Holland and Wyatt in particular; also Leverton. The work of Soane spans the eighteenth and nineteenth centuries, and many of his fine designs for the Bank of England were carried out before 1800. In the last decade of the century appears the first works of the architects of the early nineteenth century; Nash, Wilkins and Smirke, who introduced a new school of architects—good quality, but lacking the brilliance of the Adam–Chambers era.

Although almost all the architecture in Britain from the last phases of Perpendicular and Tudor Gothic in the mid-sixteenth century until 1800 was in classical vein, the **Gothic style** had not completely disappeared. There is a tenuous link appearing at intervals during this time, keeping Gothicism alive until its vigorous nineteenth-century revival.

For example, there are one or two Gothic designs by Wren in the late seventeenth century: Tom Tower at Christ Church, Oxford and some city church steeples such as St Mary Aldermanbury; and later, Vanbrugh carried out some Gothic work, notably his own fortress-style house at Greenwich. In the eighteenth century, Kent designed in Gothic at Hampton Court Palace and Gloucester Cathedral, while Hawksmoor aroused much controversy with his gatehouse towers at All Souls', Oxford; his towers at Westminster Abbey were generally accepted, however.

All these examples, different in conception as they are, have one factor in common; they lack completely the essential Medieval spirit; they are intellectual or romantic parodies of Gothic.

There is, however, one famous eighteenth-century example; the house belonging to and partly designed by Horace Walpole, called Strawberry Hill, Twickenham. Here, Walpole bought a house in 1749 and with the professional aid of his architect redesigned it as a Gothic house. The result, although amateurish in many ways, possessed some of the essence of Medievalism and had a considerable influence on much later work.

Towards the end of the eighteenth century James Wyatt carried out a number of Gothic designs in a more serious attempt to revive the style. These are described in Chapter X.

SIR WILLIAM CHAMBERS 1723–1796

Chambers was of Scottish stock, born at Gothenburg in Sweden. He spent much of his boyhood in Yorkshire but returned to Sweden where he joined the East India Company there at the age of 17. In this employment he travelled to Bengal and China and in between voyages visited England, Scotland and France. He left the Company's service at the age of 25 and went to Paris to study architecture. Here he remained for a year and made a number of French friends among the architects, notably Le Roy, with whom he corresponded for much of his life. From Paris he went to Italy where he spent five years. In 1755 he returned to England to set up in practice. He was successful almost from the beginning of his career. He progressed steadily from honour to honour. He became architectural tutor to the Prince of Wales, who, later as George III, showed his appreciation of Chambers's work and appointed him architect to the King. He became **Comptroller** in 1769, was knighted in 1770 and became **Surveyor-General** in 1782.

One of Chambers's early commissions was to lay out the **Gardens at Kew** and to ornament them with pavilions and temples in classical and oriental style. This he did between 1757–1763, designing the **Pagoda**, the **Orangery** and some temples and alcoves. These designs were published in 1763. Although Chambers later became known for his very academic approach to classical architecture, these oriental excursions show him in different mood (883).

In 1759 Chambers published his first edition of *A Treatise on Civil Architecture*. This is his most famous published work, of which the third edition appeared in 1791. Chambers compiled the work from many of his own first-hand studies in addition to many works by Italian architects. These include in particular **Bernini, Peruzzi, Palladio, Vignola** and **Scamozzi**. The work shows clearly and in detail the orders with their use and decoration, and examples incorporating them in doorways, window openings, ceilings and chimney-pieces.

Chambers was a proud, sensitive and somewhat humourless man. He was ambitious and fiercely determined that his views on classical architecture were the correct interpretation for English architects. He resisted all incursion into the Greek form of classical architecture and rigidly adhered to the pure Roman designs. His detail, ornament and proportions were meticulously correct; his work sincere, intellectual and of superbly high quality. His houses, in particular, illustrate his Palladian interests, but the work is of a more refined standard, both in general design and individual detail than buildings by Taylor or Paine. Among his town houses still extant is **The Albany, Piccadilly** (originally Melbourne House), 1771–3 (908, 975), while **Peper Harow, Surrey**, built **1765–75**, illustrates his country house style. This house, set in beautiful grounds, and now a school, is very simply designed in three storeys, with a slightly projecting centre block. There are some fine windows on the ground floor. The south front is shown in Fig. 921, some windows in Figs. 982 and 988 and the beautiful slender staircase in Fig. 991.

Chambers had a number of pupils who were strongly influenced by his work and carried on his style to the next generation of architects. These include **Gandon, Hardwick** and **Yenn**.

883 The Orangery, Kew Gardens, Surrey, 1761. Sir William Chambers

Chambers was a most successful architect and one of the first genuinely professional members of his profession. His career formed a model pattern for others who succeeded him. He was architect to the King, Surveyor-General and had close connections with the newly formed Royal Academy of Arts—he was its first Treasurer in 1768 when it was founded—and also with the 'Architects Club', another new foundation. He was the leading government architect of his day, and in this connection was the architect of Somerset House, one of the largest public buildings to be erected for many years.

Somerset House, 1778–86, is not only Chambers's principal work, but one of the few large public buildings erected in this period. It presented a number of problems which Chambers solved satisfactorily, and a first-class architectural opportunity which he grasped and carried out successfully if not brilliantly.

For a number of years a scheme had been discussed to house several government departments together in one building. Eventually the site was decided: that of the old riverside Palace. Chambers, as official government architect, was given the task of designing the new edifice. The old Palace was demolished, and the new site thus available possessed a magnificent south front, directly facing the river, of 800 feet in length, and a much narrower north front, of only 135 feet facing the Strand, and roughly in the centre of the long façade.

The problems created by these unusual site proportions were added to by the fact that the Thames lapped the actual site front (the Victoria Embankment in front of Somerset House was erected much later).

Chambers began preparing his designs in 1775 and a year later the first stone was laid. The Strand block was completed first, in 1780, the central court behind this soon afterwards, while his design of the long river façade was not finished until after his death. In fact, the two side wings were added much later; the **east wing** by **Robert Smirke** in 1828–34 and the **west wing** by **James Pennethorne** in 1852–6.

The Strand front presents a two-storey façade to the Strand, in the Corinthian order, with rusticated arches on the lower storey. The entrance is placed centrally, comprising three semicircular headed archways. A balustraded parapet surmounts the cornice. Nowadays, this comparatively small entrance front often goes unnoticed in the bustle of Strand traffic and much larger buildings which face and flank it, while opposite, Gibbs's St Mary-le-Strand provides an illustration of another but lovelier form of Italian Renaissance classical architecture (885).

The **central court**, into which this entrance leads, has three sides each with Corinthian centre pavilion. In the central façade, opposite the main entrance, is a principal feature which also forms the focal centre for the river front. It is surmounted by a pediment and dome. The latter is well proportioned when viewed from the central court, but is entirely out of scale and insignificant when set against the long river façade.

For **the River Front**, as previously mentioned, Chambers's great problem was the river itself. He dealt with this successfully by building a masonry platform above tide level, and on this constructed a basement storey for warehouses and offices. This was then fronted by a large masonry arcade, rusticated, and pierced by arches. The whole front was divided into three blocks, defined by a central archway and two side water gates, reminiscent of the York House Watergate, Strand. Before the construction of the Victoria Embankment, the water lapped the façade and the rise and ebb of the tide was controlled by the water flowing through

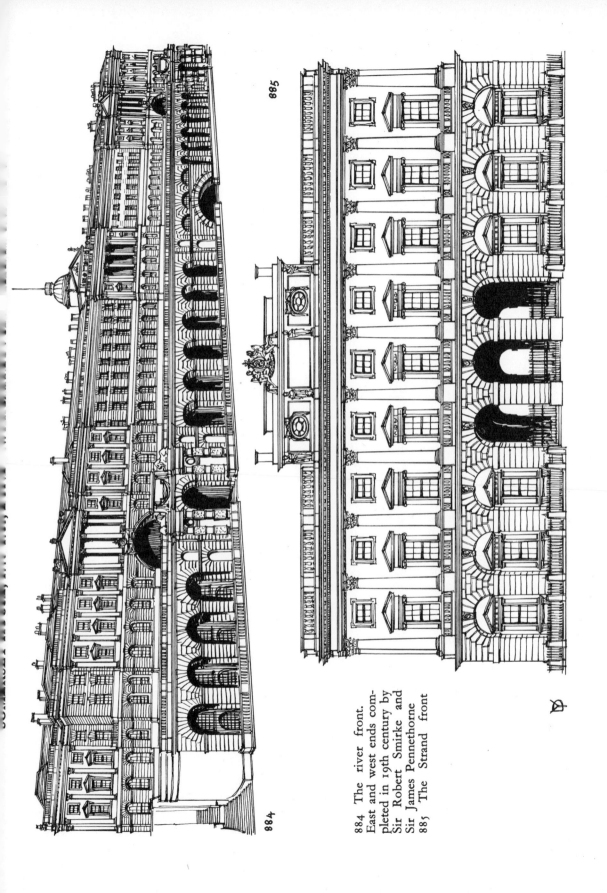

884 The river front.
East and west ends completed in 19th century by
Sir Robert Smirke and
Sir James Pennethorne
885 The Strand front

the archways. The whole appearance of the river front has obviously become much less impressive (although probably less damp) since the construction of the Embankment (884).

Portland stone was used throughout for the building of Somerset House. Chambers took
tremendous pains to maintain and supervise a very high standard of workmanship in the
carving of the classic detail, and there is no doubt that this building has added to London's
riverside a dignified, balanced, intellectual classical building of extensive proportions and
faultless execution. The work does, however, give the impression, as Sir John Summerson
suggests,* that Chambers was primarily, like so many of his contemporaries, a country-house
architect, and that this large building is of a high standard of design when viewed piecemeal,
but fails to impress with its grandeur and unity of conception when seen as a whole. Quite
certainly, the river front, in particular, has a certain monotony; it lacks vitality and is too
equally divided into its three parts. The great care and supervision which went into its design
and construction tend to present a somewhat over-studied and careful result (884–5, 953, 962,
986).

ROBERT ADAM 1728–1792

Robert Adam was born at Kirkcaldy in Fifeshire, second of four brothers, all of whom
entered the profession of architecture. Their father, **William Adam**, was one of the leading
architects of Scotland from 1730 until his death in 1748. Of the four sons, the eldest, **John**,
remained much of his life in Scotland and followed his father's example in the Palladian
tradition. The third son, **James**, most closely associated with his brother Robert, was the
family scholar, business man and draughtsman who largely organised the family firm in
London. The youngest brother, **William**, was also concerned with the family business but
primarily from a financial aspect.

Robert Adam was the architectural leader and initiator of the family. In the history of
English architecture he ranks as one of the few outstanding geniuses: an innovator and a
prolific builder. According to the fashion dictates of succeeding decades his work has been
acclaimed or derided, but, like that of Wren, it has survived and receives no longer fulsome
but sincere admiration.

Adam was educated at Edinburgh University and set off from Scotland in 1754 as a
gentleman and student on the Grand Tour. He travelled in France where he met Clérisseau
and proceeded to Italy where he spent some time. He studied at Florence and Rome, and it
was at Rome in 1756 that he became acquainted with Piranesi. In 1757 he made a journey to
Spalato (the modern Split), where he made drawings and measurements of the Dalmatian
palace of the Roman Emperor Diocletian.

During his studies Adam set out to absorb all that he could of both antique and classical
architecture and the work of Italian Renaissance architects. He endeavoured to give himself
a thorough background knowledge of the antique from first-hand study and measurement.

Robert Adam returned to England in 1758 to set up architectural practice. In 1764 was
published his lavish treatise on his work at Spalato, *Ruins of the Palace of the Emperor Diocletian
at Spalato*, and in 1773, when at the height of his fame as an architect, appeared Volume I of
The Works in Architecture of Robert and James Adam. Volume II came out in 1779 and Volume
III posthumously in 1822. (William Adam, who died in poverty in 1822, had preserved all the

* *Architecture in Britain* 1530–1830 (The Pelican History of Art).

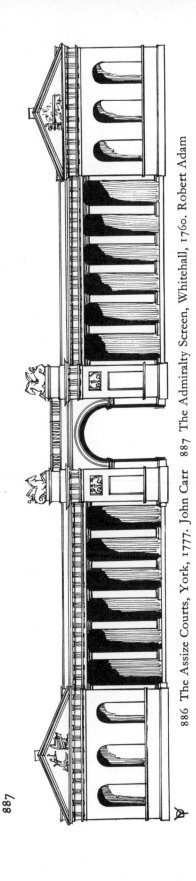

886 The Assize Courts, York, 1777. John Carr   887 The Admiralty Screen, Whitehall, 1760. Robert Adam

volumes of Robert's drawings and left them to his niece who later sold them to Sir John Soane. The drawings, some 8,000 in number, are still preserved in Soane's own museum today.)

The Adam style of architecture is a complex subject, for there is not just one Adam style, nor one source for his inspiration. Adam has been dismissed by many of his critics, particularly his contemporaries such as Chambers, as a mere decorator, not an architect. It is true that he is mostly famed today for his interiors rather than his exteriors. This is largely due to the fact that there are far more examples available of the former (for Adam was not so often, in his capacity as a domestic architect, called upon to design from the beginning or to re-design an exterior), but also because his interiors show more readily, to the casual observer, his originality of design; there is an immediate popular appeal here.

Adam was opposed to any idea of classical grammatical rigidity, and, in direct contrast to the Palladians, frequently varied his proportions and handling of classical detail according to the individual needs of the building and site. Equally, unlike the Palladians, despite this method or perhaps because of it, he had the faculty of creating the essence of classical design while altering the constituent components.

In this period there was available to the travelled architect a wealth of classical material from which to draw. Adam used nearly all of this to produce his own work, which was, in the end, intensely personal and highly original.

His favourite source of material came from his archaeological studies in Italy, Dalmatia and Greece. Especially dear to him was the Ionic order of the Erechtheum and the designs at Palmyra. In his interior work he evolved his famous 'Etruscan' style, as can still be seen at Osterley Park, although, unfortunately, many such examples have now disappeared.

Adam was also influenced in his work by French and Italian Renaissance architecture and he used ideas from these sources in his domestic schemes. In Italian Renaissance work, he was particularly interested in the creations of Michelangelo, Zuccari and Raphael. Again, this influence is seen primarily in his interior design.

In architectural form, as distinct from interior decoration, Adam's designs were delicate and imaginative. His street façades of terraces and blocks show great coherence and symmetry, but are never dull or heavy. The ornament is always elegant, in low relief and sparingly used.

In their preface to Volume I of their *Works in Architecture*, the Adam brothers claimed to have originated a new style of decoration, and that they were publishing this as so many imitators were using the style, and they wished to assert themselves as the innovators. Certainly there was considerable truth in this assertion, as can be seen in contemporary work by, for example, Wyatt or Leverton. The Adam brothers also endeavoured to explain their theory of the spirit of their external architecture, which is 'movement'. In Adam's words: 'Movement is meant to express the rise and fall, the advance and recess, with other diversity of form, in the different parts of a building, so as to add greatly to the picturesque of the composition.' In other words, Adam wants to express his intention to design architecture in tone as well as line, and his severance from the Palladian tenet of inflexibility of classical design. This sense of movement can be seen in a number of Adam's buildings still extant: at Kedleston, at Kenwood, at Mersham-le-Hatch, at Harewood despite later alterations, and even in street façades such as Fitzroy Square (888–9, 893, 895, 931).

The greatest changes made in interior design by Adam were in the decoration of plaster-work used on ceilings and walls. Here, the heavy plaster ceilings gave place to delicate stucco forms connected to painted medallions. The walls were also decorated in stucco down to wainscot level and while the ornament itself was white or touched with gilt, the backgrounds were painted in delicate shades of green, lilac or blue. Adam, like Kent, designed his own curtains and furniture to follow the scheme of the whole room. The carpets were frequently made to Adam designs which echoed the ceiling above. Examples can still be seen at Syon House.

One of Adam's greatest talents lay in his genius for the interior planning of rooms. Behind his symmetrical town façades was a tremendous variety of room shapes, octagonal, circular, square, etc., and these were all designed together as a single unit to make the greatest use of available space. Few rooms in a town house were of the same size or shape and several had apsidal ends and/or arcaded columns to break a too long or narrow room.

The inventive genius of Adam gave to the architectural profession of his day new stand-ards in interior decorative taste and employment of ornamental forms. This caused a change of attitude to such design not only in architects, but in the trades of furniture, textiles, ceramics and building as a whole. His free, almost casual, although symmetrical use of ornament closed finally the Palladian era of solemn, heavy classical forms in interior ornamentation. Such trades responded with enthusiasm to the interiors of Kenwood and Syon and followed the designs in the *Works of Robert and James Adam* with interest. A number of architects, such as Wyatt, Leverton and Crunden, owed much to the Adam style, while the ordinary builder and furniture designer showed the Adam influence in his work, especially in London, after 1775.

One of Adam's earliest works was the **screen** and **gateway** built in front of the **Admiralty** in **Whitehall** in **1760**. The screen is most successful and enhances the earlier building behind. The Doric order is used, with a central gateway and side pavilions. It has suffered some altera-tion since it was built (887). After this, the great majority of Adam's architectural contribu-tion was in the domestic sphere, both in country houses and in town houses and terraces. The first part of his career was spent mainly on altering or enlarging existing country houses. In this connection he was engaged at **Harewood House**, Yorkshire, 1759-71, **Croome Court**, Worcestershire, 1760-1, **Osterley Park**, Middlesex, from 1761, **Syon House**, Middle-sex, 1761-2, **Kedleston Hall**, Derbyshire, 1761-5, a brand-new house **Mersham-le-Hatch**, Kent, 1762-72, **Kenwood, Hampstead**, 1764-8, and **Luton Hoo**, Bedfordshire, 1767-70. During this period of work the Adam style and the family firm were created and established. The work on these houses lasted many years and it is often difficult to ascertain exact dates of commencement and completion.

From 1768 onwards for a number of years Adam was largely employed in London. In this period he worked upon the **Adelphi** speculation—a family concern; **Portland Place**, 1770, **Lansdown House, Berkeley Square**, 1762-5, houses in **St James's Square**, 1773-6 and **Fitzroy Square**, 1790. The last of these was his final venture in speculative building. He died in 1792 and was buried in Westminster Abbey.

In the late 1770s Adam worked also in **Edinburgh**, where he designed the **Record Office**, 1771, and new buildings at **Edinburgh University** in 1778.

6 Syon House, Middlesex: the ante-room. Architect Robert Adam

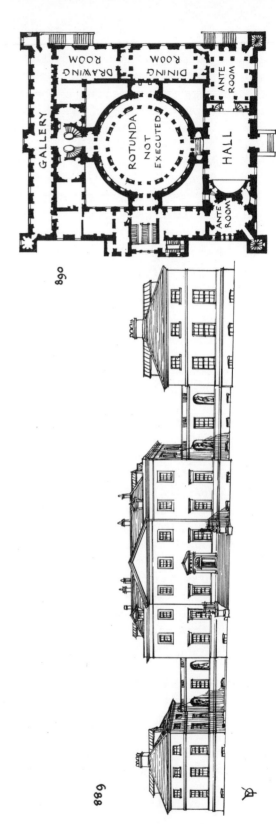

HOUSES DESIGNED BY ROBERT ADAM

888

889

890

888 Kenwood, Hampstead, London: south front 1767–8   889 Mersham-le-Hatch, Kent: south front, 1762–72   890 Syon House, Middlesex, 1762–70: plan (Great Saloon with Rotunda not carried out)

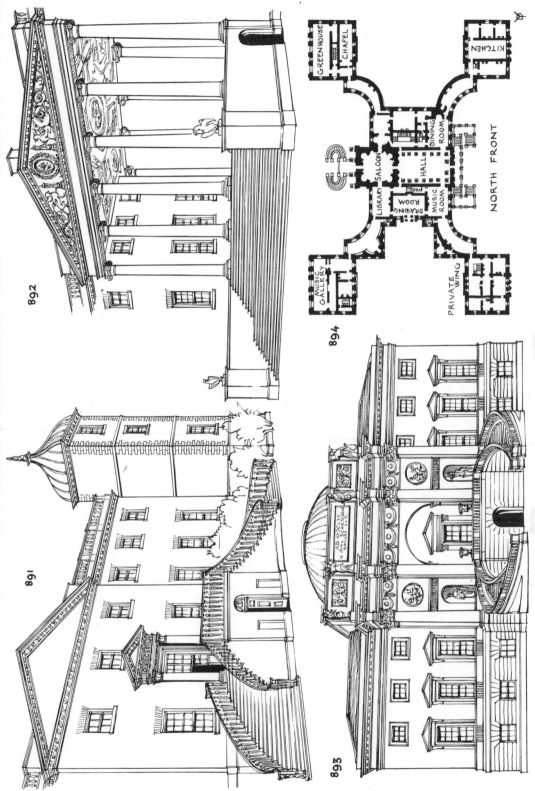

GREENHOUSE
CHAPEL
KITCHEN

MUSIC GALLERY
LIBRARY
SALOON
HALL
DINING ROOM
DRAWING ROOM
MUSIC ROOM
PRIVATE WING

NORTH FRONT

891 Osterley Park, Middlesex: south front. Begun 1761 892 Osterley: the north front, the Great Portico 893 Kedleston Hall, Derbyshire: the south front. Robert Adam from 1761 894 Kedleston: plan (side wings on south front not built)

Country Houses

The majority of existing buildings designed by Adam are country houses. In only a few of these was he given the opportunity to design a new house. Most of the work was in the form of a commission to alter or enlarge existing buildings. It is unfortunate indeed for posterity that Adam, like Inigo Jones, lived in a period and under circumstances where the opportunity to design and carry through large public works did not come to him. Like Inigo Jones, he made a number of designs for such schemes but, for various reasons, they did not materialise.

Syon House, Middlesex, ranks with Kedleston as one of the two greatest Adam master-pieces in the grand manner; they both possess rooms which compare favourably with Continental palaces. The house itself is Jacobean and is of quadrangular plan with an open space in the centre. The exterior is not interesting. Adam's terms of reference were to re-plan the interior on eighteenth-century lines. He created round the central court a progression of state rooms. Some of these were not executed but the anteroom, gallery and drawing-room show Adam at his grandest and most palatial. He planned also a great domed hall in the central court but this was not carried out.

The **entrance hall**, primarily in white, with a black and white marble floor, is not inspiring and its coolness would be more attractive in a Mediterranean climate. It is almost a double cube and spreads over two storeys. At one end is a large apse with coffered ceiling, while at the other is an exit up a flight of curved steps to the ante-room. A Roman Doric order is used on monumental scale.

The **ante-room** is one of Adam's finest interiors and sparkles with rich colour. Twelve columns and twelve pilasters decorate the walls, with shafts of *verde antique*, dredged originally from the bed of the Tiber. The capitals are gilded Ionic designs while the bases are of white marble enriched with gilt. The entablature above the columns is also of white marble with gilt enrichment. The frieze is decorated in gold and blue with honeysuckle ornament. Each section of entablature supports a gilded, plaster antique figure. The panelled ceiling is also ornamented in gold, while the floor is of multi-patterned scagliola in brilliant hues. On the walls are gilded plaster panels by **Joseph Rose**—a very high standard of relief work.

After passing through the monumental entrance hall and the richly coloured and gilded ante-room one feels that Adam must have exhausted his talents for one house. This is certainly not the case. One enters the **dining-room**—another very fine interior—in white and gold this time, with an apse at each end fronted by pillars. The ceiling is white and gold, while the walls are surmounted by a frieze of long rectangular panels by **Cipriani**.

One then arrives at the **Red Drawing-room** which, like the ante-room, is a masterpiece. It also is rich in colour and material. The coved ceiling with flat centre panel is divided into octagon and diamond shapes containing exquisite paintings by **Angelica Kauffmann**. The carpet beneath was designed by Adam to fit in with the ceiling scheme. The doors are quite magnificent in rich polished mahogany with gilded panels, while the surrounding order is in white and cream. The white marble chimney-piece is decorated with ormolu.

The **gallery** shows the Adam inventiveness at its best. Here, in proportion is a Jacobean long gallery, out of which cannot be created a Georgian interior. But Adam used all his art to adapt it and give a quite different impression. The gallery measures 136 feet in length, and

XLI *Kenwood House, Hampstead: the library, 1767–9. Arch* *Robert Adam; painter Antonio Zucchi; plasterwork by Joseph .*

is 14 feet high and 14 feet in breadth. Adam shortened it in appearance by Ionic pilaster divisions at intervals making bookshelf features. The design of the ceiling is planned to give width to the room, and is still largely Jacobean in spirit. The whole gallery abounds with delicate classical decoration in the form of arabesques and small stucco panels. The general effect is of flat linear relief in very delicate form. A plan of Syon is shown in Fig. 890 and views of the gallery and the ante-room in Plate XLII and Colour Plate 6, while detail ornamentation can be seen in Figs. 954–5.

Kenwood House, Hampstead, was remodelled by Adam from an earlier house largely from 1767 to 1768. It remains almost unchanged. The south aspect has a fine position in the grounds of the house, while there is an interesting portico on the other façade. The most outstanding room in the house is the **library** which shows Adam at his best. The coved ceiling, taking the section of a segment of a circle like a barrel vault, is in pastel shades with white and gold stucco ornament. The decoration comprises oval and rectangular panel paintings by **Zucchi** and stucco arabesques by **Rose**. At each end of the library is an apse, screened in front by Corinthian columns, above which is an entablature with richly decorated frieze. The south façade of Kenwood is shown in Fig. 888 and the library in Plate XLI. Architectural details are illustrated in Figs 987, 994 and 1002.

Kedleston House, Derbyshire, was designed by **James Paine**, who built the north front in 1761. **Adam** was called in and designed the south front and the interior. The plan of the house was a central rectangular block with four smaller side blocks connected to the central mass by curved arms. On the north façade the house was built largely according to plan, but on the south, the side wings have not been built and Adam was concerned only with the central façade. He used the Corinthian order with four giant, free-standing columns in the centre feature, which support entablatures and sculptured figures above. A central, curved staircase ascends to the *piano nobile*. Behind the façade can be seen the flattish, large dome of the **saloon** which is the chief apartment of the house. This is a beautiful stateroom with the interior of the dome coffered and decorated in gold. Paintings in this room are by **Biagio Rebecca**.

In the **dining-room** the yellowish ceiling is decorated in white relief with blue ribs. On the walls are landscapes by **Claude** and **Zuccarelli**, while the smaller paintings in the roundels are by **Zucchi**.

The **hall** is on a vast scale. It is situated on the *piano nobile* and is based on the Roman atrium. There are 20 monolithic Corinthian columns in green-veined Derbyshire alabaster. The paintings are by **Angelica Kauffmann**. There are also two very beautiful Adam chimney-pieces with stucco relief figures.

Kedleston, like Syon, represents one of the great domestic achievements of Adam's career and illustrates not only his versatile designs and his exquisite detail but also the art and craftsmanship of many of his team of painters. stuccoists and carvers; they nearly all worked at Kedleston. All the details were designed by Adam, the fenders, grates and fire-irons and most of the furniture and furnishings. The south façade is illustrated in Fig. 893, and architectural details, including the bridge in the grounds, in Figs 894, 937, 952, 983 and 1006.

Adam's work at **Osterley Park**, Middlesex, where once again he remodelled an older house, this time Elizabethan, continued over many years, and the interiors reflect his varying styles of work over this time. The exterior still has its four Elizabethan angle towers with

II Syon House, Middlesex: the gallery, 1763–4. Architect Robert Adam

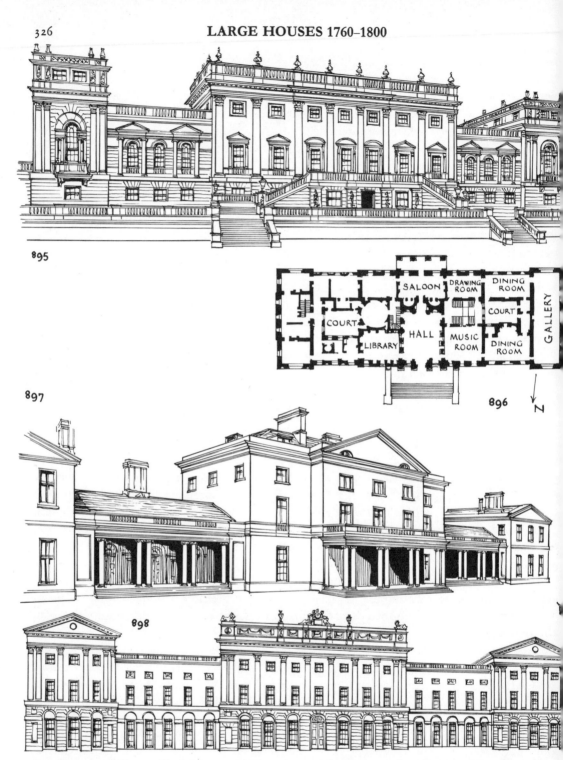

895

897

896

N

898

895 Harewood House, Yorkshire: south front, 1759–71. John Carr and Robert Adam. Façade refaced and parapet, top storey to pavilions and garden terrace added by Sir Charles Barry 1843
896 Harewood House: plan, principal floor   897 Southill, Bedfordshire: south front, 1796–1803.
Henry Holland   898 Heveningham Hall, Suffolk: north front, 1778. Sir Robert Taylor

their cupolas, but on the south side Adam built a magnificent staircase with metal balustrade, curving up to the fine entrance doorway on the *piano nobile*. On the other façade, the main entrance front, he built a great portico. This portico, inspired largely by the entrance to the Court of the Temple of the Sun at Palmyra and partly by the Erechtheum, is an impressive architectural feature, thoroughly Greek in character (891–2).

Inside the house, the **library** boasts panel paintings by **Angelica Kauffmann**, while in the **dining-room** there are some landscapes by **Zucchi** on the walls with dainty stucco arabesques in between.

The **entrance hall** is most successful with its black and white marble floor, ceiling decorated by round and oval panels and the fine detail of doorcases and window frames.

In the **Etruscan room** can be seen the only clear example of this type of Adam's work which remains. In its colours of yellow, indian red and black it illustrates the Pompeian influence of the period (891–2, 966, 968, 995, 1001).

Harewood House, Yorkshire, also shows the Adam manner on the grand scale, and much of the interior can be seen as he designed it. The exterior, however, was altered by Barry in the nineteenth century and the north façade was largely built by John Carr of York. Adam worked on the house from 1759 to 1769. The **hall** is very fine and in the Adam tradition. The **gallery** is magnificent with an impressive ceiling. Here he designed mirror and picture frames, furniture and furnishings, much of which still remain (895–6).

Mersham-le-Hatch, Kent, was the first house conceived and built by Adam from the beginning. It is modest and domestic compared with those on a palatial scale like Syon and Kedleston, but is a charming house, which illustrates the architect's versatility, and it has been very little altered. It is built of red brick and comprises a low central block with connecting side wings. It was constructed between 1762 and 1772. The long, low elevation of the south front is shown in Fig. 889 and the doorway in Fig. 969.

Other country houses by Robert Adam include **Nostell Priory**, Yorkshire, where he added a north wing with an Ionic projecting portico of such fine proportion and detail that Paine's work on the rest of the house appears stodgy by comparison (979, 1000). There is also **Croome Court**, Worcestershire, one of Adam's first commissions, where he decorated the long gallery and built a charming Doric Orangery (980), and **Saltram**, Devonshire, which possesses some fine Adam interiors with decorative ceilings and carpets in scheme. At **Bowood** in Wiltshire, 1761–71, Adam added the long Diocletian Wing. It was called this because of its slight resemblance to parts of the palace at Spalato. It has Adam capitals which he based upon a pilaster found at Spalato which has only one row of acanthus leaves encircling a fluted, bell-shaped capital.

Town Houses

Adam's houses **in London**, of which only a few remain, were planned to give adequate accommodation for lavish entertainment, and maximum privacy for the owner behind a comparatively narrow front façade. At the rear of this elevation, which was decorated in mainly linear form, was a carefully planned suite of rooms of many different shapes and sizes integrated together with an enchanting staircase and landings.

Such town houses today are converted into clubs, business, office and university accommodation, and it is not always easy to see how the original planning was arranged. Among such houses still extant are **No. 20 St James's Square, No. 20 Portman Square**, and **Chandos House, Marylebone**, all in London.

No. 20 St James's Square (now the property of the Distillers Co.) was built 1772–3. The exterior is in three storeys with entablature and balustraded parapet above. The order is Corinthian in the form of low relief pilasters spanning two floors. On the ground storey, which is rusticated, is a beautiful doorway with a leaded fanlight and curved staircase leading to the door itself. The windows of the *piano nobile* are pedimented. The whole façade is decorated in a restrained manner in low relief and exquisite taste. Inside is a pleasing stairwell giving an impression of space which does not actually exist. Its ceiling is decorated in stucco, low relief arabesques (899, 900, 970).

At **No. 20 Portman Square**, built in 1775–7 and now belonging to the Courtauld Institute, University of London, there is a rich interior with that high standard of craftsmanship redolent of the best of Adam's decoration. The exterior, which possesses some fine ironwork in its railings and standards, has been later altered by the addition of a further storey (949, 951).

Chandos House, at the end of Queen Anne Street, was built in 1770–4. Its finest exterior feature is the projecting porch (972). Inside is a magnificent staircase with wrought-iron balusters.

Terrace Architecture

The Adam brothers undertook a number of schemes of speculative building in towns, in terrace form. Apart from the famous Adelphi project (considered separately) were the houses in **Portland Place** and **Fitzroy Square** in **London**, and **Charlotte Square** in **Edinburgh**. The earliest of these was **Portland Place, W.1**, begun in 1773. At first a series of well-to-do town houses was planned here but, due to financial restrictions caused by the American War of Independence, only a limited part of the scheme was carried out, and, unfortunately, this suffered almost total destruction in World War II. The design followed the usual Adam town-house pattern, with stucco façade, a rusticated lower storey, and above, a pilastered front. All the decoration was in low relief, delicate and restrained.

Fitzroy Square, London, W.1 was begun at the end of Adam's life, in 1790. Only the east and south sides were built to his designs. Here, the elevations of the Square were planned as complete units, not merely a row of town houses. The basic principle of terrace architecture, initiated by men like John Wood of Bath, was taken up by Adam and treated in his individual manner. There is a projecting central feature with Ionic columns supporting a recessed entablature. At each end of the whole block is a terminal projecting mass, this time unbroken by a giant order. The complete terrace is in Portland stone, the decoration restrained and the projection slight; the main horizontal lines are interrupted little. The ground floor, with railings, is rusticated, and the doorways have attractive fanlights. There are four storeys in all, and the windows are plain, square-headed, sash type, except on the ground floor where semicircular arches are used. There is no balustrade (931).

At **Charlotte Square in Edinburgh** the work was also begun only a short time before Adam's death, and here again, only part of the building was completed in his lifetime. The north side, which was finished to his designs, survives in a remarkably unaltered condition and even the railings are the original work. The façade has a central feature, but this time pedimented above a giant order and a rusticated base.

XLIII   The Circus, Bath, Somerset, begun 1754. Architects John Wood, father and

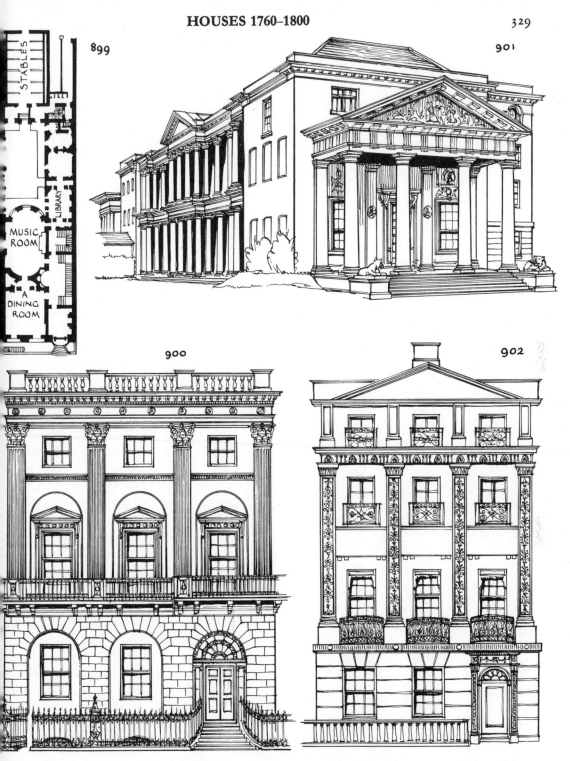

899 20 St James's Square: ground plan 900 20 St James's Square, London, *c.* 1775. Robert Adam
901 West Wycombe Park, Buckinghamshire, 1745–1773: south-east aspect. Several architects, including Robert Adam 902 7 Adam Street, The Adelphi, London, *c.* 1770. Robert Adam

IV *The Adelphi, London: the Royal Society of Arts, 1772–4. Architect Robert Adam*

The Adelphi scheme was a gigantic speculative enterprise upon which the Adam brothers embarked in **1768**. It was a financial failure, but architecturally it was most successful and it set a pattern for town terrace planning for the remainder of the century. The brothers took out a 99-year lease on a strip of land alongside the river near Westminster. They cleared the site, reclaimed the land from the Thames-side mud and embanked it to build on top streets of houses. The scheme failed financially as the government did not take over for warehouse purposes the large vaults thus created under the houses, as it had been hoped that they would do. The brothers carried on with the building work and recouped their losses by means of a lottery. The scheme brought them architectural praise, but considerable criticism for their professional and business methods.

The project as carried out comprised a riverside façade of terrace houses and another row behind with connecting side streets, constructed between 1768 and 1772. The houses were of brick with decoration in stone and terracotta. The layout was straightforward, with centre and terminal blocks slightly projecting and decorated by a giant order. The novel features of the work were in the application of the Adam style of ornament to external building in the form of very low relief projection of pilaster and entablature, also in ornamental forms of carved and terracotta decoration. Adam's idea was to provide an inexpensive prototype for town terrace building and his designs were certainly emulated by many a town builder in years to come.

This famous project was finally demolished in 1937 and all that now remains are a few houses in the back and side streets. Among these are the **Royal Society of Arts Building** and **No. 7 Adam Street**. The **former** has a fine Ionic order surmounted by a pediment and, on the ground floor, a three-part doorway (903, 964; XLIV), while the **latter**, occupied by the *Lancet*, retains a façade in first-rate condition. Here, the flat pilasters are decorated in the Adam manner as is the entablature and doorway (902, 967, 1004).

903 The Royal Society of Arts, London 1772–4. Architect Robert Adam

Apart from the two outstanding architects of the second half of the eighteenth century, Chambers and Adam, there are many others whose work should be considered in some detail. These architects may be classed conveniently together in three main groups. First, the older group, whose work was largely on Palladian lines, among whom may be mentioned **Sir Robert Taylor,**

James Paine and John Carr of York. Secondly should be considered the main body of younger architects who set the pattern and provided the ideas for the next generation, and whose work culminated in the early nineteenth century. Among them, the principal names are **George Dance II, Henry Holland, James Wyatt, Thomas Leverton** and **Sir John Soane**. Finally should be considered the work of lesser architects whose names are not as famous but whose contribution was certainly not negligible: **Robert Mylne, James Gandon, John Gwynne, Thomas Hardwick, Joseph Bonomi** and **Thomas Harrison**.

PALLADIAN ARCHITECTS

Sir Robert Taylor 1714–88

Some of the work of Sir Robert Taylor has already been discussed in Chapter VIII, for he remained a Palladian at heart all his life. His buildings show a high standard of classical architecture in the Palladian tradition, but, alongside the designs of Chambers and Adam, present a solemn, heavy appearance. Much of Sir Robert's time between 1760 and his death in 1788 was spent on designs for the **Bank of England** (XLV). Apart from this, he is noted for his smaller houses at **Ely House, Dover Street, London**, 1772, and **Asgill House, Richmond,** Surrey. His chief large country house was **Heveningham Hall**, Suffolk, the north front of which, 1760-78, is shown in Fig. 898. Here is the traditional Palladian façade with its large central, rectangular block and two side pavilions connected by slightly lower façades. A giant Corinthian order spans the two upper storeys, while the projecting masses have rusticated lower storeys. The complete elevation is impressive, dignified and extensive in faultless Palladian proportion. In 1780 Sir Robert Taylor was also responsible for the design of the **bridge** at **Maidenhead**, Surrey; a long stone bridge with balustraded parapet, now mellowed and most attractive in its Thames-side setting (946).

James Paine 1716–89, John Carr of York 1723–1807

Like Sir Robert Taylor, **James Paine** was a Palladian of the Burlington tradition and much of his work was completed before 1760. He designed a number of country houses after this date, although several of them were completed by other architects—for example, **Kedleston** and **Nostell Priory**, both continued by Adam. In 1763–9 Paine designed **Thorndon Hall,** Essex, which, based on Palladian tenets, was in the form of a large central block with side wings connected to the main mass by advancing colonnades. Of similar pattern was **Wardour**, Wiltshire, built in 1770–6. Towards the end of his life, while High Sheriff for Surrey, Paine designed a number of **Thames bridges**; those at Richmond, Chertsey, Walton and Kew. The two last-named have disappeared, but those at Richmond and Chertsey remain. **Richmond Bridge**, built 1780–3, is a five-arch bridge, faced with Portland stone. Its balustrade is articulated and it has rounded buttresses. The bridge was widened in 1929 but its character remained unaltered (938).

Although considered a provincial architect, for most of his extensive practice was carried on in the north of England, the work of **John Carr of York** was in no way inferior to that of London architects of his age. He began his career as a mason, but entered architectural practice soon after 1750. Like Taylor and Paine he was a Palladian architect and had

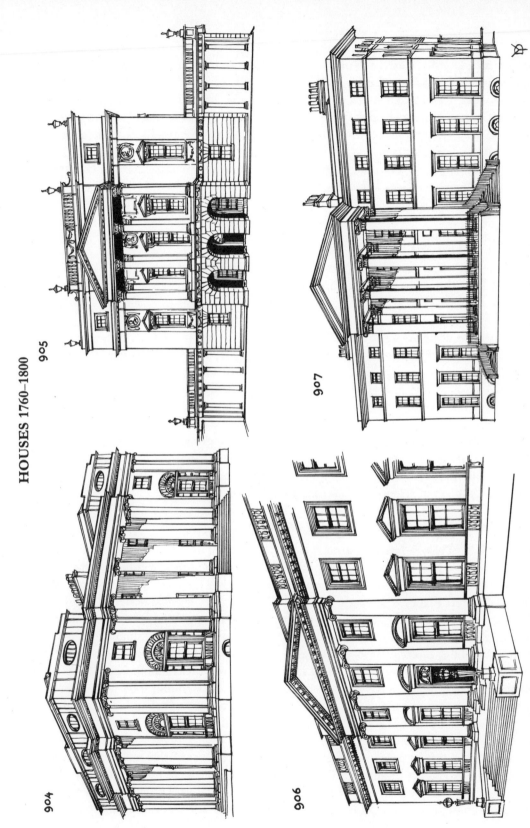

HOUSES 1760–1800

904

905

906

907

904 Southgate Grove (now Grovelands Hospital), Middlesex, 1797. John Nash   905 The Holburne of Menstrie Museum, Bath, 1795–7. C. Harcourt Masters (remodelled 1915)   906 Denton Hall, Yorkshire, 1770–80. John Carr of York   907 Attingham Park,

worked under Lord Burlington for part of his life. Much of his work is domestic in the form of country houses. He designed **Harewood House**, Yorkshire, 1760, and built the north front before Adam took over; he built the east front of **Wentworth Woodhouse**, Yorkshire, 1770, and designed **Lytham Hall**, Lancashire, 1751–64. Among his smaller houses are **Denton Hall**, Yorkshire (906), and in **York** his own house **Fairfax House**, 1770 (911). Also in **York** is his **Assize Courts**, 1776–7 (886). Among his churches is **Horbury Church**, Yorkshire, 1791, with tall, classical steeple and Ionic side porch (928, 977). Carr's work was always well-proportioned, in sound, classical tradition and he performed a great architectural service in building so much architecture of high standard in northern provincial cities.

THE YOUNGER ARCHITECTS

George Dance II 1741–1825

Dance, the first of the younger men, was the son of George Dance I, architect of the Mansion House and Clerk of the City Works in London, a post in which his son succeeded him in 1768. George Dance II was an original architect, following closely neither of the main classical factions of his day, but designing according to the individual commission in hand. Unfortunately much of his work has been damaged and destroyed, especially in London. He made a tour of Italy in his youth and returned to England in 1764. The following year, as a young man of only 24, he designed the original little church of **All Hallows, London Wall** (badly damaged in 1940–1). This church had a most interesting barrel vault pierced by large-scale lunettes. Between these, the vault was supported upon an Ionic order without full entablature above. The interior was very simple and restrained, while the decoration made use of Etruscan motifs. In 1768 Dance was elected as one of the first group of members of the new Royal Academy of Arts; also he became Professor of Architecture there.

His most famous work, unhappily demolished in 1902, was **Newgate Prison**. This building, which he designed in 1769, was one of the most original of the eighteenth century. It was built over the years 1770–82 and was an impressive work with dramatic, though austere and even grim qualities. The main composition consisted of unbroken, windowless walls, entirely rusticated; this gave an awesome appearance to the place. In the centre was the keeper's house with entrance lodges on either side. The windows here gave contrast to the enormous area of wall between. The prison was burnt by Gordon rioters in 1780, later rebuilt, but finally was demolished in 1902 to make way for the Central Criminal Courts.

Among Dance's others works are **St Luke's Hospital**, 1782–4 (now a printing works, and much altered); the **Council Chamber** in **Guildhall**, 1777 (destroyed 1906), and work in **Finsbury Square**, 1777–91, and **Bloomsbury**, 1790–1814. Some of his work was carried out in the nineteenth century and is discussed in Chapter X.

Henry Holland 1745–1806

Holland was the son of a builder and trained under him. In 1771 he went into partnership with **Lancelot (Capability) Brown**, the landscape gardener. Two years later he married Brown's daughter. In common with other eighteenth-century architects Holland undertook some speculative building in London. In 1771 he developed an area of land in Chelsea and laid it out as an estate which he called **Hans Town**. This comprised the streets known today as **Sloane Street, Hans Place** and **Cadogan Place**.

One of Holland's earlier commissions was the design of **Brooks's Club** in **St James's Street** in 1776. The Club owes more to Chambers than Adam in its treatment, but illustrates an early example of Holland's meticulous care in correctly interpreting classical form and detail. The Corinthian order is used in pilaster form; the entrance front has a pedimental, central feature (915).

By means of this commission Holland had been introduced to the aristocracy and there soon followed his largest commission, that of reconstructing **Carlton House** in **London** for the Prince of Wales. Holland produced a good design and the work was well carried out and supervised. On the north façade was built a large, central, Corinthian portico, which led into the hall decorated by Ionic columns. In front of the portico, to form a screen, was a colonnade of coupled Ionic columns. Carlton House was built during 1783–95 but was demolished in 1826. Here, as in many of his buildings, Holland used the Ionic order. He preferred a simplified treatment of Greek Ionic patterns and adhered faithfully to the ancient classical prototypes.

Another building which Holland redesigned for the Prince of Wales was the **Pavilion** at **Brighton**. Here, he made the old house into a royal residence in an attractive classical design. Later the buildings were completely replanned by Nash, as also happened at Carlton House.

One of Holland's finest country houses, happily still standing and in family hands, is **Southill** in Bedfordshire, which he built for Samuel Whitbread. The house, like all Holland's work, is tasteful, restrained, exquisite in detail and excellently planned. Here again, he used his Ionic order. It appears in the south front (897) in coupled form in the central porch and in the side colonnades which connect the central mass to the side pavilions (956, 998).

Among Holland's other works are **Berrington Hall**, Herefordshire, 1780–5 (950), **Drury Lane Theatre**, 1794, and a remodelling of **Althorp**, Northamptonshire. He had a number of pupils, the most famous of whom was Soane.

James Wyatt 1746–1813

James Wyatt was the son of **Benjamin Wyatt** the builder and architect, and came from a large family, a number of whom in the late eighteenth and early nineteenth centuries became architects of greater or lesser fame. James is the best-known and was a man of outstanding talents who designed in a number of different styles. Partly for this reason, he is sometimes criticised for being insincere in his architectural beliefs and his work described as facile and shallow. Some critics, on the other hand, have considered him to have been a genius. Perhaps, as is so often the case, the truth is somewhere in between: it does not seem to be an adequate reason to doubt a man's professional sincerity if he prefers to express himself and experiment with more than one style. So many architects, for so long, had designed classical architecture of one type or another. Wyatt presents a challenge and a refreshing interlude.

Early in his career Wyatt was hailed as a genius. At this time the Adam brothers were at the height of their fame and Wyatt designed in their manner; so much so that in their *Works in Architecture* the Adam brothers complained of plagiarism. Wyatt had spent some years in Italy, where he made measured drawings of St Peter's and the Pantheon among other buildings. He returned to England to win the competition for the rebuilding of the **Pantheon** in

908 The Albany, Piccadilly (formerly Melbourne House), 1770. Sir William Chambers   909 3 The
Terrace, Richmond Hill, Surrey, *c.* 1769   910 15 St James's Square, London, 1763–6. James Stuart
911 Fairfax House, York, 1770. John Carr of York

Oxford Street. Designed for concerts and masquerades, it consisted of a large, aisled hall under a giant cupola, with rooms underneath. The dome was shaped as a hemisphere, like its Roman prototype, but its decoration reflected that of Adam. The building created a sensation in London when it was opened after two years in 1772. Architecturally and functionally it was a universal success and Wyatt's name and reputation were made henceforth. Some of the aristocratic patronage began to come his way instead of to Adam. The Pantheon was burnt down in 1792.

Wyatt designed a number of buildings, chiefly large houses, in both the Adam manner and later in a Greek Revival style. Towards the end of the century he essayed into Gothic, but all this later work is discussed in Chapter X.

Among Wyatt's houses are **Heaton Hall**, Lancashire, where he redesigned an older building and **Heveningham Hall**, Suffolk, where he designed and carried out the complete interior. The exterior construction had been built by Sir Robert Taylor (p. 331); the internal scheme, completed largely in the 1770s, has some fine, delicate decorative craftsmanship. The beautiful **Orangery** at **Heveningham** is by Wyatt. It has a semicircular portico and tall windows with semicircular heads (915, 957, 960, 971).

From 1775 Wyatt built the **Radcliffe Observatory** at **Oxford**, originally designed by Henry Keene. This is based on the Temple of the Winds in Athens (912, 973).

Sir John Soane 1753–1837

Soane was born near Reading of a poor family—his father was a bricklayer. In his 'teens Soane determined to become an architect, and this dedication to and love for architecture stayed with him strongly all his 84 years. He was articled first to George Dance II, then worked with Holland. He won both gold and silver medals at the Royal Academy and with the travelling scholarship went to Italy from 1778–80, where he studied in Rome, Paestum, Pompeii and Sicily. After this he began practice and for eight years was almost unknown. He built country houses which were styled much on Holland's or Dance's work.

It was in 1788 that Sir Robert Taylor died and Soane was given his appointment to the Bank of England. From this time onwards Soane discovered in himself his own individual architectural style; one which was original and quite different from those which had preceded it. It was a version of neo-classicism, owing much to the Greek and somewhat to Byzantine architecture but, essentially in quality, it was Soane. His work was monumental, stripped of all non-essential decoration and fancies, and relied on its simple, pure lines and fine proportions. Sometimes the work appears cold and has a feeling of sadness. It has a geometrical quality. Soane himself was ambitious and not content with less than perfection, or as near perfection as he could attain. He paid meticulous care to detail. He dedicated his life to his profession.

Soane took over his appointment at the **Bank of England** in 1788 and carried out extensive schemes in London until his retirement in 1833. In these 45 years the work was completed in three main periods. From **1788–1800**—the time covered in this chapter—the first part of the screen wall was built, which eventually surrounded the whole site. A stylised Corinthian order taken from the Tivoli was used in column form. A different design of pilaster was introduced on the plain sections of the wall. The columns were set in pairs or in colonnades while in the projecting centre of the façade was a porch comprising eight columns. Much of

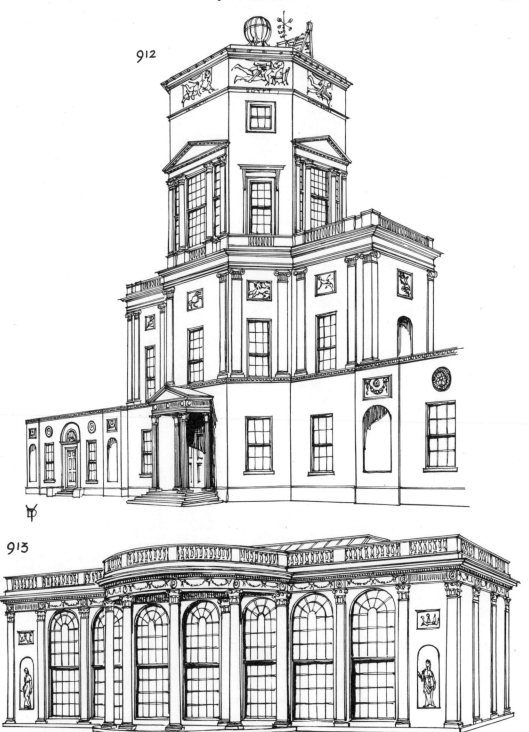

912 The Radcliffe Observatory, Oxford. Designed by Henry Keene, 1772; completed by James Wyatt after 1775   913 The Orangery, Heveningham Hall, Suffolk, 1790–5. James Wyatt

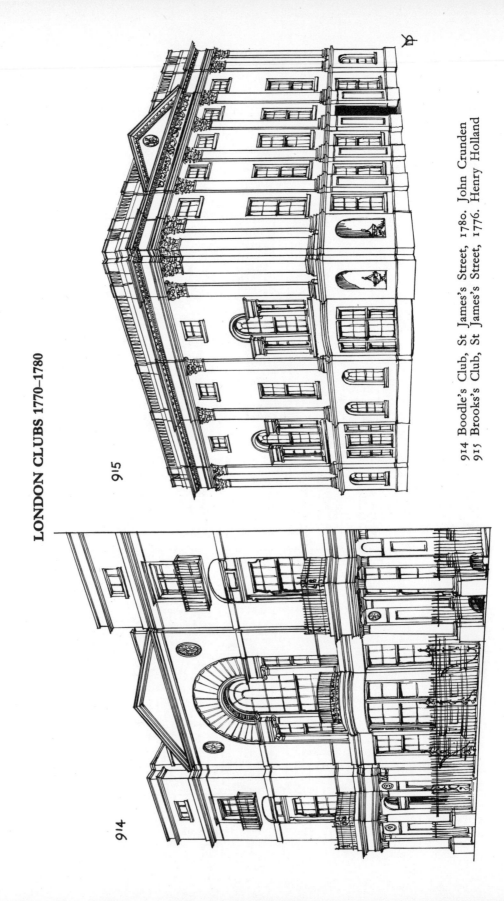

LONDON CLUBS 1770–1780

915

914

914 Boodle's Club, St James's Street, 1780. John Crunden
915 Brooks's Club, St James's Street, 1776. Henry Holland

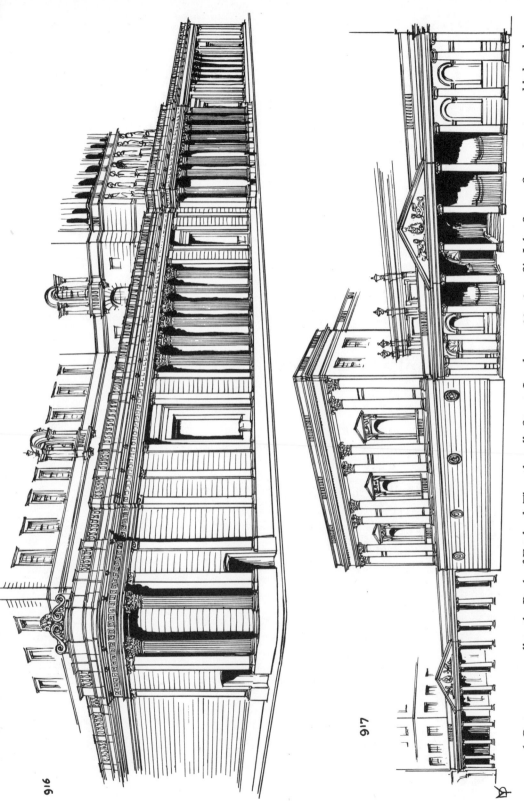

916 Outer screen wall to the Bank of England, Threadneedle Street, London, 1788–1833. Sir John Soane. Superstructure added and certain alterations made 1925–39 but screen wall left almost intact 917 The Great Pump Room, Bath, 1786–8: west front and colonnades. Thomas Baldwin

916

917

HOUSES 1760–1800

918 Woodhall Park, Hertfordshire: south front. 919 Tyringham, Buckinghamshire: entrance front,
1778–82. Thomas Leverton

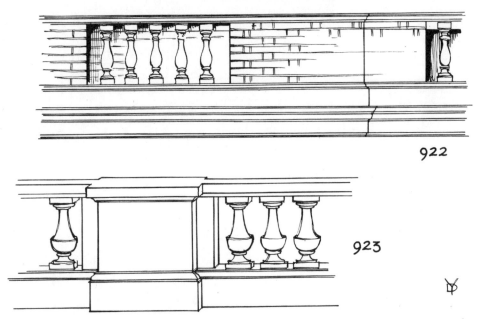

922 Parapet, Mersham-le-Hatch, Kent, 1762–72. Architect, Robert Adam
923 Parapet, Tyringham, Buckinghamshire, c. 1796. Sir John Soane

this screen wall exists today in almost unaltered form, but when the extensive rebuilding took place in 1925–39 a large superstructure towered above and behind the wall and this changes the appearance of the original design completely. The Threadneedle Street façade of the screen is shown in Fig. 916 with the superstructure merely indicated. When Soane took over as architect to the Bank he was faced with certain problems. The existing building, mainly constructed by **George Sampson** in the earlier eighteenth century and **Sir Robert Taylor** from 1766 naturally restricted some of his ideas for expansion and development. In addition, the site presented the difficulty of an acute-angled corner at Lothbury and Princes Street. The triangular screen wall thus evolved by Soane was in itself a masterpiece and a most successful solution of the problem. It was neither monotonous nor over-decorated, and even today, surrounded closely by other buildings, shows originality and dignity.

Also before 1800 Soane built the Bank Stock Office and the Rotunda. In these, his new architectural style became established. From 1800–33, several halls were constructed and the screen wall completed. A Byzantine treatment is apparent in these halls, while the vaults, walls and ceilings are handled interestingly and well (916, 1005).

In 1796 Soane designed **Tyringham House,** Buckinghamshire, one of his most famous country houses. Here he used the Ionic order in pilaster form, while the chief feature of the house is a semicircular, projecting porch, supported with giant Ionic columns, on the entrance front which extends the whole height of the house. There is a balustraded parapet above the entablature, but the present dome was added in 1907 (919, 923). The severely simple entrance gateway, using the Doric order, still survives, though in somewhat dilapidated condition (996). Soane's beautiful single arch bridge in the grounds is also still used (939).

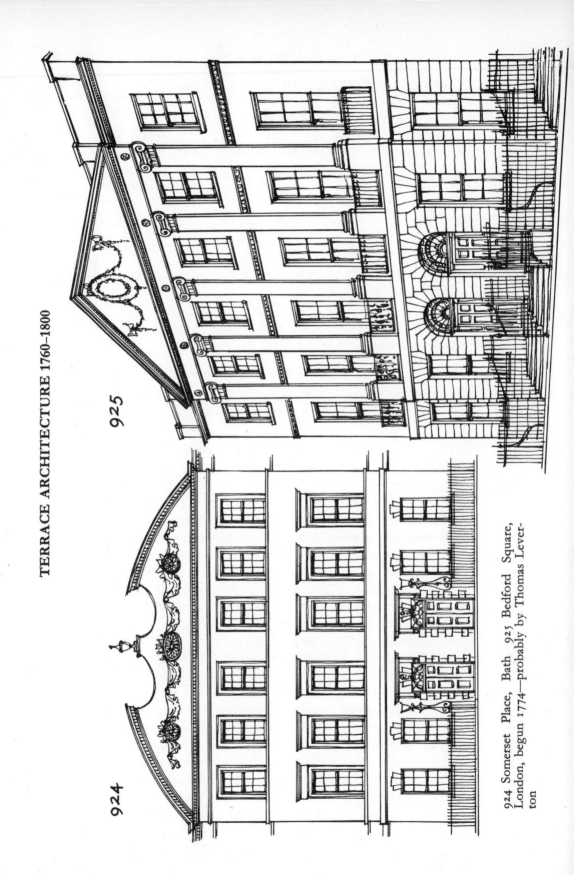

925

924

924 Somerset Place, Bath 925 Bedford Square, London, begun 1774—probably by Thomas Leverton

Thomas Leverton 1743–1824

Leverton was not classed among the great architects in his lifetime but his work, although not on the grand scale, nor great in quantity, has a delicate, tasteful quality ranking not far behind that of Adam or Wyatt, whose style he closely followed. He was the son of an Essex builder under whom he trained. Little is known of his architectural studies and there is no record of his visiting Italy or other Continental countries.

It is for his town houses in London that Leverton is best known. Here he created some exquisite interiors with fine stucco decoration, and beautiful staircases with iron balustrades.

Both **Joseph Bonomi**, the Italian, and **Flaxman**, the sculptor, were employed to decorate his interiors. Among examples of his work are several houses in **Bedford Square, London**; particularly of note is No. 1 which had a domed entrance hall and some fine stucco decoration. The staircase here was singularly attractive (925).

Woodhall Park, Hertfordshire, 1778–82, is one of his best-known country houses. A most interesting feature here was the Etruscan style entrance hall with fluted ceiling and white walls decorated with painted medallions in red, yellow and rich brown. The staircase was curved spirally and had a delicate iron balustrade. The walls of the stairwell were stuccoed in decorative panels, while the fan decoration of the dome ceiling was delicately fluted (918, 961, 984–5).

LESSER-KNOWN ARCHITECTS

Robert Mylne, 1734–1811, was a successful architect and engineer. He was born in Edinburgh and studied for five years in Italy and France. When he returned to England he won the competition for **Blackfriars Bridge** in **London**, which was built between 1760 and 1769. Two features of the bridge (which later became commonplace but which were new at the time) were the elliptical arches and the double columns mounted on each breakwater. The bridge was replaced in 1868. Mylne built several other bridges and a number of houses. Of the latter, **'The Wick', Richmond Hill**, built 1775, still survives (920). This simple neoclassic house has acted as a pattern for many later examples. His public buildings included the **Stationer's Hall, London**, and the **City of London Lying-in Hospital**.

James Stuart, 1713–88, is best known for his expedition to Athens in company with **Nicholas Revett** from 1751, which provided the material for their famous work *Antiquities of Athens* published 1762. Stuart's architectural output was not large and his best known works include **No. 15 St James's Square, London** (910), **Portman House, Portman Square** (destroyed 1941) and restoration work in the chapel at Greenwich Hospital.

Thomas Harrison, 1744–1829, was a Yorkshireman and after a number of years of study in Rome he returned to England in 1776 to spend his life designing bridges, castles and houses in the Midlands and the north of England. These include a **bridge** over the Lune at **Lancaster**, 1783–8, **Lancaster Castle**, begun 1788 and **Chester Castle**, 1793–1820. Both these very large castles were built to house gaol, courthouse and armoury. The former is in the Gothic style, the latter classical.

Joseph Bonomi, 1739–1808, was born in Rome and came to England in 1767 to work for the Adam brothers. He also worked for Leverton. In the 1780s he branched out for himself and designed a number of country houses which are Italian in conception and lack the finish of works by Leverton or Wyatt. Among these houses were **Longford Hall**, Shropshire, 1789–92, and **Eastwell House**, Kent, 1793–9.

Thomas Cooley, 1740–84, **James Gandon**, 1743–1823, and **Thomas Sandby**, 1721–98, were of Chambers's school and their work reflects his style. **Gandon** is the best-known and, like Cooley, carried out most of his commissions in Dublin. **The Custom House, Dublin, 1781–91**, is his outstanding work. This has a river-front façade which presented Gandon with difficulties similar to those experienced by Chambers at Somerset House. Much of the site was under water at high tide and a year elapsed before the foundations were completed and work could begin on the buildings. The design is masterly; one of the outstanding buildings of the eighteenth century. **Cooley**, who died prematurely, built the **Dublin Exchange** in 1779, and before this assisted Mylne on Blackfriars Bridge.

John Yenn, 1750–1821, and **Thomas Hardwick**, 1752–1829, were pupils of Chambers and exponents of his architectural style. **Hardwick** is known principally for his churches. **Wanstead Church**, Essex, was built 1787–91 in what was, at the time, a country area. It is an attractive country church with a Wren style clock tower and cupola, and a somewhat

926 Wanstead Church, Essex, 1787–1791. Thomas Hardwick

monumental porch in the Doric order (926, 976). His **St John's Wood Chapel**, 1814, and **St Marylebone Church**, 1813–17, were more imposing city churches (see Chapter X).

ARTISTS AND CRAFTSMEN

In the second half of the eighteenth century there were working in England a number of exceptionally gifted artists and craftsmen. Some worked by themselves, but the majority were employed by architects like Adam, Chambers, Wyatt and Leverton as decorators for their architectural interiors. Many of them were co-operators in the Adam brothers' team of artists. By far the majority of such artists were not English by birth and most were Italian. This was no innovation for England; artists and craftsmen had come from the Continent to work in metal, wood, plaster and paint over a period of several hundred years, but this particular half-century is noted for the quantity and quality of such artists. Together with the architects, they worked to produce the finest English interiors that have been created before or since: it was the zenith of artistic achievement in this field.

Painters

Angelica Kauffmann, 1741–1807, was Swiss, the daughter of a painter. She was a talented artist and became one of the most prolific of the Adam team. She came to England first in 1766, after spending a great deal of time in Italy. She became a friend and colleague of Sir Joshua Reynolds and was one of the two women founder-members of the Royal Academy of Arts, where she exhibited regularly. In 1781 she married Antonio Zucchi, the Venetian painter. Angelica Kauffmann lived her last years in Italy where she died in 1807 and was given an impressive funeral, under the direction of the Italian sculptor Canova. Her paintings can be seen in many Adam houses, notably Syon, Chandos House and Saltram.

Antonio Zucchi, 1726–95, was an Italian painter and also a prolific worker on the Adam interiors. Among his best paintings as a decorative craftsman are panels at Osterley, Harewood, Kedleston, Kenwood and Luton Hoo. He also carried out a great deal of work on the Adelphi scheme.

Francesco Zuccarelli, 1702–88, was born in Tuscany and later studied in Rome. He executed commissions in Italy and afterwards in England. In both countries his paintings, which were generally landscapes featuring small figures with classic ruin background, were in great demand. Zuccarelli was a founder member of the Royal Academy.

Giovanni Battista Cipriani, 1727–85, the Italian painter and etcher, was born in Florence and studied there, and later in Rome. While he was in Rome he met Sir William Chambers and Joseph Wilton the sculptor. He came to England in 1755 with them and painted a ceiling for Chambers at the Albany in London. He carried out much of his best work at Somerset House, also for Chambers, and later restored paintings by Verrio at Windsor and Rubens's ceiling at the Banqueting Hall in Whitehall. Cipriani also painted much of the Adam furniture and decorated a number of the Adam interiors, especially at Syon. He also was a founder-member of the Royal Academy.

Biagio Rebecca, 1735–1808, lived for many years in England and was elected an A.R.A. in 1771. He worked for Chambers at Somerset House and painted panels and wall decoration for Wyatt, particularly at Heveningham. His chief contribution to the Adam team was at Kedleston and Harewood.

Michael Angelo Pergolesi was an Italian decorative artist, primarily a **designer** rather

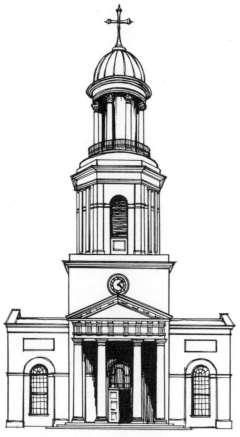

927 St Chad's Church, Shrewsbury, 1790–2.
George Steuart

than an executant in any one medium. He came to England in 1770 and worked both independently and for the Adam brothers. He designed furniture, stucco for ceilings, friezes and mural panels, also chandeliers, chimney-pieces and silverware. Many of his designs included painted panels which were carried out by Angelica Kauffmann or Cipriani.

Joseph Rose was a **stuccoist** whose work was of the highest quality. He executed a large number of designs in this medium for Adam, notably at Syon, Harewood, Kenwood and St James's Square; he also worked for Wyatt on the Pantheon.

Joseph Wilton, 1722–1803, was a **sculptor** who came to England in 1755 with Sir William Chambers and Cipriani. Most of his work was commissioned by Chambers, but he also became Sculptor to the King and, later, carried out work for Adam.

John Flaxman, 1755–1826, was an Englishman born at York. He showed early promise as a **sculptor** and exhibited at the Royal Academy at the age of 15. For 12 years, from his 20th year onwards, he worked for Josiah Wedgwood, modelling plaques, friezes, medallions and other relief decoration for the famous potter. After 1780 he devoted himself more to sculptural monuments, especially those for the dead. In 1800 Flaxman was elected an Academician and ten years later occupied the first chair in sculpture at the Royal Academy.

Josiah Wedgwood, 1730–95, cannot here be given an adequate biographical note. It is only his work in connection with interior decoration which comes within the scope of this book. Wedgwood was particularly noted for his determination to improve the standard of pottery, as distinct from porcelain, from the somewhat clumsy earthenware of his time. He produced new designs and processes; he emphasised the need for perfection of form and purity of material. Among his most famous innovations was 'Jasper Ware', and it was this ware, in its pastel-coloured forms, which was introduced into interior decorative schemes at this time. Especially to be seen were medallions and plaques ornamenting chimney-pieces and mural decoration. The bas-reliefs were generally the work of Flaxman. Both Adam and Wyatt incorporated such materials into their schemes.

CHURCHES

This was not a great period of church building. There were few if any new churches, only now and again was an architect commissioned to rebuild an old one. When a church was

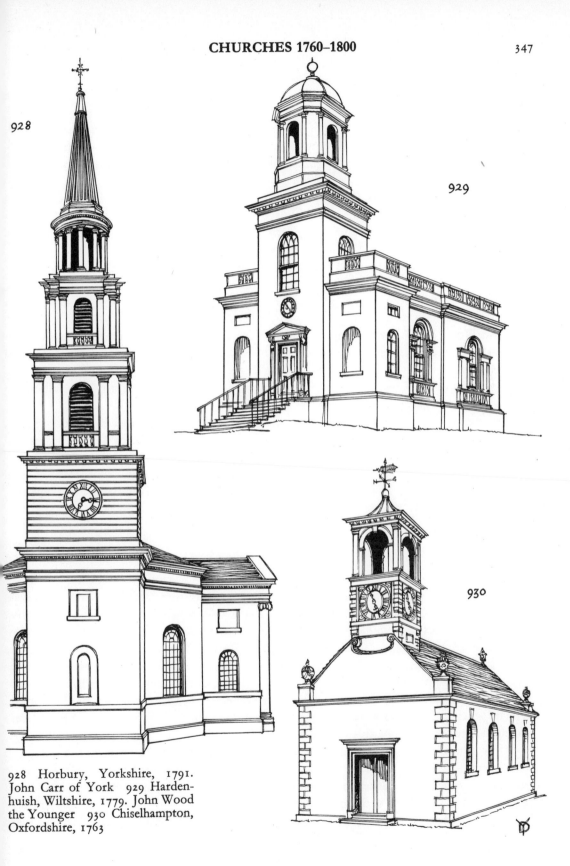

928 Horbury, Yorkshire, 1791.
John Carr of York 929 Hardenhuish, Wiltshire, 1779. John Wood
the Younger 930 Chiselhampton,
Oxfordshire, 1763

replaced its architecture reflected the secular designs of the day. The Adam style of architecture is seen as an influence, although Adam himself designed hardly any. Wyatt built some churches but most of these were later destroyed or rebuilt.

Among the interesting churches of the period is that of **St Chad, Shrewsbury**, 1790–7, designed by **George Steuart**. This church stands upon a fine site above the town and overlooking a park. It is an imposing design, dignified, a little severe, but unusual in conception. It has a circular nave and accommodates a large congregation (927).

At **Wanstead** is **Thomas Hardwick's church**, built 1787–91. This is of brick faced with Portland stone. The main body of the church is rectangular with windows on two floors while the west end has a Roman Doric porch. The church is surmounted by a small cupola in Wren tradition (926, 976).

Among the churches designed by provincial architects is **Horbury**, Yorkshire, 1791, by **John Carr of York**. This is large and very tall for a small town. At the west end is a lofty steeple in three tiers, surmounted by a spire. The Ionic order is employed in the south porch (928, 977).

John Wood II, of Bath, designed an attractive country church at **Hardenhuish**, Wiltshire in 1779. It is built upon an eminence and shows something of a Palladian influence in its design (929).

Chiselhampton, Oxfordshire, is a small country church of unpretentious but charming appearance. It has a decorative cupola at the west end (930).

Among the other classical churches of the day should be mentioned **Banbury**, 1790–7, by **S. P. Cockerell**, **Bädminton**, 1763, **Nuneham Courtenay**, 1764, by **James Stuart** and **Ayot St Lawrence**, 1778–9, by his colleague **Nicholas Revett**.

A few Gothic or strangely styled Gothic churches were erected at this time. **St Nicholas' Warwick**, is one of the best of these, built 1748–80. There is also **Tetbury**, Gloucestershire, 1777–81, designed by **Francis Hiorn** of Warwick.

TOWN PLANNING AND TERRACE ARCHITECTURE

London

The design of individual houses, both in towns and in country areas, has been discussed fully under the appropriate architect's name. There was, however, at this time, as distinct from single houses, a movement for planning terraces, crescents, streets of houses and even whole estates, particularly in urban areas. This movement had begun under the Palladians and had taken place most extensively in Bath (see Chapter VIII). In the second half of the eighteenth century these schemes were continued and largely completed in Bath, while at the same time, comparatively small areas of London were also being planned and built upon. The impetus of this movement was yet to come and the chief acceleration began in the early nineteenth century with Nash's Regent's Park layout.

Unfortunately, in **London** and in some other large cities, architecture of this period in terrace and square construction has been demolished on a widespread scale to make way for more modern accommodation and planning. While the need for this is understood, a natural regret is felt at the loss of such fine quality work.

Of such schemes initiated by the Adam brothers, both the Adelphi and Portland Place

931 Fitzroy Square, London. Two sides by Robert Adam—from 1790 932 The Paragon, Black-heath, *c.* 1790. Doric colonnades 933 Camden Crescent, Bath. Designed by John Jelly from 1788

are now lost to us and there remains only **Fitzroy Square**. Here also alterations have taken place, but something of the Adam layout and workmanship has been preserved (931).

In **Bedford Square** can still be seen some of Leverton's work. The exteriors here are almost unspoiled (925). Of Henry Holland's layouts, a few houses in Sloane Place, Sloane Street and Hans Place still remain, but it is difficult to visualise the original scheme.

At **Blackheath** among some fine Regency building is a **terrace** dated *c.* 1790. This is the **Paragon** which consists of rectangular blocks, connected by Doric colonnades. The terrace is kept in good condition, and is a peaceful oasis near the busy main road (932).

Bath

There are still many beautiful examples of terrace architecture remaining in England; this is particularly true of the spas, such as Cheltenham, Clifton and Buxton, and also in the south-coast resorts, such as Brighton and Hastings. The majority of these layouts, however, are nineteenth-century achievements, and it is in **Bath** that there can be seen a large part of a city laid out in eighteenth-century style, as one comprehensive scheme. The initiation of this civic planning under **John Wood I** was discussed in Chapter VIII. From 1755 onwards the work was carried on by his son, also **John Wood** and by men such as **Thomas Baldwin, John Jelly** and **John Palmer**. Thus, Bath is our oldest example of civic planning on a wide scale and, being constructed largely between 1750 and 1800, presents dignified, well-proportioned exteriors and tasteful, graceful interiors.

The contour of the land in Bath posed considerable problems, with its low-lying centre on the Avon and hills rising, sometimes steeply, around. The men who designed the new town layout not only dealt adequately with these problems, they took advantage of them. Thus we have curving terraces and crescents built on the edges of hill crowns, providing magnificent vistas of both town and countryside. Architecturally, in Bath, the bulk of the planning in the eighteenth century was in stone in Palladian style. The conception is on the grand scale, the whole effect is impressive, while the detail is generally good.

Apart from the Circus, planned and largely executed by John Wood I before 1760 (see XLIII and Chapter VIII), the greatest architectural achievement is the **Royal Crescent** built **1765–75** by **John Wood II**. Here, Wood shows himself, like his father and John Carr of York, not merely a provincial architect but one whose work ranks with much of the best created by London architects. The Crescent forms a gigantic arc built on the edge of the crown of a hill and arranged around a great lawn. It is high above the city, of which it provides a magnificent view set in the surrounding countryside. The Ionic order is used, with 114 columns and there are 30 houses within the terrace, presenting a uniform frontage constructed on a major axis of 538 feet. The height of the façade is 47 feet, comprising three storeys. The giant order of engaged, three-quarter columns spans the first and second floors while above this is the entablature and balustraded parapet. The return angles and the centre of the curve are emphasised by double columns. The whole crescent, although now partly internally adjusted to provide more up-to-date accommodation, is almost unchanged in the exterior façade and the stonework is in good condition. It is one of the finest examples of terrace architecture in Britain (934–6).

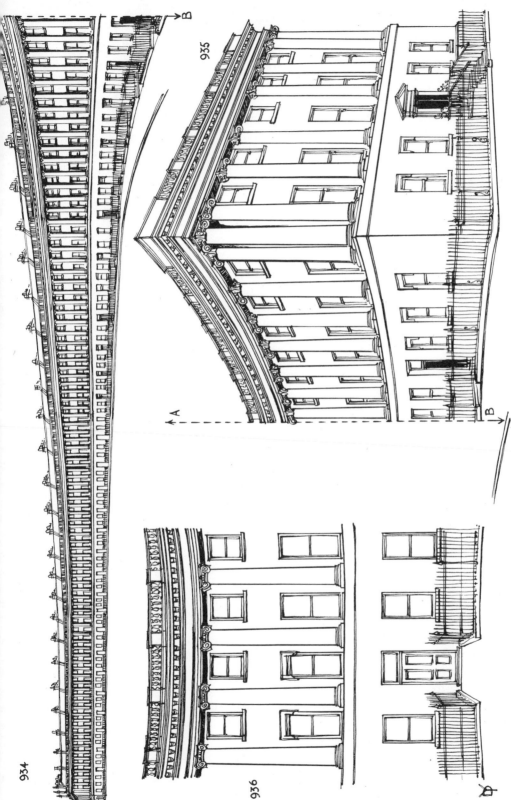

934

935

936

The Royal Crescent, Bath. John Wood the Younger, 1767–75. The complete crescent is shown in Figs 934 and 935. The dotted line A–B indicates the join, although the scale is larger in Fig. 935. The Ionic Order is used and there are 100 three-quarter engaged columns on the front façade. At each end and in the centre are double columns. Fig. 936 shows a section of the front façade

Among the many other attractive terraces and crescents in Bath are Lansdown Crescent, Camden Crescent and Somerset Place. **Lansdown Crescent**, designed by **John Palmer**, 1789–93, is, like Royal Crescent, set high up on the crest of a hill and is also on the grand scale. The 20 houses of the crescent form nearly a third of a circle, with a radius of about 300 feet. There is a central feature with Ionic pilasters and pediment above. At each end of the crescent a larger house forms a terminal pavilion. The crescent has three storeys, the lower one being rusticated. Like the Royal Crescent, the interiors were very fine with a high standard of craftsmanship on the ceilings, mural decoration, chimney-pieces and doorcases.

Camden Crescent, begun in 1788 by **John Jelly**, has also a fine view of Bath from its hill-crest position. Originally it was planned to build 32 houses here but a landslip occurred and it was decided only to build the present 18, with one wing left incomplete. However, even in this unbalanced condition, it is a beautiful terrace. The order is Corinthian in pilaster form, while the central feature uses columns, with a pediment above. Again there are three storeys with surmounting entablature (933).

Somerset Place adjoins Lansdown Crescent and, like Camden Crescent, its original scheme was not fully completed. It has an elegant, central feature which is surmounted by a curved, broken pediment. The tympanum is decorated by paterae and looped drapery (924).

Public Building in Bath

The **Pump Room** was rebuilt from 1786 to 1788 by **Thomas Baldwin**, although the interior work was completed by **John Palmer** in 1799.

The exterior, in the centre of the city, possesses a magnificent colonnade. The Ionic order is used and the colonnade is in two sections, with three building blocks. Each colonnade has a central pedimental feature, in which the tympanum is decorated by female sphinxes flanking an oval wreath which surrounds a relief head. The central block, dividing the two colonnades, is the Pump Room itself. Here the Corinthian order is used in the form of engaged columns, with entablature and parapet above, and rusticated storey beneath. The Corinthian order is also employed in the interior with gilded, foliated capitals (917).

The **Guildhall** was also designed by **Thomas Baldwin** in 1776. It is dignified and well-proportioned, while the interior is finely decorated with beautiful detailed workmanship. There is a banqueting hall of some 80 feet by 40 feet, and over 30 feet in height. Here is used the Corinthian order with fluted columns on pedestals round the room. The ceiling is elaborately patterned in stucco.

There were a number of other extensive building schemes in Bath in this period which, unfortunately, were either not carried out in their entirety or have since been demolished. Among the former schemes was that for the Bathwick Estate by **Robert Adam**. Here, only the famous **Pulteney Bridge** was completed and this has been sadly debased. There was also **Milsom Street**, planned and commenced in 1762, but now largely rebuilt. This was the social centre of Bath and is still a fine, wide shopping street. Originally the houses were uniformly designed in Palladian manner.

An interesting house in the city of Bath is that by **C. Harcourt Masters**, built in 1795. This house was altered somewhat in 1915 and is now the **Holburne of Menstrie Museum** (905).

XLV   The   Bank   of   England,   London:
court room, c. 1775. Architect Sir Robert T

BRIDGES

A considerable number of beautiful bridges were built during these years, predominantly in stone but a few in brick. Due to the increased volume of road traffic, such bridges are disappearing year by year, or are being by-passed by a modern example and left cheek by jowl with the new bridge. It is difficult to judge which is the best course of action in such cases.

Some of these existing eighteenth-century bridges were designed by famous architects of the day. A number of **Adam bridges** still survive. There is a beautiful bridge in the grounds of **Kedleston Hall**, Derbyshire, *c.* 1758–70. This is built of stone and has three segmental arches and an elegant balustrade above with finely proportioned balusters. The piers have empty niches and the restrained decoration is in the form of paterae and delicate swags (937). The **Pulteney Bridge** in **Bath** (already mentioned) had three arches bearing a row of covered shops. The actual bridge structure has not been changed a great deal but the buildings above are altered now out of all recognition. Another bridge reputed to be by Adam is the sturdy example at **Inveraray** in Scotland, over the river Aray.

In **Tyringham Park**, Buckinghamshire, is **Sir John Soane's** beautiful, single-arched stone bridge built *c.* 1796. Its simple, strong line epitomises his architectural style (939).

Sir Robert Taylor's contribution is the **Maidenhead** road bridge built in 1772. This long, many-arched bridge has prominently marked voussoirs and a pleasantly balustraded parapet. It is to be hoped that this mellowed stone landmark will not as yet, disappear from Thames-side (947).

James Paine contributed a number of **Thames bridges**, including those at Richmond, Kew, Chertsey and Walton. Two of these have been replaced but Richmond and Chertsey bridges still exist. At **Richmond** there are five spans with a larger central arch. The bridge, built in 1774–7, is faced with Portland stone (938). At **Chertsey**, built 1785, there are seven arches. Another attractive bridge by **Paine** is that in **Chatsworth Park**, Derbyshire, 1762. It has three spans and a classical parapet. Above the cutwaters are set antique, stone figures (942).

937 Bridge in the grounds of Kedleston House, Derbyshire, 1758–70. Robert Adam

VI *Fonthill Abbey, Wiltshire, 1795–1807. Architect James Wyatt*
(from an engraving by J. Lambert after G. Cattermole, 1823)

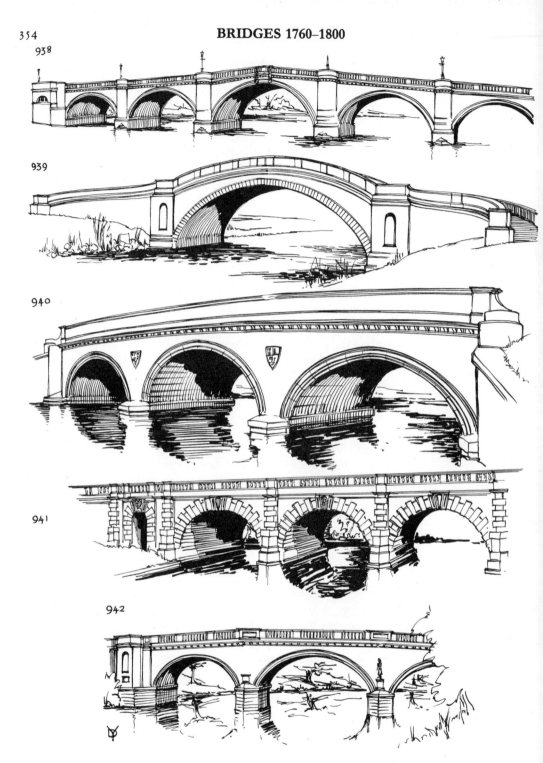

938 Richmond, Surrey, over the Thames, 1774–7. James Paine   939 Tyringham Park, Buckingham-shire, *c*. 1796. Sir John Soane   940 Trinity College, Cambridge, over the Cam, 1760. James Essex   941 Magdalen College, Oxford, 1773. John Gwynn   942 Chatsworth Park, Derbyshire, 1762. James Paine

John Gwynn built some fine bridges, among which there is the, now by-passed, bridge at **Atcham**, Shropshire, over the Severn, 1776, and scheduled as an ancient monument. This seven-span, stone bridge is well designed and the only one of Gwynn's Severn bridges in an unaltered condition (946). He did, however, build **Magdalen Bridge, Oxford**, over the Cherwell in 1773. This, his only bridge not over the Severn, is a simple one with traditional balustraded parapet and carved head keystones (941).

There is one other notable University bridge of this time: **Trinity College Bridge** at **Cambridge**. This was built over the Cam by **James Essex** in 1760. It is a stone, three-span bridge with plain, moulded decoration (940).

Other stone bridges of note, all spanning the Thames, include that at **Swinford**, built in 1777, a classical bridge still under toll; the five-span **Henley Bridge** designed by **William Hayward** in 1786 which resembles greatly Richmond bridge (944); and the interesting brick bridge at **Sonning**. This has seven arches, with the central one much larger than the others, and is in a quiet, peaceful setting despite the fact that the main road is reduced there to single-line traffic by the necessary traffic signals because the bridge is so narrow (945).

A bridge of this time which is most exceptional is the **Ironbridge** at **Coalbrookdale**, Shropshire, over the river Severn. It was the first bridge in the world to be made almost entirely of iron and the forerunner of many in the nineteenth century. It was built in 1779 and is now scheduled as an ancient monument. It is constructed of five parallel arch ribs, almost 200 feet in length. The spandrels are filled by circles and ogee arch heads, while the roadway above is made from cast-iron plates of $2\frac{1}{2}$-inch thickness. The bridge, which took only three months to build, weighs some 400 tons. Later iron bridges were less traditional in design and were adapted to the use of this newer material (943).

943 Ironbridge, Coalbrookdale, Shropshire, over the Severn, 1779. First iron bridge in the world

BRIDGES 1760–1800

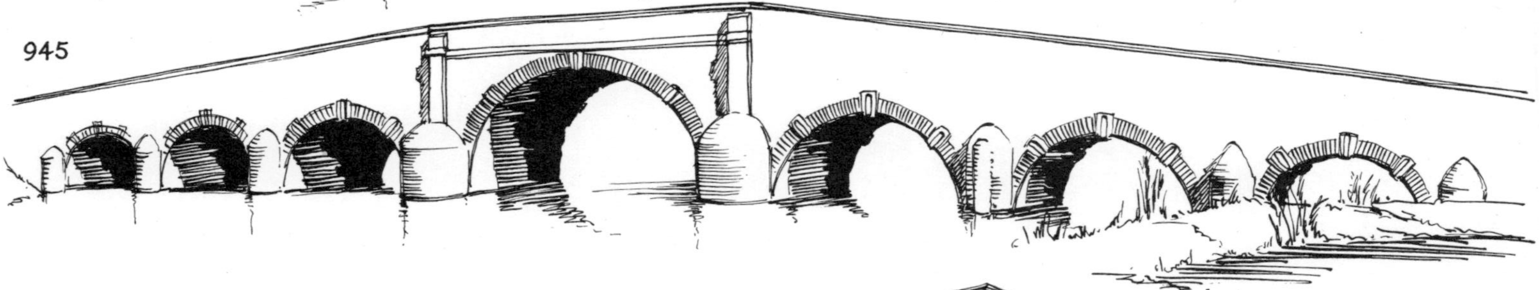

944 Henley Bridge, Oxfordshire, over the Thames, 1786. William Hayward. Stone   945 Sonning Bridge, Berkshire, over the Thames late 18th century. Brick   946 Atcham Bridge, Shropshire, over the Severn, 1776. John Gwynn   947 Maidenhead Road

944

945

946

947

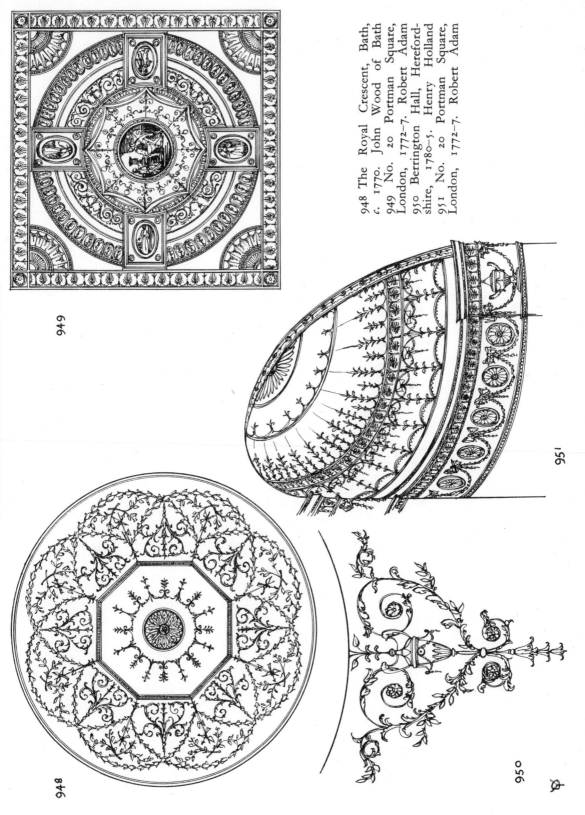

948 The Royal Crescent, Bath, c. 1770. John Wood of Bath
949 No. 20 Portman Square, London, 1772–7. Robert Adam
950 Berrington Hall, Hereford-shire, 1780–5. Henry Holland
951 No. 20 Portman Square, London, 1772–7. Robert Adam

949

948

950

951

INTERIOR DECORATION

Between 1760 and 1800 the trend in the decoration of ceiling and wall surfaces was towards lower relief. The Adam brothers were responsible for much of this great change in decorative approach and their lead was followed by Wyatt, Leverton and Holland. The heavier, deeper mouldings casting dark shadows were gradually lightened and, towards 1775–80, decoration was often merely painted and not even in relief stucco. Ceiling designs comprised isolated pictures painted by Angelica Kauffmann and her colleagues connected by stucco arabesque forms to a general ceiling pattern. The low, delicate relief was matched by the elegance of the curves and decorative forms. Mural design followed similar lines. Low sculptural relief, often in draped human figures, was utilised particularly in chimney-piece design, as also were Wedgwood plaques and medallions. Colour schemes were in white and pastel shades with delicate touches of gilt, in contrast to the Kent interiors with heavier use of gold.

The Etruscan style, popularised by Adam and followed up enthusiastically by Wyatt and Leverton, consisted of wall and ceiling paintings of Etruscan motifs: vases, urns, human figures and medallions in terracotta, chocolate, black, blue and yellow. This gave a rich contrast to the popular pastel tones. Wedgwood also used Etruscan ideas, as evidenced by the name of his factory 'Etruria'. His jasper ware, particularly his black basalt, showed Etruscan motifs and origins (948–62; XLI, XLII, Colour Plate 6).

952 Chimney-piece at Kedleston, Derbyshire. Robert Adam

The best quality **doors** were of polished mahogany, designed with six panels and moulded in low relief. The panel decoration and door furniture was in brass or ormolu. The classical form was still used for **doorways, porches** and **porticoes**. Greek motifs of decoration were used in friezes; reeding, paterae and delicate swags and looped drapery were all in general use (963–81).

Window designs followed a similar pattern. Semicircular heads often had fluted decoration or, like doorways, delicate fan tracery (982–9).

Staircases were elegant, decorative and graceful. The spiral or curving staircase was often employed. This generally had a thin mahogany handrail and a delicate, ornamental ironwork balustrade, with wood or marble stairs. These staircases were quite strong and well built but appeared often almost ephemeral in their lightness and use of iron, which, more and more, replaced wooden balusters (990). **Ironwork** generally, as used for **grilles** and **gates**, followed the same pattern. The trend was to more delicate designs in thin, elegant treatment (998–9).

The Orders and their Application

It was in the use of the orders that the controversy between Greece and Rome was illustrated most clearly. Sir William Chambers and his school adhered to the pure Roman traditions. Sir Robert Taylor and a few other architects still followed Palladian forms, while Wyatt, Holland and others tried designing in Greek Revival manner. Adam sought his inspiration from many sources, although his penchant was for the Greek more often than the Roman. In general, the interpretation and use of the orders was based accurately on the Greek, Roman and Italian, or French Renaissance originals and the architectural results in this period were superlative. A few examples are shown in Figs 1000–8.

953 Fireplace, Somerset House, London. Sir William Chambers

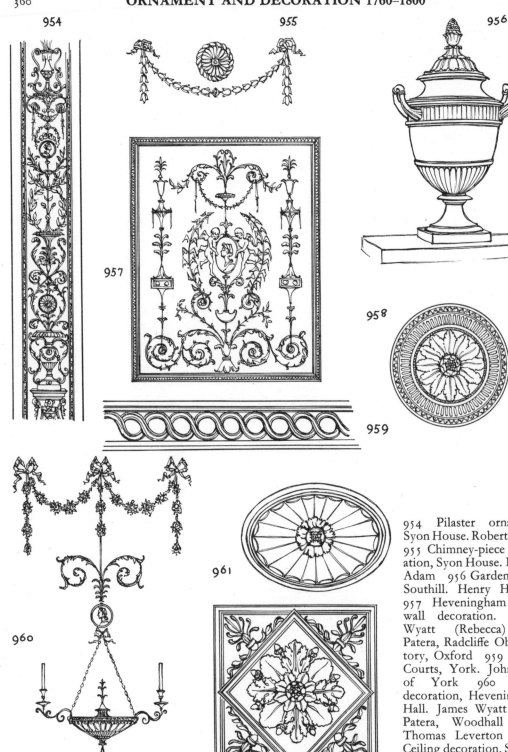

954

955

956

957

958

959

961

960

962

954 Pilaster ornament, Syon House. Robert Adam 955 Chimney-piece decoration, Syon House. Robert Adam 956 Garden finial, Southill. Henry Holland 957 Heveningham Hall: wall decoration. James Wyatt (Rebecca) 958 Patera, Radcliffe Observatory, Oxford 959 Assize Courts, York. John Carr of York 960 Relief decoration, Heveningham Hall. James Wyatt 961 Patera, Woodhall Park. Thomas Leverton 962 Ceiling decoration, Somerset House. Sir William Chambers

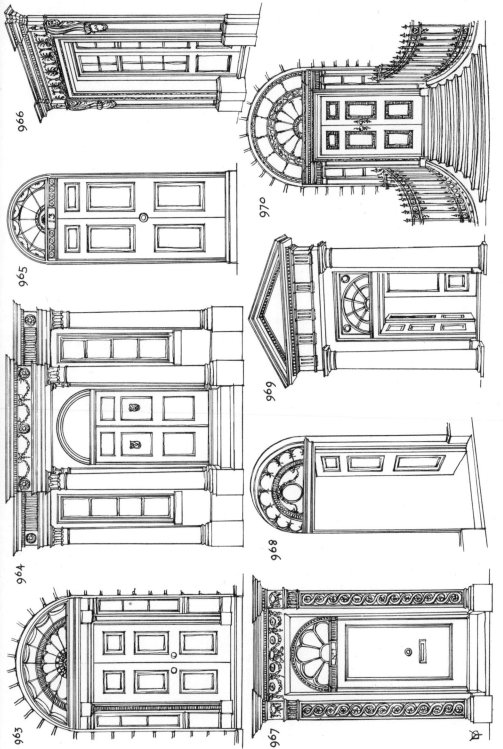

963 Bedford Square, London, 1774. Thomas Leverton 964 The Royal Society of Arts, John Adam Street, London, 1772–4 965 The Paragon, Blackheath, 1790 966 Osterley Park, Middlesex, 1761. Robert Adam 967 No. 7 Adam Street, Adelphi, *c.* 1770. Robert Adam 968 Osterley Park, Middlesex, 1761. Robert Adam 969 Mersham-le-Hatch, Kent, 1767–72. Robert Adam 970 No. 20 St James's Square, London, 1775–89. Robert Adam

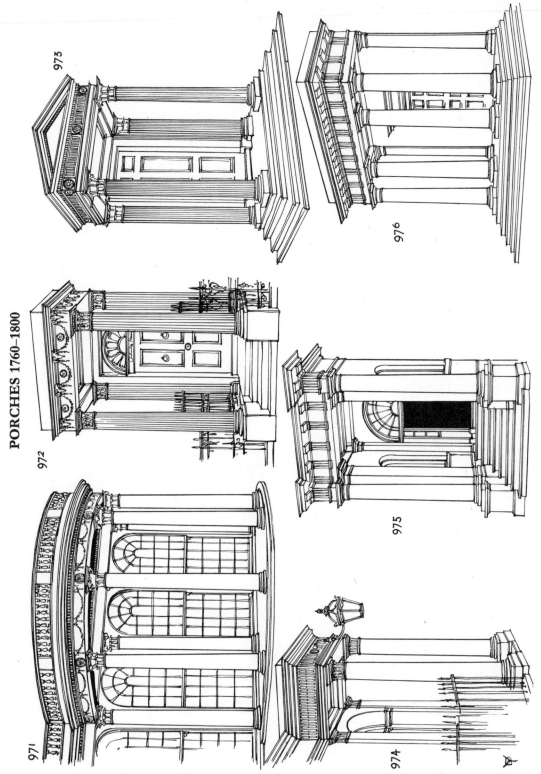

PORCHES 1760–1800

971

972

973

974

975

976

971 The Orangery, Heveningham Hall, Suffolk, 1790–1800. James Wyatt 972 Chandos House, Marylebone, *c.* 1770 Robert

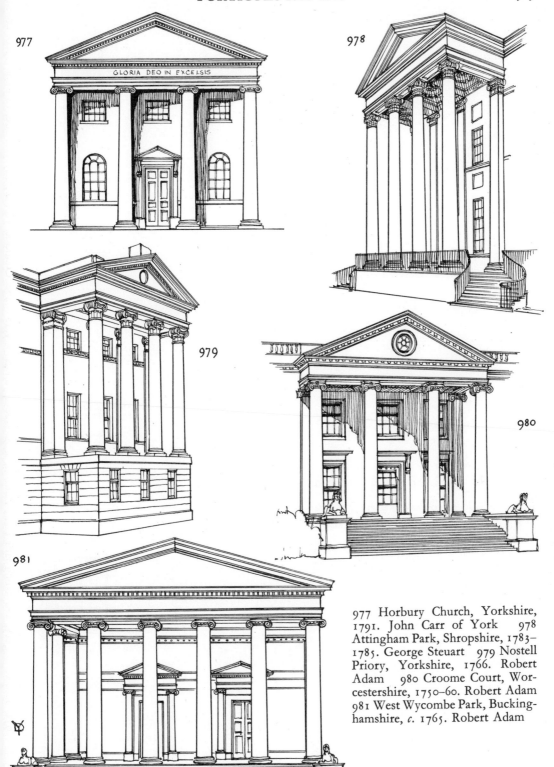

977 Horbury Church, Yorkshire, 1791. John Carr of York   978 Attingham Park, Shropshire, 1783–1785. George Steuart   979 Nostell Priory, Yorkshire, 1766. Robert Adam   980 Croome Court, Worcestershire, 1750–60. Robert Adam 981 West Wycombe Park, Buckinghamshire, c. 1765. Robert Adam

WINDOWS 1760-1800

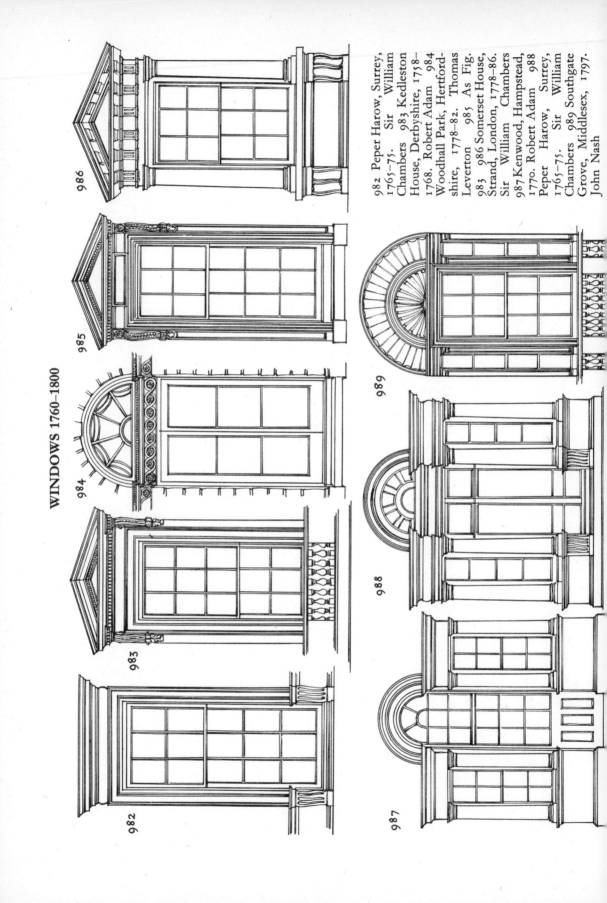

982 Peper Harow, Surrey, 1765-75. Sir William Chambers 983 Kedleston House, Derbyshire, 1758-1768. Robert Adam 984 Woodhall Park, Hertfordshire, 1778-82. Thomas Leverton 985 As Fig. 983. 986 Somerset House, Strand, London, 1778-86. Sir William Chambers 987 Kenwood, Hampstead, 1770. Robert Adam 988 Peper Harow, Surrey, 1765-75. Sir William Chambers 989 Southgate Grove, Middlesex, 1797. John Nash

990 Woodhall Park, Hertfordshire, 1778–82. Thomas Leverton 991 Peper Harow, Surrey, 1765–1775. Sir William Chambers 992 Heveningham Hall, Suffolk, 1778–84. James Wyatt 993 Serpentine scroll balustrade, late 18th century 994 Kenwood, Hampstead, 1767–8. Robert Adam 995 Osterley Park, Middlesex, 1761. Robert Adam

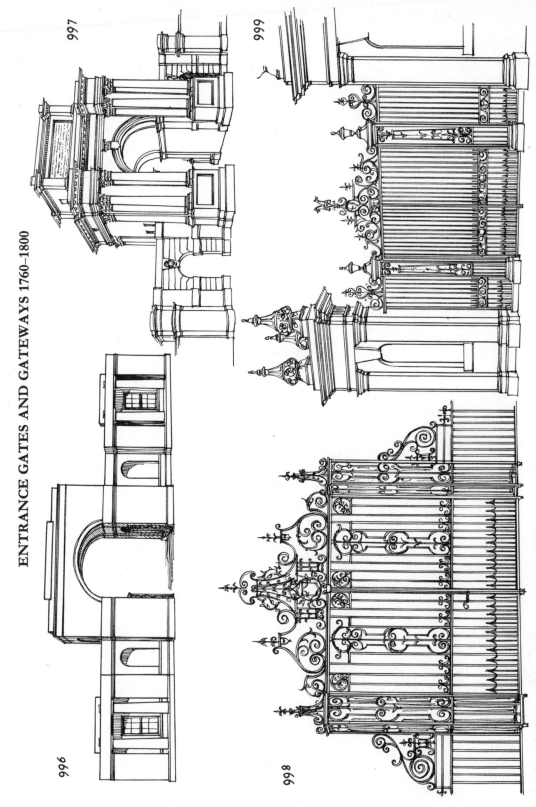

ENTRANCE GATES AND GATEWAYS 1760–1800

996

997

998

999

996 Tyringham, Buckinghamshire, c. 1796, Sir John Soane . 997 Blenheim Palace, Oxfordshire, Sir William Chambers . 998 Southill

1000 Nostell Priory, Yorkshire, 1766: Ionic Order. Adam wing   1001 Osterley Park, Middlesex, 1761: Doric Order. Robert Adam   1002 Kenwood, Hampstead, 1770: Ionic Order. Robert Adam 1003 The Paragon, Blackheath, 1790: Doric Order   1004 No. 7 Adam St, Adelphi, *c*. 1770: Doric Pilaster. Robert Adam   1005 The Bank of England, 1788–1835: Corinthian Order. Sir John Soane 1006 Kedleston House, Derbyshire, 1758–68: Corinthian Order. Robert Adam   1007 Assize Courts, York, 1780: Ionic Capital. John Carr of York   1008 Osterley, 1871: base. Adam

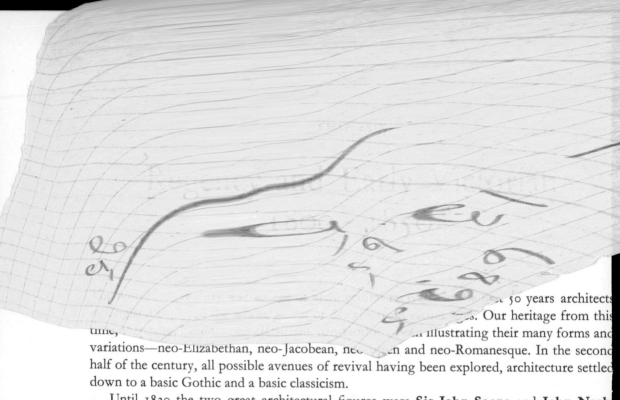

... 50 years architects ...s. Our heritage from this time, ... illustrating their many forms and variations—neo-Elizabethan, neo-Jacobean, neo-... and neo-Romanesque. In the second half of the century, all possible avenues of revival having been explored, architecture settled down to a basic Gothic and a basic classicism.

Until 1820 the two great architectural figures were **Sir John Soane** and **John Nash**. As in the instance of Chambers and Adam, here were two men of ability and individuality, almost exactly contemporary, but differing widely in their approach to their subject. Soane's work is always original, pure and in faultless taste. His detail is immaculate, his style definite and he is perhaps best known for his interior work as evidenced at the Bank of England. Nash is famed especially for his vast exterior schemes, notably the Regent's Park layout and terraces. His work was far-seeing and large scale, his sense of design fine and imaginative, his attention to detail inadequate and often sloppy. He worked in the grand manner and he turned his hand to designs which were many and varied in style and scope.

In these same years **new materials** were making their appearance and the tempo of building increased. Stucco, as a facing to brickwork, was the modern way to imitate the more costly stone. It was then painted dark in tone to imitate the stone façades. Nash's name is indissolubly linked with stucco, for he was the architect who chiefly popularised the material with his terrace town-planning schemes. Plain brick was left for cheaper buildings, but glazed brick was often employed in terrace architecture, especially on sea-front positions as at Brighton. Iron and glass, both improved by numerous technical discoveries, were employed widely, first by the great engineers then by the architects. This movement towards the use of iron and glass increased rapidly in momentum after mid century.

Since the days of Inigo Jones, nearly all English architecture had been based on the classic form. In the early nineteenth century, however, the neo-classical began seriously to split into two opposing styles: classical and Gothic. The latter aspect of the movement developed slowly and through many vicissitudes, its exponents experimenting in all forms of Gothic from Romanesque to Tudor; until 1850, the classical faction held primary place in English architecture, particularly in the field of public building.

Also from the early years of the century a preference was evinced for the Greek form of classicism. This trend had been evident in the later years of the eighteenth century, but from about 1805 onwards it became more marked. Among the chief exponents of this style were

first **George Dance II**, then both **William Wilkins** and **Sir Robert Smirke**. By 1820
and Soane were old, and Smirke and Wilkins constituted the prime architectural for[
they lacked the originality and the capabilities of their eminent predecessors. In comp
with later nineteenth-century work their contributions, especially in large, public bu
are adequate, in good taste and well designed, but only too often the chief criticism
at their work is that it is dull and lacks spirit. Some capable architects followed
classical vein, sometimes producing fine work. Especially notable are such men as
Basevi, Decimus Burton and **C. R. Cockerell**, all of whose work, while not outstandingly
original, is in the best English classical tradition, and frequently more lively, especially on
the Greek theme, than that of Smirke or Wilkins. Strangely, the public building most commonly acclaimed as the outstanding classical work of the century was not designed by one
of these architects: **St George's Hall, Liverpool**, was the creation of a young man called
Harvey Lonsdale Elmes, who unfortunately died before the work was completed. If he
had lived, England would possibly have seen more fine classical edifices.

The Gothic revival movement, also referred to as the Romantic movement, gained
ground in the early Victorian age, but played largely the role of second fiddle to the classical
theme until 1845–50. In its early years it was literary and romantic in its conception and its
architectural quality was rather in the form of a Gothic superstructure fitted on to a classical
basis. It is difficult to pin-point any one architect as the originator of the revival; there was
no Inigo Jones of the neo-Gothic movement. **James Wyatt** was one of the most vigorous
early exponents of the style. He studied it seriously and produced buildings which, if not
genuinely Gothic, were as well designed and interesting as his classical work. Like other
early neo-Gothicists, however, he used the motifs of the style in a decorative manner,
not as a means of architectural construction. In his buildings the latter quality was still
classical.

Gradually a tradition evolved that Gothic architecture was suited to ecclesiastical work,
while the classical form should be retained for public and domestic building. This was, no
doubt, due to the fact that the large majority of buildings extant in Medieval Gothic are
ecclesiastical. Such works had been fashioned from stone, and in the Middle Ages only
castles, very large houses and ecclesiastical buildings had been made from stone. Towards
1850, a number of larger country houses were designed in Gothic, generally patterned on
the Perpendicular or Elizabethan version.

Until the close of the Regency, the neo-Gothic works which were produced were designed
by the primary classic architects of the day; men like Smirke, Wilkins, Cockerell and Barry. Their
predecessors, Soane and Nash, had had little interest, but these men studied Gothic decoration and detail and, on occasion, used it. The treatment was still decorative, however, and it
was left to the next generation to design in a more valid and constructional Gothic manner.

At this time a number of books were published on Medieval architecture, with the aim
of assisting architects to interpret this style which had been largely dormant since the Middle
Ages. The best-known of these is the work by **Thomas Rickman, 1776–1841**, published in
1817, *An Attempt to Discriminate the Styles of English Architecture*. It is in this book that
Rickman laid down his suggested classifications and periods of Medieval architecture in
England. This nomenclature, of Early English, Decorated and Perpendicular, has persisted
ever since despite certain anomalies. The book was widely read and used and ran to many

...own. He known himself became an architect and specialised in Gothic study. He designed a number of churches, most of which are built in the industrial Midland areas.

Another well-known name is that of **Auguste Charles Pugin, 1762-1832**, a Frenchman who was employed by Nash as a draughtsman. In 1821-3 were published his two volumes *Specimens of Gothic Architecture*. These included exquisite drawings of Gothic buildings with measurements and details. This was one of the first works which provided the detailed information to enable a designer and builder to draw or carve the Gothic detail.

By the 1840s Gothic was being extensively used as a style for church buildings and University colleges, **William Wilkins**, in particular, carried out broad schemes at **Cambridge** where he built the entrance screen and hall at King's College to harmonise with the Medieval Chapel, and a whole new court at Corpus Christi College. At public schools also, for example Harrow and Rugby, the style was employed.

The Picturesque movement included a number of diversions or offshoots from neo-classicism which were widely indulged at this time. There developed an interest in eastern architecture: Indian, Chinese and Egyptian. Also designed were castellated houses, rustic cottages and Italianate villas. **Nash** was the well-known architect most associated with such work. He built a number of irregularly silhouetted houses, with crenellations and towers, and an even greater number of rustic cottages and Italian-style villas, for which he used timber and thatch as well as stucco and brick. With this enthusiasm for rusticity and romanticism came a flood of published designs for such cottages and houses, especially before 1820. Many of them were never used, and a number of them were architecturally wildly improbable. Their basis was predominantly seventeenth- and eighteenth-century Italian with a fanciful bias.

From the enthusiasm for **Indian designs** two large examples remain: **Sezincote**, Gloucestershire and the **Royal Pavilion, Brighton**. The former, built for Sir Charles Cockerell by his brother **Samuel Pepys Cockerell, 1754-1837**, was started in 1803. The house plan is traditionally English, but the elevations show onion domes and eastern arches. The Royal Pavilion at Brighton was originally designed by **William Porden**, 1755–1822, for the Prince Regent. His work, obviously influenced by Sezincote, later became the Dome Concert Hall at Brighton. It was Nash who designed the Pavilion which was eventually built.

By the end of this period, **1845–50**, all the various romantic styles had given way to a plain classicism and an accurate, if sombre, Gothic. The Victorians repudiated the romantic element as too frivolous. They studied Medieval Gothic with enthusiasm and care and tried earnestly to build replicas of the great age. They linked inextricably religion, morals and architecture, and worthy though their aim must have been, one regrets that somewhere by the wayside (with a few architectural exceptions) art was left behind. Within this teaching was the implied suggestion that art and beauty carried, unfortunately, a tincture of immorality. Because of this attitude and the fact that so much of the resulting architecture had a pompous, righteous and solemn air, succeeding generations have hastened to condemn with round generalisations. It should be mentioned, therefore, that it was in the early nineteenth century that the architectural profession became well established, that architectural students were soundly trained both as pupils in the offices of senior architects and with extensive study abroad, and that it was in 1837, the year of Queen Victoria's accession, that the Institute of Architects received its Royal Charter. It should also be remembered that in the nineteenth century a greater quantity of building was carried out in England than in all the earlier ages added together. Despite the two subsequent world wars and demolition of property in towns to make way for newer buildings, a tremendous amount of this nineteenth-century architecture remains. We should study it carefully, select what is worth while and not condemn out of hand. In the selection of illustrations and examples for this chapter from the extensive material available, an effort has been made to show not only famous buildings but also those which are typical. Many of the latter examples are often difficult to study *in situ* because they are overshadowed by buildings in close proximity, and the best buildings are not always readily accessible. Perhaps some of these illustrations will suggest ideas to the student so that individual judgements, not necessarily in accord with the opinion of the majority today, can then be made.

There were three prominent **architects** practising in the early nineteenth century whose earlier works have been discussed in Chapter IX. These men are Soane, Dance and Wyatt. It is convenient to begin a study of the architects of this half-century with these men, for they were leaders in setting the pattern for the following thirty years.

SIR JOHN SOANE 1753–1837

Of all architects of this period, Soane's work showed the most originality. By 1800 he had developed his extremely personal style, which was based on a number of influences—Roman, Greek, Byzantine—but remained indisputably Soane. He was a great and sincere teacher with impeccable taste who tried to raise the level of architectural appreciation in his day. He introduced a new field of thought, but this was never really taken up and developed after his death. After a long life he only retired from his work at the **Bank of England** in 1833 at the age of 80. He had completed work on the halls, much of which still remains, but his exterior façades there have now lost much of their coherence, largely due to the superstructure added in the 1920s and '30s. (916)

One of Soane's most interesting buildings of the nineteenth century is the **Art Gallery** and **Mausoleum** at **Dulwich** built 1811–14. This was largely destroyed in 1944 by enemy action but has now been rebuilt. The buildings were erected as the result of a bequest which stipulated that the mausoleum to the founder must be incorporated. Soane has made this the

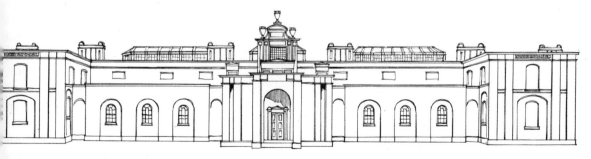

1009 Dulwich College Art Gallery and Mausoleum, 1811–14. Sir John Soane. (Badly damaged 1944, now rebuilt)

central feature of the principal elevation, with almshouses on either side and the picture gallery behind. The building is very simple but exquisitely proportioned, with elegant restrained detail (1009).

Among Soane's **houses** of this time are the country houses of Moggerhanger and Pitzhanger and his own town house in Lincoln's Inn Fields. **Moggerhanger**, built 1806–11 and now used as a hospital, is a simple, imposing house with a beautiful Greek Doric entrance portico with curved colonnade (1011, 1064, 1131, 1151). **Pitzhanger Manor**, c. 1802, which was his own country home, is now the Ealing Public Library. It is a highly individual design with an entrance façade decorated by Ionic columns supporting individual entablatures and figures above (1010, 1070). **No. 13 Lincoln's Inn Fields**, built 1812–14 for his own use, is now the Soane Museum which he left with all its contents to the nation. It also has a most original façade with incised surface decoration (1122).

Among Soane's other work are included his rebuilding of the **Law Courts** at **Westminster**, 1820–4, **entrance** to the **London Docks**, the **Infirmary** at **Chelsea Hospital** and the **churches** of **St John, Bethnal Green, Trinity Church, Marylebone**, and **St Peter's, Walworth** (1099, 1100; p. 412).

GEORGE DANCE II, 1741–1825

Most of Dance's work had been completed in the eighteenth century. His nineteenth-century contributions show a development of style with a tendency towards both Greek and Egyptian designs. In such houses as **Stratton Park**, Hertfordshire, 1803–4, Dance points the way for the Greek revivalists of the 1820s.

JAMES WYATT 1746–1813

Much of Wyatt's classical work was described in Chapter IX. **Dodington Park**, Gloucestershire, 1798–1808, however, belongs to this period. A dignified Greek classical house, it has a large Corinthian portico and inside a great hall and imposing staircase. The detail work on ceilings, friezes, doors and doorcases is of high standard in the best Wyatt tradition (1012; XLVII). Wyatt also designed the church here, on Greek cross plan, and slightly reminiscent of Soane.

Some years earlier, however, Wyatt had turned his attention to Gothic; perhaps his interest here was stimulated by his commission to restore parts of Salisbury Cathedral—work for which he later received some censure. He first built **Lee Priory** in this style in 1782, and illustrated at least his understanding of Gothic detail. After this he continued with his Gothic studies and was, during the rest of his lifetime, effective leader in England of this movement. He designed **Sheffield Place** and **West Dean** in Sussex, but his best-known Gothic houses were **Fonthill** and **Ashridge**. **Fonthill Abbey**, Wiltshire, **1795-1807**, was the most spectacular of Wyatt's essays in Gothic, and aroused tremendous interest during its erection. It was a very large house, cruciform in plan, over 300 feet in length and with a tower built over the crossing some 270 feet above ground level. The outstanding feature of the interior was a grand hall nearly 80 feet in height. At one end of this a flight of steps ascended to a saloon constructed under the tower. The Gothic detail was authentic and lavish and

XLVII   Dodington Park, Gloucestershire: the hall, 1798–1808. Architect James W

the house, unfortunately not now in existence, must have been unusual and impressive. It was built for a very rich man, Mr Beckford, whose interest in Gothic architecture was intense. He was so anxious to have the work completed that construction by shifts was carried out round the clock, and, due to inadequate supervision, specified supporting arches to the tower were not built. Some years later the tower collapsed in a gale and the house was eventually demolished (XLVI).

Wyatt's last Gothic house, **Ashridge Park**, Hertfordshire, was begun in 1806 but not completed until after his death in 1813. This building, which still exists, is less startling than Fonthill, but still irregular in silhouette. The chief feature is a central hall which takes up the whole height of the tower (1117).

Wyatt's Gothic work, like his other styles in the Adam and neo-Greek manner, was meticulous in its detail, finely proportioned and well carried out. He never fully comprehended Gothic architecture but he came nearer to doing so than any of his contemporaries, and although his Gothic buildings were still classical in basis, with Gothic clothing, he paved the way for architects such as Barry and Pugin by his careful study from original sources. Wyatt's influence both in classical and Gothic medium was considerable and his creations were always interesting and lively.

JOHN NASH 1752–1835

Apart from Soane, much of whose best work had been carried out in the eighteenth century, Nash was the outstanding original architect of the Regency. He was to this era what Barry became to the early Victorian. His architectural interests and activities were extensive and varied: they ranged from picturesque cottages and castellated houses to his great metropolitan schemes for Regent's Park and Buckingham Palace. Nash's imaginative and inventive powers were boundless; his energy and enthusiasm equally so. He had a great capacity for thinking and planning on the grand scale and if, in his great schemes, detailed supervision became a casualty, perhaps we may forgive and overlook this defect in view of the scenic, architectural layouts which he has left to us in our capital city.

As a young man Nash worked in Sir Robert Taylor's office. In 1793, with the aid of a legacy, he began architectural practice on his own, designing houses in London. He was not financially successful and became a builder of country cottages and houses on a variety of rusticated and castellated themes. Towards the end of the century, however, Nash returned to London and gained the attention of the Prince Regent. Under royal patronage he started out in the realm of town planning; a field in which his enterprising, large-scale conceptions were to have far-reaching influence, both geographically and architecturally.

Once only in the long history of the city of London has an architect's wide-scale town-planning scheme been devised and largely carried out. This was made possible for John Nash—as compared to the fate of Wren's seventeenth-century plans and Professor Abercrombie's twentieth-century designs—by the availability of land at the same time as a period of prosperity and the support of royal patronage. With this combination of circumstances Nash was enabled from the age of 60 to 80 years to carry out a fair proportion of his far-seeing planning scheme. The layout comprised a large area covering **Regent's Park, St James's Park, Regent Street and Trafalgar Square.**

VIII   *Regent Street, London, 1819–20. Architect John Nash. (a) The North end, (b) the Quadrant in engravings by Thomas H. Shepherd after Thomas Dale and W. Tombleson, 1827–8)*

COUNTRY HOUSES 1800–1835

1011

1013

1010

1012

1010 Pitzhanger Manor, Ealing. His own home designed by Sir John Soane 1802-4. 1011 Moggerhanger, Bedfordshire 1806-11

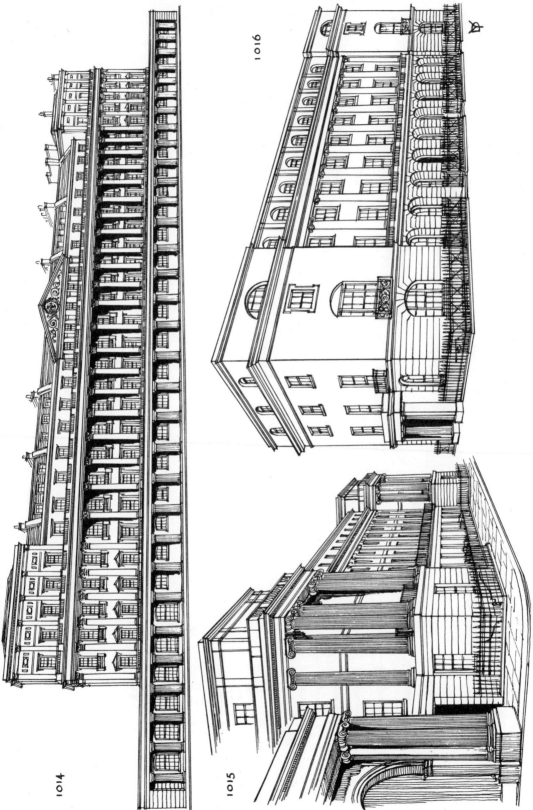

1016

1014

1015

1014 Carlton House Terrace, The Mall, 1827–32   1015 Cumberland Terrace, Regent's Park, 1827   1016 York Gate, Regent's Park, 1822

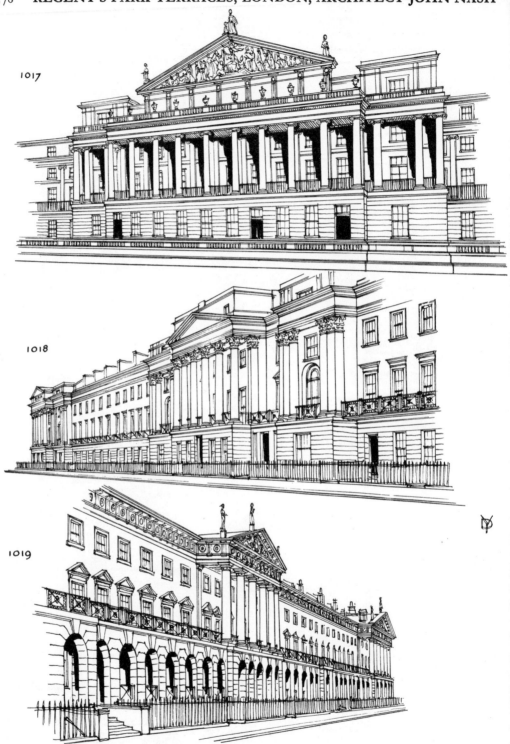

1017 Cumberland Terrace: central section of principal façade, 1827   1018 Cornwall Terrace, begun
1822. Designed by Decimus Burton under Nash's direction   1019 Hanover Terrace, 1822–3

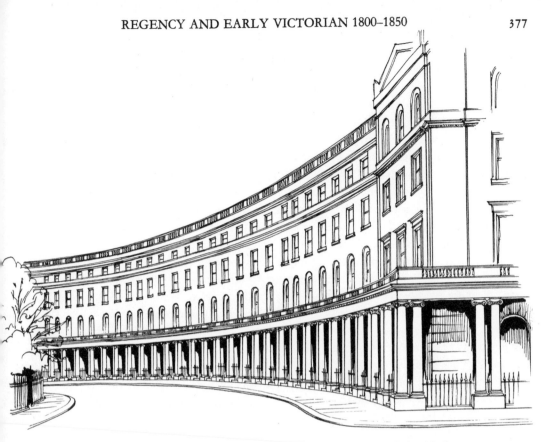

1020 Park Crescent, Regent's Park, London, begun 1812. John Nash

The opportunity arose when Marylebone Park property reverted to the Crown in 1811. This property consisted of farmland which had been under consideration for development for some time. The Prince Regent gave the proposed scheme vigorous backing, envisaging, perhaps, a plan for London which would vie with the Paris of Napoleon. Both Nash and Leverton were asked to draw up schemes. Leverton's were, however, somewhat pedantic and unoriginal, suggesting only an extension of the eighteenth-century conception of domestic squares. Nash's ideas were far more extensive and revolutionary. He set out a whole garden city for the well-to-do in the centre of the metropolis. The scheme included a park with graceful villas, a lake, a canal, crescents and terraces and focal centres such as Trafalgar Square. The *pièce-de-résistance* was to be a royal route from the Prince Regent's Park to his Palace—the future Regent Street—which would stretch from Regent's Park to Carlton House in the Mall. Nash's scheme was accepted and work began in 1812. He was then over 60 years old. When he died, more than 20 years later, much of his vast plan was complete; a plan in which he energetically participated until the end. He was forced, during this period, to forgo some of his best and cherished ideas, such as the double circus, many of the villas and their gardens, and his Summer Palace. Regent's Park today represents only a section of his original plan. But the terraces still exist and they are undoubtedly appreciated more now than they were when they were built. In that age of critical architectural appreciation, some of the slapdash detail and proportions which the builder had carried out from

Nash's sketchy drawings, and without adequate supervision were condemned and deplored. Today they present a scenic splendour against a background of twentieth-century architectural mediocrity and viewed, particularly from a distance and in sunlight, they are one of London's few remaining architectural glories.

The **crescents** and **terraces** developed gradually from 1812 over some 20 years. One of the earliest is **Park Crescent**, begun in 1812, which was planned as a circus but only half was built. It is one of the simplest layouts and has a fine colonnade of coupled Ionic columns. It suffered from war damage but is now repaired (1020). In the same area is **York Terrace**, dating from 1822, and **York Gate** which is one of the best blocks of architectural design (1016). Fronting the Park itself are the more elaborate and imposing terraces. Among these the most impressive and outstanding is **Cumberland Terrace**, 1827, originally designed as a focal point in the scheme. It is extremely long and comprises three connected blocks. It has a monumental and panoramic quality in finely proportioned architecture. It is almost impossible to illustrate the whole terrace, but two different views are shown in Figs. 1015 and 1017. Near by is **Hanover Terrace**, 1822–3, built on solid, Roman lines and also very imposing (1019). **Chester Terrace**, 1825, possesses two triumphal arches, while **Cornwall Terrace**, begun 1822, was largely built by James Burton and his son Decimus (1018). In the period 1827–32 the extensive, dignified **Carlton House Terrace** was built in the Mall and St James's Park was laid out. This was to be the southern end of Nash's royal mile (1014).

Like the Regent's Park scheme, **Regent Street** was also a most unusual and masterly undertaking. It was not planned as a direct, straight highway but took its line from Portland Place at the north end, changed direction at Langham Place and, as it approached Piccadilly Circus, curved in a quarter circle (or quadrant) to run straight down to Carlton House in the Mall. There was considerable difficulty in merging all the varied commerical interests and Nash, for this reason, only insisted on absolute symmetry in the Quadrant and lower Regent Street near Carlton House. It was, however, essential to retain perfect symmetry in his quarter circle and, in order to achieve this, Nash undertook the financial transactions in his own name and offered a speculative share in the property, instead of payment, to the builders who would create the **Quadrant.** The whole scheme was financially and architecturally successful and provided an uninterrupted curve of stucco façade into Piccadilly Circus. At the Circus itself, he let the principal site at the end of his Quadrant to an insurance firm who built a fine classical front based on Inigo Jones's Somerset House façade. This building, the **County Fire Office**, has since been replaced, as has also the Quadrant and much of Regent Street. There remain to us today only Carlton House Terrace, a few isolated buildings in the Street and **All Souls' Church** which Nash himself designed for the head of the street at Langham Place. It was a most unusual church and aroused considerable controversy during its erection. It has a circular porch and colonnade which culminates in a spiked spire. Although damaged during the war, it has been rebuilt. In the last few years its aspect has, however, become a casualty to office box building. It was created by Nash to provide a skyline feature at the top of his royal street. It is still there, but the skyline is now obliterated by the British Broadcasting Corporation so that the spiked foil against blue sky and clouds has become obscured against a background of brownish hue. Prints of Nash's original Regent Street and Quadrant are shown in Plate XLVIII and All Souls' Church in Fig. 1022.

Among near-by remnants of Nash's work still extant are the **Haymarket Theatre** built

1021 St Pancras: west front, 1819–22. W. and H. W. Inwood   1022 All Souls, Langham Place: portico, 1822–4. John Nash
1023 St Marylebone Parish Church: entrance front, 1813–17. Thomas Hardwick

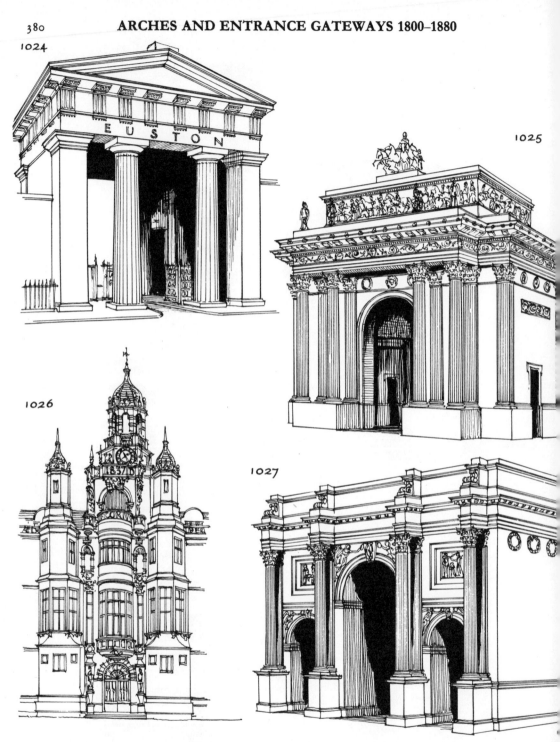

1024 Great Entrance Arch, Euston Station, London, 1838. Philip Hardwick   1025 Constitution Hill Arch, Hyde Park Corner, London, 1825–8. Decimus Burton. (Arch shown with intended ornament and quadriga. Compare with scale of present quadriga)   1026 Entrance Gateway at Harlaxton Manor, Lincolnshire, 1831–55. Anthony Salvin   1027 The Marble Arch, erected in 1828 in front of Buckingham Palace and moved to present site in 1851. John Nash

1820, and the **United Service Club** in **Pall Mall**, dated 1828 (1041). The interior of the theatre has been radically changed, but the exterior with its large Corinthian portico is almost unaltered (1033).

In 1825 Nash was creating a new scheme aimed to connect Bloomsbury and Whitehall with a link to the Regent Street layout by means of Pall Mall. A new square was formed at the top end of Whitehall, called from 1831 **Trafalgar Square**. Almost all the surrounding buildings were erected after Nash's time by other architects, with the exception of Gibbs's St Martin-in-the-Fields, which could now be viewed properly for the first time.

The ill-fated project of **Buckingham Palace** was the last of Nash's long, successful career and made a sad ending to the old man's life. In 1825 the King decided to transform the old Buckingham House into his London palace and abandon Carlton House. Nash was commissioned to do this. He was over 70 and was still engaged on his other extensive projects. It was some years before the design was settled and work was rushed because of the ageing King's impatience. Nash's design, as far as we can judge, was interesting, powerful and lively, but the building was unfinished when the King died in 1830. His patronage was thus taken away and Nash was called to account by a Select Committee set up to examine the situation. He was asked to resign from the work and Edward Blore completed the task, altering much of Nash's design and producing a building never really satisfactory, which in its turn was rebuilt by Sir Aston Webb in 1913. One relic of Nash's palace remains—the **Marble Arch**. This triumphal arch Nash had designed as an entrance to the palace forecourt. Blore had it removed, and, since 1851, it has been admired in its present position. The arch, built on the lines of the arch of Constantine in Rome, is beautifully carved and completed (1027).

The Royal Pavilion, Brighton, was yet another commission given to Nash by the patronage of the Prince Regent. Nash began his designs in 1816. The results are exciting, unusual and still cause much comment, favourable and otherwise, by visitors to Brighton. Originally planned in Indian style Nash has, however, mixed his sources of design, and parts of the building, especially the interior, are Chinese and Gothic. The exterior silhouette, in particular, is most successful; it has an ethereal quality with its delicate, pierced stonework and its onion domes. Now, floodlit on summer evenings and surrounded by attractive gardens and fountains, it is an original asset to this unique English resort (1029).

WILLIAM WILKINS 1778–1839   SIR ROBERT SMIRKE 1781–1867

It is convenient to consider the work of these two architects together as they are almost exactly contemporary and have much in common. Together they were responsible for the bulk of architectural commissions from 1825 to 1840 and are typical of their time. Their work is sound, authentic in style, well constructed and excellently executed. Both of them, though, lacked the originality of a Soane and the brilliance and sense for design in the mass and on the grand scale of a Nash. There is a tendency to consider their work as dull, particularly in reference to eighteenth-century standards, but viewed in retrospect, and considered in comparison with what followed in the Victorian age and in the twentieth century, their contributions gain in stature and accomplishment.

William Wilkins was the son of an architect and was educated at Cambridge, to which

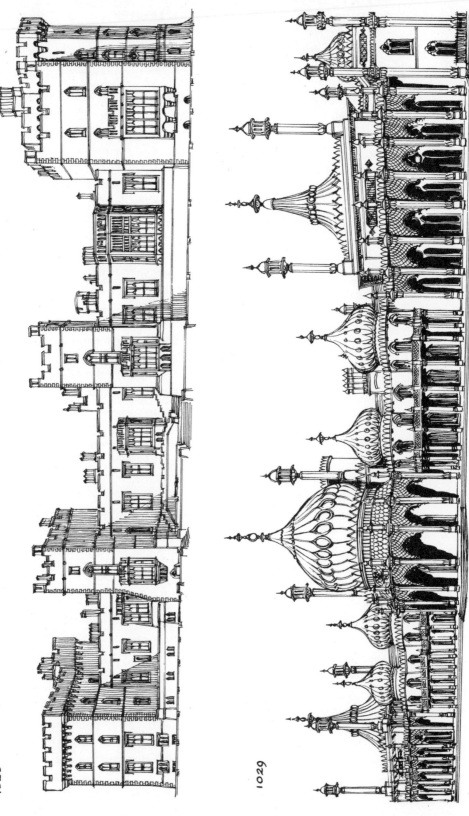

1028 Windsor Castle, east terrace, showing the Prince of Wales, the Chester, the Clarence and the Victoria Towers, from 1824. Sir Jeffry Wyattville 1029 The Royal Pavilion, Brighton, Sussex, 1815–20. John Nash

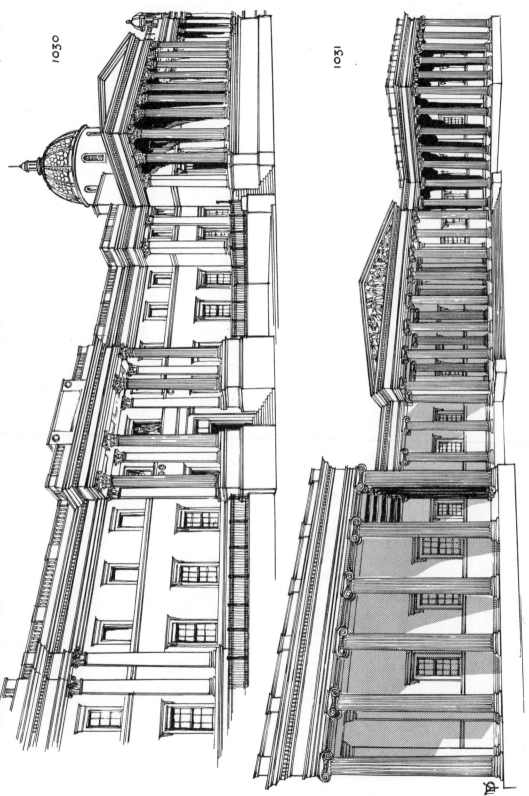

1030

1031

1030 The National Gallery, Trafalgar Square, 1832–8: entrance front. William Wilkins   1031 The British Museum, 1825–47: entrance front. Sir Robert Smirke

PUBLIC BUILDINGS IN LONDON 1800–1850

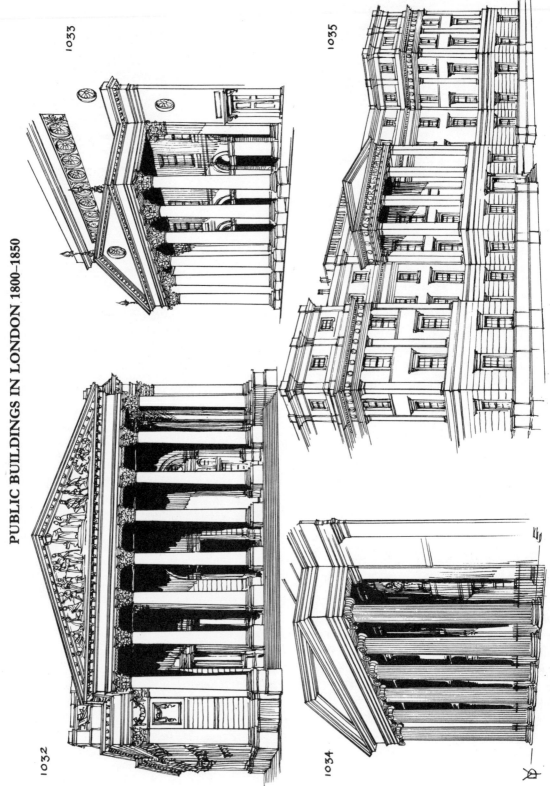

1032 The Royal Exchange: west front 1840–4. Sir William Tite   1033 The Haymarket Theatre. 1820. John Nash   1034 The College

university he returned later to carry out extensive commissions. He spent some time in Europe—in Italy, Greece and Asia Minor—and published his *Antiquities of Magna Graecia*. He settled down into an architectural career as an enthusiastic Greek revivalist and carried out much work in this style on public and collegiate buildings before turning to Gothic. His largest public works are the National Gallery, Trafalgar Square and St George's Hospital, Hyde Park Corner, both in **London**. In the commission for the **National Gallery** built **1832–8,** Wilkins was given a tremendous opportunity to show his architectural abilities. It stands on one of the finest sites in London with a long frontage overlooking Trafalgar Square and Whitehall. Here, although there is a well-designed Corinthian portico and steps, and the general standard of taste and execution is good, Wilkins showed that he was incapable of designing a large public building as a unit. The long façade is split up into numerous, fussy sections and pavilions and is surmounted by one of the silliest, petty domes ever to grace a classical building (1030). **St George's Hospital**, designed 1827–8, stands on an imposing corner site; it is an adequate though rather stodgy building, but with, again, a pleasant, well-proportioned Doric portico (1035).

Wilkins's most interesting work is in the collegiate sphere. Here, his chief contributions are University College, London, and at **Cambridge** Downing College and his work at King's College and Corpus Christi College. **University College**, designed in **1827–8** as **London University**, is Wilkins's best classical work. He built the main block with its impressive Corinthian portico raised on a great podium with steps; the dome is set above and to the rear. (Since his day have been added the side wings.) This was a new University building, erected in the centre of a great city and a break was made from the Oxford and Cambridge tradition for court planning. Here was envisaged no chapel, but a central, large assembly hall, with flanking libraries, museums and other accommodation. The portico, one of the finest in London, was built with its entrance steps and inside vestibule and grand staircase but, strangely, the Assembly hall was not carried out. The dome is much better than that at the National Gallery but it is still not quite significant enough for the giant portico in front (1036).

Wilkins's other Greek revival collegiate work was the new **Downing College** at **Cambridge** built 1806–11. Here he used the Ionic order taken from the Erechtheum. The College is austerely and conventionally designed but is very formal and uninspiring. Building has continued there until the present day and it is now an extensive layout, all planned in keeping with Wilkins's original scheme (1037).

Also at Cambridge, Wilkins made his two chief excursions into Gothic. At **King's College**, he submitted in 1822, as did many other architects, designs for the completion of the great court. Some of these designs were classical in order to fit in with Gibbs's Fellows' Building; the others were Gothic in deference to the Medieval chapel. It was decided to use Gothic and Wilkins built the long screen and main entrance gateway from the road, also the hall. The result can hardly be said to echo the Medievalism of the chapel but, viewed as a whole, the scheme has merit and interest and is not out of keeping (1092, 1146). In 1823–37 Wilkins built the **New Court** at **Corpus Christi College**, also in Cambridge. This large, new courtyard on Medieval plan in Perpendicular style is traditionally carried out with hall and chapel. Again, it lacks the genuine Medieval approach and is rather a classical undertaking with Perpendicular Gothic clothing; but it is pleasant, well designed and carried out

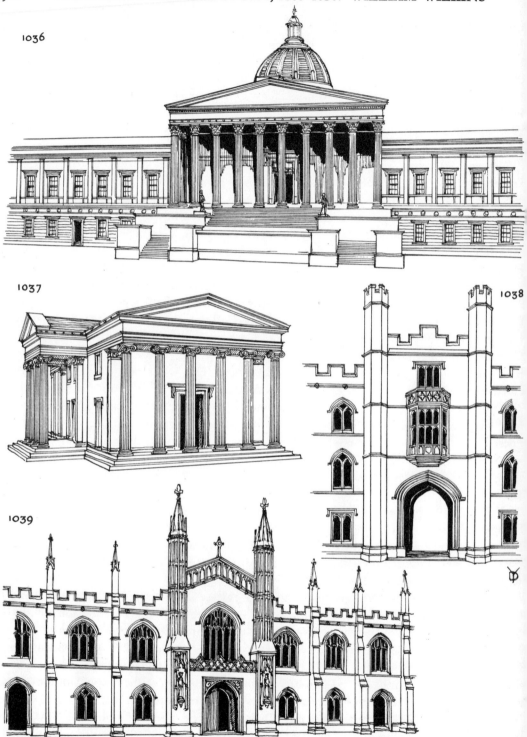

1036 The London University (now University College), 1827–8   1037 Downing College, Cambridge, 1806–21   1038–9 New Court, Corpus Christi College, Cambridge, 1823–30

(1038–9). The simple, attractive stone **bridge** forming a single arch over the Cam at **King's College** is also by Wilkins (1188).

Sir Robert Smirke was the son of an artist and began his architectural career as a pupil of Soane. Like Wilkins, he studied in Europe for some years and travelled in France, Italy, Sicily and Greece and, also like Wilkins, began his career as a convinced Greek revivalist. He became an R.A. in 1821 and was knighted in 1833. He had an exceptionally large London practice and much of his activity comprised public building. His work was academic, authentically Greek classical and well designed, but lacked the spark of outstanding architectural ability. His first important commission was the rebuilding of **Covent Garden Theatre**, burnt down in 1808. He designed a long façade with Greek Doric portico, but once again, in 1856, the theatre was destroyed by fire.

1040 St Mary's Church, Wyndham Place, London, 1823–4. Sir Robert Smirke

Smirke's largest and best-known London works are the British Museum and the **General Post Office**. The latter, built in 1824–9 was demolished in 1913, but the **British Museum**, largely erected in the years **1823–47**, still stands with its tremendous south front of 48 Ionic columns. Although the Museum has long been considered by many to be uninteresting and monotonous, with its long, uninterrupted colonnade, it is, without doubt, one of the most representative and imposing Greek buildings in London. The order is Ionic, and on the south façade there is a central entrance portico with steps, and sculptured pediment above. The building is constructed round an open quadrangle, and the Ionic colonnade is taken uninterruptedly round the whole façade. Later, in the 1850s, Sidney Smirke, Robert's younger brother, was responsible for the covering in of the central court by a cast-iron structure in the form of a dome. This created the famous reading room (1031, 1153).

Among Sir Robert's other important works were the **Royal Mint** on **Tower Hill** designed 1809, various **clubs**, including the one that he designed with **Sidney Smirke** in 1836–7; the **Oxford and Cambridge Club, Pall Mall** (1044), and the **College of Physicians** in **Trafalgar Square**, built in 1824–7. Here again is Sir Robert's famous Ionic order with finely executed Greek detail (1034). He designed a number of churches; the best-known include **St Mary's Church, Wyndham Place, London**, 1823–4, and **St George's Church, Brandon Hill, Bristol**, 1823 (1040, 1169; p. 413). Among his provincial work Smirke designed a number of **Shire Halls**, for example that at **Gloucester**, where again the Ionic order is in evidence (1056). He also carried out the **Council Offices** at **Bristol** (1137).

George Basevi 1794–1845   Decimus Burton 1800–1888
Charles Robert Cockerell 1788–1863

Again it is convenient to examine the work of these architects together. These three men were a rather younger age group than Wilkins and Smirke, although they executed some work in the 1820s. They were all architects in the classical tradition and, though perhaps not so prolific as their two predecessors, were responsible for designs of greater interest and originality.

George Basevi died comparatively young; despite this a considerable quantity of his work is still extant, mainly in London. He was a pupil of Soane for three years and, following a further three years in Europe, began private practice in 1819. His chief contribution was in town layout and terrace and square building in the Belgravia area of London; work on which he was largely engaged between 1825 and 1840. His classical terraces in **Belgrave Square** and, in **South Kensington**, terraces such as **Pelham Crescent** and **Thurloe Square**, are examples of high standard (1045–6, 1132–3). Basevi's best-known building outside these London schemes is the **Fitzwilliam Museum** at **Cambridge** begun in 1837. This is a beautifully proportioned classical building in the Corinthian order, with portico, surmounting sculptured pediment and entrance steps. Inside, there is a grand entrance hall (1048, XLIX).

Decimus Burton, so called as the tenth child of his father James Burton the builder, lived late into the Victorian age, but is never considered a Victorian architect because all his major work was done as a young man before 1850. Sponsored by Nash, he helped his father with building some of the Regent's Park terraces and, at the age of 21, actually designed **Cornwall Terrace** (1018). He is especially famed for his arch and screen at **Hyde Park Corner**, which he envisaged as a triumphal entrance and connecting link from Hyde Park to Green Park. The **screen**, consisting of three arches and a graceful Ionic colonnade, still acts as an entrance to Hyde Park. The **arch** was later moved to the top of Constitution Hill and its angle to the screen changed. It was based on the prototype of the Arch of Titus in Rome, and Burton had envisaged a sculptured quadriga on top. Instead an equestrian statue of Wellington was added in 1846 and this was replaced in 1912 by the over-large quadriga by Adrian Jones. Burton's original design is shown in Fig. 1025 and the screen in Fig. 1052. Among Burton's other work in London is the **Athenaeum Club** in **Pall Mall** built 1829–30. This finely proportioned building has a delicate, Greek, sculptured frieze and a double Doric entrance portico. An upper storey has been added later but is omitted in the drawing in Fig. 1043.

Burton also made a contribution in the field of small country houses and villas and designed a number of terraces and houses for his father at south coast resorts such as Hastings and St Leonards-on-Sea (1123). At **Hove** he designed the magnificent layout of **Adelaide Terrace** and **Crescent**.

Charles Robert Cockerell was the son of Samuel Pepys Cockerell, the architect. For

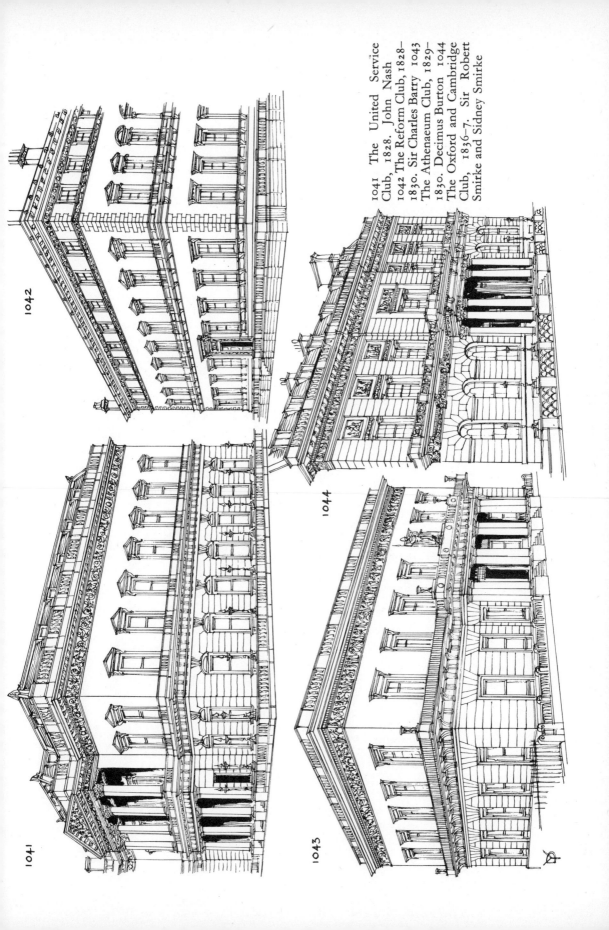

1041 The United Service Club, 1828. John Nash 1042 The Reform Club, 1828–1830. Sir Charles Barry 1043 The Athenaeum Club, 1829–1830. Decimus Burton 1044 The Oxford and Cambridge Club, 1836–7. Sir Robert Smirke and Sidney Smirke

1045 Belgrave Square, 1825. George Basevi   1046 Pelham Crescent, South Kensington, 1820–30.
George Basevi   1047 Milner Square, Islington, 1841–3. Gough and Roumieu

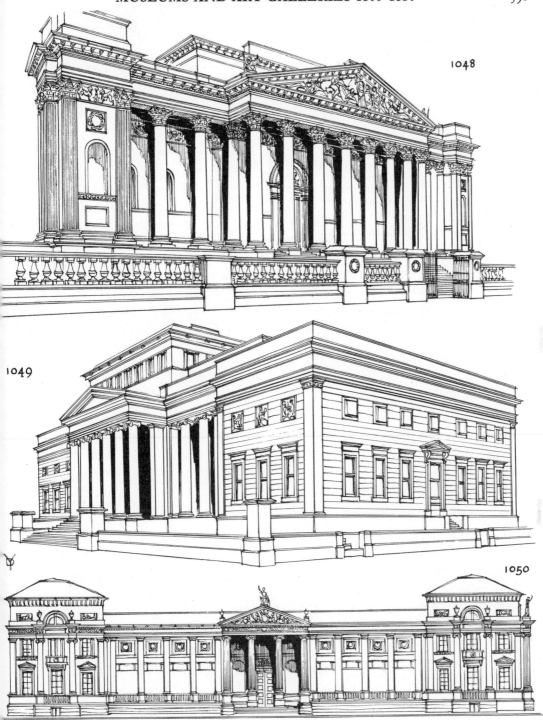

1048 The Fitzwilliam Museum, Cambridge, 1837–48. George Basevi   1049 The Royal Institution
(now the City Art Gallery), Manchester, 1824–35. Sir Charles Barry   1050 The Ashmolean Museum,
Oxford (University Galleries and Taylor Institute), Beaumont Street façade, 1840–5. C. R. Cockerell

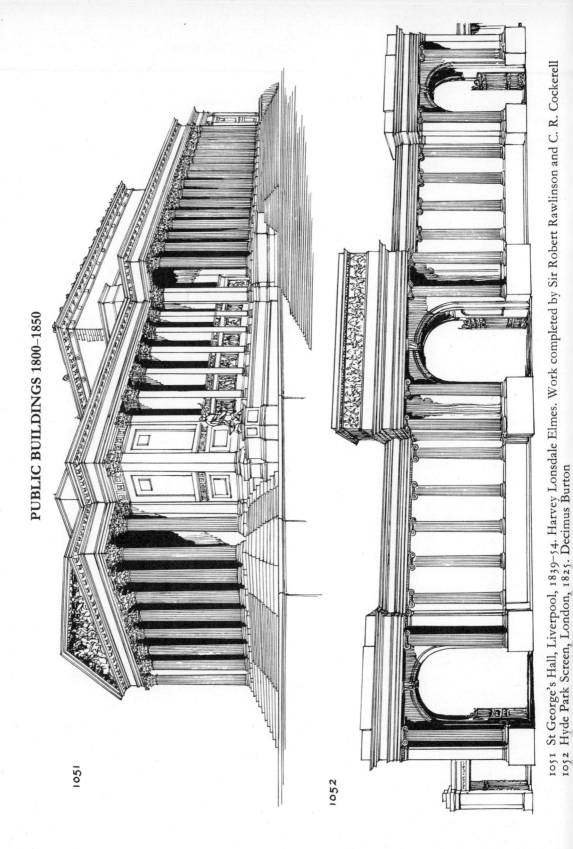

1051

1052

1051 St George's Hall, Liverpool, 1839–54. Harvey Lonsdale Elmes. Work completed by Sir Robert Rawlinson and C. R. Cockerell
1052 Hyde Park Screen, London, 1825. Decimus Burton

XLIX *Fitzwilliam Museum, Cambridge, 1837–*
entrance hall and staircase. Architect George B

1053 The Taylor and Randolph Museum (the Ashmolean), Oxford, 1840–5. C. R. Cockerell

five years he worked in his father's office, then went to Italy, Greece and Sicily to study for seven years. In 1817 he returned to England and began practice as a Greek-revival architect. Over the years Professor Cockerell—he held the chair of architecture at the Royal Academy—became the accepted authority on antique Greek architecture. He was the first President and Gold Medallist of the Royal Institute of British Architects; he was a member of academies in Athens, Rome and other Italian cities, and gained the reputation of being the 'grand old man' of the contracting classic school.

In 1825 Cockerell built **Hanover Chapel** in Nash's **Regent Street**; unfortunately now demolished. His best-known building is the **Taylorian Museum (the Ashmolean)** at **Oxford,** 1840–45. This is one of the finest of all English Greek revival buildings. The long, Beaumont Street façade has two end pavilions extended forwards to provide a forecourt, also a centre portico with steps. The Ionic order is used here, but in between, on the flat façade, Doric pilasters are decoratively applied. On the St Giles Street front the Ionic columns are free-standing and support individual entablatures and classical, sculptured figures above, as in Soane's design at Pitzhanger. The Greek detail on this building is authentic and finely executed and the whole work gives an added distinction to a city already so rich in great architecture (1050, 1053, 1152, 1168).

In 1833 Cockerell succeeded Soane as architect to the **Bank of England** and carried out

St George's Hall, Liverpool, 1841–54. Architect H. L. Elmes

PUBLIC BUILDINGS 1800–1850

1054

1055

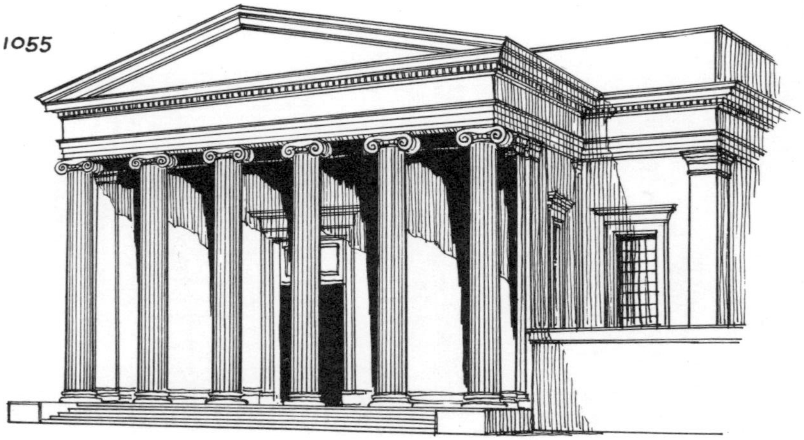

1056

1057

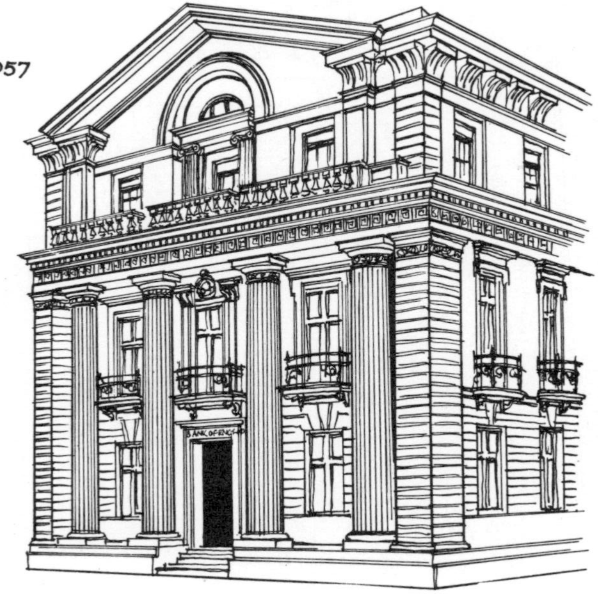

1054 The Bank of England, Bristol, 1844. C. R. Cockerell 1055 The Shire Hall, Worcester, 1834–5. Charles Day 1056 The Shire

some sound, high quality architectural improvements. Taylor and Soane before him had worked on the London headquarters. Cockerell made his name in building branch banks in the chief industrial cities. His four main banks are at **Bristol, Plymouth, Manchester** and **Liverpool**. They are similar to one another and very suitable to their surroundings and function. The Bristol and Liverpool branches are shown in Figs. 1054 and 1057. The giant Doric order is used on the main elevation and above the entablature is a central pediment. The decoration is restrained and broadly treated.

Cockerell also built a number of other banks and insurance offices. These included the **London and Westminster Bank, Lothbury**, 1837–8 and the **Sun Fire and Life Assurance Offices, Threadneedle Street**, 1840–2, while in **Liverpool** is the **Liverpool and London Insurance Offices**, 1856–8 (1227). All these were good classical buildings, eminently suited to their central city positions. Detail is limited, rustication general on lower storeys and an order is incorporated in some part of the chief façade.

SIR CHARLES BARRY 1795–1860

While Soane was the most original architect of the late eighteenth century and the Regency, and Nash the great town-planner of the age, Sir Charles Barry was unquestionably the greatest architect whom England possessed in the nineteenth century from 1830 onwards. Although he lived until 1860, and although he is often thought of as a Gothic architect because of his world-famous Houses of Parliament, he was neither a Victorian (in the architectural sense) nor solely a Gothic architect.

Barry had no family architectural background but was articled at the age of 15 to a small firm of architects in London. With a legacy left to him by his father, he set out in 1817 on an extensive tour wherein he spent three years studying in Italy, Greece, Asia Minor, Egypt and Syria. He became very interested in and knowledgeable on Egyptian and Italian Renaissance architecture. Upon returning to England he began his architectural career by designing a number of churches for the Commissioners (p. 419). He found that the Commissioners preferred Gothic or Greek classical designs, so he applied himself to studies for this purpose. He had designed more than ten churches by 1825, including his best-known example, **St Peter's Church, Brighton**, 1823–8 (1107, 1142; p. 419). In 1824 Barry won the competition for the **Royal Institution, Manchester** (now the City Art Gallery) and produced a simple, straightforward, but well-designed Greek Ionic building (1049). In 1829–31, he built the **Travellers' Club**; here he found an opportunity to design a building on the lines of the Italian Renaissance palaces which he had so much admired. His more famous club, the **Reform** in London, he won in competition in 1837. This again was on Italian palace lines, having a central court with iron and glass roofing. The façade is dignified and austere, astylar in conception, whilst the skyline is only broken by the four tall chimneys (1042).

Barry's name is inextricably associated with the **Palace of Westminster, 1836–65**, which became, and still is, the most popular neo-Gothic building in England. It is also the finest Gothic-revival construction in the country and has been imitated in several other lands. The Tudor Gothic style was chosen by Barry as suitable, particularly in reference to the Medieval buildings in the vicinity. The Palace was started before the Gothic revival

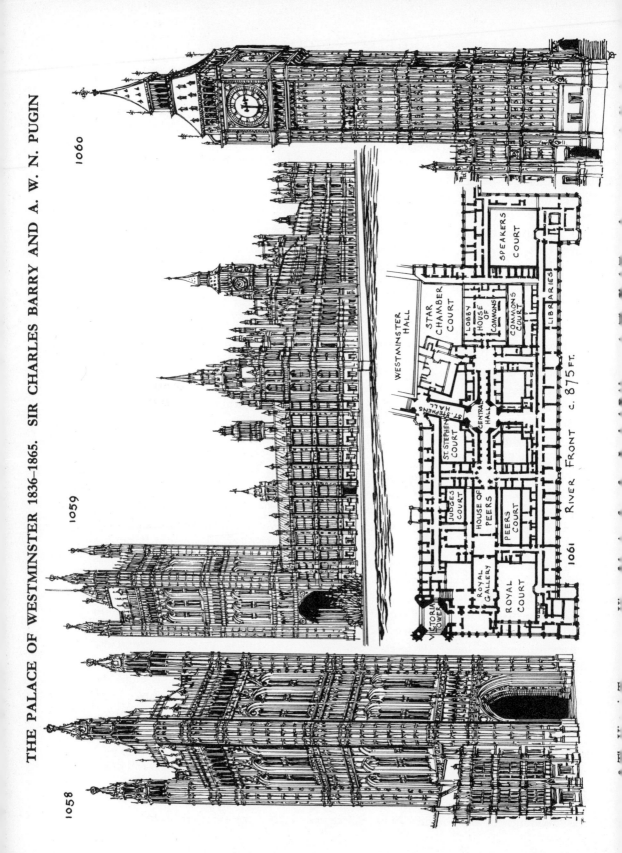

1060

1059

1058

WESTMINSTER HALL

STAR CHAMBER COURT

SPEAKERS COURT

LOBBY

HOUSE OF COMMONS

COMMONS COURT

LIBRARIES

ST. STEPHENS HALL

ST. STEPHENS COURT

CENTRAL HALL

JUDGES COURT

HOUSE OF PEERS

PEERS COURT

ROYAL GALLERY

ROYAL COURT

VICTORIA TOWER

1061 RIVER FRONT c. 875 FT.

LI *The Palace of Westminster: the river front, 1836-65. Architect Sir Charles Ba*

movement was well under way; it bears little resemblance to any of the later examples and, indeed, many of its admirers feel relieved that it was built in the 1840s and not in the '70s or '80s, when Barry's chaste, Perpendicular simplicity and cleanness of line would have been an anachronism.

In 1834 the Palace of Westminster was destroyed by fire. The Parliamentary Committee which was set up decided that the new Palace should be Gothic in design, and held a competition for the work. Ninety-six architects submitted designs. The candidates were required to consider the proximity of Westminster Abbey with its Medieval Henry VII's chapel and to incorporate the remains of the Palace which included Westminster Hall and St Stephen's Chapel.

Barry won the competition and was awarded the commission. The first stone was laid in 1840, but the work was not completed until after his death, although the House of Lords was ready in 1847 and the Commons in 1852. Barry's layout was masterly; the full appreciation of this can only be gained from an aerial view. He retained Westminster Hall and, in the centre of his new building, made an octagonal hall with lantern above; a hall which gave direct access through St Stephen's Hall to Westminster Hall. At the south-west corner he set the great Victoria Tower and, at the opposite end of the Palace, the more delicate Clock Tower. The building, which was constructed in limestone, was in Perpendicular Gothic throughout and covered a large area between the newly embanked river and Westminster Hall; behind this river façade are refreshment and common rooms and libraries.

The **central hall**, octagonal in plan, has a lofty vault decorated by over 200 carved bosses. It supports the lantern above and is itself supported by the eight arches of the octagon. The jambs of the arches are decorated by canopied, royal statues. Four of the arches enclose Perpendicular windows and four, stone screens and doorways.

The **House of Commons** was first occupied in 1852, and, owing to members' complaints about acoustic difficulties, Barry was compelled to lower the ceiling, thereby spoiling the proportion of the chamber. He also pointed out that the fire hazard was now greater—this was confirmed by the events of 1941. It was also criticised at that time for being insufficiently ornamented and dull. Present generations no doubt view this differently.

The **House of Lords** is much more lavishly decorated, with a richly ornamented ceiling incorporating the royal emblems and Medieval motifs in gold. It is illuminated by eight windows and the walls are ornately carved and panelled.

One of the most outstanding features of the Palace is the **Victoria Tower**. Here the reticulated Perpendicular Gothic character of the whole building is particularly seen to advantage. There are two deeply recessed, tall arches on the ground stage, where the spandrels are filled with carving. The four corner, octagonal turrets rise to the full height of the tower and are panelled throughout. Above the entrance arches is a storey filled with panelled niches, each of which contains a sculptured statue. Above this follow two tall storeys each with three windows. The top of the tower was completed after Barry's death by his son. Between the four turret finials is constructed a high, iron roof, partly hidden by the carved and pierced stone parapet.

The **Clock Tower** suffered from many setbacks and problems. Construction began in 1843 but had to be suspended when the height had reached 150 feet as the clock could not

The Palace of Westminster: the peers' lobby. Architect
Charles Barry; interior work by A. W. N. Pugin

be raised inside it. Further difficulties were encountered with the bells—Big Ben, the largest of these, cracked twice.

Most unfortunate and acrimonious relationships developed over the **Barry–Pugin connection** in the building of the Palace of Westminster, and this was continued more bitterly by their respective sons. The Pugin faction contended that his was the major contribution and that Barry refused to acknowledge it; the Barry faction that Pugin's contribution was negligible anyway. The architect for the building was undoubtedly Barry but equally definitely the decorative factor was Pugin's responsibility. The masterly plan and external façades were by Barry, as was also the incorporation of cast-iron in the roof construction— then an innovation—and one which saved much of the Palace from suffering the fate of the House of Commons in 1941. **Pugin** made the designs and supervised the work for the interior wall decoration, the decorative art, the stained glass, the fittings, furniture and all ornament. He made the most exquisite working drawings for exterior ornament also, including sculpture and carved, decorative mouldings. He is thought to have had a hand in the design of the Clock Tower, which bears a resemblance to that at Scarisbrick Hall (1078). If the construction, design and silhouette of the Palace is Barry's, the clothing is by Pugin. (Illustrations of the Palace of Westminster can be seen in Plates LI and LII and in Figs. 1058–61. Details are shown in Figs. 1072, 1079–80, 1082, 1086–7, 1125, 1141, 1147, 1154 and 1158.)

Barry designed several houses, and, among others, he remodelled **Highclere Castle**, Hampshire, 1842–4. This was done in Elizabethan style, with four corner towers and a

1062 Highclere Castle, Hampshire. Remodelled by Sir Charles Barry, 1842–4

1063 1064 1065 1066 1067 1068 1069

1070 1073 1071 1072 1074

1063 St Peter's Church, Cheltenham, 1847–9.
S. W. Dawkes 1064 Moggerhanger Bedfordshire,
1806–11. Sir John Soane 1065 Highclere Castle,
Hampshire, 1842–4. Sir Charles Barry 1066
Nelson Monument, Trafalgar Square, London, 1839. William Railton. (Lions later date) 1067–8,
1071 Church of St Mary and St Nicholas, Wilton, Wiltshire, 1840–6. Wyatt and Brandon 1069
The Promenade, Cheltenham 1070 Pitzhanger Manor, Ealing, 1802–4. Sir John Soane 1072 The
Clock Tower, Palace of Westminster. Sir Charles Barry 1073 St George's Hall, Liverpool, 1839–54.
Harvey Lonsdale Elmes 1074 Christchurch, Cheltenham. The Jearrads

larger one, near the centre. The treatment of strapwork and ornament is restrained but the whole effect is one of controlled richness (1062, 1065, 1088, 1156). In **London**, Barry designed **Bridgewater House** in **Cleveland Square**, 1847–57. This is in similar vein to his clubs and is built on the grand scale for town houses. At **Cliveden** in Buckinghamshire he carried out a rebuilding after the fire. This is similar to his work at **Harewood House**, Yorkshire, where he altered Adam's south front. At Cliveden also, he laid out an extensive balustraded terrace with flights of steps leading down to the gardens and the river. The house itself is decorated by Ionic pilasters along the façade while the ground floor is planned with rusticated arcades (1208).

Among his other public works, Barry laid out part of **Trafalgar Square**, continuing Nash's enterprise; in particular, he constructed the embanked terrace in front of the National Gallery. **Nelson's Column** by **William Railton** was erected in the centre of the square in 1839, but the lions were added later (1066). In 1846 Barry designed the **Treasury Buildings** in **Whitehall** which contrast favourably with Scott's more ornate Foreign Office near by.

AUGUSTUS WELBY NORTHMORE PUGIN 1812–1852

A. W. N. Pugin was the son of the French refugee Auguste Charles Pugin who had worked for Nash and published books of carefully drawn Gothic detail and building. Pugin the son spent his all too short life in passionate denunciation of Renaissance architecture and, through his immense output of drawings, publications and architecture, established the rule of Gothic in England. Pugin became a Catholic in 1834 and in devoting his life to this faith was bitterly disappointed in the preference of the Church of Rome for Renaissance architecture which he considered to typify the embodiment of sin.

Pugin regarded the Middle Ages as the greatest era in human history; a time when men were inspired to live and work for the glory of God, and when buildings such as the great cathedrals were erected in this spirit. Since that age, Pugin felt, mankind had walked the broad and easy road to sin and immorality. As the finest era for man had been in the Middle Ages, so he reasoned, the Medieval architecture created by such men must furnish the right style for building. Thus, he attempted to wipe away the previous 300 years and start afresh. He held firmly to the view, supported by many a Victorian after him, that only a man moral and good in heart could design good architecture; an immoral man could only create inferior work. As is only too unfortunately apparent, this principle illustrates the inconsistency and illusory quality of Pugin's thinking on this subject, although we cannot doubt his own intense sincerity and dedication.

In order to prove his theories Pugin spent several years touring the country and making beautiful drawings of Medieval and Renaissance buildings. He then published his famous book: *Contrasts; or a Parallel between the noble edifices of the fourteenth and fifteenth centuries and similar Buildings of the present day. Showing the present decay of Taste.* (Like many of his contemporaries, Pugin loved lengthy, pedantic titles.) In this work he sought to prove the inferiority and immorality of Renaissance architecture. Although the book contains fine drawings, the choice of pairs of buildings to contrast is highly prejudiced. He would, for example, compare a great Medieval cathedral with a poor standard, early nineteenth-century classical work. A few years later he published *True Principles of Pointed or Christian Architecture.* Here, in his

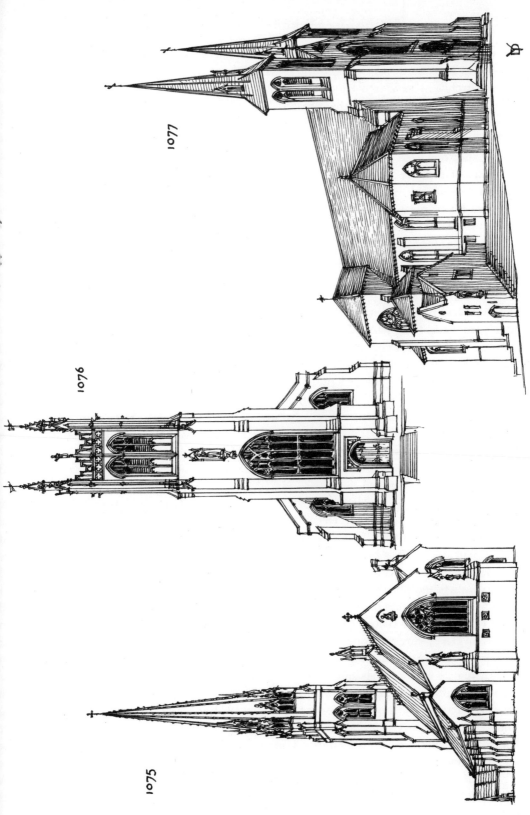

1075 St Giles', Cheadle, Staffordshire, 1841–6   1076 St Marie's, Derby, 1838–9   1077 St Chad's (now the Roman Catholic Cathedral), Birmingham, 1839–41

six true principles, he expounded the glory of Gothic architecture and his hatred of sham. He was an inveterate enemy of the eighteenth-century and early nineteenth-century Gothic by such architects as Wyatt. He complained that, not only was their work not authentic in style, but that they employed sham materials; for example, plaster to repair stone vaulting or iron as a supporting medium.

Pugin worked unceasingly; his output was tremendous. He was imaginative, desperately sincere and somewhat cynical. His vision of the Middle Ages was romantic and coloured by 300 years of distance. If it had been possible to have transported him to fifteenth-century England, he would have been horrified by the cruelties of the day and by the secular uses to which his beloved churches had been put. In 1852, at the age of 40, he died from over-work, insane.

Pugin designed a number of houses and many churches. His completed buildings, apart from the Palace of Westminster (p. 398) which is his great monument to posterity, are largely disappointing. Although his designs and drawings for these were good and his detail always of a high standard of Gothic perfection and feeling, he did not seem to have the ability (as had Barry to a marked extent) to visualise the entire building in three dimensions. As a Catholic in Protestant, Victorian England, he suffered numerous setbacks in his eccle-siastical work and his churches were generally Catholic and built in the rapidly expanding, black industrial towns of Britain. A number of them remain undamaged and though the exteriors are generally covered by a black film, the interiors are as rich, dark and over-decorated—yet exquisitely so—as ever.

One of Pugin's churches is now a Roman Catholic Cathedral—**St George's Cathedral, Southwark**, built in 1848. It was badly damaged in World War II and is now rebuilt. Though appearing a fine design in Pugin's drawings, in reality it has a chilly, sombre quality. Of fourteenth-century Gothic style, it has a long nave and short chapel. The lofty tower and spire were never completed.

The finest of Pugin's ecclesiastical works is the **Roman Catholic Cathedral (St Chad's), Birmingham**, 1839–41. It is in Decorated Gothic and constructed of red (now black) brick. It has two west towers of Rhenish quality. It is difficult to appreciate the cathedral's merit at the present time as it is built on a steep incline and is surrounded by uncleared bomb sites and damaged industrial buildings, but perhaps in the future Birmingham will award it more gracious surroundings (1077).

Two other churches designed by Pugin which are of interest are **St Marie's, Bridgegate, Derby**, 1838, and **St Giles', Cheadle**, Staffordshire, 1841–6. The former is a Perpendicular church in Derbyshire gritstone, now black, with a lofty tower containing a large Perpendicular window (1076). St Giles' is a fine church designed originally for Lord Shrewsbury and it was extremely costly. It has an elaborate, tall spire, over 200 feet high, which is elegant and well-proportioned in itself but perhaps rather large for the rest of the church, which is built of weathered, warm brown sandstone. The carved detail is of Pugin's usual high standard and the interior is particularly richly decorated with gold and colour on most surfaces including the floor, which is tiled in red, cream and blue. It is very dark and has the richness of a Byzantine interior (1075, 1084, 1145).

Among Pugin's other churches are **St Augustine's, Ramsgate**, 1846, **St Marie's Uttoxeter**, 1839 and **St Oswald's, Liverpool**, 1840–2. St Augustine's was Pugin's mode church where he endeavoured to express his ideals and conception of true Medievalism. It was to be built of genuine materials on the Medieval pattern and without sham. The results, unhappily, are mediocre, and one feels that he tried too hard. The peaceful, simple beauty of a small village Medieval church has evaded him and here is a squat, solid building evincing an unmistakeable air of revival. At St Oswald's he also aimed for a model church, this time in Decorated Gothic. The interior was exceptionally gloomy, even for Pugin, owing to the small window area, and was extremely uncomfortable and uninviting. It gave the impression, so common to much Victorian ecclesiastical building, that to be spiritually good man must suffer physical discomfort.

Of his houses only one large example is well known today and that is **Scarisbrick Hall**, Lancashire (built 1837–67, and completed after his death). It is an extensive, Gothic house with a tall tower at one corner, surmounted by a four-sided flat spire. Now used by Liverpool University, this house has some excellent Gothic detail and carved ornament, particularly evident on the porch, bay windows and lantern (1078, 1127, 1160–1, 1172).

Just before his death Pugin was still working on the **Palace of Westminster** to which he gave a tireless devotion and fine scholarship (1072, 1079–80, 1082, 1087), and in 1851 he arranged the **Medieval Court** for the **Great Exhibition**. He undertook this work with his usual passionate enthusiasm, although he did not scruple to make clear his scorn and contempt for the building itself: 'a greenhouse', he called it.

LESSER-KNOWN ARCHITECTS

The work of **Thomas Harrison, 1744–1829,** was discussed in Chapter IX. In the early nineteenth century he continued his work on **Chester Castle**; a giant project, which was not completed until 1820. His career

1078 Scarisbrick Hall, Lancashire, 1837. A. W. N. Pugin

1079–80, 1082, 1086–7 Palace of Westminster, London: details. A. W. N. Pugin   1081, 1083 Church of St Mary and St Nicholas, Wilton, Wiltshire, 1840–6. Wyatt and Brandon   1084 St Giles', Cheadle, Staffordshire, 1841–6. A. W. N. Pugin   1085 St George's Hall, Liverpool, 1839–54. H. L. Elmes   1088 Highclere Castle, Hampshire, 1842–4. Sir C. Barry   1089 St George's Ramsgate, Kent. H. E. Kendal

1090 Lonsdale Square, Islington, London, 1838. R. C. Carpenter

finished as it had commenced, with the design of a bridge. This was the **Grosvenor Bridge**
at **Chester** spanning the River Dee with the, at that time, unusual single span of some 200
feet (1186).

    Richard Cromwell Carpenter, 1812–55, like Pugin and Elmes, was short lived. Into
his 43 years, however, he crowded a considerable quantity of work of a Gothic character. A
disciple of the Camdenian doctrine (see Churches), he designed a number of churches, the
best-known of which are **St Paul's, Brighton**, 1846–8, **All Saints', Hove,** 1848–52, **St
Stephen's** and **St Andrew's, Birmingham**, and, in **London, St Mary Magdalene, Munster
Square**, 1849–52. St Paul's, Brighton, now hedged in by commercial buildings, was completed by his son, and the tall spire intended by Carpenter did not materialise. His best
church was the London example, built in Decorated Gothic on ecclesiologist principles
(p. 416). In the domestic field Carpenter built an attractive Gothic Square in **Islington—
Lonsdale Square**—in 1838. Now the district has an air of having seen better days, but the

pleasant, Medieval peacefulness is still apparent in this Perpendicular backwater behind the busy main road (1090, 1144). Carpenter's finest work, **Lancing College Chapel**, was started in 1854 only just before his death. It is discussed in Chapter XI.

Thomas Rickman, apart from his connection with the nomenclature of Medieval architecture, had a deep interest in Medieval churches. He was first trained for medicine and then became an insurance clerk, but in his thirties he began to travel the country drawing churches. He then set up in architectural practice and was busily employed building churches (p. 419). He also designed the **New Court** at **St John's College, Cambridge**, in co-operation with **Henry Hutchinson**. This large, new court was built in the years 1827–31 and is in Perpendicular Gothic; it consists of a traceried screen and gateway with central blocks and cupola. The stone **bridge** over the Cam at St John's, also in Perpendicular style, was erected in 1826 (1091, 1189).

PUBLIC BUILDINGS

The first half of the nineteenth century was a time of extensive and energetic construction of public buildings. These are predominantly classical in form, both Roman and Greek, and those listed in this paragraph have been discussed in context under the appropriate architect's name. The remainder are described in this section.

Barry: Palace of Westminster
  Royal Institution, Manchester
Basevi: Fitzwilliam Museum, Cambridge
Burton: Arch and Screen, Hyde Park Corner
Cockerell: Ashmolean Museum, Oxford
Nash: Marble Arch
  Regent Street and Park Scheme
  Royal Pavilion, Brighton

Smirke: British Museum, London
  Shire Hall, Gloucester
  College of Physicians, London
Soane: Bank of England, London
  Dulwich Art Gallery and Mausoleum
Wilkins: National Gallery, London
  University College, London
  St George's Hospital, Hyde Park Corner

The outstanding classical building of the nineteenth century is **St George's Hall, Liverpool**, designed by **Harvey Lonsdale Elmes, 1814–47**. Elmes studied at the Royal Academy Schools in 1831–4 and then entered the office of H. E. Goodridge, where he worked for three years. In 1839 he won the competition by his design for St George's Hall in Liverpool, and, in 1840, the competition for the new Assize Courts in the same city. It was then decided to combine the two buildings in one large design and Elmes redesigned the scheme as it stands in the present building. This was to include a great central hall for concert performances with, at one end of the building, the crown court and at the other, the civil court. The design was approved in October 1840 and work began in 1842. However, after working for a few years on the project, Elmes's health deteriorated and he had to go to Jamaica to try to recuperate, and there he died at the age of 34. In common with so many of his contemporaries in the arts, he was a victim to tuberculosis, and a great loss to his generation. Work on St George's Hall was completed on the exterior, and also on the interior vault, by Sir Robert Rawlinson, to Elmes's designs, between 1847 and 1851, and C.R. Cockerell was responsible for the remaining interior work after this date. Elmes's reputation rests, therefore, on this one building; an outstanding creation by so young and inexperienced an architect, and one who had never visited Italy or Greece. It is, as Sir Hugh Casson* describes it 'the noblest classical

* *An Introduction to Victorian Architecture* (Art and Technics, London, 1948).

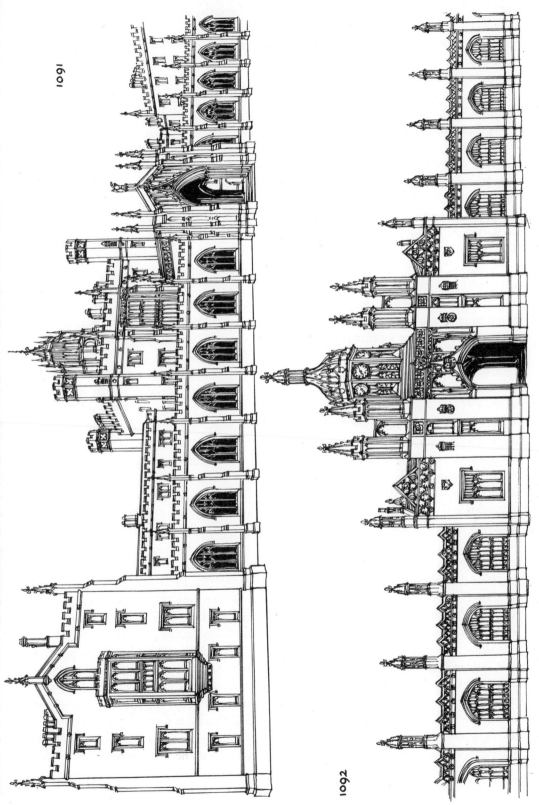

1091

1092

1091 St John's College, Cambridge, 1827–31: New Court. Thomas Rickman and Henry Hutchinson 1092 King's College, Cambridge, 1822–4: screen and entrance gateway. William Wilkins

building of the nineteenth century'. It occupies a fine site in the centre of a great square in the city of Liverpool, and one reflects how much more it could be appreciated if the layers of soot were removed.

The exterior of St George's Hall is of Greek classical design using the Corinthian order. The long façade has a great portico of Corinthian columns, while the remainder of this elevation is decorated by Corinthian pilasters which are square in section and are partly free-standing. The south end of the building is completed with a portico and pediment—set on a flight of steps, while the north is semicircular in section. Above the entablature of the building rises an unbroken attic which covers the main vault over the central hall.

Inside the building, the Great Hall (not very good acoustically) is the essence of Roman grandeur. The great vaulted roof was constructed in hollow bricks based on the design of the Baths of Caracalla in Rome. This work was carried out by Rawlinson, but the remainder of the interior of the hall was decorated by Cockerell from 1851 to 1854. It has heavy piers with shafts of polished grey granite and the spandrels above the piers are decorated by high relief, huge, winged figures. The original colour scheme (since altered) was chiefly in white with gold decoration and the grey columns. The small hall was elegant and beautifully decorated in low relief and essentially early Victorian with its cast iron, papier mâché and plaster carried out in a colour scheme of gold, grey and cream. The hall was opened in 1854 with a performance of Handel's *Messiah* (1051, 1073, 1085; L).

Two other well-known classical buildings which should be mentioned are the Royal Exchange and the Fishmongers' Hall, both in **London**. The old **Royal Exchange** was destroyed by fire in 1838 and a new Exchange was built in 1841–9 by **Sir William Tite**, an architect also well known for his railway station construction. The predominating feature of the Royal Exchange is its gigantic, though traditional eight-column Corinthian portico facing the circus at the Mansion House. Flanked by the Bank of England on one side and the Mansion House opposite, it is essentially Victorian, lacking in grace, its detail blatant though correct, in comparison with these two more refined, subtle buildings. The best exterior elevations are the long sides of the triangular site which are decorated almost their whole length by a giant Corinthian order in pilaster and column form. At the opposite end from the portico is a tall clock tower (1032). The **Fishmongers' Hall**, a smaller building, is much more attractive; it can be seen to advantage from the centre of London Bridge. Its designer was **Henry Roberts**, and the building with its decorative Ionic portico was erected 1841–3.

Two famous London landmarks were erected at this time. The **Duke of York's Column** (Doric) in **Waterloo Place** was designed by **Benjamin Dean Wyatt** in 1831–4 and **Nelson's Column** (Corinthian) in **Trafalgar Square** by **William Railton** in 1839 (1066).

One of the large Gothic structures not yet discussed is the extensive rebuilding operations at **Windsor Castle** in the nineteenth century. By 1800 Windsor Castle had become an unsightly and incongruous mass of accumulated building much of which was in a useless and even dangerous condition. **Sir Jeffrey Wyatville**, 1766–1840, nephew of James Wyatt, won the competition in 1824 to transform the castle and this he did, making a picturesque, castellated mansion of it. At the cost of half a million pounds he created a scheme of considerable grandeur, romantic in silhouette and congruous in its unified conception. He was knighted for this work (1028).

Two familiar Gothic memorials of this time have long excited criticism favourable and otherwise, more commonly otherwise, being out of fashion in the twentieth century. One of these is the **Scott Monument** in **Princes Street, Edinburgh**, constructed in 1840–6. In an open competition won by Rickman, the commission was, however, given to the third contestant; a Scottish carpenter who had become an architect. The memorial, at a cost of over £15,000, is an unusual monument and its wealth of Medieval sculptured detail, as well

as excellent views of Edinburgh and East Lothian, can be seen to great advantage by the energetic climber who ascends to the top. In contrast, the **Martyrs' Memorial** in **Oxford**, designed in 1841 by **George Gilbert Scott** is on a much smaller scale and is less ambitious. It is based upon the Medieval Eleanor cross pattern (1093).

CLUBS, THEATRES AND HOTELS

Many of **London's club-houses** were built or rehoused in this period. A number of the prominent architects of the day designed one or more of these, which are nearly all situated in one small area of London; Pall Mall or St James's Street.

The most outstanding of these designs is the **Athenaeum** by **Decimus Burton**, 1829–30. This is decorated by a continuous frieze of Athenian low-relief sculpture all round the building below the cornice. It has a fine porch, while inside is a grand staircase (1043). **Sir Charles Barry** was responsible for the other beautifully designed clubs—notably the **Travellers'** and the **Reform**. Both are patterned on Italian Renaissance palace design inspired predominantly by those in Venice and Rome. Barry was imitated widely after his establishment of this new mode. The principal rooms are placed at the front and rear of the site while the centre is lit from a covered (in Italy open) court. The

1093 The Martyrs' Memorial, Oxford, 1841. Sir George Gilbert Scott

HOTEL AND SPA ARCHITECTURE 1800–1850

1094 The Bedford Hotel, Brighton, Sussex, late Regency 1095 The Queen's Hotel, Cheltenham, 1837–8. E. W. and C. Jearrad 1096 Brunel House, Bristol (originally The Royal Western Hotel). 1828–40. R. S. Pope 1097 The Pittville Pump Room, Chelten-

designs have a robust quality and are eminently suitable for their purpose (1042). **Nash's** contribution was the **United Service Club** (situated opposite to the Athenaeum across Waterloo Place, although both buildings front Pall Mall). The design (remodelled in 1858) has much in common with the Athenaeum, particularly a sculptured frieze, but the Pall Mall entrance has a two-storey portico with the Doric order employed on the ground stage and the Corinthian above, with pediment (1041). The **Smirkes** were active in club-house building; **Sir Robert** combined with his brother on the **Oxford and Cambridge Club** in 1836–7 and **Sidney Smirke** built the **Carlton Club House** in 1847–55, and, with **George Basevi**, the **Conservative Club** in 1843–4 (1044).

Unfortunately little remains of the extensive **theatre building in London** of this period mainly owing to the hazards of fire. The new **Covent Garden Theatre**, rebuilt by **Sir Robert Smirke** in 1809, was destroyed again in 1857. The present building is by E. M. Barry. Smirke's theatre had a Greek Doric portico and was a good design. **Drury Lane Theatre**, burnt down 1809, was rebuilt by **Benjamin Wyatt**. The interior has been largely altered but much of his Corinthian rotunda, with its approach staircases, survives. **Nash's Theatre Royal, Haymarket**, which he rebuilt 1820–1 has continued to exist much as he designed it on the exterior. The interior was reconstructed in 1879 (1033).

With the railway era under way and the improved road conditions the need for **hotels** began to be felt. Most of the famous hotels were built in the second half of the nineteenth century, but from this period one or two should be mentioned. The **Queen's Hotel** at Cheltenham at the top of the Promenade was designed in 1837–8 by **E. W.** and **C. Jearrad**, the Cheltenham architects, as part of the whole Promenade scheme (see p. 424). It is an attractive, well-proportioned and finely sited classical building with a Corinthian, two-storey portico and pediment above (1095). In **Brighton**, on the sea-front is the **Bedford Hotel**, decorated now in white, grey-green and black, but still showing its late Regency characteristics of a bastard but individual classicism (1094). At **Bristol** there is the **Royal Western Hotel** (now Brunel House), designed 1838–40 by **R. S. Pope**. It has a long, Ionic arcade in front of the two lower storeys and the Corinthian order is used for the two upper floors (1096).

ECCLESIASTICAL BUILDINGS

Comparatively little church building had been carried out since the impetus given by the 1711 Act providing for the erection of churches, in which Hawksmoor had been the leading spirit. By the early years of the nineteenth century the population had increased and had been redistributed. The Industrial Revolution had caused a great migration of workers to urban areas, many of which were new centres of population. To meet this situation in 1818, the Church Building Society was formed and, with Parliamentary support, a Church Building Act was passed which provided that one million pounds should be spent on the building of new churches. The money would be allocated under the supervision of the Church Commissioners, since which time these churches have been referred to, generally in a derogatory manner, as the Commissioners' Churches. Some few years later another half-million pounds was allocated and the total number of churches constructed was eventually 214, of which 174 were Gothic. The majority of these churches are in London suburbs and in the industrial areas of Yorkshire, Lancashire and the Midlands. Few of them are aesthetically or architecturally attractive; they are nearly all large, capable of holding big congregations, and most were cheaply built. In the years 1818–30 there were no terms of reference as to style and the early examples were in Greek classical form. Later the Gothic revival movement gained ground, especially for ecclesiastical building; also, a Gothic church was generally cheaper, being often of brick instead of stone and needing no costly storeyed tower and portico. The Church Commissioners were advised in their selection by a board of three architects: Nash, Smirke and Soane. All of these built one or more churches, although only Smirke contributed any outside the London area. But none of these architects was very interested or helpful in this project of mass-production churches. They were individualists, successful and busy. No real leader emerged and it is inevitable that later generations should compare this situation and its results with the two previous opportunities which had occurred; the first after the Fire of London in the seventeenth century when Wren had designed his 50-odd churches, and the second in 1711, when Hawksmoor and his fellow architects had stepped into the breach. Here, lamentably, was no Wren or Hawksmoor, and at the same time the Commissioners were asking for as large a church as could be built for as little of the taxpayers' money as possible. This injunction (so familiar today) was hardly likely to produce a St Bride or a St Martin-in-the-Fields.

Classical Churches

Of these churches erected between 1800 and 1850, some examples stand out in contradistinction to the preceding remarks, and indeed some of the churches were built before the Act of 1818. Among the exceptions to the rather uninspiring mass of churches of the time are those designed by the Inwoods, in particular, **St Pancras', London**, 1819–22, by **H. W. and W. Inwood.** The design for this church was by H. W. Inwood, who had travelled for a short while in Greece and returned to win the competition at the age of 24, and he and his father, who were partners, built it together. This building is one of the few really fine Greek-revival churches and ranks with St Martin-in-the-Fields as a successful design. Many churches during the eighteenth century had been modelled on the steeple of St Martin's and the Greek revivalists felt that they needed a new pattern, but few satisfactory ones emerged. Inwood based his tower on the Tower of the Winds in Athens; he adapted the design and repeated it, having one tower with a smaller edition placed on top of it. The church, in general, is largely based on the Erechtheum in Athens, with fine detail ornament. The design comprises a large hall with an apse at one end and the tower and portico at the other. Inside is a simple, galleried hall with flat ceiling and rich, Greek decoration. The church was costly—some £70,000—over four times the cost of an average Commissioners' Church (1021).

Another delightful **Inwood church** is **All Saints'** at **Camden Town**, 1822–4. This has a tall, semicircular portico, still with Greek Ionic order, and a slender cylindrical tower. Here too the detail is delicate and finely executed (1098).

Sir John Soane's contribution to the Commissioners' Churches is somewhat disappointing and does not show his work at its best. There are three examples: **Holy Trinity, Marylebone**, 1824–5, **St Peter's, Walworth**, and **St John's, Bethnal Green**, 1824–5. **Holy Trinity** has pleasant proportions when viewed in two parts: the tower and the body of the church. However, one is not harmoniously connected to the other and there is a division between the verticality of the tower and the horizontal mass of the church. The portico has no pediment but is of pleasing design in the Ionic order (1099). **St Peter's, Walworth,** is very similar, but **St John's** is of different design with a solid, squat tower, surmounted by an insignificant cupola (1100).

Apart from the Inwood's churches, the most original and attractive example is **Nash's All Souls' Church, Langham Place,** 1822–4, which he designed to act as a terminal feature to his Regent Street and to close the vista. It is unconventional, having a circular porch built at a tangent to the church. This porch, of Roman Doric design, has a spiked spire rising out of the upper stage, which aroused caustic comment at the time. The church was built of Bath stone at a cost of some £18,000. Broadcasting House, next to the church, was designed to harmonise with All Souls' but the same cannot be said of the large rectangular blocks which have risen behind it in the last few

1098 All Saints' Church, Camden Town, 1822–4. W. and H. W. Inwood

years (1022). Also in **Regent Street** were two good examples of classical, ecclesiastical architecture, both now unfortunately demolished. One was **Cockerell's Hanover Chapel,** 1823–5, which had a Greek Ionic portico with flanking towers and a dome-covered atrium. The other was **St Philip's Church,** designed by **Repton.**

Also in Marylebone, not far from Soane's Holy Trinity, is the **parish church** of **St Marylebone,** designed 1813–18 by **Thomas Hardwick.** This is an imposing classical church on a large scale, with pedimented Corinthian portico and a square tower topped by a circular colonnade and cupola (1023).

Sir Robert Smirke designed a greater number of churches for the Commissioners than either of his two colleagues. They are all in Greek revival vein and have considerable similarity. The best of these is probably **St Mary's, Wyndham Place, London,** 1823–4. The church is built on a terminal site on the Portman Estate and has a fine semicircular Greek Ionic

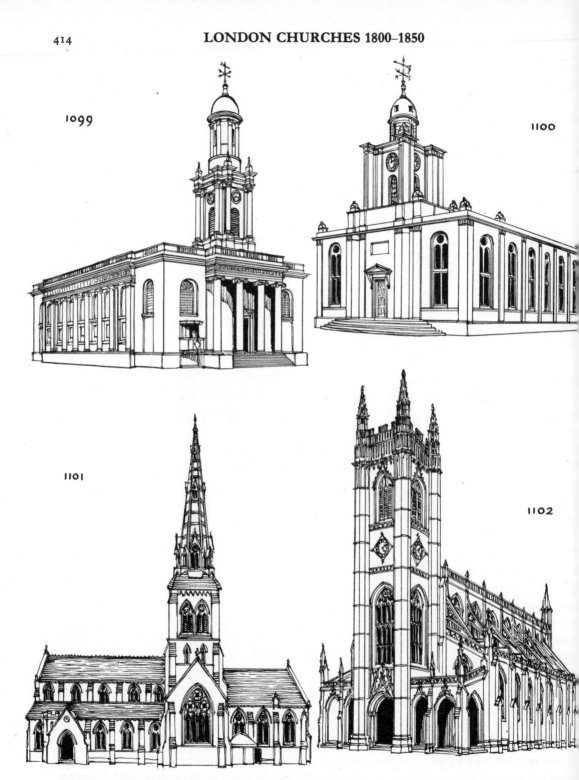

1099 Holy Trinity, Marylebone, 1824–5. Sir John Soane   1100 St John's, Bethnal Green, 1824–5
Sir John Soane (interior altered)   1101 St Giles', Camberwell, 1842–4: south front. Scott and
Moffatt   1102 St Luke's, Chelsea, 1820–4. James Savage

portico. The tower is too lofty
and somewhat repetitive (1040).
Smirke also designed **St Anne's,
Wandsworth,** 1820–2, **St
Nicholas', Strood,** and **St
George's, Brandon Hill,
Bristol,** 1823. At this last the
Doric order is used, while in the
circular tower are flat Doric
pilasters (1169).

James Savage designed a
number of good churches for
the Commissioners, both Gothic
and classical. His church of **St
James** in **Bermondsey,** 1827–9,
is an attractive design in traditional classical form (1103).

Before turning to the Gothic-
style churches, two unusual
classical examples should be
mentioned, both showing Italian
influence. The first is the church
of **St Mary and St Nicholas** at
Wilton, Wiltshire, designed
1840–6 by **Wyatt** and **Brandon.**
This is an impressive large-scale
edifice built in stone in Italian
Romanesque style. There is a
campanile at the side, free-standing except for a short arcade,
and the principal front is decorative with large, central rose
window and a richly decorated,

1103 St James's Church, Bermondsey, 1827–9. Architect,
James Savage

Romanesque doorway below. Both exterior and interior are sumptuously carved and ornamented; one has the feeling that here is an Italian church which has lost some of its colour
and has strayed into a typically English village (1067–8, 1071, 1081, 1083, 1104, 1149). **Christ
Church, Streatham,** 1840–2, by **J. W. Wild** is quite different. Here is a large but not costly
church, built in yellow brick with decoration in red and white brick. The design is very
simple and modern, well ahead of its time, but there is also an Italian influence in the side
campanile and restrained polychrome decoration.

Among the more average products of the Commissioners' Churches in classical vein
should be noted **St Matthew's, Brixton,** by **C. F. Porden, St Mark's, Kennington,** by
A. B. Clayton, both Greek Doric (1167) and **St Peter's, Hammersmith,** by **Edward
Lapidge,** Ionic (1105), also **St Mary's, Greenwich,** by **George Basevi.**

Gothic Churches

It is difficult to discuss the Gothic-revival ecclesiastical architecture of the nineteenth century without first explaining the term 'ecclesiology' and introducing the ecclesiologists. However much we, at a distance of more than 100 years, may feel aversion towards this well-intentioned but excessively prejudiced group of people, we must study their beliefs in order to understand the architecture of the period, for their influence was powerful and lasting.

The **ecclesiological movement** had its roots both in Oxford and Cambridge. From Oxford came first the Tractarians: Anglicans inspired by the tracts of Pusey and Newman. From Cambridge came the Camden Society founded in 1839. From 1841 onwards the Camden Society published a monthly magazine called *The Ecclesiologist*, which laid down instructions on ritual, architectural ecclesiastical interiors, etc. The two movements became one and grew apace. It gained in authority in both ecclesiastical and architectural matters. Medieval churches were carefully studied, measured, drawn and the conclusion was reached that not only was Gothic the only true style for church architecture, but it must be fourteenth-

1104 Church of St Mary and St Nicholas, Wilton, Wiltshire, 1840–6. Wyatt and Brandon

century Gothic or, as they termed it, 'Middle Pointed'. The ecclesiologists tried to monopolise church building in England by appointing only architects who would build to their orders. This fortunately failed, but far too many architects did permit themselves to be cajoled, bullied or threatened.

The ecclesiologists' method of deciding the value of a Gothic building was not on architectural merits but on moral ones. Like Pugin, they firmly believed that only a good man could design a good building. Like Pugin also, they had a horror of architectural sham. Thus, any material which did not exist or was not understood in the Middle Ages, could not be employed in nineteenth-century building. In this the church builders cut themselves off from modern structural development. The movement became widespread after 1840. It included influential members of the Church and government, and was powerful enough to dictate to much of the architectural profession and to establish a practical architectural dictatorship in ecclesiastical building. Classical architecture was sinful and must be destroyed, as must also Norman, Early English and Perpendicular Gothic. Much restoration of Medieval Cathedrals and churches was carried out by these well-meaning but bigoted people, and this entailed destruction of all which did not comply with their narrow view. They did not seem to comprehend the gradual process of evolution from Norman to Perpendicular visible in most English Medieval parish churches.

Fortunately, in this period, a very large number of Commissioners' Churches were built before the ecclesiologists became powerful enough to have great effect and, although few such examples are outstanding architecture, they were not stultified by the cloak of righteousness with which the ecclesiologists endeavoured to cover architecture from 1840 onwards. **Pugin's contribution** has already been described and examples of his work can be seen in Figs. 1075–7. An early Gothic church which is interesting and largely successful is **St Luke's, Chelsea, 1820–4**, designed by the same **James Savage** who had built a number of Greek revival churches for the Commissioners. Although there is shown here a lack of experience in building in Gothic, it is a serious attempt to construct

1105 St Peter's Church, Hammersmith. Edward Lapidge

1106 St Peter's, Cheltenham, 1847–9. S. W. Dawkes   1107 St Peter's, Brighton, 1823–8. Si
Charles Barry   1108 St. George's, Ramsgate. H. E. Kendall   1109 Theale, Berkshire, 1820–30
Edward Garbett

a Perpendicular Gothic church with stone not plaster vaults, and the necessary supporting buttresses. It is a large, costly church with pleasing silhouette and good detail (1102).

Sir Charles Barry made some adequate Gothic contribution to the Commissioners' Churches in the early days at the start of his career, although he later professed distaste for them. He designed two churches in Manchester and then won the competition for **St Peter's, Brighton**, built 1823-8. Here, like Savage, he showed his lack of experience in handling Gothic but he produced a good, stone church, sited as a terminal block to the Steyne. To strengthen this impression, Barry erected a screen wall to the lower part of the tower; he buttressed the corners and provided flying buttresses to the tower itself. This tower is slender and tall, with admirable proportions (1107, 1142). Barry then designed **St Andrew's, Hove**, 1824, an example in Italian Renaissance style; also three churches in **Islington**, 1825-6.

In the first 40 years of the nineteenth century, Gothic church building was, in general, reasonably authentic. The romantic aspect of the eighteenth century had disappeared and architects understood Gothic construction well enough but were not fully at home in the style and used it tentatively. They lacked the feeling for Medieval building and proportion. Even architects who were capable of designing an elegant and refined building in classical style seemed to find it difficult to transpose this ability to their Gothic work. One such architect was Decimus Burton.

Two of the most prolific Gothic church architects were Goodwin and Rickman. They both designed primarily for the provinces and in the new urban areas of the Midlands and the north.

Francis Goodwin, 1784-1835, carried out designs, like so many of his colleagues, in classical or Gothic vein. His practice was large; it included an output of work varying from the Greek Town Hall at Manchester (old Town Hall) and designs for an extensive London cemetery to the Commissioners' Churches which were generally in Gothic. His most important of these were **Holy Trinity, Bordesley, Birmingham, St Matthew's, Walsall**, and **St George's, Hulme, Manchester**, all built in the 1820s. His work was capable and sound, sometimes extravagant, and generally noted for its tall towers and cast-iron decoration.

Thomas Rickman, 1776-1841, employed all his considerable knowledge of Medieval Gothic architecture in his church building, but the results are generally disappointing. In this field he showed himself more apt as an antiquarian scholar than as a Gothic architect, although later, at St John's College, Cambridge, he illustrated that he was capable of designing well in Gothic. Among his Gothic churches, which in Midland areas have suffered greatly from dirt, war damage and town replanning, are **St George's, Edgbaston**, Birmingham, 1819-22, **Christ Church, Coventry**, and **St Peter's, Preston**. The **Ombersley** Church and that at **Hartlebury**, both in Worcestershire, have more rural settings and belong to the 1830s, rather later than the others. All these examples have the common traits of their time; plaster vaults and cast-iron columns and tracery, but they illustrate Rickman's sincere attempt to follow the traditional Medieval pattern. He generally worked in Perpendicular Gothic and was one of the last early Victorian architects to do so before the power of the ecclesiologists was felt (1126, 1157).

Typical Gothic churches of the period are examples such as **St George's, Ramsgate,** by **H. E. Kendall**, a design based on the Medieval Boston church (1089, 1108, 1180); **St Peter's, Leeds**, 1839-41, by **R. D. Chantrell**, which has a fine tower but is now badly damaged;

St Michael's, Stockwell, in Early English vein by **W. Rogers** (1162) and the church at **Theale**, Berkshire, 1830-2, by **Edward Garbett**. This large building with side campanile is also in Early English design, with pairs of tall lancet windows. There is a projecting porch and, above, a decorative rose window (1109, 1130, 1165).

In **Camberwell** stands a large, costly church, **St Giles'**, 1842-4. This was one of the first commissions of the youthful **George G. Scott** and built by him and his partner **Moffatt**. The exterior is good, with a lofty, stone tower and spire, forming a well-known South London landmark. The church is cruciform in plan, over 150 feet in length, and the style is Decorated Gothic. It became a prototype for both Scott and his fellow architects in the next 20 years (1101, 1128).

Cheltenham, although famed primarily for its classical terraces, also possesses three Gothic churches of this period. The best of these is the neo-Norman church of **St Peter**, built in 1847-9 by **S. W. Dawkes**. It is a cruciform church with a circular tower and lantern over the crossing. One of the best Gothic churches of the period, it has a wealth of well-carved and authentic Norman detail on windows, doorways and arcades (1063, 1106, 1164, 1173). There is also **Christ Church, Cheltenham**, 1837-40, designed by the **Jearrads**, on the Lansdown Estate. This has a tall, sad-looking tower sited as a terminal at the end of a tree-lined road (1148). Less satisfactory is the gaunt church of the **Holy Trinity** in the same town, 1820-2, by **G. A. Underwood**, whose classical contributions there are much more pleasing.

TOWN PLANNING IN ESTATES

London

From 1800 began the growth—steady but at ever-increasing speed—of London, which transformed the capital from a normal city surrounded by pleasant villages into the sprawling metropolis that we see today. When the nineteenth century opened, most of the suburbs which we now consider to be near Central London were yet villages: Hampstead, Highgate, Blackheath, Wimbledon, Chelsea. Between 1800 and 1835 were developed much of London's present West End, Bloomsbury and Belgravia. In general, the architectural standard was good, the quality of building and amenities excellent. The classical form of architecture in **terrace** construction prevailed. These terraces varied in length from whole streets to small blocks and were curved or straight. Flats were almost unknown. Apart from Nash's widespread schemes in the Regent's Park area, described on pp. 377-8, the two men largely responsible for the building enterprise of these years were firstly James Burton, then Thomas Cubitt.

James Burton, 1761-1837, a Scotsman, was the most enterprising and successful builder of his time. He developed much of Bloomsbury, taking over sites and letting out some of the work to other builders, although supervising the whole himself. By this means he kept up a high standard of building. His son, **Decimus**, designed much of the work for him and he also built a great deal for **Nash**, including many of the **Regent's Park Terraces**, parts of **Regent Street** and **Waterloo Place**. In recompense, Nash sponsored Decimus early in his architectural career. James Burton was largely responsible for laying out **Russell Square**, 1800-14, and surrounding area, part of **Tavistock Square, Burton Street** and **Bloomsbury Square**. He also played a large part in layouts at **Tunbridge Wells** (see p. 424), and from

1828 onwards developed much of **St Leonards-on-Sea**, where again Decimus designed terraces and houses for him.

Thomas Cubitt, 1788–1855, who continued Burton's work in London from the 1820s onwards, is perhaps more famous, particularly as the founder of the first modern-style building firm. Until Cubitt's time, work in different trades had been sub-contracted—bricklaying masonry, carpentry, etc.—and, whereas the scheme had worked well enough until 1800, when large-scale development was involved, as the nineteenth century required, the system showed itself inefficient and slow. Cubitt thus bought land and workshops and set up a firm which included all craftsmen necessary to the building trade, on a permanent wage basis. To keep his firm financially solvent he had to provide continuous work for them. This he did by large-scale speculative building. Thomas Cubitt was the first of our modern builders. His standards in building, architecture and drainage were high, far above those of the men who followed him. Sometimes he had to sacrifice aesthetic needs to financial and domestic ones; here was the beginning of the devaluation of architectural and building standards; a devaluation which has continued almost uninterruptedly ever since. But, on the whole, Cubitt performed a great service to London. Many of his houses, squares and terraces still stand; as fine, elegant and sound as they were over 100 years ago. They expose as inferior indeed the later phases of development which now surround them.

Cubitt began his building activities at **Highbury Park** and at **Stoke Newington**, then, in 1824, in the **St Pancras** area in **Tavistock Square, Woburn Place** and **Euston Square**. His houses were in blocks of Greek classical stucco; they were all well designed and built. His most extensive and best known enterprise was his creation of **Belgravia** in south-west London. When Buckingham House was redesigned as Buckingham Palace, he realised that this area was suitable for development. He leased an area of swampy ground from Lord Grosvenor and converted it into the aristocratic squares of Belgravia. **Belgrave Square** itself was designed by **George Basevi** for Cubitt, who built it. It consists of four classical blocks, one on each side of the square, while at three of the corners are built single, large houses. The Corinthian order is used throughout except for the individual entrance porches which are varied (1045, 1133). In the remainder of the Belgrave scheme Cubitt and his brother Lewis the architect made the designs. From 1836 to 1849 Cubitt laid out **Lowndes Square** in which there was a five-storey block designed by **Lewis Cubitt** in Italian palace style with astylar façade. From Belgravia, Cubitt went on to **Pimlico** and then further into the suburbs to **Clapham Park**.

Cubitt was the first of the large-scale speculative builders but, unlike so many of his successors, he used his influence all his life to combat the abuses of architecture, building and living standards to which speculative building is heir. He was particularly interested in drainage and London's sewage arrangements and constantly worked to improve these. His own houses were soundly built, pleasant to live in and created for a period of years, not just for the moment. He supplied first-class amenities in the way of land drainage, sewage, lighting and roads.

Apart from Thomas Cubitt's building enterprises many other schemes were being developed from 1825 onwards. The Gloucester Road–South Kensington area was extended rapidly. **George Basevi** had designed **Pelham Crescent, South Kensington**, in 1825 (1046, 1132), and by 1850 **Gloucester Road** and **Kensington Gate** were being built. In **Paddington,**

1110 The Promenade, Cheltenham, 1825–30 (some later alterations)   1111 Lansdown Terrace, Cheltenham, *c.* 1825. J. B. Papworth   1112 Lewes Crescent, Kemp Town, Brighton. H. E. Kendall

Westbourne Terrace was constructed *c.* 1845 (1134) and the **Bayswater** district extended. **Hyde Park Gardens** were laid out in 1836-8 by **John Crake**, and **Oxford, Cambridge** and **Gloucester Squares** in 1837-50. All this building was classical in pattern, only varying in treatment. With the onset of the Victorian age, Gothic began to intrude in domestic building. In **Islington** are two squares differing widely from one another but also from the classical pattern evolved by Nash, Burton and Cubitt. **Milner Square**, 1841-3, was designed by **Gough** and **Roumieu** with brick façades decorated all round the square by flat, plain pilasters (1047). **Lonsdale Square** near by is the work of **R. C. Carpenter** and is late Gothic in conception. Its Perpendicular treatment is almost Tudor and the façades are simple brick (1090, 1144). Another well-designed layout is in the **Ladbroke Grove** area, 1845-53, by **Thomas Allom**.

The Victorian age has often been accused of building the nation's slums. Indeed much of the industrial area building, especially in the north by speculative builders, was inexcusably bad and quickly created slum-conditions. But many so-called nineteenth-century slums are in reality eighteenth-century building which, in the overcrowded urban conditions of the nineteenth-century Industrial Revolution, became slums. The Victorian standards of building construction may have been aesthetically inferior to those of their predecessors but in soundness of domestic habitation were often better both in material and workmanship. The Georgian and Regency periods both produced their quota of jerry building and shoddiness, but the Victorians with their infinitely larger quantity of building are too often held responsible for the sins of all generations.

Cheltenham

Outside London in this period there was also much urban expansion. In a number of towns, particularly spa resorts and sea-coast towns, can be found a quantity of architecture in terrace and block form of as high a standard as that in the capital. Indeed, from 1825 onwards the speculative builder had begun to replace the architect in this field, and in other cities finer architecture may be found than in London. Bath was largely laid out in the eighteenth century, although further expansion continued in the nineteenth (see Chapter IX). The most outstanding development in quality and quantity in the first half of the nineteenth century was probably in **Cheltenham**. Here, a number of good architects were working and creating public buildings, terrace architecture and villas for the rapidly expanding spa. Two names in particular stand out: Papworth and Forbes.

John Buonarotti Papworth, 1775-1847, carried out architectural commissions in London and elsewhere but the majority of his work was for Cheltenham. His name is so linked with the town's Regency development that much is often ascribed to him without foundation. He was the son of a builder and after his apprenticeship in London in an architect's office he developed into a most versatile and capable architect. In Cheltenham he laid out the **Montpellier** and **Lansdown estates** which included the **Montpellier Pump Room**, 1827. This building was designed with a circular domed hall, after the Pantheon in Rome. The interior decoration of the hall was exceptionally attractive. Papworth's work in Cheltenham was versatile but predominantly Greek classical. **Lansdown Terrace**, *c.* 1825, is very simple, consisting of four-storey houses with an order and pediment at second-floor level (1111).

The other strong architectural influence at Cheltenham in the Regency was that of **John B.**

Forbes, whose chief work was for **Joseph Pitt**, the great landowner. For Pitt, Forbes laid out the basis of the **Pittville estate** which was built round the **Pittville Pump Room**. Forbes designed this Pump Room in 1825–30; it was erected on a rise of ground below which the surrounding area was landscaped with a lake and bridges. The Pump Room itself is a first-class classical building. Like Papworth's Montpellier Pump Room, it has a front colonnade and behind it a rotunda. Unfortunately, Papworth had to build his Pump Room behind an earlier colonnade, but Forbes designed the whole building from the beginning and his rotunda is in better proportion to the colonnade than Papworth's. The Pump Room was a great assembly hall based on the Roman bath plan. In style it is Greek revival, using the Ionic order in a fine colonnade. The interior, now put to different use, was beautifully decorated with exceptionally fine ceilings. From the exterior it is still the finest Regency building in Cheltenham. The remainder of the Pittville estate was built after Forbes and Pitt had died, but theirs was the inspiration and initial achievement (1097).

After Forbes and Papworth came other good architects. Between 1830 and 1850 further terraces, villas and public buildings were designed, almost all in Greek classical vein by, among others, **R. W.** and **C. Jearrad, G. A. Underwood, Dangerfield** and **Knight**. The **Queen's Hotel**, at the head of the Promenade, 1837–8, was built in dignified style by the **Jearrads**. It has a central, six-column portico in the Corinthian order and a rusticated ground floor. It shows more of a Palladian quality than Greek revival (1095). **The Promenade** itself was largely laid out from 1825 as a broad, tree-lined road. At the upper end, near the Queen's Hotel, it is lined mainly by plain terraces and attractive villas. Lower down, nearer the centre of the town, is a long, imposing terrace of large houses with municipal offices beneath. Although it has suffered some alteration, it still presents an impressive stucco façade (1110). The ironwork in the canopied balconies and railings of the Promenade is some of the best in Cheltenham, a town which possesses in quantity high-quality craftmanship in iron (1069, 1176).

Among the many great terraces of Cheltenham should be noted the **Royal Crescent**, 1805–12, an early, simple but large-scale example; **Lansdown Parade** and **Crescent**, and **Wolseley Terrace** (1181).

Tunbridge Wells

This town developed as a resort in the seventeenth century, but much of its architecture is Regency. The chief influence here is that of **Decimus Burton** who designed the **Calverley Estate** for his father James Burton. **Calverley Park** is laid out with detached and grouped houses on a curve which faces the actual park. Local sandstone is used for building. The scheme is not severe or stately classicism, but more romantic and informal with delicate balconies and verandas. The houses have curved bay fronts. **Calverley Crescent** behind is more severe with a thin iron colonnade.

Brighton and Hove

This seaside resort popularised by the Prince Regent from the village of Brighthelmstone gives the lie to the theory that all good classical architecture ceased with the Regency. From Hove to Kemp Town, some three miles of sea-front, stands a magnificent tribute to the period of 1800–50. Much of the layout was erected in the 1820s and '30s but both Adelaide

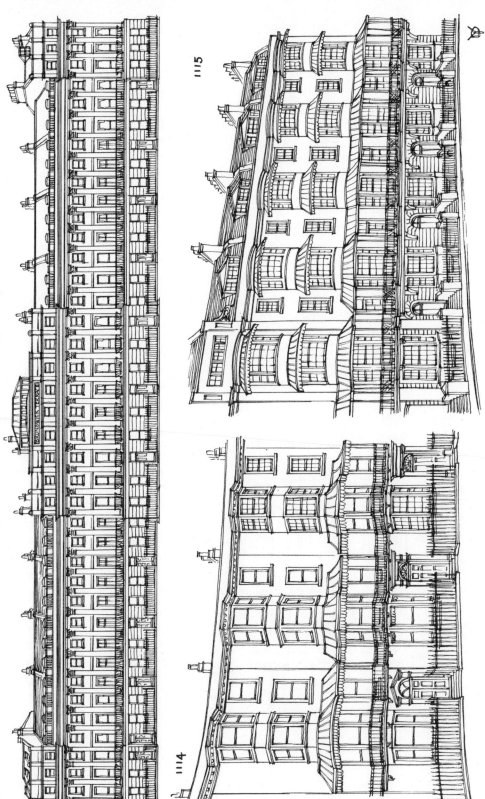

TERRACE ARCHITECTURE IN SEASIDE TOWNS 1810–1850

1113

1115

1114

1113 Brunswick Terrace, Sea Front, Hove, Sussex, 1825. H. Wilds and Charles Busby   1114 Royal Crescent, Sea Front, Brighton, Sussex: white paint and glazed, black brick   1115 Sea Front Terrace, Hastings, Sussex

Crescent at the Hove end and Kemp Town at the opposite extremity of the front were not completed until after 1850. Here is the culmination and extension of Nash's Regent's Park terraces; there is no local feeling present. The work is predominantly in painted stucco as was common in London and Cheltenham.

Two of the prime movers in the Brighton scheme were **Charles Busby** and his partner **Amon Wilds**, and later Wilds's son, **Amon H. Wilds**. Their finest work was the magnificent sea-front enterprise **Brunswick Terrace**, dating from 1825. The tremendous length of this façade is split into two sections at Brunswick Square, also by the same architects. One section of the terrace is shown in Fig. 1113; it has a central feature and end pavilions. The giant Corinthian order is used throughout; the ground floor is rusticated and, above the entablature, is a balustrade and attic storey. **Brunswick Square** is made up from large, stucco-faced houses with curved bay fronts. Ionic and Corinthian orders are used here, spanning the first and second floors. Each house is separate although the square has a unified appearance (1116, 1139). Near by is **Adelaide Crescent** designed by **Decimus Burton**; another fine layout. At the other end of the sea-front, **Kemp Town** was built over a long period from 1800 to 1855. Here again are some magnificent terraces and squares reminiscent of Nash's schemes. Particularly noteworthy is **Lewes Crescent**, 1828–30, by **H. E. Kendall**, also **Sussex Square, Arundel Terrace** and **Clarendon Terrace** (1112). There are many other attractive, well-designed houses and terraces on this front and behind it towards the town. Some of the more interesting include **Regency Square, Bedford Square, Marine Square** and **Portland Place. The Royal Crescent** should be especially praised; its simple, black-brick facing, with white painted woodwork and canopied iron balconies and railings, is most pleasing even for so exceptional a resort (1114). Like Cheltenham, Brighton and Hove have numerous examples of beautiful ironwork, wrought and cast, from this whole period. The variety of design is infinite and the majority of the craftsmanship is well appreciated and kept in good condition (1177, 1179).

At **Hastings** and **St Leonards** there was also considerable expansion at this time. **James Burton** and his son **Decimus** designed and built much of the fine architecture there, although far less remains today than at Brighton. Among extant examples is **Pelham Crescent, Hastings**, *c.* 1823; another sea-front terrace with bow windows and canopied iron balconies now, unfortunately, in poor condition.

1116 Brunswick Square, Hove, *c.* 1826. Architects, Wilds and Busby

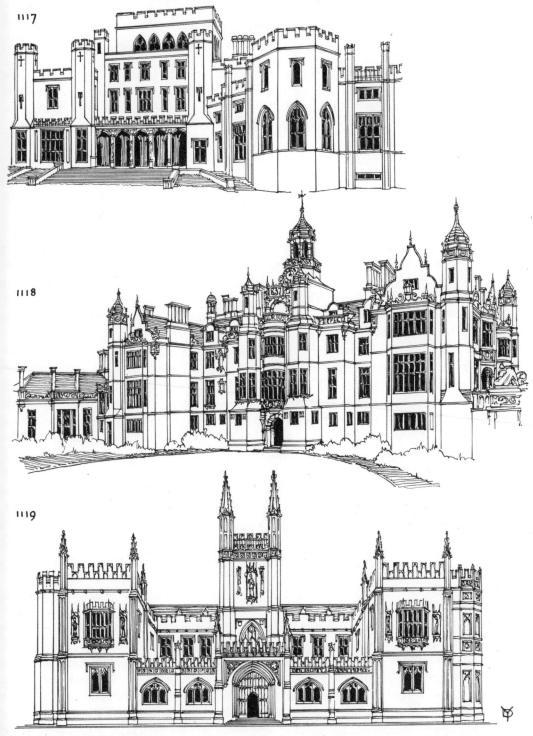

1117 Ashridge Park, Hertfordshire, begun 1806. James Wyatt. Work finished by his nephew, Wyatville 1118 Harlaxton Manor, Lincolnshire, 1831–55. Anthony Salvin 1119 Toddington Manor, Gloucestershire, 1819–40. Lord Sudeley

DOMESTIC BUILDINGS

Large Country Houses

The first half of the nineteenth century was the last phase in the building of genuinely large English country mansions. Great houses were erected after 1850, but never again in quite so untrammelled and large-scale a manner. There was no actual architectural style common to the country houses of this date; it can only be said that a similar approach was made—picturesque and informal approach—to many styles: Greek or Roman classical, Gothic Elizabethan, Jacobean, Indian or Egyptian. Up to 1830 classical, castellated Tudor and Eastern styles predominated; after this, Gothic in its many forms was in more common use Most of the well-known architects of the day built such houses; there are examples by Salvin Barry, Pugin, Wilkins, Wyatt, Blore, Soane and Hardwick.

On the classical pattern there are **Soane's** houses at **Moggerhanger** and **Pitzhange** (1010–11; p. 372). There is also the interesting house at **Ickworth, Suffolk**, built 1796–183 to the design of **Francis Sandys**; on the entrance front is a concave curving, lower store with projecting Ionic portico, while behind is the unusual oval centrepiece in Corinthia manner with a sculptured relief frieze (1013). Before turning to Gothic, **Wyatt** designed **Dodington Park, Gloucestershire**, 1797–1817: a straightforward classical house with enormous Corinthian portico (1012).

In Elizabethan and Gothic are many examples including **P. C. Hardwick's Aldermaston Court, Newbury**, 1848–51, **Pugin's Bilton Grange, Rugby**, 1841–6, and **Wilkins' Tregothnan, Cornwall**, 1816–18. Five houses have been selected here for illustration a being typical of the range of designs of the time. First there is **Wyatt's Ashridge Park** Hertfordshire, begun 1806 (1117; p. 373) and then one of the greatest houses of the nine teenth century, **Harlaxton Manor**, Lincolnshire, 1831–55, by Salvin. **Anthony Salvin** designed many houses on different themes. He was a good architect and understood hi Medieval architecture well. Harlaxton is a magnificent house on Elizabethan pattern. I is a beautiful building, very complex in design and built from a warm stone in authenti sixteenth-century manner; the south-west side is particularly impressive. The house i constructed on Elizabethan E plan and bears considerable resemblance to Burghley. In the centre of the entrance front is an enormous gatehouse with flanking towers and a central semicircular oriel window. Behind this rises a square tower and above it an octagonal cupola The skyline is made lively and interesting by chimney-stacks, turrets, finials and gables in Elizabethan tradition. The decoration also is authentic, with strapwork and heraldic beasts although in general it is restrained. The whole effect is rich and well proportioned (1118 1159, 1166; LIII). The third example is by **Barry, Highclere Castle**, Hampshire, which he remodelled in Elizabethan/Jacobean style in 1842–4. Here is quite a different approach to Elizabethan architecture from that of Harlaxton. The work is less picturesque and more austerely symmetrical. The four-sided house is built round a court with corner towers and one larger tower placed centrally behind one of the sides. The whole effect is of dignity graciousness and wealth (1062, 1065, 1088, 1156). **Pugin's** principal contribution was **Scarisbrick Hall**, Lancashire, begun 1837 and finished after his death. Pugin remodelled and enlarged the half-timber Tudor house there and retained parts of the original work The tower was completed by his son, E. W. Pugin, after Pugin's death. The house and some

1120 Apsley House, Hyde Park Corner, London, 1828. Benjamin Wyatt 1121 Charles Russell House, 23 Park Lane, London, 1846–8. W. B. Moffatt 1122 The Soane Museum, Lincoln's Inn Fields, London (originally designed as his own town house by Sir John Soane), 1812–14 1123 Crown House, 57 Marina, St. Leonards-on-Sea, Sussex. Probably by Decimus Burton

1120

1121

1122

1123

of the finely executed details are illustrated in Figs. 1078, 1127, 1160, 1161, and 1172. The last example, **Toddington Manor**, Gloucestershire, was designed for himself by **Lord Sudeley**, 1819–40 (although sometimes attributed to Barry). It is built in Perpendicular Gothic in yellowish stone and in collegiate manner. The house is constructed in three quad rangles connected together on a diagonal axis. There is a central tower which shows well in silhouette from a general view. Two aspects of the building are symmetrical; the remainder is somewhat haphazard in placing. Like the Palace of Westminster, it has an all-over pattern of panelled stone tracery with decoration in the form of castellations, sculpture and heraldic animals and motifs. The detail is authentic; the work illustrates a serious attempt to present the popular Gothic style in the form of a large country house. It is reasonably successful in this although aesthetically it is less pleasing than Harlaxton or Highclere (1119, 1129, 1150).

Town Houses

Town houses, as distinct from those built as part of a terrace or general scheme for layout in squares, were almost entirely built in classical idiom. Gothic and picturesque, informal silhouettes may lend themselves to country-house design where adequate building land is available, but are markedly less suited to limited town sites. Apart from **Barry's house** (p. 400), two other houses of note in London were designed by **Benjamin Wyatt**, 1775–1850, son of James Wyatt: Apsley House and York House. **Apsley House, Hyde Park Corner, Piccadilly** was enlarged and remodelled by Wyatt for the Duke of Wellington in 1828. He cased the house in Bath stone and added a central, Corinthian portico over a rusticated lower storey. **York House, St James's** (now Lancaster House) was built for the Duke

1124 White marble chimney-piece with carved decoration; fire opening black with gilt ornament, steel grate, 1811–25

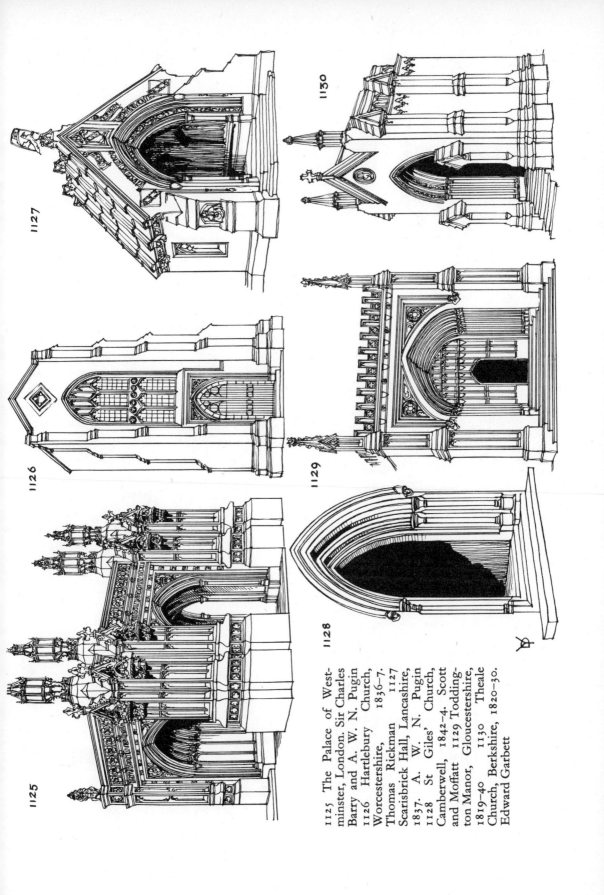

1125 The Palace of West-
minster, London. Sir Charles
Barry and A. W. N. Pugin
1126 Hartlebury Church,
Worcestershire, 1836–7.
Thomas Rickman 1127
Scarisbrick Hall, Lancashire,
1837. A. W. N. Pugin
1128 St Giles' Church,
Camberwell, 1842–4. Scott
and Moffatt 1129 Todding-
ton Manor, Gloucestershire,
1819–40 1130 Theale
Church, Berkshire, 1820–30.
Edward Garbett

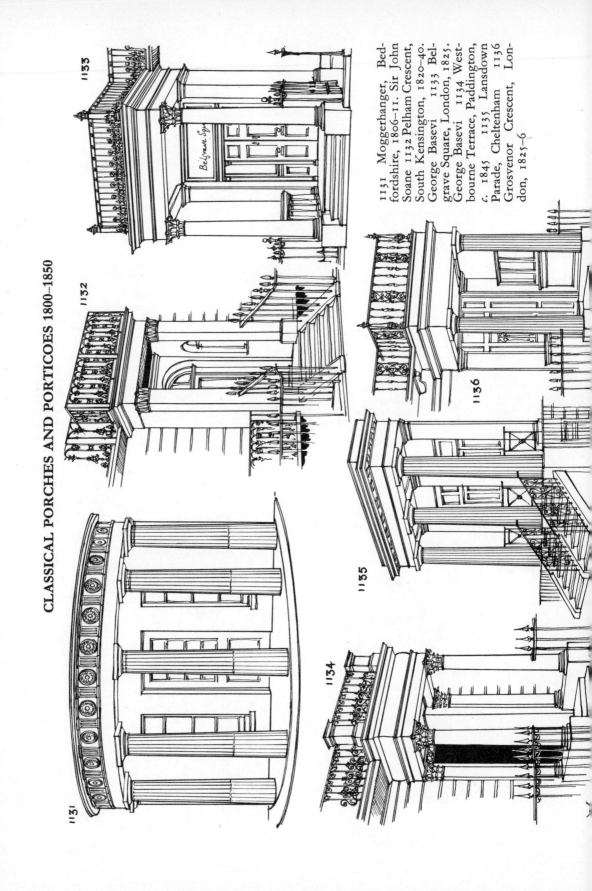

CLASSICAL PORCHES AND PORTICOES 1800–1850

1131 Moggerhanger, Bedfordshire, 1806–11. Sir John Soane 1132 Pelham Crescent, South Kensington, 1820–40. George Basevi 1133 Belgrave Square, London, 1825. George Basevi 1134 Westbourne Terrace, Paddington, c. 1845. 1135 Lansdown Parade, Cheltenham 1136 Grosvenor Crescent, London, 1825–6

Belgrave Sqr

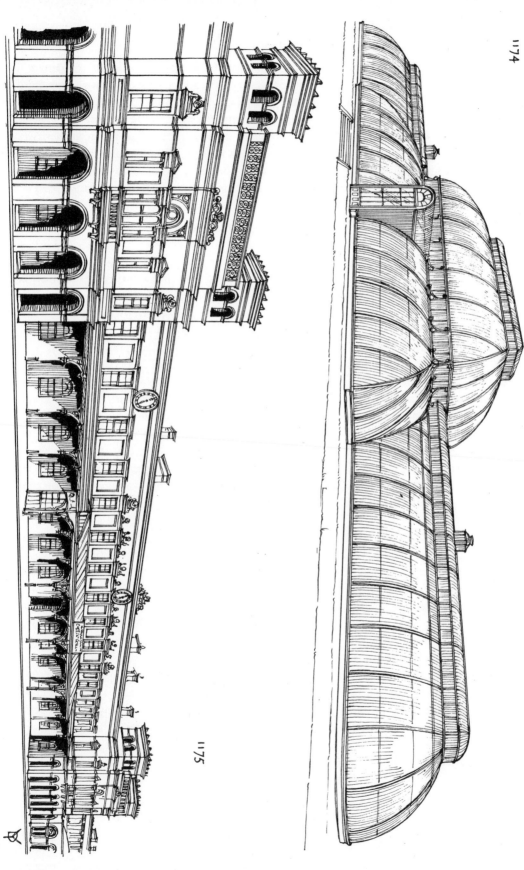

1174

1175

1174 Palm Stove, Royal Botanic Gardens, Kew, 1844-7. Cast iron and glass units, 362 ft total length, Decimus Burton, 1175 Chester

DOORS AND DOORWAYS 1820-1850

1144 Lonsdale Square, Islington, London, 1838. R. C. Carpenter
1145 St Giles' Church, Cheadle, Staffordshire, 1841–6. A. W. N.
Pugin 1146 King's College, Cambridge: screen gateway, 1822–
1824. William Wilkins 1147 Victoria Tower entrance, Palace of
Westminster. Sir Charles Barry and A. W. N. Pugin 1148
Christ Church, Cheltenham, 1837–40. The Jearrads 1149 Church
of St Mary and St Nicholas, 1840–6. Wyatt and Brandon

1154

1151

1155

1152

1156

1150 Toddington Manor, Gloucester-
shire, 1819–40   1151 Moggerhanger,
Bedfordshire, 1806–11. Sir John Soane
1152 The Ashmolean, Oxford, 1840–5.
C. R. Cockerell   1153 The British
Museum, London, 1827–45. Sir Robert
Smirke   1154 The Palace of West-
minster, London. Sir Charles Barry and
A. W. N. Pugin   1155 Regency bow
window, Brighton   1156 Highclere
Castle, Hampshire, 1842–4. Sir Charles
Barry   1157 Hartlebury Church, Wor-
cestershire, 1836–7. Thomas Rickman

1157

of York in 1825, Wyatt continuing Smirke's work there. It is similar to Apsley House and both are conventional, well-built but rather dull town houses (1120). A more original and interesting example is **Soane's** own house in **Lincoln's Inn Fields** (1122; p. 372).

In the Gothic vein is (or was, for it is now demolished) **No. 23 Park Lane, Charles Russell House**, built in 1846–8 by **W. B. Moffatt** (partner in his early days to G. G. Scott). This was a medium-sized terrace house, rather tall and narrow in Perpendicular or Tudor Gothic. Much of the façade was covered by a large, rectangular, oriel window which was almost the width of the house and compassed the first and second storeys. Below this was a Tudor doorway on one side and a window on the other with a central buttress between. Above, on the third floor, was another window and, higher still, dormer windows behind a carved, pierced parapet. This is an unusual house for this date, but it makes satisfactory and successful use of the style for a town terrace house (1121).

Smaller Houses

The external façades of **Regency** houses were much plainer than in the eighteenth century. Painted, stucco-covered brick with bow or segmental bay windows was most common. The sash windows themselves were curved in section and had rectangular panes, large and small (1155). Some small villas were of plain, almost severe, brick.

Gothic began to have an effect in middle-class housing after **1840**. Coloured brick with Bath stone dressings was employed and the house was much less symmetrical in design than its Regency counterpart. The roofline bristled with gables and chimney-stacks, whereas in the 1820s the roof had generally been hidden by a plain parapet or balustrade. The windows were Gothic, chiefly in lancet form, singly or in groups, with Early English shafts and capitals between. Stained glass began to make its appearance in domestic architecture.

THE UNIVERSITIES

At **Cambridge** four colleges carried out extensive building schemes in the first half of the nineteenth century, and three of these were designed by the same architect, **William Wilkins**.

At **King's College** Wilkins won the competition for the new Gothic work, comprising the entrance screen and gateway and the hall. Both were planned to harmonise with the great Medieval chapel which, after 140 years, they do to a large extent, although Wilkins's screen lacks the essential dignity and fine proportions of the chapel. The work was largely completed in the years 1822–4. In his Gothic hall, Wilkins has set his great oriel window midway down one side of the building instead of at the daïs end, as was traditional. His simple classic bridge over the Cam was built 1819–20 (1092, 1145, 1188; p. 385).

At **Corpus Christi College** Wilkins designed the **New Court** 1823–30 in Perpendicular Gothic style. The whole new, large quadrangle is laid out as one unified scheme which comprises library, hall and chapel. It is here that Wilkins's Gothic can best be judged as he had a free hand in a completely new court. The results are well proportioned and pleasing and the Medieval spirit is not lacking (1038–9, 1171; p. 385).

Still in Gothic vein is **Rickman** and **Hutchinson's New Court** at **St John's College**, built in 1827–31. This also is in Perpendicular design, but is warmer and more romantic than Wilkins's rather classical Perpendicular. There is a screen wall with central gateway and

1159

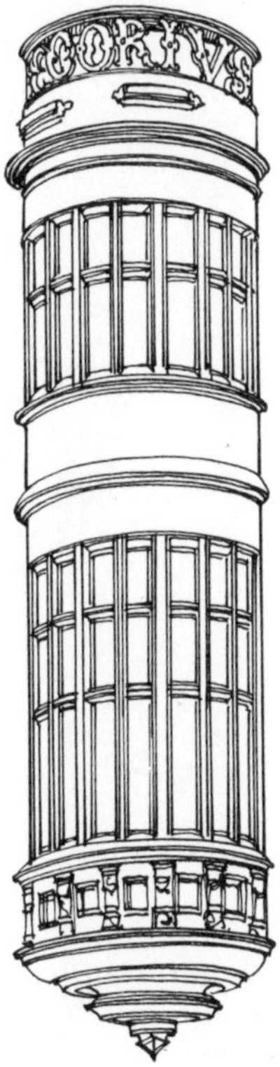

1160

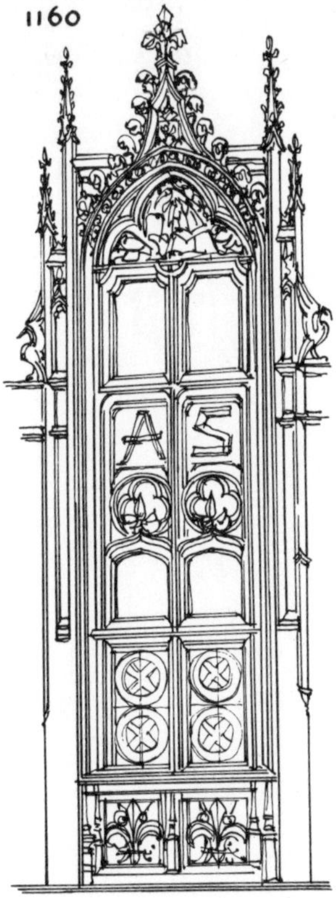

1161

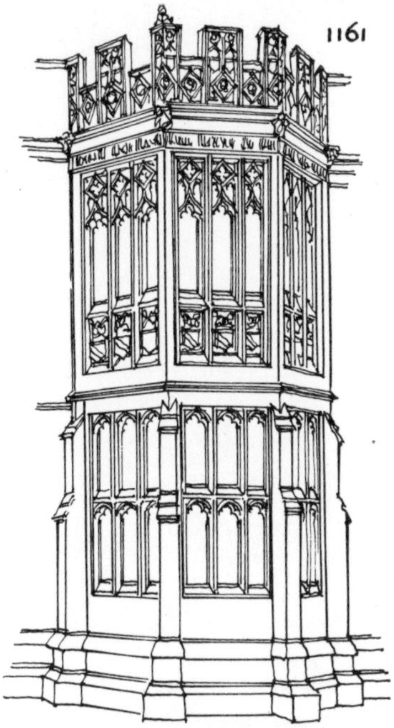

1165

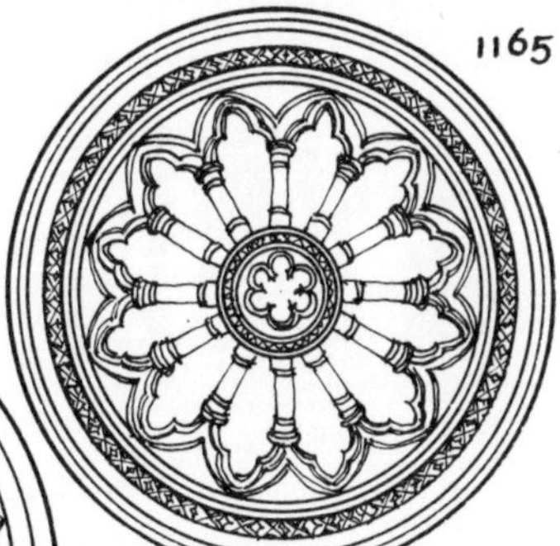

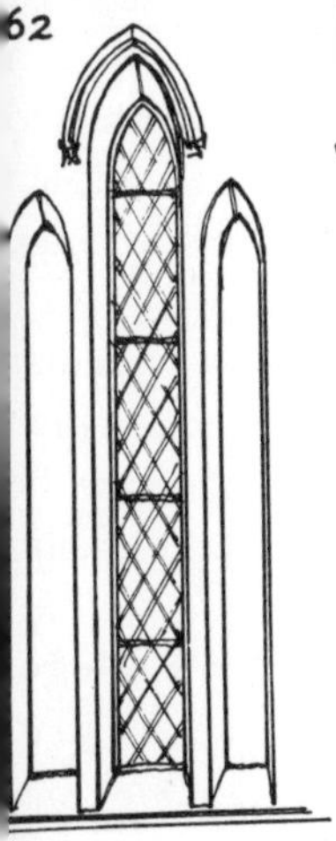

1163

1164

1162

1158 Palace of West-
minster, London: oriel. Sir
Charles Barry and A. W. N.
Pugin 1159 Harlaxton
Manor, Lincolnshire, 1831–
55: oriel. Anthony Salvin
1160 and 1161 Scarisbrick
Hall, Lancashire, 1837:
bay. A. W. N. Pugin
1162 St Michael's Church,
Stockwell, London. W.
Rogers 1163 Richmond
College, 1841–3. A. Trimen
1164 St Peter's Church,
Cheltenham, 1847–9. S. W.
Dawkes 1165 Theale
Church, Berkshire, 1820–
1830. Edward Garbett

ARCHITECTURAL DETAILS 1800–1850

1166

1167

1168

1169

1170

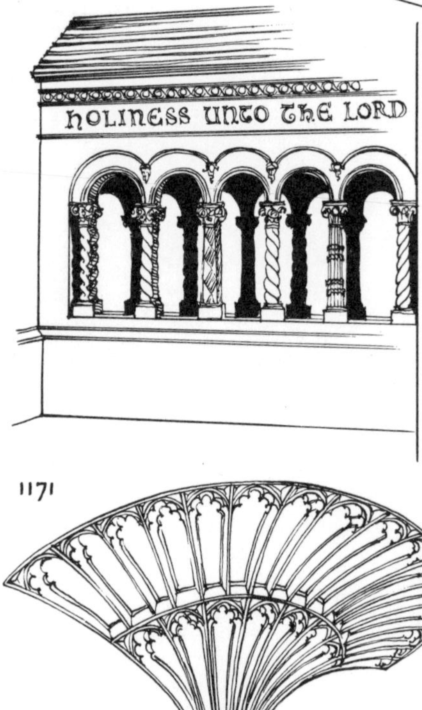

HOLINESS UNTO THE LORD

1172

1171

1173

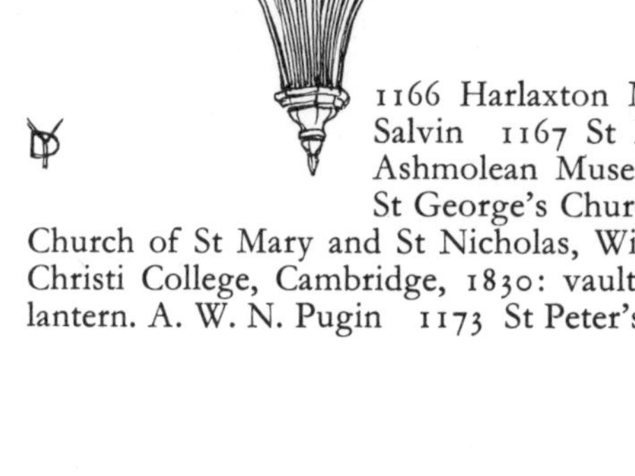

1166 Harlaxton Manor, Lincolnshire, 1831–55: chimney-stack. Anthony Salvin 1167 St Mark's Church, Kennington. A. B. Clayton 1168 The Ashmolean Museum, Oxford, 1840–5: balustrade. C. R. Cockerell 1169 St George's Church, Brandon Hill, Bristol, 1833. Sir Robert Smirke 1170 Church of St Mary and St Nicholas, Wilton: 1840–6: arcade. Wyatt and Brandon 1171 Corpus Christi College, Cambridge, 1830: vault. W. Wilkins. 1172 Scarisbrick Hall, Lancashire, 1837: lantern. A. W. N. Pugin 1173 St Peter's Church, Cheltenham, 1847–9: arcade. S. W. Dawkes

erminal features with centrally placed Perpendicular oriel windows. Behind is a square block
vith surmounting cupola. The Perpendicular Gothic bridge, 'the Bridge of Sighs', so called,
fter its Venetian prototype, is by the same architects. It is a single-arched bridge and has a
imilar quality to the court. This scheme is undoubtedly Rickman's most successful Gothic
chievement (1091, 1189).

Classical architecture is represented at Cambridge by Downing College, also by Wilkins
nd Basevi's Fitzwilliam Museum. At **Downing**, where **Wilkins** won the competition to
lesign buildings for a new college, a large site was provided and work started in 1807. He
mployed the Greek classical style with the Ionic order and had built the hall block by 1821.
Downing is a spacious college and its buildings are now very extensive as work, in similar
vein to Wilkins's original design, has gone on intermittently until the present day, adding
nd enlarging the buildings (1037; p. 385).

George Basevi won the competition for the **Fitzwilliam Museum** and the work was
carried out between 1837 and 1848; it was completed by Cockerell after the death of Basevi.
t is a monumental classical building with a fine large portico in the Corinthian order. Inside
s an impressive entrance hall decorated by Cockerell (although the staircase is Victorian).
The whole building is in Roman classical style with good quality, though over-heavy, decora-
ion (1048, XLIX; p. 388).

At **Oxford** the outstanding building in this part of the nineteenth century is the **Ashmolean Museum** designed 1840–5 by **C. R. Cockerell**. This is one of the finest designs of
he Greek revival period in England. It was built as the Taylor and Randolph Museum, but
s generally called the Ashmolean after its principal collection. It stands on a corner site and
ts main façade (Beaumont Street) has two projecting end wings and a central portico, also
set forward. The rest of the elevation is in low relief but the wings and the portico are bolder;
he contrast is interesting and original in treatment. The St Giles Street front has typical
Cockerell free-standing columns supporting their individual entablatures and sculptured
figures above. The Greek Ionic order is used, taken from Cockerell's own drawings from
Greece. The detail is finely executed and beautifully placed. The building comprises a library,
art gallery and lecture rooms (1050, 1053, 1152, 1168; p. 393).

Other work at Oxford in this period includes the **University Press** in Corinthian classical
design by **Blore** and **Robertson**, and **Scott's** Medieval style **Martyrs' Memorial**, 1841 (1093).

The **London University** building (now University College) by **Wilkins** has already been
described (1036; p. 385).

RAILWAY ARCHITECTURE

The nineteenth century was the age of the great engineers, the railways and of **cast iron and
glass**. These factors are inextricably linked together. Early railway stations were unpretentious, often just open sheds. Soon, however, especially at great termini, the railways required
buildings which in turn involved them in architecture and the battle of the styles. Much of
the construction of this architecture was in cast iron: railings, footbridges, brackets, trusses
and cantilevers. Classical units such as entablatures, columns, capitals, etc. were simply transferred to the new medium, only with somewhat attenuated columns. Most railway stations
were built under the direction of a principal architect and a principal engineer. The architect
simply wanted to transpose his classical, and later Gothic architecture, into iron. It was the

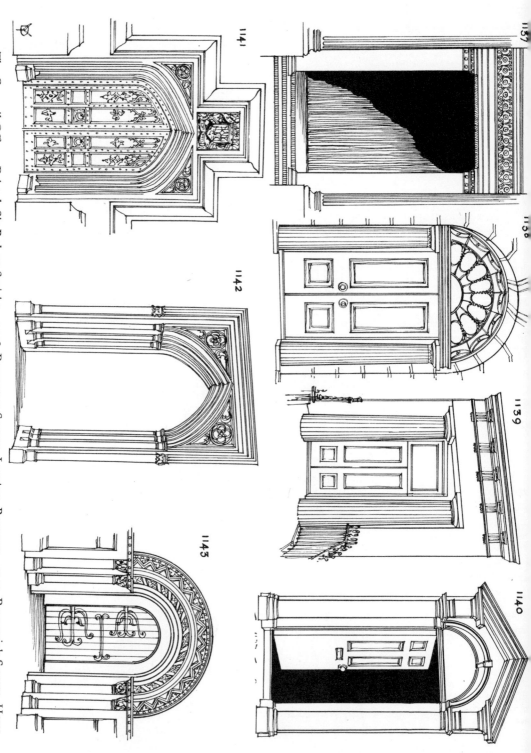

1137 The Council Offices, Bristol. Sir Robert Smirke 1138 Bryanston Square, London, Regency 1139 Brunswick Square, Hove, 1826. Wilds and Busby 1140 Royal Crescent, Brighton 1141 Palace of Westminster, London. Sir Charles Barry and A. W. N. Pugin 1142 St Peter's Church, Brighton, 1823–8. Sir Charles Barry 1143 St Peter's Church, Cheltenham, 1847–9. S. W. Dawkes

engineer—men such as George and Robert Stephenson and I. K. Brunel—who opposed this. They evolved a new design based on the practical needs of the task in hand and the qualities of the new material. They led the way in the exploitation of this material as applied to architecture, but did not do this consciously, only as needs dictated. The opposing views of engineer and architect, then often violently in conflict, still exist at the present day, though in a quieter key.

Many great railway stations were built between 1800 and 1850. Most of them remain, but the majority have received one or more new façades and exterior buildings, generally in the later nineteenth century, and we can only rely on drawings in order to see the stations as they were constructed.

One of the most famous of these 'cathedrals of the nineteenth century', as they are some-times called* is **Euston Station, London**. This monumental station was designed largely by the **Hardwicks**, father and son, but all that until recently remained of their work now was the vast imposing Doric arch outside the station, built 1838 (1024).† The whole façade was equally impressive and the great hall, built in 1849, was 60 feet in width and had a coffered ceiling.

Among other stations now altered beyond recognition or totally demolished are **Brighton**, designed 1841 by **David Mocatta**, a pupil of Soane; **Dover**, built 1843-4 by **Lewis Cubitt**; **London Bridge**, 1844 by **Henry Roberts** and **George Smith; Carlisle**, designed in 1848 by **Sir William Tite**, the well-known railway architect and one of the finest examples ever built, and **Lime Street, Liverpool**, 1839 by **John Franklin**, built to harmonise with St George's Hall. The **Nine Elms Station** at **Vauxhall, London**, also built by **Sir William Tite**, in 1838-40, has been retained as the Transport Museum for British Railways, but suffered badly from damage in World War II. One station which remains comparatively un-altered is the enormous 1000-feet façade at **Chester**. This design by **Francis Thompson** and **Robert Stephenson**, 1847-8 is built in Italian manner and, despite the grime, is still most interesting and impressive (1175).

IRON AND GLASS

Ironwork, generally wrought iron, had been used as a building material for a long time, but it was only in the late eighteenth and early nineteenth century that architects began to find use for it on a large scale. The Regency style of terrace house with its canopied balconies and railings provided infinite scope for ironwork and cast iron was manufactured in mass-produc-tion patterns. These generally originated at the foundry (apart from individual cases where architects designed their own). Particularly fine ironwork was incorporated in buildings by Smirke, Nash and the Cheltenham and Brighton architects. Designs up to 1825 were delicate, original and beautifully made. After this ironwork was heavier and, in larger buildings, more ornate; although, in less costly schemes, plain verticals and lattice railing was employed. By 1830 iron was being used constructively as well as decoratively and had been accepted as

---

* *Early Victorian Architecture in Britain* by Henry-Russell Hitchcock (The Architectural Press).

† In spite of protests and advice against its destruction by the Royal Fine Arts Commission, the Historic Buildings Advisory Committee, the London County Council Planning Committee and leading architects, art historians and engineers, the arch was demolished on 6th November 1961 by Government edict, to make way for 'improvements'.

IRON GATES, BALCONIES AND RAILINGS 1800–1850

1176

1177

1178

1179

1180

1181

1176 The Promenade, Cheltenham 1177 New Steyne, Brighton, Sussex 1178 Gates to Hyde Park at Marble Arch, London, 1841 1179 New Steyne, Brighton 1180 Gates to St George's Church, Ramsgate, Kent. H. E. Kendal 1181 Wolseley Terrace, Cheltenham

a building material; it was employed for columns, brackets and roof construction. It was, however, the engineers who used the material most widely in their bridges, railways and general industrial development. Towards 1850 the growing Gothic revival lent itself to increased use of iron as a structural medium in public buildings and particularly churches. It was used for tie beams, principals, columns and arches (1176–81).

The combination of **iron and glass** was only in its infancy before 1850; it was the Crystal Palace which provided the great inspiration to this type of construction. However, glass and cast iron was used a great deal for glasshouse construction. **Nash** designed the conservatory at the **Royal Lodge, Windsor** in 1814 and **Paxton** his great **Conservatory** at **Chatsworth** in 1837; this latter example was nearly 300 feet long. **Decimus Burton** became interested in the possibilities of the medium. He designed the **Winter Gardens** in **Regent's Park** (since demolished) with the engineer **Richard Turner** and, a more famous example, the **Palm Stove** in **Kew Gardens** in 1844. This, for the period, remarkable construction is 362 feet long and 62 feet high in the centre. Inside is a gallery reached by an iron spiral staircase. The glasshouse contains 45,000 square feet of glass, slightly tinged with green, and was the largest edifice of this type to date (1174).

THE GREAT ENGINEERS

From the early nineteenth century onwards the role of the **engineers** in architecture has increased, until in the post-war period there is only a small percentage of architecture which is not almost entirely a concept of engineering. This revolution was brought about from 1770 onwards, by the development and expansion in the coal and iron industries; a field in which Britain led the world for over a century.

The academic, scholarly approach of the great eighteenth-century architects gradually disappeared as the nineteenth century advanced; here the products of the industrial revolution—coal, iron and cheap labour—provided a new means for building and construction. With the dissolution of the age of great architecture came the new, and in its way, equally great age of the engineer. Prodigious feats of construction were evolved and mastered; and, strangely, some of the finest aesthetic designs of the age were produced by these men whose chief aim was to create a practical construction. The attraction, grandeur, and even beauty of the finished work was the product of the understanding that these men possessed of their materials; of their needs, limitations and possibilities. The architects were many years in gaining this experience and continued to use the materials unwisely and unattractively.

Several fundamental discoveries were made in this period which were instrumental in making the use of **cast iron** desirable, cheap and widespread. Among these were, in 1784, the new process for producing wrought iron—whose tensile strength is greater than that of cast iron—from pig iron by means of a vibrating puddling furnace; in 1856 Henry Bessemer's process to produce cheaper mild steel in quantity and the Open Hearth invention by Siemens and Martin in 1865. These innovations made the use of iron in bridge building, in particular, much more widespread. Spans could be wider; bridges were cheaper and quicker to build; piers were safer and the suspension bridge was developed. Among the greatest of the engineers who built our bridges, railways and canals in Britain at this time were **Rennie, Telford, Brunel** and **Stephenson**.

BRIDGES 1800-1850

1182

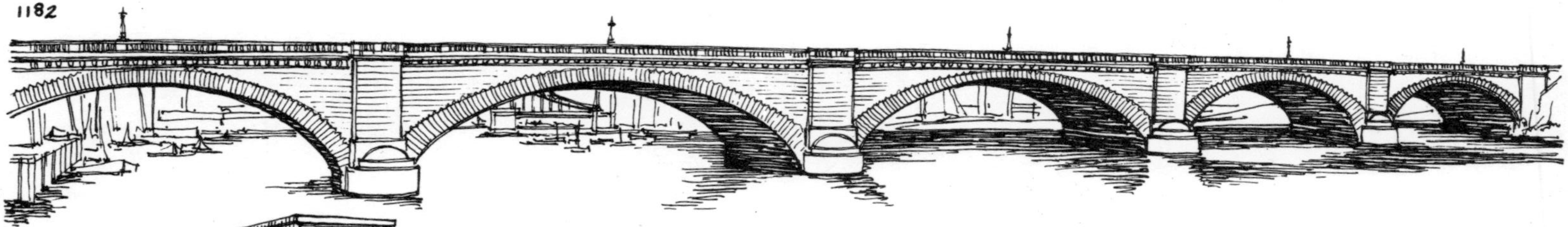

1183

1184

1182 London Bridge, 1831. John Rennie 1183 Clifton Suspension Bridge, Bristol, over the Avon Gorge, 702 ft span, 1836–64. I. K. Brunel 1184 Conway Road Suspension Bridge, North Wales, 1826. Thomas Telford

John Rennie 1761–1821

John Rennie, like so many of the engineers, was a Scot and studied at Edinburgh University. He built his first bridge at Leith and later, a more important example, at Kelso. He is best known for his great bridges over the Thames in London of which, unfortunately, only one remains. The greatest of these was **Waterloo Bridge**, opened in 1817 and freed from toll in 1878, but regretfully demolished to make way for the present concrete structure. Rennie's bridge was a magnificent design on the grand scale. It consisted of nine semi-elliptical arches, each with a 120-foot span, and on each pier was set a pair of Doric columns supporting a continuous entablature. It had radiating granite voussoirs and a granite balustrade. The bridge was well constructed, but even this workmanship could not for ever stand up to the scour of the Thames. In 1923 one of the piers settled badly and in face of an acrimonious battle for repair and retention by both the public and Parliament the London County Council demolished and replaced it. The bridge was named the Waterloo Bridge after the then recent battle and was opened by the Prince Regent in 1817. The Italian sculptor Canova described it as 'the noblest in the world'. Rennie designed three other London bridges over the Thames: Vauxhall, Southwark and London. **Vauxhall** was considered too expensive and a cheaper one by James Walker was built. **Southwark**, 1811, was constructed with an enormous central arch of 240-feet span and 42 feet above the high water level in order to accommodate the river traffic. To make this possible the arches were very flat and the voussoirs made of bolted, cast iron. The piers were of stone and the roadway was constructed of iron plates like the Ironbridge at Coalbrookdale. The bridge was an engineering feat for the time but was aesthetically less satisfactory than Waterloo. It was opened in 1819 and replaced a century later.

    London Bridge, the only one of Rennie's bridges in London to survive, was designed in 1831. It has been widened but otherwise is much as Rennie conceived it. He did not live to see the bridge built; this was carried out by his son, while Smirke was responsible for the façade. The bridge, which is of stone, has a centre arch span of 150 feet; the adjacent arches are 140 feet in span and the end ones 130 feet. In design it is simple and well proportioned but lacks the magnificence that Waterloo had, and was less of an engineering feat than Southwark. Eric de Maré* tells us that the bridge cost £2 million and 40 lives (1182).

1185 Section of the Pont-Cysylltau Aqueduct, Vale of Llangollen, Wales. Carries Shropshire Union Canal over the Dee. Stone piers, iron superstructure. Completed 1805, 127 ft high, with 18 piers and approx. 1,000 ft in length. Thomas Telford

* *The Bridges of Britain* (B. T. Batsford, Ltd, 1954).

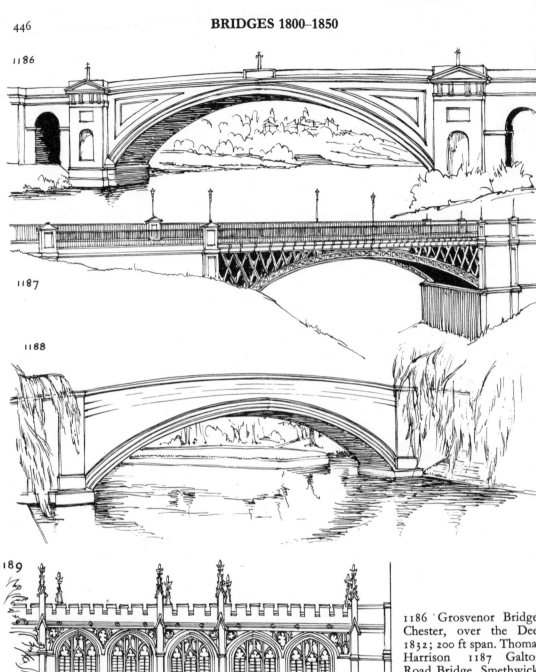

1186 Grosvenor Bridge, Chester, over the Dee, 1832; 200 ft span. Thomas Harrison 1187 Galton Road Bridge, Smethwick, Birmingham, 1829; cast iron. Thomas Telford 1188 King's College Cambridge: stone bridge over the Cam, 1818–20. William Wilkins 1189 St John's College, Cambridge: stone bridge over the Cam, 1826. Rickman and Hutchinson

Thomas Telford 1757–1834

Thomas Telford, also a Scotsman, was apprenticed to a mason and worked on Somerset House in that capacity. Later he became the County Surveyor for Shropshire. He is especially known for his roadway and waterway construction and also for building docks, harbours and bridges. His output of work was prodigious, his technical standards high and he became the world's leading engineer in his day. He carried out extensive work on **roads** in **Wales** and **Scotland**, on the **Caledonian Canal**, on the **harbour** at **Aberdeen**, and at **St Katharine's Dock, London**. He was the first president of the Institution of Civil Engineers.

His cast-iron bridges are his most famous and his best designs. His **masonry bridges**, of which there are a considerable number, are inclined to heaviness of design and unfortunate proportion. Among them are the **Tongueland Bridge** over the Dee in **Scotland**, 1805, the **Dean Bridge** in **Edinburgh** and the **Over Bridge** near **Gloucester** over the Severn.

In **cast iron** Telford surpassed all other designers at the time. He built a great number of bridges in this medium and exploited it to the full. His designs are courageous and inspiring. His first iron bridge, one of the very early examples in Britain, was at **Buildwas** over the Severn. This was a tremendous advance over the eighteenth-century Ironbridge, as Telford exploited the assets of the medium and produced a bridge of great strength for a much smaller weight of iron.

In 1805 he built the colossal **aqueduct** at **Pont-Cysylltau** which carries the Shropshire Union Canal over the River Dee in the vale of **Llangollen.** The aqueduct of 18 masonry piers is 127 feet high and over 1,000 feet long. It has cast-iron segmented arches and railing parapet (1185).

His **Waterloo Bridge** over the Conway at **Bettws-y-Coed**, Caernarvonshire, was built in 1815. It has a 105-foot span and is made of cast iron based on masonry abutments. He constructed the **Galton Bridge** over the **Birmingham Canal** in 1829; a cast-iron bridge capable of bearing great loads (1187). A more beautiful example is his cast-iron bridge at **Craigellachie** over the river Spey, with trussed arch and ribs.

Telford's two great enterprises were the **road bridges** over the Menai Straits and the Conway, both in **North Wales.** The **Menai Bridge** carries the A5 London to Holyhead road and was built when the road was continued on to Anglesey. This was a tremendous project for its day, both for the distance to span and the navigation of the Straits. Telford was asked to submit a design in 1801. He provided two, but the project was left in abeyance. In 1815 the matter was raised again and Telford designed a third bridge, a design which was adopted. It was a suspension bridge, not then an original idea, but the largest project of its type undertaken to date, and although some reconstruction has been carried out in order to increase the load-bearing capacity for present-day traffic, the bridge remains today one of Britain's prime structural achievements. Work was begun in 1820. By 1825 the two 153-foot pylons had been built and the 15 chains fixed. The bridge was opened to traffic in 1826 and freed from toll in 1940. It is nearly half a mile in length and has a central span of 579 feet. Its cost was £120,000 (1190).

The **Conway road suspension bridge** is almost equally famous. This is built over the estuary of the river Conway in the town of the same name. It is also a suspension bridge with iron chains, but Telford here designed the towers in castellated form to harmonise with the Medieval Conway Castle which provides the background to the bridge. It is a smaller example

1190 The Menai Straits (road) Bridge, North Wales, 1820–6. Designed by Thomas Telford

than the Menai one but attractive, although now it is not only compassed by Stephenson's adjacent railway bridge but also by a modern road bridge (1184).

Isambard Kingdom Brunel 1806–1859

I. K. Brunel was also responsible for the building of many bridges and docks; he was one of the most famous of all the railway engineers and this despite a comparatively short life

1191 The Britannia (rail) Tubular Bridge over the Menai Straits, completed 1850. Robert Stephenson

and far less robust health than Telford. He was the son of the engineer Sir Mark Brunel.

Among his bridges are the **railway bridges** over the Thames at **Basildon** and at **Maidenhead**, and the beautiful iron bridge over the river Wye at **Chepstow**. His two great feats of engineering were the **Royal Albert Bridge** over the Tamar in **Cornwall**, completed 1859, and his **Clifton Bridge** over the Avon Gorge at **Bristol**. Several engineers, including Telford, submitted designs for the Clifton Bridge, but the young Brunel's was accepted. The project, however, was dogged by ill-luck and delays. The foundation-stone was laid in 1836,

then the plans were shelved for lack of money. Eventually the bridge was completed to Brunel's design, but after his death, in 1864. The bridge is set in a glorious background 245 feet above the River Avon, with the rocky gorge descending precipitously on both sides. The approach is at Clifton over a 702-foot span suspension design. It possesses similarities in construction to the Menai Straits road bridge with its Egyptian-style pylons and great suspension chains (1183, 1192).

Robert Stephenson 1803–1859

Like his father **George Stephenson**, Robert was a great railway engineer and, like Brunel, built many railway bridges. He was responsible for the construction of the tremendous **Tweed Valley Viaduct** at **Berwick** which is 126 feet above the river and extends by means of 28 60-foot span arches over a length of 2,160 feet. The construction is of stone and brick and was opened in 1850. Stephenson designed the **High Level Railway Bridge** at **Newcastle** which spans the river Tyne 130 feet above the water. The bridge is built in two levels, a railway above a road. It has little aesthetic merit, but is functional and imposing.

1192 Clifton Suspension Bridge over the Avon Gorge, Bristol, 1836–64; 702 ft span. Isambard Kingdom Brunel

Stephenson's most famous work, as with Telford, is his bridge over the **Menai Straits**, but in this case to carry the railway not the road traffic. His **Britannia Bridge**, some distance up the Straits from Telford's, was also of iron, but in tubular form to withstand the weight and vibration of the trains. Stephenson's problems here were the same as Telford's: the great distance to span and the difficulty of keeping navigation open during construction. Work began in 1846 and the red sandstone piers were built. The two great iron rectangular

1193 Cressbrook Mill, Monsal Dale, Derbyshire, 1815: cotton mill

1194 Former silk mill, Macclesfield (now a card factory). Henry and Leigh Slater

tubes (or beams) to take the trains, each 1,511 feet long, were supported in five places: at each end on the banks, and with three piers in the Straits. The central one, the Great Britannia Tower, was built on rock in the centre of the Straits and is 230 feet high. This was the first example of the use of such beams in modern bridge building. The bridge was completed in 1850 (1192).

At **Conway**, Stephenson also built his **railway bridge** parallel to Telford's road bridge, but this time very close alongside. This was another tubular construction in a single span; each of the two tubes is 412 feet long.

There are a number of well-designed bridges extant built by architects and other engineers. At **Cambridge** is **Wilkins's** stone single-arched bridge at **King's College** (1188; p. 436) and **Rickman's 'Bridge of Sighs'** at **St John's College** (1189; p. 439). There is also **Thomas Harrison's** ambitious stone construction at **Chester** over the river Dee (1186; p. 405). Among the iron bridges of the time is the Gothic style **iron bridge** at **Cambridge** over the Cam, built 1823, and **William Tierney Clark's** two Thames **suspension bridges**. One of these was at **Hammersmith** (now replaced) and was built in 1824–7. The other example, which still exists, is at **Marlow** and was completed in 1832. In **Hyde Park** in London is **George Rennie's** bridge over the **Serpentine**. This is a masonry construction and has five segmental arches.

CHAPTER XI

Victorian 1850 - 1900

The history of architecture in the Victorian England of the second half of the nineteenth century is largely that of the Gothic Revival. This is not to say that buildings were never, at this date, erected in any other pattern, but the great mass of building—and, indeed, the quantity was prodigious—was on Gothic lines. It was generally accepted that public building, particularly in towns, was more suited to the classical form, as also was terrace house construction, but in the ecclesiastical field Gothic was supreme and its influence extended to schools, colleges, town halls, industrial fabrics, hospitals and numerous other classes of work.

Earlier in the century, the revival had been confined largely to English Medieval architecture, particularly, under the jurisdiction of the Ecclesiologists, of 'Middle Pointed' Gothic. After 1850, a greater number of architects travelled abroad more widely and an increasing number of buildings at home were based upon Italian, Venetian, French or German Medieval designs. Materials also invaded England from the Continent. The extending railway systems facilitated the transport of Italian marbles and French and Belgian stones, granites and marbles to this country. Polychrome architecture, so much admired by our architects in the Italian sunlight at Siena and Pisa, came to Manchester and London to receive its deposit of grime from the coal-burning hearths and factories of industrial England.

The fundamental spirit of the Gothic Revival was a religious one, and it was in ecclesiastical building that the revivalists were most at home. Building was still largely in private hands and the well-to-do, middle-class Victorian builders and speculators were strongly influenced by the religious fervour of the day. The success of the movement was largely due to its religious and moral tenets, which found sympathy with the whole population and made the architectural style one acceptable to the nation, not only for its churches but for nearly all its architecture.

The question is often asked: 'What is the difference between architecture of the Gothic Revival period and that of the Medieval Gothic?' It is obvious that there are differences: these are clearly visible to the eye, but less simple to define. One of the primary differences is that of craftsmanship. In the Middle Ages the style evolved slowly over several hundred years, during which time a large body of craftsmen was trained and their skills and knowledge were handed on and developed, as did the architectural styles. In the early nineteenth century, when the Gothic Revival began, there were no such Gothic craftsmen. For several hundred years masons, carvers, carpenters, etc., had been working in the classic medium and, often, with different materials. It was for this reason that Barry and Pugin had to gather and train a new school of craftsmen in order to build the Palace of Westminster. As the movement grew and as, after 1850, the pace of building increased so phenomenally, the numbers of craftsmen were not available and detail was mass-produced. It is this manufactured appearance of capitals, ornament, and detail which gives the hard, repetitious feeling to so many Gothic Revival buildings. After all, in the Middle Ages many buildings were in wood and plaster; those in stone took many years of loving care to build. In the nineteenth century, architects were in charge of large numbers of buildings: Sir George Gilbert Scott, for example, is credited with overseeing more than 700 constructions. Is it surprising that the detail often has a factory-made appearance? Another fundamental difference is that of spirit. In the Middle Ages, the Gothic way of architecture arose from the religion of the period. This was a basic tenet and at the centre of life at the time. In the nineteenth century the religious fervour was strong indeed, but it was not the be-all and end-all of existence. Its place in the life of the people was different; the architecture reflects this. Sir Kenneth Clark* expresses this feeling most vividly: 'Although the saints in a modern Catholic image shop are extremely virtuous, they are obviously the product of an utterly worldly civilisation, whereas the gargoyles of a Medieval cathedral, though monsters of vice, are alive with the spirit of a truly religious age.'

During this half-century, however, other, smaller movements were afoot. A number of public buildings were erected in basically classical style. Even Sir George Gilbert Scott was prevailed upon to build a classical Foreign Office. At the same time, several men were endeavouring to re-establish the art of the genuine craftsman, and the use of genuine, as opposed to the sham, material. William Morris was a prime mover in this idea, as were his friends and associates like Philip Webb. In the 1880s, a number of architects began to create buildings on these lines, of whom Norman Shaw and Nesfield were leaders. Towards the end of the century came men like Ernest George, Sir Guy Dawber, C. F. A. Voysey and the young Giles Gilbert Scott and Edwin Lutyens. The work of these men was, at this time, still somewhat in the revival stage, but it was a revival with a difference and one which brought simplicity where there had been ornateness and crisp, clear lines where there had been confusion.

JOHN RUSKIN 1819–1900

Ruskin was not an architect, but an art critic. His gifts were literary and considerable. He used these to further the cause so dear to his heart—that of the Gothic Revival. Because his prose was magnificent and because his arguments were enthusiastic, though fallacious, and above all, because he was firmly Protestant and not Catholic, his influence over the Gothic Revival and the architecture of his age was widespread and far, far greater that Pugin's had been. Both these men, to a large extent, preached the same things: a hatred of sham, a love of all things Gothic, a disgust of classicism and Renaissance art and architecture, and the theory that goodness of spirit and greatness of architecture must go hand in hand. Ruskin, as a good Protestant, did not, indeed could not, bring himself to acknowledge his debt to, and agreement with Pugin—a Catholic, and so beyond the pale. However, because he was a Protestant, Ruskin was *au fait* with the British public and they devoured his writings whole and uncritically.

Born of well-to-do, middle-class parents, who regarded him as a literary genius, Ruskin lived over 50 years with them in a protected, rather isolated atmosphere with all facilities

* *The Gothic Revival* (John Murray Ltd., 1962).

given to him for work, travel and leisure. The religious atmosphere of the home was strict, with regular times each day for prayer and Bible reading and an extreme Puritan Sunday ritual. Ruskin's conscience was deeply disturbed by the poverty and distress of so many Victorian citizens. An attempt to alleviate this, together with a fervent desire to establish Gothic Revival architecture in England, were the two burning passions of his long life.

Ruskin's two most famous works of artistic and moral criticism were the *Seven Lamps of Architecture* and the *Stones of Venice*. His *Seven Lamps*, those of Sacrifice, Truth, Power, Beauty, Life, Memory and Obedience, was published in 1849 only a few years after Pugin's *True Principles*. Ruskin's was one of the most influential books published on the study of taste and went to many editions. Many years later, however, in the 1880s, Ruskin was disgusted by what he had written in his more youthful enthusiasm. He helped to establish the Gothic Revival; he was one of its most fervent prophets and protagonists. When it came to maturity he was horrified by it. Often he entered with enthusiasm with its architects into the creation of a building. When it was completed, he was bitterly disappointed. The most famous example of this reaction is the University Museum at Oxford on which he advised and took great pains (1224). The result caused him great regret. What he really loved was Medieval Gothic. The Gothic Revival which he extolled so much never satisfied him.

In his *Stones of Venice*, published 1851–3, Ruskin drew attention to the architecture of Venice which for a long period had been largely by-passed by English critics. The work was very popular despite its 450,000 words, especially for the section entitled 'The Nature of Gothic'. It introduced Venetian Gothic architecture to Britain and from this time onwards buildings appeared illustrating details from the Doges Palace or the Ca' d'Oro, and Byzantine work inspired by that on the island of Torcello in the Venetian lagoon. However, in this work, as in his others, Ruskin was both prejudiced and illogical. Classicism, especially Renaissance classicism, was anathema and he denigrated it all as pagan and evil. He regarded as permissible or desirable pure Venetian Gothic, Pisan Romanesque and Italian early Gothic, but thought of classical architecture as 'an architecture invented to make plagiarists of architects'. It does not seem to have occurred to him that there was more than a hint of plagiarism about the Gothic Revival.

In his introduction to the new edition of the *Stones of Venice*,* Ruskin writes off architecture resulting from the Renaissance and quotes, as examples, St Paul's in London, St Peter's in Rome, and in Venice and Vicenza the works of architects such as Palladio and Longhena. All these, according to Ruskin, result from the mighty change in architecture due to the Renaissance, that is, the age of degradation in the art of architecture. The change is symptomised, he says, by a loss of truth and vitality in architecture and then corruption—a state which corresponded to that of religion all over Europe at the time. This change, in Ruskin's view, includes all Perpendicular Gothic in England and he refers to Henry VII's Chapel at Westminster Abbey as one of the 'sundry blunders' throughout the world at this time.

SIR JAMES PENNETHORNE 1801–1871

A majority of the numerous Victorian **architects** may be conveniently discussed in groups, but Sir James Pennethorne, being the principal government architect of the mid-Victorian period, was therefore chiefly concerned with buildings in classical style. He had been a pupil

* Ed. and abs. by J. G. Links (Collins, 1960).

1195 London University Buildings, Burlington Gardens, 1866. Sir James Pennethorne

of Nash and his work, in many respects, belongs primarily to the early Victorian period. In 1852 he added, for example, the **west wing** to **Somerset House**, which illustrates a respectful continuation of Chambers's work. One of his outstanding contributions was the **University of London Building** in **Burlington Gardens**, now part of the Royal Academy, built in 1866. Typical of its period in a certain floridness of style, it is nevertheless well designed, dignified and monumental, and well suited to its position (1195). Much of Sir James's architectural life was passed at the Office of Works. Among his other commissions were included the **Stationery Office, Westminster**, 1847, and the **Record Office** of the same date.

THE GOTHIC REVIVAL

G. E. Street, Alfred Waterhouse, Sir George Gilbert Scott, and **William Butterfield** constituted the backbone of Gothic Revival architecture in the High Victorian period. There were many others, but most of the larger commissions were apportioned between these four men.

CATHEDRALS 1850–1900

1196

1197

1198

1196 Bristol Cathedral, 1868–88: west front. G. E. Street 1197–8 Cathedral Church of the Most Precious Blood, Westminster, begun 1895. John F. Bentley

LIII *Harlaxton Manor, Lincolnshire, 1831–55. Architect Anthony S*

George Edmund Street 1824–1881

G. E. Street was perhaps the most outstanding. His work was strong and uncompromising with a fondness for colour and polychrome work; he was a deeply religious man and believed wholeheartedly in the theory of the indissolubility of a clear conscience and great architecture. He was intellectually honest and an untiring worker and student. He was born in Essex, and after studying at Winchester under Mr Carter, at the age of 20 he entered Scott's office. He travelled extensively on the Continent: to France and Germany in 1850–1; to Italy in 1853; and later in 1861–3, to Spain. In 1855 he published *The Brick and Marble Architecture of Northern Italy*, a work which, like Ruskin's publications, had a strong influence on the architecture of his time. In 1865 *The Gothic Architecture of Spain* appeared; this work was finely illustrated with his own drawings. Street built many churches. He was a member of the Ecclesiologist Society, but his work in this field, though uncompromising, is varied and shows Italian influence as well as 'Middle Pointed' English Gothic. His best-known church is **St James the Less**, at **Westminster**, built 1858–61. This church has a tall, square tower with steeple, set aside as a campanile. It is decorated by coloured bricks in deep red and black, both on the exterior and in the interior. Inside the church is vast and gloomy, with rich decoration (1264, 1315; LIV). He also designed **All Saints', Clifton**, 1863, **St Paul's, Herne Hill**, 1858, **St John's, Kennington**, 1870–4, **St Peter's, Bournemouth, St John's, Torquay**, 1861–71, and **St Philip and St James, Oxford**, 1862. Street carried out much restoration work, particularly on **Bristol Cathedral**. Here he built the nave and the west front 1868–88. In Decorated Gothic there are now two west towers and a central rose window above a complex Decorated central doorway. The façade is solemn and heavy, basically good in detail, but the whole effect is uninspiring (1196, 1303).

Street became a Royal Academician in 1871 and was also Professor of Architecture at the Royal Academy and President of the Royal Institute of British Architects. He received a number of recognitions for his studies in French and other Continental Gothic architecture.

Street's greatest and best-known work is the **Law Courts** in the **Strand**, 1868–82 (1200, 1259, 1294, 1305). He was unfortunate in this commission which dragged on for many years, and twice the site was changed before work could begin. In the end Street died before the building was finally complete. The Strand front was a difficult one, very long and narrow, and Street's irregular façade is successful here in splitting up and making interesting what would otherwise be a dull elevation. The work is severely Gothic in Street's favourite thirteenth-century castellated style, carried out in stone. It is a dignified building, not perhaps fully appreciated today with the bustling noisy traffic outside its doors, and like so many of London's buildings, only on Sunday mornings can it be viewed in tranquillity. Inside, Street's treatment of the Great Hall is very fine indeed.

Alfred Waterhouse 1830–1905

Waterhouse is an architect whose reputation still stands somewhat low in the opinion of most historians and critics. It has, however, risen considerably in the last 15 years and doubtless will continue to do so until he, like so many of his contemporaries, takes his considered place in the history of architecture. The style of his work is still unfashionable; most of his buildings stand in sooty, overcrowded industrial cities and he was indubitably heavy-handed and often lacking in refinement of taste. This represents the debit side of his work. On the

St James the Less, Westminster, 1858–61. Architect G. E. Street

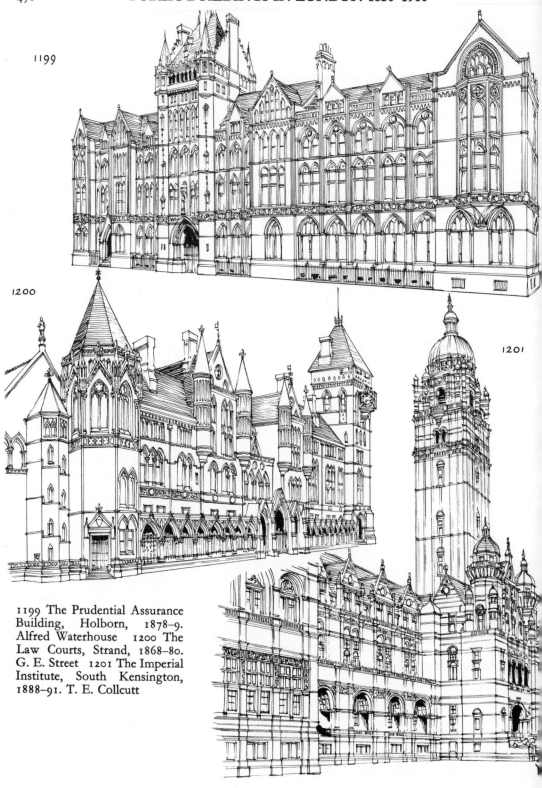

1199 The Prudential Assurance Building, Holborn, 1878–9. Alfred Waterhouse 1200 The Law Courts, Strand, 1868–80. G. E. Street 1201 The Imperial Institute, South Kensington, 1888–91. T. E. Collcutt

credit balance is, firstly, his innate and extensive skill in planning and controlling the design of a large-scale, complex building (much of his work falls into this category), and in producing interesting, varied skylines and masses. Waterhouse thought of architecture in a three-dimensional way and his work is always fiercely individual and therefore easily recognisable for its weight, dignity and power. Like many of his contemporaries, he liked to employ polychrome methods, particularly terracotta and coloured brick; his use of the vivid, harsh red, yellow and black bricks has been vigorously condemned. When first constructed, some of his buildings, such as the Prudential Assurance Building and the Metropole Hotel at Brighton, must have given offence to the eye. Time and weathering have improved this but even so, with the exception of the Natural History Museum which is now quite pleasant in tone, much of his work is enhanced when illustrated in a black and white photograph or drawing.

Waterhouse's two finest works are the **Natural History Museum** at **South Kensington, London**, 1873–9, and **Manchester Town Hall**, 1869. The impressive principal façade of the **Museum** along Cromwell Road, with its two central towers and doorway and terminal bastion towers, is Romanesque in style, and in material is brown and yellow brick with terracotta decoration. A century after it was first constructed, the Natural History Museum now appears to possess a timeless quality, while its decoration and sculpture still enchants a large public, children and adults alike (1202, 1228, 1297, 1302, 1304, 1306). Much of Waterhouse's work arouses controversial opinion and no building perhaps more than **Manchester Town Hall**. Some critics describe it as his best work and a fine achievement, others as inferior. Despite its heavy layer of industrial soot, it still stands impressively in a huge square in the centre of Manchester, magnificently situated, unlike the twentieth-century Town Hall extension which is huddled on to a narrow site not far away. Like all Waterhouse's buildings it is Gothic in style, with a complex roofline of gables and chimney-stacks and a soaring, central tower and steeple which dominates the city centre (1236).

Among Waterhouse's red-brick Gothic, large-scale buildings are three well-known examples: the **Prudential Assurance Building, Holborn in London**, 1878–9, the **Metropole Hotel** on the sea-front at **Brighton**, 1888–9, and **St Paul's School** at **Hammersmith**, 1881–5. These are all Waterhouse at his least tasteful; the strong red colour offends the eye even after so many years of weathering, whilst the terracotta decoration is at once fulsome and overbearing. St Paul's School is the most pleasing of the three examples and from the rear, viewed across the green playing fields, has a good skyline and attractive massing. **The Metropole Hotel** is out of key with the, even now, predominantly early nineteenth-century, classical sea-front (1199, 1269, 1312).

Waterhouse's other work includes extensive university rebuilding (pp. 495, 498) and public buildings such as **University College Hospital, London**, the **Manchester Assize Courts** and his most flamboyant and elaborate creation, the rebuilding of **Eaton Hall, Cheshire**, in 1867 in complex, romantic Gothic style.

Sir George Gilbert Scott 1811–1878

Sir George Gilbert Scott represents to us today the epitome of High Victorian Gothic architecture; he led his age in the Gothic Revival and he was responsible for the largest and most varied number of buildings in his lifetime. His work had not the individuality of his

PUBLIC BUILDINGS IN LONDON 1860–1880

1203

1202

1202 The Natural History Museum, South Kensington, 1873–9. Alfred Waterhouse   1203 The Albert Memorial, Kensington, 1863–72. Sir George Gilbert Scott

contemporaries: of Street or Butterfield or Waterhouse. Their architecture is always immediately recognisable from this quality; Scott's is not, but it is recognisable for its typification of the Gothic Revival of his day. He popularised the movement; he believed in it implicitly; he worked industriously to further its ends because he sincerely thought it the best and most suitable of styles of architecture for all buildings. He was an ardent disciple of Pugin and in his book *Remarks on Secular and Domestic Architecture, Present and Future,* published 1857, he propounds these views. However, Scott was no Pugin. He was not a Catholic, nor a Medievalist, and he was not prejudiced or brilliant as was his mentor. He was capable, knowledgeable, very hard-working, sincere and the founder of an architectural dynasty which spanned more than a century in Britain.

Among Scott's tremendous output of buildings—he was responsible for the initiation, creation and rebuilding of some 730 in his lifetime—he designed many **churches**, and restored a number of cathedrals and large churches. His own ecclesiastical building tends to dullness and respectability. His endeavour to present a truthful picture of Medieval Gothic was rarely successful. His churches were sterile and lacked the vitality and warmth of the original. Among examples of his work in this field are **St Giles', Camberwell**, 1844, one of his best (1101), and **St Matthias', Richmond**, Surrey. His restoration work has long been the subject of great controversy, and for many years he was condemned roundly for destroying what could have been retained and for rebuilding undesirably. In latter years, however, evidence has shown that this was not necessarily so and we owe the existence of considerable areas of our great cathedrals to his timely intervention and skilled supervision and workmanship. His attitude was different from ours in this matter. He believed that one should restore the Medieval craftsmanship as nearly as possible to the original work. We endeavour to preserve as far as possible, but not to imitate more than is necessary. Taking into account this fundamental difference, our debt to him for his restoration of our Medieval heritage is greater than our grounds for denigration. He was no Ecclesiologist or Camdenian and his work in this respect was infinitely better and more reverent than theirs would have been. Among the cathedrals where he carried out restoration work are **Hereford, Winchester, Ely, Salisbury, Lichfield** and **Peterborough**.

Scott came of a religious but not wealthy family. He entered an architect's office when quite young and studied under several different architects. For financial reasons he had difficulty in starting practice and much of his early work was in building gaols and workhouses. Before 1850 he built the **Martyrs' Memorial** at **Oxford** (1093), and **Reading Gaol**. Later, he went to the Continent where he studied French Gothic cathedrals and churches. All his life he preferred to design in Gothic where he could and his work in this field included some 26 public buildings, 25 schools, over 40 large houses and over 450 churches and restorations and additions to over 30 cathedrals and 25 colleges.

Whilst the veil of disapproval has now been lifted partially from such architects as Street, Pearson and even Butterfield, the work of Scott has not yet received more than qualified appreciation except in one or two controversial instances. Two of these are the **Albert Memorial** and **St Pancras Hotel**. In 1861 the Prince Consort died and it was decided to hold a competition for a national monument to house his shrine in Hyde Park. Scott won this competition and the **memorial** was built between 1863 and 1872. He considered it his most successful work and it has always represented the essence of High Victorian taste in this field:

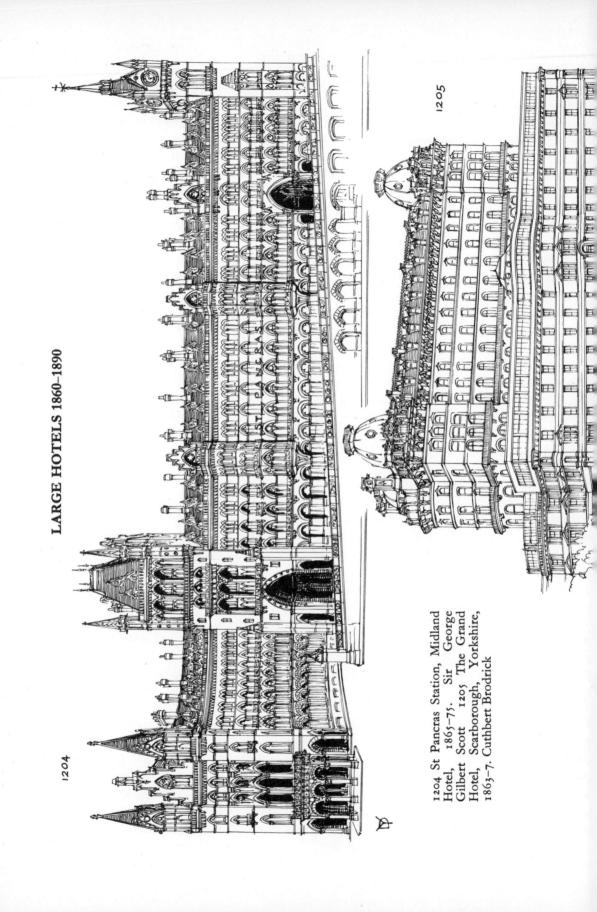

LARGE HOTELS 1860–1890

1204

1205

1204 St Pancras Station, Midland Hotel, 1865–75. Sir George Gilbert Scott 1205 The Grand Hotel, Scarborough, Yorkshire, 1863–7. Cuthbert Brodrick

at first with unqualified approval and later, in the earlier twentieth century, with contempt and derision. Now it is returning to favour, or at least it is beginning to be appreciated for its merits if not for its deficiencies. Scott based his design on a Medieval shrine and encrusted the monument with fine workmanship but perhaps an excess of ornament in inlay, gilt, precious metals, marbles and enamels. In the early morning sunshine, the colours of these materials shine and glint iridescently across the park and give an impression of a jewel set amongst the solemn buildings of London—perhaps the effect for which Scott strived. The bronze seated figure of Prince Albert (by J. H. Foley, 1876) is covered by a Gothic canopy and pinnacled steeple, while supporting the pedestal are corner, sculptured groups and sculptured friezes all round the memorial (1203).

In 1865, two years after R. M. Ordish and W. H. Barlow had begun work on the sheds of the new Midland Station at **St Pancras, London**, Scott won the competition to build the fronting hotel. The station itself was a nineteenth-century achievement in engineering (LVIII). The hotel is one of the largest High Victorian Gothic structures in the world, the epitome of all large European Gothic works. The style appears unsuitable for the function of the building; its colour, a deep red covered by a patina of London dirt, is unsatisfactory, its position in the overcrowded Euston Road is highly unfortunate, but its quality of magnificence, interest and rumbustiousness combined with propriety, so redolent of the age, cannot be denied. Perhaps it is not surprising that having lost the battle for the Euston arch, informed, cultured Britons are wondering how to preserve the remainder of their London station heritage at St Pancras and King's Cross. An anachronism St Pancras may be, but would it not be a tragedy to see it replaced by yet another curtain-walled, gigantic box (1204)?

In 1856 a competition was held for the design of the **Foreign and War Offices** in the **Whitehall** Government buildings. After winning this, Scott designed first a Gothic building, then one in Byzantine style, both of which Lord Palmerston and the government rejected. Reluctantly Scott turned to classicism and gave us the present buildings which harmonise with the rest of Whitehall and are suitably dignified as government façades but compare unfavourably with Barry's Treasury Buildings and Inigo Jones's Banqueting Hall a little further up the thoroughfare. Scott is then said to have used his rejected design for St Pancras Hotel and classicists heaved a sigh of relief that this façade did not appear in Whitehall. Certainly it would have seemed an incongruous intruder there.

From the considerable number of large houses which Scott designed, **Kelham Hall,** Nottinghamshire, is illustrated here. It is typical in its irregular, romantic plan, profusion of chimney-stacks and gables, its red brick walls and Gothic headed doorways and oriels (1207). Scott, like Waterhouse, was a prolific restorer and rebuilder of the **universities**. This work is discussed in that section.

William Butterfield 1814–1900

Butterfield was a reserved, arrogant and deeply religious man. His religion was one with his architecture and he was one of the most fervent disciples of the theory that a good man creates good architecture. Above all other architects of the nineteenth century Butterfield was the most revered by the Ecclesiologists: he was tailor-made for them. The majority of his work was ecclesiastical and he built a large number of churches. The pattern for these was set by his early examples, in which he developed his highly individualistic style. This was

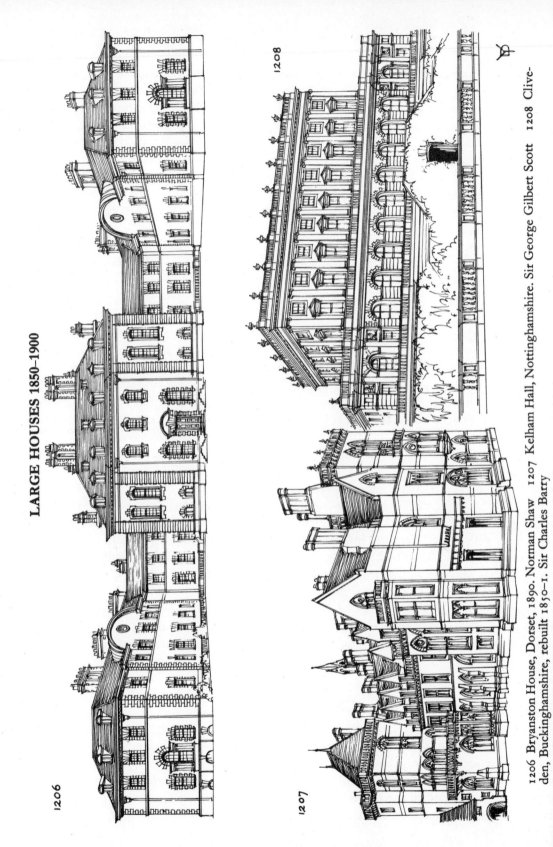

LARGE HOUSES 1850–1900

1206

1207

1208

1206 Bryanston House, Dorset, 1890. Norman Shaw   1207 Kelham Hall, Nottinghamshire. Sir George Gilbert Scott   1208 Cliveden, Buckinghamshire, rebuilt 1850–1. Sir Charles Barry

LV   *Truro Cathedral, 1879–1903. Architect J. L. Pear*

characterised by strong massing of shapes, lofty towers and steeples and an abiding love for polychrome design. He was one of the first architects to follow this method of decoration in the nineteenth century in England, and he used stronger, harsher colours than anyone else and left few surfaces undecorated. He did not believe in painted or stained colour, but in durable materials, so he made up his coloured ornament by use of mosaic, tile, brick, marble, stone and alabaster.

Butterfields best-known church is that of **All Saints, Margaret Street, London,** 1849–59. It is an original and, even today, breathtaking church when one sets foot inside for the first time. Sponsored by the Ecclesiologists, it was to be the model church. Unfortunately, unlike some of its contemporaries in other capitals, it was given a poor site, narrow and cramped in a side street behind Oxford Street. The only possible direction for expansion was upwards, and upwards All Saints went, with a lofty steeple stretching skywards. The church was built of red brick and decorated with black brick and bands of stone. Today the exterior, except for the steeple, is so hedged in by tall commercial buildings that it is hardly visible at all, but the interior remains. Here, Butterfield created a vividly rich effect by patterning almost every surface with marble and tile marquetry, gilt, stained glass, carving, semiprecious stones and alabaster. Like the tower, the nave and chancel are also lofty and cavernous. This church led the way both for Butterfield and for polychrome architecture in Britain. Butterfield's polychrome became harsher and louder, and this is the most unfortunate quality in his work and one which most stands in the way of our appreciation today.

Among the many other churches that he designed were **St Matthias', Stoke Newington,** 1850–2, and **St Alban's, Holborn,** 1858–61. Both of these churches were badly damaged during the war and St Alban's is now a fragmentary shell. In 1856 he designed the church at **Baldersby St James',** Yorkshire, which still survives. This also has a square tower and lofty, pyramidal spire, but is softer in colouring than All Saints.

In addition to his churches Butterfield carried out much ecclesiastical work in collegiate buildings. His best-known examples in this field are Keble College, Oxford, and the chapels at Rugby School and **Balliol College, Oxford.** The **chapel** at **Rugby**, built 1868–72, is of most violent and repellent polychrome and does not even appear to have mellowed with time. The university work is discussed in that section, but it should be mentioned here that **Keble College** is Butterfield's finest work. The chapel here, 1868–70, has aroused fierce controversy for many years, and for a long time was indiscriminately condemned. Its brilliant, almost harsh polychromy has mellowed greatly; it is finely proportioned and individualistic in design (1229, 1265, 1267; LVI).

Butterfield went on designing churches and schools for many years, but after 1875 such violent polychromy became much less fashionable and little is heard of his later work.

FURTHER VICTORIAN ARCHITECTS

Most of the work of **John Loughborough Pearson, 1817–97,** was ecclesiastical. He built many churches (a number of which were destroyed during the late war), and his career culminated in the building of **Truro Cathedral**. From 1870 to 1880 he was one of the leaders of Victorian Gothic architecture and set the pattern for large, rather gaunt churches, generally in thirteenth-century Medieval style. The best known of these is **St Augustine's, Kilburn,**

Keble College Chapel, Oxford, 1868–70. Architect William Butterfield

1870–80. This church has a lofty steeple and, facing the main road, a gable with twin towers and a large rose window (1244, 1298, 1311). His other churches include **St Peter's, Vauxhall,** 1864 (destroyed), and **St Michael's, Croydon,** 1885, which is a good red-brick example of his work. He also built **St John's, Upper Norwood,** 1887, and **St Barnabas', Hove,** 1882.

Truro Cathedral itself, **1879–1903,** is built in granite in traditional manner. It is one of the chief monuments of the later Gothic Revival and the last large-scale work of imitative Gothic in England. The cathedral was consecrated in 1887 and finally completed, in 1903, by Pearson's son after his father's death. The design, in thirteenth-century Gothic with a French flavour, is lofty, with soaring towers and spires. There are two western towers and a central tower; the plan is traditional, a nave and aisles of nine bays, choir and transepts with aisles and a circular baptistery. The interior is rather monotonous and chastely cold. The cathedral is finely built and displays a masterly planning of towers and spires but, by 1903, it could not fail to be merely a copy and, to a certain extent, an anachronism (LV).

John Francis Bentley, 1839–1902, is primarily known as the designer of the **Westminster Roman Catholic Cathedral.** Here is a complete contrast to that at Truro. In deference to Roman Catholic desires, Bentley studied in Italy for this work and decided on a polychrome structure on the lines of the cathedrals at Siena and Orvieto, but in the Byzantine style of architecture. His handling of the polychrome materials in brick and stone is subtle and masterly, and the cathedral has beauty and grandeur. Its tall, elegant, central tower is one of London's finest landmarks. Work was begun on the building in 1895 and the shell was finished by 1903. It was many years, however, before the interior was largely complete (1197–8, LX).

The work of **Richard Cromwell Carpenter, 1812–55,** was discussed in Chapter X. Because of his untimely death in 1855, only one building of his was designed in this period, that of **Lancing College Chapel** in Sussex, 1854–5. This was Carpenter's finest work and building had only commenced when he died. It is a beautiful chapel, built on a hill above the sea in Decorated Gothic Style. It is a lofty, three-storey, single unit chapel with flying buttresses all round (1271, 1316).

William Burges, 1827–81, was widely travelled and had studied particularly in Belgium, Italy, France and Germany. He is well known for his rebuilding of **Cardiff Castle;** an immense structure which still dominates the centre of the city. In **Cork** he designed the **Church of Ireland Cathedral,** 1865–76, on a beautiful site. It is a fine, complex building in twelfth-century Gothic, reminiscent of French designs of that period. It has three towers, two on the west and one over the crossing. Burges also built a number of churches, including **Studley Royal Church** and **Skelton Church,** both in 1871. Both designs are ornately decorated with coloured marbles.

George Frederick Bodley, 1827–1907, like Burges, is famed for one of his commissions outside England; he was the designer of **Washington Cathedral.** At home, his work was in Gothic, predominantly in the Decorated style, and the majority of it was church building. Among these are **St Michael's, Brighton,** 1862, and **St Martin's-on-the-Cliff** at **Scarborough,** 1863. Bodley was a pupil of Scott and a close friend of a number of the Pre-Raphaelites, including Rossetti, Burne-Jones and William Morris.

George Gilbert Scott, 1839–97, was the son of Sir George Gilbert Scott and, though a much less famous architect than his father, built some well-designed Gothic churches which had more of the Medieval quality about them than those of Sir George. These churches included **St Agnes, Kennington**, 1877, and **All Hallows** at **Southwark**.

William Morris 1834–1896   Philip Webb 1831–1915

Morris was not an architect; although he did spend a year in Street's office training to be an architect, and here he met Philip Webb, but, like Ruskin, he had a considerable influence on the architecture of his day. Also like Ruskin, he was a crusading reformer and tried to put into practice Socialist ideas which he felt urgently necessary to improve the standards of life for the majority in his time. He approached this problem primarily through the arts. He abhorred the trend towards mechanisation and mass-production, and felt strongly that man could only express himself in the arts by individual craftwork. He achieved a great deal in this sphere by giving an example of fine design in many fields, carried out to its ultimate conclusion in the finished article, but in his crusade to put over individual craftsmanship to the common man he was doomed to failure; mass-production had come to stay; Morris could not put the clock back.

It was when he married in 1859 and commissioned his friend Philip Webb, the architect, to build his new home, that he discovered it to be difficult to find the designs of textiles and furniture that he wanted; so he designed these himself and, with his friends, carried out the workmanship. From this beginning, Morris and Co. was born. This was the firm which became famous for its design and production of fabrics, wallpapers, furniture, glass design, murals and weaving. The name Morris became synonymous with that of good design, vivid, beautiful colouring and first-class, individual craftsmanship. The well-to-do flocked to buy his work, but the mass of people were unmoved. Morris never realised his ambition to elevate the craftsman once more to his original position in society—indeed he would be horrified today to find that such workers are becoming an extinct species in many trades—but his influence on design was profound, particularly in the later nineteenth century.

Webb, who was born at Oxford, entered the office of G. E. Street there and met William Morris. In 1856 he set up practice in London and designed many houses. The first of these was for Morris himself, the **Red House, Bexley Heath**, 1859. Not a large or pretentious building, this house nevertheless represents a milestone in English domestic architecture of the nineteenth century. It was built of plain, red brick, very simply and with no polychromy. It was irregular and informal in plan, but practical and well designed. Webb endeavoured, as Morris did also in his field, to return to English materials and craftsmanship and here pointed the way for architects of the late nineteenth century such as Shaw and Voysey.

Webb produced many designs for Morris and Co. in the form of interior decoration, floor coverings and furniture. Among his later houses are **Rounton Grange, Northallerton**, 1872–6, **'Clouds', East Knoyle**, Wiltshire, 1880, and **Benfleet Hall, Cobham**, Surrey, 1861. His work was always sincere, with good lines, and plain, in strong contrast to the houses by other architects at this time. The roofs were generally steeply sloping and of red tile. The windows were sash styled, painted white.

RICHARD NORMAN SHAW 1831–1912

Shaw was the most influential architect of the last three decades of the nineteenth century. He did not design original architecture, indeed he worked in many styles all derived from

HOUSES 1870–1900

1209

1210

1211

1209 'Wispers' 1876, St Cuthman's School, Midhurst, Sussex, 1876, Norman Shaw. 1210 'Grim's Dyke', Harrow Weald, Middle-

the past, but his designs were good in the different media which he employed. He cast aside the harsh colouring, over-ornamentation and sham materials of the High Victorian architects and returned to simpler lines and earlier designs based upon Wren, Jacobean work and Medieval half-timber building. He specialised principally in domestic architecture and his practice became the largest of his day. Through this large, but good-quality, output his influence on the raising of the standard of taste in architecture was very great. In the early years of the twentieth century his reputation was at a peak; today it is valued less highly but more realistically, as the passage of time has reassessed his considerable contribution to English architecture.

Shaw was born in Edinburgh but came to London with his family as a boy. He studied for a number of years under Burn, the Edinburgh architect, then at the Royal Academy, where he won gold and silver medals and the Travelling Scholarship. He travelled on the Continent in 1853–4, to Italy and France in particular, where he made many drawings. He published some of these in 1858 in his *Architectural Sketches from the Continent* which showed his high standard of architectural draughtsmanship. In 1858 he entered the office of G. E. Street and remained there for four years, becoming Street's principal draughtsman. Then he set up practice in partnership with **William Eden Nesfield**, 1835–88, who shared his views of rebellion against the High Victorian architectural style. Together they designed some country houses, for example, **Cloverly Hall**, Shropshire, 1865, and **Leys Wood**, Sussex, 1868. Both houses are Tudor in inspiration, whilst Leys Wood was early Tudor or late Medieval in half-timber design with very tall chimneys. It was built round a courtyard in Medieval manner and had gatehouses and early Tudor timber decoration.

The partnership was then dissolved and Shaw went on to build up his large domestic practice. He built many country houses of different sizes but predominantly large, and a number of town houses, particularly in London. He used a variety of style and materials, moving from one to another with consummate skill and rarely abandoning any one style completely. He used half-timber, brick, stone and combinations of these. His earlier work is generally more Medieval and informal, his later work more classical, based on Jacobean, Wren and Queen Anne periods.

Among the best of Shaw's **country houses** are **Grim's Dyke, Harrow Weald**, 1872, and **'Wispers'** (now St Cuthman's School), **Midhurst**, Sussex, 1875. Both these are early Tudor, half-timber houses with tall, brick chimneys, barge-boarded gables and deep oriel and bay windows with mullions and transoms. They are well built, very picturesque and have a rambling and informal plan (1209–10, 1313). Other houses of this period include **'Merrist Wood', Guildford**, 1877; **Adcote**, Shropshire, 1877, and **Pierrepont, Farnham**, Surrey, 1876. Shaw then turned to the more classical idiom and his two famous houses in this mode are **'Bryanston'**, Dorset, **1890**, and **'Chesters'**, Northumberland, **1891**. **Bryanston** is a symmetrical country house on an eighteenth-century scale. It has a central block and two side wings. The central mass, rather reminiscent of Coleshill, has a large entrance hall, 54 by 24 feet and a further hall of 44 by 36 feet. The house is built of brick with stone angle and window dressings. It is two storeys in height, above which is the cornice and dormer windows in the roof. The chimney-stacks are set in eighteenth-century fashion to dominate and enhance the skyline. The detail is good and the whole design is well planned, spacious and rewarding. It was one of the last English country houses to be built on such a scale and is now used as a well-known school (1206, 1266, 1299). **'Chesters'** is also a very fine house on magnificent scale. It also has a central block with two side wings. Stone is the chief material here and the roof is of slate without dormers. On the entrance elevation the side wings advance round a forecourt.

Shaw also designed many **houses in London** for varying types of site. One of his early houses was **Lowther Lodge, Kensington**, 1875, now occupied by the Royal Geographical Society. A pleasant, large house, once sited on open ground, it is now crowded in by surrounding buildings. Near by are his **Albert Hall Mansions**, built in 1879. Here is a large, brick block of flats, a rarity in London at this date, with considered proportions and an interesting skyline; not a mere box as are so many of its successors (1257). In **Hampstead** Shaw built his own house, **No. 6 Ellerdale Road**, 1875. This three-storeyed house still stands in pleasant, ordered surroundings and retains its air of graciousness. In **Chelsea** are **Swan House** on the embankment, 1876, **Cheyne House**, 1876, and **Clock House**, 1879; all charming London houses, still distinctive and possessing the quality of taste. **Queen's Gate, South Kensington**, still boasts several Shaw houses despite the inroads made by the Imperial College of Science. In particular are Nos 196, 180 and 170, illustrated in Figs. 1212–13, 1215, 1260, 1300 and 1314. **No. 196** has a rather ornate façade, tall and surmounted by a gable. It is decorated by brickwork strips and terracotta sculptured panels. **Nos 180 and 170**

1212 170 Queen's Gate, London, 1888. Norman Shaw

1213 196 Queen's Gate, 1875. Norman Shaw   1214 14–16 Hans Road, Kensington, 1891. C. F. A.
Voysey 1215 180 Queen's Gate, 1885. Norman Shaw   1216 63-4 Sloane Street, 1897. Fairfax Wade

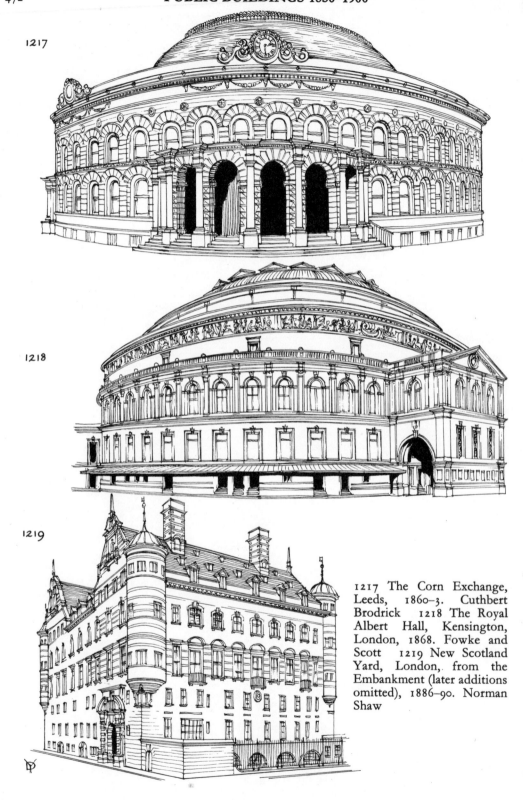

1217

1218

1219

1217 The Corn Exchange, Leeds, 1860–3. Cuthbert Brodrick 1218 The Royal Albert Hall, Kensington, London, 1868. Fowke and Scott 1219 New Scotland Yard, London, from the Embankment (later additions omitted), 1886–90. Norman Shaw

are corner sites. The former is a simple, brick block with tall chimneys and semicircular arched recesses and doorway. No. 170 is the most distinguished house of the three on plain, classical lines. The façades are only decorated by white-painted sash windows with wood shutters and the pedimented doorway. There is a row of dormer windows in the roof and a centrally placed, curved gable. The house is of red brick with stone quoins; the roof is tiled while the beautiful entrance doorway is of carved stone.

As with his domestic architecture, Shaw tried in his **ecclesiastical work** to get away from the High Victorian ideal. He reverted to the simple church, plain and built of local materials where possible. His early example at **Bingley**, Yorkshire, of **Holy Trinity Church**, 1866–7, still shows the High Victorian influence, particularly of Street, with whom Shaw so recently worked. The church has a very tall, central tower and steeple, finely proportioned, strong, but rather gaunt. The carved details are good and the colour sombre and plain. At **Ilkley, St Margaret's**, 1878, provides a different type of example. This is also simple, in Gothic design but low and long with an immense, traceried window in the end wall. The stonework is beautifully handled and treated. **Swanscombe Church**, Kent, 1873, is a flint and stone example, whilst **All Saints', Leek**, Staffordshire, 1886, is a typical, plain parish church with a low, square tower over the crossing.

The best-known work of Shaw's **public buildings**, apart from the Quadrant which is discussed in Chapter XII, is **New Scotland Yard** in **London**, built **1887–90**. The original building, shown in Fig. 1219, is a single, large block and was completed in 1890. Subsequently, in 1900, another part was added, but this upsets the balance of the original design. The main block he planned in castellar form, like a Medieval keep with corner turrets. It is built of Dartmoor granite with dressings of stone and bands of brick which present an attractive colour composition; a more subtle polychromy than Butterfield's, for example. The roof is steeply pitched with banded chimney-stacks and rows of lights in Flemish Medieval tradition. The roofs are gabled at the ends with curved, stepped, Flemish treatment while the corner turrets are circular in section and are corbelled below. The main doorway is plainly handled in the Doric order. The whole building is very fine, especially when viewed from the embankment or Westminster Bridge. It has a quality of strength and solidity and appears admirably suited to its purpose.

In St James's Street Shaw designed two insurance buildings. On the corner site with Pall Mall the **First Alliance Assurance Building** was built in 1882. This is a notable example of Shaw's use of brick and Portland stone, with complex, Flemish gables and a corner, sided turret. The effect is impressive and cannot pass unnoticed. On the lower storey are large, semicircular arches containing windows, with voussoirs of brick and Portland stone (1220). The **other Alliance Assurance Building** is quite different. Of later date, 1903, this is in traditional classic style in Portland stone. In his plans for the **New Zealand Chambers** in **Leadenhall Street** Shaw astonished the city by designing for this highly traditional area a façade of red brick decorated by ornamental plaster work in Jacobean manner. Instead of the usual large, plate-glass windows he used lead framed panes. The whole façade was split into three bays with oriel windows in between. The deep, cove cornice above was pargetted with plaster swags and strapwork. This amazing building, conspicuous at first, soon lost its brilliance of red and white colouring and is now, unfortunately, destroyed.

1220 First Alliance Assurance Building, Pall Mall, London, 1882. Norman Shaw   1221 Bishopsgate Institute, London, 1893–4. C. Harrison Townsend   1222 Martin's Bank, Bromley, Kent, 1898. Ernest Newton   1223 Whitechapel Art Gallery, London, 1900. C. Harrison Townsend

C. F. A. Voysey 1857–1941   William Richard Lethaby 1857–1927
Charles Rennie Mackintosh 1869–1928

These three architects, together with **C. Harrison Townsend** who designed the **White-chapel Art Gallery**, 1900, and the **Bishopsgate Institute**, 1893–4, both in **London** (1221, 1223), were prime movers in the trend away from High Victorian towards modern architecture. This movement, which in England was slow to develop, had begun with Webb and his colleagues, passed on through Shaw and Nesfield, and at the end of the nineteenth century and early years of the twentieth was taken up by Voysey and his contemporaries.

Voysey was not only an architect but also designed wallpapers, fabrics and furniture. In the architectural field his participation was domestic. His style varied from commission to commission according to individual needs, but his work was always very simple and un-ornamented. The elevations were not symmetrical and the plan was informal; the walls were rough cast, plaster-covered or in brick—no half-timber like Shaw—the ceilings were low and the roofs long and sloping with lean-to buttresses. The casement windows were small and lead-framed. Houses typical of his work include his own home **The 'Orchard'** at **Chorley Wood**, Hertfordshire, 1898–9 (1211, 1301), **'Broadleys'** on **Lake Windermere**, 1898, **'Perrycroft'**, Cornwall, 1893, and **'The Pastures'**, **North Luffenham**, Rutlandshire, 1901 (1411). Among his town houses is one at **Bedford Park** and the pair of terrace houses in brick, **Nos 14–16 Hans Road** near **Sloane Square**, London, built 1891. These have five storeys and dormer windows in the roof; the chief features of the plain façade are the window openings in oriel and lantern design, with the usual leaded lights. Like all Voysey's work the houses are unpretentious but possess the quality of charm (1214).

Lethaby's architectural contribution was chiefly in literary form and he designed few buildings. In 1879 he won the Soane travelling studentship of the Royal Institute of British Architects and later worked in Shaw's office for 12 years. He was a great admirer of Webb, Shaw and Morris and was influenced by their work. In 1906 he was appointed Surveyor to the fabric of Westminster Abbey. Earlier he became the first Principal of the Central School of Arts and Crafts in London and remained there from 1893–1911. He was Professor of Design at the Royal College of Art from 1900–18. Among his numerous publications are *Mediaeval Art*, 1904, *Architecture*, 1912, *National Architecture and Modernism,* 1918–21 and *Westminster Abbey re-examined*, 1925.

Mackintosh was a Scottish architect working chiefly in Glasgow, whose most famous building is the **Glasgow School of Art**, begun 1898–9. This school, which is simply and practically designed for its purpose with large windows and an economy of decoration, represents a link between Victorianism and the modern movement of the twentieth century, in the same way that Voysey's houses do. In the 1930s its importance was often magnified and it was described as the first modern building. This is not so, but it was original at its time and does point the way to modernism in a similar manner to the earlier designs of men like Gropius and Mendelsohn.

OTHER VICTORIAN ARCHITECTS

Both **Sir Ernest George** and **Sir Ernest Newton** were strongly influenced by the work of Norman Shaw, indeed Newton was one of his pupils. They both worked mainly in the domestic field, using similar materials and basic designs to those of Shaw himself.

1224 The University Museum, Oxford, 1855–60. Deane and Woodward   1225–6 Selwyn College, Cambridge, 1882–95; chapel and entrance gateway. Sir Arthur Blomfield

Sir Ernest George, 1839–1922, carried out much work on Shaw's **Bedford Park scheme**, in conjunction with May and Adams. His firm of George and Peto was responsible for a number of building projects in London, in particular, **Collingham Gardens**, 1881–7, and **Harrington Gardens**, 1882. Further building was carried out in **South Audley Street** and **Cadogan Square**. Sir Ernest's work was frequently in brick with terracotta decoration; he used Flemish, stepped gables and decorative bay windows, very reminiscent of Shaw's 196 Queen's Gate and his First Alliance Assurance Building. His influence on his contemporaries and successors was considerable; both Sir Guy Dawber and Sir Edwin Lutyens studied under him.

Sir Ernest Newton, 1856–1922, excelled in country-house design, following in Shaw's footsteps here, although his work was generally more symmetrical and with less decoration. He designed in brick and stone also using tile and weather-boarding. His work was always well considered, gracious and tasteful. Among his houses are **'Feathercombe'**, near **Godalming**, Surrey (1412), **Flint House, Goring-on-Thames**, and **Anderson Place**, Surrey.

Sir Arthur Blomfield, 1829–1899, was an influential architect of his day and his large practice was primarily devoted to ecclesiastical and collegiate work. He began practice in 1856 and became President of the Architectural Association in 1861; he was knighted in 1889 and won the Royal Institute of British Architects' Gold Medal in 1891. He designed many churches, particularly in the 1880s. Many of these were in brick; some were plain and inexpensive, others more elaborate; nearly all were Gothic. Among examples of his work in this field are **St Mary's, Portsea**, 1854, **St Matthias', Croydon**, and **St John's, St Leonards-on-Sea** (1242). In his collegiate work he designed the **Whitgift School** at **Croydon**, the **King's School** at **Chester** and **Queen's School, Eton**. Much of **Selwyn College, Cambridge**, is by Sir Arthur (p. 498).

The majority of **Basil Champneys'**, 1842–1935, work was for the universities, both Oxford and Cambridge, and is discussed in that section. His architecture was pleasant, soundly designed but not original. He used both Medieval and Renaissance patterns and excelled in his approach to either. Apart from collegiate architecture, he also was responsible for **Rylands Library** in **Manchester**, a Gothic building of 1885, the **Harrow Museum** and the **Indian Institute** at **Oxford**, 1882.

J. J. Stevenson, 1832–1908, was a domestic architect and a friend of William Morris. His best-known work is the **Red House** (not Webb's design) in **Bayswater**.

The work of **John D. Sedding**, 1839–1891, was predominantly ecclesiastical. For many years he lived in the west country and restored and built churches there; for example, **All Saints', Falmouth**. In London he is best known for **Holy Trinity, Sloane Square, Chelsea**, built in 1890. Like much of his work this is in fifteenth-century Gothic style; a good example, while the interior boasts craftsmanship by famous pre-Raphaelites such as William Morris and Burne-Jones.

PUBLIC BUILDINGS

The undermentioned buildings have been discussed under the appropriate architect's name:

Bentley: Westminster Cathedral
Pennethorne: London University Buildings

Scott: St Pancras Hotel
The Albert Memorial

Shaw: New Scotland Yard   **Waterhouse:** The Prudential Assurance
    First Alliance Assurance Building   Building
Street: Bristol Cathedral   Manchester Town Hall
    The Law Courts   The Natural History Museum

The Crystal Palace, 1850–1. Designer, Sir Joseph Paxton

A competition was held in 1850 for a structure to house the proposed Great Exhibition. A Building Committee was appointed which included the architects Barry and Cockerell and the engineers and builders Brunel, Robert Stephenson and William Cubitt. Out of the 245 designs submitted Paxton's was eventually decided upon. A number of the entries were from the Continent, but many of these and the British ones were eliminated because they did not comply with the essential conditions of limited funds available and of the necessity of being able to dismantle and re-erect the building elsewhere. The committee's own design had to be abandoned for these reasons. Paxton had been working for some years for the Duke of Devonshire and had built his giant glasshouse at Chatsworth (see Chapter X). He considered that he could apply these principles to a building for the exhibition. The result was a glass and iron structure of enormous dimensions which, by prefabricated methods (the first time that these had been employed on a large scale in the world) could be erected cheaply and quickly. The site was some 20 acres in **Hyde Park** and the building had to house an immense number of exhibits of considerable size and complexity.

Paxton, who was neither an architect nor an engineer, made a sketch of his idea. It was supported by Robert Stephenson, Prince Albert and Robert Peel. Meeting only lukewarm reaction from the Committee, Paxton published his design in the *London News*. Public response was overwhelmingly in favour; the Committee capitulated. In *Punch* it was first called 'The Crystal Palace'. The name stuck and as this it has always been known. It was immensely popular with the public and visiting foreigners admired it greatly.

Artistically the building had considerable merit, although many architects then and later criticised it bitterly. At the time Pugin and Ruskin were scathing in their criticisms. A prefabricated building constructed on mass-production methods was alien to all their principles. However, from a constructional point of view the Crystal Palace was an innovation both for the use of the materials—iron and glass—and for the methods employed in it. It pointed the way to modern techniques and the details of its dimensions and construction are incredible to read, even today.

The site was taken over by the contractors on the 1st August 1850. The Exhibition was opened on 1st May 1851. The actual building itself was erected in just over half that time. Its length was 1851 feet, its width 450 feet. The glass panels, as large as could possibly be made at the time, were 49 inches long and there were 900,000 square feet of glass in the whole erection. 3,300 iron columns supported the building, together with 2,224 girders. The original design was built in tiers from the ground; there were three storeys in all and above this there rose the barrel roof of the transept, 135 feet above ground level. The building, constructed on standard units to a detailed timetable, was a ferro-vitreous triumph.

In 1852 the building was taken down and re-erected at Sydenham in South London, 1852–4. Alterations were made and the Sydenham Palace, which remained until its spectacular destruction by fire in 1936, was considerably different from its predecessor. Water towers designed by Brunel were built at each end, giving vertical terminals to the composition, and the central part of the building was higher with two smaller transepts added (LVII).

The **Royal Albert Hall, 1868**, is an interesting building of no little merit, though derided in modern times for its acoustic deficiencies and for its over-ornamentation. It was designed by the engineers **Fowke** and **Scott** who were responsible for the construction of the vast dome. Many sculptors were employed for the frieze encircling the exterior and for the interior decoration. Viewed from the Albert Hall Mansions, the elegance of the building can still be appreciated although the terracotta colouring is rather too harsh. Inside, the

1227 The Liverpool and London Assurance Offices, Liverpool, 1856–8. C. R. Cockerell

tiers of boxes rising around the vast, circular auditorium, ornamented by classic orders, are most impressive. If only there could be the same standard of ventilation, heating and acoustics as in the modern Royal Festival Hall, how different it would be for music lovers (1218).

At the same period further development was taking place in South Kensington in the same area. **Fowke** also designed the **Museum for Science and Art** (later known as the Victoria and Albert Museum) and building was begun in 1866. Fowke had died the year before this but Scott carried on the work. The museum was erected in brick with cream-coloured terracotta. In similar vein, Scott also built the **Royal College of Science**, 1868–71.

The **Imperial Institute** in **South Kensington** was designed by **T. E. Collcut, 1840–1924**, in 1887 and built 1888–91. A catholic mixture of styles were incorporated into its design—Romanesque, Byzantine, Renaissance—but they all blended harmoniously and most successfully into a beautifully proportioned whole. The dominating feature is a tall, elegant tower, rising above the cupola-crowned towers of the entrance hall front (all that is now extant). There is a subtle, pleasing use of polychromy in the building in the form of red brick and Portland stone masonry, finely blended to give an appearance of grandeur and dignity (1201).

The **Bishopsgate Institute**, 1892–4 and the **Whitechapel Art Gallery**, 1900 were both designed by **C. Harrison Townsend** on awkward, restricted sites in congested parts of

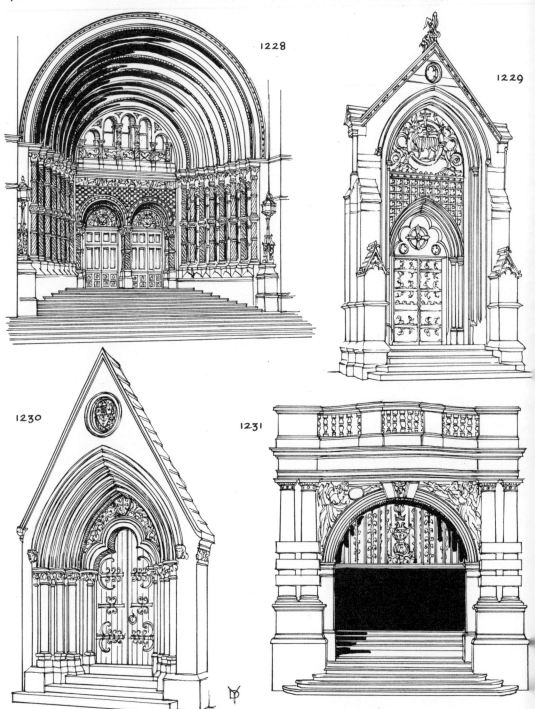

1228 Natural History Museum, London, 1873–9: main entrance. Alfred Waterhouse   1229 Keble College Chapel, Oxford, 1868–82. William Butterfield   1230 University College, Oxford: library entrance, 1861. Sir George G. Scott   1231 Sheffield Town Hall, 1891–6: main entrance. E. W. Mountford

1232 Royal Holloway College, Surrey, 1886   1233 Newnham College, Cambridge, from 1880.
Basil Champneys (Gates illustrated in Fig. 1280)   1234 Windsor and Eton Riverside Station: royal
porch, 1850. Sir William Tite   1235 Battersea Town Hall, 1891: entrance porch. E. W. Mountford

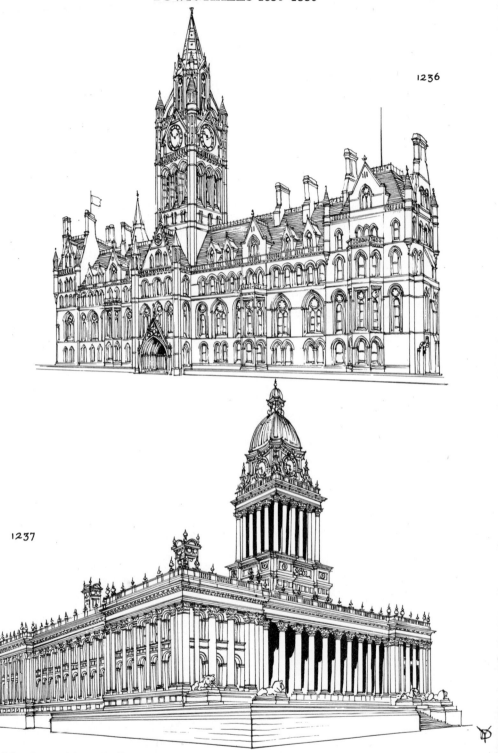

1236

1237

1236 Manchester Town Hall, 1869. Alfred Waterhouse   1237 Leeds Town Hall, 1855–9. Cuthbert Brodrick

1238 Congleton Town Hall, Cheshire, 1864–7. E. W. Godwin
1239 Sheffield Town Hall, 1891–6. E. W. Mountford

1238

1239

1240 Halifax Town Hall (only tower shown here),
1860–2. Sir Charles and E. M. Barry

London. Both designs are original and revolutionary for their time. The **Bishopsgate Institute** has a tall, narrow façade with flanking towers; the **Art Gallery** is wider and simpler, but both buildings possess a wide semicircular arched entrance of simple but majestic proportions which enclose a plain doorway and entrance hall (1221, 1223).

The **University Museum, Oxford**, 1855–60, designed by **Sir Thomas Deane** and his colleague **Benjamin Woodward**, is, to a large extent, a memorial to **Ruskin**. Woodward won the competition to design the museum but Ruskin took tremendous interest in it and made drawings and supervised its erection. It was to be the expression of his whole doctrine. However, when it was completed, very much according to his ideas, he was chagrined that the result, in tangible form, was not what he had hoped and envisaged. The museum still stands today, very much a monument to the ideals of the Gothic Revival which rarely, in practice, measured up to the vision of those who extolled it as a religion. A well-built and constructed edifice, it has no more Medieval feeling about it than a modern office block, but is an interesting survival to us of a bygone age and inspiration (1224, 1296).

Town Halls

The second half of the nineteenth century saw a tremendous rise in population figures for England and Wales; this was partly due to the larger Victorian families and partly to the lower mortality rate for infants, mothers and children. In the same period there was an acceleration in the movement of population from country to industrial areas. Whole new urban communities were

1241 Northampton Town Hall, 1864. E. W. Godwin

created and the colossal building drive of Victorian society towards catering for these was stepped up. While housing for these families often lagged far behind their needs, two forms of building construction proceeded apace: town halls and churches. In general, Victorian town halls are today decried or ignored and, indeed, many are ugly, dirty and unfortunately sited in our present-day towns. However, among the large numbers of new civic buildings of this time there are several which present very fine architectural examples of their period.

Apart from **Manchester Town Hall** already discussed (1236; p. 459), two public buildings stand out as masterpieces: those at Leeds and Halifax, both of which were built at the mid-century. **Leeds Town Hall,** 1855–9, was designed by that capable, lively northern architect, **Cuthbert Brodrick,** who was also responsible for the **Corn Exchange,** 1860–3, in the same city (1217). The town hall is classical in design, a baroque type of classicism on the grand scale. An immense, rectangular building, it is ornamented by the Corinthian order in pilaster and column form all round the block. The clock tower rises on a square plinth with a Corinthian column middle stage and above this a cupola; it is finely proportioned and handled. The interior shows some resemblance to the earlier St George's Hall in Liverpool; the exterior surfaces of both buildings are of the same neglected, black sooty appearance. This is a building based on classical principles but illustrating the vigour and power of the Victorians (1237).

Halifax Town Hall, 1859–62, was one of **Sir Charles Barry's** last works; he died before its completion and his son finished it in 1862. Again, it is a very large building dominated by an impressive, well-proportioned tower, set in one corner. This tower, illustrated in Fig. 1240, is again classical, but in its stepped, rising stages there is more than a little Gothic quality about the design. It has a lofty steeple, a landmark for many miles around. Like Brodrick's Town Hall in Leeds, this building illustrates the best in Victorian architecture, which owes something to the past but which is architecture in its own right also.

Two more interesting and well-designed Town Halls were built by **E. W. Godwin, 1833–86**; those at Northampton and at Congleton, Cheshire. The two buildings have much in common, but, although they are totally different from the examples at Halifax and Leeds, they too are particularly Victorian buildings which possess character and charm. **Northampton Town Hall**, 1861–4, is the larger, more pretentious building; it is in Romanesque and Gothic tradition, with rich, sculptured ornament on the façade and window openings. There is a simple, satisfying clock tower and, further along the façade, a gable flanked by two turrets (1241). The **Congleton** example, 1864–7, is plainer and smaller, but has a more imposing, castellated tower with clock turret above. It is Early English in derivation and has an attractive row of dormers in the roof (1238).

Towards the end of the century came more large town halls, but differing in style. The later examples were often classical, but an early classical, almost Elizabethan or Jacobean, with strapwork and swags as well as the orders. **Oxford Town Hall**, 1892, built by **H. T. Hare** is an example of this type of design. A stately town hall of the same period, 1891–6, is that at **Sheffield**, designed by **E. W. Mountford**. This is in early Renaissance design, simply ornamented with pedimented windows and an oriel and gable feature at each end of the principal façade. There is a lofty, slender, corner clock tower terminating in a parapet, hipped roof and, above, diminishing turrets (1231, 1239). Another, much less pretentious, example by the same architect is the **Town Hall** at **Battersea, London**. This is a very typical pattern of its period, built in 1891 for the expanding, but not wealthy, suburbs of London, in brick and stone with lively but often coarse detail. The semicircular, Ionic porch is illustrated in Fig. 1235.

LARGE HOTELS

With the establishment and consolidation of the railway system, a chain of comfortable, spacious hotels was now required in many parts of the country. Many of these were enormous constructions, illustrating a lively disregard for such modern problems as domestic staff and cleaners. The **St Pancras Hotel** and the **Metropole Hotel** at **Brighton** are two such examples, and have already been discussed (1204; pp. 463, 459). By far the most typical, original and capably designed hotel in this class is the **Grand Hotel** at **Scarborough**, built in 1863–7 as

1244

1243

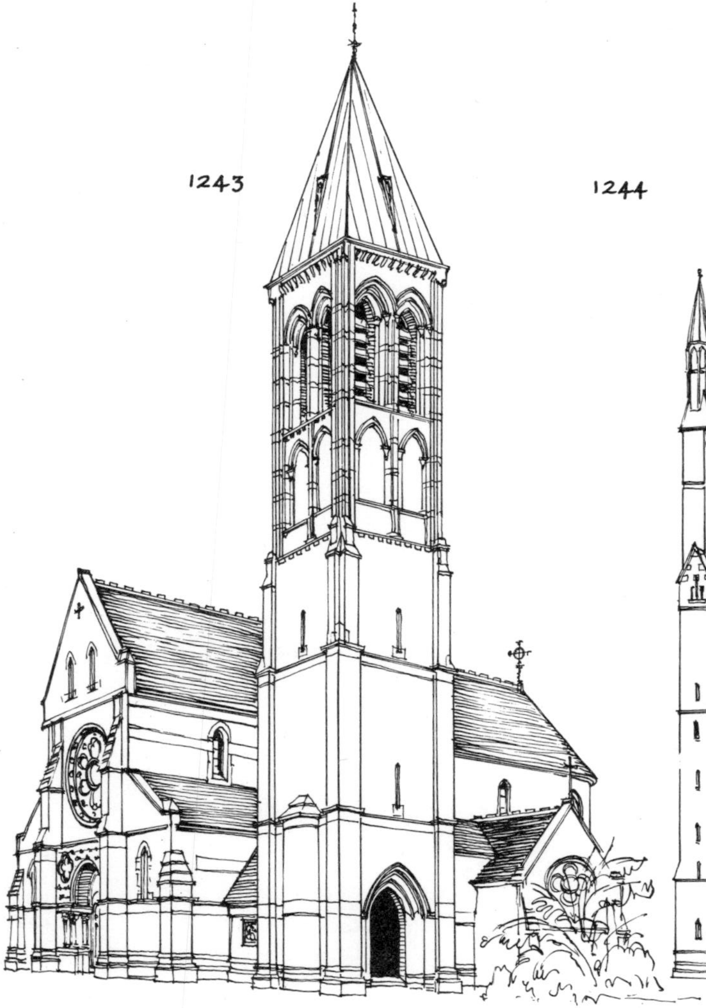

1242

1242 St John's, St Leonard's-on-Sea, Sussex. Sir Arthur Blomfield   1243 St Peter's, Leamington Spa, Warwickshire, (shown here with original pyramidal roof, not now existing) 1861–5. Henry Clutton   1244 St Augustine's, Kilburn, London, 1870–80. J. L. Pearson

the Cliff Hotel by **Cuthbert Brodrick**, on a wonderful site on the top of the cliffs overlooking the sea. This is a style of hotel seen in this period in many cities in different Continental countries; it is a true design of its time and though today something of a 'museum piece', it is an attractive and friendly one. It is built on the massive scale like a keep, with brick walls decorated with terracotta. It has four corner, domed pavilions joined by a deep, projecting cornice, and roof with dormers above (1205).

In **London** there are, in particular, two large examples of this type of hotel, but neither is so pleasantly designed as Scarborough. **The Grosvenor Hotel** at **Victoria Station** was built 1859–60 by **Sir James T. Knowles**, who also designed much of the Hove sea-front. The design here is interesting and powerful, with a convex, mansard roof and higher terminal pavilions. However, the detailed ornament is profuse, coarse and even crude, and is permanently impregnated with the black dirt from Victoria Station. The hotel possesses a certain vigour and gusto but there is more to offend than please. **The Langham Hotel** in **Portland Place**, 1864, designed by **John Giles**, is different. Here is a much better site and a better quality, if enormous, hotel. It has two strongly decorated end pavilions to its main façade, but the original tower became a casualty to war-time bombing.

ECCLESIASTICAL BUILDINGS

The two **cathedrals** of this period, **Westminster** and **Truro**, have already been discussed (1197–8, LV, LX; pp. 466).

The number of **churches** built all over the country to accommodate the expanding population was phenomenal, but at no period of English architecture has there been such a paucity of examples of well-designed, attractive churches. They were nearly all built in Gothic style, most commonly Early English or Decorated Gothic. A sincere and earnest attempt was made to study and reproduce the original, Medieval plan, silhouette, detail and materials, but rarely did a Gothic Revival church of this period approach the original for quality. The carved detail tends to be too hard and mechanical and has a mass-production appearance. The materials are often too garish in hue or, quite soon, too black from industrial smoke. The theory that good men should labour to build good, ecclesiastical architecture was widely and strongly held, but seldom have so many good intentions failed so lamentably. The results were gaunt, forbidding or merely dull, cavernous, dark and gloomy and almost always unprepossessing. Among the better examples of the time are the following: **Christ Church, Kennington**, and **Roehampton Old Church** by Benjamin Ferrey; **The Transfiguration, Lewisham, St Michael's, Shoreditch, The Annunciation, Chislehurst**, and **The Ascension, Battersea**, by James Brooks; **St Bartholomew's, Brighton**, by Edmund Scott; and **St Peter's, Leamington Spa**, by Henry Clutton (1243). St John's at St Leonards-on-Sea, St Augustine's, Kilburn, St James the Less, Westminster, and All Saints, Margaret Street have already been discussed (1242 and p. 477; 1244, 1298, 1311 and p. 465; 1264, 1315, LIV, and p. 457; p. 465.

HOUSING AND TOWN PLANNING

Vast areas of open country were built upon in this century to house the increasing population. The bulk of such building was in industrial, urban areas. Some of it was soundly, if not always attractively, built and many a middle-class Victorian house, considered merely

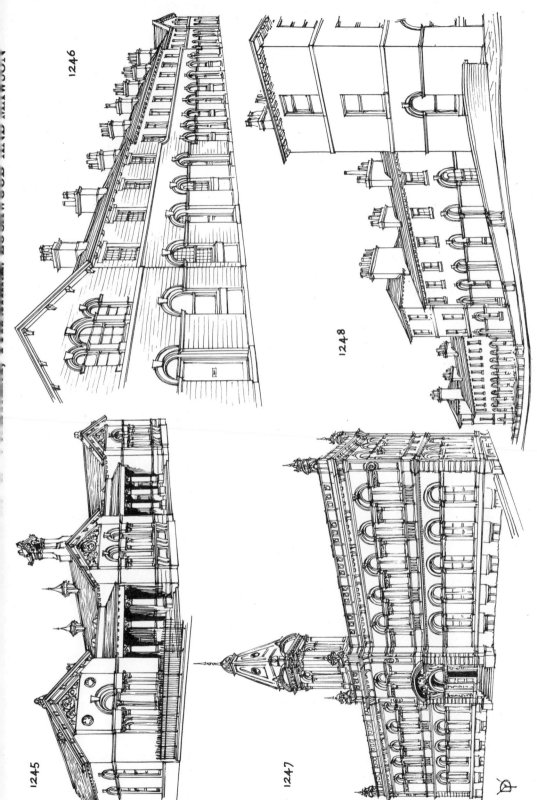

1245 Salt Boys' High School, 1867–8 1246, 1248 Stone terrace houses built on the steep slopes above the mill. Titus Street and George Street, 1854–70 1247 The Saltaire Institute, 1867–71

adequate in its day, is thought of as a mansion today and is split up into a number of flats. However, on the darker side, back-to-back houses were built in nearly all industrial towns, constructed 50 to the acre in row upon row, facing and backing into one another: a jungle of black, damp brick, housing underfed, often tubercular families in close confinement.

However, not all the blame should be laid on the Victorians. They created the immense population and it was often these great numbers of people crowding into the earlier dwellings which turned them into slums. Not all the mean houses of the mid- and later-nineteenth century had been built by the Victorians. Yet, theirs was the responsibility and this was not accepted until far too much time had passed. In the nineteenth century it was the rare individual who realised that the only satisfactory answer to the problem was town planning on a large scale, with safeguards for landowner, landlord, tenant and the individual. Eventually this need produced the twentieth-century garden cities and new towns. In the nineteenth century, however, there were some examples of this, carried out by individuals, necessarily on a small scale, but it was an important beginning in the solving of this great problem.

One very early example of this kind of idea was the town of **Saltaire** in Yorkshire. **Sir Titus Salt** decided in 1850 to move out of Bradford and set up his new mill for manufacturing alpaca cloth on the banks of the river Aire near Shipley. He built a mill and homes for his workpeople, a chapel, a school, almshouses, a hospital, an institute and a school of art. The architects who were responsible for the whole project were **Lockwood** and **Mawson**, both Yorkshiremen, and this complete scheme, organised by its founder Sir Titus Salt, was then unique in architectural history in England. The **mill**, which has since been added to, is an imposing Italianate design in stone: a long building broken by towers, and very symmetrical in treatment. The **earliest houses**, also of stone, were erected near the mill in 1852–1856 in terrace form. The design is simple and in keeping with the mill. The accommodation included a parlour, kitchen, pantry and cellar, three bedrooms and outside, a privy and coalplace. The streets were named after Sir Titus's large family of children; Titus, Caroline, George, William Henry, etc. Although somewhat deficient in the amenities which a working family expects today on a new town estate, the Saltaire houses are solidly built, reasonable in size, pleasant, if simple in appearance, and palaces compared to the hovels in Bradford from where these workers had come in 1852. The **chapel** was built in 1858–9, also of stone and near to the mill; it has a circular porch with Corinthian columns. In 1867 the **Salt Boys' High School** was begun, quickly followed by the **Saltaire Institute** and **School of Art**. From 1870 onwards more houses were built; the later ones were larger, more elaborate and more Victorian in design, but less original than the earlier examples. The whole scheme, which covered many years in the building, was of one spirit and treatment, all in the local stone, mainly Italian in inspiration but English Victorian in execution. Saltaire is a remarkable monument to its founder (1245–8, 1254, 1262, 1317).

A similar scheme but on a much smaller scale was initiated at **Copley** village near **Halifax**, Yorkshire, where a Grecian-styled mill and about **100 houses** were built to the designs of **W. H. Crossland** in the 1860s. The houses are simple, basically late Gothic in design and are also of stone.

A little later in the century a parallel experiment was carried out at **Bedford Park**, **Turnham Green**, in the London area. Here, however, was no industrial centre or an industrialist founder. In 1876 Mr J. T. Carr initiated the construction of a housing estate centred

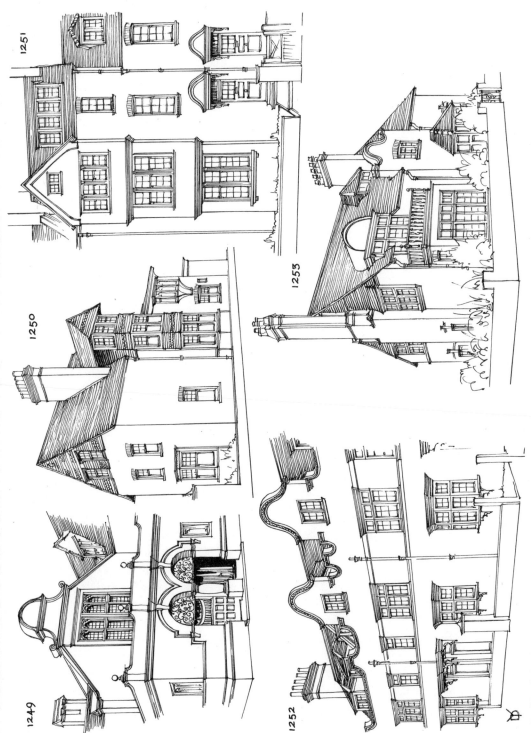

1251

1250

1253

1249

1252

Bedford Park, London, from 1876. Principal architect, Norman Shaw   1249 St Michael's Church porch   1250–3 Terrace and detached houses chiefly built in brick

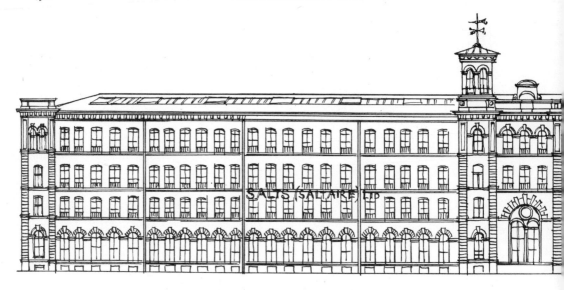

1254 Salt Mill, elevation facing Saltaire, near Bradford, 1851–3. Lockwood and Mawson

round a church, general stores and a club. **Norman Shaw** was appointed to design the church and some houses and was assisted by **Maurice Adams** and **E. J. May**. The building was carried out in brick and most of the houses were semi-detached, three- or four-bedroomed homes with two reception-rooms, suitable for families of moderate income. The designs were unpretentious in Shaw's Queen Anne and Dutch styles, using white-painted window and door openings and gabled roofs. Building continued over a long period and several architects participated later. The designs are good, with simple, clean lines, well in advance of their time (1249–53, 1261, 1318–19).

TOWN HOUSES AND FLATS

In large towns, particularly London, the urban area grew rapidly, and suburban building acquired a similarity of appearance whilst local character in houses became less marked. The bulk of such building was in brick, in plain red or yellow or, more often, in polychrome treatment, using black bricks for banded decoration. The medium-sized house was of this material, perhaps banded or dressed with stone; the front door was generally approached up a flight of steepish stone steps and was covered by a porch, supported on Gothic columns and capitals. The window and door openings were commonly in Gothic; windows were generally decorated with stained glass and the houses comprised a number of storeys including basement or cellar and, at the top, attics and dormers. Most rooms had fireplaces and a quantity of coal was burnt, causing a smoke pall over urban areas. Woodwork was generally painted brown, commonly grained, and both exterior and interior surfaces were liberally decorated. On the outside, panels of fruit and flower decoration were common, in terracotta or stone.

In more fashionable town areas larger houses were built; in **London** the districts of **Kensington, Paddington, Victoria** and **Holland Park**, for example, were developed. In

such areas the designs were generally still classical, with porticoes and classical columns. The brick was usually covered with stucco and painted. The lower storeys were rusticated; windows were sash-styled and pilastered orders decorated the façades. Above the cornice was a balustrade and hipped roof. Particular thoroughfares developed in the 1850s and '60s include **Princes Gate, Kensington; Exhibition Road, South Kensington; Cleveland Square Gardens, Paddington; Victoria Street, Queen's Gate** and the **Cromwell Road**. Towards the end of the century, plainer houses were built, still predominantly in red brick, but less polychrome was seen and a smaller quantity of ornament. Architects such as Shaw and Voysey exercised a considerable influence in this development. There was a great deal of terrace building in this period for all classes of the population in towns, from the working class rows of slums in heavily industrialised areas to the façades of South Kensington and Victoria; a range from the small, two-storeyed blocks to six-storeyed schemes in the centre of big cities. Few blocks of flats were erected until towns became crowded towards the end of the century. There were well-designed examples like Shaw's Albert Hall Mansions, but more commonly such buildings were tenement blocks of mean and ugly appearance to house the poorer sections of the population. Examples of town housing accommodation are illustrated in Figs. 1213–16, 1255–7, 1260, 1300 and 1314.

EDUCATIONAL BUILDINGS

The Universities

At **Oxford**, by the mid-nineteenth century, a large part of the Medieval college building was in dire need of restoration or rebuilding. It is considered unfortunate, even tragic, by many critics that this happened in this particular period, for it fell to the earnest Gothicists of the time, Butterfield, Waterhouse and Scott, to carry out the work. Earnestly and thoroughly

1255

1256

1257

1255 Blenheim Terrace, Manningham Lane, Bradford, Yorkshire. Stone terrace, *c.* 1855   1256 Nos 1–5 Grosvenor Place, London, S.W.1. Large-scale terrace architecture, *c.* 1867–75 (now partially replaced by modern building)   1257 Albert Hall Mansions, Kensington, London. Brick block of flats, 1879. Norman Shaw

1258 Exeter College Chapel, Oxford, 1864. Sir George Gilbert Scott

hey did so. The new work was in Gothic to match the old but, as was the case in ecclesiastical
building, somehow it so often did not succeed in this endeavour. It jarred, and even after a
century of weathering, in many cases it still does. Three colleges which received a large dose
of this treatment were Balliol, Exeter and University. At **Balliol, Butterfield** built a new
chapel to replace the old; this is described by some critics as a 'pink obscenity', by others
as 'the best feature of the college'. Much of the remainder, including the street façade, is by
Waterhouse, built 1867–8. This is forbidding, overbearing and gloomy, divided at intervals
by baronial turrets and gatehouses. The **hall**, built in the 1870s, is also by Waterhouse. At
Exeter, the most interesting feature of this time is the new **chapel** by **Sir George Gilbert
Scott.** The seventeenth-century chapel was demolished in 1856 and Scott's Decorated
Gothic design was based on the Sainte Chapelle in Paris (1258, 1263, 1307–8). At **University
College, Scott** also carried out considerable work on the **chapel** and designed the **Library
**(1230).

DOORWAYS 1850–1900

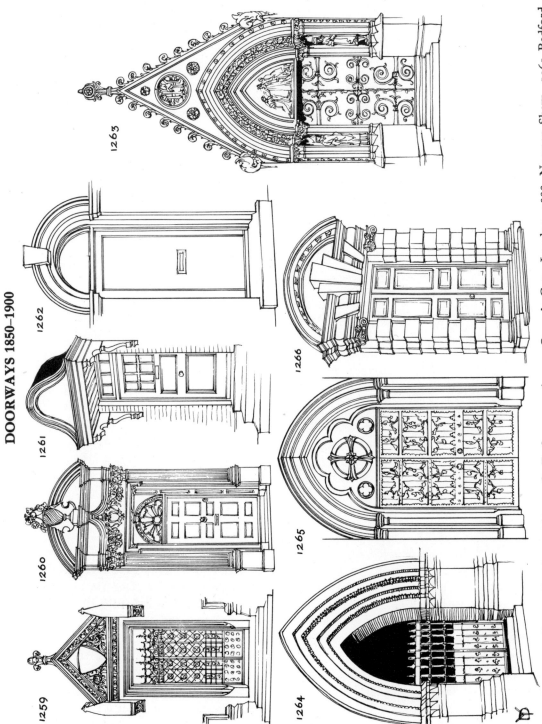

1259 The Law Courts, London, 1868–74. G. E. Street 1260 170 Queen's Gate, London, 1888. Norman Shaw 1261 Bedford Park, London, 1876. Norman Shaw 1262 House at Saltaire, Yorkshire, 1854–60. Lockwood and Mawson 1263 Exeter College

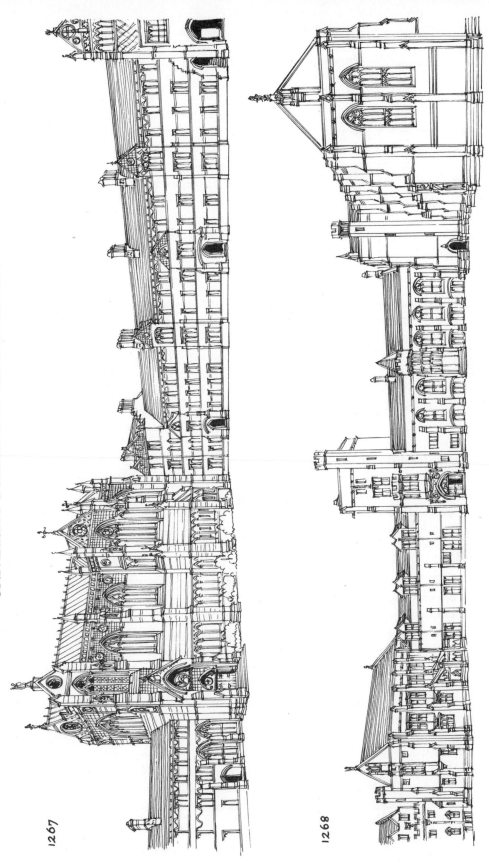

1267

1268

1267 Keble College, 1868–82: chapel and quadrangle. William Butterfield   1268 Mansfield College, 1886: general view. Basil Champneys

A number of new colleges were founded in this period and these are more successful architecturally: although still in Victorian Gothic, there is no disharmony of styles within a particular college. Among such foundations are those of Keble, Mansfield and Manchester. **Keble College** was opened in 1870 and the college architect over the period 1868–82 was **William Butterfield**. Keble is one of the most striking monuments to Victorian Gothic and has for many years aroused critical controversy. Like all Butterfield's work, it is an exercise in polychromy. He used red brick decorated in stripes and checks with stone and brick in black and white. Fortunately the college is situated away from the early collegiate building on the outskirts of the town and does not therefore clash with other architecture. It has mellowed greatly with time and now has a more pleasant colouring, attractive in the sunlight and fortunately uncontaminated by urban soot. The **chapel** built 1873–6, is the finest building of the college; it is monumental, finely proportioned and richly decorated. The interior is very typical of its period and therefore less pleasing to many of us. It is over-decorated with very little plain surface left anywhere. In the small memorial chapel here is the famous painting by Holman Hunt entitled 'The Light of the World'. The quadrangle is large and also contains the hall and library which are not on quite so monumental a scale (1229, 1265, 1267; LVI). **Mansfield College** founded in 1886, was designed by **Basil Champneys**. It presents a satisfactory Gothic layout built on three sides of a very large quadrangle, with central gatehouse and prominent side wings. The hall has a roofed, oriel window extending the full height of the building. Modern additions are now being constructed on available land opposite the main quadrangle (1268). **Manchester College**, built 1891–3, is by **Worthington**. It is also in the Gothic tradition but is less successful than Champneys' Mansfield College.

At **Cambridge** the Medieval buildings suffered less than those at Oxford from Gothic restoration and enlargement. Work had already been carried out in a number of colleges in the eighteenth century and early nineteenth century. At **Pembroke College, Waterhouse** built a new façade to Trumpington Street in 1871: a Gothic-turreted design which harmonises ill with Wren's chapel. At **St John's, Scott** built a large **chapel**, and at **Jesus, Waterhouse** added new blocks.

The more interesting work here in this period was in the **new foundations**, among which are Girton, Newnham and Selwyn colleges. **Girton college** is an unfortunate architectural essay, largely in strong red brick by **Waterhouse**. The college was built on a magnificent site several miles outside the town, and has fine trees and lawns. **Newnham College**, the other new foundation for women at this time, was designed largely by **Champneys**, and is a most pleasing example of his work towards the end of the century. There are a number of buildings arranged around lawns and gardens, in red brick with tiled roofs and white-painted window frames. The steeply sloping roofs have dormers, a high balustrade and tall chimneys, whilst at the ends of the blocks are curved gables and semicircular-headed window groups (1270, 1295, 1321). The main gateway, also of red brick, is in robust, early Renaissance pattern, with flanking towers and a sloping roof. The bronze gates were designed in commemoration of the first principal, Miss Clough (1233, 1280). **Selwyn College**, dating from 1882, is also largely in brick, and is built around a huge quadrangle in Tudor Gothic style. It was designed mainly by **Sir Arthur Blomfield** between 1895 and 1908. The chapel is built with a large Perpendicular Gothic window flanked by cupola-topped towers, on the quadrangle elevation;

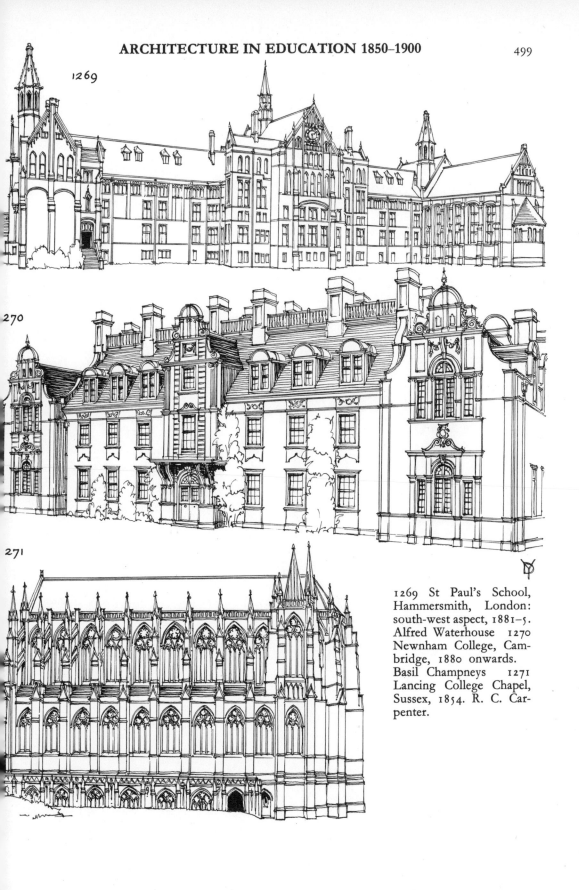

1269 St Paul's School, Hammersmith, London: south-west aspect, 1881–5. Alfred Waterhouse 1270 Newnham College, Cambridge, 1880 onwards. Basil Champneys 1271 Lancing College Chapel, Sussex, 1854. R. C. Carpenter.

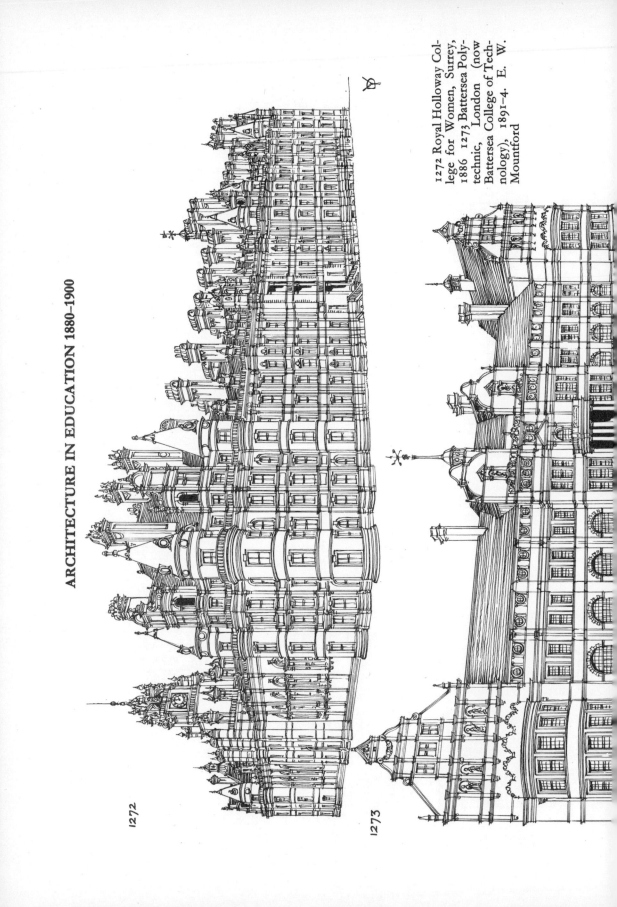

ARCHITECTURE IN EDUCATION 1880–1900

1272 Royal Holloway College for Women, Surrey, 1886 1273 Battersea Polytechnic, London (now Battersea College of Technology), 1891–4. E. W. Mountford

1272

1273

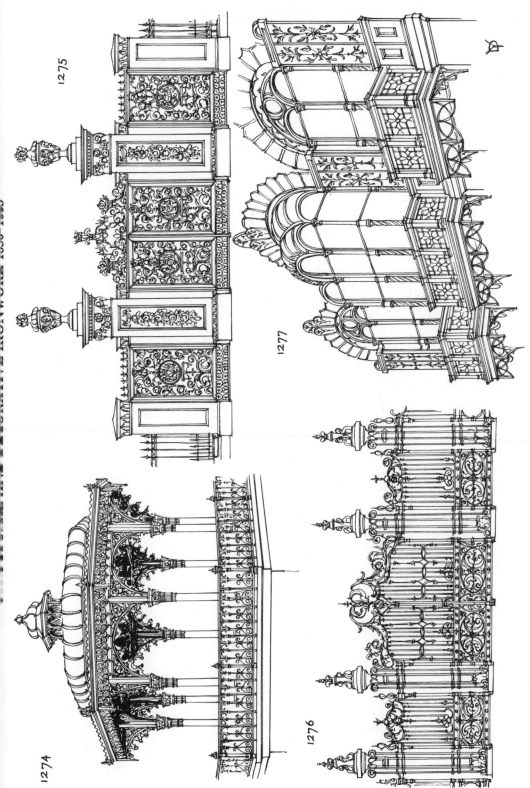

1274

1275

1277

1276

1274. Seaside ironwork, Brighton, Sussex   1275 Kew Gardens: entrance gateway, *c.* 1866   1276 Hyde Park, London: iron gates
(originally designed for the 1851 Exhibition)   1277 Station-master's office, Paddington Station, London: oriel window, 1852–4.
I. K. Brunel and M. D. Wyatt

1278 Kew Gardens: entrance gates, *c.* 1866   1279 Paddington Station, London, 1852–4. I. K. Brunel and M. D. Wyatt   1280 Newnham College, Cambridge: main gate, *c.* 1893. Basil Champneys   1281–2 Iron lamp standards, London: Fig. 1281 at Westminster and Fig. 1282 on the Embankment

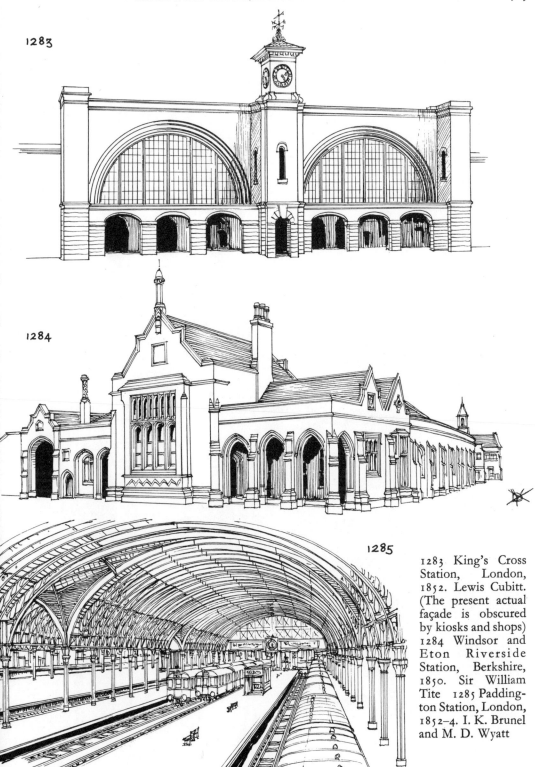

1283

1284

1285

1283 King's Cross Station, London, 1852. Lewis Cubitt. (The present actual façade is obscured by kiosks and shops) 1284 Windsor and Eton Riverside Station, Berkshire, 1850. Sir William Tite 1285 Paddington Station, London, 1852–4. I. K. Brunel and M. D. Wyatt

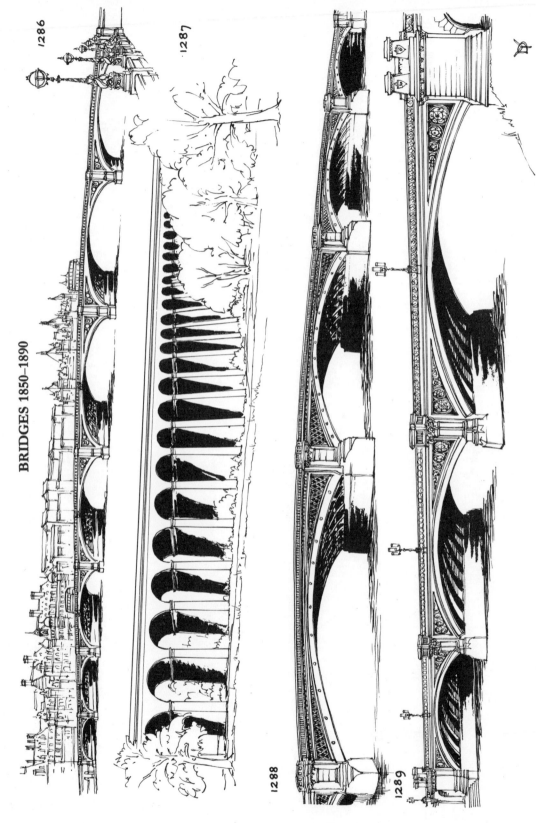

BRIDGES 1850–1890

1286

1287

1288

1289

1286 Westminster Bridge, London (Thames), 1857. Thomas Page 1287 Digswell Viaduct, Welwyn, Hertfordshire, c. 1850 1288
Trent Bridge, Nottingham (Trent), 1871. M. O. Tarbotton

1290

1291

1292

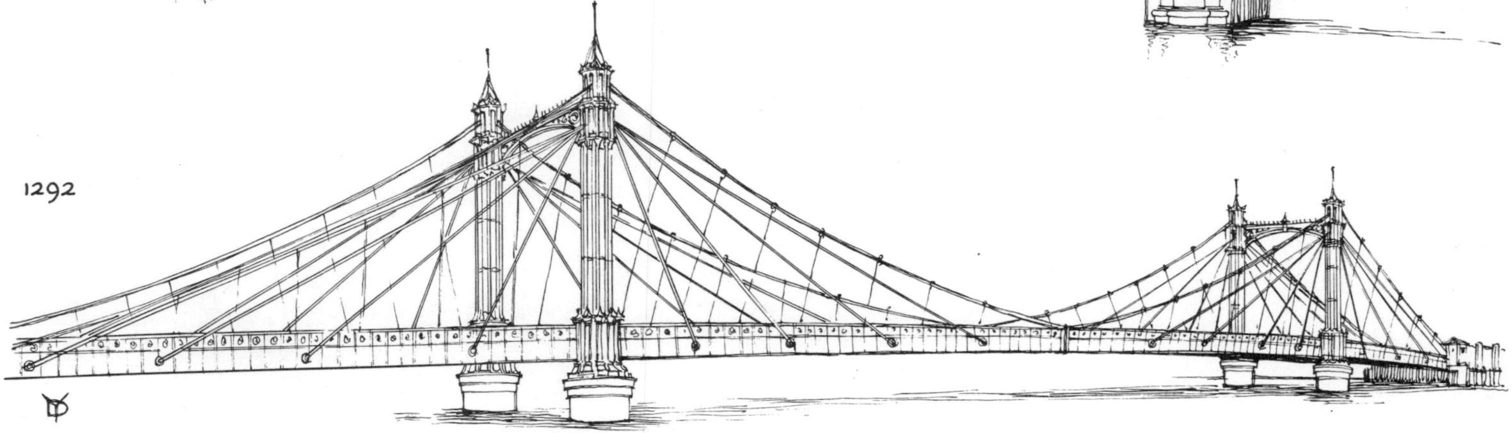

1290 Tower Bridge, 1894. Sir John Barry and Sir Horace Jones 1291 Hammersmith Bridge, 1887. Sir J. Bazalgette
1292 The Albert Bridge, 1872-3. R. M. Ordish

1293 The Forth Railway Bridge, 1882–90. Sir John Fowler and Sir Benjamin Baker

the gatehouse, in similar vein, has one turret tower and a central, oriel window over the carved Tudor Gothic doorway. The hall, which is early Renaissance in conception, is rather later, being built in the early twentieth century. The whole layout is attractive and peaceful, redolent of the wealth and security of its age (1225–6).

Schools and Colleges

A number of schools and colleges were built at this time; also, in towns, the newer evening institutes and polytechnics. **Cheltenham Ladies' College** was opened in 1854. It was extended bit by bit and now covers a large area. The main buildings are Gothic in design. **St Paul's School, Hammersmith, Lancing College, Sussex**, and **Rugby School** have already been discussed (1269, 1271, 1316; pp. 459, 466, 465). Typical of the **polytechnic** type of design of the 1890s is that at **Battersea** (now Battersea College of Technology), designed in 1891–4 by **E. W. Mountford**. Built in a mixture of brick and stone, with tiled roof, it has terminal gabled blocks and a complicated central gabled feature with a Doric entrance portico of stone. The windows are of sash design and at each end is a curved two-storey bay window. As is standard practice now, modern additions are being erected adjacent to the building, architecturally most incongruous and lacking the 'individuality' of the older building (1273). Near Virginia Water in Surrey in 1886 was designed the **Royal Holloway College for Women** (now a part of London University). Situated in beautiful, sheltered grounds, this is a very large, most Victorian, and quite amazing example of architecture. Of brick and stone, it is built round an enormous rectangular plan in French château style, with innumerable pointed turrets and decorative chimney-stacks. Over the main entrance on the principal façade is an elaborate clock tower, balustraded and decorated by scrolls and vase-shaped urns. It is a museum piece indeed, but a fascinating one. Considered in the light of the ubiquitous rectilinear building of the mid-twentieth century, here is a refreshing, if exhausting contrast (1232, 1272).

BUILDING AND DECORATION IN CAST IRON

Iron, cast or wrought, was used more and more in the second half of the nineteenth century for building construction and decoration. Steel began to be made also, but it was many years before it was produced in large quantity. Its use did, however, make new designs in bridges possible, for the greater tensile strength of steel permitted larger spans. The iron used in constructional work was commonly wrought, but cast iron was in ubiquitous use for decorative work in the form of railings, gates, balconies, seats and even furniture. At holiday resorts, particularly at the seaside, its employment was widespread in piers, seaside shelters, bandstands and arcades. The designs became much more ornate than those of the first half of the century. Flowers, fruit, animals, birds and cherubs decorated seats and shelters. There was vigour and robustness in these patterns and they are distinctive of their age. Some of the lamp standards, for instance, and railings, are fine examples of the craft, and it is a matter for regret that so many of these have been removed in favour of the concrete, sodium lamp-holders of the present day. Much of the ironwork was in the form of standardised mass-production articles and much of it was crudely and badly designed. There are, however, exceptions to the general rule, and it is to be hoped that some of these will survive modernisation. Typical interesting examples are illustrated in Figs. 1274–82.

RAILWAY ARCHITECTURE

This was the culminating period for the great railway age: a tremendous number of railway stations were constructed, large and small, in country and in town. Comparatively few of these survive in the condition in which they were built. In many instances, especially in towns, a later hotel façade has obscured the original station front. In **London** two of the finest stations of the period still exist largely in their original condition: King's Cross and

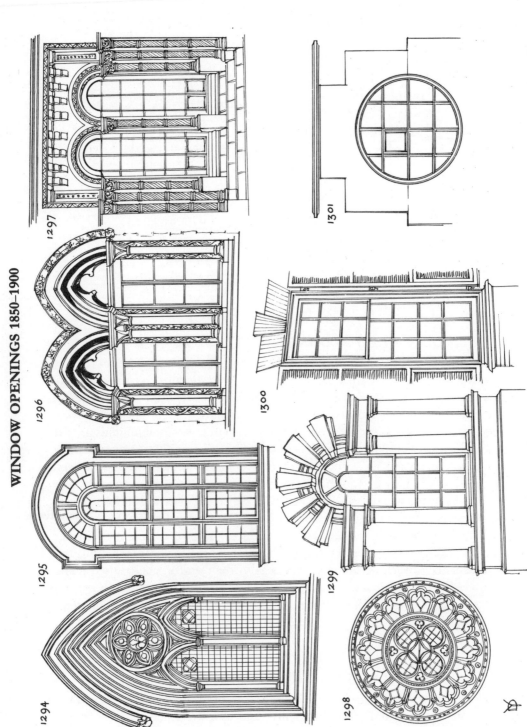

WINDOW OPENINGS 1850-1900

1294 The Law Courts, 1868–74. G. E. Street 1295 Newnham College, Cambridge, 1880. Basil Champneys 1296 The University Museum, Oxford, 1855–60. Deane and Woodward 1297 The Natural History Museum, London, 1873–9. Alfred Waterhouse 1298 St Augustine's Church, Kilburn, 1870–80. J. L. Pearson 1299 Bryanston House, Dorset, 1890. Norman Shaw 1300 170 Queen's Gate, London 1888. Norman Shaw 1301 The Orchard, Chorley Wood, Hertfordshire, 1900. C. F. A. Voysey

Paddington. **King's Cross** was built 1850–2; its façade was designed by **Lewis Cubitt** and it is a great example of its time. Unlike **Scott's** neighbouring Gothic hotel façade, it is simple, powerful and unpretentious. There are two tremendous semicircular arches boldly projecting and a finely proportioned central, clock tower. The lunettes are glazed and, below these on the lower storey, are six segmental-arched openings and a central porch. In front of these there is now, unfortunately, a hideous conglomeration of kiosks, shops and huts. In the drawing in Fig. 1283 these have been omitted. The station itself possesses a fine double shed, 800 feet in length. **St Pancras Station** is illustrated in Plate LVIII.

Paddington Station, built 1852–4, was designed by **Matthew Digby Wyatt** and **Isambard Kingdom Brunel**. Wyatt was responsible for the fine craftsmanship and pattern of the ironwork in roofing, columns and decoration, whilst Brunel was the station engineer. The remarkable roof, with its cast-iron trusses and columnar supports, still exists, as does also the wall decoration, as for example, the station-master's oriel office window. At Paddington, the use of cast iron is artistically and functionally at its best, not merely a copy of earlier designs in different materials (1277, 1279, 1285).

A completely different type of station façade can be seen in the rural design at **Windsor and Eton Riverside Station**, designed in 1850 by **Sir William Tite**. Here is a simple, brick and stone, Gothic façade with its royal porch still intact opposite the gates to Windsor Castle (1234, 1284).

BRIDGES

The majority of late Victorian bridges are not noted for their beauty, but most of them were well constructed and advantage was taken of new discoveries in the use of cast and wrought iron and steel. Among such examples, three are illustrated on page 504, Trent Bridge, Nottingham, and two London examples, Westminster and Blackfriars. **Trent Bridge**, a road bridge, was built in 1871 by **M. Tarbotton**. It has three 100-foot spans and is constructed with balustrade, cornice and arches in cast iron (1289). **Westminster Bridge**, with seven arches, was designed by **Thomas Page** in 1857 (1286). **Blackfriars**, by **Joseph Cubitt**, was built in 1863–9 and has three cast- and wrought-iron arches with cast-iron parapet above. The central arch has a span of 185 feet (1288).

Many **suspension bridges** were built at this time. Two **London** examples are illustrated on page 505. **The Albert Bridge**, designed 1872–3, was by **R. M. Ordish**. Here, both suspension and cantilever principles are incorporated. Each river pier consists of two cast-iron columns filled with concrete. The towers are of cast iron and tie bars radiate from the top of these towers to the deck sides. The central span is 400 feet. This bridge, together with the **Hammersmith** suspension design, built 1887, constitute London's two oldest surviving suspension bridges (1291–2).

Among many examples, two famous bridges in particular do not fall into any obvious category and merit more detailed discussion. Neither is beautiful but both are impressive and are feats of engineering. These are the Forth Bridge in Scotland and Tower Bridge, London. The statistics for the **Forth Railway Bridge**, built over the Firth of Forth near Edinburgh between 1882 and 1890, are astonishing. A labour force of 5,000 men was employed over this period, working day and night. The cost was over £3,500,000. The bridge consists of two spans of 1,710 feet and two of 690 feet; the length, including approach

III   St Pancras Station, London, 1866–70

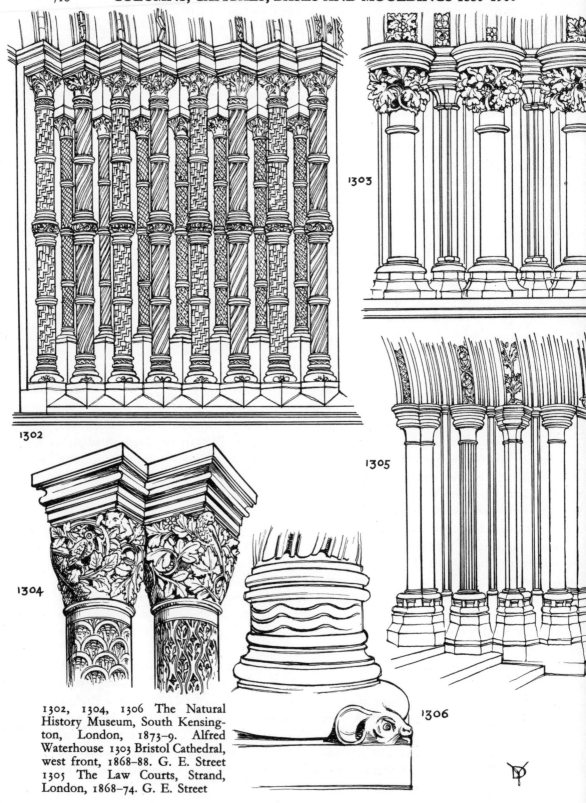

1302

1303

1304

1305

1306

1302, 1304, 1306 The Natural History Museum, South Kensington, London, 1873–9. Alfred Waterhouse 1303 Bristol Cathedral, west front, 1868–88. G. E. Street 1305 The Law Courts, Strand, London, 1868–74. G. E. Street

1307–8 Exeter College, Oxford, 1857–64: chapel doorway. Sir G. G. Scott 1309 Grosvenor Place: corbel, *c.* 1867 1310 Iron lamp standard, Brighton 1311 St Augustine's Church; Kilburn, 1870–80: doorway, tympanum. J. L. Pearson 1312 Prudential Assurance Building, Holborn: oriel window. Alfred Waterhouse 1313 Grim's Dyke, 1877: corbel. Norman Shaw 1314 196 Queen's Gate, London, 1875: ornament. Norman Shaw

1315 St James-the-Less, Westminster, 1858–61.
G. E. Street 1316 Lancing College, 1854: flying
buttress. R. C. Carpenter 1317 Saltaire Church,
Yorkshire, 1866–71: tower 1318 St Michael's
Church, Bedford Park, 1876–7: lantern. Norman
Shaw 1319 St Michael's Church: buttress
1320 Grim's Dyke, 1872: brick chimney. Norman
Shaw 1321 Newnham College, Cambridge:
lantern, c. 1880. Basil Champneys 1322 Gros-
venor Place, London, c. 1867: balustrade

viaducts, is over 1½ miles; the viaduct is 158 feet above water level and its width is 27 feet. The largest tubes are 12 feet in diameter. 54,000 tons of steel were used in the construction and 109,000 tons of concrete. The bridge, designed by **Sir Benjamin Baker** and **Sir John Fowler**, has been in continuous service since 1890, taking trains at express speed, and it is only now, in the 1960s, that a road bridge is being built alongside to take the motor traffic. The bridge was built on cantilever principles, and there are three giant cantilever elements linked together by short trussed spans. Each cantilever element consists of an iron framework tower rising to 360 feet above high water level. The four 12-foot diameter tubes of each skeletal tower are supported on four separate masonry piers; the dead weight on each pier is 16,000 tons. From these towers the cantilever arms extend; the extreme ends rest on granite pylons. The saying that the painting of the Forth Bridge is a continuous process is justified; there are 145 acres to paint, and the painters take three years to do this, by which time work restarts (1293).

Tower Bridge was built in 1886–94 to the designs of the city architect **Sir Horace Jones** and the engineer **Sir John Barry**. It is a complicated structure which was planned to harmonise with the near-by Tower of London. It does not really do so and has a typical Victorian quality, with two massive towers in a highly decorated hybrid style partly Medieval, partly Renaissance. It has now been accepted as an essential part of the London landscape and is affectionately regarded as a monument. From the engineering point of view it is a remarkable movable bridge, which has been operated efficiently and unceasingly since its construction. The central span is 200 feet whilst the two side spans from tower to shore are 270 feet each. The piers are of granite on concrete foundations, and the towers have a framework of steel, faced with granite and stone. They are 206 feet high above road level and are linked 140 feet above the water by two steel footways reached from the towers, but these are not now in use for foot passengers. The bascules are raised by hydraulic machinery and each weighs over 1,000 tons. The operation can be carried out in four minutes (1290).

CHAPTER XII

The Twentieth Century 1900 - 1945

To attempt to sum up and delineate the trends and styles of architecture in the England of these years is a much more difficult task than for previous centuries. For one reason, we are still too near in time to be able to accord to the buildings their due place in the history of architecture. Secondly, this half century has witnessed social, economic and political upheavals which have no parallel in the past. There have been two world wars causing an almost complete cessation of building and an uprooting of the population, together with widespread destruction of property; there have been several economic depressions—largely resulting from these wars—of which the most formidable hindered building in the years 1929–33. The economic factor has gradually become more dominant: during this period and increasingly as time passes the reason for the choice of a design is economic and cost-saving rather than architectural, aesthetic or functional. Thirdly, the actual styles of architecture have been revolutionised by two outstanding influences: the modern discoveries and developments in building materials, leading to steel-frame construction and use of concrete and allied substances; and the desire of architects in many parts of Europe, America and England to get away from derivative and evolutionary design founded on the two primary styles of classical and Gothic architecture and to create a new style owing nothing to what has preceded it, and to be based on and to use fully these new materials. These fundamental factors—the economic and political upheavals, the need for economy, the new materials and the modern movement in architecture—present a very broad basis for the study of architecture in England in the twentieth century up to 1945. To understand how these factors have influenced the architectural designs of these years, there must be further study of many allied and alternative movements which subdivide and affect the larger ones.

At the beginning of the century and until 1914, when the First World War virtually put an end to building expansion, the trend was largely a continuation of late Victorian work. Many of the buildings erected to Edwardian designs were based on classical or Gothic lines, more often the former, and there was still a considerable use of ornamental and sculptural decoration. Such works as the **Cardiff City Centre** and the **Central Hall, Westminster**, both designed by the firm of **Lanchester, Stewart and Rickards** (1355–6, 1367), illustrate a robust, baroque classicism closely allied to the Petit Palais in Paris, which had been built a few years earlier, in 1900, by Charles Girault. The designs are good, the detail finely carved and, though to mid-twentieth century eyes a little over-decorated, they have stood the test of time well and set a high standard for civic buildings in our cities. In these years steel framing for building construction was used in a number of instances, not as a basis for architectural form, but simply to produce a more economic, sounder structure. This was then clothed in a stone façade of similar type to that used on constructions without steel framing. The possibilities of a new architectural style based on steel-girder construction were not realised or, at least, were not explored.

At this same time the movement of l'Art Nouveau enjoyed its brief flowering in England. This was one of the first of the numerous attempts in this century to break with the Gothic/classical tradition and to produce a new architecture. It was very much a minority movement, especially in England, where it has had no real permanent effect. Its influence was strongly decorative rather than architectural and was more profound upon painting, stained glass, mural decoration, for example, than upon three-dimensional arts. The origins were Continental, primarily Belgian, but also from Germany, Austria and Spain. One of its chief aims was an achievement of aesthetic beauty; it is a sad paradox that in England, at any rate, the results were so often unbeautiful, sometimes bizarre and, in the domestic field, frequently uncomfortable. By 1914 the movement had largely died out.

When the building impetus gathered force after the war there was tremendous activity in the years 1920–9. In both Europe and England buildings damaged and destroyed during the war had to be replaced; urban communities were expanding and populations increasing. In England, the vast majority of such building, and especially that for civic purposes, was in the classical/Gothic tradition. However, it was not a straightforward imitation of the work of earlier ages. There was a marked and increasing trend towards simplification, larger plain wall areas, less decoration and less sculptural ornament. In towns, especially London, the common materials were brick or Portland stone; after 1918 more commonly based upon steel-framed construction, but still designed on the same classic lines. These traditional patterns were set and exampled by such architects as **Sir Reginald Blomfield** as in, for instance, his Quadrant and Piccadilly Circus, by **Sir Edwin Lutyens** in a more original but basically traditional form in his numerous banks, and other civic work, and by **E. Vincent Harris** with his many town halls. In the domestic sphere the brick or stone country house was also still on traditional lines when designed by such architects as **Sir Guy Dawber** or **Sir Ernest Newton**. This movement was also, like so much of the architecture of the period, led by **Sir Edwin Lutyens**. The principal exponent in the parallel simplification of the Gothic motif was **Sir Giles Gilbert Scott** who set the pattern with his Liverpool Cathedral (1344, LIX), and followed this with many churches and much collegiate work.

From 1929 to about 1933, building work received a severe set-back. The depression, both in England and on the Continent, took a severe toll of building schemes which had been planned or started. From 1933 the industry got under way once more and a considerable quantity of work was carried out before 1939 when, once again, building virtually ceased for a second World War. In the years 1933–9 the same trends continued: a further simplification, less decoration, larger plain areas of wall, especially on the exterior of buildings. A large proportion of the buildings of this period are extremely dull. An emptiness, a vacuous plainness had replaced the Victorian and Edwardian fondness for over-decoration. This was a negative approach. If decoration and ornament are taken from architecture, to achieve an aesthetically pleasing result it is essential to create an exquisite proportion to the building, a subtlety of line, a refinement of three-dimensional shape. Rarely did this happen, and all over our country today are solid, solemn blocks of stone or brick, unadorned, dull. Among such mediocrity cannot be included the activities of **Sir Edwin Lutyens**. His work continued to be traditional, largely classical, simplified but always finely proportioned and exquisite in its sparing detail. Aesthetically it may be chilly, a little too intellectual for everyone's taste, but it is never dull.

Together with this basic, simplified traditional movement in England were many under-currents. It was from these hidden factors that modern architecture was born and evolved. It was not, however, until after 1945 in this country that this movement broke through and became the architectural style, the established vogue. One of the strong 'opposition' factors in the inter-war years was that generally described as 'functionalism'. Like most of the modern architectural themes its admirers and exponents were much more active on the Continent and in the U.S.A. than in England. Also, like all other such breakaway movements from the classical/Gothic tradition, its aim was a new architecture which was beholden to nothing from the past. As the name suggests, the basic tenet was that the building should be designed primarily to fulfil a given purpose. A worthy aim; surely no one could dis-agree and, many would feel, one which had inspired architects for centuries, even if the results could not always be justified by such a criterion. However, the endeavours of the functionalist did not end here. It was divined that, if the building was planned so that its structure was perfect for its required use, there was only one way this could be achieved and, as a natural corollary, only that way could be correct; most important of all, that way must result in a design pleasant to the beholder. This theory contains obvious deficiencies. Utilitar-ian building naturally has great uses, but to say that it is automatically architecture omits the need of humanity for beauty in this art. Beauty does not necessarily follow functional design, although it can, of course, do so. This theory, that what is perfectly functional must also be aesthetically satisfactory, has a parallel in the Ecclesiologist view in the nineteenth century that only a good man could design beauty in architecture. Architectural design which fully pleases the eye is a much more complex and elusive quality than either of these facile theories would purport. One of the earliest functionalists in England was Professor W. R. Lethaby, but the strongest influence of the movement was much later, in the years 1920–35, when it enjoyed a considerable following, on the Continent in particular. This revival and enthusiasm was largely brought about by its new leader in this period, **Le Corbusier**, a Swiss architect practising in France.

The extreme view that fitness for purpose must be the be-all and end-all of architecture was held by only a few architects, but in a modified form the movement presented a solid basis for modern architecture. When the fitness includes siting, landscaping, materials, construction, style and decorative treatment, together with the intellectual and spiritual approach to the design it is, of course, an admirable precept. In its narrow form, the theory would exclude many of the great works of architecture in the world; of what use, for example, are the seventeenth- and eighteenth-century church steeples?

THE MODERN MOVEMENT

The principal source, as opposed to the derivatory expression, for this movement towards a new architecture came from the Continent. Here was the strongest determination and enthusiasm to break away from the traditional shackles and the chief centre for this was in central Europe. Representative architects of many countries felt this desire and worked separately and, in some cases together, to evolve a new architecture. Among such men were

Walter Gropius, Peter Behrens and **Erich Mendelsohn** from **Germany, Le Corbusier** working in **France** and **Frank Lloyd Wright** in the **U.S.A.** The movement began before the First World War but was primarily built up between 1918 and 1939. These men were united by a belief in the prime importance of a building's functional purpose, a desire for a new architecture to reflect the new industrial age of the twentieth century, a distaste for ornament *per se*, and the feeling that the aesthetic qualities of the new age should find co-operation and meaning in the scientific characteristics of this period. A favourite maxim of the time was that a machine designed for an engineering or a scientific purpose was not built with any idea of aesthetic quality but only for its essential purpose, yet, when complete, it was beautiful. Architecture should evolve in a similar manner. Art purely for the sake of art was outmoded. Art must exist only for the new age, for its science, its technical achievements such as vacuum cleaners, television sets, refrigerators, aircraft and engineering plant; here was the new field for art; as an expression of beauty only, art was archaic. Early essays in the twentieth century on these principles, especially in housing, were disappointing. The results showed plain concrete blocks relieved only by a railing, a lone tree or a gate. Stark simplicity was the order of the day. Undoubtedly a new approach to architecture was needed; classical columns and Gothic pinnacles had been used too long as the only possible architectural expression for all classes of building. But was this new architecture the answer? It was not. But it was new, and needed time to re-evaluate and develop. In the 1930s it began to do this. However, there was a strong feeling that such modern architects must make use of all the new materials and fabrics. A praiseworthy concept, but one which, in practice, led often to inefficient, unfunctional buildings and, certainly equally often, to unaesthetic ones.

It is, nevertheless, easy to criticise and much more difficult to do what these men were trying to do. For centuries architectural proportions and design had been governed by struc-tural means. Steel and concrete building meant that many of the old concepts of weight, support and strength were invalid. The architect was now freer than ever before to design heights, spans and loads far greater than had previously been known. The problem was how to take advantage of this. The consequent freedom of design created a challenge not easy to accept and make the most of, especially to men trained in certain precepts of proportion and plan. Experience by trial and error was necessary with the qualities of these new materials. For example, steel has to be covered as it will rust if left open to the atmosphere; concrete weathers most unpleasantly, not like stone; columns need not be of a certain diameter in proportion to height now, but what proportion is desirable if a designer has a free choice? These and many other problems needed a long time to be solved satisfactorily and even today many concrete walls are left uncovered, and after several years present a very poor appear-ance, simply because the cost of facing them with ceramics, glass or faïence is considered too costly.

Meanwhile in this period in England the modern movement was evolving far more slowly than in Europe and it is noteworthy that nearly all the architects who constructed or designed architecture in the modern vein in England before 1939 were men of foreign extraction. Because of dictatorships and oppression in Europe during the period 1920–39, many such men of great talent came to France, England and the U.S.A. to make their homes in the greater peace and security which these countries had to offer and to contribute by their gifts and ideas to the architecture of their adopted lands. Because of various difficulties, political, economic or personal preference, a number of the men who came to England in the 1920s and '30s went on later to make their final homes in the U.S.A. and have left with us only fragmentary examples of their work.

Among such men who led the modern architectural field in England were **Wells Coates**, who had been born in Tokyo but had lived in Canada, **Amyas Connell** and **Basil Ward** from New Zealand, **Serge Chermayeff** from the Caucasus, **Erich Mendelsohn, Walter Gropius** and **Peter Behrens** from Germany and **Berthold Lubetkin** from the Caucasus who had also lived for some time in Paris. One of the very few truly English architects of this group was **E. Maxwell Fry** who carried out a good deal of work with Walter Gropius as, for example, the **Village College** at **Impington**, Cambridgeshire (1417). Fry also designed **Kensal House, Paddington** (1414), and **Sassoon House, Peckham**. In the 1930s much fine modern work, which has since been universally acclaimed, was carried out by the firm of **Tecton** which was founded by **Lubetkin**. Among the best-known works of this firm are the **Highpoint flats** at **Highgate** (1415), the **Finsbury Heath Centre** and the Penguin Pool at the **Zoological Gardens, Regent's Park**.

In addition to Le Corbusier, whose work has kept him primarily in France, and who has long been regarded as one of the chief originators of modern architecture, is an equally famous architect—**Walter Gropius**. Gropius, who was born in Berlin in **1883**, was trained in Germany and set up practice in Berlin in 1910. He is primarily known as the **Director** of the **Bauhaus** (*Das Staatliche Bauhaus*) at Weimar. In response to the invitation by the town council, he designed a Bauhaus at **Dessau** to which the School of Design was moved in 1923. Here he evolved a new approach towards the teaching of his students. He taught them the mutual relationship of building, architecture, equipment, furniture, interior decoration and lighting, and established a close connection between the mass-production crafts and the fine arts, always illustrating how one was needed and should dovetail into the other. Unlike William Morris, who had tried to hold back the era of mass-production, Gropius accepted it and he believed that architecture must adapt itself to an industrial age but must not suffer by so doing; it must inspire and assist. He tried to take every advantage of modern methods and materials, especially glass and steel. He built one of the first glass curtain-walled buildings in his **Fagus factory** in 1911. Gropius is widely travelled and is one of the most dynamic and visionary architects of the twentieth century. He is teacher, builder and designer and is working still in America. One of the émigrés from Nazi Germany, he came to England in 1934, where he designed buildings with Maxwell Fry. He left for America in 1937, where he had been appointed Professor of Architecture at the Graduate School of Design at Harvard.

Another émigré from Nazi Germany was **Erich Mendelsohn** who was born in East Prussia in **1887**. He studied architecture at the Technische Hochschule in Berlin and in Munich and set up practice in 1912. He was well known as a pioneer of modern architecture in Germany and for the use of glass, steel and ferro-concrete. Among his buildings there were the Department Store for Schoeken at **Chemnitz**, his gigantic Luxor Palast in **Berlin** and, in **Jerusalem**, the University Medical Department. One of his early works was his design in concrete for the Einstein Tower at **Potsdam**; a physical laboratory and observatory designed especially for Professor Einstein's research work. Mendelsohn then built the power station at **Haifa**, the Textile Trust Factory at **Leningrad** and in 1933 finally came to settle in England. He went into partnership with **Serge Chermayeff**. Their best-known work in England is the **De la Warr Pavilion** at **Bexhill-on-Sea**, Sussex (1396). Mendelsohn later went to the University of California and he died in the U.S.A. in 1953.

SIR EDWIN LUTYENS 1869–1944

Like Sir John Soane a century earlier, Lutyens early dedicated himself to architecture and was absorbed by it and contributed to it all his life, remaining at work almost until his death. During this working life he dominated the English architectural scene; there were several outstanding architects in this period, but only to Lutyens can the label of genius be deservedly applied. He was above all things an artist; his taste was impeccable and one of his greatest architectural qualities was his innate sense of proportion in the relationship of line, tone and mass. Like Sir William Chambers, his attention to detail was infinite and he was satisfied only with the best which he could achieve. He treated architecture as an art and in this respect he is unsurpassed in the twentieth century. He has been criticised in late years for this view, as it is now often said that architecture is a science not an art. Regrettably, this is now largely so, and it is sometimes difficult to know where civil engineering ends and architecture begins. Lutyens' work is criticised by some for its traditional quality, for its use of traditional materials and for his adherence to established proportions and methods. However, although he designed much of his work in the classical and Renaissance idiom, he transposed the styles to his own conception and a Lutyens Doric Order or Roman ornament is always readily recognisable as such; he had Wren's faculty of making these motifs and ideas peculiarly his own.

Lutyens was born in 1869, the eleventh child in a large family. Owing to delicate health in childhood he spent much of his time at home and learnt early to study for and by himself. At the age of 16 he began his studies at the Royal College of Art, and in 1887 became an articled pupil to the office of Sir Ernest George. When barely 20 he set up his own practice in London. At this time, in 1890, there were still enough people in England with money to build their own houses and to employ an architect to design them. In this Lutyens was fortunate, and from then until 1914 he built up a large country-house practice. He was much influenced by the work of Norman Shaw and by that of Philip Webb, and his early country-house designs show this influence. They were irregular in plan, informal, and he used brick and half-timber in Shaw's Elizabethan and Queen Anne manner.

After 1905 his work turned more to the austere and the classical. He used stone where possible, although one of the features of Lutyens' work has always been his feeling for material, and his desire, like that of Webb, Voysey and Shaw, to employ a wide range of materials, local if possible. After 1914, for architects, country-house building was never quite the same again. Never again have they been able to build such houses reasonably untrammelled by thought of cost, land and space. Not many private houses of any size were built between 1918 and 1939, but Lutyens built a fair proportion of them. From 1920 onwards his civic practice was growing. He built blocks of offices, housing estates, memorials and a number of large banks. Of his two principal achievements, only one has been carried out—the extensive civic work at New Delhi, which is beyond the scope of this book. The other, the Roman Catholic Cathedral at Liverpool, fell a victim to lack of funds and the

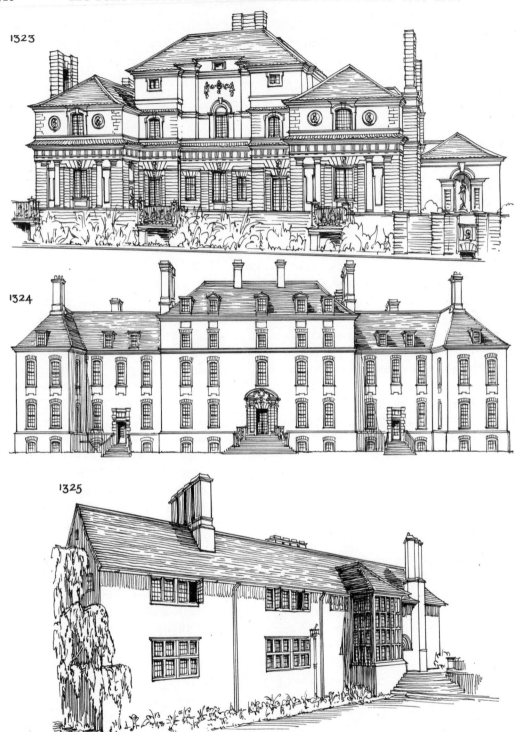

1323 'Heathcote', Ilkley, Yorkshire, 1906. Stone   1324 Great Maytham, Rolvenden, Kent, 1910. Brick   1325 The Deanery, Sonning, Berkshire, 1899–1901. Brick

Second World War, and then the architect died. Lutyens' cathedral will now never be built.

Lutyens felt very strongly about the changing position of the architect in twentieth-century professional society. He thought that architecture was becoming too much a mass-production machine, with its aim efficiency not art. To him, beauty in architecture was an essential quality and the 1920s and '30s were providing architecture aesthetically vulgar. His disagreement and disapproval were so strong that in 1929 he resigned from the Royal Institute of British Architects because he felt that it was becoming a trade union and not a learned society.

Lutyens was elected a Royal Academician in 1920. He became President of the Royal Academy in 1938. He was awarded the Royal Gold Medal for Architecture in 1921. He died in 1944 and his ashes were interred in St Paul's Cathedral.

Lutyens' first important commission was the **country house** at **Munstead Wood, Godalming**, Surrey, which he designed in 1896. The unusual feature of this design is the first-floor gallery which, in order to provide extra breadth, he constructed to overhang the hall below by nearly six feet. The house is built of local stone and has plain, gabled, steep roofs and a massive brick chimney. Here, in this simple, clean-lined but romantic house he set out on his career of building his so-called Surrey-styled houses. There followed in 1899 **'The Orchards', Godalming**, and **'Goddards', Abinger Common**, both a mixture of rough-cast and moulded brick and with tall chimneys and gables. **The Deanery Gardens, Sonning**, Berkshire, was built in 1899–1901. This also is in brick with tall, grouped chimneys and a brick semicircular arched and stepped doorway. There is a Medieval flavour to the hall, with timber roof and leaded light bay window. The house is set in delightful surroundings near the river in a beautiful garden landscaped on more than one level (1325, 1427). In the same period—1899—came **Tigbourne Court, Hambledon**, Surrey. This is a larger house and more symmetrical, although the tall chimneys are still much in evidence. There is an entrance colonnade and impressive, curved flanking walls. Here, Lutyens used Bargate stones and brick quoins, also horizontal bands of tiles; tile voussoirs appear in the arches. The entrance façade is most striking (1328).

After 1900 a greater variety of design can be seen in Lutyens' houses. A notable example of this is **'Heathcote'** at **Ilkley** in Yorkshire, built in 1906 of the local stone to suit the quite different landscape and colouring of the Pennines in contrast to the Surrey Hills. At Heathcote he employed the classical medium. The house is strictly symmetrical with a large central block (46 feet square) and two rectangular side wings. On the garden front he has used the Roman Doric order and has concentrated the focal point of the design on the ground floor. The house is most successful and illustrated at the time that Lutyens' versatility extended far beyond his romantic country-house blueprint (1323). Also in this period Lutyens built **'Marshcourt'**, Hampshire, 1902, a Tudor design in chalk and stone, **Little Thakeham**, Sussex, 1903, a more symmetrical house in local stone, and **Overstrand Hall**, Norfolk, built round a court. In 1909 followed the very large house of **Great Maytham, Rolvenden**, Kent. This has a very symmetrical brick principal façade, with central block and side wings, regularly spaced sash windows and a central, decorative doorway, approached by a flight of steps (1324, 1383, 1426). **Nashdom Abbey, Taplow**, Buckinghamshire, was built in 1910. This is another large house, in stone, in the classical manner, most beautifully handled (1373). Lutyens' last large country house was **Middleton Park**, Oxfordshire, built in 1935.

HOUSES 1900–1945

1326

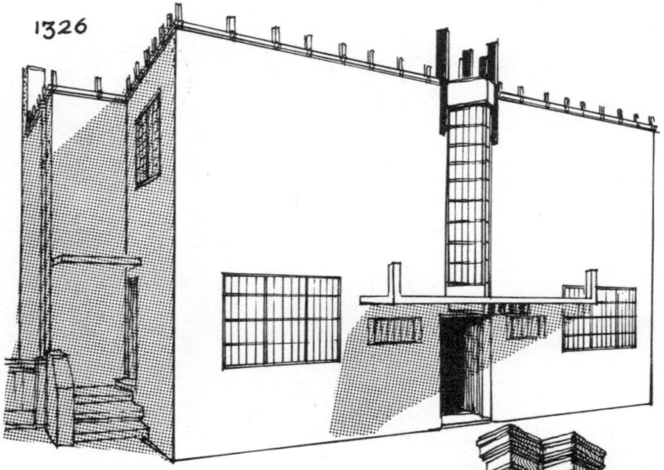

1327

1328

1326 'New Ways' Northampton 1924 Peter Behrens. 1327 'Sun House' Hampstead 1935 E. Maxwell Fry. 1328 'Tichbourne

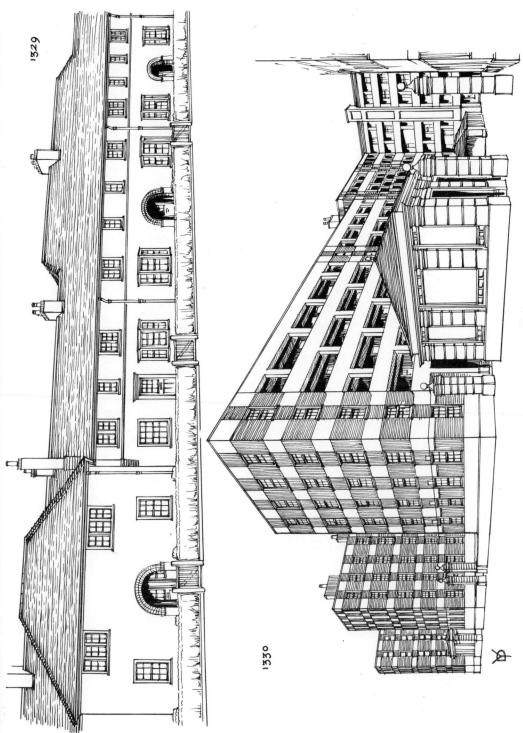

1329

1330

1329 L.C.C. Becontree Estate, Essex. Built mainly 1920–30. Red brick 1330 Page Street Estate, Westminster, 1928. Grey brick and Portland stone. Sir Edwin Lutyens

Here, on H plan, is a finely designed, gracious home with good, classical detail, set in beautiful grounds and redolent of a past age of refined living (1368). Among Lutyens' smaller houses is the charming **Cedar House** at **Chobham**, Surrey, built in 1934 entirely of cedar wood, and the two cottages at **Plumpton Place**, Sussex, built in 1928 (1430).

Lutyens built comparatively few **town houses** and they were nearly all restrained and formal. Typical is **No. 36 Smith Square, Westminster**; a rectangular corner block of three storeys and attics in eighteenth-century style.

Lutyens worked on two large **housing schemes**, quite different from one another in purpose, conception and construction. One scheme was the **Hampstead Garden Suburb**, for which he carried out a large proportion of the early work, including the main Central Square. This is discussed in the section dealing with Garden Cities (1404–6). The other example is a working-class rehousing scheme undertaken in 1928 at **Page Street, Westminster**. This has a most original treatment and design, particularly for its period. Lutyens used light grey bricks, Portland stone and white Portland cement to form a chequer-board pattern which would remain durable and clean. The effect is austere and plain but quite remarkable. The chequer-board design covers the entire flat wall surfaces in an unbroken line from top to bottom, including the rectangular, white-painted sash windows. The roofs, of greenish slate, are low pitched and therefore invisible from street level. The construction is in standard block units with an open end to each court, facing south. Each block is of six storeys and contains 96 flats with accommodation varying from one to four rooms. Small shops are part of the scheme. Today the area is dingy and the novelty of the design is no longer remarkable. Even so these blocks hold their own well with the ubiquitous housing blocks now erected in all parts of London (1330).

In the early 1920s Lutyens embarked on his **career of public building** and developed his classical style. This, however, became simpler, and more individualistic as time passed, so that by the 1930s his work contained a smaller proportion of classicism. In 1923, in collaboration with other architects, he began to carry out work for the **Midland Bank**. His first essay was the **Piccadilly** branch which is sited next to Wren's St James's Church. Lutyens has designed the bank in a similar style; a small, low building, using Wren's ornamental swags and classical doorways. Then followed the colossal edifice of the chief offices of the Bank in **Poultry**, begun 1924 and completed in 1937. This is a building impossible to photograph or to illustrate and even difficult to view. It has a tremendous façade and is so lofty that it disappears up into the narrow sky between the two sides of Poultry. Like most City of London buildings it is erected on an irregular site with its main elevation of 188 feet fronting Poultry. It is a very plain building in Portland stone on steel framing. The façade is largely rusticated and there is a Doric base and entrance. There are six storeys of which the top one is set well back. Despite its plainness, the magnificent proportions make the façade alive and exciting. The corner groups of sculpture depicting a boy and a goose—the emblem of Poultry—were designed by Sir William Reid Dick. They are somewhat dwarfed by the immense building towering above them (1424). Among the other Midland Bank branches, Lutyens built the example in **Leadenhall Street**, a tall, narrow façade without orders (1388), and that in **King Street, Manchester**, which has a fine, island site. This is also an immense block, nearly symmetrical on all four sides and decorated by a Corinthian order at the top.

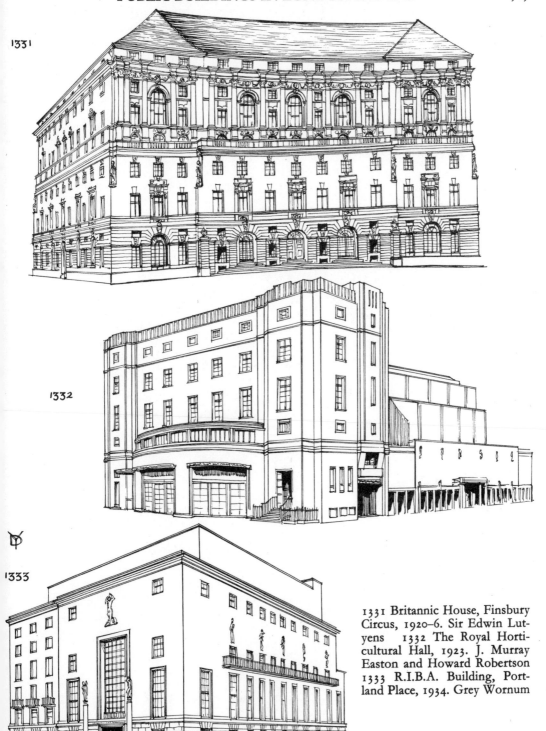

1331 Britannic House, Finsbury Circus, 1920–6. Sir Edwin Lutyens   1332 The Royal Horticultural Hall, 1923. J. Murray Easton and Howard Robertson   1333 R.I.B.A. Building, Portland Place, 1934. Grey Wornum

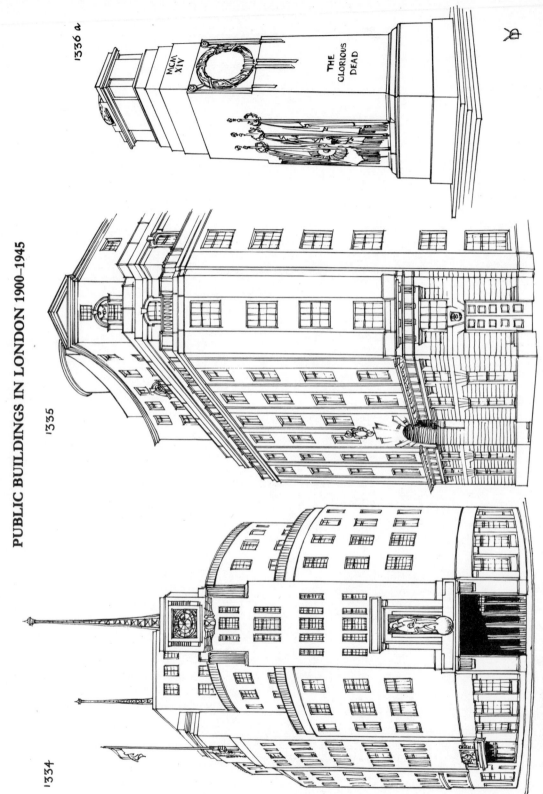

1334

1335

1336 a

MCM XIV

THE GLORIOUS DEAD

1334 Broadcasting House, 1929. G. Val Myer 1335 85 Fleet Street. Headquarters of the Press Association and Reuter Building,

Lutyens also designed a number of massive **office blocks** of which two at least are justly famous. The first is **Britannic House, Finsbury Circus**, London which was built 1920–6. Here are the offices of the Anglo-Iranian Oil Company in an impressive seven-storey building on one corner of the circus. The block has one curved façade which forms part of the circus and has a frontage of 140 feet. This, the dominant façade, has a three-arched entrance. The lower storey is rusticated all round the building. The fifth and sixth storeys are treated together architecturally as one on the circus façade, decorated by the Corinthian Order. The roof, of Westmorland slate, curves round in an unbroken sweep above the upper storeys which are set back from the building line above the third floor. There are a number of decorative sculptured figures. It is easily the finest building in the circus and one of London's best of this period. It has dignity, interest and solidity (1331). The second example is the **Headquarters** of the **Press Association** and **Reuter Building**, No. 85 Fleet Street, London, built in 1935. Like the Midland Bank in Poultry, it is difficult of access for illustration purposes. Built on a corner site, this tall building of nine storeys is set back at the top and curved on the Fleet Street elevation. The seventh floor is also set back and is partly hidden by a balustrade on the sixth floor. The building, of Portland stone, is classical, but is typical of Sir Edwin's later work of this type. It is very subdued and plain, relying on its proportions, line and recessing for its effect. The main doorway, enclosing two storeys, uses the Doric order in rusticated form but the pilasters do not follow through; only the capitals and bases are indicated. This same treatment can be seen in the Middleton Park porch of the same date (1335, 1368).

Two other large office blocks designed by Lutyens are situated in **Pall Mall: No. 120**, built in 1928, and **No. 68**, built in 1929. These are traditional classical buildings suited to their position here. No. 68 has a corner site and is the more imposing; Lutyens has used his favourite Doric order, finely proportioned and detailed as always.

Among other works by Lutyens in London is the **Y.W.C.A. Central Club** in **Great Russell Street**, which was opened in 1932. This is a modern styled, severe building with, however, classical fenestration and a decorative doorway; the latter—the focal point of the design—is approached from a double flight of steps with iron balustrade. The building comprises some 90 bedrooms, a restaurant and concert hall and is entered through a lofty entrance hall (1370).

Lutyens was also one of the principal architects to design our ill-fated **National Theatre**. He made one design in 1937 which was planned for the triangular island site in the Cromwell Road at South Kensington; a site still unused and enclosed by unsightly hoardings in one of London's most impressive thoroughfares. In 1942 he made another design for the theatre, this time on the South Bank. This was a larger site and Lutyens made a more ambitious plan. The theatre has not yet progressed beyond this point.

Lutyens, like other leading architects in the 1920s, designed a number of war **memorials,** but to him we owe one of the most famous yet one of the simplest—the **Cenotaph** in **Whitehall**. In 1919 this was erected in wood and plaster for the peace procession of that year. The design immediately impressed both the public and artistic critics and it was decided to perpetuate it in Portland stone. Lutyens himself called it the Cenotaph, intending to convey thereby a description of an empty tomb lifted up on a high pedestal. It is very plain, its only decoration being the flags and carved wreaths. The very simplicity of the design is misleading;

A fanciful perspective view of the Metropolitan Cathedral, Liverpool 1960's

it is a simplicity born of subtle and thoughtful conception. There are no true vertical or horizontal planes in the monument. The 'verticals', if produced upwards, would actually meet at a point 1,000 feet above ground level; the 'horizontals' are imperceptibly curved in a similar manner to those on the Parthenon, their common centre is some 900 feet below the monument (1336a). Among his other memorials is the **Memorial Arch** at **Leicester**, a much larger construction set pleasantly in the Victoria Park. This has four arches, one on each face, and again the decoration is in the carved flags and wreaths.

The Metropolitan Roman Catholic Cathedral, Liverpool was to be Lutyens' monument. In the design he incorporated all his principal ideas on the adaptation of classicism to modern architecture. If it had been built it would have been the greatest monument to modern neo-classicism in Britain, in much the same way as Scott's Liverpool Cathedral, near by, is a last great monument to neo-Gothic architecture. The Roman Catholic Archbishop of Liverpool intended to build a cathedral second to none save St Peter's in Rome in size and greatness. Lutyens—an Anglican—made the first designs in 1929. There was much enthusiasm among Catholics in the area and the necessary £100,000 was raised. The plans and elevation were published the following year and in 1933 the foundation stone was laid. The crypt and sacristy were built and then, in 1941, work stopped because of the Second World War. It has never begun again. For some time after the war it had been hoped to continue building, but with the tremendous depreciation in the pound sterling the complete estimated cost of the cathedral was much too high. Eventually hope was abandoned and a competition held for a cut-price £1 million cathedral. This competition has now been won by Frederick Gibberd for a modern construction. A greater contrast to Lutyens' enormous classical pile can hardly be envisaged, but the design appears to be excitingly original.

A quarter-inch-scale detail model was made of Lutyens' Cathedral and exhibited in the Royal Academy. From photographs of this and from his detail drawings, upon which he worked almost until his death in 1944, we can envisage what a tremendous shrine to Catholicism this cathedral would have been. It was a domed cathedral and the domed space, though lower than St Peter's in Rome, would eventually have had a greater diameter than that of the great cathedral church. The nave was short and not wide but was immensely tall, giving a Gothic appearance to its proportions. The total height of the building to the summit of the cross was to be 509 feet, considerably higher than St Peter's and only 21 feet lower than the Minster at Ulm, the highest spire in Europe. The materials to be used were grey granite and warm, brown brick, giving a subtle polychrome effect to the building. Some four million bricks have actually been laid. The whole design was literally a classical pile, each architectural member supporting the one above to culminate in the immense lantern and cupola. It would have been a monument of which to be proud and one which England is the poorer for not having built (1336b).

SIR GILES GILBERT SCOTT 1880–1960

From the considerable number of deservedly well-known architects of this period, the name of Scott stands out as the most famous and second only to Lutyens in his ability to handle masses and to produce finely proportioned buildings. Scott's training as an architect followed more an eighteenth-century pattern than a modern one. He was never an architectural student

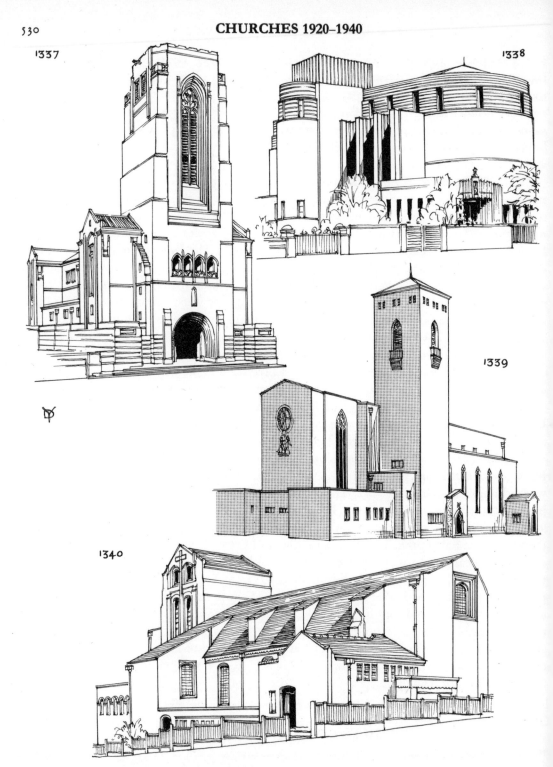

1337 Church of Our Lady, Northfleet, Essex. Sir Giles Gilbert Scott   1338 St Nicholas', Burnage, Manchester, 1931. Welch, Cachemaille-Day and Lander   1339 St Thomas's, Hanwell, Middlesex, 1933. Sir Edward Maufe   1340 St Wilfred's, Brighton, 1933. H. S. Goodhart-Rendel

in the usual meaning of the term. He was a young prodigy, having inherited great talent from his father and grandfather (Sir George Gilbert Scott of Victoria Memorial fame), and he learnt his profession in an architect's office and in practice. By the time he had attained 50 years of age he had received every honour that a member of the English architectural profession can receive. In 1922 he was elected a Royal Academician. In 1924 he was knighted, in 1925 he received the Royal Gold Medal for Architecture and from 1933 to 1935 was President of the Royal Institute of British Architects. He was awarded the Order of Merit in 1944. He was a Roman Catholic and early became interested in ecclesiastical architecture. He became an articled pupil in 1898 at the age of 18, in the office of Mr Temple Moore, the church architect. His name was quickly brought to professional and public notice when as a young man of 21 he won outright the competition for the new **Liverpool Cathedral**, a work to which he gave considerable time and study during the whole of his long life.

Scott was not entirely a traditionalist; his work was too varied for this, but equally he was no true modernist. Thus, despite an enormous practice extending over 60 years, and a diversity of achievement which extended from his Gothic cathedral to Battersea Power Station and Waterloo Bridge, his work never found unqualified favour with modern architects nor with the more romantic adherents to past centuries.

Scott carried out a quantity of ecclesiastical work and by many is remembered chiefly for his **churches** and **chapels**. This is a pity, for most of this work, except the cathedral, is very traditional, generally in Gothic vein and, in the majority of instances, dull. Typical among his churches are **St Alban's, Golders Green**, 1932, **St Andrew's, Luton**, 1932, the **parish church, Stoke-on-Trent**, 1928, **St Paul's, Liverpool**, and the **Church of Our Lady** at **Northfleet** (1337). He commonly used brick for these churches and the exteriors, at least, as was common in the 1930s, showed large areas of plain wall and massive, stodgy towers. The interiors were better, though often dark.

His **collegiate work** was much more interesting and original, although still generally on a Gothic basis in modern dress. An exception was his large scheme for the **University Library** at **Cambridge** and, adjoining it, **Clare College Memorial Court**. He also carried out designs for the Byzantine chapel at **Lady Margaret Hall, Oxford**; the chapel at **Charterhouse School, Godalming**; the nave at **Downside Abbey, Bath**; the Ampleforth Abbey **Chapel**, Yorkshire; **Westfield College** and **Whitelands College** at Putney; additions to **Magdalen College, Oxford**, and new buildings at the **Bodleian Library, Oxford**. These works are discussed more fully under University and School Building and can be seen in Figs. 1382, 1418, 1419, 1420 and 1421. Like his grandfather, Scott carried out much **ecclesiastical restoration** work as, for example, at **St George's Chapel, Windsor**, 1926, and at **Chester Cathedral**.

Among Scott's very varied commitments, he designed additions to the **County Hall** in **London**, 1937; the **Guinness Factory, Park Royal**, 1936; the **Phoenix Theatre, Charing Cross Road**, 1930 and **Cropthorne Court, Maida Vale**—a modern, rather uninspired block of flats, 1930. Of much higher standard and greater interest was his **rebuilding** of the **House of Commons** and the **Guildhall** after war-time damage. Here, his Gothic work is impeccable and the Guildhall roof, in particular, a fine reconstruction.

In 1929 Scott set the pattern for **power stations** all over Britain by his brick design at **Battersea** fronting the Thames. The work was carried out in stages and it was not until

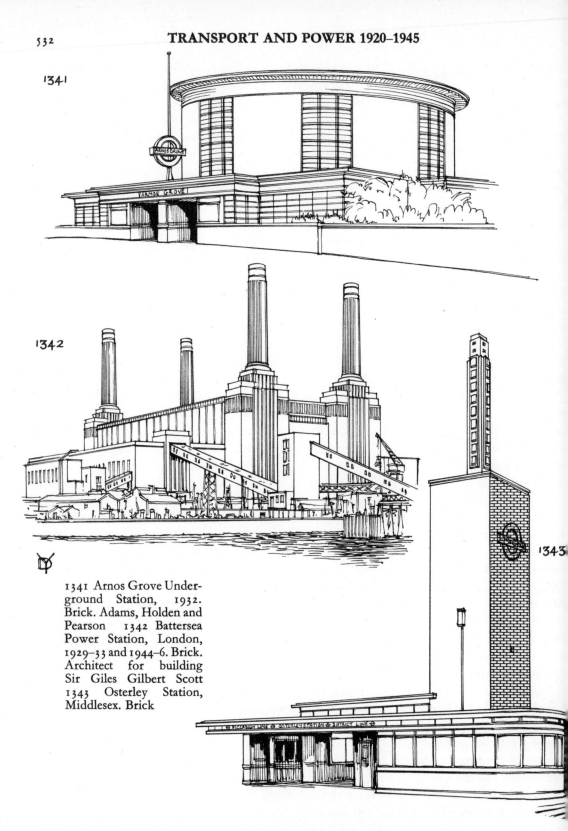

1341 Arnos Grove Underground Station, 1932. Brick. Adams, Holden and Pearson   1342 Battersea Power Station, London, 1929–33 and 1944–6. Brick. Architect for building Sir Giles Gilbert Scott   1343 Osterley Station, Middlesex. Brick

LIX   Liverpool Cathedral, 1903– . Architect Sir Giles Gilbert Scott

1946 that all four chimneys were belching forth over London. Nowadays Londoners are familiar with Battersea Power Station but when it was first erected it was considered modern, original and an interesting and satisfactory union of architecture and civil engineering (1342). Scott continued his connection with power stations and bridges until the end of his life. At the age of 79 he was still advising on the design of the **nuclear power station** at **Berkeley**. He was also, at this time, active consulting architect for the new **Forth suspension road bridge** (1508–10, 1512). In the period 1937–42 he constructed the controversial **Waterloo Bridge**. The chief controversy had been over the destruction of the old Waterloo Bridge. Scott's new one, finished during the war, can hardly be described as traditional (1434; p. 576).

Liverpool Cathedral

Liverpool Cathedral is unquestionably Scott's greatest work and a magnificent monument to his life as an architect. It is also, undoubtedly, the last cathedral which we shall ever see in England built on these dimensions and in masonry in this manner. Despite the fact that Scott designed it as such a young man and that he lived to be nearly 80, he did not live long enough to see it completed. The work has been held up many times for lack of funds and skilled craftsmen, especially masons, and no doubt will be again, though it is hoped to complete the cathedral in the 1980s—80 years of building, truly a Medieval counterpart.

In 1901 a competition was held for the new Anglican Cathedral of Liverpool. The principal assessors who chose the young Scott were Norman Shaw and G. F. Bodley. The cathedral commissioners, somewhat apprehensive at leaving a young man with so little architectural experience to carry out so enormous a task, appointed Bodley as joint architect. However, Bodley died a few years after and the cathedral has been in Scott's sole charge since 1907. After this Scott realised that his original design did not give him full satisfaction. This had been a cruciform cathedral with twin towers over the single transepts and with a very long nave. He altered his design a number of times and the cathedral was eventually built as we see it now, with a single, central, massive tower, and a choir and nave of equal length (only one bay of the nave is yet completed and this was dedicated by the Bishop in 1961).

Work was begun on the cathedral in 1903. The first part to be completed was the Lady Chapel, which was opened in 1910. This is the most traditional part of the cathedral, probably because it was completed before Scott had fully developed his modern Gothic theme. The choir was finished in 1924 and the tower in 1925. There were then great gaps in the building programme, but work is now continuing.

The cathedral is built of local sandstone, of a soft red colour, set with wide, white joints. Its foundations are of brick and concrete; the exterior roofing is of reinforced concrete beams, some of which are hollow for circulation of warm air. The Roman method of under-floor heating is used.

The design is Gothic, but a modernised, streamlined version of the style. Its source of inspiration is obviously traditional Gothic, but there is a classical feeling to the whole conception despite the Gothic detailing. The exterior is powerful and dignified. It is set on a fine site on high ground overlooking the Mersey and miles of industrial England. It is a landmark from any part of the city of Liverpool and its environs. The interior, however, is more striking and impressive than the exterior. Here is the true feeling of a cathedral; silence, grandeur, soaring simplicity. Here is space and plainness. The piers ascend upwards into the darkness

Roman Catholic Cathedral, Westminster, begun 1894. Architect J. F. Bentley

1344

1345

1344 Liverpool Cathedral, begun 1903 (nave on left of drawing, still incomplete). Sir Giles Gilbert Scott   1345 Guildford Cathedral, Surrey, begun 1936. Consecrated 1961 (tower still not completed). Sir Edward Maufe

with no break for the arch springing. The vault is very high, much loftier than in other Gothic cathedrals. It rises to 176 feet above ground level in the central space. These piers emphasise the vertical lines as in traditional Gothic design, but there is a classical horizontal emphasis as well. The poorest feature of the cathedral, and one which is unfortunately common to Scott's work, is in the decoration and figure sculpture. Here the craftsmanship is slipshod and ordinary. This is the principal criticism which can be levelled at this great work which displays so proudly the imaginative power and design of its creator.

Liverpool's cathedral is one of the finest buildings of the twentieth century, but it is not typical of the century to date, only of the period in which it was designed. It belongs to the era of 1900–14 and is something which we shall not see again—the economic difficulties are too great. Guildford Cathedral, built of brick, has taken 25 years, including a world war, to reach completion except for its tower. Coventry Cathedral has been completed in less than 10 years, but Liverpool, after more than half a century of building is still nowhere near completion. This is because it is a traditional cathedral, of cathedral not parish church proportions, and built in the cathedral tradition of masonry. The labour force of skilled masons has diminished alarmingly; the craft of masonry is dying fast. There is always difficulty in finding men for restoration work as, for example, at the House of Commons and at Bath Abbey. In 1939 the labour force on Liverpool Cathedral was 266; 120 of these were masons. Today there are less than 75 men working on the cathedral and only some 20 of them are masons. The work slows down and so it will be the last of its kind. It is, however, even incomplete a magnificent memorial to Scott and a cathedral worthy of the Gothic tradition (1344, LIX.)

Sir Aston Webb 1849–1930   Sir Reginald Blomfield 1856–1942
Sir Guy Dawber 1862–1938   Henry Vaughan Lanchester 1863–1953
Edwin Rickards 1872–1920

It is convenient to examine the work of these men together because, although their individual achievements are different, they were all traditional in their approach to architecture, basing their designs on past styles though with a modern bias, and they all carried out the major part of their work in the period 1900–30.

Sir Aston Webb's designs are in classical vein, sometimes introducing early Renaissance features. Much of his practice was in large civic schemes of which the most famous were, in London, the completion of the Victoria and Albert Museum and the Royal College of Science and the layout of the Mall from Buckingham Palace to Trafalgar Square. The **Victoria and Albert Museum** had been begun in the nineteenth century. In 1899 Queen Victoria laid the foundation stone for the Cromwell Road façade in South Kensington and the building was opened in 1909. The dominant feature of this elevation is the decorative entrance doorway and, above, the tower, with its arched superstructure crowning the central space. The façade, in red brick with stone dressings and sculptured decoration and figures, is carried out in Renaissance style (1348). In the same period Sir Aston Webb built a new front to **Buckingham Palace**, laid out the architectural settings in front of the Palace for the **Victoria Memorial** and the **Mall** and built the **Admiralty Arch** at the head of the thoroughfare as a terminal feature into Trafalgar Square. The arch, like the palace, is in straightforward classical design, though in the former instance the Corinthian order has stylised capitals.

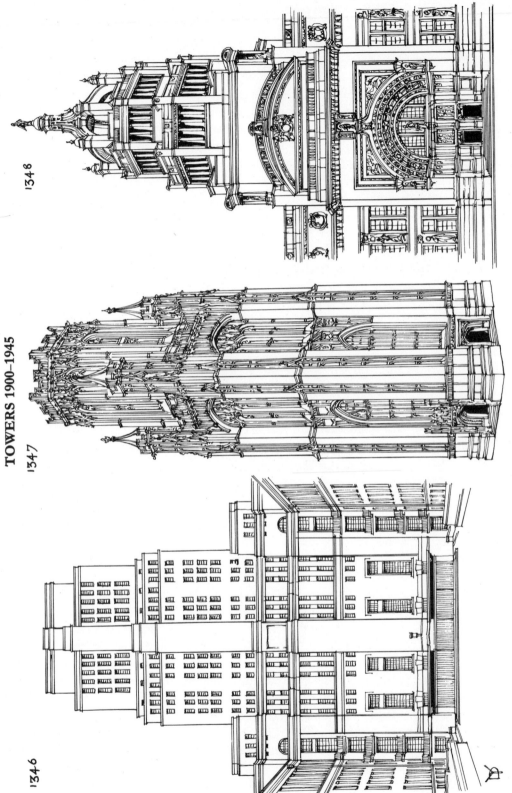

TOWERS 1900–1945

1346

1547

1348

1346 Senate House, London University, 1933–7. Sir Charles Holden 1347 The University Tower, Bristol, 1925. Sir George Oatley
1348 The Victoria and Albert Museum, London, 1899–1909: entrance Cromwell Road façade. Sir Aston Webb

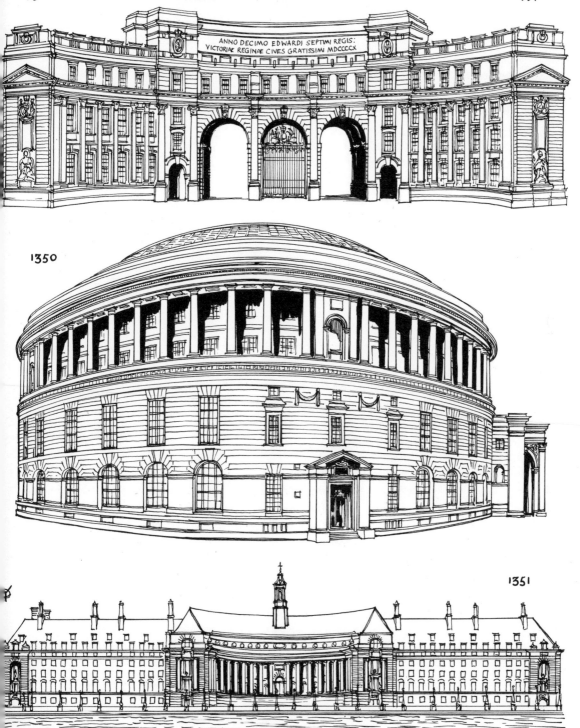

ANNO DECIMO EDWARDI SEPTIMI REGIS:
VICTORIAE REGINAE CIVES GRATISSIMI MDCCCCX

1349 The Admiralty Arch, The Mall, London, 1910. Sir Aston Webb   1350 The Manchester City Library, 1929–34. E. Vincent Harris   1351 The County Hall, Westminster, London, 1912–22. Ralph Knott

The royal entrance is pierced by three semicircular arches and the central gate is normally kept closed (1349, 1372). Among Sir Aston's other work are the **Law Courts** and **University** at **Birmingham** and the **Dartmouth Royal Naval College**. He was President of the Royal Institute of British Architects 1902–4, was knighted in 1904, won the Royal Gold Medal for Architecture in 1905 and became President of the Royal Academy in 1919.

Sir Reginald Blomfield was a vigorous, intelligent and capable man, an intellectual and a believer in stating firmly without fear or favour his views on architecture. He was a Devon man, born of an ecclesiastical family, and was educated at Haileybury and Exeter College, Oxford. At university he distinguished himself outstandingly both scholastically and in sport. Rather later in life than is usual he began his architectural career and became a pupil in his uncle's (Sir Arthur Blomfield) office in 1880.

Blomfield had a very large practice and his work ranged over a wide field including houses, bridges, monuments, civic architecture and collegiate building. His greatest achievements were the Memorial at Ypres, the Quadrant layout and Lambeth Bridge. He was principal architect to the Imperial War Graves Commission and in this capacity designed many memorials on the Continent of which his **Menin Gate**, 1923–6, at **Ypres** is the most famous. This is a massive memorial, movingly suited to its conception.

At the turn of the century it was decided to rebuild Regent Street and much of Piccadilly Circus, but to retain the curve of the Quadrant. **Norman Shaw** was asked to design the new **Quadrant** and **Piccadilly Circus** which would include Regent Street as far as Vigo Street, Swan and Edgar's and the County Fire Office. He produced his designs in 1905 at the age of 75. The scheme was planned in Italian classical idiom and was a worthy successor to Nash's Quadrant. The colonnaded section, forming the northern façade of the Piccadilly Hotel, was completed by 1908 and then the scheme foundered on the subject of costs and disputes with the interested business factions. Shaw died in 1912, most of his scheme incomplete. A Quadrant Committee was established but nothing much was done until after the war when Blomfield was asked to present a new design. This he did and the present **Quadrant, County Fire Office** and **Swan and Edgar's façades** are his, carried out between 1918 and 1930. Blomfield's design, though still classical, was plainer and much less interesting than Shaw's, but it avoided the strictures on cost on which Shaw's scheme had foundered. Blomfield himself was a life-long admirer of Shaw's work and modelled much of his own upon it. He had, however, a more intellectual approach and lacked the warmth and inspiration which motivated Shaw.

Among the best known of Blomfield's numerous works are **Lambeth Bridge**, designed 1929 and built 1935–7 in conjunction with Topham Forrest, architect to the London County Council (1432); **Stratford-upon-Avon Bridge**, 1932; **Shepperton Bridge**, Surrey, 1921; the **Public Library** at **Lincoln**, 1913; the new façade to the **Middlesex Hospital, London**, 1928, and the **Cottage Hospital, Rye**, 1929. He carried out a great deal of work on the new buildings at **Lady Margaret Hall, Oxford** between 1896 and 1930 (1416). He built many houses in London and in other parts of the country.

Blomfield was also well known as a critic and writer on architecture and art. His famous two-volume *History of Renaissance Architecture in England 1500–1800*, published 1897, has been the standard work for many years, as is also his *History of French Architecture 1494–1661*, published 1911, and *1661–1674*, published 1920. Both these productions are lavishly illustrated

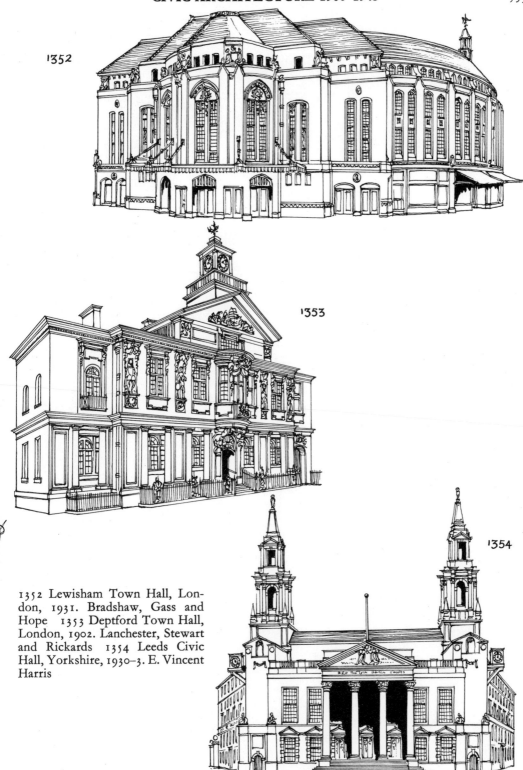

1352 Lewisham Town Hall, London, 1931. Bradshaw, Gass and Hope 1353 Deptford Town Hall, London, 1902. Lanchester, Stewart and Rickards 1354 Leeds Civic Hall, Yorkshire, 1930–3. E. Vincent Harris

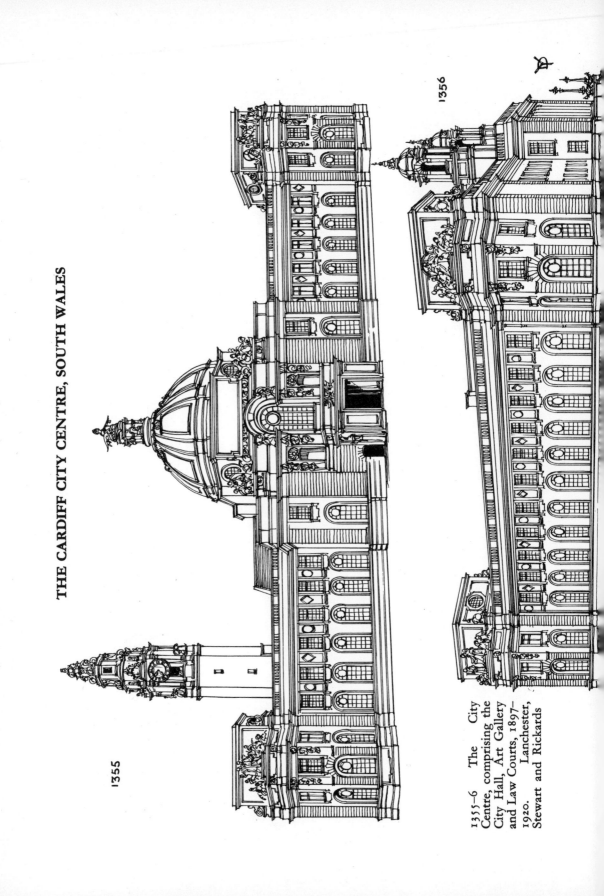

THE CARDIFF CITY CENTRE, SOUTH WALES

1355

1356

1355–6 The City Centre, comprising the City Hall, Art Gallery and Law Courts, 1897–1920. Lanchester, Stewart and Rickards

by his own drawings and by contemporary illustrations and engravings. His *Life of R. Norman Shaw*, published in 1940, though now seemingly prejudiced in favour of his mentor, is a valuable work.

Blomfield won the Royal Gold Medal for Architecture in 1913, was elected Royal Academician in 1914, became President of the Royal Institute of British Architects in 1912 and was knighted in 1919.

Sir Guy Dawber was almost entirely a domestic architect following in the tradition of Newton. He was an ardent worker for the preservation of England's rural areas and created the Council for the Preservation of Rural England. He was born at King's Lynn in Norfolk and studied at the Royal Academy Schools. He became an articled pupil in King's Lynn, then assisted Sir Thomas Deane in Dublin and later entered the office of Sir Ernest George.

Dawber designed houses all over England; in Gloucestershire, Wiltshire, Norfolk and Somerset in particular. Among these are **Stowell Hill**, Somerset; **Burdocks**, Gloucestershire, and **Wiveton Hall**, Norfolk. He also published many books and articles and painted wate-rcolours. He was President of the Royal Institute of British Architects from 1925 to 1927 and won the Royal Gold Medal for Architecture in 1928.

Henry Vaughan Lanchester was one of the pioneers of modern town planning. He was a Founder Member of the Town Planning Institute and became its President in 1922. Of the firm of Lanchester, Stewart and Rickards, he was the planner and **Edwin A. Rickards** was the brilliant draughtsman and designer, famous for his baroque architectural decoration and sculpture. The partnership of these men began in 1899 and it was in the Edwardian age that their fine works were carried out. The first of these to be completed was **Deptford Town Hall, London**, won in competition in 1901. This is not a large building and it is now hemmed in by indifferent commercial work, but it still shows its quality and is a beautiful example of its kind (1353, 1366).

The largest scheme carried out by the firm was the **Cardiff City Centre**, won in competition in 1897. They built the **Town Hall** and the **Law Courts** between 1897 and 1906, and the scheme has later been extended widely in keeping with the original buildings. In a baroque classicism, these two buildings are reminiscent of Charles Girault's Petit Palais in Paris and constitute one of the finest city layouts in the country. The planning, grouping, detail and execution are all of very high standard (1355–6, 1367, 1378, 1386, 1431).

Stewart died in 1904, but Lanchester and Rickards won the competition for the **Central Wesleyan Hall, Westminster**, in 1905. In very similar vein to their work at Cardiff, the Westminster Hall is a larger, simple unit, sumptuous in decoration and grandiose in conception. It is one of London's fine pieces of monumental architecture (1357). Rickards died in 1920 and Lanchester concentrated more and more on civic planning and design. He was awarded the Royal Gold Medal for Architecture in 1934.

E. Vincent Harris 1879–   Herbert J. Rowse   Sir Herbert Baker 1862–1946

These three architects designed most of their work in the years between the two World Wars. The style is largely a plain, simplified or modernised classicism and, except in a few instances, uninspiring and lacking in vitality. Much of the work is in monumental civic architecture.

1357

1358

1357 Central Wesleyan Hall, Westminster, London, 1906–12. Lanchester and Rickards
1358 Broadway House, Westminster, London. London Transport Offices, 1929. Adams, Holden and Pearson

Vincent Harris was born in Devonport. He was articled to a Plymouth architect and also studied at the Royal Academy Schools. He worked for a number of years with the London County Council. He has won many competitions, chiefly for civic architecture. Typical of his work in this respect are the **Glamorganshire County Hall, Cardiff**, 1909–11; **Headquarters Fire Station, Cardiff**, 1929; the **City Hall, Sheffield**, 1920–9; the **Leeds Civic Hall**, 1931–3 (1354); the **Manchester Town Hall Extension**, 1927, and **Essex County Hall**. His best-known work, which is a fine classical building, is the **Manchester City Library**, 1929–34. This is circular, with a projecting porch. The third and fourth storeys are fronted by a Doric colonnade. The Library is well proportioned, finely detailed and has a beautiful interior (1350).

In 1914 Harris won the competition for new Government Offices on the Thames Embankment. Building was twice postponed due to World Wars and the work was finally carried out after 1945. The finished layout is plain, modern but achingly dull.

Much of **Herbert Rowse's** best-known work is in **Liverpool**. Here he was the architect for the **Mersey Tunnel Scheme** and designed the great ventilator shafts and dock areas 1934–42. He built the **Philharmonic Hall, Birkenhead Hall, Martin's Bank**, 1926–32, and the **India Building**, all in the same city. He has been responsible for many other schemes in housing, hospital building and libraries. His work is modern and plain, generally in stone, with restrained or non-existent decoration, but it belongs to the empty, flat architecture so typical of the 1930s.

Much of **Sir Herbert Baker's** work was carried out **abroad**; he was associated with Lutyens in the New Delhi scheme, he built cathedrals in South Africa and Rhodesia and designed the Rhodes Memorial, Cape Town, and the Government Houses at Mombasa and Nairobi. In **England**, he was responsible for the unfortunate superstructure extension to Soane's **Bank of England**, he built **Martin's Bank** in **Lombard Street** and **Rhodes House** at **Oxford**. Perhaps his best-known works were India House and **South Africa House** in **London**. **India House, Aldwych**, built 1929, is a large building with a curved façade to Aldwych. It is plain, with restrained decoration; the focal centre being the entrance doorway. On either side of this are Indian columns with elephant bases and, perched on top of the columns, seated tigers (1375, 1379).

Sir Percy E. Thomas 1883–   Sir Edward Maufe 1883–

The work of these two architects, although belonging to the same period as the last three described, is much more modern in conception, particularly that of **Sir Percy Thomas**. Sir Percy was born in South Shields but spent his childhood in Cardiff. In 1911 he set up architectural practice there with Ivor Jones. He was one of the principal builders of modern South Wales. He built the **Technical College** at **Cardiff** (now the Welsh College of Advanced Technology), the **University College, Swansea**, and carried out further collegiate work at the **Universities** of **Bangor** and **Aberystwyth**.

Sir Percy's most original work, and one which has brought him general acclaim, is the **City Hall** layout at **Swansea**. Here, on a new site outside the old city centre, is a modern civic centre in contrast to the baroque layout at Cardiff, but equally fine in its individual approach. There is a suggestion of the Stockholm Town Hall in the design which is dignified,

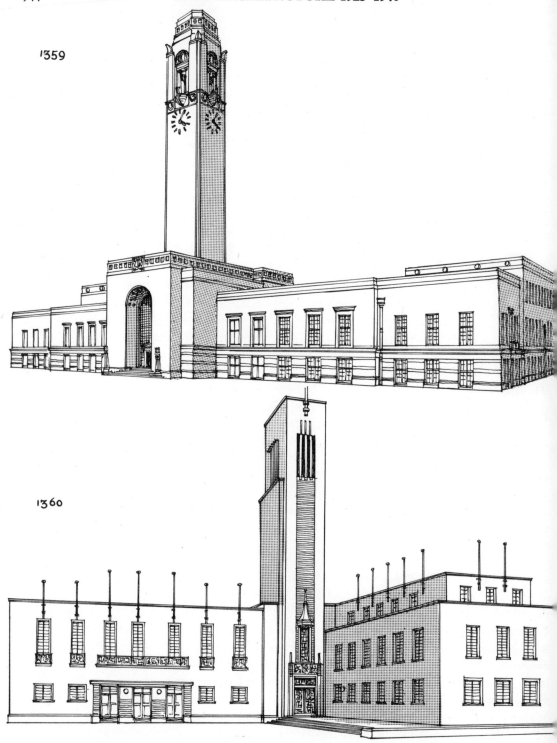

1359 City Hall, Swansea, South Wales, 1930–4. Sir Percy E. Thomas　1360 Town Hall, Hornsey, London, 1933. Reginald H. Uren

simple and effective (1359, 1380). Sir Percy had an extensive industrial practice and acted as **consulting architect** for the Steel Company of Wales works at Abbey and Margam, for the Carmarthen Bay Power Station and the British Nylon Spinners Factory at Pontypool. Now, at the age of 79, he is the consulting architect for the new **Severn Bridge** project. He was awarded the Royal Gold Medal for Architecture in 1939 and is almost unique in having been President of the Royal Institute of Architects twice, in 1935–7 and 1943–6. He only retired from his firm of Sir Percy Thomas and Son in 1961.

Sir Edward Maufe is primarily known as the designer of Guildford Cathedral. Apart from this, much of his work has been ecclesiastical, although he has built a number of country houses, for example, **Broadstone,** Dorset and **Kelling Hall**, Norfolk; also the **Playhouse Theatre, Oxford**, and the **Festival Theatre, Cambridge**. He built a number of branch banks for **Lloyds Bank**, such as those at Putney, Cheam and St Albans and designed **Morley College** in **Westminster Bridge Road, London**.

Maufe was born in Ilkley, Yorkshire, and was educated at St John's College, Oxford. He was articled to W. A. Pite before setting up in practice for himself. He was a Silver Medallist at the Paris Exhibition of 1925 and was awarded the Royal Gold Medal for Architecture in 1944. Among his better-known **churches** are **St Saviour's, Acton**, and **St Thomas's, Hanwell**. St Thomas's has much in common with Guildford Cathedral, though on a smaller scale; its window and door openings are particularly similar. The church is of brick with large areas of plain wall and narrow lancet windows. The tower is tall and square. The window at the east end is circular and the cross is formed by Eric Gill's carved crucifixion (1339, 1390).

Guildford Cathedral

A competition was held for a cathedral to be built in the new diocese of Guildford in 1930. This was won by **Sir Edward Maufe**. The foundation-stone was laid by the Archbishop of Canterbury in 1936 and work continued until its interruption due to the war. Building did not recommence until 1948—priority for building houses being insisted upon by the government until that time—and the cathedral was consecrated by the Bishop of Guildford in the presence of H.M. the Queen on 17th May 1961. Apart from the tower and the east end, upon which building is still continuing, the cathedral is largely complete.

Guildford Cathedral occupies an exceptionally fine site on the summit of Stag Hill outside the town. On three sides the ground falls away sharply; on the west aspect there is a long, grassy, sloped approach giving a vista up to the west front. From Guildford and from the surrounding countryside the cathedral is clearly silhouetted.

The design is based upon the Gothic idiom but it is a modernised Gothic. The exterior is very simple with enormous areas of plain brick walling interrupted only by tall lancet windows. The tower is to provide the focal centre of the design and at present the building has a truncated appearance due to its absence. In the illustration on page 534, the proposed tower, to be 175 feet above ground level, has been included to give an adequate impression of the cathedral, although the remainder of the building is depicted as it stood in late 1961.

The west front, approached up a dignified flight of steps, is in tripartite form with three doorways below three tall lancet windows. The doors are of bronze and the decorative glasswork, finely incised by John Hutton, represents angels playing musical instruments.

The south entrance possesses two interestingly decorated bronze doors. The ornament is in relief, depicting elemental occupations in individual designs. Above these doors is a large window and a crude, carved stone statue of St John the Baptist by Eric Gill.

The interior of the cathedral is more interesting and successful than its exterior and it is beautifully lit by the tall lancet windows—largely filled by plain glass—of the nave aisles. The nave itself is broad, long and high; this width is made possible by the vault of reinforced concrete which is simply and effectively constructed. There is no choir screen and the altar is visible to everyone. The heating, which is most effective, is by hot water in copper piping under the floors. These are paved with freestone and marbles. The cathedral is 365 feet long.

Inside, the decoration is restrained but adequate. Much of it, in stained glass, engraved glass, carved stone and wood is well done and, in some instances illustrates fine craftsmanship. But some of the sculpture and wood-carving is poor and depreciates the general good standard (1345, 1369, 1389; LXI).

PUBLIC BUILDINGS

Of the large number of **halls, clubs, hotels, hospitals** and **offices** erected between 1900 and 1945, it is proposed to discuss a representative few. In the period up to 1914 might be considered, for example, the Ritz Hotel, Piccadilly; the Royal Automobile Club, Pall Mall; the *Morning Post* Building, Strand; the Central Wesleyan Hall, Westminster; Adelaide House,

1361 Shell Mex House, London, 1929–32. Messrs Josephs

London Bridge and the Kodak Building, Kingsway, all in **London**. These examples present a diverse picture of the architectural scene, although all except the two last named are traditional in design. The **Ritz Hotel**, built 1906, the *Morning Post* **Building**, 1906, and the **Royal Automobile Club**, 1911, were all constructed by the same architects—**Mewès and Davis**. Mewès was a Frenchman and these three buildings show something of the French elegance of that period. The architects used steel framing in the Ritz and the *Morning Post* Building but in design the stone façade indicates nothing of this. The Ritz, in particular, is faced with a heavy stone façade more in Renaissance tradition than modern. The *Morning Post* Building occupies a narrow, triangular site in the Strand; it is surmounted by a dome which, from this view-point, accentuates its tall, narrow appearance. **The Central Wesleyan Hall**, 1906–12, by **Lanchester and Rickards**, with its French baroque design, large square dome and spacious interior, has already been discussed (1357, p. 541).

Adelaide House, London Bridge and the **Kodak Building, Kingsway**, 1911, are in modern dress and were both designed by the firm of **Sir John Burnet, Tait and Lorne**. Here steel framing is used, but this is shown in the façades of the buildings in the vertical emphasis of the design. These are two of the earliest examples in London of non-traditional architecture.

Between 1920 and 1930 there are several examples of modern, less derivative architecture, for instance: Broadway House, Westminster; the County Hall, Westminster; Bush House, Aldwych; Shell Mex House, Embankment; Broadcasting House, Portland Place, and the Royal Horticultural Hall, Westminster, again all in **London. Broadway House**, the giant office headquarters of the London Transport Executive, built 1927–9, was a prototype for the massive block type office architecture which has continued to be built since that date. The architects, **Adams, Holden** and **Pearson**, constructed the building over St James's Station and incorporated this into the design. The plan is shaped on a cross in order to accommodate the station and to provide adequate lighting to all the windows of this enormous pile. Portland stone was used for facing and for the decorative sculpture, Epstein's 'Night' and 'Day'. There is a strong sense of power in the design which piles upwards in a triangular manner towards the solid clock tower in the centre. The chief decoration is in the rectilinear fenestration. On the ground floor the triangular plan is retained (1358).

The London County Hall, Westminster, is quite different. This was won in competition by **Ralph Knott** and was built 1912–22. The main façade fronting the river at West-minster Bridge almost opposite the Palace of Westminster occupies a wonderful site and, though partially successful, insufficient use has been made of the opportunity which it gives. The building is classical in approach and the central mass is curved in a recessed colonnade. The roof is steeply pitched with tall decorative chimneys and a too insignificant lantern in the centre (1351). **Bush House**, with elevations on the **Strand** and **Aldwych**, was built 1925–8 by **Helmle, Corbett** and **Harrison**. This very large building also has a fine site and once again, but even more strongly, one feels that the opportunity has been missed. There is a central block with four wings. The main mass is the focal centre of the building and the most interesting part, presenting a terminal feature to the wide thoroughfare of Kingsway. Despite unusual columns (1429) and its general plan, the building is extremely dull with a relentless monotony to both the fenestration and the spaces between. In Broadway House the repetition is intentional and studied; in Bush House it seems to have just happened and is unsuccessful.

Shell Mex House, facing the **Embankment** near Waterloo Bridge, was built as an ultra-modern office block in 1929 by **Messrs Josephs**. Today, in the light of post-war architecture and the ubiquity of block building, it seems dated, but when it was first erected it caused controversy. It presents a vast façade to the river, set well back and constructed on an arcade at ground floor level. The building, with its 200-odd windows, is then stepped upwards to culminate in a massive block clock tower visible on London's skyline for some distance. Here again is a prototype for many later schemes (1361).

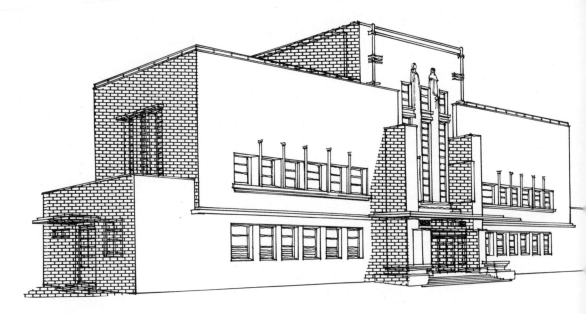

1362 Royal Masonic Hospital, Ravenscourt Park, London, 1932. Architects, Sir John Burnet, Tait and Lorne

Broadcasting House, the British Broadcasting Corporation's centre, built at the end of Portland Place in 1929 to the designs of **G. Val Myer**, was one of the most original modern buildings of its time in England. The site was a difficult shape but full advantage has been taken of its possibilities as a terminal feature to Regent Street, although its juxtaposition to All Souls' Church is unfortunate. The chief façade is curved and stepped back, culminating in a square clock and the slender aerial mast. The principal entrance is simple, rectangular in shape and crowned by the single, sculptured group by Eric Gill (1334).

The **Royal Horticultural Society Hall, Westminster**, built in 1923–6 by **J. Murray Easton** and **Howard Robertson** is, in contrast to the stone of the previous buildings described, constructed chiefly in brick. It is modern in treatment, with a plain, balanced principal elevation and a softly curving entrance feature (1332).

A simple but picturesque brick building of the 1930s is the **Royal Masonic Hospital** at **Ravenscourt Park**, built 1930–3 by **Sir John Burnet, Tait and Lorne**. The hospital, which was awarded the R.I.B.A. Medal as the best building of its year, was one of the few hospitals built in the inter-war years. It combines a pleasant exterior with a highly functional interior. The floors and roof are of concrete and the flat roofing is available for open-air accommodation. There are also large semicircular shaped sun balconies (1362).

In the realm of **department-store construction** in the inter-war period, England lagged far behind the Continent in the modern approach to such stores, where a large number were erected, especially in Germany. Two examples in London, should, however, be mentioned. In 1910–14 **Heal's** of **Tottenham Court Road** was built and this has since been extended in similar style to increase the frontage. The design is simple, especially for its date, with vertical strip pilasters at intervals, decorative coloured panels and, above the parapet, a

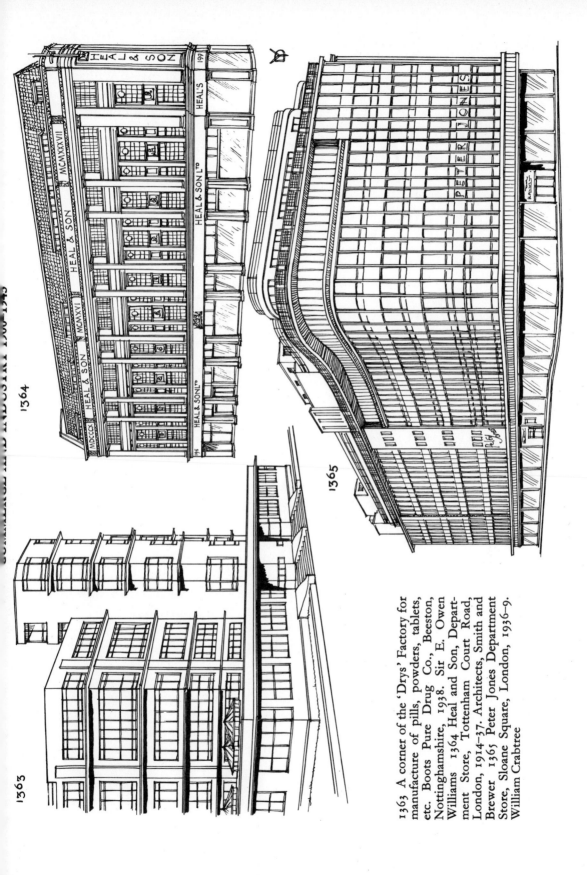

1363 A corner of the 'Drys' Factory for manufacture of pills, powders, tablets, etc. Boots Pure Drug Co., Beeston, Nottinghamshire, 1938. Sir E. Owen Williams 1364 Heal and Son, Department Store, Tottenham Court Road, London, 1914–37. Architects, Smith and Brewer 1365 Peter Jones Department Store, Sloane Square, London, 1936–9. William Crabtree

1363

1364

1365

sloping roof. The architects were **Smith** and **Brewer** (1364). In 1936–9 **William Crabtree** built the new **Peter Jones** store in **Sloane Square**. This was a very up-to-date façade of glass curtain walling curving round the two elevations and set the pattern for future development in post-war stores (1365).

Civic Centres and Town Halls

Many town halls were built in this period to meet the continued adjustment and urbanisation of population. Most of these were designed on a traditional basis, usually in the classical idiom. The motive was dignity, power and solidity. To assist in giving this impression the majority of designs were built with a prominent tower feature.

Two of the most elaborate and successful of the **civic-centre** schemes of this date were in **South Wales** and have already been briefly referred to. The earlier example, at **Cardiff**, was begun in 1897 by the firm of **Lanchester, Stewart** and **Rickards** who built the two main blocks to this layout in 1906—the **Town Hall** and the **Law Courts**. These blocks are sited side by side in one extensive façade divided by a wide avenue and in front of them is a very large open space of lawns and flower beds so that the elevations can be viewed as a whole. The theme is baroque classical, in stone, with a horizontal emphasis of line. Both blocks have terminal pavilions with bay windows and sculptured decoration above the parapet. There are twin towers to the Law Courts on the side elevation where the entrance portico is reached up a flight of steps. The Town Hall block has a very tall, elegant tower on the side elevation and a large decorative dome on the main façade, reminiscent of the same architects' dome at the Central Hall, Westminster. The standard of carving, ironwork, fenestration and sculpture is very high, the design interesting and the whole layout impressive (1355–6, 1367, 1376, 1378, 1431).

The second example at **Swansea** is quite different but equally successful. It was laid out to the designs of **Sir Percy Thomas** in 1930–4. The scheme comprises an assembly hall, the administrative offices and law courts, forming the **civic centre** on a pleasant, spacious site in a park outside the centre of the town. The buildings are grouped round a courtyard on an extensive plan. The exterior facing walls are faced with Portland stone while those looking on to the inner courtyard are of brick finish. The chief entrance hall to the council suite forms a large, square, central block on the main elevation, projecting forward and upwards from the general building line. The entrance arch is immensely high with a semicircular head, in the lower part of which is set the classical doorway. The tall slender clock tower rises from the block to 160 feet. It is very simple in design and is decorated by pierced, round arches on all four sides to emit the sound of the chimes (1359, 1380).

Two further town halls can be mentioned as examples of the traditional and modern styles respectively. In classical vein is **Leeds Civic Hall**, designed by **E. Vincent Harris** and opened in 1933. It is built on a rise of ground in the centre of the city of Leeds, and in front of it, on the narrow end of the triangular site, are gardens and flower-beds. The principal façade is severely symmetrical, with twin towers, clocks and a central Corinthian portico and flight of approach steps. The towers soar up to 170 feet and made an impressive silhouette from the front until the new technical college began to rise immediately behind the city hall. The building is of Portland stone and is roofed with Westmorland slate. It is capable, traditional, eminently suitable but unexciting (1354).

1366 Deptford Town Hall, London, 1902. Lanchester, Stewart and Rickards 1367 City Centre, Cardiff, South Wales, 1897–1906. Lanchester, Stewart and Rickards 1368 Middleton Park, Oxfordshire, 1935. Sir Edwin Lutyens 1369 Guildford Cathedral, 1936–61. Sir Edward Maufe

1370 Y.W.C.A. Central Club, 1932. Sir Edwin Lutyens   1371, 1374 London Life Assurance Building, 1924. W. Curtis Green   1372 Admiralty Arch, 1910. Sir Aston Webb   1373 Nashdom Abbey, Sir Edwin Lutyens   1375 India House, Aldwych, 1929. Sir Herbert Baker   1376, 1378 Cardiff City Centre, 1897–1906. Lanchester, Stewart and Rickards   1377 Hornsey Town Hall, 1933. Reginald Uren

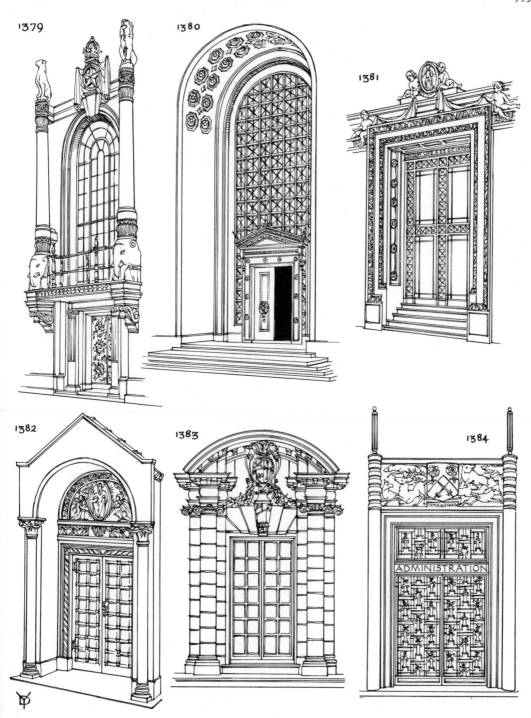

1379 India House, Aldwych, 1929. Sir Herbert Baker   1380 City Hall, Swansea, S. Wales, 1930.
Sir Percy Thomas   1381 London Life Assurance Building, London, 1924. W. Curtis Green   1382
Lady Margaret Hall, Oxford: chapel, 1931. Sir Giles G. Scott   1383 Great Maytham, Rolvenden,
Kent. Sir Edwin Lutyens   1384 Hornsey Town Hall, London, 1933. Reginald H. Uren

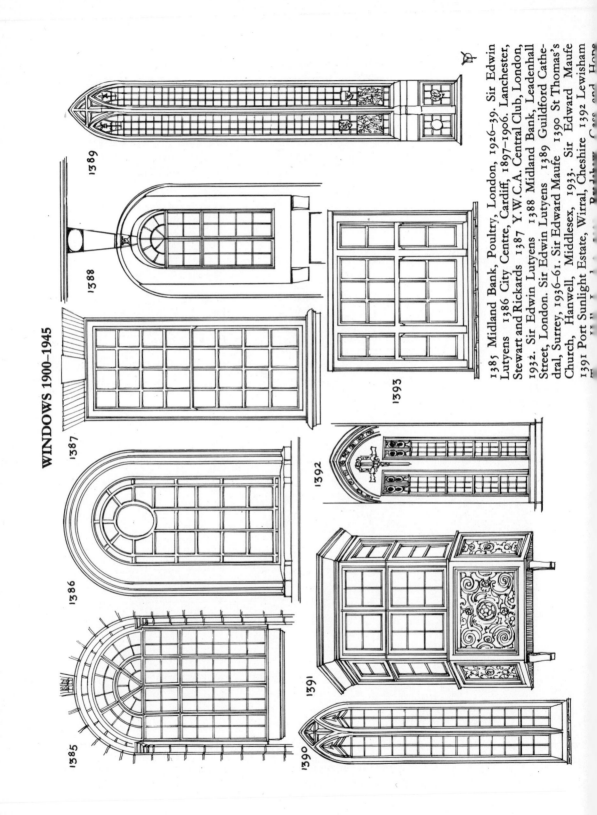

WINDOWS 1900-1945

Equally typical and dignified and perhaps a shade more interesting is the modern-styled town hall at **Hornsey, London**, built in 1933–5 by **Reginald H. Uren**. This is well situated in an average London borough, with an L-shaped frontage facing on to gardens. The building is of brick on steel frame construction and has a tall, slender, square tower. The principal entrance, at the foot of the tower, provides the focal decorative centre with a carved Portland stone surround and ornamental metal gates with animal motifs (1360, 1377, 1384).

Deptford Town Hall, that small but interesting design by **Lanchester, Stewart and Rickards** of 1902, has been mentioned (1353, 1366; p. 541). Another unusual example is that at **Lewisham, London**. Designed in 1931 by **Bradshaw, Gass and Hope**, this town hall occupies a prominent position in the wide main thoroughfare on a curving site. There is no lofty tower here, only a lantern feature. The sloping roof plays a prominent part in the design, whilst the stone façade is split into many faces, projecting and angled round the building. The windows, of Gothic origin, are decorative and tall; a supported canopy shadows the entrance floor (1352, 1392).

Three interesting examples of **libraries** should be mentioned. The **Manchester City Library**, designed and built 1929–34 by **E. Vincent Harris**, is the largest municipal library in the country. On the first floor is the chief feature: the reading room. The library is circular, with a domed roof. The main entrance is in the form of a Corinthian portico which leads into a large vestibule. The building is encircled by a Doric colonnade at third and fourth floor level. This is a fine building and Harris's greatest architectural success (1350). The other two examples are university libraries, that at **Cambridge** by **Sir Giles Gilbert Scott** and that at **London** by **Sir Charles Holden** (1346, 1420; p. 569).

BUILDINGS FOR ENTERTAINMENT

Of the **theatres**, one in particular stands out for its design: the **Royal Shakespeare Memorial Theatre** at **Stratford-upon-Avon**, Warwickshire, 1928–32. A competition was held for the design of this theatre. It was won by **Elizabeth Scott** (cousin of Sir Giles), who carried out the work in collaboration with **Chesterton** and **Shepherd**. The theatre is sited most attractively, with one elevation on the river's edge and the main façade fronting a pleasant garden layout. The design is modern in treatment and the theatre is built of brick. It is simple and unpretentious, but has a quality of Tudor charm which harmonises with the town. On the principal elevation there shows the fan-shaped auditorium with the curved foyer in front. At the rear, the square mass incorporating the stage grid can be seen above. Some years later, glass-walled terraces, including a café and a restaurant, were added on the river front. Inside the theatre, beyond the foyer, is a circular staircase hall; here is a central fountain and the wall staircase leads up to the dress circle foyer. In the auditorium there is a painted plaster ceiling, while the walls are wood lined; many different woods are used, richly veneered: ebony, laurel, oak, maple. The interior has a functional appearance but is not too cold or ascetic (1395).

A number of **pavilions** for use as concert halls, cafés, restaurants, sun lounges, etc., were built during these years, especially at seaside resorts. Two of these are of particular interest. The **De la Warr Pavilion** at **Bexhill-on-Sea**, Sussex, was designed in 1935–6 by the firm of **Erich Mendelsohn** and **Serge Chermayeff**. This is a most remarkable building

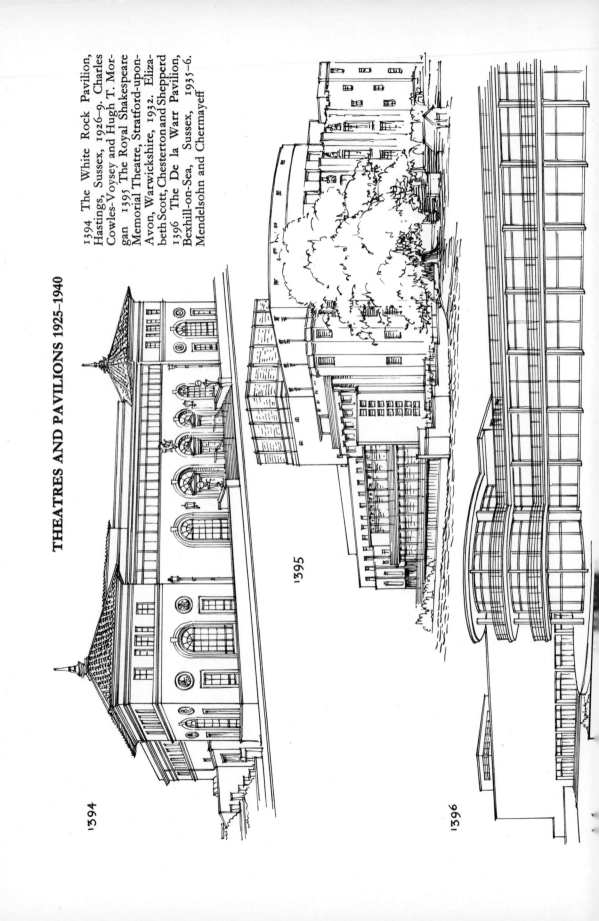

THEATRES AND PAVILIONS 1925–1940

1394 The White Rock Pavilion, Hastings, Sussex, 1926–9. Charles Cowles-Voysey and Hugh T. Morgan 1395 The Royal Shakespeare Memorial Theatre, Stratford-upon-Avon, Warwickshire, 1932. Elizabeth Scott, Chesterton and Shepperd 1396 The De la Warr Pavilion, Bexhill-on-Sea, Sussex, 1935–6. Mendelsohn and Chermayeff

1394

1395

1396

1397

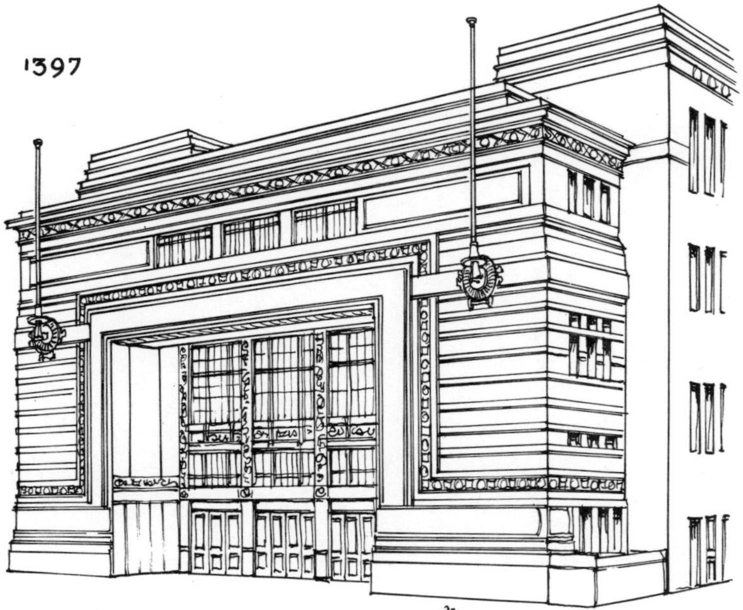

1398

1399

1400

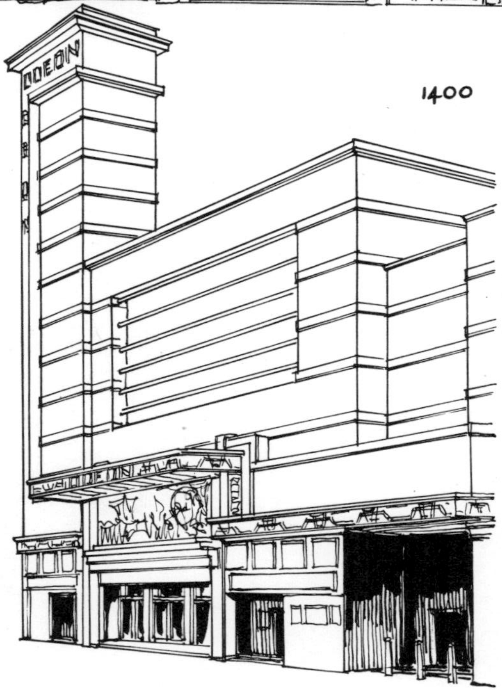

1397 Kensington Cinema, London (now Odeon), 1924–5. J. L. Leathart and W. F. Granger 1398 Regent Cinema, Bournemouth (now Gaumont), 1927 1399 New Victoria Cinema, London, 1929–30 1400 The Odeon Cinema, Leicester Square, London

for its time. It contains a theatre and restaurant and various rooms, while, on the seaward side, are glass-fronted lounges. One can sit in shelter from the cold and wind or, if preferred, outside on the deck with the projecting roof of the floor above as protection and shade. The curved section of the building in the centre of the façade is one of the chief architectural features of the design and enables one to gain the benefit of the sun's rays all day long. The whole exterior structure is in glass, concrete and steel, foreshadowing the common use of these materials (1396).

Another interesting example is the **White Rock Pavilion** at **Hastings**, Sussex, also built on the sea-front. This was designed by **Charles Cowles-Voysey** and **Hugh T. Morgan** in 1926. The site was limited, particularly in depth from front to rear, but the architects succeeded in overcoming the difficulties and achieved a fine concert hall with a broad, wood-panelled auditorium and balcony on three sides. The principal source of daylight is from the large skylight set into the ceiling. The exterior is in white cement finish with coloured roofs. The sea elevation is symmetrical with two end pavilions and a central, three-arched entrance. The general theme is classical but it is adapted to be suitable for light-hearted seaside entertainment (1394).

The **cinema** created a special kind of architecture typical of the inter-war years. Before 1920 most cinemas were converted music halls or theatres, but after this date the cinema was more often built especially for its function. The tempo of building increased until 1930 when the depression curtailed construction for some years, but in the later 1930s building was again in full swing. The years 1927–37 were the age of the super cinema, built larger and larger to accommodate more and more people, with cantilever balcony construction and lavish interior decoration, often in execrable taste. The quantity of cinema construction in England was second only to that in America; in every town and village cinemas were being built. Often it was only a plain brick or concrete building covered with painted decoration and coloured posters depicting next week's attraction. The most lavish and the most interesting examples of cinema building were in Germany, but in England, among thousands of tasteless marzipan cinemas there were a few which had architectural merit. Two of the best of these, both still functioning, are the **New Victoria Cinema**, 1929–30, and the **Kensington Cinema**, 1925 (now Odeon). The latter, designed by **J. R. Leathart** and **W. F. Granger**, was in its day one of the largest cinemas in London. It is set well back from the road and has a dignified, suitable exterior (1397, 1399). Among other appropriate, pleasant and meritorious designs are the **Regent Cinema, Brighton**, 1921: the **Empire, Leicester Square**, 1929 (now demolished); the **Regent** (now Gaumont) **Cinema, Bournemouth**, and the **Gaumont Palace, Lewisham** (1398, 1400).

CHURCHES

From 1900 onwards the tendency in ecclesiastical design was to simplification. Gothic remained the chief source of inspiration until 1920, when architects sought ideas from earlier periods—Byzantine and Romanesque, for example. Between 1925 and 1939 a large number of churches were built to cater for the expanding communities in the suburbs of towns. Brick was the most common material and the exteriors of most of the churches of this period are either dull and solid or gaunt and grim. The interiors are more interesting: in a number of instances these are well-lit and spacious, and diverse means of devising simple vaults and ceilings were employed such as the parabolic concrete ribs in **St Philip's, Osmondthorpe**,

Leeds, built 1932 by **F. R. Charlton,** where the ribs spring from floor not arch level. The traditional, cruciform plan gave way in many cases to a plainer, rectangular layout; such basilican churches were often without aisles and arcades.

One of the principal ecclesiastical architects of this period was **Sir Giles Gilbert Scott.** An example of his church building, the **Church of Our Lady, Northfleet,** is illustrated in Fig. 1337. This is typical of his work in this field. The church is in brick; the fenestration is Gothic, whilst the main doorway is semicircular headed in stepped, brick mouldings. Two churches by the firm of **Welch, Cachemaille-Day** and **Lander, St Saviour's, Eltham,** 1932, and **St Nicholas', Burnage, Manchester,** 1931, are typical of this time. These are built of brick and have weighty, grim exteriors, giving a castellar quality in their dramatic light and shade. The only exterior decoration is in patterned, self-coloured brick (1338). Less dramatic, more traditional brick churches can be seen in the two examples by the firm of **W. A. Pite, Son and Fairweather: St John's, Beckenham,** and the **Church of the Holy Cross, Hornchurch,** both built 1932. The former is constructed on a rectangular plan, whilst the church at Hornchurch is cruciform; both are very simple in design and austere in treatment.

Sir Edward Maufe was another leading church designer of the period. Representative of his work are **St Thomas's, Hanwell,** Middlesex, 1933, and **St Saviour's, Acton,** London (1339, 1390; p. 545). Other principal ecclesiastical architects include **H. S. Goodhart-Rendel,** whose church of **St Wilfred, Brighton,** 1933, is illustrated in Fig. 1340. There was also **Bernard Miller** who designed **St Christopher's, Norris Green, Liverpool,** and **Robert Atkinson** with **St Catharine's, Hammersmith.**

DOMESTIC ARCHITECTURE AND TOWN PLANNING

Garden Cities and Housing Estates

Several such schemes were propounded and established in the years 1900–45; some were started by industrial concerns, others as Garden City Trusts, and some were created by borough councils, although these last-named were generally only dormitory suburbs. The general idea was to create new centres of population in a planned housing area which would also contain amenities such as churches, shops, schools, clubs, etc., and thus produce a self-supporting community in the cleaner rural air, and with a higher proportion of open space per house than had been the case in nineteenth-century industrial towns.

One of the original protagonists for this idea was Ebenezer Howard, who enunciated his plans in a book published in 1898. He felt strongly that towns should be built to provide healthy living conditions on land owned or held in trust for the community concerned and that there should be adequate land space to provide a rural belt between this town and any other towns. It was an attempt to call a halt to the ever-increasing urban sprawl of cities like London, Liverpool, Manchester and Birmingham. The Garden City Association was formed and a company established called Garden City Ltd. This led to the Garden Cities of Letchworth and Welwyn.

At the same time, industrialists like Lord Leverhulme were establishing their own model housing estates. Port Sunlight was Lord Leverhulme's conception, Bournville came from Messrs Cadbury, and Messrs Rowntree built theirs near York. In the towns themselves, Hampstead Garden Suburb provided a better-class housing estate in North London and borough councils were building their extensive dormitory suburbs.

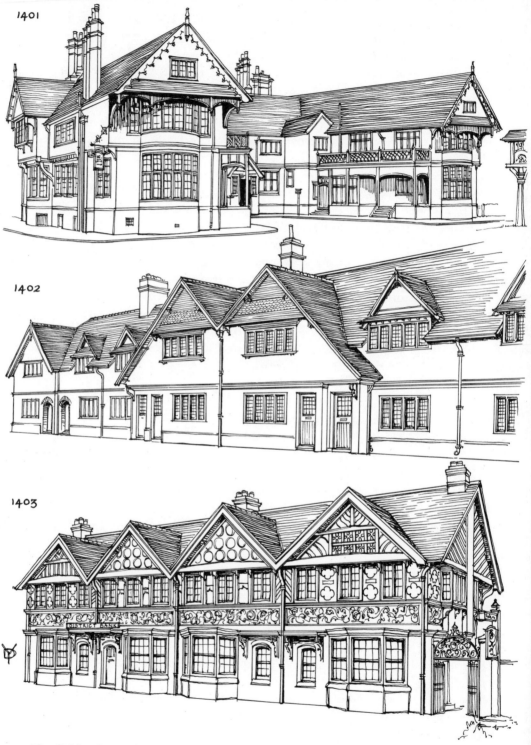

1401 The Bridge Inn 1402 Terrace Houses. Brick, stone and tile 1403 Brick and half-timber block containing bank and library

The **London County Council** was the largest organisation in the field and contributed a number of **cottage estates**. The largest of these, and typical of the inter-war years, is that at **Becontree**, on the east side of London. The largest municipal housing estate in the world at that time, it comprises 2,784 acres of which only a small area—500 acres—is open space. This is very far below Ebenezer Howard's suggested figures. The aim and achievement of this estate is to rehouse people from the slum areas of east London in houses better than those from which they came. Not very much more, however, can be conceded to it. It is a dormitory suburb and so its workers have to travel, many long distances, to work. It covers an enormous area, including parts of the boroughs of Ilford, Barking and Dagenham, in a sprawling brick and concrete jungle of unrelieved architectural suburban monotony. There are some 25,000 dwellings, housing 112,000 people. To give a picture of the low standard of amenity provided at Becontree, Welwyn Garden City, for example, covers much the same area of land, houses only one-third of the population, and is surrounded by countryside; Becontree, on the other hand, is encompassed by more suburbs. Amenities such as shops and clubs, etc. are still not adequate. There is no central community life, the estate has no corporate meaning, it is quite featureless and very much of one class of society. Building still continues at Becontree, but much of the estate was constructed between 1920 and 1930. The cottages have three to six rooms and there are some cottage flats. Among the public buildings so far built are 30 schools, 27 churches, two cinemas and nine public houses. A typical terrace block in one of the main thoroughfares at Becontree can be seen in Fig. 1329.

Port Sunlight, Wirral, Cheshire, is most interesting and, with Bournville, was the first actual successful outcome of the Garden City ideal. The Lever factory was built in 1888 and the housing estate has developed since then. On 160 acres the estate was planned for a population of 10,000. The tenancies of the houses are restricted to the firm's employees. Most of the 1,500 houses are now built. The whole plan is formal, with good roads and avenues, gardens and open spaces. There is a church, an art gallery, schools, a cottage hospital, swimming bath, village inn, stores and shops, library, bank, fire station and post office. There are several halls and clubs. Architecturally the estate is most successful. There is tremendous variety in materials and styles, so there is no overall architectural monotony. The roads and vistas are carefully planned to give pleasant views in different directions. A number of well-known domestic architects contributed to the scheme: for example, Sir Ernest George, W. Owen and Wilson and Talbot. Most of the houses are simple, but are not austere or undecorated. Brick, stone, half-timber, pargeting are all used. Examples of these can be seen in Figs 1391 and 1401–3.

Bournville Village was founded by George Cadbury, who moved his factory some five miles out of Birmingham in 1879 and established a new urban area. The present housing estate was begun in 1895 and building still continues. Since 1900 it has been administered by the Bournville Village Trust. It now covers some 1,000 acres, planned less formally than Port Sunlight, with more curving roads and a larger area of open space and sports grounds. There are now about 2,500 houses and a population of nearly 9,000. There are five churches, three village halls, and several schools including one for arts and crafts. Unfortunately, unlike Port Sunlight, the garden city was planned too near its parent town, Birmingham, and is now a suburb of it with little open land in between.

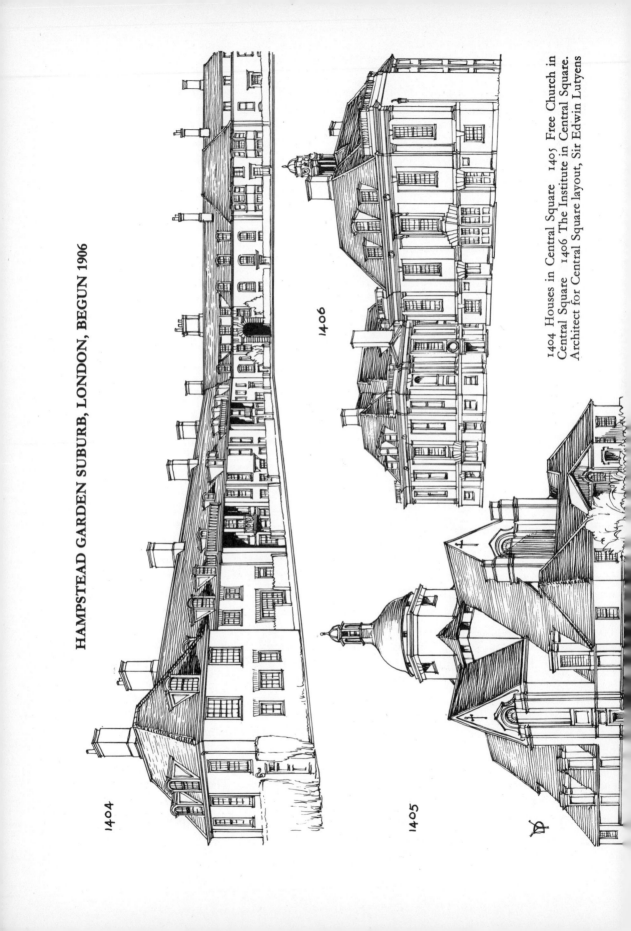

HAMPSTEAD GARDEN SUBURB, LONDON, BEGUN 1906

1404

1405

1406

1404 Houses in Central Square 1405 Free Church in Central Square 1406 The Institute in Central Square. Architect for Central Square layout, Sir Edwin Lutyens

1408

1407

1410

1409

1407 The Council Offices 1408 House, The Parkway, Louis de Soissons 1409 Roche Products Factory, 1938. Salvisberg and Brown 1410 Terrace Houses. Louis de Soissons and A. W. Kenyon

HOUSES 1900–1914

1411

1412

1411 'The Pastures', North Luffenham, Rutland, 1901. C. F. A. Voysey   1412 'Feathercombe', Hambledon, Surrey. Sir Ernest Newton

Hampstead Garden Suburb was planned as a good-quality architectural layout to provide a high-class housing area in north London. The Garden Suburb Trust was founded in 1906. The chief planning experts were **Sir Reginald Unwin** (later Chief Town Planning Officer to the Ministry of Health) and **Barry Parker**. By 1908 the scheme was thought out and **Sir Edwin Lutyens** was asked to prepare designs for **Central Square**, the proposed hub of the community. This he did, and created a formal, symmetrical centre in Renaissance tradition. Here, on the top of the hill, are two churches, balancing one another in the design, on opposite sides of the square, which is an open green space. One is the **Anglican Church** of **St Jude**, with a tall spire, and the other the domed **Free Church**. Around the square are large terraced houses and the **Institute buildings** (1404–6). The remainder of the estate, covering 317 acres, is less formally laid out in a variety of architectural styles. The predominant material for the whole scheme is brick and red tiles, with white-painted woodwork. The architectural standard is high and the workmanship equally so.

The ideal **Garden City** propounded by Ebenezer Howard was largely embodied at **Letchworth**, Hertfordshire, which was planned by **Sir Raymond Unwin** and **Barry Parker**. It is a social success, though not outstanding architecturally. It is an industrial area and a residential town with a high proportion of surrounding agricultural land. The total area comprises about 4,500 acres of which about 1,500 are used by the town and about 3,000 are kept as a green belt. The factory area is apart from the town but readily accessible to it. The town centre is formally planned, while the remainder is laid out irregularly. The plan is spacious but the architecture generally is indistinctive. Over a period of some 40 years have been built about 5,000 houses, nearly 200 shops, about 145 factories and many schools, churches, cinemas and hotels. The population is now over 20,000.

Welwyn, also in Hertfordshire, is near Letchworth and similar in conception though smaller in area. It covers some 2,500 acres, surrounded by a green belt, and will be limited to a population of 40,000. Building began in 1920 and much of the architecture and layout was by the architect **Louis de Soissons**. There is a factory area adjacent to the residential part and readily accessible to it. The centre of the town is formally planned with broad avenues, shops, a theatre, the Council Offices and civic buildings. The residential part is less formal and, in many parts, quite rural in appearance. Like Letchworth, the houses have gardens, but architecturally, Welwyn has more in common with Port Sunlight. There is great variety in size and style of house, from terraced cottages to large, detached villas. Brick is the most usual medium, but clapboard and half-timber is also used to great effect. Much of the residential layout makes use of the cul-de-sac planning motif, rather in the same way as at the Dover House Council Estate at Putney, S.W.15. There are many tree-lined roads and these are often wide enough to permit broad grass central and side verges. In general, the architectural standard at Welwyn is high and shows ingenuity and diversity of design. Some examples of this are illustrated in Figs. 1407–10.

Houses

Before 1914 many attractive houses were built by such architects as **Lutyens** (1323–5, 1328; p. 521), **Voysey, Newton, Dawber** and many others. A proportion of these were still on Georgian plan; others, like Voysey's were very plain with small window openings and steeply pitched roofs. Most of them were spacious, pleasant to live in and soundly built. Examples of these are **Voysey's 'The Pastures', North Luffenham**, Rutland, 1901 (1411), and **Newton's 'Feathercombe', Hambledon, Surrey** (1412).

The modern house of much less traditional approach, as was built in Germany and France by men like **Gropius** and **Le Corbusier** in the 1920s, was rare in England until 1930; and, even in the period 1930–9, the majority of such examples were designed by foreign architects. The increased use of steel and concrete construction made new design in houses possible, but English architects were slower in the domestic field to take advantage of this than even in other spheres of building. It was possible in the 1930s to design such houses with walls largely of glass and with a reduction in the number of dividing walls inside the house. Many examples were a compromise between traditional and modern; the plainness of the house was accentuated and there was a larger area of glass; flat roofs became a feature of the modern house. Among examples of such houses are **Sun House, Frognal Way, Hampstead**, 1935, by **Maxwell Fry; High and Over, Amersham**, 1929, by **Amyas Connell** and **New Ways, Northampton**, 1926, by **Peter Behrens** (1326–7).

All these, of course, were architect-designed houses, and as such, were a minority. Most of the housing accommodation (apart from the estates already described) was built by the speculative builder. Those erected before 1914 were soundly built if dull. In industrial towns they were commonly in terrace form, but were more often designed with bathroom facilities than in the nineteenth century. From 1920 to 1939 much speculative building was a disgrace. This was the age of the jerry-builder and of ribbon development along our expanding arterial road system. The plan was more or less standardised on two floors with accommodation including three bedrooms, two reception rooms, bath and kitchen. The variety was an economic and social one: the cheapest houses were generally in terrace form, the better quality, semi-detached and the best, detached. It was in the last-named of these categories that the fashion for pseudo half-timbering and Elizabethan brickwork was so popular in the 1930s in the so-called 'stockbroker belts'.

Blocks of Flats

It was after 1930 that the congestion became so acute in London and other large cities that it was realised that flat accommodation represented the only way to begin to solve the problem; the garden city had only touched the fringe of this. Municipal authorities were responsible for building a number of these schemes; many of the tenement block layouts of this period are unutterably depressing and show little imagination. In addition, two of the main problems in designing good accommodation in flats are to permit adequate ingress of light and to cut out noise. Most London County Council schemes, for example, did neither of these. The usual layout was for access by galleries, that is, an open corridor along one façade of the block. Each corridor was reached by intermittent staircases. There is no privacy from the noise of people approaching other flats and the gallery above cuts out the light from the windows on the gallery below.

Lutyens and **Wells Coates** both designed schemes for flats in this period, and both layouts were in corridor-access design. Architecturally, however, both were of higher standard than the average. Lutyens' working-class flats at **Page Street, Westminster**, have already been described (1330, p. 524). **Wells Coates** designed the luxury flats at **Hampstead** in

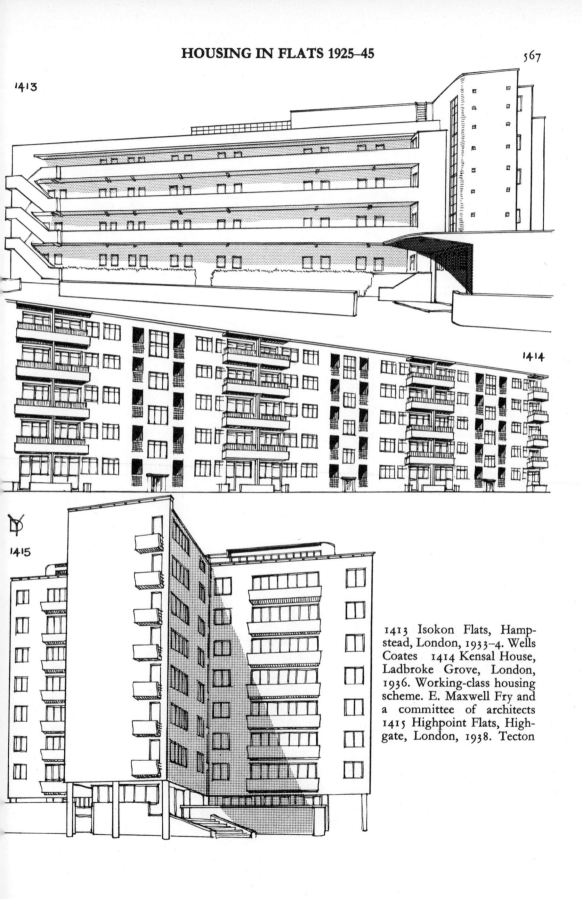

1413 Isokon Flats, Hampstead, London, 1933–4. Wells Coates 1414 Kensal House, Ladbroke Grove, London, 1936. Working-class housing scheme. E. Maxwell Fry and a committee of architects 1415 Highpoint Flats, Highgate, London, 1938. Tecton

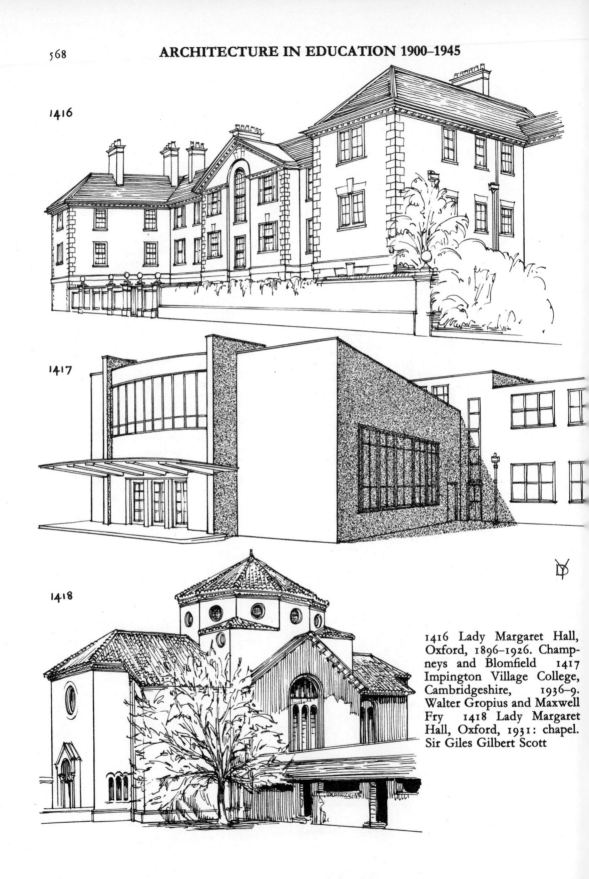

1416 Lady Margaret Hall, Oxford, 1896–1926. Champneys and Blomfield   1417 Impington Village College, Cambridgeshire, 1936–9. Walter Gropius and Maxwell Fry   1418 Lady Margaret Hall, Oxford, 1931: chapel. Sir Giles Gilbert Scott

1933–4—**Isokon Flats**—which are constructed in concrete in simple, balcony pattern (1413). Among the balcony style of flats with different approach was **Maxwell Fry's Kensal House** at **Ladbroke Grove**, London, built in 1936, as a working-class housing scheme (1414). A more unusual design, quite new in England at this date, was the tall block construction by **Tecton** at **Highgate**, the **Highpoint flats**, built in 1938. These are in the luxury class and are laid out with pleasant gardens behind. Today, these flats do not appear to be very high, but in the 1930s, with reluctance to build high, they were most unusual. The flats have rectangular fenestration and projecting balconies (1415).

BUILDINGS FOR EDUCATION

The Universities

The principal architectural work at **Oxford** in the period was at Somerville College and at Lady Margaret Hall. **Somerville College** had been established in 1879 but much of the building was after 1900. **Basil Champneys** was responsible for much of this, which was mainly constructed before the First World War. **Lady Margaret Hall**, also a college for women, had been established in 1878 in a Victorian house. The present college buildings are twentieth century and were built over a long period between 1896 and 1931. Much of this work is in red brick with white painted windows. Several architects took part in the scheme, but the main part of the earlier work was by **Sir Reginald Blomfield** and the later by **Sir Giles Gilbert Scott**. Scott also designed the attractive Byzantine-style **chapel**, based on a Greek cross plan. This is one of the best buildings of the period in Oxford (1382, 1416, 1418).

The principal work at **Cambridge** at this time was all by **Scott**, and comprised one large layout of the University Library and Clare College New Court. The **University Library**, which was opened in 1934, was a large, new building on symmetrical plan. It is a steel-framed construction and is built with a long front block from which rises a massive, square tower over the central entrance. The frontage is 420 feet and the tower ascends to 160 feet. The building is faced with fawn-coloured brick and, though basically classical, is modern in treatment. The vertical lines of the shafts between the windows and of the uprights in the tower give emphasis to this. Behind this block are others which enclose two square courts. The library is finely equipped and houses primarily scientific books (1420). **The Memorial Court** of **Clare College** was built by Scott adjacent to the library between 1922 and 1934. Like the library it has a classical foundation in design, but is modern in its approach and treatment. It is the most attractive and successful work at Cambridge in this period (1419, 1421).

At **London University** the new construction of **Senate House** and the **University buildings** were undertaken by **Sir Charles Holden**, designer of the London Transport Offices at St James's, in 1931. The foundation-stone was laid in 1933 and Senate House was completed in 1937. The principal feature of this extensive layout is the Senate House tower which houses the University Library. The construction is of masonry and brick. The lower part, up to the first floor, is of brick faced with Cornish grey granite. Above this, the facing is of Portland stone. The building is essentially modern and bears great similarity to Holden's Broadway House. There are the same rectangular window openings and the same diminishing stages of massive, rectangular prisms but, this time, no clock tower (1346).

UNIVERSITY ARCHITECTURE AT CAMBRIDGE 1918–1940

1419   1420   1421

1419, 1420 Clare College, Cambridge; Memorial Court, entrance, 1922–24   1420 University Library, 1931–4. Architect for both

Work on the new **University** buildings at **Bristol** was begun in 1915. The architect, a Bristol man, was **Sir George Oatley, 1863–1950**, and he designed the University in traditional Gothic pattern. The most noteworthy feature is the University tower, visible from all parts of Bristol. It is constructed on monumental scale and is in careful, Perpendicular Gothic. It was completed in 1925 (1347).

Colleges and Schools

Technical college building in this period did not really get under way before all such schemes were severely curtailed by the depression. In the mid-1930s work began again, but only a small number were completed before the beginning of the Second World War. Among these were the **South-West Essex Technical College** at **Walthamstow** and the **South-East** at **Dagenham**, Essex, also those at **Guildford**, Surrey, and **Hendon**, Middlesex. None of these buildings have particular architectural merit.

In a slightly different field there was proposed in the 1920s a scheme for village Colleges in Cambridgeshire. The idea came from Henry Morris, the Secretary for Education to the Cambridgeshire County Council. The village Colleges were intended as centres of cultural and social life in the rural districts and were to cater for all age groups. The first of these at **Sawston** was opened in 1930. Then came the depression and, by 1939, only four of the proposed 11 colleges had been built. Among these was the **Village College** at **Impington**, built 1936–9, for which Mr Morris commissioned **Walter Gropius** and **Maxwell Fry** to carry out their designs. The college is a prototype for today's schools and rural colleges. It was the first such college built on modern lines. It is very simple, in the form of low rectangular blocks with horizontal rectangular window frames and with covered ways along the blocks. The entrance is subtly curved and has a wide window above and a projecting canopy over the tripartite doorway below (1417).

In **school** building the usual plan, after 1900, was to construct the school around a playground or quadrangle. This stemmed from the older public school conception, but most of the schools were a poorer version of this. The buildings were several storeys high, especially in towns, with many stone staircases. The layout was generally symmetrical and the architectural appearance often stark and gloomy. After 1930 a less rigid approach employed. The tendency towards one- or two-storey buildings began, but there were very few schools built in the modern idiom in England before 1945.

INDUSTRIAL BUILDING

Since there was little town planning organisation before 1945, and building for both housing and industry was largely a free-for-all, many factories, like the houses, were built along busy, arterial roads on plots fronting the roads themselves. This had the obvious advantage of facilitating transport problems for the factory itself but, of course, as is now painfully apparent, the tremendous disadvantage of heavy vehicles queuing up to disgorge on to already overburdened trunk roads. From the architectural viewpoint this idea was also generally fatal. The offices and showrooms were constructed to face the road, whilst the factory was behind. The former building was generally symmetrical and often classical or traditional, whilst the factory itself was of as cheap a construction as possible, which meant steel and concrete—an incongruous and unharmonious mixture. One of the worst areas in England for this practice was London, particularly its artery the Great West Road.

An outstanding example of a large modern factory building enterprise of this period is that of **Boots Pure Drug Company** at their factory at **Beeston,** Nottinghamshire The site of 236 acres was acquired in 1927, some 3½ miles from Nottingham near the River Trent. The two principal buildings there are the two sections of the pharmaceutical factory, the 'wets' and the 'drys'. Both were designed by **Sir E. Owen Williams.** The 'wets', which was finished in 1932, is the factory for liquids, creams and pastes. This is a glass and concrete structure on the unit dimension system and has a cantilever roof construction (1422). The 'drys', which is for powders, tablets and lozenges, was finished in 1938. A corner of it is shown in Fig. 1363. The factory covers an enormous area and Sir Owen Williams's buildings marked a new stage in factory design at the time. They are functional and light, with a tremendous area of glass curtain-walling. There were few such examples in Britain before 1945.

In **power-station** design, **Scott's** construction at **Battersea** has already been referred to (1342, pp. 531–3). Several new **underground railway stations** were built in this period on

1422 Pharmaceutical Production 'Wets' Factory, Boots Pure Drug Co., Beeston, Nottinghamshire. Glass and concrete structure, 1932. Sir E. Owen Williams

1423 Heathcote, Ilkley, Yorkshire, 1906. Sir Edwin Lutyens 1424 Midland Bank, Poultry, 1926–30. Sir Edwin Lutyens 1425 Nashdom Abbey, Taplow, Buckinghamshire, 1905. Sir Edwin Lutyens 1426 Great Maytham, Rolvenden, Kent, 1910. Sir Edwin Lutyens 1427 'Goddards', Abinger Common, 1899. Sir Edwin Lutyens 1428 Downing College, Cambridge 1429 Bush House, Aldwych, London, 1925–8. Helmle, Corbett and Harrison 1430 Plumpton Place, Sussex, 1927. Sir Edwin Lutyens 1431 Law Courts, City Centre, Cardiff, 1897–1906. Lanchester, Stewart and Rickards

the lines extending out of London. Among the modern designs, two contrasting examples are illustrated in Figs 1341 and 1343, showing those at **Osterley** and **Arnos Grove**. Other interesting designs include those at **St John's Wood** and **Hanger Lane**.

IRON AND STEEL

From 1900 onwards steel has been used in ever-increasing quantities, with a corresponding diminution in the employment of cast iron. The high tensile strength of steel, manufactured after 1920 in large quantities, made it particularly suitable for metal-constructed framed buildings and for engineering projects such as bridges, tunnels, etc. However, cast iron still had its uses; among these in this period were, for instance, the road setts in the flooring of the Mersey Tunnel (engineer, Sir Basil Mott), lamp standards, bollards, post boxes and telephone boxes. Sir Giles Gilbert Scott designed a new G.P.O. telephone kiosk which was made in vast numbers in cast iron. This was a simple, prefabricated construction which was cheap to produce and pleasant to look at. One great problem with iron and steel has always been that they are liable to rust. The Victorians painted it for exterior use and black-leaded it for interiors. Modern methods include treatments like bonderising and parkerising. Chromium-plating has been widely used since the 1930s.

Metal Bridge Construction

Among the large-scale bridges of this type built before 1945 are the Tyne Road Bridge, the Connel Ferry Bridge and the Middlesbrough Transporter Bridge. These are typical of the construction of their time. The **Tyne Bridge** at **Newcastle-upon-Tyne** is a steel construction designed by **Messrs Mott, Hay and Anderson** and completed in 1930. It possesses a huge steel arch span of 531 feet. This type of construction was deemed suitable to the heavy, industrial traffic which the bridge constantly has to bear (1433 a, b and c).

The **Middlesbrough Transporter Bridge** is a much earlier type in design and appearance. It spans the River Tees and was opened in 1911. It is a large, unprepossessing construction of movable design, permitting ships to pass up and down the river. The **Connel Ferry Bridge**, on the other hand, is of steel cantilever design and is both elegant and powerful in appearance. This construction, near **Oban**, spans Loch Etive and was a much-needed Edwardian enterprise.

REINFORCED CONCRETE

This has become such a common material in present-day building construction that we are apt to forget that its wide-scale use is comparatively recent. Concrete had, of course, been employed extensively by the Ancient Romans, but the art of its use and mixture had been, like so many other crafts, lost after the fall of Rome. It was not until the eighteenth century that this was rediscovered and only in the later nineteenth century that it was used much at all. Reinforced concrete, that is concrete with metal strengthening, is a material of the twentieth century. From 1920 onwards it was widely used and the more costly stone and brick retained more and more for facing and decoration. However, in this period until 1945, designs did not change radically, only the materials. It was left to the post-war period to

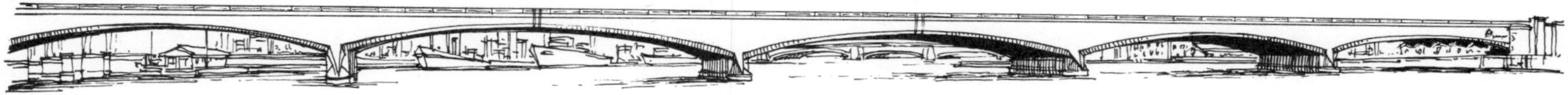

1434

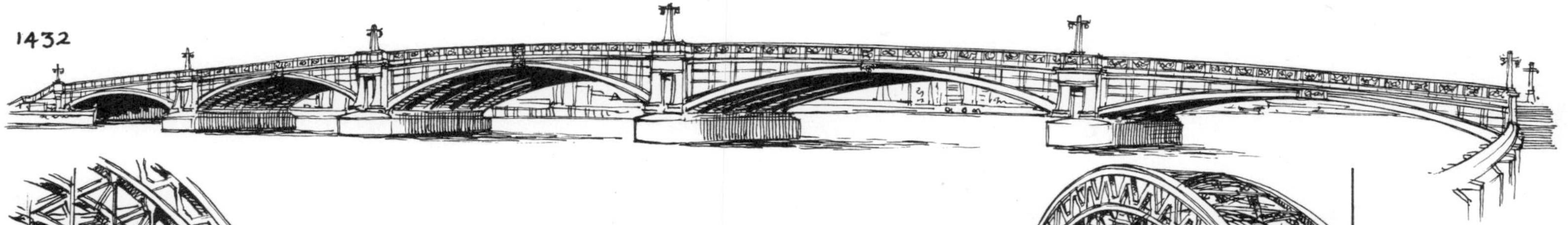

1432

1433 a

1433 b

1433 c

1432 Lambeth Bridge, London, 1935–7. Sir Reginald Blomfield 1433a, b, c Road Bridge, Newcastle-on-Tyne, 1930. Architect, R. Burns Dick; engineers, Messrs Mott, Hay and Anderson 1434 Waterloo Bridge, London, 1939–45. Sir Giles Gilbert Scott

adapt architecture to the medium. In the 1920s and '30s concrete was used primarily for industrial building; warehouses, factories, railway stations, etc., and for bridges.

Reinforced Concrete Bridges

By 1850 Portland cement was being produced in quantity, but this material alone has little tensile strength. Steel, on the other hand, is strong in this capacity, so that when steel rods are inserted into the concrete an ideal new plastic material is created for bridge building. Modern construction uses pre-stressed concrete which makes possible lighter and more economical bridges,

One of the principal examples of this type of construction in this period is the new **Waterloo Bridge**, designed by **Sir Giles Gilbert Scott** and built 1939–45. The engineers were **Rendel, Palmer** and **Tritton** in association with **Sir Pierson Frank**. The bridge is constructed of two parallel, continuous, reinforced concrete beams each of five 240-foot spans. It is faced with slabs of Portland stone laid vertically. The design of the bridge has aroused controversy. Some critics deem it a beautiful example of modern bridge building, others consider it to be an inferior successor to the original. There is no doubt, however, that due to the material from which it is constructed, it has a more elegant and light-weight appearance than its Victorian neighbours, and, though completely plain, is pleasant to look at (1434).

CHAPTER XIII

Modern Architecture 1945 onwards

The post-war period presented a magnificent architectural opportunity in England and in Europe. No building had been carried out for nearly six years. Vast areas of destroyed and damaged property needed rebuilding. Within a decade a new problem emerged and crystallised: the struggle between pedestrian and motor vehicle for space in the city streets. New building materials and methods of construction also suggested a different approach.

That a new look has been given to the architecture of the mid-century is undeniable. Modern architecture owes little or nothing to its predecessors in classical or Gothic vein, whether in style, three-dimensional form, materials or building methods. It is undoubtedly new. Equally it is not in any way national. Certain characteristics do appear, in specific countries, due largely to climatic conditions. For example, glass curtain walling is ubiquitous in England, North America, Northern France and Germany. In the hot sun of Greece and Italy it would be impracticable, and the open, balcony style with shuttered windows takes its place. Far more colour is apparent too in these countries which enjoy a high percentage of sunshine during the year. Basically, however, architectural design is depressingly, but inevitably, similar from London to Chicago and from Berlin to Athens.

There can only be praise that at last, after so many centuries, mankind has evolved a new architecture. It was sadly overdue. Whether it is a style which will develop into something fine and beautiful is not yet clear. As yet, the potentialities of the new building methods, materials and design have only begun to be explored. Whether man has in the present mode reached the end of the line or whether he will advance to greater heights is yet to be seen. We who are living in this age cannot yet evaluate or criticise the complete pattern. The author attempts only, therefore, in this last chapter, to comment on typical completed or proposed schemes, and trends which have impressed her while travelling the length of Britain.

Three factors strongly and continuously present themselves, all of which are causing concern to thinking people both inside and outside the architectural profession. One of these is the feeling that the profession of architecture itself is becoming rapidly an adjunct to that of civil engineering, and that the aesthetic quality of a building has become a luxury which can seldom be afforded. Many of the outstanding building schemes of the last ten years have been, in fact, triumphs not of architecture but of civil engineering. To the engineer has gone the excitement, interest and success in solving problem after problem in increasing the height of buildings, in abandoning columnar support for ceilings, in providing floors of tremendous area, in heating, ventilating and supplying the manifold facilities of vast schemes. There are a few exceptions to this thesis, where grace of line and shape, the quality of fine proportion and the use of materials of attractive aesthetic qualities have been of great importance in the building and successful in the completed project. They are, unfortunately, too rare.

A second disturbing feature in modern building is its monotony. With mid-twentieth-century communications, transport, mass-production and prefabrication of units and materials, a sameness of design in windows, doors, roofing, ceiling materials, lighting, floor covering, etc. is, in the interests of economy, no doubt inevitable. But, when seen in town after town and country after country, the monotony disturbs profoundly and, as years pass and more old buildings—which at present provide a leavening—are demolished, it will become insupportable. Humanity needs variety. Will modern architecture develop and change quickly enough to provide this?

The third unfortunate aspect of modern architecture is the quality of the finished article. This is a criticism not just of architecture but of building. It is, no doubt, an economic factor in these days of high cost of labour and transport, but comparatively few buildings of whatever type are erected where, within a few months, there are not complaints of doors and windows which do not fit, hot water pipes placed in inconvenient positions, paint which is peeling, plastic and floor coverings which are cracking or bulging and handles and fastenings which break in the hand. These criticisms come equally from occupants of technical colleges, universities, schools, houses and office blocks. Excessive areas of glass window— still used after building in this way for fifteen years—result, when it is sunny, in overheated and dazzled occupants, who are destined to be frozen during the cold weather. Every word uttered by a headmaster in remonstrating with a pupil in his study of a new school can be heard by the occupants of the classroom next door; sinks and washbasins in new university hostel accommodation are set at back-breaking level. This list can be extended indefinitely. The implication is one of lack of thought, care and supervision by the architect who designs and the firm who builds and installs. Insufficient responsibility is accepted at all levels.

There are, however, a number of factors to the credit of modern architecture. One of these is the modern interior of hotel, office, schoolroom or drawing-room. New materials and a fresh approach to design and living have brought more light, better heating methods, surfaces which are gaily coloured yet clean easily and, in general, far more pleasant surroundings in which the average person can live and work. In comparing the typical schoolroom of, for instance, 1960 with that of 1900, the former is infinitely more pleasant to inhabit, as also is its office counterpart. Staircases, courtyards, foyers are all treated much more imaginatively and with an expanding utilisation of light, artificial and natural.

Another great benefit of modern design is the planned new town or city centre, particularly where, as at Stevenage or at Coventry, the traffic and the pedestrians are completely segregated, and the shopper with perambulator can window-gaze in safety and comfort. This type of planning which, though fantastic in cost, seems likely to extend to city centres such as Birmingham and traffic nightmares like Piccadilly Circus and Hammersmith Broadway, is well worth while, though difficulties and problems besetting its completion seem almost insuperable. In conjunction with the extension of the clean air zones, our cities are gradually becoming better places to live in than they were in the late nineteenth century— provided that a solution to the ever-increasing traffic problem can be found in time.

PROFESSOR SIR LESLIE PATRICK ABERCROMBIE 1879–1957

Planning of areas of town and country is largely a twentieth-century conception. There were nineteenth-century examples on a comparatively small scale as were described in Chapter XI but the more urgent need for such planning has been brought about by the large population centres of modern times.

Today, an increasing number of architects, economists, university lecturers and politicians are calling for more large-scale planning as it becomes apparent that it is the only way in which can be met the imperative needs of citizen, motorist, pedestrian, business-man and the problems of commerce and of the local authorities resolved. It is all too clear, however, that admirable plans involving architects, town planners, local council and central government mean little unless there is also power to control and purchase land. The growing demand for central space, in particular in cities, has led to taller and taller buildings, but this is only a partial solution. Segregation from traffic becomes daily more necessary; off-street parking is an urgent requirement, yet commercial access to buildings must be maintained.

The best-known pioneer in this field of modern town planning was **Sir Patrick Abercrombie**. He established his reputation in 1913 by his scheme for the replanning of **Dublin** with which he won the international competition. He later devised plans for many other cities including **Bath, Bristol, Stratford-upon-Avon** and **Sheffield**. From 1915 to 1935 Abercrombie held the chair of civic design at the University of Liverpool, but in 1935 he came to London and occupied the chair of town planning at London University until 1946.

Sir Patrick was best known for his extensive work in replanning Britain's bombed cities, particularly **Plymouth** and **London**. Here he illustrated that his ideas were years ahead of his time, and he anticipated traffic and road problems which are now urgently with us. Yet, much of his planning has not been implemented.

During the war the London County Council prepared its plan for the reconstruction of London. Sir Patrick Abercrombie sent in his report in 1943. At this time he was convinced that London's traffic problem was an integral part of the necessary replanning and should be dealt with as such. This advice was not taken and today we are faced with the situation which he visualised 20 years ago. In 1944 he presented his Greater London Plan, emphasising the need for decentralisation and planning for an overspill from the Metropolitan area. From this scheme developed the New Towns policy and many of his proposals on green and agricultural belts and regional planning were put into operation in later years. The London County Council's 1951 Development Plan is largely based on Abercrombie's ideas. Much of his plan for London, in particular, his proposals for road redevelopment and replanning, were shelved as too costly and are pigeon-holed still, probably never to see the light of day. Like Wren's plans of the seventeenth century, they fell victim to commerce and economy. In the end, this procrastination may well prove more costly than the schemes themselves.

Sir Patrick established the profession of town planning in Britain and he trained the next generation to continue his work. He was famed far beyond this country and his assistance and advice were sought by many countries as far apart as Russia, Abyssinia, Palestine and Ceylon. He was Vice-President of the Royal Institute of British Architects, 1937–9; Royal Gold Medallist 1946, also Gold Medallist of the American Institute of Architects. He was knighted in 1945.

SIR BASIL SPENCE 1907–

Best known among the names of post-war British architects is that of Sir Basil Spence, largely because of his position as architect to the new Coventry Cathedral. Since 1951, when he won the competition for the cathedral, he has carried out a prodigious quantity of work from his three offices, one in Edinburgh and two in London. Unlike so many architects with large practices he has never permitted himself to become solely an administrator, and still carries out a quantity of drawings and takes active responsibility for the architecture erected and completed in his name.

Spence is a Scot; he was educated at George Watson's College in Edinburgh, then studied at the Architectural Schools in Edinburgh and later at London University. In 1931 he became the Royal Institute of British Architects' Recognised Schools Silver Medallist and, in 1933, the Pugin Student. Early in his career he spent a year in Lutyens' office, where he worked on drawings for the Viceroy's House in Delhi. After his army service during the war, he was in 1947 elected F.R.I.B.A., in 1948 awarded the O.B.E., and in 1953 elected to the Royal Academy. He was President of the Royal Institute of British Architects 1958–9. Apart from the Coventry Cathedral competition in 1951, he also won the Festival of Britain award by the Council of Architecture, Town Planning and Building Research for his **housing estate** at **Sunbury-on-Thames**. In 1962 he was awarded the O.M.

Spence's work has been of varied scope: it includes blocks of flats, churches, houses and housing estates; industrial work including exhibition sites; university and other educational and laboratory designs; theatres and hospitals. His quantity of **exhibition work** includes the Imperial Chemical Industry's Pavilion for the Glasgow Exhibition, 1938; he was chief architect for the Britain Can Make It Exhibition in 1946; he designed the Imperial Chemical Industry's Stand for the British Section in 1948 at the Copenhagen Exhibition; in 1951, for the Festival of Britain he designed the Sea and Ships Pavilion.

In **educational work**, he was responsible for the Comprehensive School at Sydenham and St Martin's School at Shrewsbury. In **university building** he has been planning consultant at Edinburgh and consultant architect at Southampton and Nottingham. He designed the new Physics buildings at Liverpool and Durham, the Chemistry building at Nottingham, the Engineering block at Southampton, the Department of Natural Philosophy at Glasgow and the Physics and Chemistry building at Exeter. His largest and most interesting project in this field is the new **University of Sussex** at **Brighton**.

Spence has designed a number of **churches**, among them examples at Manchester, Edinburgh, Coventry and Sheffield.

In modern housing he has carried out work at the **New Towns** of **Basildon** and **Hatfield**. A large transformation scheme has been carried out under his direction in **Glasgow** where Gorbals slums are being turned into a new residential neighbourhood.

Spence is an up-to-date architect using modern methods and materials but he is no extremist. His work is admired by his colleagues and the layman but probably less by the young student who finds it too traditional. He has met tremendous success in the last 11 years following upon his designs for the new Coventry Cathedral. His warmth and charm of personality, his enthusiasm for his profession and his pleasant and unpatronising manner in dealing with the layman have won him liking and approval from all with whom he has come into contact.

Coventry Cathedral

Like Guildford Cathedral, the new Cathedral of Coventry is a product of its age. Although the Cathedral at Guildford was consecrated only recently, in design and execution it belongs

LXI   Guildford Cathedral, 1936–   . Architect Sir Edward Ma

to the 1930s. So Coventry belongs to the '50s and '60s. It is a modern building wherein have been employed modern methods of construction, lighting, heating, planning and modern artists and craftsmen have carried out the glasswork, metalwork, stained glass and carvings with which the cathedral is decorated. It is, however, as the architect himself has stated, a traditional cathedral in plan and treatment. It is not shocking, abhorrent or revolutionary. Although the original design published in 1951 was criticised strongly, the majority of opinion has, since the consecration, veered overwhelmingly in favour of the finished product. Coventry cathedral is a resounding success. It is totally different from its Medieval and Renaissance predecessors but its interior has that quality essential to all cathedral churches: the power to move and uplift the human spirit.

When the old Cathedral of St Michael was bombed in 1940 the tower and spire were preserved. It was early decided to retain these and the ruined walls of the old cathedral as a memorial and to incorporate them into the new cathedral site. The problem thus given to architects who entered the competition for the new building included the necessary harmonisation of their design with the fifteenth-century ruins. There has been considerable controversy as to whether Sir Basil Spence's design, planned with the axis at right angles to the axis of the old cathedral, has succeeded in this respect. In the author's view, it has not. It is, one feels, the chief criticism which can be levelled at the finished building. Despite the use of the pinkish sandstone, there still seems to be no point of contact, spiritually or aesthetically, between the beautifully proportioned, blackened fifteenth-century tower and the new, pinkly glowing, attractive, but modern cathedral. The site too does less than justice to Sir Basil's design. There is no position yet from which the cathedral can be adequately viewed. It is surrounded by parked cars, too closely adjacent buildings and a new technical college. No doubt a further clearing of the site will take place, but it still seems very cramped in comparison with Guildford's magnificent position on Stag Hill, approached by a fine carriageway and viewed in its entirety from the town of Guildford. Perhaps a cathedral should be in the heart of its city, but at what cost to its appearance and peace. All our Medieval cathedrals do not now possess the hallowed calm of Salisbury's Cathedral close, but should we not, when building a new one, set it, as at Guildford, apart from the clamour of a modern industrial city?

Sir Basil Spence has made the cathedral appear larger than it really is. In fact it is not large—the interior is under 300 feet in length and 80 feet in width—and approximates to the old cathedral which was actually the parish church of St Michael raised to cathedral status in 1918. On the exterior, the sheer walls, lofty windows and almost stark simplicity have increased the apparent dimensions. Inside this effect is greater still; the slender piers, the high springing of the vault, the masterly treatment of light—natural and artificial—together with the breaking of the line of vision from one end of the cathedral to the other by the 'thorns' and stall canopies, give the impression of a spacious, almost limitless church.

The **cathedral exterior** is simple and effective. Built in pinkish-grey sandstone it is contrasted in colour and shape with the rounded, greenish slate chapels. The **Chapel of Unity** on the south-west is joined to the cathedral by a short cloister. It is composed of a circle of tall buttresses or winged flanges and has a low conical roof of copper covered concrete. The **Guild Chapel** at the other side on the east is also circular but less exciting in form. It is patterned with mullions and transoms and includes the chapter-house beneath. The general

II   Coventry Cathedral, 1954–62. Architect Sir Basil Spence

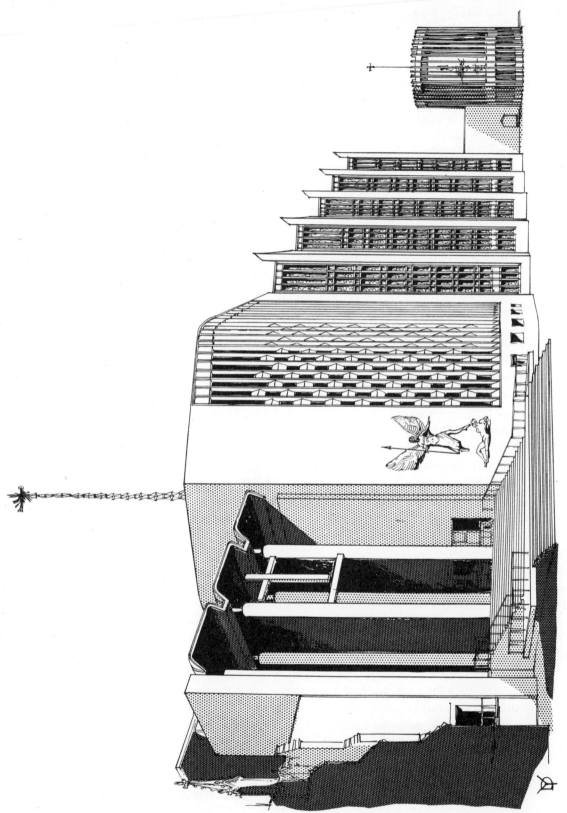

14353a Coventry Cathedral (showing principal entrance and Lady Chapel), consecrated 1962. Sir Basil Spence

silhouette of the cathedral from the principal entrance elevation is interesting, comprising the zig-zag of nave windows, the upwards surge of the magnificent baptistry window and the flat planes of the main entrance decorated only by **Sir Jacob Epstein's** bronze, 25-foot-high sculpture of **St Michael and the Devil**. This massive work is reduced to ideal proportions by the enormous expanse of plain sandstone above and around it. The sculpture is one of Epstein's last but finest works. The cathedral has no tower but is surmounted by a flèche set over the crossing, topped by Geoffrey Clarke's weather vane (set in position by Royal Air Force helicopter at the second attempt). The flèche itself is weak, lacks substance and is too reminiscent of the radio aerials on Broadcasting House. The principal entrance—the **porch**—is not only an impressive, spacious and lofty approach set in its sandstone columns, but acts also as the link between the cathedral and the atrium and ruined walls. A general view of the exterior is shown in Fig. 1435a.

Inside the cathedral there is a strong impression of unity. The light and the general design are focused forward towards the altar. The tall, full height, nave windows are set at an angle to shed light in this direction and are grouped in colour combinations reflecting different moods, seasons and times of day. One group is in browns, greens and blues, the next in reds and yellows, a third in purples and greys, etc. Each contrasts with the others but the whole creates a complete scheme. The stained glass was designed and made by **Lawrence Lee** at the Royal College of Art. The mullions are splayed in one direction in order to project the light forward towards the altar. The transoms, however, are equally splayed to keep the light level horizontal. As one enters the cathedral none of these windows can be seen for they are set forward away from the viewer. Behind him is the magnificent **glass screen** engraved by **John Hutton** (as at Guildford), which gives a fairy-like quality to the end of the cathedral. It screens and protects from the outside but does not cut off or obscure. There is no full stop here, only a gossamer barrier between the new cathedral and the old—a most impressive and successful motif.

On the left-hand side of the cathedral, on entering, is the approach to the **Chapel of Unity**, which leads off the nave. Here the greenish slate contrasts attractively with the pinkish sandstone. The lighting is handled magnificently. It splays off the cathedral into the narrow entrance of the circular chapel. Opposite, on the right-hand wall of the cathedral is the most beautiful feature of the building: the **baptistery window**. Designed by **John Piper**, the coloured glass in its 195 lights is handled superbly to give an impression of brilliance in central yellows and oranges which radiate outwards and downwards into the other colours of the spectrum. The window depicts the glory of baptism and is the greatest single successful unit in the cathedral. Standing below this window is the font made of the rough-hewn rock from Bethlehem.

The nave is 270 feet in length and seats 2,000 people. The walls are faced simply with white plaster. The floor is of polished dark inlaid marble. From the seats near the entrance and towards the centre of the nave one receives an impression of complete symmetry of perspective. The colouring is cool, subtle and pleasing with the light walls, grey pillars, golden brown of the vault and the pale wood of the chairs. The thorn screen, of wood with gilt candle holders in the ends, and organ pipes are also muted in colour. The focal centre above the altar is the famous **tapestry** designed by **Graham Sutherland**. The whole concept of the cathedral appears to be focused here and, regretfully, it is an anti-climax. There is so much green—a green which is crude and jars—the only strong colour note in this view of the cathedral; but, unlike Piper's window or the nave windows, its effect is not richness and glory but inadequacy and a sense of unease. Viewed from the far end of the cathedral it is not unimpressive, but, upon closer inspection, although the workmanship of the tapestry itself is exquisite, the design appears unworthy. Also poor in standard are the carved and lettered panels which decorate the nave walls, with ugly benches below them. The stained glass in the ambulatory at the sides of the altar is equally undistinguished. Of high quality, however, is the woodwork of the chairs, clergy choir stalls, pulpit and lectern. These are finely finished and constructed.

The **vaulted ceiling** is most successful. From floor level it appears as golden brown slats allowing the artificial light to come through in rays. The actual ceiling is an immense canopy of reinforced concrete with a structural pattern, giving an impression of star-shaped ribbing— a Medieval conception but modern in treatment and construction. The canopy is supported on two rows of seven narrow columns which taper towards the bottom and do not obscure the light or view. Heating is by under-floor hot-water pipes.

At the end of the cathedral to the right of the altar is the **Chapel of Christ in Gethsemane**. This is a chapel for private prayer, quite small, with rough-cast cream walls and gilt background to the end wall with a relief figure. The entrance screen is a circle of bronze thorns. The **Lady Chapel** beyond is circular, very light, with plain glass between the mullions.

A competition was held for the new Cathedral in 1951. There were 219 designs. The assessors were Sir Percy Thomas, Sir Edward Maufe and Sir Howard Robertson, all men whose reputations were made in pre-war days. To their immense credit, they chose an architect of today. Sir Basil's design not only complied with the requirements, it was competent, workable and, above all, forceful and original. Building started in 1954 and the foundation-stone was laid by H.M. the Queen in 1956. Her Majesty returned for the Consecration Service on 25th May 1962, since when thousands of people have visited the cathedral. Interest, quite rightly, shows little sign of diminishing. The cathedral is, with the individual exceptions mentioned, successful both architecturally and artistically (1435a, LXII).

SIR HUGH CASSON 1910–

The name of Sir Hugh Casson is probably best known for his work at the 1951 **Festival of Britain**. He was the **Director of Architecture** in this venture from 1948 to 1951 and some 40 architects co-operated under his direction to reclaim the South Bank. In particular, he was responsible for the 1851 Centenary Pavilion.

Casson, who was educated at Cambridge, later became Reader in Interior Design at the Royal College of Art. He has published a number of books and his architectural work covers a wide field. Among these are banks, restaurants and houses.

With his partner **Neville Conder**, Casson was responsible for the **Coronation Decorations** for the City of Westminster and later, for **University building** at **Birmingham** (Halls of residence); **Oxford** (residence for students at **Worcester College**) and the new Faculties and Lecture rooms in Sidgwick Avenue at **Cambridge** (1476).

FREDERICK GIBBERD 1908–

Frederick Gibberd, who was born in Warwickshire, studied at the Birmingham School of Architecture and later spent four years as an articled pupil. Before the war he designed a number of buildings among which were several blocks of flats notably **Pullman Court, Streatham**, 1934–5, **Park Court, Crystal Palace**, 1935–6 and **Ellington Court, Southgate**, 1937. Among his published works at this time were *The Modern Flat* written with F. R. S. Yorke, 1937, and *The Architecture of England*, 1938. In 1943–4 Gibberd was Principal of the Architectural Association School and in 1950–1 was Vice-President of the Royal Institute of British Architects.

It is in the post-war period, however, that Frederick Gibberd has achieved a considerable reputation. He was appointed **Architect Planner** to the **New Town** of **Harlow Development Corporation** (1474), and has recently completed the new long-distance terminal building at **London Airport**. This building, in severe modern style, is decorated on the exterior by a series of large abstract murals by **Stefan Knapp**, the artist who carried out a smaller but similar mural at St Anne's College, Oxford. These murals are an integral part of the architecture and not just decoration, and consist of sheets of steel on to which have been fused weatherproof glass in brilliant hues. The effect is impressive if startling as one arrives in the airport coach.

Gibberd has recently won the open competition for the new **Metropolitan Roman Catholic Cathedral of Liverpool** which is to succeed Lutyens' design, and which will incorporate the crypt which has already been built. The scale model of Gibberd's cathedral was exhibited at the Summer Exhibition of the Royal Academy in 1962 and showed a large, original and striking design, circular in form upon a rectangular base, reminiscent of a marquee which soars up into the heavens. It will be interesting indeed to see the new cathedral when it is finished (1435b).

PROFESSOR SIR WILLIAM G. HOLFORD 1907–

Sir William Holford's name has been in the news in recent years for his town-planning schemes and in particular for his suggested layout for the thorny problem of Piccadilly Circus. He has had a varied and outstanding career both in architecture and town planning. Born in Johannesburg, South Africa, he was educated at the Diocesan College in Cape Town and came to study architecture at the Liverpool School of Architecture from 1925 to 1930. He was a Rome scholar in 1930 and spent three years at the British School in Rome until 1933. In this year he returned to England and was appointed Lecturer at Liverpool University. In 1936 he succeeded Sir Patrick Abercrombie as Lever Professor of Civic Design at Liverpool University.

During the war Holford made a name for himself designing hostels for war workers whilst chief architect to the Ministry of Supply. He was also adviser to Lord Reith from 1940. Among his post-war appointments he became, in 1946, Planning Consultant, with the late Charles Holden, to the Corporation of the City of London. In the same year he was appointed Planning Consultant to the University of Liverpool. In 1948 he again succeeded Sir Patrick Abercrombie, this time as Professor of Town Planning at the University of London. At the same time he became Planning Consultant, with H. M. Wright, to the County of Cambridge, also to the City of Pretoria, South Africa. From 1950 to 1954 he was architect and consultant

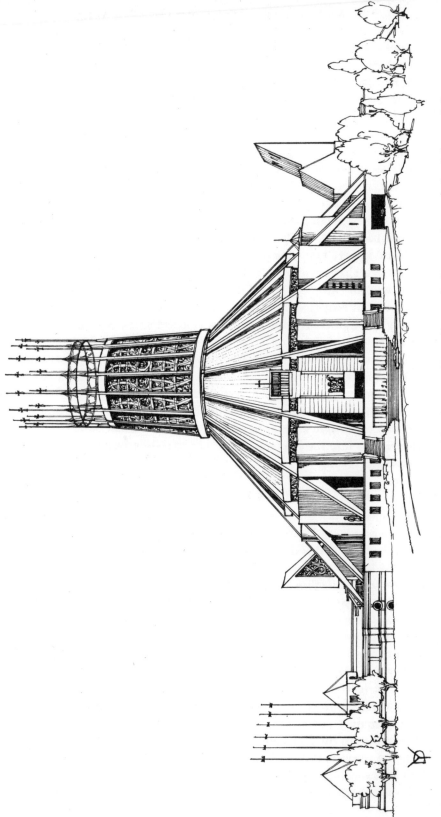

METROPOLITAN CATHEDRAL OF CHRIST THE KING, LIVERPOOL

1435b General view from the west. Frederick Gibberd, 1962. (Drawing made from a photograph of the model)

to Corby New Town Development Corporation. From 1951 to 1957 he was Consultant to the Commonwealth Government of Australia on regional development plans and on the future of the Federal Capital, Canberra.

Sir William has been a member of the Royal Fine Art Commission since 1944 and of the Historic Buildings Council since 1953. He is vice-chairman of the Centre of Urban Studies and president of the Housing Centre, London. He is chairman of the Advisory Committee for Buildings of Historic and Architectural Interest.

His architectural achievements include Farrer House at **Eton College**, to which he is the architect; the **Jeremiah Ambler Factory** at **Peterlee**; the **Woolworth building, Oxford**; the Market Square at **Corby New Town**; the Administrative Building at **Team Valley** and the Wholesale Markets at **Sheffield**. He has carried out a considerable quantity of **university** architecture. He has been architect and consultant for **Exeter** where he was responsible for the Queen's Building (Arts faculties), for the Senate Chamber, the Administrative Building and the Refectory. At **Liverpool** he designed the nuclear laboratory group. At **Nottingham** he is engaged with G. A. Jellicoe and Mrs G. Heyward on the extensive scheme for new buildings in the University Park.

Sir William has published a number of articles including among many others, works such as *The Future of Canberra, Cambridge Planning Proposals* (with H. M. Wright) and *The City of London: a record of Destruction and Survival* (with C. H. Holden). He has been awarded the Royal Institute of British Architects Distinction in Town Planning; he is a past president of the Town Planning Institute and of the Royal Institute of British Architects. He was knighted in 1953.

It is not surprising with such a varied and successful career in town planning that Sir William Holford was asked to make definite and extensive proposals for the future development of **Piccadilly Circus**. These proposals were published in April 1962 and the model and drawings of the plan were on show to the public at County Hall at that time. Sir William's plans, which include the controversial Monico building, are ambitious, long-term and comprehensive. The circus would become a rectangle of 260 by 220 feet, with a broad paved piazza for pedestrians at each side. Eros would be moved a few yards northwards and the focal point would be indicated by a high tower which would carry neon advertisements (some of the newspaper reports of the time, likening this tower and square to St Mark's Campanile in the Piazza San Marco in Venice do not appear quite apt!). The open central space would be surrounded by buildings of similar height to the present building line, whilst taller blocks would be set further back so as not to crowd this area and to give scale to the complete scheme. The aim would be to reconcile the opposing functions of the present circus, which is a busy traffic junction and a place filled with pedestrian sightseers and shoppers. The new plan would segregate the two factions considerably and still permit the traffic to keep moving. The scheme appears an interesting one, and would be a vast improvement upon the present circus which Sir Patrick Abercrombie once described as 'a neon hell imposed upon a Blomfield heaven'. Whether all the private developers of the sites will co-operate remains to be seen. The London County Council, which refused permission to the earlier application to develop the Monico site, has some powers in the matter, but since it does not own all the land, these powers are limited. It is to be hoped that Sir William's plans will eventually come to fruition.

SIR ROBERT HOGG MATTHEW 1907–

Sir Robert Matthew, elected President of the Royal Institute of British Architects in 1962, has held many appointments in architecture and town planning. From 1946 to 1953 he was Architect to the London County Council, and in this capacity was responsible for an enormous programme of post-war building and town planning. This included primarily schools and housing. Among the **housing projects** were the large estates of Alton and Ackroyden at **Roehampton** (1449–51, 1455, 1499, 1500, 1503). In 1949 Sir Robert was awarded the Royal Institute of British Architects Distinction in Town Planning.

Sir Robert, who was educated in Edinburgh at the Architectural School in the Edinburgh College of Art and began his career in his father's office in Edinburgh, has, apart from his period with the London County Council, spent much of his life in Scotland. In 1945 he was chief architect and planning officer in the Department of Health for Scotland. He also acted as Deputy Consultant to Sir Patrick Abercrombie in preparing the post-war report on the Clyde Valley region. In 1953 he was appointed Professor of Architecture at Edinburgh University and since this time has entered into private practice with offices in Edinburgh and London. Among the buildings which he has designed in this period are the **Edinburgh Airport Terminal**, the Arts Faculty building at **Edinburgh University** and the almost completed **New Zealand House** in **London** (1436).

One building with which Sir Robert's name is strongly linked is that of the **Royal Festival Hall, London,** which was built during his term of office at the London County Council. The building was proposed in 1948 and was completed in record time for the opening of the Festival of Britain in 1951. The Architect's department of the London County Council was responsible for its building with **Sir Robert Matthew** in charge. **Sir Leslie Martin, Peter Moro** and **Edwin Williams** were among those closely concerned in its design and erection.

The site was occupied by derelict buildings but has a fine view of the riverside, of which full advantage has been taken by the architects. It is adjacent to the railway and to Waterloo Station—highly convenient but extremely noisy. The Festival Hall, to be built for the enjoyment of fine music, had to keep out this noise. This has been done: the sound insulation is remarkable. Through a glass screen the trains can be seen thundering by, but not a sound can be heard. The acoustics are equally remarkable. From every part of the large auditorium (seating nearly 3,500) can be heard the softest of violin notes, and this includes the boxes, which are designed both as a decorative, interior feature and to be suitable for both seeing and hearing. The auditorium is the principal feature of the Royal Festival Hall. The site was restricted, so the auditorium is raised on stilts and has two foyers below it on two different levels, and walls of glass all round so that concert-goers can stroll about during the intervals and view the river outside. The lighting is excellent as also are the heating and air-conditioning. On a cold winter's evening or in a heat-wave the auditorium is still fresh and comfortable. It is rectangular in shape and both its construction and decoration have been determined by acoustic needs. It has heavy, double walls, floors and roof. The auditorium is sealed within an outer envelope which contains restaurants, bars, a theatre and the foyers. Despite the site restrictions, there is always room to stroll or sit. For pleasant weather there are exterior terraces and gardens.

LXIII	*Royal Festival Hall, London, 1951. Ar*
tects Sir Robert Matthew and Sir Leslie Ma

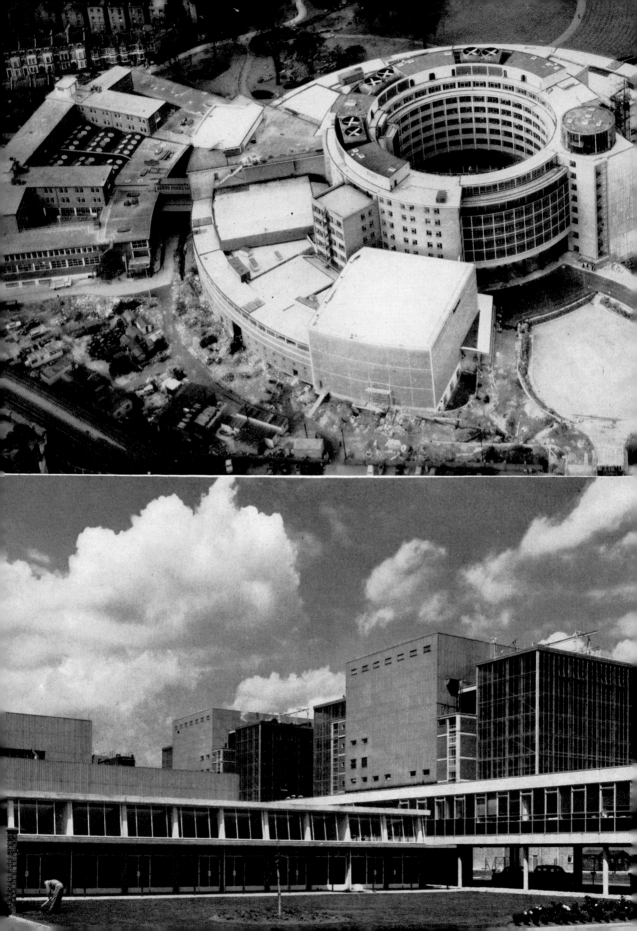

1436 New Zealand House, Pall Mall, London (as in August 1962, not yet complete). Sir Robert Matthew

The Festival Hall was a new venture in 1951: the first post-war place of public assembly in London to be designed in the modern idiom and using modern constructional methods to achieve good sound, light, heat and comfort. As such, it is an overwhelming success. Architecturally and aesthetically it has since been felt to be lacking in interest, particularly from the exterior viewpoint. Even the interior of the auditorium has a somewhat clinical appearance but it is pleasant and supremely functional and is one of London's most used and popular buildings (1442, LXIII).

XIV(a) *The B.B.C. Television Centre, London, 1949–60. Architect Graham Dawbarn*
Bradwell Nuclear Power Station, Essex, 1957–61

SIR JOHN LESLIE MARTIN 1908–

Sir Leslie Martin has also held a number of architectural appointments, and in 1953 succeeded Matthew as Architect to the London County Council, after being in the Architect's Department since 1948 as Matthew's Deputy.

Martin was educated at Victoria University School of Architecture at Manchester. In 1930 he was appointed Lecturer in Art at Manchester University and left there in 1934 to become Head of the School of Art at Hull College of Arts and Crafts. From 1939 to 1948 he was Principal Assistant Architect to the L.M.S. Railway where he designed railway buildings. In 1948 he came to the London County Council where he did a great deal of work on the **Royal Festival Hall** with Matthew. Also during this period, up to 1956 when he left the London County Council, Martin carried out work on the designs for the National Youth and Sports and Exhibition Centre being built at **Crystal Palace**. In 1954 he received the Royal Institute of British Architects London Bronze Medal for his **housing scheme** in **Wandsworth**. He was responsible for many London schools between 1948 and 1956, particularly in the field of comprehensive school building.

In 1956 Sir Leslie was appointed Professor of Architecture at Cambridge.

OTHER ARCHITECTS

The bulk of architecture today is designed not by individual architects, but by **firms** and combines of architects. Most of these names do not become generally known outside the profession but many of them have carried out good work and sound designs in the post-war period. Among such architects and firms should be mentioned: Gollins, Melvin, Ward and Partners; Powell and Moya; Norman and Dawbarn; Richard Sheppard and Partners; Peter Moro (L.C.C. Architects Department) Russell Diplock Associates; Ley, Colbeck and Partners; Professor R. Llewelyn Davies and John Weeks; Drake and Lasdun; F. R. S. Yorke (the late); E. Rosenberg and C. S. Mardall and Lyons, Israel and Ellis.

CIVIC BUILDINGS AND HOTELS

From a number of such buildings which have been executed, the following examples have been selected as being interesting and/or typical.

The **Trades Union Congress Memorial Building**, Great Russell Street, **London**, 1957, was the result of an open competition which was held for this building in 1948 and was won by **David du R. Aberdeen**. The site is very restricted for a large public building, with three open sides and the fourth immediately adjacent to the Y.W.C.A. Building. The seven-storey main entrance front consists largely of glass curtain walling with an open portico below. The only exterior decoration is a single sculptured group set on a plain pedestal. On the side elevation are some attractive glass balconies. Inside, the chief feature is the marbled memorial hall with its Epstein sculpture. Further accommodation includes a conference hall at basement level, a dining hall and above, a public foyer. The structure is in reinforced concrete faced on the exterior by polished Cornish granite (1437–8).

The **Manchester Courts of Law**, 1957–61, gleam gold and white in the heart of this industrial city. The rectangular principal façade is largely glass-fronted and is delicately

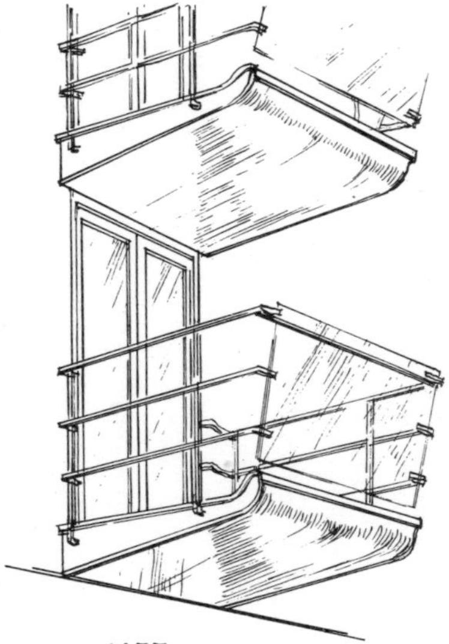

1438

1437

1439

1437-8 Trades Union Congress Building, London, 1957. Architect, David du R. Aberdeen 1439 Manchester Courts of Law, 1957-61. City Architect, Leonard C. Howitt

1440 Manchester Courts of Law, 1957–61: principal entrance. City Architect, Leonard C. Howitt

decorated in gilt and black. The entrance steps and three-part portico are the focal feature, with tripartite canopies over the doorway. A most successful modern exterior (1439–40).

Goodenough House, Old Broad Street, **London**, 1960, is the new head office building for Barclays Bank and is one of several such large banking headquarters to be erected in the city in recent years. Streets such as this one, typical narrow city thoroughfares, present difficult sites for tall buildings and tend to shut out the light completely from the principal façades. This design has been most successfully handled in this respect for, despite its great height, the block has been split up so as to admit the sunshine and present an interesting balance of mass and form. The simple panel decoration is by the sculptor **Gilbert Ledward** —unfortunately, his last work before his death.

City by-laws in the area insist on stone façades for new buildings so, although this erection is steel-framed, it has a thin stone facing. Unlike its pre-war predecessors, there is nothing classical in its design but it is dignified and impressive nevertheless. There are 12 floors above ground level. Below this is accommodation for safe deposits, dance floor, dining-rooms and car garaging. The building was designed by **Ley, Colbeck and Partners** (1441).

The **B.B.C. Television Centre, London**, 1949–60, designed and carried out by the architect **Graham Dawbarn**, of the firm of Norman and Dawbarn, and the civil engineer **M. T. Tudsbery** (B.B.C.), was the first attempt to provide studios specially built for television. Previously, existing buildings had been adapted for the purpose. The site of 13 acres was acquired in 1949 at Shepherd's Bush. The large area made it possible to incorporate in one place all the necessary buildings and equipment.

The layout comprises a large, circular main building, with three subsidiary blocks for scenery, restaurant and general works, which radiate from the central mass. The circular building is in fact a multi-storey ring of steel-framed construction and concrete flooring.

Inside the ring is a 150-foot-diameter court and central garden, entered via a colonnade. Its surrounding walls of 82 feet in height are set back at the upper levels. The garden, which is largely paved, has a circular central lawn and a fountain. The main feature of this is a 10-foot high, gilded bronze figure representing Helios the Greek Sun God, set upon an obelisk. Around this is a free-standing bowl supported on four legs. Underneath is a pool with reclining sculptured figures. The sculptor is **T. B. Huxley-Jones**.

The material for the exterior work is largely brick, but in contrast to this is the mosaic and coloured glass of the colonnade and court. Inside, there is variety and richness of colour and texture, showing off modern wall and floor decoration to its best advantage. The entrance hall is 60 feet long and 25 feet wide and follows the curve of the building. Its principal feature is the west wall mural, 25 by 14 feet in mosaic, designed by **John Piper**. This is an abstract design in beautiful colouring. The remaining wall surfaces are in plain glass, wood and marble (1443–4, 1493; LXIV).

1441 Goodenough House, Old Broad Street, London, Barclays Bank DCO, 1960. Architects, Ley, Colbeck and Partners. Sculptor, Gilbert Ledward

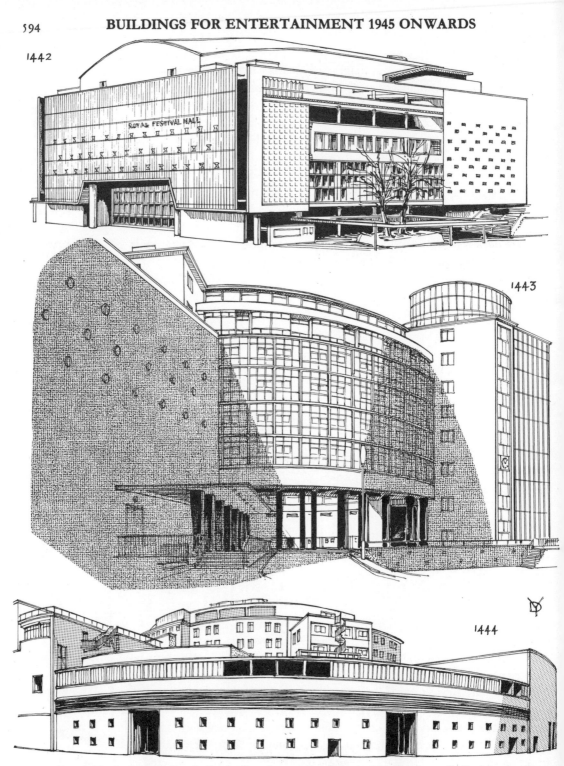

1442 Royal Festival Hall, South Bank, London, 1951. Robert H. Matthew, J. L. Martin, Peter Moro and others 1443-4 B.B.C. Television Centre, Hammersmith, London, 1949-60: general view and principal entrance. Graham Dawbarn of Norman and Dawbarn

1445 The Ariel Hotel, London Airport, 1961. Russell Diplock Associates

Of the few hotels that have been built in Britain since the war the **Ariel Hotel, London Airport**, 1961, is the most interesting. Erected by the side of the Great West Road near the entrance to London Airport, it suffers the double noise problem of traffic and jet aircraft. It was essential, therefore, to insulate its accommodation thoroughly. This in part was the reason for its unusual shape, which is a circle of 176 feet in diameter and 48 feet in height. Erected in 18 months to the designs of the architects **Russell Diplock Associates**, it comprises a ground floor divided by a projecting parapet from the three storeys above. The lower part is of reinforced concrete faced with purplish brick. Above this the facing is of white Italian glass mosaic, decorated by glass-panelled windows and rich teak strips. The windows are of double construction with metal frames within teak sub-framing. There are Venetian blinds between the panes (1445).

CHURCHES

From the number of churches built in Britain since 1945 five examples have been selected for illustration; three are new churches erected to serve communities in the new towns, and the other two have been built to replace churches destroyed by bombing during the war. It is one of the latter group which is the most interesting example. This is the **Punshon Memorial Methodist Church** at **Bournemouth**. The old church was bombed in 1943 and the new building, which was dedicated in 1958, was designed by **Ronald H. Sims**, and was awarded the Royal Institute of Architects Bronze Medal for Architecture. It is an entirely modern church with an interesting and pleasing exterior. The walls are faced largely with multi-coloured brick and the shallow pitched roofs are copper covered. The tower, of brick and glass, is 60 feet high and is surmounted with a cross which rises to 132 feet above ground level. The interior, which is also modern in treatment, illustrates a very high standard of

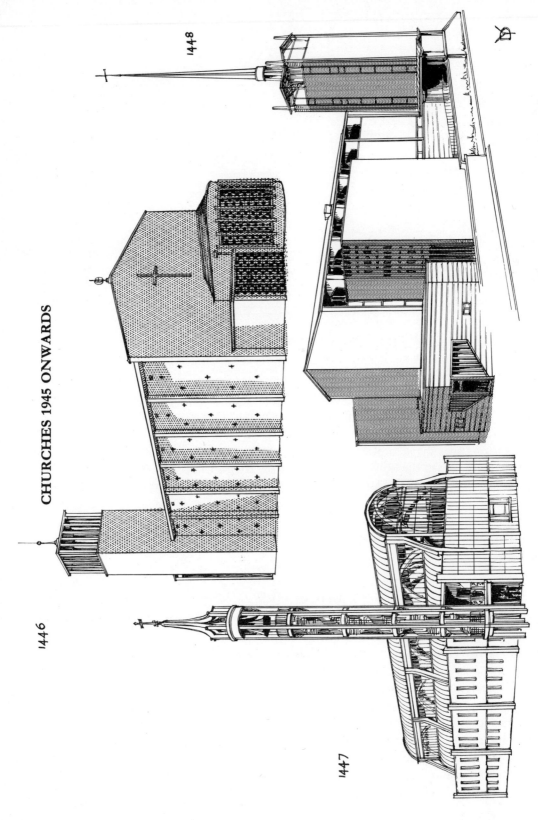

CHURCHES 1945 ONWARDS

1446

1447

1448

1446 St Ethelreda's Church, Fulham, London, 1956–7   1447 Parish Church of St George, Stevenage New Town, Hertfordshire, 1956–61.   1448 Punshon Memorial Methodist Church, Bournemouth, Hampshire, 1958. Ronald H. Sims

craftsmanship in the woodwork, coloured glass windows and furniture. The lighting is most effectively handled (1448). The other rebuilt church is that of **St Ethelreda** in **Fulham, London** (1446). A much plainer and less ambitious example, this has a pleasing, though simple exterior in brick with a square tower at one end and an apsidal feature at the other.

In **Stevenage New Town** the parish church of **St George** is built in slabs of flint and concrete with glass panels. It has a free-standing concrete campanile at the west end which, like several of Berlin's new churches, is open to show the central newel staircase leading to the belfry. The campanile is surmounted by a cross. This is an unusual and modern design but lacks the quality finish of the Bournemouth example. The foundation-stone was laid in 1956 (1447).

A complete contrast in design but equally modern is **St Richard's** in the **Three Bridges** residential area of **Crawley New Town**, built in 1953–4 to the designs of **N. F. Cachemaille-Day**, who is well known for his many pre-war ecclesiastical designs. This church has a drum tower rising from the square mass and this is surmounted by a tall, slender cross. The front porch is high and semicircular in projection (1466).

Another example with a most interesting and finely finished interior is the Catholic church of **Our Lady of Fatima** in **Harlow New Town**, built 1958–60 to the designs of **Gerald T. Goalen**. The structure is of reinforced concrete with the aisle walls and the walls of nave and transepts faced with brick. The plywood flèche, surmounted by a cross reaching to 131 feet above ground level, is sheathed in copper. The windows, which occupy some 60 per cent of the wall area, have mullions and transoms in white concrete in startling contrast to the vivid and telling coloured glasswork. The glass, which was designed and made at Buckfast Abbey in Devon, is in one-inch-thick coloured slabs, joined by concrete instead of the more usual lead. This is an effective new method; the windows glow and glitter in the sunshine. The interior is plain but the standard of craftsmanship is high. The church is very light inside due to the large window area, some of which is in plain glass. The artificial lighting is also ingeniously designed. The walls are plain, the floor largely terrazzo and the decoration simple in metal and wood (1473).

HOUSING

Estates

Before the war a considerable proportion of homes were built by the private builder or speculator. Since 1945 a far larger amount of housing has been the responsibility of local authorities. This has been partly due to shortage of building land, to town overspills and consequent new town development. In already overcrowded cities the modern approach is to build high and to retain a larger space between blocks. In many instances, quite large areas have been laid out with different types of building on one estate; perhaps one or two high multi-storey blocks, some two-storey terrace houses and some individual homes. Larger estates have been designed with their own amenities which include shops, schools, church and community centre.

London County Council, having the largest housing problem on its hands, has, naturally, built some of the largest and most comprehensive of such schemes. A good example of this is the **Alton Estate** at **Roehampton**. The open site is a magnificent one: on high ground

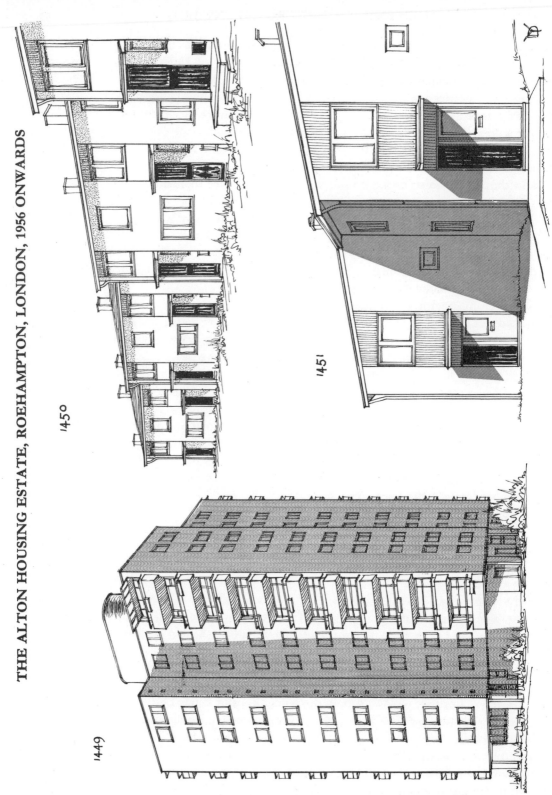

THE ALTON HOUSING ESTATE, ROEHAMPTON, LONDON, 1956 ONWARDS

1449

1450

1451

1449 Eleven-storey block of flats, 100 ft high 1450–1 Two-storey terrace houses. Housing Division, London County Council Architects Department

with views in all directions it adjoins Roehampton village and Wimbledon Common. The estate is planned with mixed development in an informal layout wherein the old trees have been retained to landscape the site and prevent too clear a view from the road. There are 11-storey flats, two-tier maisonettes and several types of terrace house. Nine of the 11-storey blocks are planned, built on to the highest part of the site and each nearly 100 feet in height and with a base 60 feet square. The plan of each block is cruciform with one flat on each floor in each of the four wings. Each flat has two bedrooms and a living room with balcony. Each block is served by a lift, central heating and hot water and there is a communal laundry and workshop. The four-storey maisonette blocks also have balconies, and small gardens. The terrace houses are stepped up and down the undulating site and each has a garden. The overall planning and layout is good and not overcrowded; due to the hilly landscape and the trees, monotony of design does not offend and the quality and finish of the estate is good. A criticism which should be made is that insufficient forethought appears to have been given to the problem of car parking, and the site is overcrowded with cars for which there is not adequate space. The estate was designed and built by the **Housing Division** of the **London County Council Architect's Department**, represented especially by **J. L. Martin** and **Whitfield Lewis** (1449–51, 1455, 1499, 1500, 1503).

Another scheme, also by the Housing Division of the London County Council Architects Department, is the **Loughborough Road Estate** in **Brixton**, 1955. Here also is mixed development with nine 11-storey blocks, but of a different type of design. There are also terraces of two-storey houses with gardens, a two-storey block of one-room flats, a three-storey block with shops and several six- and four-storey maisonette blocks. The 11-storey blocks are 260 feet long and 30 feet wide. The structure is of reinforced concrete with plain concrete ends. From a distance the designs are effective but on closer inspection the external finish is not good (1453).

Also in London, two other schemes should be mentioned. One is the 'cluster block' layout at **Bethnal Green**, built by **Drake and Lasdun**, 1958. This is an interesting and effective plan for housing in a densely populated area. Four rectangular blocks are connected to a core by bridges. The structure is in reinforced concrete. The advantage of the 'cluster' over a solid block is that light and air are admitted more freely and the appearance is more interesting and less clumsy. No doubt due to economy the external surfaces have the drab semblance of discoloured concrete (1454).

In another part of London is an estate with a quite different standard of workmanship and finish. The firm of **Philip Powell** and **Hidalgo Moya**, while still young men in their twenties, won the competition for the **Pimlico Housing Estate** on the Embankment opposite Battersea Power Station. The estate, which won the Royal Institute of Architects London Bronze Medal, is attractively laid out, well finished, interestingly designed and decorated in colour and form. Its heating system is original in that exhaust heat from the Power Station opposite is used to supply the whole housing estate of 1,600 dwellings. The green glass tower, some 140 feet high, is the centre of the plant for this heating system (1452).

Outside London there is an estate at **Sheffield**—the **Park Hill Estate**—developed by the City Architect's Department. In published photographs this scheme, built on rising ground behind the railway station, appears to be interesting and unusual. The site is sloping so that at one end the buildings are composed of some 14 storeys and at the other end only

1452

1452 Thames-side, Pimlico, London, 1951. Powell and Moya 1453 Loughborough Road, Brixton, London, 1955. Housing Division, London County Council Architects Department 1454 Claredale Street, Bethnal Green, London, 1958. 'Cluster Design'. Drake and Lasdun

1454

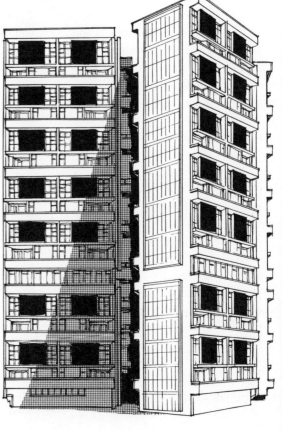

1453

1455

1456

1455 Maisonette block, Alton Estate East, Roehampton, London, 1956. Housing Division, London County Council Architects Department 1456 Park Hill Development Scheme, Sheffield, Yorkshire, 1961. City Architect, J. L. Womersley

1457

1458

1459

1457 and 1459 The Parkeleys Estate, Ham Common, Surrey, 1955: shops and flats. Eric Lyons
1458 Village Housing, Rushbrooke, Suffolk, 1957. R. Llewelyn Davies and John Weeks

four or five. Included in the plan are shops, pedestrian walks and play spaces. The structure is of reinforced concrete with brick panels. Unfortunately upon inspection of the actual site the plain concrete looks monotonous, particularly in its constantly recurring horizontal and vertical bands and the general colouring is drab and uninspired; 20 years hence, one feels, this will be a grim tenement block layout. It appears to be yet another example of economy first and attractive living conditions second (1456).

Among smaller, more intimate development schemes, might be quoted the admirable village reconstruction at **Rushbrooke**, Suffolk, by **Professor R. Llewelyn Davies** and **John Weeks**, where the village is being rebuilt with attractive white houses which are modern but have a rural character quite in keeping with their surroundings; a most successful enterprise (1458). There is also at **Ham Common**, near **Richmond**, Surrey, the **Parkeleys Estate**, built in 1955 by **Eric Lyons**. This is planned in two- and three-storey blocks with most attractive garden layout and a row of shops. The general scheme is spoilt only by its poor quality of finish (1457, 1459).

New City Centre Coventry

As is well known, due to large-scale destruction during the war, the area of replanning in the city of Coventry is vast and it will be some years before the scheme is fully complete. The new cathedral has already been discussed. Here, perhaps we may refer to the new central area of the city: **the shopping precincts**. This appears to be the most interesting and successful design, not excluding the new towns, for a central shopping area without traffic. The precincts at Coventry are a roughly rectangular area built on two levels. The shops almost surround the rectangular space and can be entered from the paved ground level or from the terraced upper storey reached by staircases at each end of the precinct. One end is approached from the main square of the town, near to the famous equestrian statue of Lady Godiva by Sir William Reid Dick, and behind this can be seen a fine view of the old cathedral steeple. At the other end is a circular restaurant at first-floor level. Under the staircase approaches are sculptured panels and flower decoration, while trees, shrubs and flowers are laid out in all parts of the square—in all a pleasant and attractive retreat for quiet shopping, window gazing or merely resting in the centre of a busy industrial city. **Arthur G. Ling** has now succeeded **D. E. Gibson** as city architect and planning officer (1460–2, 1492, 1495, 1498).

The New Towns

In October 1945 a New Towns Committee was appointed with Lord Reith as its chairman to suggest guiding principles upon which the new towns might be developed. The idea was that these communities should be quite different from the pre-war dormitory suburbs. They were each to be built by a separate, public corporation. In August 1946 the New Towns Act was passed. It provided for a plan of 20 such towns to take the overspill of large cities, especially London, and that they should not adjoin the city in question. In the 10 sites recommended in his Greater London Plan of 1944, Sir Patrick Abercrombie had suggested that these satellite towns should take an overspill of a million of London's population. He had envisaged a similar scheme for cities like Manchester, Birmingham and Liverpool.

Planning was quickly started on the first sites at **Hatfield**, Hertfordshire; **Crawley**, Sussex; **Stevenage**, Hertfordshire; **Harlow**, Essex, and **Hemel Hempstead**, Hertfordshire.

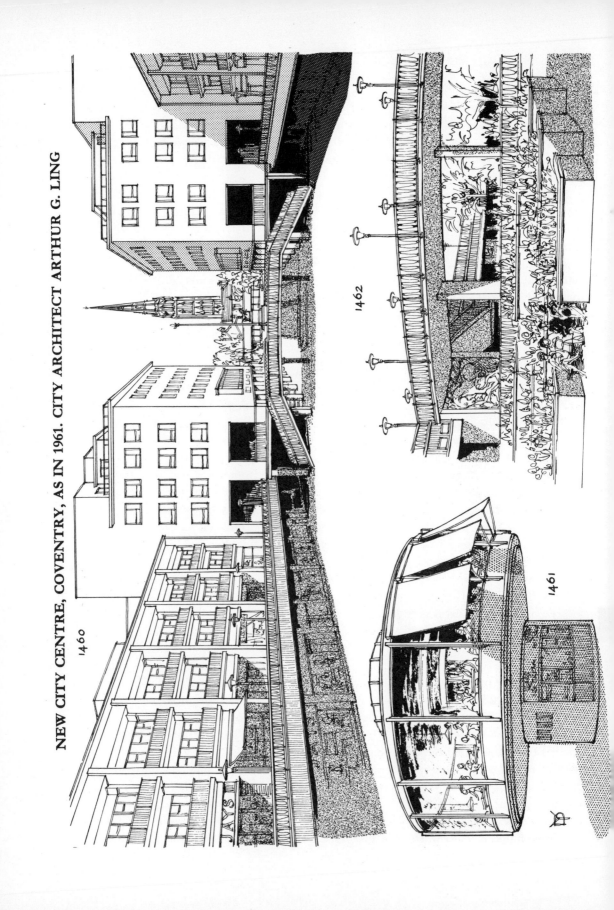

NEW CITY CENTRE, COVENTRY, AS IN 1961. CITY ARCHITECT ARTHUR G. LING

1460

1461

1462

CRAWLEY NEW TOWN, SUSSEX, AS IN 1961

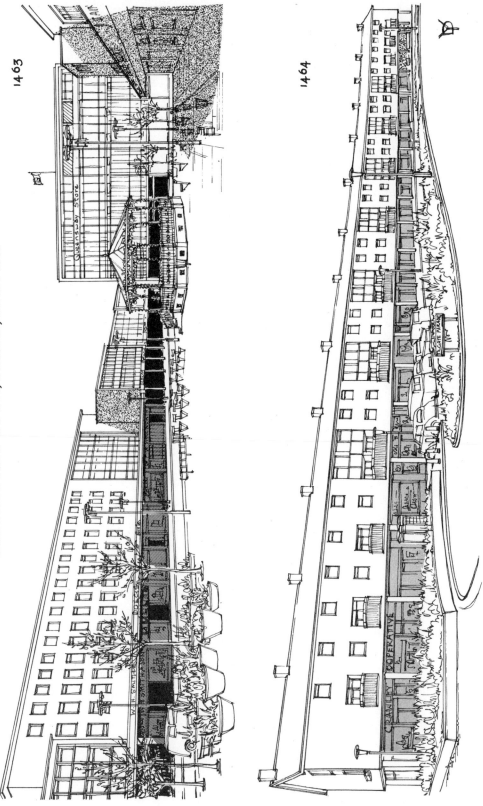

1463

1464

1463 Town Centre, Crawley, showing shops, stores, Victorian bandstand, flowers and trees, 1956–8. H. S. Howgrave-Graham, K. C. Bourne, J. Chitty and Gaby Schriber and Associates 1464 The Shopping Parade, Tilgate residential area, 1956–7. H. S. Howgrave-Graham and E. M. Bourne

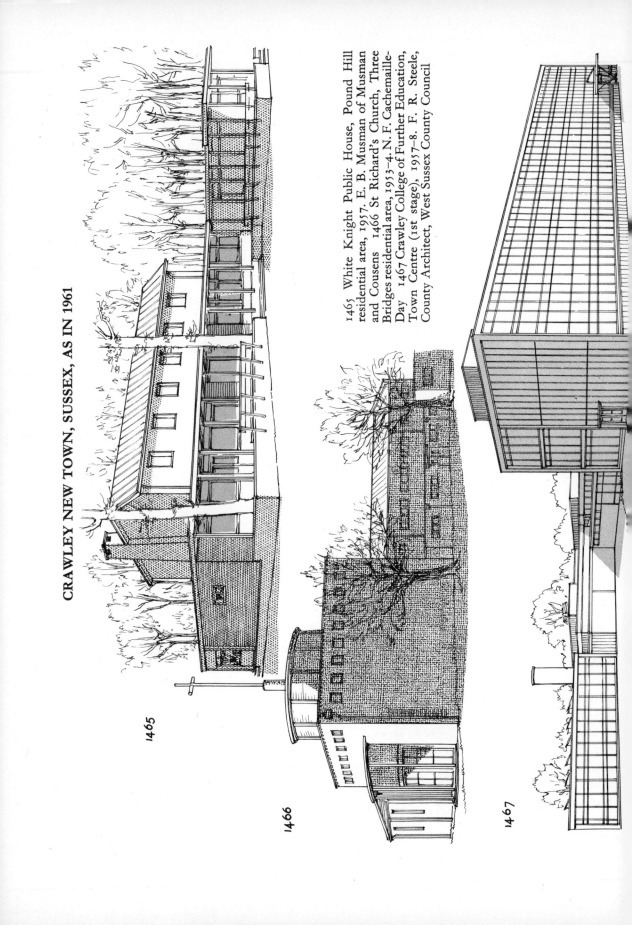

CRAWLEY NEW TOWN, SUSSEX, AS IN 1961

1465

1466

1467

1465 White Knight Public House, Pound Hill residential area, 1957. E. B. Musman of Musman and Cousens 1466 St Richard's Church, Three Bridges residential area, 1953–4. N. F. Cachemaille-Day 1467 Crawley College of Further Education, Town Centre (1st stage), 1957–8. F. R. Steele, County Architect, West Sussex County Council

The New Town was to be a complete unit comprising industry and homes and shops for the workers in these industries. The industrial and domestic parts of the town would be adjacent but would be kept separate. This has been done in all the above-named towns and general lines of planning common to all have been developed, although individually they have acquired character of their own.

The layout comprises a town centre in which there are the larger shops, near-by car-parking facilities, civic and cultural buildings, services such as fire station, police station, post office, grammar or comprehensive school, college of further education, hospital, etc. There are then several residential areas planned with different forms of housing separated from one another by agricultural land or sports and playing fields. In each area are local shops, church, primary school, public house and community centre.

As all building in these towns is new, there is a certain monotony about living in one and there is considerable similarity between one new town and another. But, particularly for families with children and for elderly people, it is incomparably more pleasant to live in one of these towns rather than in the London inner suburbs whence most new town dwellers have come. After talking to a number of such families the author received a very strong impression of this feeling of thankfulness that at last the children could go to school safely without fear of traffic; at last mother could shop easily by walking down the road and not having to queue for a 'bus; the air was purer, the countryside accessible, and now there were no longer always far too many people waiting for all the amenities. There are drawbacks of course. Cultural amenities and entertainment cannot be of London standard. But much is being done in this respect and for most people it is a great improvement in living.

To live in, **Crawley New Town**, Sussex, is probably the most attractive of the new towns built so far, not because its plan or layout is so much superior to the others—although it is of high standard—but the Sussex woodland and hills provide such a pleasant and varied background to the town. The **chief architect** of the **Crawley Development Corporation, H. S. Howgrave-Graham**, and his staff have certainly taken every advantage of this country-side and have laid out their nine residential areas with fine views over the rolling hills. The flat land has been used for the industrial sites and for the **town centre**. This incorporates the old Crawley High Street and the new focus is now Queen's Square, which contains large shops, a Victorian bandstand (to offset the modernity), fountain, mosaic and floral decoration and adequate car-parking facilities. Its public buildings include the police headquarters, post office, fire station, library, hospital, technical college and comprehensive school. The residential areas are generally in the form of individual houses and gardens; there are no tall blocks of flats. Each area has its church, public house, shops and primary school. Illustrations of the town centre, technical college and area shops, church and public house are shown in Figs. 1463–7, and 1497.

Like Crawley, **Stevenage New Town**, Hertfordshire, will cover some 6,000 acres of land and will eventually house about 50,000 people. The town centre here, which was built rather later than Crawley and some of the other new towns, has taken advantage of this and is, like Coventry, completely segregated from the motor traffic, which is kept in parking areas outside the centre. This is an immense improvement and should be compulsory in all new town development. The **central square** is on two levels and contains a rectangular clock tower set in a pool with a fountain. Leading out from the main square are further

TOWN CENTRE, STEVENAGE NEW TOWN, HERTFORDSHIRE

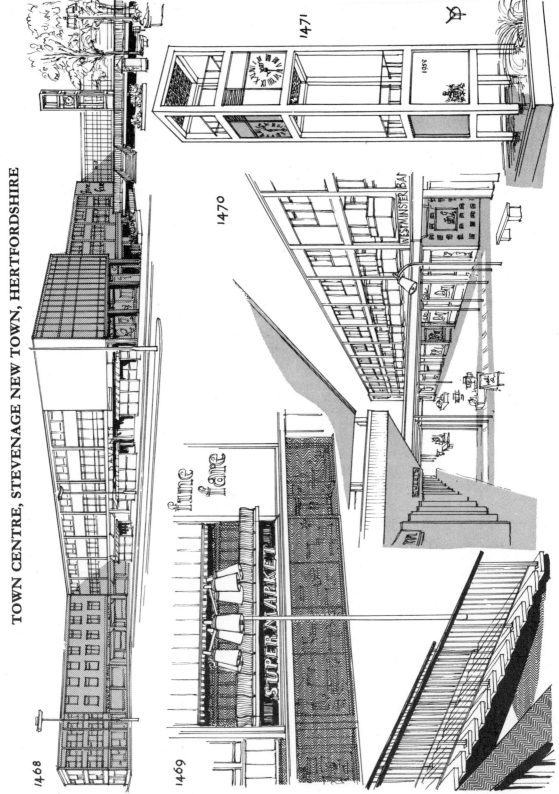

1468   General view   1469   Terrace steps   1470   Pedestrian shopping way   1471   Tower and fountain. Town centre as in 1960

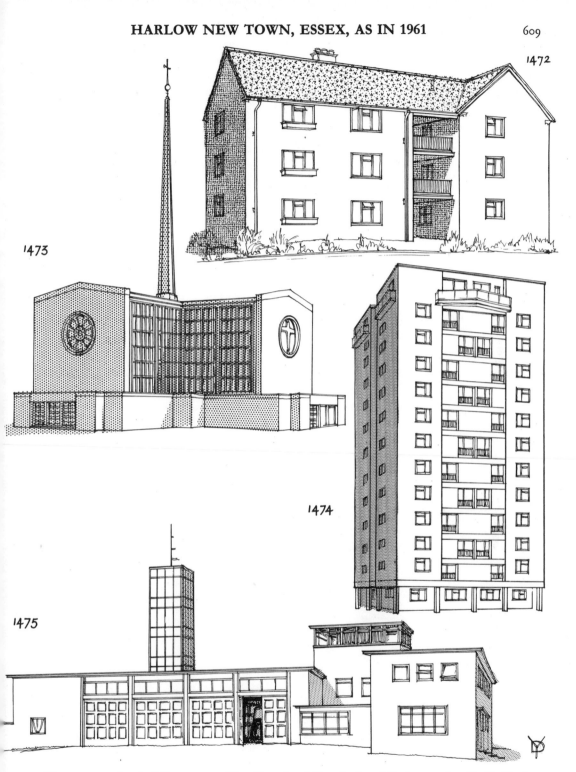

1472 Three-storey flat building   1473 The Church of Our Lady of Fatima, 1960. G. T. Goalen
1474 Thirteen-storey block of flats   1475 The Fire Station, Town Centre. Architects for town
centre Frederick Gibberd and Victor Hamnet

pedestrian shopping ways. There are to be five residential areas, planned in similar manner to those at Crawley. The **chief architect** and **planner** to the Stevenage Development Corporation is **C. Holliday**, and a number of architectural firms are working on the project including Messrs. Yorke, Rosenberg and Mardall (1468–71, 1494).

Harlow New Town, Essex, is a larger project than the other two examples and is being built to house some 80,000 people. The **architect planner** to the Corporation is **Frederick Gibberd**, and the **executive architect** is **V. Hamnet**. The site, of some 6,300 acres, was entirely rural and there is no old town to form a nucleus of the new. There are two industrial estates and the housing is planned in four clusters; three are built around neighbourhood shopping centres and the fourth in association with the town centre. There has been forward thinking in Harlow with regard to the motor car, and in some of the housing areas plans are made to allow for one car per family—a different approach from the Alton Estate, Roehampton.

Marking the gateway to the town centre is a 13-storey block of flats which provides variation from the rather low level building of much of the housing and civic area (1472–5).

At **Hemel Hempstead New Town**, Hertfordshire, the problem was different from the others in that there was already a sizeable town before new building commenced. It has proved a complicated task to integrate the new town with the old, also to build a new town centre on land already occupied by buildings. The new town is at last emerging from its chrysalis and is proving more successful than it appeared would be possible. The task of the **chief architect, H. Kellett Ablett**, is to provide accommodation and amenities for a population increase from 20,000 to 60,000 and to create an industrial area. The new town centre is off the old High Street and is in the form of a pedestrian court.

ARCHITECTURE IN EDUCATION

The Universities

At **Oxford**, in 1950–1, Hartland House was extended as **St Anne's College**. The buildings, designed by **Sir Giles Gilbert Scott**, are solemn and appear old-fashioned. There is, however, a more recent addition, **the hall**, which adjoins Hartland Hall. This dining hall for 312 persons was built 1958–9 to the designs of **Gerald Banks**. It is also used for concerts, lectures and dances. Both the acoustics and lighting are good and the hall is of an attractive design and treatment. The exterior, apart from its large window area, is stone faced. The chief decoration is a vividly coloured abstract panel by **Stefan Knapp** (1478).

At **Cambridge** new **Arts Faculty buildings**, to comprise lecture and seminar rooms, libraries and museums, are being built in **Sidgwick Avenue**. The general plan is on courtyard lines to conform to the remainder of Cambridge University design; wheeled traffic will be excluded from the central areas. The external facing materials are of high quality and give a sparkling black and white impression in the sunshine. The general line is of long, low blocks set on stilts, built round a quadrangle. The architects are **Sir Hugh Casson** and **Neville Conder** (1476).

A tremendous quantity of new university building is taking place all over the country, both in new universities as at Brighton, or in the form of extensions to almost all established universities. An interesting example of the latter type of development is the new **University**

1476

1477

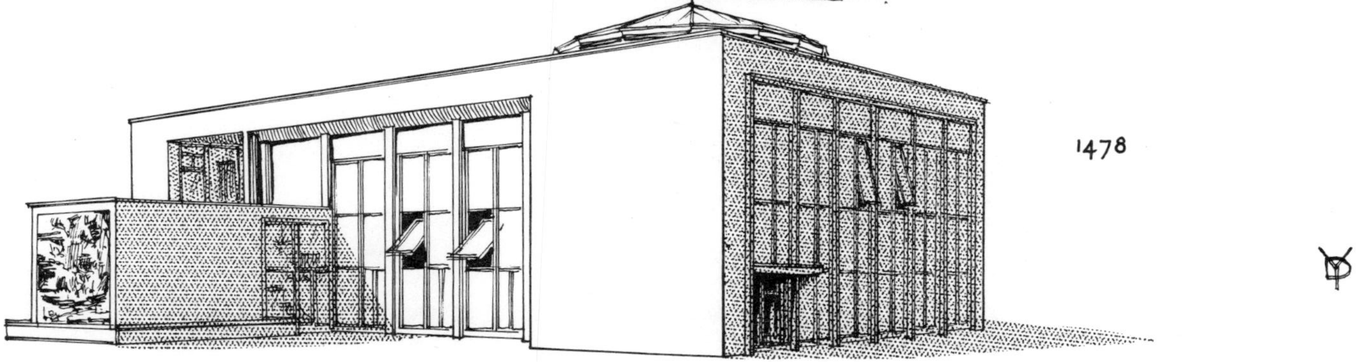

1478

1476 New buildings for Arts Faculties, Sidgwick Avenue, Cambridge, 1961: courtyard view. Sir Hugh Casson and Neville Conder 1477 University Library, Sheffield, 1955–61. Gollins, Melvin, Ward and Partners 1478 New Hall, St Anne's, Oxford, 1958–9. Designed by Gerald Banks. Mural abstract by Stefan Knapp

TECHNICAL COLLEGES 1950 ONWARDS

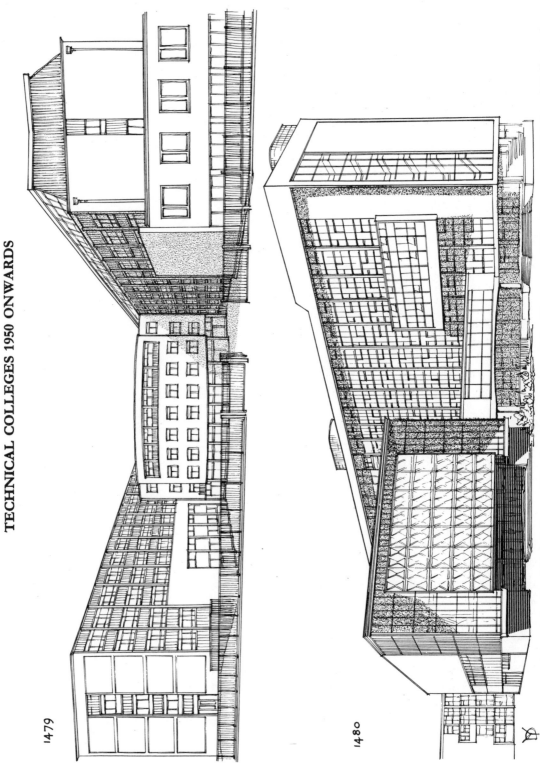

1479

1480

1479 Luton and South Bedfordshire College of Further Education, 1956–61. Norman and Dawbarn   1480   The Royal College of

Library at **Sheffield**, which adjoins the remainder of the buildings in the Park. The library is in the form of a square, low block and contains, on the upper floor, one large reading room of 8,000 square feet. The glass is tinted most effectively. The interior decoration and materials are of very high quality and interest. The architects, who won this commission in competition in 1953, are **Messrs Gollins, Melvin, Ward and Partners** (1477).

Technical Colleges

While a large-scale building extension plan has been in operation for some years in universities, the situation with regard to technical colleges is even more radical. Traditionally, the technical college (or 'college of technology', as the senior ones are now called) has always been the poor relation of the university. But, although even today larger sums of money are allocated to the university, the change in the status of the technical college, particularly in regard to the science and engineering departments, has been revolutionary. Only a small quantity of building in this field was carried out between 1918 and 1939. Since 1950 this situation has altered considerably.

Immediately after the war the urgency of building in the educational field was for schools. Later came the drive for technical and after-school further education. The White Paper of 1956 on Technical Education marked a new phase in this development. It was decided to establish a number of Colleges of Advanced Technology and to allocate £100 million for buildings and equipment. At the same time, the National Council for Technological Awards, with Lord Hives as its Chairman, was set up to establish the Diploma of Technology, with particular reference to sandwich courses in co-operation with industry. This qualification provides an alternative, in a technical approach, to the university degree. Colleges have been classified in four categories: at the top, Colleges of Advanced Technology, followed by Regional Colleges, Area Colleges and, at the bottom of the scale, Local Colleges. These were designated by the Ministry of Education according to standard of work, number of students, area involved, local industrial needs, etc.

This tremendous expansion, however, is primarily in the sciences and engineering, which raises an important question: that of the broad purposes of further education. In her admirable book on technical colleges,* Miss Barbara Price asks most pertinently, 'How is the narrowing of the scope of the work to be reconciled with the repeatedly expressed need for broadening technical education?' She points out that 'commerce and art education form an integral part of the present functions of many technical colleges. In the proposed Colleges of Advanced Technology there seems to be no place for them.' The matter has become of concern to Ministry and local education authorities, and the answer so far has seemed to be in the form of 'liberal studies', compulsorily administered to the science and engineering student in the form of lectures. This 'applied' method of culture broadening is unlikely to prove very effective, and certainly less so than the spontaneous interest aroused in the student by natural contact in the college with his colleagues in the arts subjects, as is the case in a university or old-type technical college.

Many existing technical colleges all over the country are now building new accommodation. The problem of choosing suitable sites has not been easy. The majority of existing

* *Technical Colleges and Colleges of Further Education* (B. T. Batsford Ltd, 1959).

1481 Central College of Technology, Leeds, Yorkshire, 1955–61. F. R. S. Yorke, E. Rosenberg and C. S. Mardall   1482 Laboratory and workshop blocks, Sheffield College of Technology, 1956–61. Gollins, Melvin, Ward and Partners

technical colleges are in busy industrial towns and cities and the question arises of whether to erect the new building in the centre of the town as before, or to build outside on the outskirts where the land is cheaper and a larger site can be chosen. Most universities are built outside the town, but hostel accommodation forms part of the majority of university schemes, also the students are generally carrying out full-time studies. The technical college serves the town community and, apart from full-time and sandwich-course students for whom there is at present rarely any hostel accommodation and who live at home or in lodgings, the college often provides evening and recreational classes for any adults who require further studies. For easy accessibility, therefore, most colleges have decided upon a central site for their new buildings, and this has, in most cases, restricted their available building area. In consequence, such colleges have been built high and not entirely in low blocks as are most new university buildings.

From among the many examples four colleges have been selected here for illustration. Of these, the most interesting and successful exterior design is the **Royal College of Advanced Technology** at **Salford**, Lancashire, designed by Lancashire County Council County architect, **G. Noel Hill**, and opened by Her Majesty the Queen in May 1961. Here, in tremendous contrast to the blackened, Victorian town of Salford, adjoining Manchester, is a colourful, exciting college of technology. The scheme is not yet complete but the multi-storey teaching block and the unusual great hall are in use (1480).

At Luton, the **Luton and South Bedfordshire College of Further Education** is largely complete. It is designed by **Messrs Norman and Dawbarn** and consists of two four-storey blocks for laboratories and lecture rooms linked by a curving block which contains the entrance hall, administrative offices, library and common rooms (1479, 1496).

At Leeds and Sheffield, both congested city centres, have been erected tall blocks. The sloping **Leeds** site is of nine acres near the Civic Hall. The scheme is about three-quarters completed and the design by **F. R. S. Yorke** (the late), **E. Rosenberg** and **C. S. Mardall** includes an eight-storey laboratory block and tiered workshops (1481). The **Sheffield** design is by **Messrs Gollins, Melvin, Ward** and **Partners** in conjunction with **J. L. Womersley** the city architect. It occupies a 7-acre site on a steep slope, in the centre of the city, unfortunately near the main railway station. (Due to this proximity it was necessary to clean the glass curtain walling of the eight-storey building immediately before opening.) The scheme is an ambitious one and will comprise an 11-storey block, an eight-storey one and single-storey workshops (1482).

Schools

Of all forms of education, a greater quantity of building has been carried out since 1945 at school level than in any other field. This was urgently essential after the war, for several reasons. Partly, there was the increased birth rate of the years immediately following the war; partly, it was made necessary by the raising of the school leaving age to 15; in addition, many school buildings had been damaged or destroyed by enemy action, and the 1944 Education Act had to be implemented. For these reasons the start was made on the most urgent level—primary schools. Then came secondary modern schools and later comprehensive schools. Very little has been done for the secondary grammar school because, before the war, these schools were in the best position and were adequately catered for. This has now altered and

COMPREHENSIVE SCHOOLS 1950 ONWARDS

1483 1484 1485

1483 Mayfield Girls' Comprehensive School, Putney, London, 1955. Powell and Moya 1484–5 Churchfields Comprehensive School, West Bromwich, Staffordshire, 1958–60. Richard Sheppard and Partners

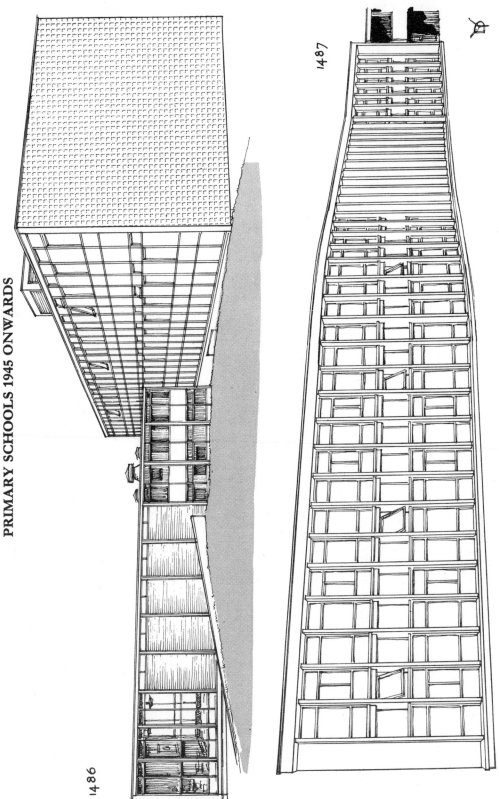

1486 Fairlawn Primary School, Honor Oak, London, 1957. Peter Moro   1487 Hallfield Primary School, Paddington, London, 1955. Drake and Lasdun

1486

1487

the pendulum has swung in the other direction. Our most gifted children are often now being taught in the worst conditions and there are not enough grammar schools available for those children able to take advantage of such education. In view of the publicity given to the pressing need for scientists and engineers, and for teachers of science and mathematics, it seems to be putting the cart before the horse to create large technical colleges but not enough grammar schools to supply them with students.

In comparing the three types of buildings erected for educational purposes in this postwar period, the most interesting of the designs are for schools. These buildings suffer from similar defects to those of technical college and university: too much glass, not enough blinds, walls through which every sound can be heard, paint which is peeling, doors and windows which do not shut, badly designed wash basins, tables, desks, kitchens and blackboards. Apart from this, imagination has been shown in the external design of school buildings, in general layout, in the use of materials and colour, and in the functions and placing of rooms and halls. Some schools are a joy to teach in, and the contrast between them and their nineteenth-century predecessors is startling and gratifying.

Four schools have been selected for illustration here: two comprehensive and two primary schools. **The Mayfield Comprehensive School for Girls** at **Putney**, designed in 1955 by **Powell and Moya**, is a London County Council Comprehensive School which has been evolved from the Girls' Grammar School already on the site. The area of 9 acres has accommodated the new buildings in long, low development and still leaves pleasant wooded surroundings. The exterior walls are chiefly glass. The assembly hall is supported on columns. The standard of finish is high (1483). **The Churchfields Comprehensive School** at **West Bromwich** was designed by **Richard Sheppard and Partners** in 1958–60. Here, the house block system has been planned, with separate blocks for gymnasia, assembly hall and library. The houses are one- or two-storey designs while the science blocks are in four-storey style (1484–5).

The **Hallfield Primary School** at **Paddington**, designed in 1955 by **Drake and Lasdun**, has an interesting elevation in vertical mullions and louvres. The general colour scheme is mainly in black and white, in brick, with small areas of bright colour (1487). At the **Fairlawn Primary School** at **Honor Oak**, designed 1957 by **Peter Moro**, the buildings are carefully arranged to take advantage of the steeply sloping site. Decoration at the rear is in brightly coloured panels in glass and ceramic (1486, 1502).

COMMERCIAL AND INDUSTRIAL BUILDING

Commercial building design in the form of offices and shops is generally not inspiring. Four smaller but typical examples are illustrated in Figs. 1488–91.

Many new **factory** buildings have been erected in the post-war years. Designs, on the block system, are very similar to one another. Three of the less uninteresting examples have been illustrated here. In particular, the **Seed Factory** of Messrs Cooper, Taber and Co. at **Witham**, Essex, designed 1956 by **Chamberlin, Powell and Bon**, has character. This is provided chiefly by coloured glass and ceramic arranged in rectangular panels (1504–6).

A great deal of work has also been done in **airport design**, especially at London and Gatwick. At **Heathrow** there is, in particular, the passenger handling building, 1955, by

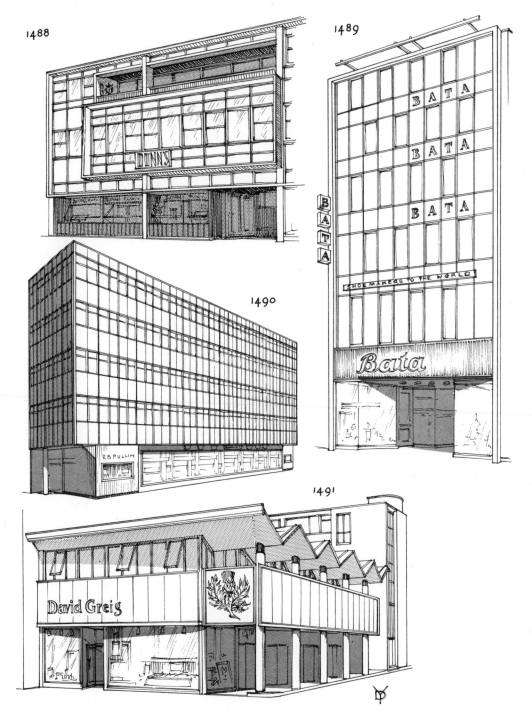

1488 H. G. Dunn and Sons Ltd, Bromley, Kent, 1957. Bertram Carter   1489 Bata, Oxford Street, London, 1956. Bronck, Katz and R. Vaughan   1490 Office block, New Cavendish Street, London, 1957. Gollins, Melvin, Ward and Partners   1491 David Greig Ltd, Canterbury, 1954. Robert Paine and Partners

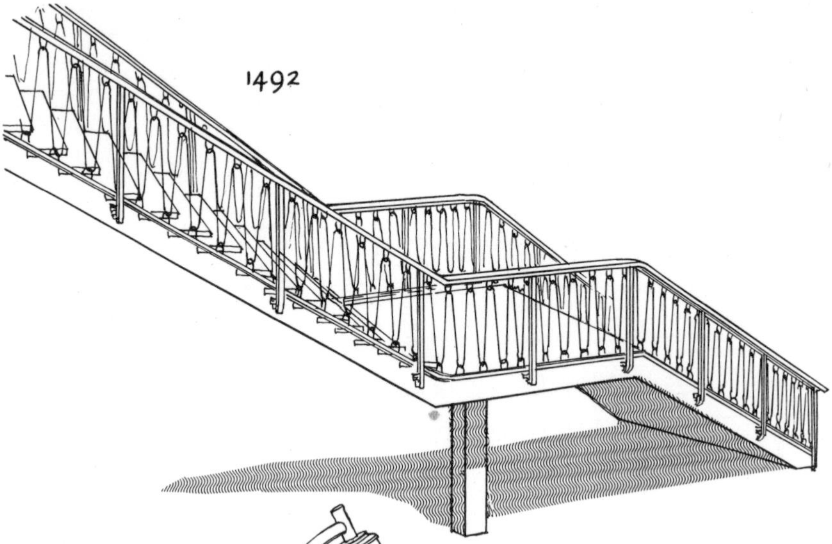

1492

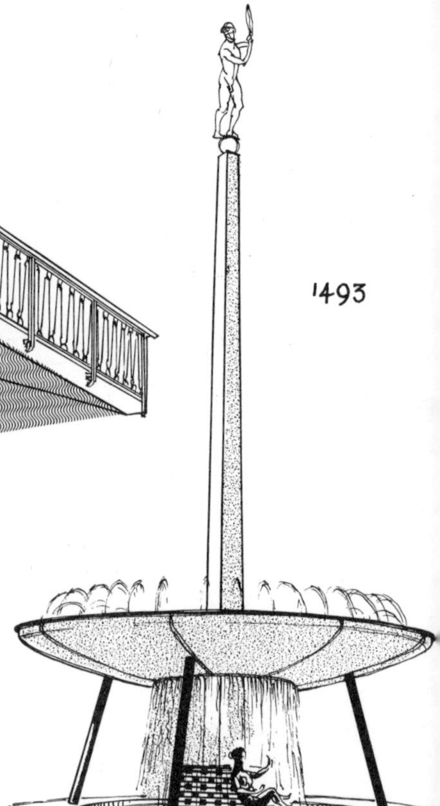

1493

1494

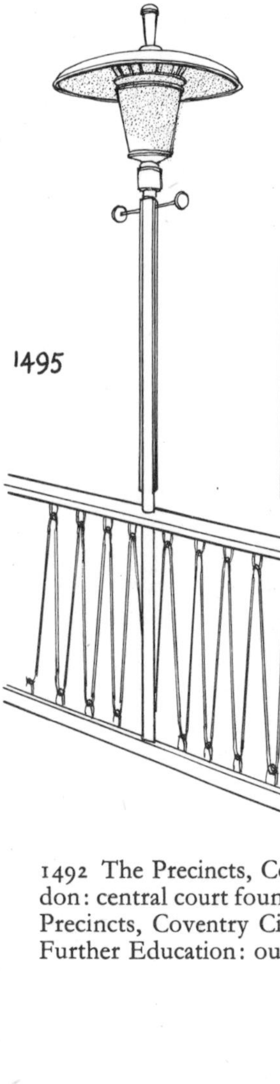

1495

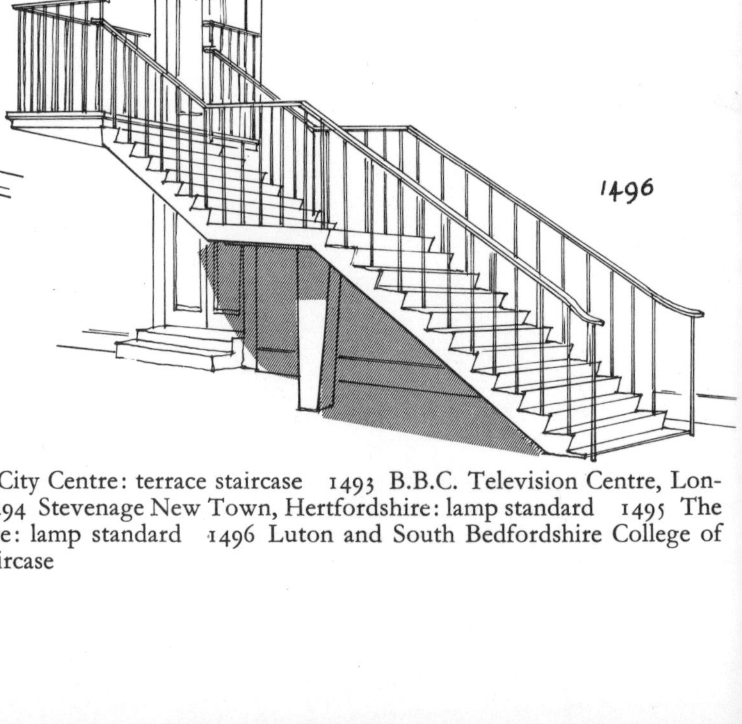

1496

1492 The Precincts, Coventry City Centre: terrace staircase   1493 B.B.C. Television Centre, London: central court fountain   1494 Stevenage New Town, Hertfordshire: lamp standard   1495 The Precincts, Coventry City Centre: lamp standard   1496 Luton and South Bedfordshire College of Further Education: outside staircase

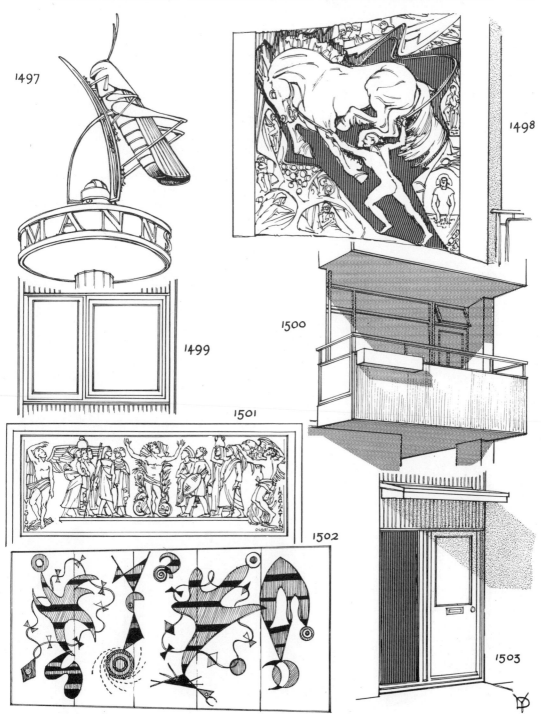

1497 Crawley New Town, Sussex: public house emblem 'The Grasshopper', Tilgate area   1498 The
Shopping Precincts, Coventry: sculptured panel   1499, 1500, 1503 Alton Estate, London, S.W.15
1501 Goodenough House, London, Barclays Bank Head Office: sculptured panel. Sculptor, Gilbert
Ledward   1502 Fairlawn Primary School, London, S.E.23: colour panel

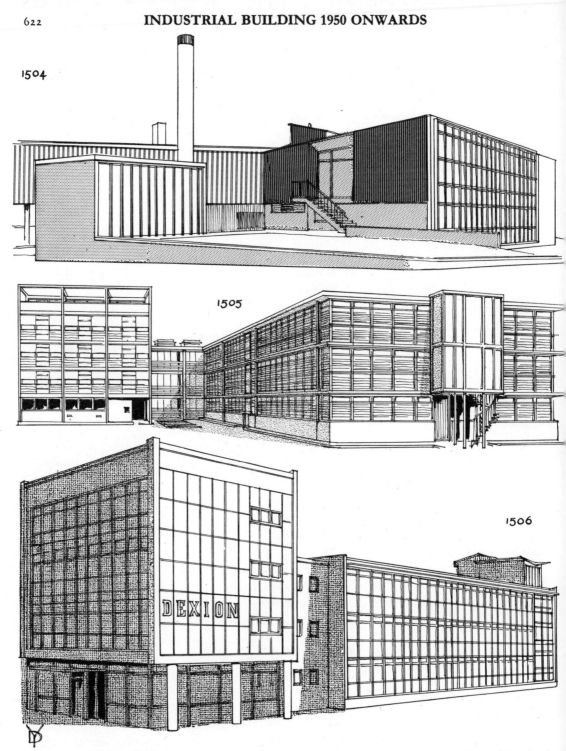

1504 Chemical Building Products Factory, industrial area, Hemel Hempstead New Town, Hertford-shire, 1956. Ove Arup and Partners   1505 Seed factory, Messrs Cooper, Taber and Co. Ltd., Witham, Essex, 1956. Chamberlin, Powell and Son   1506 Dexion Factory, Hemel Hempstead New Town, industrial area

Frederick Gibberd, also his new terminal building, already mentioned, and the B.O.A.C. Headquarters, 1955, by **Sir Owen Williams and Partners. Gatwick** was a pre-war airport which has been greatly extended and replanned. The principal architects are **Yorke, Rosenberg and Mardall.** There is a large new terminal building, reached either from the new railway station or from the road below. At a lower level still, the A23 London–Brighton road runs through the airport. The terminal building is supported on columns above this road. From this terminal building stretch out three long, low masses. The control tower is of reinforced concrete construction with glazed panels and brick facing.

POWER STATIONS

Since so much of modern architecture is in the form of civil engineering, modern power stations are representative of the most interesting designs of this age. A large number have been built since 1945 of which **Marchwood Generating Station** on **Southampton Water** is typical of the modern approach. It was designed by **Farmer and Dank** and built in 1957–9 by the engineers **Sir William Halcrow and Partners.** It was constructed to run on oil or solid fuel, though so far only oil has been used. The structure is of steel framing with brick for the ground-floor walls and glazed and solid covering above. It is well proportioned, light and colourful and has two slender chimneys. In comparison with Battersea Power Station, designs of this type have advanced considerably since the 1930s (1507).

Nuclear Power Stations

Calder Hall, Seascale, Cumberland, near the river Calder and the north-west coast of England, was the site of the first **nuclear power station** in the world to operate on an industrial scale. The plant, which was opened by Her Majesty the Queen in 1956, was constructed alongside the existing Windscale plutonium factory (now dismantled). The tallest features of the Calder Hall design are the cooling towers (traditional in pattern); the general building scheme is in the form of simple, steel-framed structures with colour used for piping. Each reactor building with its shield rests on a reinforced concrete raft which is 11 feet thick, 130 feet long and 104 feet wide. The necessary biological shield, octagonal in cross-section, for each reactor is also of reinforced concrete, some 88 feet in height and 46 feet across inside. An exceptionally high degree of accuracy was essential in the construction: massive quantities of reinforced concrete were set in place to a precision hitherto unapproached; indeed the way in which problems of civil engineering were solved, quite apart from those in mechanical and nuclear engineering, is most likely to have important influences on the design and erection of large-scale buildings for other than nuclear enterprises.

From each of the reactors heated carbon dioxide gas at a pressure of 100 pounds per square inch is passed through heat exchangers where water is heated to generate steam. Each of the four heat exchangers per reactor has a steel pressure shell with an interior height of 80 feet. The superheated steam from the heat exchangers passes to the turbine-driven electric generators of virtually conventional pattern. The reactors also produce plutonium for the manufacture of nuclear weapons. Nearly 150 million gallons of water per day circulate the plant; each cooling tower is a large chimney built over a shallow pond and is 300 feet in

CONVENTIONAL POWER STATION DESIGN 1945 ONWARDS

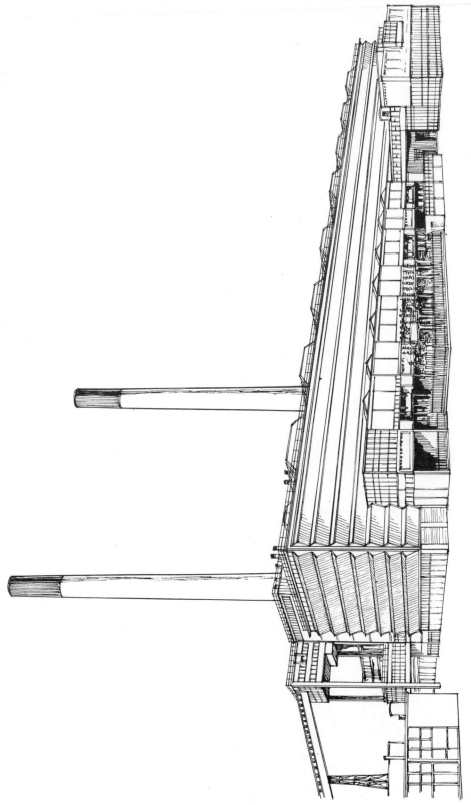

1507 Marchwood Generating Station, Southampton Water, Hampshire, 1957–9. Oil fired (designed to be run on oil or solid fuel). Architects Farmer and Dank. Consulting engineers, Sir William Halcrow and Partners

BERKELEY NUCLEAR POWER STATION, GLOUCESTERSHIRE, 1957–1962

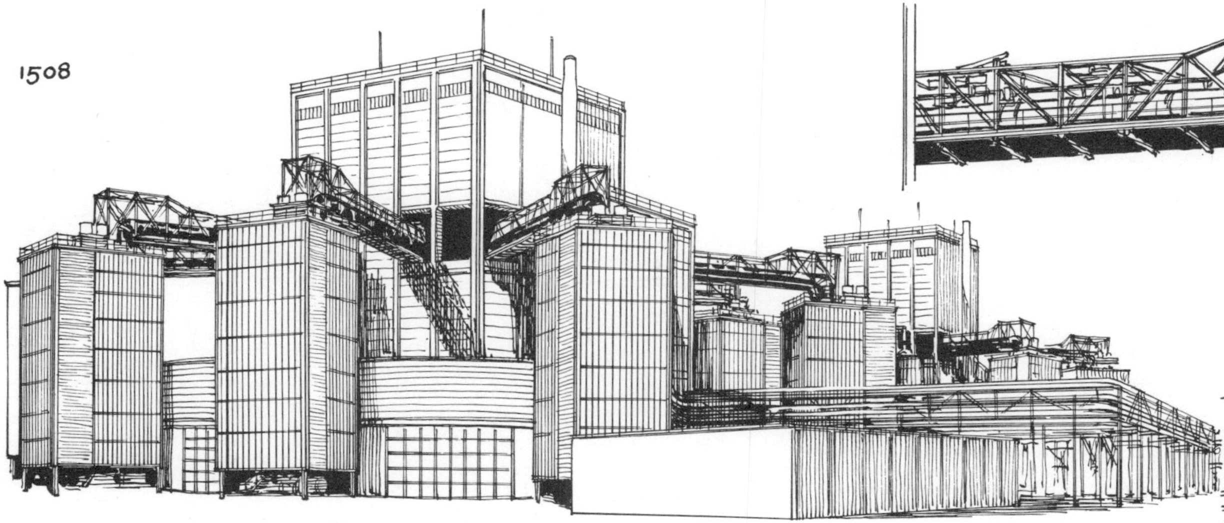

1510

1508

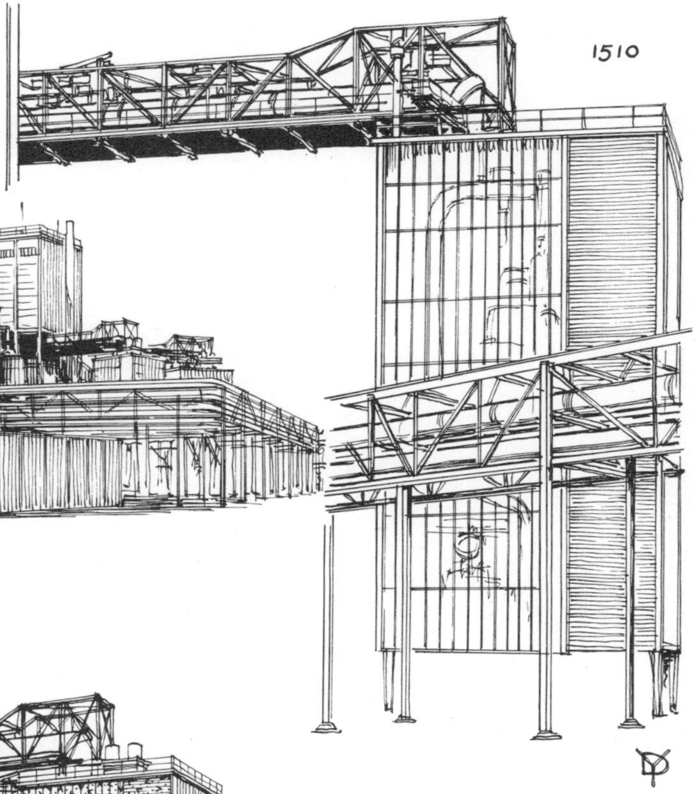

1509

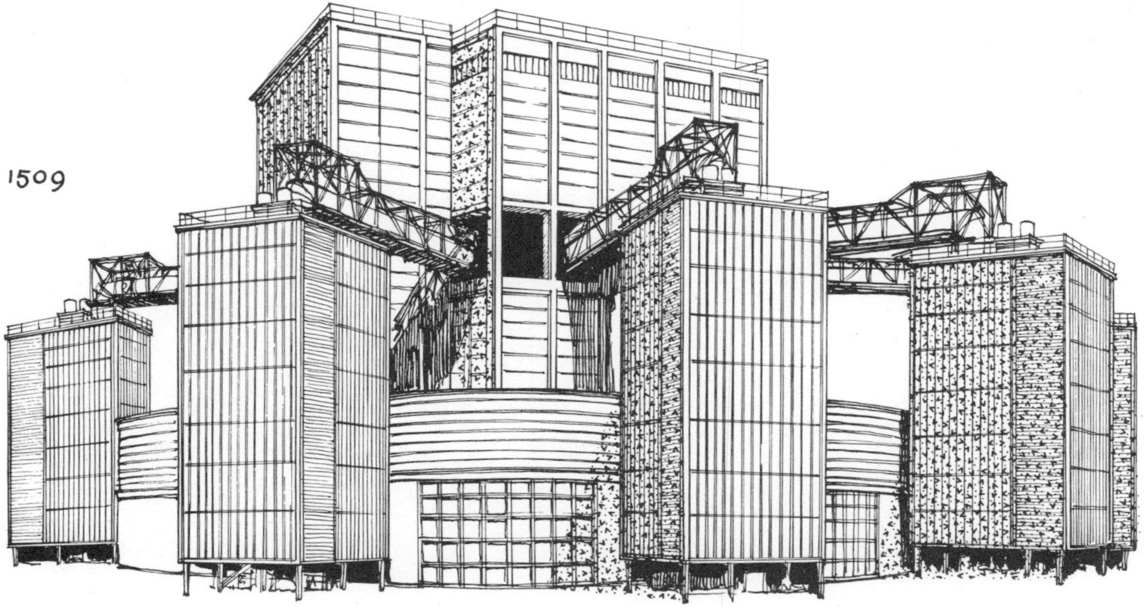

1508 General view of Power Station showing both reactors 1509 A view of one reactor showing five of the eight heat exchangers 1510 Detail of heat exchanger showing duct connecting to reactor

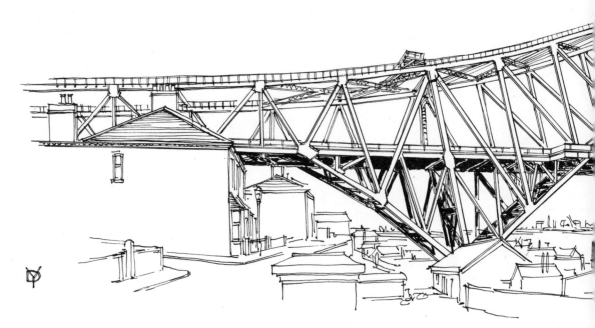

1511 The Runcorn–Widnes road bridge spanning the Mersey and the Manchester Ship Canal.

height and 190 feet in diameter at the base, with a reinforced concrete shell of 16 inches thickness at the bottom and $4\frac{1}{2}$ inches at the top.

The civil engineering contractors for Calder Hall were Taylor Woodrow Construction Ltd; the steelwork was undertaken by Alexander Findlay and Co.

Very much more interesting from the architectural and aesthetic viewpoints are the **nuclear power stations** built for the **Central Electricity Generating Board**. A 10-year programme for building power stations was announced in the Government White Paper of 1955. This envisaged the construction of 12 nuclear power stations built by private industry for the Board at a cost of £300,000,000. A number of these are now functioning or being constructed. Those at Bradwell and Berkeley came into operation in 1961, and at **Hinkley Point**, Somerset, in 1962. Construction continues at **Trawsfynydd**, Merionethshire, and at **Dungeness**, Kent.

Work began on the site of **Bradwell Nuclear Power Station**, Essex, in January 1957. Two natural uranium, carbon dioxide gas-cooled, graphite-moderated reactors were planned. Unlike Calder Hall, there is no need to shut down the plant in order to change periodically the fuel in the reactors. This station is situated on the Blackwater Estuary near the sea, near also, in considerable contrast architecturally, the Anglo-Saxon church of St Peter-on-the-Walls. The site was originally a marsh below high tide level. All the land in the vicinity of the main buildings had to be raised to $3\frac{1}{2}$ feet above the maximum recorded flood level.

Under each reactor is a heavily reinforced concrete raft, 9 feet thick and 200 by 100 feet

Opened 1961. Consulting Engineers, Messrs Mott, Hay and Anderson

in area. On this, which is 45 feet below finished ground level, is constructed a series of reinforced 'box' structures to take the load of three boilers at each end of the reactor. The central bay comprises the reactor vault which has an internal diameter of 77 feet and is 81 feet in height. It is enclosed by a biological shield 8 to 10 feet thick.

Twenty-one million gallons of cooling water per hour are taken from the Blackwater Estuary and are discharged back. The plant was built by the Nuclear Power Plant Co. Ltd. (LXIV).

Like Bradwell, work was started on the **Berkeley Nuclear Power Station**, Gloucestershire, in January 1957, and there are again two reactors. The plant was constructed by the John Thompson Nuclear Energy Co. Ltd.

The site is on the east bank of the Severn Estuary near the new Severn Bridge. Figures are similar to those for Bradwell, but the arrangement and design of the plant is rather different in that the heat exchangers are not enclosed as at Bradwell. This makes a much more interesting design (1508–10).

In all cases where these nuclear power station sites are being constructed, huge development schemes of raising land levels, road construction and building of accommodation are required first, and all the stations built so far have enhanced, and not been detrimental to, their respective landscape settings. Immense care and thought have been taken in this respect. Sir Giles Gilbert Scott concerned himself with each stage of construction and design until his death. The sites are well organised, tidy and controlled and the administration of the Central Electricity Generating Board is most helpful and co-operative.

1512 The Forth road bridge, due to be completed 1964. Engineers, Messrs Mott, Hay and Anderson

BRIDGES

Of the bridges built since 1945 there are three large-scale engineering constructions which are particularly noteworthy and which represent feats of engineering in the 1950s and '60s reminiscent of Telford and Brunel. All three are road bridges and all have been or are being designed and their construction supervised by the engineering firm of **Messrs Mott, Hay and Anderson.**

The Runcorn–Widnes Road Bridge

This is a gigantic, single-arched, steel bridge spanning the river Mersey and the Manchester Ship Canal. It has a main span of 1,082 feet and is the third longest span of its kind in the world (the other two longer spans being the Bayonne Bridge, New York State, U.S.A., and the Sydney Harbour Bridge in Australia). Situated next to the railway bridge, the new construction is not only a triumph for modern engineering, but is also beautiful and impressive. The steelwork, painted in light green, stands out in the murky Mersey landscape in a delicate subtle curve from bank to bank (1511). The project was begun in 1947 and the bridge was opened by Princess Alexandra of Kent in 1961. Approach roads and viaducts of considerable length were built at each end of the main structure.

The Forth and Severn Road Bridges

The engineers, **Messrs Mott, Hay and Anderson**, were first asked for a report on a **Forth Road Bridge** in 1926. Work was finally begun after the war and the bridge will be completed in 1964. The present site chosen is about half a mile upstream from the old railway bridge.

3300 FT.

associated with Freeman Fox and Partners, Consulting Architect, Sir Giles Gilbert Scott

The new bridge will be rather longer than the older example; it is of suspension design and will be the fourth longest in the world. It will have a main span of 3,300 feet and side-spans of 1,340 feet each. There will be two 24-foot carriageways, two 9-foot cycle tracks and two 6-foot footpaths. These will be carried on a grid of steel beams and girders which, in turn, will be slung from vertical steel ropes, at intervals of 60 feet, from the main suspension cables.

The north pier site is fixed by Mackintosh Rock which provides a firm base in shallow water. The south pier site is in much deeper water. The towers are of steel and are over 500 feet in height. There are also two side towers constructed of reinforced concrete and which rise to deck level. The suspension cables are supported on the main towers and are about 24 inches in diameter. Each of the two cables is made up from 12,000 high-tensile steel wires run parallel to one another and clamped together in sections on the site. Each wire has a diameter of 0·196 inch. The cables are anchored at each end in concrete-filled tunnels cut in rock.

In the achievement of aerodynamic stability, the principal factor is the proportion and disposition of the components of the bridge; this is particularly assisted by the separation of the carriageways from each other and from the cycle tracks by open spaces in the deck. In addition to the bridge, there will be approach viaducts on each side of 17 spans, and there will be also 12 miles of approach roads.

Except for the deck the bridge is now largely completed. It is a delicate structure in appearance, making it difficult to credit its massive proportions when viewed against the background of the Firth of Forth. Though it lacks the majesty of the companion railway bridge it is more graceful. Perhaps this quality is reflected in the quantities of steel in the two bridges: the longer road bridge contains over 10,000 tons less than its old neighbour. Apart from its immense span, the construction of this modern bridge is a new venture for British engineers as it involves the American cable spinning method for making suspension cables. Though 'spinning' is a misnomer, an interesting process is involved whereby each steel wire is passed individually across the river above the 500-foot towers. When a number of these parallel wires has been strung across and the tensions in them carefully adjusted, they are clamped together. These groups of wires are then finally compressed together to give one 24-inch diameter cable. It is a remarkable structure and one which enhances the Firth of Forth and does not detract from the achievement of its railway predecessor. The engineers for the bridge are **Messrs Mott, Hay and Anderson** associated with **Freeman Fox and Partners**. The consulting architect was the late **Sir Giles Gilbert Scott**.

The Severn Road Bridge

A railway tunnel has linked the two banks of the river Severn for many years, but the Severn Road Bridge is the first bridge to be built across the Bristol Channel. It will constitute a tremendous saving of time for road users between Wales and Gloucestershire. The task is not easy: the Severn here has the fastest tide in Britain and a rise and fall of 40 feet. The Severn Bridge, although of the same magnitude as the Forth Road Bridge, will differ strikingly in appearance because of the aerfoil form of the deck and the arrangement of the hangers in an inclined pattern. It will be a little shorter with a main span of 3,240 feet. The bridge is being built near the present ferry route, from Aust to Beachley. It is hoped to complete the work in 1966. **Messrs Mott, Hay and Anderson** are also building this bridge, but the consulting architect is **Sir Percy Thomas**.

Glossary

Abutment—Solid masonry acting as support against the thrust or lateral pressure of an arch.

Adze—Tool like an axe for cutting wood surface. It has an arched blade at right angles to the handle.

Almonry—A room in a monastic establishment where alms were distributed.

Arabesque—Ornament used in Renaissance classical art and architecture. Generally describes delicate, flowing ribs or lines, decorated by flowers or leaves and terminates in scrolls.

Arcade—A series of arches, open or closed with masonry, supported on columns or piers.

Arch—A structure of wedge-shaped blocks over an opening which support one another by mutual pressure.

Architrave—Lowest section of classical entablature which passes horizontally across the columns. Expression also applied to door and window frames.

Ashlar—Hewn and squared stones prepared for building.

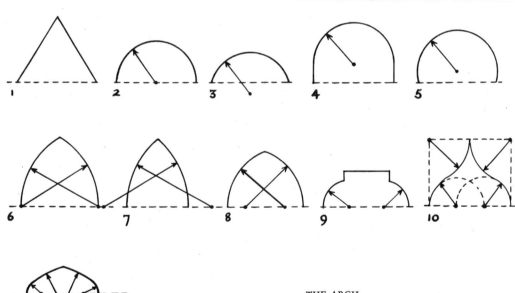

THE ARCH

1 Triangular	5 Round—horseshoe	9 Shouldered
2 Round—semicircular	6 Pointed—equilateral	10 Ogee
3 Round—segmental	7 Pointed—lancet	11 Four-centred
4 Round—stilted	8 Pointed—obtuse	

Astragal—A small, semicircular moulding, generally at the top of a shaft or column and below the capital.

ASTRAGAL

Astylar—A classical façade designed without columns.

Bailey—A court enclosed by inner or outer walls of castle, or by any of its defensive circuits.

Barbican—Outer defence to a city or castle. Generally a double tower over a gate or bridge.

Barge board—Ornamental, carved wood boards on the exterior gable beams of a roof.

BARGE BOARD, OCKWELLS MANOR HOUSE

Barrow—see Tumulus.

Bascule—A type of drawbridge raised or lowered with counterpoise.

Bay—Compartment or division in a building. Term particularly applied to cathedrals where bays are marked by vaulting shafts and pillars.

Bolection moulding—A curved moulding generally used to raise one surface, such as a panel, above the remainder.

Cantilever—Bracket used to support cornice or balcony, etc. of considerable projection. Cantilever Bridge—principle used for large spans such as the Forth Railway Bridge. Cantilever is the beam supported above and carrying the weight at free extremity. In the Forth Bridge, girders connect up the ends of the huge cantilevers (1293, p. 509).

Cartouche—Ornament in the form of elaborate scrolled forms round shields, tablets or coats of arms.

CARTOUCHE

Cathedral or large church, parts of—

Aisle	Lady chapel
Apse	Nave
Chapter house	Presbytery
Choir (quire)	Transept
Cloisters	Vestry (Sacristy)
Crossing	*See also* Chapter II,
Crypt	p. 32

Caryatids—Sculptured female figures in the form of supports or columns. Employed particularly in chimney-piece design (1124).

Chamfer—An angle which is cut off diagonally. The cut can be straight or concave; in the latter instance, it is termed a hollow chamfer.

Chancel—Eastern arm of a church.

Cinquefoil—Five-leaf tracery opening.

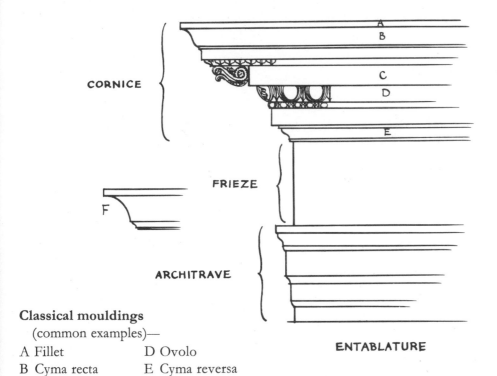

CORNICE

FRIEZE

ARCHITRAVE

ENTABLATURE

Classical mouldings
(common examples)—

A Fillet	D Ovolo
B Cyma recta	E Cyma reversa
C Corona	F Cavetto

ACANTHUS LEAF

ANTHEMION

ANTHEMION (HONEYSUCKLE)

PATERA

EGG AND DART

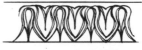

LEAF AND DART

BEAD AND REEL

Classical ornament—

Acanthus leaf
Anthemion (honey-
suckle decoration)

Bead and reel
Egg and dart
Leaf and dart
Patera

Coffer—Panel or caisson sunk in ceiling, dome or vault. Often ornamented.

Collar beam—Horizontal tying beam in timber roof.

CINQUEFOIL

Corbel—A projecting block of stone or timber supporting a cornice or other mouldings of a vault. Such blocks are often elaborately carved (300).

Cornice—The horizontal, moulded projection which crowns an architectural feature such as a parapet, entablature or wall.

Cornucopia—The 'horn of plenty'. Ornament in the form of a horn, often twisted and filled with fruit and flowers. A symbol of prosperity.

Crocket—A projecting block of stone carved in Gothic foliage on the inclined sides of pinnacles and canopies.

CROCKET

Cromlech—A large, flat stone laid horizontally on upright stones. Prehistoric workmanship.

Cupola—A spherical roof covering a circular or polygonal form.

Cusp—Point forming the foliations in Gothic tracery.

Dormitory—Sleeping apartment in a monastery.

CUSP

Drawbridge—Bridge hinged at one end so that it can be drawn up in order to prevent passage.

Drum tower—Round tower.

Dry-stone building—No mortar or filling used in construction.

Entablature—The top portion of an architectural order which consists of horizontal mouldings. These are divided into architrave, which surmounts the column, then the frieze, and last and uppermost, the cornice.

Entasis—A slight fullness or outward curve given to a column to correct the optical illusion which makes the column silhouette appear concave when the lines of the shaft are straight.

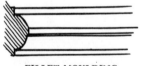

FILLET MOULDING

Fillet moulding—A small, flat band between mouldings to separate them from each other. Also used as the top member of cornice.

Finial—Ornament finishing off the apex of the roof, gable, pediment, pinnacle, newel, canopy, etc.

FINIAL

Hammerbeam—Horizontal beam in timber roof situated as a tie-beam but in two sections with main opening in the centre.

Hammer post—Rests on the inner side of the hammerbeam.

Impost—The horizontal stone or mouldings on top of a pier from which the arch springs.

Foil—Spaces between cusps in Gothic tracery. Trefoil, quatrefoil, etc., indicate the number of foils in the window light.

Frieze—The middle division of the classical entablature.

Frontispiece—The two- or three-stage entrance feature applied to the principal façade of a court or building.

Galilee—A porch used as a chapel in some Gothic cathedrals and churches.

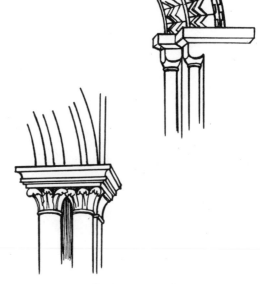

IMPOST MOULDINGS

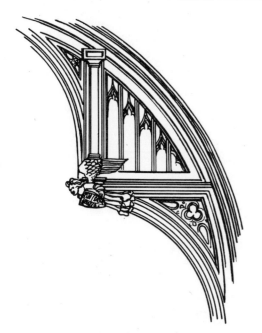

HAMMERBEAM AND HAMMER POST,
WESTMINSTER HALL

LANTERN, ELY CATHEDRAL

King post (also **queen post**)—Vertical post extending from ridge to tie-beam centre to support the latter. Queen posts are in pairs (see Timber Roof diagram).

Lantern—Structure for ventilation and light. In classical architecture, generally placed on top of a dome. In Gothic architecture it generally takes the form of a tower.

Lintel—Horizontal piece of stone or timber over a door or window opening.

LINTEL

Louvre (Louver)—Turret or lantern on roof with openings for emission of smoke and admission of air. Placed above central hearths and fireplaces. Louvre boards keep out the rain whilst permitting free passage for air and smoke (311).

Lunette—A semicircular panel, often ornamented, in the form of stone, wood or glass.

Monolith—Single, standing stone.

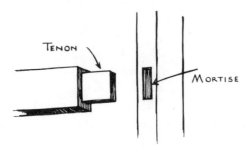

MORTISE AND TENON JOINT

Mortise and tenon—Mortise piece of timber has a hole into which the tenon or tongue on another piece of timber is made to fit. Stone and other materials also suitable.

Mullion—Vertical bar dividing the lights in a window.

Mural tower—Tower set in the castle walls.

Necking—Space between the astragal of a shaft or column and the actual capital.

Niche—A recess in the wall hollowed out to receive sculpture.

Ogee moulding or **scroll**—A moulding incorporating a convex and a concave curve.

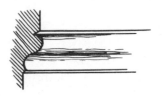

OGEE MOULDING

Oolite—Granular limestone.

Order—In classical architecture the order comprises a column and the entablature which it supports. The column is divided into base, shaft and capital (p. 186).

Parapet—Part of wall above guttering; sometimes battlemented (392–6).

Pediment—The triangular feature in classical architecture which resembles the Gothic gable. Supported on the entablature over porticoes, doors and windows.

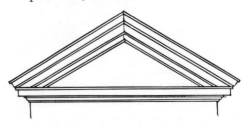

PEDIMENT

Pier—A solid mass of masonry between windows, also support for a bridge and masonry from which an arch springs.

Pilaster—Column of rectangular section often engaged in wall.

Pillar—Column supporting an arch.

Pinnacle—A termination to buttresses, parapets and gables in the form of a small turret and spire.

Plinth—Lowest member of base or wall: sometimes divided into stages.

Portcullis—A strong, heavy frame or grating of oak or iron, made to slide up and down in vertical grooves at the sides of a castle gateway.

QUATREFOIL DECORATION

Quatrefoil—Four-leaf tracery opening.

Quoin—External angle of a building.

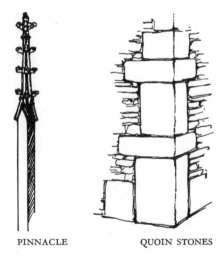

PINNACLE   QUOIN STONES

Ragstone or **rag-work**—Stone varies from county to county. Flat-bedded and broken up into about brick size or smaller. Thick mortar in between.

Refectory—Dining hall of a college or monastery.

Ridge-crest—Exterior ridge or upper angle of roof.

Ridge pole or **piece**—A long piece of timber extending along the internal ridge of a roof on which the upper ends of the rafters rest (see Timber Roof diagram).

Roll moulding—A plain, round moulding, also sometimes known as a round or bow-tell.

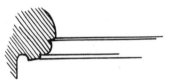

ROLL MOULDING

Rubble work—Stones of most irregular shape and size used, although generally roughly in cube or block form.

RAG-WORK

RUBBLE WORK

Rustication—Used in classical architecture, particularly in Renaissance work, wherein masonry joints are grooved and some sections are raised and left or made rough.

Sanctuary (Presbytery)—Eastern part of the choir of a church where the altar is placed.

Scroll moulding—Resembles a roll of parchment, the end of which projects beyond the remainder.

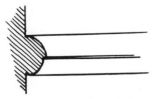

SCROLL MOULDING

Set-off—Part of a wall which is exposed horizontally when the portion above it is reduced in thickness.

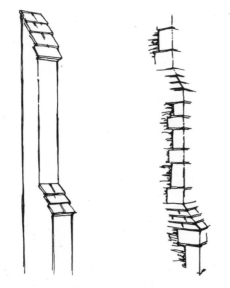

BUTTRESS SETS-OFF   WALL SETS-OFF

Shingle—Oak tile.

Sill—Horizontal timber or other material placed at base of building, partition, window or door opening.

Spandrel—Triangular space formed between an arch and the rectangle of outer mouldings as in doorway construction. Generally decorated by carving.

Starling—Pointed mass of masonry or wood projecting from the pier of a bridge.

SPANDREL, THAXTED CHURCH

Steeple—Tower including any superstructure such as spire or lantern.

Strapwork—A form of ornament using straps or lines of decoration, intertwined and forming panels. The straps are flat with raised, fillet edges, and might be pierced with circular or diamond-shaped holes. All the work is in one plane, i.e. as in ceiling or wall decoration.

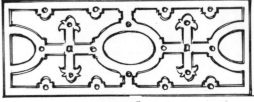

STRAPWORK

Swag—A drop type of decoration composed of flowers and fruit.

SWAG

Tablet or **table**—Medieval term applied to all horizontal bands of mouldings. Most commonly used for cornice.

Tie-beam—A horizontal or slightly arched beam connecting the principal rafters of the roof (see Timber Roof diagram).

Tracery—The ornamental stonework in the upper part of a Gothic window.

Transom—Horizontal bar of wood or stone across a window, or a door top.

Trefoil—Three-leaf decoration used in Gothic architecture, particularly in window tracery and in panelling.

TREFOIL

Tumulus—Burial mound.

Turret—Small tower often containing a staircase.

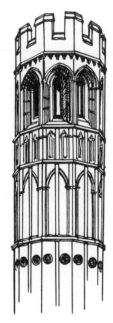

TURRET, ELY CATHEDRAL

Tympanum—The triangular space between the horizontal and sloping cornices of a pediment (classical architecture). Also (in Medieval architecture), the name given to the space between the lintel and arch of

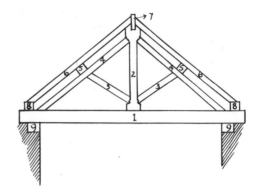

SECTIONAL DIAGRAM OF MEDIEVAL TIMBER ROOF

1	Tie beam	6 Common rafters
2	King-post	7 Ridge-piece
3	Braces	8 Pole plates
4	Principal rafters	9 Wall plates
5	Purlins	

a doorway (1083, 1311).

Vault—Arched covering in stone, brick or wood.

TURRET, ROCHESTER CASTLE KEEP

Wall plate—Horizontal timber on top of wall immediately under roof (see Timber Roof diagram).

Wattle and daub—Walling made from vertical timber stakes woven horizontally with branches and reeds. The whole is then covered by mud.

Bibliography

GENERAL (AND PRE-MEDIEVAL)

ALLSOPP, B., *A General History of Architecture*, Sir Isaac Pitman and Sons Ltd, 1960

BATSFORD, H. and FRY, C., *The English Cottage*, B. T. Batsford Ltd, 1950
    The Cathedrals of England, B. T. Batsford Ltd, 1960

BRAUN, H., *The Story of the English House*, B. T. Batsford Ltd, 1940

BRIGGS, M. S., *Th English Farmhouse*, B. T. Batsford Ltd, 1953

BRITTON, J., *Christian Architecture in England*, Longman, Rees Orme, Brown and Green, 1826

CLARK, G., *Prehistoric England*, B. T. Batsford Ltd, 1948

CLIFTON-TAYLOR, A., *The Pattern of English Building*, B. T. Batsford Ltd, 1962

COLVIN, H. M., *The Biographical Dictionary of English Architects 1660–1840*, John Murray Ltd, 1954

The Connoisseur Period Guides (several volumes), 1957

COX, C. and FORD, C. B., *The English Parish Church*, B. T. Batsford Ltd, 1954

CROSSLEY, F. H., *Timber Building in England from Early Times to the end of the Seventeenth Century*, B. T. Batsford Ltd, 1951
    The English Abbey, B. T. Batsford Ltd, 1949

DUTTON, R., *The English Country House*, B. T. Batsford Ltd, 1949

FELTON, H. and HARVEY, J., *The English Cathedral*, B. T. Batsford Ltd, 1956

FLETCHER, SIR BANISTER, *A History of Architecture on the Comparative Method*, The Athlone Press, 1960

GARDNER, A. H., *Outline of English Architecture*, B. T. Batsford Ltd, 1946

GASQUET, Cardinal, *English Monastic Life*, Methuen and Co., 1924

GLOAG, J., *Guide to Western Architecture*, George Allen and Unwin Ltd, 1958

GLOAG, J. and BRIDGWATER, D., *A History of Cast Iron in Architecture*, George Allen and Unwin Ltd, 1948

GODFREY, W. H., *A History of Architecture in and around London*, Phoenix House Ltd (new ed.), 1962

HARTLEY, D. and ELLIOT, M. M., *Life and Work of the People of England*, (6 Vols.), B. T. Batsford Ltd, 1925–31

HUTTON, G. and SMITH, E., *English Parish Churches*, Thames and Hudson, Ltd, 1952

JORDAN, R. FURNEAUX, *A Picture History of the English House*, Edward Hulton, 1960

KERR, R., *The Gentleman's House*, John Murray Ltd, 1865

KERSTING, A. F. and DUTTON, R., *English Country Houses in Colour*, B. T. Batsford Ltd, 1958

KIDSON, P. and MURRAY, P., *A History of English Architecture*, George G. Harrap and Co., 1962

LLOYD, N., *A History of the English House*, Architectural Press Ltd, 1931

LUTYENS, R., *Six Great Architects*, Hamish Hamilton Ltd, 1959

MARÉ, E. de, *The Bridges of Britain*, B. T. Batsford Ltd, 1954

MEYER, P. and HÜRLIMANN, M., *English Cathedrals*, Thames and Hudson Ltd, 1950

MORGAN, T., *Romano-British Mosaic Pavements*, Whiting and Co., 1886

NASH, J., *The Mansions of England in Olden Time*, The Studio, 1906

NICHOLSON, C. B., *England's Greater Churches*, B. T. Batsford Ltd, 1949

OGILVIE, V., *The English Public School*, B. T. Batsford Ltd, 1957

PARKER, J. H., *A Concise Glossary of Terms used in Grecian, Roman, Italian and Gothic Architecture*,
    James Parker and Co., 1846

QUENNELL, M. and C. H. B., *Everyday Life in Prehistoric Times*, B. T. Batsford Ltd, 1959
    Everyday Life in Roman Britain, B. T. Batsford Ltd, 1951

RUSKIN, J., *The Stones of Venice*, Wm Collins Sons and Co., 1960
    The Seven Lamps of Architecture, The Noonday Press, U.S.A. (new ed.), 1961

SALZMAN, L. F., *Building in England*, Clarendon Press, Oxford, 1952

SPIERS, R. P., *The Orders of Architecture*, B. T. Batsford Ltd, 1893

STATHAM, H. H., *A History of Architecture*, B. T. Batsford Ltd, 1950

STRATTON, A., *The Styles of English Architecture*, B. T. Batsford Ltd, 1949
    The Orders of Architecture, B. T. Batsford Ltd, 1931

SUMMERSON, J., *Architecture in Britain 1530–1830*, Penguin Books Ltd, 1953

TIPPING, H. A., *English Homes* (9 Vols 1066–1820), Country Life, 1921

TOY, S., *The Castles of Great Britain*, William Heinmann Ltd, 1953

TREVELYAN, G. M., *Illustrated English Social History* (4 Vols), Longmans, Green and Co., 1949

TURNOR, R., *The Smaller English House 1500–1939*, B. T. Batsford Ltd, 1952

UHDE, C., *Baudenkmaeler in Grossbritannien* (2 Vols), Ernest Wasmuth, Berlin, 1894

VALE, E., *Churches*, B. T. Batsford Ltd, 1954
    Abbeys and Priories, B. T. Batsford Ltd, 1955

MEDIEVAL AND TUDOR

BALDWIN BROWN, G., *Ecclesiastical Architecture in England from the Conversion of the Saxons to
    the Norman Conquest*, John Murray Ltd, 1903

BLAIR, P. H., *An Introduction to Anglo-Saxon England*, Cambridge University Press, 1956

BOND, F., *Gothic Architecture in England*, B. T. Batsford Ltd, 1905

BOWMAN, H., *Specimens of the Ecclesiastical Architecture of Great Britain from the Conquest to the
    Reformation*, John W. Parker, 1846

BRAUN, H., *An Introduction to English Mediaeval Architecture*, Faber and Faber Ltd, 1951

BROWN, R. A., *English Medieval Castles*, B. T. Batsford Ltd, 1954

CESCINSKY, H. and GRIBBLE, E. R., *Early English Furniture and Woodwork* (2 Vols), George
    Routledge and Sons Ltd, 1922

CLAPHAM, A. W., *English Romanesque Architecture Before the Conquest*, Clarendon Press, Oxford,
    1930
    English Romanesque Architecture After the Conquest, Clarendon Press, Oxford, 1934

CLARK, G. T., *Medieval Military Architecture in England* (2 Vols), Wyman and Sons, 1884

GARNER, T. and STRATTON, A., *The Domestic Architecture of England during the Tudor Period* (2 Vols), B. T. Batsford Ltd, 1929

HARVEY, J., *Henry Yevele*, B. T. Batsford Ltd, 1944
    English Medieval Architects, B. T. Batsford Ltd, 1954
    Gothic England, 1300–1550, B. T. Batsford Ltd, 1948

PARKER, J. H., *An Introduction to the Study of Gothic Architecture*, James Parker and Co, 1849

PUGIN, A., *Specimens of Gothic Architecture* (2 Vols), M. A. Nattali (original edn J. Taylor, 1821), 1835

RICKMAN, T., *An Attempt to Discriminate the Styles of Architecture in England from the Conquest to the Reformation*, John Henry and James Parker, 1862

SHARPE, E., *A Series of Illustrations of the Window Tracery of the Decorated Style of Ecclesiastical Architecture*, John Van Voorst, 1849

TURNER, T. H., *Domestic Architecture in the Middle Ages* (3 Vols 1066–15th Century), John Henry Parker, 1851–9

WEST, G. H., *Gothic Architecture in England and France*, George Bell and Sons Ltd, 1927

STUART AND GEORGIAN

ADAM, R. and J., *The Works in Architecture of Robert and James Adam*, Alec Tiranti Ltd, 1959

BIRNSTINGL, H. J., *Sir John Soane*, Ernest Benn Ltd, 1925

BLOMFIELD, R., *A History of Renaissance Architecture in England 1500–1800* (2 Vols), George Bell and Sons, 1897

BRIGGS, M. S., *Wren the Incomparable*, George Allen and Unwin Ltd, 1953

Burlington Magazine, Monograph III, *Georgian Art*, B. T. Batsford Ltd, 1929

DAVIS, T., *The Architecture of John Nash*, Studio, 1960

DUTTON, R., *The Age of Wren*, B. T. Batsford Ltd, 1951

EDWARDS, A. T., *Sir William Chambers*, Ernest Benn Ltd, 1924

FIELD, H. and BUNNEY, M., *English Domestic Architecture of the Seventeenth and Eighteenth Centuries*, George Bell and Sons Ltd, 1928

FLEMING, J., *Robert Adam and His Circle*, John Murray Ltd, 1962

FURST, V., *The Architecture of Sir Christopher Wren*, Percy Lund Humphries and Co., 1956

HUSSEY, C., *English Country Houses, Early Georgian 1715–60*, Country Life Ltd, 1955
    English Country Houses, Mid-Georgian 1760–1800, Country Life Ltd, 1956
    English Country Houses, Late Georgian 1800–1840, Country Life Ltd, 1958

JOURDAIN, M., *The Work of William Kent*, Country Life Ltd, 1948

LEES-MILNE, J., *The Age of Inigo Jones*, B. T. Batsford Ltd, 1953
    Tudor Renaissance, B. T. Batsford Ltd, 1951
    The Age of Adam, B. T. Batsford Ltd, 1947

RICHARDSON, A. E., *An Introduction to Georgian Architecture*, Art and Technics Ltd, 1949
    Monumental Classic Architecture in Great Britain and Ireland during the Eighteenth and Nineteenth Centuries, B. T. Batsford Ltd, 1914

SEKLER, E., *Wren and his Place in European Architecture*, Faber and Faber Ltd, 1956

SITWELL, S., *British Architects and Craftsmen 1600–1830*, B. T. Batsford Ltd, 1948
STROUD, D., *The Architecture of Sir John Soane*, Studio, 1961.
WHIFFEN, M., *Stuart and Georgian Churches, 1603–1837*, B. T. Batsford Ltd, 1948

NINETEENTH CENTURY

BARMAN, C., *An Introduction to Railway Architecture*, Art and Technics Ltd, 1950
BLOMFIELD, Sir R., *Richard Norman Shaw*, B. T. Batsford Ltd, 1940
BRANDON, R. and J. A., *An Analysis of Gothick Architecture* (2 Vols), David Boque, 1849
CASSON, H., *An Introduction to Victorian Architecture*, Art and Technics Ltd, 1948
CLARK, Sir K., *The Gothic Revival*, John Murray Ltd, 1962
CLARKE, B. F. L., *Church Builders of the Nineteenth Century*, Society for Promoting Christian Knowledge, 1938
GOODHART-RENDEL, H. S., *English Architecture since the Regency*, Constable and Co., 1953
HITCHCOCK, H. RUSSELL, *Early Victorian Architecture in Britain* (2 Vols), Architectural Press Ltd, 1954
Architecture, Nineteenth and Twentieth Centuries, Penguin Books Ltd, 1958
MEEKS, C. L. V., *The Railway Station*, Architectural Press Ltd, 1957
PILCHER, D., *The Regency Style*, B. T. Batsford Ltd, 1948
PUGIN, A., *Pugin's Gothic Ornaments*, drawn by J. D. Harding, Auguste Pugin, 1831
REILLY, P., *An Introduction to Regency Architecture*, Art and Technics Ltd, 1948
RICHARDS, J. M. and MARÉ, E. de, *The Functional Tradition in Early Industrial Buildings*, Architectural Press Ltd, 1958
TURNOR, R., *Nineteenth Century Architecture in Britain*, B. T. Batsford Ltd, 1950
Villa and Cottage Architecture, Blackie and Son, 1868

TWENTIETH CENTURY

BENNETT, T. P., *Architectural Design in Concrete*, Ernest Benn Ltd, 1927
BUTLER, A. S. G., *The Architecture of Sir Edwin Lutyens* (3 Vols), Country Life Ltd, 1950
DANNATT, T., *Modern Architecture in Britain*, B. T. Batsford Ltd, 1959
FITCH, J. M., *Walter Gropius*, Mayflower Books Ltd, 1960
GALE, S., *Modern Housing Estates*, B. T. Batsford Ltd, 1949
GROPIUS, W., *Scope of Total Architecture*, George Allen and Unwin Ltd, 1956
HATTRELL, W. S. and Partners, *Hotels, Restaurants and Bars*, B. T. Batsford Ltd, 1962
HARVEY, W. A., *The Model Village and its Cottages, Bournville*, B. T. Batsford Ltd, 1906
HOWARTH, T., *Charles Rennie Mackintosh and the Modern Movement*, Routledge and Kegan Paul, Ltd, 1952
HUSSEY, C., *The Life of Sir Edwin Lutyens*, Country Life Ltd, 1950
JAY, K., *Calder Hall, Britain's First Atomic Power Station*, Methuen and Co. Ltd, 1956
LUTYENS, R., *Sir Edwin Lutyens*, Country Life Ltd, 1942
MCALLISTER, G. and E. G., *Homes, Towns and Countryside*, B. T. Batsford Ltd, 1945
MUTHESIUS, H., *Die englische Baukunst der Gegenwart*, Cosmos, Leipzig and Berlin, 1900
PARK, J., *Houses and Bungalows*, B. T. Batsford Ltd, 1958

PRICE, B., *Technical Colleges and Colleges of Further Education*, B. T. Batsford Ltd, 1959

RICHARDS, J. M., *An Introduction to Modern Architecture*, Penguin Books Ltd, 1940

RICHARDSON, A. E., *Robert Mylne, Architect and Engineer*, B. T. Batsford Ltd, 1955

WHITTICK, A., *European Architecture in the Twentieth Century* (2 Vols), Crosby Lockwood and Son Ltd, 1950–3

    Erich Mendelsohn, Leonard Hill Ltd, London, 1956

YERBURY, F. R., *Small Modern English Houses*, Victor Gollancz Ltd, 1929

REGIONAL

BETJEMAN, J., *An Oxford University Chest*, John Miles, 1938

BULLEID, A., *The Lake Villages of Somerset*, The Glastonbury Antiquarian Society, 1949

COBB, G., *The Old Churches of London*, B. T. Batsford Ltd, 1948

COOK, G. H. *Portrait of St Alban's Cathedral*, Phoenix House Ltd, 1951

    Old St Paul's Cathedral, Phoenix House Ltd, 1955

    Portrait of Canterbury Cathedral, Phoenix House Ltd, 1949

    Portrait of Durham Cathedral, Phoenix House Ltd, 1948

COURLANDER, K., *Richmond*, B. T. Batsford Ltd, 1953

EDWARDS, T., *Bristol*, B. T. Batsford Ltd, 1951

FYFE, T., *Architecture in Cambridge*, Cambridge University Press, 1942

HIND, A. M., *Wenceslaus Hollar and his views of London and Windsor in the Seventeenth Century*, The Bodley Head Ltd, 1922

ISON, W., *The Georgian Buildings of Bristol*, Faber and Faber Ltd, 1952

    The Georgian Buildings of Bath, Faber and Faber Ltd, 1948

JESSUP, R. F. and F. W., *The Cinque Ports*, B. T. Batsford Ltd, 1952

JOWITT, R. L. P., *Salisbury*, B. T. Batsford Ltd, 1951

KENYON, K. M., *The Roman Theatre of Verulamium*, St Albans and Hertfordshire Architectural and Archaeological Society, 1934

KERSTING, A. F. and DICK, M., *Portrait of Oxford*, B. T. Batsford Ltd, 1956

KERSTING, A. F. and LITTLE, B., *Portrait of Cambridge*, B. T. Batsford Ltd, 1955

LITTLE, B., *The Three Choirs Cities*, B. T. Batsford Ltd, 1952

    Cheltenham, B. T. Batsford Ltd, 1952

MOULD, D. D. C. POCHIN, *Scotland of the Saints*, B. T. Batsford Ltd, 1952

    Ireland of the Saints, B. T. Batsford, 1953

NEWALL, R. S., *Stonehenge, Wiltshire*, H.M. Stationery Office, 1955

POPE-HENNESSY, J. and WILD, HANS, *The Houses of Parliament*, B. T. Batsford Ltd, 1945

RODGERS, J., *York*, B. T. Batsford Ltd, 1951

Royal Festival Hall, Max Parrish Ltd in conjunction with the London County Council, 1951

SHEPHERD, T. H. and ELMES, J., Metropolitan Improvements, Jones and Co, 1828

SMITH, R. A. L., *Bath*, B. T. Batsford Ltd, 1948

SPENCE, Sir Basil, *Phoenix at Coventry*, G. Bles Ltd, 1962

SUMMERSON, J., *Georgian London*, Pleiades Books, 1945

TANNER, L. E., *A History and Treasures of Westminster Abbey*, Pitkin Pictorials Ltd, 1953

WILLIS, R., *An Architectural History of the University of Cambridge*, Cambridge University Press, 1886

GUIDE BOOKS, INFORMATION LEAFLETS AND BOOKLETS

Prehistoric, Roman, and Early Times

Stonehenge, Wiltshire, Ministry of Works
The Lake-Villages of Somerset, Arthur Bulleid
London in Roman Times, London Museum Catalogue
Roman Britain, B.B.C. Pamphlet
The Roman Theatre of Verulamium, Kathleen M. Kenyon

Cathedrals

Canterbury, Canon John Shirley, D.D., F.S.A.
Chester, Frank Bennett
The New Coventry Cathedral
Exeter, Rev. Wilfred Westall
Gloucester, Dr Henry Gee, F.S.A., the late Dean
Guildford, Philip Crawford
Liverpool, Vere E. Cotton, C.B.E.
Oxford, The Dean and Chapter
Peterborough, Rev. R. E. Sibthorp, M.A.
Ripon, Rev. J. M. Cunningham
Rochester, Rev. Francis Underhill
Winchester, The Dean and Chapter

Abbeys and Priories

Bolton Priory, Yorkshire, Arthur Raistrick
St Mary and St Blaise Priory, Boxgrove, Edgar Popham
Fountains Abbey, Yorkshire, Arthur E. Henderson
Glastonbury Abbey, Somerset
St Mary's Abbey, West Malling, Kent, Alan Maycock
Abbey Church of St Mary the Virgin, Tewkesbury, Gloucestershire, Lionel Gough
Tintern Abbey, Monmouthshire, Ministry of Works

Churches

Church of St Giles, Cheadle, Staffordshire, The Catholic Records Press
Priory Church at Christchurch, Hampshire, E. Russell Oakley
Greensted Church, Essex
Church of St Mary the Virgin, Iffley, Oxford
The Abbey Church of St Mary the Virgin, Sherborne, Dorset, Friends of Sherborne Abbey

Universities

Exeter College, Oxford
Mansfield College, Oxford
Corpus Christi College, Cambridge
Trinity College, Cambridge

Castles

Carisbrooke, Isle of Wight, Ministry of Works
Deal, Kent, Ministry of Works
Dover, Kent, Ministry of Works
Harlech, N. Wales, Ministry of Works
Lewes, Sussex, Sussex Archaeological Society
The Tower of London, Ministry of Works

Royal Residences

Hampton Court Palace, Ministry of Works
The Abbey and Palace of Holyroodhouse, Edinburgh, Ministry of Works
Windsor Castle, and St George's Chapel Windsor Castle, H. W. Blackburne and M. F. Bond

Houses

Blenheim Palace, Oxfordshire, The Blenheim Estate Office
Chatsworth, Derbyshire
Haddon Hall, Derbyshire
Ham House, Surrey, H.M. Stationery Office

Hardwick Hall, Derbyshire
Harewood House, Yorkshire
Hatfield House, Hertfordshire
Old Soar, Plaxtol, Kent, Ministry of Works
Penshurst Place, Kent
Sutton Place, Surrey
West Wycombe, Buckinghamshire, Francis
  Dashwood

National Trust Publications

Bateman's, Sussex
Bodiam Castle, Sussex
Charlecote Park, Warwickshire
Ellen Terry Memorial, Smallhythe, Kent

Knole, Sevenoaks, Kent
Little Moreton Hall, Cheshire
Montacute, Somerset
Petworth House, Sussex
Stoneacre, Otham, Kent
Uppark, Sussex

Miscellaneous

The City of Bath, Somerset, Official Guide
Crawley New Town, Sussex, Crawley Development Corporation
Harlow New Town, Essex, The Church of Our Lady of Fatima
Leeds Civic Hall, Yorkshire

Index

Page references are printed in ordinary type; figure references in **heavy type.**